Roz Chast
Cartoonist
Page 240

Hester Mundis
Humor Writer
Page 132

Glenn McCoy
Cartoonist
Page 284

1993 Humor and Cartoon Markets

Distributed in Canada by McGraw-Hill,
300 Water Street,
Whitby Ontario L1N 9B6.
Also distributed in Australia by Kirby Books,
Private Bag No. 19, P.O. Alexandria NSW
2015.

Managing Editor, Market Books Department:
Constance J. Achabal; Assistant Managing Editor:
Glenda Tennant Neff

Humor and Cartoon Markets.

International Standard Serial Number
1043-240X
International Standard Book Number
0-89879-559-1

1 9 9 3

HUMOR AND CARTOON MARKETS

Edited by
Bob Staake
and
Roseann Shaughnessy

Writer's Digest Books

Cincinnati, Ohio

Contents

From Bob Staake

If you recall, past editions of *Humor and Cartoon Markets* have been released in the spring. After carefully examining the needs of our readers, we decided to release the book in the fall so readers can get a jump on the coming year.

But forget about juggling your calendar—the important thing is that the long-awaited, newly-updated edition of *Humor and Cartoon Markets* is finally here, and it's by far the best edition we've put out.

By now, you know the book from front cover to back. Basically, the book is filled with detailed listings from markets with specific humor needs. Happily, we have 150 *new* markets in this edition. Also important, we update the listing information every year so you don't send material to markets that have shut down, art directors or editors who have moved on, or markets with dramatic changes in their freelance needs.

Whether you specialize in comedy writing, caricature, gag cartooning or humorous illustration, *Humor and Cartoon Markets* will help you locate markets for your work.

You'll notice a couple of big changes with this edition. For example, we've dropped the Agents/Representatives chapter. The decision wasn't mine, and when I heard of the change, my hellish screams emanated from the cracked tuckpointing in my circa 1890s studio in Webster Groves, Missouri and carried all the way to Cincinnati. But instead of screaming back, Writer's Digest Books explained they were dropping the Agents/Representatives chapter to add the Playwriting chapter. They reminded me that they publish a terrific book called *Guide to Literary Agents and Art/Photo Reps*. If you're looking for an agent, it's an invaluable resource and I recommend it highly.

You'll also stumble upon my major article, The Art of Self-Promotion. While some of the strategies in the article can be used by freelance writers, the piece was written primarily to help cartoonists and humorous illustrators market their work on a more "sophisticated" level. I cannot stress enough the importance of self-promotion, and because so many young cartoonists send me pro-

Bob Staake *is a freelance cartoonist/writer based in St Louis, Missouri. He describes his drawing style as a "marginally wacky mix of sophisticated zaniness against a backdrop of wacky." He has done work for such clients as* The Washington Post, USA Today, *"Children's Television Workshop,"* Playboy, Parents, The Los Angeles Times, *MGM, Warner Brothers, Paramount Pictures, AT&T,* Premiere, *Anheuser-Busch, Coor's, Sunkist, to name a few. He has illustrated or authored a total of seven books including* Headlines *(by Jay Leno),* True and Tacky 2 *and* The Complete Book of Caricature.

motional packages that would benefit from a little professionalism, I thought it was time to write a comprehensive article on the subject.

Of course we've kept the regular *Humor and Cartoon Market* features enjoyed by our readers. This year's Humor Roundtable includes participation from cartoonists and writers, but there's also the fascinating input of three top syndicators. Before you sit down to create the next "Far Side" or "Bloom County," read the Humor Roundtable and acquire some uncommon insight into the business of syndication.

With the amount of mail I receive, it's apparent that *Humor and Cartoon Markets* continues to be an invaluable tool for freelancers interested in marketing their humorous work. Indeed, it's very encouraging when a cartoonist, humorous illustrator or writer takes the time to pick up the phone to thank us for publishing this book. When I was starting out in this business, no book existed that even remotely resembled *Humor and Cartoon Markets*. Therefore, I learned about freelancing the usual way—by *stumbling* through it.

If I've been able to succeed as a freelancer, it's because I've done three things: I've nurtured what *talent* I've had; I've *worked harder* than the next guy; and I've learned as much as I possibly could about the *business* of freelancing. After all, having talent and working hard doesn't automatically mean that you'll be able to tuck away a few dollars in the bank.

The reason for this book being so solid is that the objectives of Writer's Digest Books have always been aligned with mine. I have always felt that if *Humor and Cartoon Markets* was anything, it was the one book that *no* freelance cartoonist, humorous illustrator, animator or humor writer should be without. It's really that simple. The funny pictures are nice, but if you *read* this book, you'll learn more about freelancing than you ever dreamed possible. I absolutely guarantee that.

So many people help me crunch out this book each year. Naturally, there's my agent, Susan Schulman, and Connie Achabal and Roseann Shaughnessy at Writer's Digest Books, who I simply couldn't do without. Roseann handles the editorial details and makes sure that I turn in my materials when I'm supposed to. When I don't, Connie snarls at me. But it's a *good* kind of snarl. Lots of other people to thank as well—Mary Vieth, Paulette Fehlig, Jack Dickason, Miles Walters—and I'll tip my hat again to the professionals who graciously participated in the Humor Roundtable and those who allowed me to reprint their art in the book. Were it not for the magnanimous involvement of these people, *Humor and Cartoon Markets* wouldn't be as special as it is.

I also wanted to take a moment to respond to all the people who send letters to me. Unfortunately, it's getting increasingly difficult to respond promptly to everyone who writes to me, but I *do* respond to every letter I receive. And while the popularity of *Humor and Cartoon Markets* continues to grow, more and more cartoonists and humorous illustrators send in examples of their work in the hope that they will be reprinted in this book. Understand that space limitations prohibit me from reprinting as much material as I would like to, so if I *didn't* reprint your work, it's not that I'm a jerk or anything, it's just that I ran out of room. I'm sure you understand.

Enjoy the book. And the best of luck to you in the coming year!

How to Use Your Humor and Cartoon Markets

Targeting appropriate markets for your work requires a bit of research on your part, but using *Humor and Cartoon Markets* makes it relatively painless. We've compiled listings of markets seeking work from brilliantly funny freelancers. The listings include specific types of materials sought, submission procedures, payment information and helpful tips. All you need to do is read through the listings and find the markets buying your brand of humor. But read the listings carefully! Editors, art directors, producers and creative directors dislike wasting precious time with inappropriate submissions from careless freelancers.

In addition to the listings, there are informational articles, detailed section introductions, Close-up interviews and a major article on self-promotion. This material is provided to help you better understand the business of humor and, hopefully, give you the professional edge you will need as a freelance humorous writer or illustrator. We've also included samples of freelance humorous writing and illustration to demonstrate the type and quality of work being bought today. You'll also find—and enjoy—caricatures and cartoons by Bob Staake, who has been a successful freelancer for some 17 years. Read his introductory piece, From Bob Staake, for his opinions on the industry and the use of this book.

Where to start

It's easiest when working with this book to move from the very general to the very specific. The first step is to refer to the sections in the book that correspond to the specific area in which you work. For example, if you are a humorous illustrator, you will want to go directly to the major markets for this work: Advertising/Public Relations, Art/Design, Greeting Cards and Paper Products and Publications. If you are a cartoonist, you will want to refer immediately to Animation, Comic Books and Syndicates. Finally, if you are a humor writer, you will want to seek out listings in Book Publishers, Gags/Entertainers, Playwriting, Publications, Syndicates and Television/Radio. Humor writers should refer to the Subject Indexes beginning on page 319 for a breakdown of subject areas sought by various publishers of humorous writing.

Remember that this is just a preliminary search. You will want to check out areas you haven't worked in before, in order to expand your markets. Most sections of the book contain markets whose needs "cross over"—that is they need both illustrations and writing.

Interpreting the markets

You've identified the market categories you're thinking about sending work to. The next step is to research within each section to identify the individual markets that will be most receptive to receiving your work.

Most users of *Humor and Cartoon Markets* should check three items in the listings: location of the organization, the types of material the organization is interested in considering, submission requirements and rights and payment policies of the organization. Depending upon your personal concerns, any of these items could be considered the deciding factor for you as you determine which markets to send your humorous writing or illustration to.

It's important to remember that when you see "SASE" within a listing it refers to a self-addressed, stamped envelope to ensure return of your work. For unsolicited submissions, you should always include a SASE whether or not one is requested in the listing. A "ms" or "mss" refers to "manuscript" or "manuscripts" respectively. See the Glossary at the end of this book for complete explanations of terms.

Whenever possible, obtain writer's/artist's guidelines. Depending upon what the market wants to see, your actual submission may include a query or cover letter, resume and/or client list, synopsis or complete manuscript, and cartoon or illustration samples. Since they may be held indefinitely (or even lost), never send originals of your work.

For specific information about promoting yourself and your work, see The Art of Self-Promotion, by Bob Staake on page 25.

Listing formats (or style) vary from section to section since they are designed to incorporate all the requirements for working within a specific market. For this reason, it is important to read the introductions at the beginning of each section to familiarize yourself with the unique aspects of each market.

Corner-Free Discussion: Our Ever-Popular Humor Roundtable

It *would* be pretty cool to book a table at a Five Star Restaurant in Cincinnati at which to hold our Humor Roundtable. Imagine two top cartoonists, two seriously hysterical comedy writers and three respected syndicate bigwigs all sitting at the same table. The cartoonists would doodle on their linen napkins, the comedy writers would attempt to impress waitresses with groan-provoking one-liners, and the syndicate guys would order lobster knowing that *we* were picking up the tab. Why, Fox has built an entire sitcom on a lesser premise.

Of course in the middle of all this (and after six bottles of chardonnay), the conversation would be pithy, insightful and marvelously revealing. These guys would know their stuff, and they would freely exchange inside humor info like most people exchange expired gallons of milk. Better yet, the info wouldn't look like cottage cheese.

And while a face-to-face schmooze-fest at a non-cornered table would be perfectly idyllic, we don't live in a perfect world (this explains taxes and Cher). So what's the next best thing? We use fax machines.

To conduct the Humor Roundtable, we provide the participants with questions and then ask them to fax back their responses. No touching, no hugging — simply transmitting back pages of scribbled notes is sufficient contact. Not even an agoraphobic could contest those game rules. *This* is why so many top professionals agree to participate in our Humor Roundtable.

We want to thank our seven participants for devoting their time, input and knowledge. Read their words, heed their advice. There *will* be a test at the end.

Humor Writing

Jerry Dumas is a humor writer who has written material for such strips as "Beetle Bailey," "Hi and Lois" and "Benchley."

© Jerry Dumas

Mark Evanier is a Los Angeles, California-based comedy writer. His writing credits include "Cheers," and the "Garfield" and "Mother Goose and Grimm" Saturday morning cartoon shows.

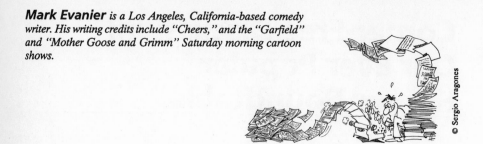

© Sergio Aragones

When did your writing career really begin to take off? What are some reasons for this?

Dumas: It never took off. It crawled along on all fours, ducking occasionally. I started writing "Beetle Bailey" and "Hi and Lois" in 1956. For two years Mort Walker and I also did (the legendary!) "Sam's Strip," which I wrote half of and drew all of. It is considered legendary because it was unusual and cruelly short-lived. Along the way I wrote some books, lots of magazine pieces (some with pictures) and created other comic strips, like "Benchley" (drawn by Mort Drucker), and "Rabbits Rafferty" (drawn by Mel Crawford). If you like doing a thing, you tend to do it a lot. If you do a thing a lot, you should get better and better at it, if there is any justice in the world.

Evanier: My career started in 1969 and has expanded since ... a little more every year. I wrote for local magazines, started writing comic books in 1970, started writing for stand-up comedians in 1974, started doing live-action TV in 1975 and animation a few years later. I think judicious diversification is important to a career, meaning that you succeed in one area and then expand into another, *not* that you try to succeed on ten fronts at once. What you learn in one area can usually be applied to another. Moreover, those who hire writers usually like to hire the guy who never seems to be out of work.

Besides the ability to write funny, what other skills must the humor writer possess?

Dumas: One of the best ones to have is—as Hemingway said—a built-in shit detector. Just a colorful, crude way of saying it is necessary to see through the pompous and the dishonest and the vain, whether in others or in yourself. Seeing into the truth of things leads to a great deal of humor. It helps also to not be narrowly focused, to have a wide-ranging interest in the world and its people. It helps to read a lot.

Evanier: The two skills every writer needs are (a) the ability to produce under tight deadlines and (b) the ability to cut and edit. These are both especially important when one is writing humor since our "muse" is sometimes a bit more difficult to summon on demand . . . and we usually work in small spaces or time slots. When you write something and the audience doesn't laugh at it, you can't waste a lot of time arguing; you have to ruthlessly cut and rewrite. Fast typing can also be handy.

For gag writers, what are the challenges of tailoring your writing to a particular performer's technique? How important is topicality?

Dumas: As one who has made most of his living doing comic strips, I have to tailor gags to pen and ink characters who, over time, seem to become real. I've done "Sam and Silo" for 13 years now, and I know those guys as well as I know "Beetle" or "Sarge" or "General Halftrack." I know right away whether Sarge is likely to say a certain thing, and exactly how he would phrase it. If a thought is too sensitive or complex or sophisticated for him, you give the line to someone else, someone it fits. We don't do topical gags, we do character.

Evanier: The best comedians do not, for the most part, do interchangeable material: They speak in unique "voices" and those who write for them have to be able to write for those "voices." Usually, this is just a matter of understanding someone's sense of humor. But when you do a good job of this, you render yourself invisible; everyone assumes the performer made it up. So you must also have the selflessness to tolerate that. I've written for a number of stand-up comedians who, even though they uttered my words and paid me for them, have convinced everyone—including, often, themselves—that they write their own material. Topicality is important for certain performers in certain venues. It's a matter of each performer's individual style.

How do you organize the business side of your craft, i.e., target appropriate markets, set fees, submit material, etc.?

Dumas: I have no organization. My books go to my agent, strips go to the syndicate (my lawyer having handled negotiations when the strip was sold), magazine pieces go to editors, and I more or less accept what is offered. The only time this varied was when I sold the first of seven straight offerings to *Connoisseur*. The editor phoned and said, "Your "Van Gogh's Ghost" is great." Pause. "I can't believe this came to me." Pause. "How much do you want for it?" I told him what *The New Yorker* would have paid me. "We're not as rich as *The New Yorker*," he said. "How about $1,800?" I accepted.

Evanier: I generally let my agent handle anything that involves dollar signs and I strenuously avoid talking money with anyone. I rarely submit material. I like to get my name and work out there and to allow it to "sell" me and cause folks to come to me. I intend to keep following this approach until, any day now, it starts working, at which time I'll be especially interested in others' answers to this question.

What are some obstacles you encounter as a humor writer? How do you solve them?

Dumas: The main obstacle is that I am my own boss, and a lenient one at that. Another obstacle, after more than 30 years of work, is the nagging worry that someone else may have already done this idea, even I may have done it, and I don't want to repeat it. Another problem is that I don't like gags that are too simple—I want the reader to make that little jump. Then someone at a party whom I deem intelligent will say that my gags are too subtle. That person would not like the comedian Steven Wright, whom I admire. As for solving obstacles. I don't. I wait for them to go away.

Evanier: The toughest thing about writing humor is that you often have to do it when you don't feel particularly funny. When deadlines loom, you have to get "in the mood" in a hurry. There used to be a saying in the newspaper game that the toughest part of being a daily columnist was that, "No one has something to say every day." Most comedy writers not only have to say something every day, it has to be something funny and pointed. "Pointed" is the key word here, and it's my usual solution to the problem. I ask myself, "What's bugging me? What is there out there that I have an opinion about?" Writing about that—whatever it is—can put a spark of passion/inspiration behind the work. It can be a lot of fun to trash something that's become a pet peeve of yours.

If you could do it all over again, what things would you do differently that would directly help your writing career?

Dumas: I would carry a pencil. I have lost thousands of gags over the years, saying to myself, "That's a terrific idea, I'll write that down when I get home. I won't forget it. How could I forget such a great idea?" But I do. Not as much lately, though, since I began to make 'mental keys.' I don't try to remember the whole idea, just a key word. I think also that I wish I had made a determined effort not to let a day go by without getting a certain amount of work down on paper. Despite having turned out many thousands of comic strip gags, and two fairly long books, it saddens me sometimes that many days passed—quite actively, full of physical work and play and happy times with my sons and friends and nature—with no real work, the thing I do, getting accomplished. But on the other hand, I think maybe I chose the best course after all. I ask, which would I prefer to have done—write ten books of fairly decent quality, or one really great book? Forty years worth of so-so comic strips, or five years worth of great comic strips?

Evanier: Early on, it was enormously helpful to me to do a lot of writing that was anonymous, for magazines where it didn't matter how bad I was. If I had it to do all over again, I'd spend more time in those venues, making my mistakes in places where I didn't have my byline clearly affixed. I always suggest to new writers that they try this for a time and not be so eager to get on to the visible, "Big Name" projects. This is excellent advice and I intend to keep giving it until some day, someone somewhere follows it.

Cartooning

Chon Day *has been drawing gag cartoons for (a staggering) 62 years. He lives in Rhode Island.*

© Chon Day

© Mell Lazarus

Mell Lazarus *is the creator of "Momma" and "Miss Peach." He is also President of the National Cartoonists Society (NCS).*

How long was it before your first big break in cartooning? What made it happen?

Day: I joined the Art Students League in 1929 and sold my first cartoon in 1930 for five dollars. The crash on Wall Street made it happen; many humor magazines appeared and they crashed, too.

Lazarus: At age 24 I started a 3-year run of sales to *Saturday Evening Post*, *Colliers*, etc. (gag cartoons). At age 30 I sold "Miss Peach" to N.Y. Herald Tribune Syndicate. That really kicked it off.

What are some typical obstacles you encounter in your career as a cartoonist? How do you solve them?

Day: Editors holding submissions long after they have considered them. To solve this problem, honk your horn!

Lazarus: Trying to please a general audience can be a problem. The solution is to please yourself.

What do you see as trends in cartooning, comic strips or humor in general?

Day: It's sad: the belly-laugh humor is out. People need to laugh at "the funnies." The belly-laugh in *Collier's* is just as funny today as it was then.

Lazarus: More sophisticated, relevant material, and cartoons that inform and amuse.

Do you agree or disagree that the most important component of a cartoon is the idea rather than the physical drawing? Should aspiring cartoonists concentrate more on the drawing of cartoons or the writing of them?

Day: Cartoons should fit the written gag.

Lazarus: It seems obvious that what one says is more important than how he or she illustrates it. The combination of both, however, is dynamite.

What is the best piece of advice you could give to aspiring cartoonists who want to be successful in this industry?

Day: Get into syndication. The freelance business is mighty risky. I was lucky.

Lazarus: Have something to say.

Syndicates

Steven Christensen *has worked in the field of syndication for seven years. He is executive editor of the Los Angeles Times Syndicate.*

Alan Shearer *is general manager/editorial director for The Washington Post Writers Group.*

Jay Kennedy *is the comics editor of King Features Syndicate.*

Are you more apt to consider for syndication a cartoon/strip/panel if it is exceptionally well drawn or if it is exceptionally well written?

Christensen: All things considered, I think concept, characterization and writing are more important than art skills. Many strips and panels that are not particularly well drawn have succeeded on the strength of excellent writing. On the other hand, it's rare to find a successful cartoon where the art work is terrific and the writing is weak.

Kennedy: I think you'll find industry-wide unanimity on this question. Good writing is more important than good art. The truism goes "Good writing can carry bad art, but good art can't carry bad writing."

If a reader reads a new strip and likes the joke, he will feel rewarded and continue trying out the new strip each day until he becomes a regular reader. If the jokes are too frequently disappointing, the reader simply begins to skip over the new strip.

The importance of good art, however, is not to be ignored. It can make an enormous contribution to a strip's popularity, especially when the strip is establishing itself in a newspaper. Good art has the power to entice a reader to try a new strip. Word of mouth recommendations can eventually get the same number of people to try a new strip, but good art is an excellent short cut and these days it is important to develop loyal readers as fast as you can.

Shearer: A strip that is well-drawn probably will catch my eye faster, but in the end it is the writing, the message and the humor that will carry it.

When a strip/panel is presented to you, how important is its storyline or premise?

Christensen: It's very important. The competition in syndicated cartooning is extremely tough, and a strip or panel based on a weak premise has little chance of winning the support of either newspaper editors or readers.

Kennedy: While undeniably important, the premise of a comic strip or panel is not the critical factor that most aspiring cartoonists seem to think it is. The quality of the humor is far and away the most important factor in our deciding whether or not to syndicate a strip. The premise is important to the extent that it contributes to or detracts from our ability to sell the comic into an already crowded marketplace.

A unique, appealing or pointed premise can contribute to the chances of an already humorous strip. A premise can detract from a comic's chances if it overlaps too directly with the premise of a successful existing strip, is depressing or is too elaborate.

Continuous storylines, more often than not, hurt a strip's syndication chances, because they need to be read virtually everyday. Few people manage to stay with new story strips long enough to become hooked.

Within the context of humor strips, short story lines of two weeks or less are OK if the bulk of the strips also contain a joke each day. A common mistake in submissions is to tell an origin story—a story of how the characters all met and why they are the way they are. Most people will never see the first few weeks of a strip, so they have to be able to tell what the strip is about without such a story. I suggest that people pretend that the samples they are sending are taken from their comic as it will apppear after it has already been in syndication for two years. If a reader can't understand the basics of the comic by reading any four weeks worth of a strip, then the basis of the comic is too complicated.

Shearer: I never read the storyline or premise first. I go right to the strips, just as a newspaper reader would do. Then I usually scan the attending material, unless I find no appeal in the strips whatsoever.

Are you more interested in seeing strips/panels that have ongoing characters, or that consist of one-shot "gags?"

Christensen: There's no one answer to this question. Both approaches can work. But I think it would be fair to say that strips or panels with ongoing characters have a better chance of building reader loyalty because readers develop personal affinities for the characters. They develop relationships with the characters that bring them back to the comics pages day after day. On the other hand, one can't deny the success of such "gag" cartoons as "The Far Side." In these cases, I think readers develop an affinity with the cartoonist rather than with the characters.

Kennedy: King Features is open to either kind of submission. It has been our experience that strips and panels with regular characters have a better chance of survival than strips and panels without them. It is impossible to be truly funny 365 days a year. If readers care about a strip's characters, they will get something out of the strip by touching base with them—even if the cartoonist is having an off-day.

If a comic doesn't have regular characters and the day's joke is a poor one, then that day's comic falls entirely flat. Cartoonists who work without regular characters must maintain a higher level of consistency in their humor than cartoonists who have ongoing characters. It is more difficult to succeed this way, but if you are capable of maintaining a consistently high level of humor without regular characters, King Features is open to syndicating your comic.

Shearer: I don't put any parameters on what I would or wouldn't like to see. I believe comic strips are an art form. I wouldn't think of telling an artist what to draw, or a columnist what to say.

If you feel a cartoon/strip/panel shows potential, how do you and the cartoonist develop it for syndication? Is the cartoonist paid for his/her development efforts? What happens if after developing the cartoon/strip/panel the syndicate declines to pick the feature up?

Christensen: It's a case-by-case situation. In some instances, cartoonists are paid for their work in development. In others, they are not; they work on the speculation that their cartoon will eventually be syndicated. I think it's important, therefore, that syndicates be honest and up-front with cartoonists as development progresses so that no one is misled. Some cartoons require little development because they're outstanding to begin with. Others may take a year of back-and-forth to get them to the point where everyone thinks they are ready for the market.

Kennedy: It is a rare occasion that we see a comic and immediately offer the cartoonist a syndication contract. The years are gone when newspapers were willing to hold onto a weak new strip to allow it to hit its stride in print. Today, a strip has to find its voice before it enters syndication. Too much is at stake to launch a strip without a period of development during which weaknesses are strengthened and the cartoonist's understanding of his or her own strip matures.

More often the path to syndication begins with our seeing talent in a person's work and becoming excited about his ability to create a marketable comic feature. When that happens, we give the cartoonist encouragement, critique his work and request additional samples. If the additional samples continue to excite us, we may offer an option/development contract.

During this development period the cartoonist does sample strips, exploring solutions to weak points in the comic. When the cartoonist and syndicate are satisfied that the cartoonist has a full understanding of his or her strip and of the syndication process and its needs, then the artist begins doing strips on a daily basis as would be the case in regular syndication. The best of these strips will be used to convince newspaper editors to add the comic to their comics page line-up.

The development period lasts for less than a year and the cartoonist does receive some payment. If at the end of the development period the syndicate decides the comic isn't one that it can successfully sell, the cartoonist is free to show it around without any obligation to King Features.

Shearer: Since the Writer's Group carries only a few comics, I would most likely be interested in a strip or panel that shows polish when it arrives. We are less likely to take something in the rough and bring it along. Under certain circumstances, a development advance is possible, with the advance deducted from future revenues.

Can you describe the special combination of things that convince you that a cartoon/strip/panel has the potential to become syndicated?

Christensen: My first consideration is: Am I dealing with a pro? It isn't hard when reviewing a submission to tell if I am dealing with someone who falls in, say, the top 5 percent of those submitting ideas. Then, is it a concept that can find its hold in the marketplace? Finally, is it a concept that can work in the long term rather than running out of gas in a few months?

Kennedy: I can't easily describe the core of what we are looking for in great detail, because what we are most interested in is the cartoonist's sense of humor and what he or she chooses to focus that humor on.

We want a cartoonist whose work embodies a humorous outlook on life, not presently found on the comics pages. We can teach someone to construct a gag better or to give his art more impact, but we can't teach a sense of humor or an outlook. That's what best sets one strip apart from another and that's a hard quality to pin down in words.

On a mechanical level, I look for comics with original jokes. I look to see that the cartoonist hasn't too narrowly defined the scope of his or her comic. I look for likeable characters. I look for attractive and distinctive art. I look for comics that are easy to read (far too many cartoonists don't take the time to letter their comics neatly). I look for comics that aren't cluttered. I look for comics that focus my eye on the elements crucial to conveying the joke. I look to see if the cartoonist knows how to draw for reproduction. I look to see if the cartoonist has presented his work with care.

Shearer: There is no answer to this question. I believe, though, that the best comics impart a universal truth through humor. It is this truth that will give a strip broad appeal. Berkeley Breathed perhaps said it best in the introduction to one of his "Bloom County" books: ". . . the most important dynamic in a comic strip is not shock and satire, but character and truth: the truth of Charlie Brown's anxiety, for example—a mirror of our own. The truth of Calvin's protective manipulations of his world. The truth of Opus' vanity and naivete."

How difficult is it for a cartoonist to get his/her feature syndicated? How can the cartoonist who desires to be syndicated beat the odds?

Christensen: It's extremely difficult, and unfortunately becomes only more so as more and more talented people seek syndication. I think persistence is the key—not necessarily persistence in "nagging" syndicates, but persistence in developing art and writing skills, in trying different ideas and approaches, and in refusing to get discouraged.

Kennedy: Getting syndicated involves a great deal of work, so it is never easy. Numerically, we get nearly 7,000 submissions a year, out of which we syndicate two or three. Those odds are deceptive however, because they don't account for talent. The bulk of those submissions are from people indulging a momentary fantasy of becoming a professional cartoonist. They haven't taken the time to put together a thorough presentation of their work or include an adequate number of samples.

No one with talent should be discouraged by the number of other aspiring cartoonists. If you have talent, the biggest step you can take towards beating the odds is to prepare a thorough submission package as outlined in the King Features submission guidelines.

Shearer: It's always been difficult to become syndicated and there is no formula for beating the odds. But every aspiring cartoonist should realize that timing plays a large role. And timing is something the cartoonist rarely controls. If the Writers Group has just introduced a new comic strip, we are less likely to be interested in a new one immediately. Also, I chose our last strip because it was different from anything I had seen in quite some time. Most of the submissions seemed to revolve around family situations, almost like TV sitcoms. Had our new strip, "Non Sequitur" by Wiley, appeared two years earlier, the market may not have been as receptive to something so nontraditional.

What are the trends in syndication today and how important is "licensing potential?"

Christensen: Syndicates are always interested in the "licensing potential" of a feature because of the revenues that can be generated. But licensing is a very broad term, and there's almost always a way for a successful product to be branched out into different areas. In terms of trends, I think a quick glance at today's comics pages shows that there really are no trends. Today's pages are filled with wonderfully eclectic work that covers the whole spectrum of subject matter, art styles and approaches. What they have in common is that each comic is written and drawn by a top cartoonist who is really in touch with his characters and has something worth saying.

Kennedy: For every trend that someone points out, there will always come along an exception to that trend that will break away and become successful, in part because it does break the trend. I wouldn't presume to cite a trend that would increase someone's chances at syndication.

Licensing potential is not something that is heavily weighed in our decision to syndicate one strip over another.

Shearer: Licensing is secondary to me at the outset. I will be the first to try to develop licensing potential but that is never the overriding reason for introducing a particular strip. I want the comic strip to succeed on the newspaper page as an art form and draw readers to the papers that publish it. So many submissions talk at length about licensing potential. Cartoonists should produce what satisfies *them*; the rest will take care of itself.

Has the recession altered the criteria you use to consider a cartoon/strip/panel for syndication? For example, do poor economic times mean that syndicates must look to strips/panels that are traditional rather than groundbreaking?

Christensen: More than anything else, poor economic times prompt syndicates to be especially careful in launching new projects. Properly rolling out a comic is not an inexpensive proposition, so syndicates want to be reasonably certain that it can succeed in a market where editors are on tight budgets and will probably have to drop another strip to make way for a new one.

Kennedy: The simple answer is, "No, the recession hasn't changed our criteria for selecting comic features." The criteria has always been to select features that editors will buy because people will want to read them.

Shearer: I'm not sure I can easily define "traditional" and "groundbreaking." But "Non Sequitur" was different from anything I had seen before and we grabbed it. If anything, the recession should make all of us look for something new and different. A strip that offers "more of the same" is less likely to catch the attention of the skeptical editor whose budget is in tatters.

The Business of Humor

by Roseann Shaughnessy

To stay ahead of the competition in the humor business is no laughing matter. It requires more than just talent and a unique style. It requires determination, discipline and perseverance. And it demands professionalism in the way you submit your work and handle your business details.

Packaging your work

When sending a manuscript five pages or less in length, fold it in thirds and send it in a #10 (business-size) envelope. For a self-addressed, stamped envelope, fold another #10 envelope in thirds or insert a #9 reply envelope, which fits neatly into a #10 without folding. For larger manuscripts, use a 9 × 12 envelope for mailing and another as a SASE for return of the manuscript. The return SASE may be folded in half. Protect book manuscripts and long scripts by sending them in a typing paper or envelope box. Be sure to include a self-addressed mailing label with appropriate return postage.

When sending out cartoon and illustration samples, your goal is obviously to get them to their destination unscathed. Keep slides, transparencies, photostats, photocopies or photographs in your file at home in case your samples are lost, or you need to make changes on an assignment. Package flat work between Styrofoam or heavy cardboard. Cut the material slightly larger than the piece of artwork and tape it closed. To ensure the return of your artwork, include your business card or a piece of paper with your name and address on it on the outside of the packaging material in case the outer wrapper and inner packaging become separated.

Types of mail service

The two classifications of mail you will be utilizing most as a freelance writer or illustrator are First Class (for letters) and Fourth Class (for packages). While First Class mail receives better handling and is delivered more quickly, there are no guarantees of when your work will arrive with either class.

Certified mail includes a mailing receipt and provides a record of delivery at the deliveree's post office. The charge for this service is $1, in addition to the required postage and $1 charge for a return receipt. With registered mail, a package is signed in and out of every office it passes through, and a receipt is returned to the sender when it reaches its destination. The minimum charge

Roseann Shaughnessy *is editor of* Humor and Cartoon Markets *and* Guide to Literary Agents & Art/Photo Reps.

I.WRIGHT
222 Tudor Street
Toonerville TX 01100
Telephone: 111-555-1234

June 20, 1988
Mr. Rod Rambeau, Editor
Courage Magazine
999½ Beacon Way
Boston, MA 02222

Dear Mr. Rambeau:

I am enclosing my short story *The Secret of 'Gator Grandy: America's Unknown Hero*. I feel certain your readers will enjoy reading this story, which although fiction, is based on a legendary character who supposedly lived in the Louisiana swamps and, with his mysterious concoctions, helped save the lives of hundreds of people with yellow fever.

My story runs approximately 7,500 words.

I am a published writer. My mystery novel will soon be brought out by Jones Publishing. I have also published stories in *Valor Times* and *Glory Review*.

I have enclosed a stamped, self-addressed mailer.

I look forward to hearing from you.

Sincerely,

I. Wright

Encl.

This is a cover letter for a short story sent to a magazine. Notice it is brief. Information about the story is mentioned early—within the first paragraph. Publishing credits are mentioned in the third paragraph and the author points out an SASE is enclosed. This and the following sample were taken from the book, **The Writer's Digest Guide to Manuscript Formats,** *copyright © 1987, by Dian Dincin Buchman & Seli Groves, (Writer's Digest Books).*

I. WRIGHT
222 Tudor Street
Toonerville TX 01100
111-555-1234

January 5, 1987
Jones Publishing Co.
888 E. 57th Street
New York, NY 10166

Dear Ms. White:

What if a series of brutal murders were being committed in Paris, Texas, and everyone thought a maniac was responsible, but the real culprit wasn't even human? My book, *The Rueful Murders in the Morgue*, shows how several women were torn apart by the creature until brilliant detective work ended the rampage.

Today's readers have shown they want to read books that combine the classic elements of mystery with the modern techniques available for solving them. My book provides the experience of horror that comes with the realization that terrible murders are being committed. The book also shows how a detective's observations and his scientific expertise solve the mystery.

Readers also appreciate carefully introduced subplots that add different textures to the story. I have included a love story that grows out of the experiences of two of the characters, and I have also shown how the sailor came into possession of the ape that plays a major role in the way the murders are committed and in the way they are solved.

Enclosed is my proposal, along with three chapters of the book, and synopses of these chapters. I have thoroughly researched the material on which my book is based, including the actual case, which occurred in Paris, France, in 1832. I have studied both the psychology of humans facing the terrors of the unknown and the behavior of primates in a frightening environment.

The book will run 250 pages and can be ready for submission one year from contract.

Also enclosed: A post card on which I would appreciate your noting that you received this material, as well as a stamped, addressed envelope in which this material can be returned to me if necessary.

I look forward to hearing from you.

Sincerely,

I. Wright

Encl.

This is a cover letter accompanying a book proposal. The first paragraph is like a story lead. It pulls the reader (the editor) into the story immediately. Paragraph four includes details on research. This is where qualifications and experience might be mentioned. Notice the letter includes much information about the story, but is confined to one page.

for this service is $4.40 in addition to postage. If you choose to insure the package, the cost begins at $4.50.

United Parcel Service may be somewhat cheaper than First Class postage if you drop the package off at UPS yourself. Your cover letter must be mailed separately since UPS cannot legally carry First Class mail. Rates vary depending upon the package's weight and the distance of its destination.

If your work must be at its destination by a certain time, you may want to consider utilizing Priority Mail, Express Mail Next Day Service or Special Delivery, all available through the post office. Another option is to utilize a freight service, the most familiar one being Federal Express.

Copyright

In order to protect your creative works, you must be familiar with the copyright law. Copyright protects the *expression* of an idea, not the idea itself. It provides its owner the exclusive rights to reproduce, sell, distribute, display and publish his work.

What can you copyright?

You can copyright any work that has sprung from your creative efforts and is fixed on paper or any other tangible medium such as canvas or even in computer memory. Reproductions are copyrightable under the category of compilations and derivative works.

What can't be copyrighted?

Ideas are not copyrightable. To protect an idea, you must use nondisclosure agreements or apply for a patent. Copyright protects the form but not the mechanical aspects of utilitarian objects.

How do you get copyright protection?

Your work is automatically protected from the date of completion until the date of publication. When your work is published, you should protect it by placing a copyright notice on it.

What is a copyright notice?

A copyright notice consists of the word "Copyright" or its symbol ©, the year of first publication and the full name of the copyright owner. It must be placed where it can easily be seen, preferably on the first page or front of your work. You can place it on the back of an illustration as long as it won't be covered by a backing or frame. Always place your copyright notice on slides or photographs sent to potential clients or studios. Affix it on the mounts of slides and on the backs of photographs (preferably on a label).

If you omit the notice, the work may still be copyrighted if you have registered it before publication and you make a reasonable effort to add the notice to all copies. If you've omitted the notice from a work that will be published, you can ask in your contract that the notice be placed on all copies.

When is a work "published?"

Publication occurs when a work is displayed publicly or made available to public view. Your work is "published" when it is exhibited, or reproduced in a magazine, on a poster or on your promotional pieces.

How long does copyright protection last?

Once registered, copyright protection lasts for the life of the creator plus 50 years. For works created by two or more people, protection lasts for the life of the last survivor plus 50 years. For works created anonymously or under a pseudonym, protection lasts for 100 years after the work is created or 75 years after publication, whichever is shorter.

How do I register work?

Write to the Copyright Office, Library of Congress, Information and Publications, Section LM-455, Washington DC 20559 for information, forms and circulars. You may call the Copyright Office information number (202)479-0700 if you need assistance after receiving the forms. Return the completed form to the Copyright Office with a check or money order for the required amount, a deposit copy or copies of the work and a cover letter explaining your request. For almost all artistic works, deposits consist of photographs, either transparencies (35mm or $2\frac{1}{4} \times 2\frac{1}{4}$) or prints (preferably 8×10). For unpublished works, send one copy; send two copies for published works. You will receive a certificate of registration which offers you more indepth protection than the copyright notice can.

Do I have to register my work?

You can register either before or after publication. The only time you must register your work is when you are planning to sue for infringement. However, it is always better to be protected from the start. You will not be entitled to attorney's fees or statutory damages if the infringement occurs before the date of registration (unless, in the case of the published work, registration is made within three months after publication).

What is a transfer of copyright?

Ownership of all or some of your exclusive rights can be transferred by selling, donating or trading them and signing a document as evidence that the transfer has taken place. When you sign an agreement with a magazine for one-time use of a work, you are transferring part of your copyright to the magazine. The transfer is called a license. An exclusive license is a transfer that's usually limited by time, place or form of reproduction, such as first North American serial rights. A nonexclusive license gives several people the right to reproduce your work for specific purposes for a limited amount of time. For example, you can grant a nonexclusive license for your hippopotamus design, originally reproduced on a greeting card, to a manufacturer of plush toys, to an art publisher for posters of the hippopotamus, or to a manufacturer of novelty items for a hippopotamus eraser.

What constitutes infringement?

Anyone who copies a protected work owned by someone else or exercises an exclusive right without authorization is liable for infringement. In an infringement case, you can sue for an injunction, which means you can stop the infringer from reproducing your work; for damages (you must prove how much money you've lost); and to prevent distribution of the infringing material.

Contracts

In simplest terms, a contract is an agreement by which two parties bind themselves to perform certain obligations. Contracts may be written, oral or tacit, but to protect yourself from misunderstandings and faulty memories, make it a practice to have a written contract signed and dated by you and the party you are dealing with.

The items you want specified in your contract will vary according to the assignment and the complexity of the project, but some basic points are: your fee (the basic fee, possibly a kill fee, payment schedule, advances, expense compensation, etc.); what service you are providing for the fee; rights; deadlines; how revisions will be handled; and return of work or original art.

Read carefully any contract or purchase order you are asked to sign. If the terms are complex, or if you do not understand them, seek professional advice before signing. If it is a preprinted or "standard" contract, look for terms which may not be agreeable to you. Because of a 1989 Supreme Court decision, "work for hire" is not as ominous as it once was—when it meant losing all rights to the work created. Now a freelance artist working at someone else's direction will still own rights to the work unless the type of work fits into the law's enumerated categories and the artist agrees in writing to transfer those rights.

Further information for artists on contracts is available in *Business and Legal Forms for Illustrators*, *Business and Legal Forms for Graphic Designers* and *Legal Guide for the Visual Artist*, all by Tad Crawford; *The Artist's Friendly Legal Guide*; *Graphic Artists Guild Handbook of Pricing and Ethical Guidelines*; and *Contracts for Artists*, by William Gignilliat. For writers, see *The Writer's Essential Desk Reference* and *A Writer's Guide to Contract Negotiation* (both published by Writer's Digest Books).

Keeping records

In order to gauge your personal profit and substantiate your income and expenses to the IRS, you must keep accurate records of your business transactions. Be sure to save all invoices, cash receipts, sales slips, bank statements, and cancelled checks plus receipts related to travel and entertainment expenses. You will want to maintain a separate bank account and ledger apart from your personal finances.

You will need to establish an accounting period, which determines the time frame you will use to report income and claim deductions. The easiest route is to elect a calendar year accounting period, beginning January 1 and ending December 31. An accounting period other than a calendar year is known as a fiscal year.

Having selected your accounting period, you will need to determine which accounting method best suits your business. Your accounting method will determine what income and expenses will be reported during a particular accounting period.

There are two basic accounting methods, the cash method and the accrual method. The cash method, used more frequently, records income when it is received or when a gallery or agent receives it for you. Similarly, expenses are recorded when you pay them. Expenses paid in advance can only be deducted in the year in which they occur. This method typically uses cash receipts and disbursement journals, which record payment when received and monthly paid expenses.

The accrual method is more complicated. In this method, income is reported at the time you earn it rather than when you receive it. Also, you deduct expenses at the time you incur them rather than when you pay them. If you use this method, which lists projects as they are invoiced or expenses as they are incurred, you will probably keep accounts receivable and accounts payable journals. The accrual method is best for artists with huge inventories.

You may choose any accounting method you wish, but once you've made the decision, you may only change your accounting method with the approval of the IRS. To request a change of accounting method, you must file Form 3115, Application for Change in Accounting Method, with the Commissioner of the Internal Revenue Service in Washington DC not more than six months after the beginning of the year in which you wish to make a change.

Here are a few tips for establishing an effective recordkeeping system. The first thing you should do is divide your income and expense records into separate headings. Then you should divide each into various subheadings. A handy method is to label your records with the same categories listed on Schedule C of the tax form. That way you'll be able to transfer figures from your books to the tax form without much hassle. Always make an effort to keep your files in chronological order.

There are various bookkeeping systems at your disposal. A single-entry bookkeeping system records expenses as they are incurred; you add them up at the end of the year. This can be recorded in a journal or diary. A double-entry system is more complicated, involving ledgers and journals in which every item is entered twice—once as a debit and once as a credit—so the books are always in balance.

Taxes

Before you know what income you should report and deductions you can claim, you must prove to the IRS that you are in business to make a profit, that your writing or illustrations are not merely a hobby. Under the Tax Reform Act of 1986 it was determined that you should show a profit for three years out of a five-year period to attain professional status. What does the IRS look for as proof of your professionalism? Keeping accurate financial records (see previous section on business records), maintaining a business bank account separate from your personal account, the time you devote to your profession and whether it is your main or secondary source of income, and your history of profits and losses. All are considered. The amount of training you have invested in your field is also a contributing factor to your professional status, as well as your expertise in the field.

If your business is unincorporated, you will fill out tax information on Schedule C of Form 1040. If you're unsure of what deductions you can take, request the appropriate IRS publication containing this information. Under the Tax Reform Act, only 80 percent (formerly it was 100 percent) of business meals, entertainment and related tips and parking charges are deductible. Other deductibles allowed on Schedule C include: capital expenditures (such as a computer), car expenses for business-related trips, professional courses and seminars, depreciation of office equipment, dues and publications and miscellaneous expenses, such as postage used for business needs, etc.

If you're working out of a home office, a portion of your mortgage (or rent), related utilities, property taxes, repair costs and depreciation can be deducted as business expenses. To qualify, though, your office must be used only for business activities. It can't double as a family room during nonbusiness hours. To determine what portion of your home expenses can be taken, simply divide the square footage of your business area into the total square footage of your house. You will want to keep a log of what business activities occur each day; the IRS may want to see records to substantiate your home office deduction. For more information on home office deductions, consult Publication 587 (Business Use of Your Home) from the IRS.

The method of paying taxes on income not subject to withholding is your "estimated tax." If you expect to owe more than $500 at year's end and if the total amount of income tax that will be withheld during the year will be less than 90% of the tax shown on the previous year's return, you will generally make estimated tax payments. Estimated tax payments are made in four equal installments due on April 15, June 15, September 15 and January 15. For more information, request Publication 505, Self-Employment Tax.

Depending on your net income you may be liable for a Social Security tax. This is a tax designed for those who don't have Social Security withheld from their paychecks. You're liable if your net income is $400 or more per year. Net income is the difference between your income and allowable business deductions. Request Schedule SE, Computation of Social Security Self-Employment Tax, if you qualify.

If completing your income tax return proves to be a complex affair, call the IRS for assistance. In addition to walk-in centers, the IRS has various publications to instruct you in the facets of preparing a tax return.

The Art Of Self-Promotion: Strategies for the Cartoonist and Humorous Illustrator

by Bob Staake

Muhammad Ali could have been a great freelancer.

It's not that Ali was particularly good at creating laugh-inducing cartoons or awe-inspiring humorous illustrations, but he did have a talent for self-congratulatory *braggadocio*. The only thing bigger than the boxer's bravado was his right cross, and when Ali declared "I am the GREATEST," he almost always backed up such lofty, if not arrogant, statements with actions. Indeed, Muhammad Ali was great at *self-promotion*.

And while few successful freelancers have needed to use their fists to get work, almost all understand the critical importance of self-promotion. The only way to ensure that work is being seen by art directors, creative directors, editors and art buyers is by *putting it out there*.

"Self-promotion" can best be described as a freelancer's all-inclusive marketing *strategy*. The flow chart illustrates the specific elements which constitute self-promotion

Direct mail

Perhaps the most effective element of any self-promotional marketing strategy is the direct mail approach. This is because the freelancer can target specific individuals (magazine art directors, for example) to familiarize them with his art. And because direct mail self-promotion is relatively inexpensive and potentially very successful, more and more freelancers are utilizing their mailboxes to market their work. Given this fact, freelancers must constantly ensure that *their* self-promotional missives stand out amidst a sea of mail.

A freelancer can do many things to make sure an art director looks at his work, from filling envelopes with cleverly written cover letters and oversized color posters, to stuffing in animated flip books or sending pop-up postcards (would *you* toss a flip book into the trash?).

While gimmicks can snag the attention of even the most jaded art buyer and attest to your cleverness, there is no substitute for a self-promotional direct mail package that's filled with truly great samples of your work.

Printed samples of work

Essentially, any printed material bearing examples of your cartoon or humorous illustration work can be described as a "self-promotional piece" (a "promo-piece," for short).

This flow chart shows the essential elements of a freelancer's self-promotion campaign.

A typical black and white promo piece will measure 8½ × 11 and will include anywhere from 4 to 7 printed samples of your work. A typical color promo piece will measure 9 × 12 and will include the same number of samples. It goes without saying that *all* promo pieces should include your name, address and phone number if you *ever* expect to snag an assignment.

The price of printing 2,500 quality, 8½ × 11 black and white promo pieces will vary slightly from printer to printer, and you should expect to pay anywhere from $140 to $200 (this does not include typesetting, stats, PMTs or halftone work).

Most freelancers who are just getting started, incorrectly assume that publishing a *color* promo piece will be too expensive to even consider. This simply isn't so. If you don't mind waiting up to three months to receive your color promo pieces from a Southern California-based print broker, Serbin Communications (804)963-0439 will supply you with 2,500 9 × 12 color promo pieces for the amazing price of $680 (that's no typo, and that includes 6-color separations).

These days, postcards (black and white or color) seem to be the hottest self-promotional medium. The reason is simple: they're extremely inexpensive to print and mail, and they don't require being folded and stuffed into envelopes (just think of all the saliva you save). To qualify for the 19¢ postal rate, a postcard must be no smaller than 3½ × 5 and no larger than 4¼ × 6, which means you can print four different 4¼ × 6 postcards on a 9 × 12 sheet of card stock (2,500 black and white cards would cost you approximately $70, and 2,500 color cards (through Serbin) would set you back $1,000). Simple arithmetic tells you that it will cost $95 to mail 500 of these self-promotional postcards. However, many freelancers feel that a small postcard doesn't do justice to their work. If you agree, you may want to consider printing a large format postcard. In this case, you can get two 5½ × 8½ black and white postcards from a standard sheet of 8½ × 11 card stock, and two 6 × 9 color postcards (using Serbin) from a sheet of 9 × 12 card stock. Cost would therefore be approximately $125 for 2,500 black and white postcards or $1,075 for 5,000 color postcards (2,500 of each postcard design). These large format postcards cost 29¢ each to mail, so sending 500 of them will cost $145.

Of course this article cannot discuss every printing option (large format posters, 12-month calendars, specially die-cut configurations, etc.) but a freelancer can get as fancy as he wants when printing self-promotional pieces — you're only limited by your imagination and budget.

Printed letterhead, envelopes, business cards, etc.

A potential client forms an immediate opinion of you and your work as soon as your envelope crosses his desk. You are, after all, a *business* and you should present yourself as such. Therefore, if your envelope is imprinted with your name and address next to your snazzy logo, you instantly project *professionalism*. You can project the same professionalism with printed, gummed labels for oversized envelopes.

As long as we've got the presses rolling, let's print up some stationery, business cards, a client list, a resume/bio and 2-part invoices. These printed support materials reinforce your promo pieces. See the sidebar for what you can expect to spend.

Large format black and white postcard. 5½ × 8½ on coated card stock. Self-promo for Ron Coddington.

One-color letter envelope. Black ink on yellow stock. 4¼ × 9½. Self-promo for Oliver Christianson (aka Revilo).

One-color business card. 2 × 3½. Self-promo for Andre Noel.

Small format black and white postcard. 4¼ × 6 on uncoated card stock. Self-promo for Jeff Shelly.

JARED D. LEE STUDIO, INC.
2942 Hamilton Road/Lebanon, Ohio 45036

Two-color, pregummed mailing label. 4½ × 3½. Self-promo for Jared Lee.

Print Support Materials for Freelancers

(Unless indicated, all printing quotes are for black ink on white bond)

Item	Size	Units	Costs
Stationery	8½×11	1,000	$ 35
Business Card	2×3½	*1,000	$ 30
#10 Envelopes	4×9½	1,000	$ 50
Envelope Labels	4¼×5½	1,000	$ 50
Client List	5½×8½	1,000	$ 22
Resume/Bio	5½×8½	1,000	$ 22
2-Part Invoices	8½×11	1,000	$135
		Total: (A)	**$344**

Printed Samples of Work			
Color Promo Piece	9×12	*2,500	$680
B&W Promo Piece	8½×11	*2,500	$170
		Total: (B)	**$850**

GRAND TOTAL of Lines A and B $1,194

* indicates coated paper
(NOTE: Above prices are only approximated. Prices do not include typesetting, PMTs, stats, camera costs, etc.

Sending out your message

Now that your promo pieces, support materials and stationery have been printed, you'll want to draft a cover letter to go along with your promotional package. While it is by no means a mandatory component of a self-promotional package, enclosing a well-written, cover letter is a professional way to acquaint a client with your work—especially if this is the first time you are contacting the client.

A good cover letter is a substitute for a warm handshake (gee, that sounds like a Hallmark card), and you should keep the tone of the letter informative, but on the light side. Unfortunately, I have read many cartoonists' and humorous illustrators' cover letters that attempt to induce laughter, but instead generate painful groans. While you may be able to *draw* funny, you may not be able to *write* funny. If you find yourself tripping over your forced, marginally-pithy allusions and hackneyed segues, you may want to get back to the original intent of your cover letter—to introduce yourself and your work to a potential buyer. See the sample of the succinct, conversational cover letter that I send to art directors at advertising agencies.

Because I work on a word processor, I don't have to send generic cover

January 4, 1993

Mr. Scott Kidman
Art Director
Edge Advertising
11326 Pier Avenue
Santa Monica, California 90255

Dear Mr. Kidman:

Enclosed please find a few samples of my cartoons and humorous illustration.

While I do a considerable amount of work for editorial, packaging and publishing clients, my first love is advertising. Simply put, it's what I'm best at.

I work fast, conceptualize well, meet deadlines and floss after meals (and isn't that what people look for in a cartoonist these days?).

Over the years I have created work for major advertising agencies and such diverse clients as MGM, Anheuser-Busch, Ralston Purina, Mattel, Turner Broadcasting System, Paramount Pictures, Coors, National Football League, Southwestern Bell, Dewar's Scotch, Hallmark Cards, Sunkist, HBO, Volkswagen, Jose Cuervo, Tyson Chicken, Everready Batteries, AT&T, Warner Brothers and countless others.

But what I'd really like is to work for **you**.

To that end, please keep me in mind when you have a project that requires my special brand of humorous illustration.

Hope to hear from you soon!

Best,

Bob Staake

cc:
BS/pf

letters to potential clients. While the above cover letter states that my "first love" is advertising, I have other letters in my system that make the same claim about greeting cards, magazines, books, etc. (so I'm a *loving* king of guy!). Therefore when I send a cover letter to an art director at a greeting card company, I am able to make specific references to my greeting card/paper product clients.

Time does not allow me to generate hundreds of "personal" letters like the sample as part of a mass self-promotional campaign. Yet when I come across a client who I feel will be responsive to my work, I do crunch out one of these "original" cover letters to include with a large self-promotional package. Nevertheless, when it comes to a *mass* self-promotional mailing (in the hundreds or thousands), you certainly could *print* a generic cover letter to accompany your samples.

Formulating a mailing list of potential clients

Happily, you hold in your hands the beginnings of one terrific mailing list. Within the pages of *Humor and Cartoon Markets* you'll find over 600 potential buyers of your work. Better yet, the detailed listings will help you eliminate inappropriate markets and discover markets best suited to you.

Once you've selected perhaps 300 potential markets from the book, you'll save yourself hours of work by inputting the names and addresses into your computer or word processor and creating a simple database from which to generate mailing labels. Even if you don't own a word processor or computer, you can manually type names and addresses onto easy-to-use 8½ × 11 Avery label guides. Once you've typed out your addresses, simply take the guides to your local copy center where the list can be copied directly onto pre-cut, gummed Avery label sheets. The only thing left to do is peel off the labels and stick them onto your envelopes, mailers or postcards.

While it's considerably easier to update a database, you can amend Avery label guides by simply pasting up a new address over an old one without re-typing an entirely new guide sheet.

There are many ways to assemble a mailing list. If you're interested in doing humorous illustration work (editorial) for magazines, you're best served by going to your local library or bookstore to look at publications that you feel will be receptive to your particular brand of work. Magazines have mast heads so it's a relatively simple process to find out who the art director is. But if you're interested in doing work for greeting card companies and decide to spend a few hours researching in an *independent* greeting card shop, it's likely you'll only walk away with a few addresses. It then becomes a time-consuming process of tracking down the company's phone number in hopes that you'll be able to pry an art director's name out of a receptionist's tight lips.

However, if you do a little homework, you'll find a trade organization or publication that specifically covers the area you're interested in. For example, *Greetings Magazine* publishes an annual directory that lists approximately 80 percent of all U.S.-based greeting card publishers. If you poke your nose around, you'll find similar directories covering advertising agencies, newspaper syndicates, book publishers, animation houses, design studios, etc. Unfortunately, some of these directories can be incomplete and contain old (or incorrect) information, and I have yet to find one that lists art directors and other "plebians" by name. Again, to find out the name of an actual art director, you'll almost certainly have to call the company directly.

Sendin 'em out and waiting for work

Today's the big day. You've gathered up all the neighborhood kids and they're stuffing promo pieces into envelopes at 25¢ an hour. You've even been able to persuade your dog to lick the envelopes. When everything's done, you'll take your envelopes down to the post office, kiss 'em goodbye and hope the phone rings.

Well, it's been a week, and nothing. You've even called the phone company and had them check your line. Don't panic (yet). *Any* self-promotional activity must be viewed over the long term. At best, you'll nab two or three assignments that will essentially pay for the self-promotion itself. But more importantly, you're putting into motion the self-promotional machinery. If your *first* self-promotion doesn't result in a call from an art director, perhaps your *second* self-promotion will. And if that one doesn't, maybe your *third* self-promotional missive will cross the art director's desk at the moment he's making art assignments. Timing, after all, is everything.

When it comes to self-promotion, I like to make an analogy to Midas Muffler. You may not be in the need for a muffler *today*, but if you're in the market for one *tomorrow*, the name "Midas Muffler" will probably pop into your head. A freelancer's self-promotional strategy can work the same way. An art director may have no need for your work today, but tomorrow may be another story. Yet the only way to help the art director remember you at the proper time is to consistently remind him that you're out there. Indeed, a freelancer and Midas Muffler must do the same thing: They must self-promote on a fairly regular, long-term basis if they are to spark a memory at the critical time.

What constitutes "regular" self-promotion?

You'll get a lot of different answers to that question. Some freelancers send a new self-promotion out every three months to 2,000 potential clients, while others send one a year to 250 "prime" clients. I also know illustrators who send monthly color tearsheets of past jobs to 25 to 50 of their "core" clients.

The kind of freelance work you want to go after should greatly determine the frequency and content of your self-promotions. If, for example, you are going after advertising work, you may want to do a yearly mailing of self-promotional materials to a couple thousand agency art directors (this would *augment* your illustration directory advertising—see page 35). But if you're interested in doing work in a specialized area (let's say humorous character design for animation), you will probably want to send out three or four different self-promotions per year because the animation market is considerably smaller than the advertising market.

If you can't afford to send out 2,000 promo pieces at a time, you may want to develop a "staggered," alphabetical self-promotional plan. There's really nothing mystical about such a plan. Simply divide the year into four quarters and send out 500 promo pieces in January (A-G), April (H-N), July (O-T) and October (U-Z). However, if you assemble a mailing list of 2,000 potential clients in January, you have to make sure that those addresses are still correct by the time July or October rolls around. Of course you can always use the phone to verify and correct your listings, but that's an expensive, time-consuming proposition. By assembling quarterly lists immediately *prior* to your quarterly mailings, you can better ensure their accuracy.

Portfolio

After seeing your promo pieces, a client may call and ask to "see your book." No, it's not your diary he's after, he merely wants to examine your portfolio. When a client requests your book, it usually means that he's considering you for a project and he wants to get a better look at your work. If he likes your book, he'll probably give you the job, so you can see just how important your portfolio is.

Simply speaking, your portfolio should be a professional presentation of anywhere from 10 to 25 *printed* examples of your work. Under no circumstances should your portfolio contain original artwork. While tearsheets of published work are ideal, your portfolio can also include Cibachromes(™), color photographic prints, and you can even get away with quality color photocopies. Most freelancers keep at least two different portfolios on hand—one that shows more examples of their advertising work and one that shows more of their editorial work. It's worth checking with the client who requests your portfolio to see if he will be responsible for the cost of shipping it. In most cases, this would mean that you overnight the portfolio to him via Federal Express under his account number. He would then also be responsible for the cost of returning the portfolio to you.

Advertising

After consistent direct mail successes and increased freelance assignments, you may be ready for the next level of self-promotion—advertising your work.

Unfortunately, I have seen too many freelance humorous illustrators and cartoonists prematurely advertise in the expensive, highly sophisticated illustration directories such as *American Showcase*, *Creative Illustration* and *The Workbook*. Before sinking your hard-earned cash into one of these national directories, you have to be *ready* to make that leap; thankfully, the high cost of advertising in these directories helps dissuade freelancers who aren't.

To determine if you're ready to advertise in a national illustration directory, ask yourself these questions:

1. Is my work as polished, professional and sophisticated as the work I see in these illustration directories?

2. If a top art director came across my ad in an illustration directory, would he hire me over another humorous illustrator in the book?

3. Did I make over $16,000 last year from my freelance illustration? If I did, am I prepared to spend over 25% of that money on a single advertisement?

Granted, these are very tough questions to answer. If you answered "yes" to all three, then you're as ready as you'll ever be for the illustration directories. But if you answered "no" to two of the questions, you really have to reevaluate your tugging desire to place an ad in an illustration directory. And just because you're not ready to advertise this year doesn't mean you won't be ready next year. As your work matures and becomes more sophisticated, you will be able to justify this expensive, risky next step in self-promotion.

Self-promotion via an illustration directory

An illustration directory is really a visual "Yellow Pages" for an art director. Generally speaking, all of the top illustration directories contain hundreds of ads promotiong everyone from airbrush artists to sculptors, medical illustrators to cartoonists. With few exceptions, an illustrator buys a page on which to advertise his particular style. This ad may be comprised of a single large color illustration or as many as 10 different color illustrations.

When working on a project that requires a special illustrator or graphic style, an art director will refer to these directories to find an appropriate illustrator for the project. Each year new volumes of the directories are sent to tens of thousands of art directors, creative directors, design studios, publication designers and other art buyers primarily in North America, although some directories boast circulation in Europe, Asia, etc. And while the circulation of such books is extremely high and protracted, many illustrators disdainfully report that the directories do not live up to their glowing hype. With a mean price of $2,762.50 per page of color advertising (not including color separations and/or filmwork), ads in illustration directories aren't for every freelance illustrator. However, the illustrator is provided with anywhere from 2,000 to 2,500 free color reprints of his ad that can then be used with his direct mail self-promotional efforts.

Before committing to any illustration directory, pick up the most recent volume. Select three to five humorous illustrators and give them a call. Explain that you're considering advertising in a directory, and you want to know if they have been pleased so far with the response to their ad. You may be surprised to learn that some of these illustrators *have yet to receive a single assignment as a result of running their ad*! Indeed, illustration directory advertising is by no means a guarantee of success for the freelancer.

Advertising via trade publications

Occasionally, a freelance humorous illustrator or cartoonist can benefit from a properly placed ad in a trade magazine that has a strong circulation to art directors, creative directors and other art buyers. If you scan the pages of such publications as *Art Direction, Adweek* or *Advertising Age*, you may come across a small classified or display ad promoting someone's freelance abilities. The price of these ads can be as little as $1,325 and as high as $4,200.

While there is potential in this form of advertising, the success of it seems dependent on an art buyer literally *stumbling* upon the ad itself. And if the ad piques someone's attention, then the next logical step would see the freelancer sending a promo package off to the interested art buyer who would then keep the materials on file. The problem, of course, is that the ad is flashed in front of the art buyer's eyes at a time when he's leafing through a magazine, and not necessarily in the mind-set of making art assignments.

If a freelancer *must* test the trades, certain times are better than others. Most trade magazines know well in advance what special issues they'll be publishing in the coming year. Therefore, if a freelance illustrator wants to buy a trade ad, he should do it when the publication has a special *illustration* issue, not when they come out with that stellar *photography* issue.

High profile assignments

With every illustration assignment comes a certain degree of "exposure," which essentially acts as free advertising for the freelancer. A savvy freelancer is aware of who potentially will see the work he is assigned to produce and will thereby seize the promotional benefit(s) of the assignment. For example, freelancers who specialize in creating illustration for advertising will gladly accept editorial assignments not for the relatively small money they bring, but for the high exposure they provide. Exploiting this situation ensures that the advertising illustrator remains "visible."

Editorially, the adage works the same way. Even if you are able to snag an illustration assignment with a moderate-size trade magazine, there's a reasonably good chance that an art director somewhere else will see your illustration. Increase the circulation numbers of the magazine and you increase the number of art directors who will see your illustration. Things *really* take off when (make that *if*) you're lucky enough to snatch some illustration assignments at the big consumer magazines. At that point, your illustration in *Rolling Stone* could net *Esquire* which in turn cound snag *TIME*. Just ask Elwood Smith, Robert Risko or Steven Guarnaccia.

It then stands to reason that when creating high profile art, the freelancer must be cognizant that people are looking at it. Needless to say, the same people see the good *and* bad illustrations. The only difference is that they don't *call* when they see bad stuff. Never forgetting that fact will keep your work on its best promotional behavior. After all, *Big Art Director Is Watching You*!

Calls for entry

Once you hit your stride and begin to consistently produce solid humorous illustration or cartoon work, you may want to respond to the "Calls for Entry" put out by various design publications.

Each year, magazines such as *Print*, *Communication Arts*, *Graphis*, *How* and *Art Direction* publish special editions which exhibit state-of-the-art illustration, photography and design. To compile these voluminous editions, the magazines solicit tearsheets from thousands of illustrators, photographers and designers by sending them a "Call for Entry."

The Call for Entry is nothing more than a flyer that informs the recipient of the eligibility requirements for submitted illustrations (usually they must have been published within the previous year), the deadline date for submissions and the entry fees.

Not only does it cost *you* to respond to Call for Entry, submitting work (along with your check) is by no means a guarantee that your illustration(s) will be published in the design annual. And because entry fees seem to be going up each year, responding to all the Calls can be an expensive endeavor. Understand that the design annuals receive thousands of highly sophisticated submissions from the top freelancers in the business. Before wrapping up your tearsheets and signing that check, study the various design annuals to determine how realistic your chances of making the cut really are.

To ensure that you receive the regular Calls, your should write to each publication and ask that you be put on its Call for Entry list.

The self-promotional value of being in the annuals should be obvious. These annuals are anxiously awaited for (especially *Print's Regional Design Annual*) by art directors, creative directors and other art buyers. Under ideal conditions, a freelancer's *consistent*, year after year exposure in the annuals can result in a number of assignments. However, it's wise not to count on that. Instead, a freelancer should accept inclusion in a design directory as a single success in his cumulative self-promotional plan.

Print, TV and radio interviews

For some odd reason, the media (and the general public) seem fascinated with artists—particularly cartoonists. Given this fact, a freelancer will occasionally be called upon to impart a few words into an interviewer's spongy microphone. Excited beyond his wildest dreams, the freelancer predicts that being interviewed in the local paper, during a drive-time radio show or on the evening news will result in a flood of business. Wrong.

Having been interviewed by magazines ranging from *People* to *TIME*, booked as a guest on such shows as *Good Morning America* and *Sally Jessy Raphael*, and wired for live radio call-in shows from Bangor to San Diego, I can tell you from personal experience that such media interviews do not result in illustration assignments. I have never received a *single* job as a result of my being interviewed. At best, these fleeting interviews "legitimatize" you and your work, but do little beyond that.

I touch on this subject because I have seen a number of young, green freelancers come to my studio and explain their grand plan of "getting publicity." Many will pull out an interview they gave to the local weekly shopper, and assure me that the interview should "bring in lots of work" for them. When it doesn't, they can't seem to figure out why.

The only time I *have* snagged work as a result of a media interview was when the interview was published in a trade magazine. For example, a recent interview in *HOW* resulted in a surprising amount of phone calls and even three assignments. However, this is very unusual.

Instead of devoting excessive amounts of time and energy sending press releases and PR kits to media sources, a freelancer is more apt to grab illustration assignments if he directs his hyperbole-laden mail to those who *pay* illustrators rather than those who merely *interview* them.

Agents/representatives

Once a humorous illustrator or cartoonist has established himself as a marketable freelance talent, he may contract with an agent or representative to promote his work. Ideally, an agent handles the bulk of promoting an illustrator so that the artist has more time to illustrate.

The illustrator/agent relationship works this way: The illustrator is represented by an agent usually within a predetermined geographical territory for a certain duration of time (usually one year). The agent is then largely responsible for promoting the illustrator and subsequently securing work for him within the agent's geographical territory. The agent or representative then receives a 25 to 30 percent commission from the gross fee paid to the illustrator.

While an illustrator may *want* to acquire an agent, it doesn't mean that he's ready to be represented by one. Freelance illustration is a highly sophisticated, money-motivated business, and an agent has no interest in representing unpolished, unprofessional or *unsaleable* illustrators. Better yet, it doesn't make economic sense for an agent to handle an illustrator who is only able to command a couple hundred dollars for a magazine illustration.

For those humorous illustrators and cartoonists who *are* credible candidates for representation, potential agents can be found. Writer's Digest Books publishes *Guide to Literary Agents & Art/Photo Reps*, which provides detailed listings on various artist representatives. Another way to find an appropriate agent for humorous illustration, cartooning or for that matter *any* graphic medium, is by referring to the illustration directories. Over 50 percent of the directory ads are placed by agents. By looking at the ads, you *see* what kind of illustrators the various agents represent and get a better sense of whether or not they would be interested in the possibility of representing you. For example, an agent who represents predominantly serious illustrators and realistic artists would probably agree to represent a *chimney sweep* before agreeing to represent a cartoonist, so don't waste postage by sending them samples of your work.

Important Marketing Listing Information

- *A word about style: This book is edited (except for quoted material) in the masculine gender because we think "he/she," "he or she," "him or her" in copy is distracting. We bow to tradition for the sake of readability.*
- *Listings are based on questionnaires, phone calls and verified copy. They are not advertisements nor are markets reported here necessarily endorsed by the editor of this book.*
- *Information in the listings comes directly from the company and is as accurate as possible, but companies and staff come and go, and needs fluctuate between the publication of this directory and the time you use it.*
- **Humor and Cartoon Markets** *reserves the right to exclude any listing that does not meet its requirements.*

The Markets

Advertising /Public Relations

If you don't believe that anything can happen, simply look at advertising. Cars fly; soap sings; cheeseburgers dance and even donuts march.

Yes, advertising is pretty bizarre. This is a business where grown adults sit in rooms thinking of ways to give sex appeal to laundry detergent, friendly personalities to tubes of zit cream, and even facial expressions to pepperoni pizzas. Conjure up those ideas *outside* of an ad agency, and you may be institutionalized!

Yet for all its faults, freelancers still want to get into the wacky world of advertising. A chief reason, of course, is money. When you understand that advertising pays 10, 15 even 20 times more than editorial work, the attraction is obvious — and extremely compelling.

While a major portion of an advertising campaign's budget is used to buy print space or TV time on which to air the message, the message itself must first be created. It is at this primal stage that the freelancer is brought in.

In advertising everything has its price, from the $2,000 cost of having a freelance copywriter crunch out some boastful words about the glory of oat bran, to the $8,000 it takes to have a humorous illustrator render a group of teens gleefully chug-a-lugging sugar-laden soda. When you toss around these obscene figures, it's not surprising why many freelancers are attracted to the mega-money advertising profession.

However, it is important to note that at this writing, advertising continues to suffer a tremendous hit from the economic recession. Big and small ad shops have collapsed like dominoes, and clients have drastically scaled down their advertising expenditures. The "trickle down" effect has been widespread. Because agencies place fewer advertisements, layoffs have become common in the advertising *and* editorial departments of radio and TV stations, newspapers, magazines and larger trade publications.

Freelancers who work primarily in advertising have felt the tightening pinch of the current recession as well. Many freelance photographers, illustrators and writers have seen their billings drop as much as 50 percent this past year. Hardly a week goes by that I don't receive at least one phone call from a panicky freelancer looking for advice in weathering this relentless recession.

After he finishes crying on my shoulder, I usually advise him to kick his "advertising jones." When advertising prospers, it can be very good for the freelancer, but when advertising goes through its inevitable dry periods, it can wreak havoc on a freelancer's very business survival. If a recession teaches anything, it is that the freelancer should not *depend* on advertising. If he becomes better diversified (working in magazine editorial and greeting cards and books, for example), he has a stronger chance of braving the slings and arrows of economic chaos within a single industry such as advertising.

The market for the freelance cartoonist and humorous illustrator

A highly-polished, savvy humorous illustrator who draws in a *marketable* style and understands how to promote his work can make a yearly six figure income in advertising. (Did you ever think you could pull in those kind of bucks without a law or medical degree?)

Indeed, successful humorous illustrators in this field are the ones who understand the paramount importance of advertising their work, promoting it, employing agents or representatives to sell it, securing high-profile projects and, of course, developing and nurturing a sophisticated illustration style that the market is receptive to in the first place.

If you're tantalized by the big bucks and want to get into advertising, the direct mail approach should be your first step. In assembling a package of work for an agency art director, it is advisable to send material that he can hang on to. The *last* thing you want is to have this material returned to you. Rather, you should suggest that the art director retain these materials in his files so that when an appropriate project surfaces, he can refer to your work—and subsequently call on you with an assignment. I have even seen humorous illustrators who send actual manila files stuffed with their work. This way a busy art director need only shove the pre-assembled file into his bulging file cabinet.

A professional presentation of cartooning or humorous illustration consists of the following: a color self-promotional piece, a black and white promo page, your client list, business card, resume and cover letter. Under absolutely no circumstances should you send original art, and if you must send printed tearsheets, transparencies or slides, enclose a SASE so they can be returned to you with little hassle for the potential art buyer.

However, don't fool yourself into believing that just because you have sent direct mail promotions to 500 clients the phone will be ringing off the hook. At best you'll get a job, even two, which will essentially cover the cost of the direct mail promotion itself. For more comprehensive information on self-promotion, please refer to the detailed article on page 25.

Repeatedly, the most common misconception among humorous illustrators and cartoonists who do a reasonable amount of work for consumer or trade magazines is that they'll be welcomed with open arms into advertising. Not true! With few exceptions, humorous illustrators and cartoonists who successfully draw for editorial clients aren't necessarily applicable for advertising assignments.

The market for the freelance writer

The writer will also be pleased to learn that when it comes to copy, advertising has a healthy sense of humor. While a humorous illustrator's specialized, graphic style may pigeonhole him and limit the work he can do for a particular agency, writers seem more able to *nurture* ongoing professional relationships with agencies by being able to flex and bend their humor writing style from account to account.

When assembling a promotional package of your work, show a broad range of your writing ability and various applications (ideally, you'd be able to show writing examples for print, TV and radio applications). Keep your presentation clean and professional, and provide the potential buyer (usually the creative director) with tearsheets (or copies), your client list, resume, business card and, of course, a witty yet concise cover letter. You'll either sink or swim with this presentation, so it's important to carefully analyze the message that your package projects.

It seems that most agencies prefer to hire in-town writing talent. Therefore, you should approach local agencies with a simple phone call. Ask the creative director what types of copy he might be interested in seeing and then mail a few fitting examples. You might even get approval from the creative director to fax in those samples. If the creative director likes what he sees, chances are good that you'll be able to wrangle a face-to-face meeting. It's therefore important that you hang on to a couple of extra-special, wonderfully-witty examples of your writing to show when you're sitting across from the creative director.

Usage and rights

Usage and rights negotiated for freelance advertising work are extremely varied. This is where an agent or representative becomes important. One time rights, first time rights, all rights (for which a work-for-hire contract must be signed to legally transfer copyright), per usage fees and, in the case of humorous illustration, the sale of the original artwork, are terms that must be specified at the inception of the project so that neither freelancer nor client is surprised down the road.

If you are a freelance illustrator, I highly suggest you get a copy of the most recent edition of *Handbook of Pricing & Ethical Guidelines* (published by the Graphic Artist's Guild, (212)463-7730). This book will give comprehensive guidelines on rights and usages. For the freelance writer, I suggest you pick up the most recent edition of *Writer's Market* (published by Writer's Digest Books, 1-800-289-0963).

A note on faxing

Thanks to fax technology and fiber optics, it is now much easier for the freelance humorous illustrator or writer in Miami, Ohio to work with the ad agency in Miami, Florida. In fact, agencies *expect* to do business with freelancers who have fax capabilities. Prices for the machines have dropped dramatically (you can pick up one for less than $400), and units now come with special switches so you need not have the phone company install a costly "dedicated" fax line into your work space. If you don't already have a fax machine, get one as soon as possible. And if you can't afford one, find a local copy center with fax capabilities.

*AD AGENCY, 314 E. Curling Dr., Boise ID 83702. (208)344-7770. Estab. 1979. Advertising agency that provides brochures, catalog sheets, yellow page display ads, magazine ads and TV for corporations and law firms. Current clients include Bonner Chasan Walton & Bauer, Smith & Ardussi and The Gellert Co. Needs humorous illustration and cartoons for print.
Illustration: For first contact send b&w promo piece to Ed Gellert, President. Reports back only if interested. Keeps materials on file. Buys all rights. Pay $100 by the project; negotiated with artist. Payment is based on skill of illustrator and ability of illustrator to work well under our art direction.

THE AD WORKS, INC., 4 Gorham Ave., Westport CT 06880. (203)454-2388. FAX: (same, call first). Estab. 1984. Advertising agency that provides print ads, brochures and promotional pieces for hotels, restaurants, retail stores and professionals. Needs humorous illustration and copywriting, caricature and cartoons for print and radio. 20% of freelance humorous illustration is for print ads. Prefers to work with freelancers with fax capabilities.
Illustration: Works with approximately 6 freelance humorous illustrators/month. Looking for freelancers who are "flexible and not 'prima donnas.'" For first contact send cover letter and b&w tearsheets (or photocopies) to Dick Commer, President. Reports back within 1 week. Returns materials if accompanied by a SASE. Keeps materials on file. Negotiates rights purchased. Pays $30-85 by the hour; $100-500 by the project.
Writing: Works with approximately 2 humor-oriented writers/month. Looking for freelancers who are "light" in approach. For first contact send cover letter, client list, tearsheets, writing samples and audiotape to Dick Commer. Reports back within 1 week. Returns materials if accompanied by a SASE. Negotiates rights purchased. Pays $40-60 by the hour; $200-400 by the day; by the project depending on time considerations. *Inside Tips:* "Cartoonists have excellent possibilities for advertising work. The problem is knowing who is available."

 The asterisk before a listing indicates that the listing is new in this edition. New markets are often more receptive to freelance submissions.

ADVANCE ADVERTISING AGENCY & ART STUDIO, Suite 202, 606 E. Belmont, Fresno CA 93701. (209)445-0383. Estab. 1951. Advertising agency and art/design studio that provides direct mail, newsletters, mailing pieces, illustration, flyers, folders, TV production, vocal talent, photography, logo design, cartoons, copywriting, radio shows, commercials and business specialties for retail stores, musical societies, service businesses, clubs, independent merchants, jazz bands, etc. Current clients include Howard Leach Auctions, Fresno Dixieland Society, High Sierra Jazz Club, Mr. G's Carpets, Windshield Repair Service and Club Casino. Uses humorous illustration, cartoons and music-related humorous items. 100% of freelance humorous illustration is for print.
Illustration: Works with approximately 12 freelance humorous illustrators/year. Looking for freelancers who are "priced for our market and clients." For first contact send "appropriate samples of versatility" to Marty Nissen, Production Manager. Reports back only if interested. Returns materials if accompanied by a SASE or keeps materials on file. Negotiates rights purchased. Pays $30 minimum by the hour.
Writing: Looking for freelancers who "fit the needs of particular client or campaign." For first contact send demo cassette. Reports back only if interested and if accompanied by a SASE. Pays $30 minimum by the hour. *Inside Tips:* "Important to keep in mind that markets vary greatly in sophistication, pay scale, usage, etc. What might be considered a 'good buy' in San Francisco may be out of the question in our market. Local union situations may also be a factor."

*THE ALDEN GROUP, 535 Fifth Ave., New York NY 10017. (212)867-6400. FAX: (212)986-5988. Estab. 1956. Advertising agency, PR firm that provides annual reports, collateral, print ads to corporations, banks, department stores, restaurants. Current clients include Gucci Eyewear, Sharp Watches, Bahamas Air and Bounty Resorts. Needs humorous illustration and copywriting, cartoons, animatics, storyboards and slide shows for print, TV, radio, audiovisual, video tape and presentations. 50% of freelance humorous illustration is for print ads. Prefers to work with freelancers who have fax capabilities.
Illustration: For first contact send cover letter, color tearsheets and color promo piece to Jack H. Casper, CEO. Reports back only if interested. Returns materials if accompanied by a SASE or keeps materials on file. Negotiates rights purchased. Payment is based on complexity of project, skill of illustrator, turnaround, business manner and professionalism of illustrator, ability of illustrator to work well under our art direction, client's budget and possibility of a long term agency/illustrator relationship.

AM/PM ADVERTISING, 196 Clinton Ave., Newark NJ 07108. (201)824-8600. FAX: (201)824-6631. Estab. 1962. Advertising agency that provides marketing, advertising, national ads, TV commercials and sales promotion for consumer package goods companies in food, health and beauty aids. Current clients include J & J, Nabisco, Revlon, P & G, American Cyanamid, Carter Wallace, Bristol Myers and Lever Brothers. Needs humorous illustration and copywriting, animation, humor-oriented comprehensives, caricature, animatics, cartoons and storyboards for print, videotape, TV, radio and audiovisual. 50% of freelance humorous illustration is for print ads.
Illustration: Works with approximately 10 freelance humorous illustrators/year. Looking for freelancers "who have the talent to fit the project." For first contact send resume to Robert Saks, President. Reports back within weeks only if interested. Returns materials if accompanied by a SASE. Keeps materials on file. Buys one-time rights. Pays $50-150 by the hour.
Writing: Works with approximately 6 humor-oriented writers/month. Looking for freelance humorous writers "who have the talent to fit the project." For first contact send resume to Robert Saks. Reports back within weeks. Returns materials if accompanied by a SASE. Buys first rights. Pays $50-150 by the hour. *Inside Tips:* "Creative ability is

solving the problem successfully, within budget/time restraints, and following professional instructions/directions."

*ASAP ADVERTISING, P.O. Box 7268, Thousand Oaks CA 91359-7268. (818)707-2727. FAX: (818)707-7040. Estab. 1981. Advertising agency serving business to business advertisers with print ads, collateral materials and marketing strategies for industrial, high tech, business to business and corporations. Current clients include American Nucleonics Corp., Aleph International, Downs Crane & Hoist, Evolutionary Concepts, Inc., The Wilkinson Corp., J.J. Mauget and Quality Concepts, Inc. Needs humorous illustration and humor oriented comprehensives for print. 90% of freelance humorous illustration is for print ads.
Illustration: Works with approximately 1 freelance humorous illustrator/month "depending on current projects. Sometimes months pass with no requirement at all." Looking for freelancers who can interpret concept objectives effectively. For first contact send cover letter, resume and client list ("photocopies of work samples acceptable") to Brian Dillon, President. Reports back only if interested. Returns materials only if requested and accompanied by SASE. Keeps materials on file. Buys all rights. Pays $20-35 by the hour; $150-600 by the project (depends on project). Payment depends on complexity of project, ability of illustrator to work well under our art direction and client's budget.

*THE ATKINS AGENCY, 1777 N.E. Loop 410, San Antonio TX 78101. (512)826-5500. FAX (512)826-1247. Estab. 1966. Advertising agency that provides advertising, marketing and public relations for tourism bureaus, hospitals, banks and automotive aftermarket. Needs humorous illustration, storyboards and humorous copywriting for print, TV, radio and outdoor ads. 90% of freelance humorous illustration is for print ads. Prefers to work with freelancers with fax capabilities.
Illustration: Works with approximately 5-6 freelance humorous illustrators/year. "Can illustrate in a style of humor that we cannot do well. (Special area expertise)." For first contact send cover letter, resume, client list, b&w tearsheets and color promo piece to Becky Benavides, Associate Creative Director. Reports back only if interested. Returns materials only if requested. Keeps materials on file. Negotiates rights purchased. Pays $25-5,000 by the project ("depends entirely on the project.") Payment is based on complexity of project, turnaround and business manner and professionalism of illustrator.

*LEWIS BENEDICT BEDECARRÉ, 1333 Willow Pass Rd., #204, Concord CA 94520. (510)825-5555. FAX: (510)825-5555. Estab. 1971. Full service advertising agency for hotel, entertainment and home-building clients. Needs humorous illustration and copywriting, animation and caricature for print and radio. 75% of freelance humorous illustration is for print ads.
Illustration: Works with 2-4 freelance humorous illustrators/year. For first contact send cover letter, resume, client list, b&w and color tearsheets, b&w and color promo pieces and slides to Jay Bedecarré, President. Reports back only if interested. Returns materials if requested and accompanied by a SASE. Pays $15-50 by the hour; $150 minimum by the project.
Writing: Works with 1-2 humor-oriented writers/year. For first contact send cover letter, resume, client list, tearsheets, writing samples, ½″ demo tape and audio tape to Jay Bedecarré, President. Reports back only if interested. Returns materials if interested and accompanied by a SASE. Negotiates rights purchased. Pays $15-35 by the hour; $150 minimum by the project.

*THE BENJAMIN GROUP, 2323 Bascom Ave., Campbell CA 95008. (408)559-6090. FAX: (408)559-6188. Estab. 1988. PR firm. "Our main thrust is PR and strategic marketing; however, we do collateral and advertising as well" for high tech industry and business to business. Current clients include Integrated Measurement Systems, Verilog and Brooktree. Needs humorous illustration and copywriting and cartoons for print. Prefers to work with freelancers who have fax capabilities.

Illustration: Works with approximately 1 freelance humorous illustrator/month. Looking for freelancers who are local. For first contact send portfolio to Cher Cultrona, Art Director. Returns materials only if interested. Negotiates rights purchased. Payment is based on complexity of project and client's budget.

Writing: Works with approximately 2 humor oriented writers/year. Looking for freelancers who are local. For first contact send writing samples to Cher Cultrona, Art Director. Reports back within matter of weeks. Returns materials only if interested. Negotiates rights purchased. Payment is based on complexity of project and client's budget.

*BLUMENFELD AND ASSOC., 130 W. 42nd St., New York NY 10036. (212)764-1690. Estab. 1980. PR firm that provides publicity for corporations. Current clients include DuPont, American Mensa and Cigna. Needs humorour illustration, slide shows and humorous copywriting for print. Prefers to work with freelancers who have fax capabilities.

Illustration: Works with approximately 1-5 freelance humorous illustrators/year. For first contact send cover letter to Jeff Blumenfeld, President. Reports back only if interested. Returns materials only if interested. Buys all rights. Pays $500-1,500 by the project. Payment is based on complexity of project and client's budget.

Writing: Works with approximately 1-2 humor oriented writers/year. For first contact send cover letter and writing samples.

*CHALEK & CHALEK, 380 Lexington Ave., New York NY 10017. (212)972-3222. FAX: (212)557-7585. Estab. 1985. Advertising agency that "produces advertising and promotional materials for various packaged goods and service advertisers. We specialize in the food industry but also service clients in the areas of education, health and beauty and soft goods." Current clients include Geisha brand, Steakwich, Casa di Bertacchi, Caesar's Pasta, North American Training Schools, Coast Manufacturing. Needs humorous illustration, animations humor oriented comprehensives and humorous copywriting for print, TV and radio. 90% of freelance humorous illustration is for print ads. Prefers to work with freelancers who have fax capabilities.

Illustration: Works with approximately 3 freelance humorous illustrators/year. For first contact send b&w and color promo pieces to Mitch Chalek, President. Reports back only if interested. Returns materials only if interested. Keeps materials on file. Buys all rights, negotiates rights purchased. Pays $50-1,500, by the project. Payment is based on complexity of project, skill of illustrator, turnaround, client's budget and usage.

*COAKLEY HEAGERTY, 1155 N. First, San Jose CA 95112. (408)275-9400. FAX: (408)995-0600. Full service ad agency serving banks, food service, grocery, real estate, insurance and high tech. Current clients include Shea Homes, Citation Insurance, California Banc Corp., Wm. Lyon Co., Ampex and Cosentino's. Needs humorous illustration, cartoons, animation, animatics and storyboards for print TV and video tape. 85% of freelance humorous illustration is for print ads. Prefers to work with freelancers with fax capabilities.

Illustration: Works with approximately 5 freelance humorous illustrators/year. For first contact send b&w and color promo pieces to Susann Rivera, Creative Director. Does not report back. Returns materials if accompanied by a SASE. Negotiates rights purchased. Pays by the project. Payment is based on skill of illustrator and ability of illustrator to work well under agency's art direction.

Close-up

Marty Chapo
Art Director
Ralston Purina

"Art directors in this organization wear a lot of different hats," says Marty Chapo, who, as an art director and buyer at Ralston Purina, hires out illustration, works with copywriters, develops and designs concepts for sales promotion and packaging, and is involved in "anything to help sell the product outside of strict advertising."

Of the many products developed at the St. Louis-based corporation, Chapo is responsible for promoting Hostess Snack Cakes, Cat Chow brands and several of their cereals for kids. In addition, she is involved with the annual "Pets for People" program sponsored by Purina that matches cats and dogs in animal shelters with lonely senior citizens wanting pets.

Chapo says that humorous illustration, 99 percent of which is used for print ads, is an ideal promotional tool for the Hostess and kids' cereal lines because kids find humor particularly appealing. She works with an average of three illustrators per month, and "the most appropriate illustrator for each project is chosen," be they a freelancer or an illustrator on staff. Since deadlines tend to be very short, Chapo admits that budget is not always the most significant factor in choosing an illustrator. "We are very busy and therefore are not constantly 'cutting it to the bone,'" she says.

Above all, she looks for "a thinker, someone who can take the project along to the next step, someone who thinks about the project carefully—looks at every angle—looks at it differently." Work that reflects "strong conceptual thinking and a really knockout illustration style that is interesting and fresh," stands the greatest chance of consideration.

The illustrator's work, not the resume, is the most important component of the portfolio, according to Chapo. She does not accept ideas only—she must see work to back them up. In addition, unsolicited ideas are not considered at Ralston Purina, so Chapo requests freelancers write a letter of query before submitting material. She will look at both personal and commercial portfolios, and admits she sees "a lot of portfolios that are filled to the brim, yet in a shabby manner. It's disappointing. It is better for an illustrator to go in and show a few really good pieces—only their best."

Chapo offers the following advice to freelancers: "Keep the portfolio tidy. Put it together in a professional manner. What is in there will be remembered. The manner in which your material is presented is 50 percent of the perception on the part of the client. The more you can cut through the clutter, the better—

keep it streamlined! Have a uniformity to the entire presentation. Don't let your portfolio distract from the work itself."

During a time when advertisers must work more diligently than ever to generate consumer spending, Ralston Purina has risen to the challenge by focusing its advertising efforts on creating deals for the consumer. "Consumers are taken by 'freebies'," says Chapo. As companies like Purina focus on the quick-hit sale, advertising remains a busy field. "Business is booming in the areas of sales promotion and packaging," she says.

— Roseann Shaughnessy

reprinted with permission of Ralston Purina Inc.

Get a Bite of These: This packaging incorporating humorous illustration was designed under the direction of Marty Chapo for Ralston Purina.

*STAVROS COSMOPULOS, INC., 200 Clarendon St., Boston MA 02116. (617)437-1600. FAX: (617)572-3400. Estab. 1991. Advertising agency that provides advertising, marketing and design services for food, shoe, technical, restaurant, corporation and banks. Needs humorous illustration, caricature, cartoons, animatics and slide shows for print, TV and audiovisual. 10% of freelance humorous illustration is for print ads. Prefers to work with freelancers who have fax capabilities.

Illustration: Works with approximately 4 freelance humorous illustrators/year. For first contact send b&w and color promo pieces to Stavros Cosmopulos, President. Reports back only if interested. Does not return materials. Buys all rights or negotiates rights purchased. Pays $500-2,500. Payment depends on client's budget.

CRANFORD JOHNSON ROBINSON WOODS, 303 W. Capitol Ave., Little Rock AR 72201. (501)376-6251. FAX: (501)376-4241. Estab. 1961. Advertising agency that provides full-service advertising for insurance companies, utilities, banks and hospitals. Current clients include Baptist Medical Center, First Commercial Bank, Arkansas Parks and Tourism and the Energy Corporation. Needs humorous illustration, animation, animatics, storyboards and slide shows for TV, radio and audiovisual. 30% of freelance humorous illustration is for print ads. Prefers to work with freelancers with fax capabilities.

Illustration: Works with approximately 6 freelance humorous illustrators/year. Looking for freelancers who "have great portfolios and references." For first contact send "best work, print and broadcast" to Boyd Blackwood, Creative Director. Reports back within days. Keeps materials on file. Negotiates rights purchased. Pays $35-60 by the hour.

Writing: Works with approximately 2 humor oriented writers/month. Looking for freelancers "who have great portfolios and references." Send all humor writing materials to Boyd Blackwood, Creative Director. Reports back on submissions in days. Keeps materials on file. Negotiates rights purchased. Pays $35-60 by the hour; $150-300 by the day $150-300. **Editor's note: After deadline, this listing asked to be deleted.**

CREATIVE DIMENSIONS, 2369 Park Ave., Dept. HC, Cincinnati OH 45206. (513)961-4400. FAX: (513)961-5400. Estab. 1971. Advertising agency that provides full service radio, TV, direct mail, print, collaterial, P.O.P. outdoor, etc. for financial institutions, auto dealers, Anderson Windows, furniture companies and cabinet companies. Needs humorous illustration and copywriting for print, TV and radio. 10% of freelance humorous illustration is for print ads.

Illustration: Works with 1-8 freelance humorous illustrators/year. For first contact send b&w and color tearsheets to Sam McClausland, Art Director. Reports back within a few days. Returns materials if requested. Buys all rights. Pays by project. Payment is based on client's budget, possibility of a long term agency/illustrator relationship and usage.

Writing: "To date, everything has been inhouse, but we are changing this. Looking for freelance humorous writers who can write material for a long-running campaign we presently have. Also, if they can come up with campaign ideas of their own." For first contact send writing samples, demo tape (if possible) and audio tape to Arnold R. Barnett, CEO. Reports back within days. Returns materials if requested. Buys all rights. Pays varied amounts by the project according to client's budget, usage and possibility of a long term agency/writer relationship. *Inside Tips:* "We are primarily interested in humorous radio campaigns. We are the largest radio agency in this area. Many of our campaigns are humorous. Because of the number of spots we are responsible for creating each month, we are increasing our dependence on freelancers."

CROSS KEYS ADVERTISING, INC., 329 S. Main St., Dept. HC, Doylestown PA 18901-4814. (215)345-5435. Estab. 1981. Advertising agency that provides full service advertising dealing in all forms of media for automotive, retail stores, banks, developers and

Regal Raspberry: *Told to follow his "best instincts," Skip Morrow of Wilmington, Vermont created this visually-slapstick poster/ad for Virgin Atlantic Airways showing the "human side of the Royal Guard." Given a verbal outline for the three panels, Morrow then had a two-week deadline to create the final art.*

industries. Current clients include Porsche Motorsport North America, The Thompson Organization (automotive dealerships) and Penns Grant Corporation (commercial and industrial developers). Needs humorous illustration, animation and humorous copywriting for print, video tape and radio. 60% of freelance humorous illustration is for print ads. Prefers to work with freelancers with fax capabilities.

Illustration: Works with approximately 4 freelance humorous illustrators/year. For first contact send cover letter, b&w tearsheets and promo piece to Laura Thompson, President. Returns materials only if requested. Keeps materials on file. Negotiates rights purchased. Payment is based on complexity of project, turnaround, business manner and professionalism of illustrator, ability of illustrator to work well under our art direction, client's budget and skill of illustrator.

Writing: Works with approximately 4 humor oriented writers/year. For first contact send cover letter, writing samples and audio tape to Laura Thompson. When establishing payment considers complexity of project, skill of writer, turnaround, ability of writer to work well under our creative team, business manner and professionalism of writer and client's budget.

JOHN CROWE ADVERTISING AGENCY, 1104 South 2nd St., Springfield IL 62704. (217)528-1076. Estab. 1954. Advertising agency that provides full service media, printing, promotion, production, direct mail, design, full graphics service, art work (commercial and fine art), photo retouching and illustration art to industrial, commercial, retail, banking, publishing, aviation, architecture, city, state, federal and medical clients. Needs humorous illustration and copywriting, caricature, animatics and cartoons for print, videotape, TV and radio. 10% of freelance humorous illustration is for print ads.

Illustration: Works with approximately 3 freelance humorous illustrators/year. Looking for freelancers who are "requested by clients." For first contact send cover letter, resume, client list and b&w tearsheets to Bryan J. Crowe, Art Director. Reports back within 10 days if interested. Keeps materials on file. Negotiates rights purchased. Pays $25 maximum by the hour.

Writing: Works with approximately 3 humor-oriented writers/year. For first contact send cover letter, resume, client list, tearsheets and writing samples to Bryan J. Crowe. Reports back within 10 days. Keeps materials on file. Negotiates rights purchased. Pays $25 minimum by the hour.

R.I. DAVID & COMPANY, Dept. HC, 3601 W. Devon Ave., Chicago IL 60659. (312)478-7481. FAX: (312)478-7482. Estab. 1950. Advertising agency that provides advertising and sales materials in foreign languages to all markets. Needs humorous copywriting for print, videotape, TV, radio and audiovisual. 75% of freelance humorous illustration is for print ads. Prefers to work with freelancers with fax access.

Writing: Looking for freelance humorous writers who are "native born with foreign language capacity." For first contact send resume, client list and tearsheets to Alicia Adams, Vice President. Reports back only if interested. Does not return materials. Keeps materials on file. Buys all rights. Pays 10¢ minimum by the word.

DEDONATO, GLADSTONE & QUINN ADVERTISING, INC., Suite 500, 1225 King St., Wilmington DE 19801. (302)575-0606. FAX: (302)575-0648. Estab. 1985. Advertising agency that provides marketing, full media and advertising, print, radio, TV, outdoor, collateral, and video for corporations, banks, manufacturers, hotels, service businesses and insurance. Current clients include Heritage Cablevision, Delmarva Power, Himont Plastics, DuPont, AIG Insurance and Beneficial National Bank. Needs humorous illustration and copywriting, humor-oriented comprehensives, animation, caricature, animatics, cartoons, storyboards, and slide shows for print, TV, radio, audiovisual and videotape. 5% of freelance humorous illustration is for print ads.

Illustration: Works with approximately 8 freelance illustrators/year. Looking for freelancers with "distinct style, cooperation, ability to work with humor." For first contact send b&w and color tearsheets and b&w and color promo pieces to Rick DeDonato, Creative Director. Reports back only if interested. Returns materials only if requested. Keeps materials on file. Buys all rights or negotiates rights purchased. Pays $100 minimum by the project.

Writing: For first contact send writing samples, ½" demo tape and audiotape to Rick DeDonato, Creative Director. Reports back only if interested. Keeps materials on file; returns materials only if requested. Negotiates rights purchased. Pays $100 minimum by the project.

*DETROW AND UNDERWOOD, 1126 Cottage St., Ashland OH 44840. (419)289-0265. FAX: (419)289-3390. Estab. 1945. Advertising agency that provides collateral, direct mail and trade advertising for corporations—building materials, toy. Current clients include Mansfield Plumbing Products, National Latex and Swan Hose. Needs humorous illustration, caricature and humorous copywriting for print. 80% of freelance humorous illustration is for print ads.

Illustration: For first contact send resume and b&w tearsheets to Don Hubacher, Sr. Art Director. Reports back within days. Keeps materials on file. Payment depends on the complexity of project, schedule of illustrator and client's budget.

Writing: Send all humor writing materials to Pat Snyder, Copy Writer. Reports back within days. Keeps materials on file. Buys all rights. Payment depends on complexity of project, client's budget and schedule of writer. *Inside Tips:* "We do a lot of humor illustration and writing but it is almost always handled within our agency. However . . . at times we might need to go outside. Good sources would be welcomed."

DGS GROUP, 5948 N. College Ave., Indianapolis IN 46220. (317)575-9910. Estab. 1985. Advertising agency that provides full service to restaurants, banks, carpet companies, service companies, manufacturers, business-to-business and corporate. Current clients include Long John Silvers, Rent-A-Center, USA Funds and Lilly. Needs humorous illustration, animation, humorous copywriting, animatics, storyboards and slide shows for print, videotape, TV and radio. 50% of freelance humorous illustration is for print ads. Prefers to work with freelancers with fax capabilities.

Illustration: Works with approximately 2 freelance humorous illustrators/month. For first contact send cover letter, client list, b&w and color tearsheets and b&w promo piece to Dean Glascock, VP Creative. Reports back only if interested. Returns materials only if requested. Keeps materials on file. Negotiates rights purchased. Payment is based on complexity of project, client's budget, skill of illustrator and usage.

Writing: Works with approximately 4 humor oriented writers/month. For first contact send cover letter, tearsheets, writing samples, audio tape and ½" demo tape to Dean Glascock. Reports back only if interested. Returns materials only if interested. Keeps materials on file. Negotiates rights purchased. Pays $100 minimum by the project.

DIEGNAN & ASSOCIATES, P.O. Box 298, Oldwick NJ 08858. (908)832-7951. Estab. 1977. PR firm that provides services for corporations. Current clients include Cerberus Pyrotronics, Newark Wire Cloth, Croll Reynolds, Liquiflo and UC Industries. Needs humorous illustration and copywriting, animation, humor-oriented comprehensives, caricature, animatics and cartoons for print, videotape and TV. 100% of freelance humorous illustration is for print ads.

Illustration: Works with approximately 6 freelance humorous illustrators/year. For first contact send b&w tearsheets to N. Diegnan, President. Reports back within 1 week. Keeps materials on file. Negotiates rights purchased. Pays $50 minimum by the hour.

Writing: Works with approximately 6 humor-oriented writers/year. For first contact send writing samples to N. Diegnan. Reports back within 1 week. Keeps materials on file. Negotiates rights purchased. Pays $50 minimum by the hour.

CHARLES EDELSTEIN ADV., INC., 92 Austin Drive, Dept. HC, Holland PA 18966. (215)355-5015. Estab. 1971. Advertising agency that provides annual reports, collateral and print ads to corporations, banks and stores. Needs humorous illustration, humor-oriented comprehensives, humorous copywriting, caricatures, cartoons and storyboards for print, video tape, radio and audiovisual. 75% of freelance humorous illustration is for print ads.
Illustration: Works with approximately 6 freelance humorous illustrators/year. For first contact send b&w tearsheets and promo piece to Charles Edelstein, President. Does not return materials. Keeps materials on file. Negotiates rights purchased. Pays $15-30 by the hour or $75-200 by the project.
Writing: Works with approximately 6 humor oriented writers/year. For first contact send resume and tearsheets to Charles Edelstein. Does not return materials. Keeps materials on file. Negotiates rights purchased. Pays $15-30 by the hour or $120-240 by the day.

EGD—EDWARD G. DORN & ASSOCIATES, INC., 1801 H Hicks Rd., Rolling Meadows IL 60008. (708)991-1270. FAX: (708)991-1519. Estab. 1971. Advertising agency and art/design studio that provides full service advertising, marketing, sales promotion, PR, graphics and printing to business-to-business, consumer, industrial and service companies. Current clients include Goulding, Jeycom, Airphone and Bostic/Emhart. Needs humorous illustration, caricature, cartoons, storyboards and slide shows for print and audiovisual. 50% of freelance humorous illustration is for print ads. Prefers to work with freelancers with fax capabilities.
Illustration: Works with approximately 1 freelance humorous illustrator/month. Looking for freelancers who have "fresh ideas and top drawing ability." For first contact send cover letter, resume, client list, and b&w and color tearsheets to Kathleen Dorn, VP Personnel. Reports back within 1 week if interested. Returns materials if requested; otherwise keeps materials. Buys all rights. Pays by the project. Payment is based on complexity of project, client's budget, possibility of a long-term agency/illustrator relationship and skill of illustrator.
Writing: Works with approximately 2 humor-oriented writers/year. Looking for freelance humorous writers "who can also illustrate." For first contact send cover letter, resume, client list and writing samples to Kathleen Dorn.

ERWIN-PENLAND, INC., 131 Falls St., Dept. HC, Greenville SC 29601. (803)271-0500. (803)235-5941. Estab. 1986. Advertising agency and PR firm that provides full-service marketing, advertising and PR services for auto dealer associations, chain restaurants, jewelers, cellular phone company, real estate firm and hospital. Current clients include Metro Mobile, Motor Mile, Wellspring Hospital and Ryan's Family Steakhouse. Needs humorous illustration and copywriting and storyboards for print, radio and audiovisual. 70% of freelance humorous illustration is for print ads. Prefers to work with freelancers who have FAX capabilities.
Illustration: Works with approximately 3 freelance humorous illustrators/month. Looking for freelancers who "exhibit strong conceptual ability: matches work well to our copy/selling strategy." For first contact send cover letter and photocopies to Joe Erwin, Creative Director. Reports back only if interested. Returns materials only if requested if accompanied by a SASE. Negotiates rights purchased. Pays $25 minimum by the hour; $100 minimum by the project.

Writing: Works with approximately 1 humor oriented writer/month. Looking for free-lancers who "show strong advertising ability—humorous spots that clearly communicate the copy strategy." For first contact send cover letter, writing samples, audiotape to Joe Erwin, Creative Director. Reports back only if interested. Returns materials only if interested. Negotiates rights purchased. Pays $40 minimum by the hour; $300 minimum by the day.

FITZSIMONS ADVERTISING & PUBLIC RELATIONS, 750 Midland Building, Cleveland OH 44115. (216)241-5656. FAX: (216)241-5658. Advertising agency that provides full service advertising and public relations to investment, industrial and retail. Needs humorous illustration and humorous copywriting for print and videotape. 75% of freelance humorous illustration is for print ads. Prefers to work with freelancers with fax capabilities.
Illustration: Works with approximately 2 freelance humorous illustrators/year. Looking for freelance humorous illustrators who can work within a budget. For first contact send b&w tearsheets to Mike Guyot, Art Director. Negotiates rights purchased. Payment is based on complexity of project, turnaround, client's budget and skill of illustrator.
Writing: For first contact send writing samples and 3/4" demo tape to Mike Goyot or Eric Klosky. When establishing payment considers complexity of project, ability of writer to work well under our creative team and client's budget.

*GLAZER DESIGN, 2 James Rd., Mt. Kisco NY 10549. (914)666-4554. Estab. 1988. Art/design studio that provides collateral and print ads for agencies and corporations. Current clients include Jill's Merchandise Mart, Laura Lox Publishers and Northern Westchester Hospital. Needs humorous illustration and copywriting, cartoons and slide shows for print and audiovisual. 10% of freelance humorous illustration is for print ads. Prefers to work with freelancers with fax access.
Illustration: Works with 8 freelance humorous illustrators/year. For first contact send b&w and color tearsheets, b&w promo piece to Art Glazer, President. Reports back only if interested. Returns materials if accompanied by a SASE or keeps materials on file. Negotiates rights purchased. Pays $10-100 by the hour; $100-500 by the project. Considers complexity of project, turnaround, client's budget and skill of illustrator when establishing payment.

GROUP ATLANTA, Box 566725, Atlanta GA 30356. (404)442-1100. FAX: (404)442-1118. Estab. 1980. Full service Advertising agency. Needs humorous copywriting for radio.
Illustration: Reports back only if interested. Returns materials if accompanied by a SASE. Keeps materials on file. Negotiates rights purchased. Payment is based on complexity of project, turnaround, client's budget and usage.
Writing: Looking for freelancers who "can write great radio spots." Reports back only if interested. Returns materials if accompanied by a SASE. Keeps materials on file. Negotiates rights purchased. Pays by the project. Payment is based on complexity of project, turnaround and client's budget. *Inside Tips:* "We look for great radio humor. No nonsense—we want super-intelligent concepts."

*HACKMEISTER ADVERTISING & PUBLIC RELATIONS CO., 2727 E. Oakland Park Blvd. #205, Ft. Lauderdale FL 33306. (305)568-2511. FAX: (305)568-2577. Estab. 1979. Advertising agency, PR firm that provides business-to-business technology advertising, industrial press relations, collateral materials and user manuals to electronics manufacturers. Current clients include Optoelectronics, Inc., Raltron, Sun Electronics Corp., Monicor, Sabtech Industries Inc. Needs humorous illustration, caricature and cartoons for print. 100% of freelance humorous illustration is for print ads. Prefers to work with freelancers who have fax capabilities.

Illustration: Looking for freelancers who understand electronics/radio/computers. For first contact send cover letter, resume, b&w tearsheets (photocopied tearsheets acceptable) to Dick Hackmeister, Owner. Reports back only if interested. Keeps materials on file. Negotiates rights purchased. Pays $300-2,000. Payment depends on complexity of project, skill of illustrator, business manner and professionalism of illustrator and client's budget.

HANCOCK ADVERTISING AGENCY, 5032 Justin St., Nacogdoches TX 75961. (409)564-9559. FAX: (409)560-0845. Estab. 1973. Advertising agency that provides collateral, radio/TV, annual reports, outdoor, newspaper, magazine ads for retail clothing stores, corporations, manufacturers, banks, insurance companies and car dealers. Current clients include Fredonia State Bank, Mike Perry Motor Co., Temple-Inland, Conquest Airlines, Nacogdoches Chamber of Commerce. Needs humorous illustration and copywriting, caricature, cartoons and slide shows for print, TV, radio, audiovisual, videotape. 90% of freelance humorous illustration is for print ads. Prefers to work with freelancers who have FAX capabilities.
Illustration: Works with approximately 4 freelance humorous illustrators/year. Looking for freelancers who "are in Texas." For first contact send cover letter, resume and copies of work to Judith Butler, Creative Director. Reports back within 2 weeks only if interested. Returns materials only if requested. Keeps materials on file. Negotiates rights purchased. Pays $30-75 by the hour.
Writing: Works with approximately 4 humor oriented writers/year. For first contact send cover letter, writing samples, audiotape to Judith Butler, Creative Director. Reports back on submissions in 2 weeks. Reports back only if interested. Negotiates rights purchased. Pays $15 minimum by the hour; $120 minimum by the day; $50 minimum by the project.

THE HITCHINS COMPANY, 22756 Hartland St., Canoga Park CA 91307. (818)715-0510. Estab. 1984. Advertising agency that provides full service advertising to various clients. Needs humorous illustration and copywriting, caricature and cartoons for print. 100% of freelance humorous illustration is for print ads. Prefers to work with freelancers with fax capabilities.
Illustration: For first contact send cover letter, resume and b&w tearsheets (if available) to W. E. Hitchins, President. Reports back only if interested. Does not return materials. Keeps materials on file. Negotiates rights. Pay depends on job and client and is based on client's budget.
Writing: For first contact send cover letter, resume and writing samples if available to W. E. Hitchins. Reports back only if interested. Returns materials only if interested. Keeps materials on file. Negotiates rights purchased. Pays according to project and client. When establishing payment considers client's budget.

BERNARD HODES ADVERTISING, 1101 Embarcadero Rd., Palo Alto CA 94303. (415)856-1000. Estab. 1970. Advertising agency that provides recruitment advertising and employee communications for high tech, finance, health care, retailers, apparel manufacturers and aerospace. Current clients include Sun Micro Systems, Ford Aerospace, National Semiconductor, American Savings, Wells Fargo Bank, Seagate Technologies, Community Hospitals of Central California, S. Agnes Med Center, Levi Straus and Clorox. Needs humorous illustration and copywriting for print. 100% of freelance humorous illustration is for print ads. Prefers to work with freelancers with fax capabilities.
Illustration: Works with approximately 2 freelance humorous illustrators/year. For first contact send cover letter, resume, client list, b&w and color tearsheets to Doug DeCarlo, Creative Director. Reports back only if interested. Does not return materials. Keeps

Taking the Dive: *Madison, New Jersey-based humorous illustrator Larry Ross uses his "loose, shaky-line style" to create this shaky-kneed diver for a Biotrol USA collateral postcard. Ross was granted the illustration assignment after showing his portfolio to Biotrol's advertising agency. To promote his work, Ross advertises in* **American Showcase** *and does "one or two mailings a year."*

materials on file. Buys all rights or negotiates rights purchased. Pays $150-2,000 by the project.

Writing: Works with approximately 6 humor oriented writers/year. Looking for freelance humorous writers who have "prior advertising copywriting experience with a major ad agency." For first contact send cover letter to Mike Doyle, Senior Copywriter. Reports back only if interested. Does not return materials. Does not file materials. Buys all rights. Pays $15-50 by the hour; $250-2,000 by the project.

*THE KAMBER GROUP, 1920 L St., NW #700, Washington DC 20036. (202)223-8700. FAX: (202)775-0203. PR firm that provides annual reports, 4-color magazines, brochures, newsletters, print ads and posters for labor unions, local universities and corporations. Current clients include Corporation for Public Broadcasting, SWMIA, LIUNA, BCTD, American University and The Nature Conservancy. Needs humorous illustration for print.

Illustration: Works with approximately 1-2 freelance humorous illustrators/month. For first contact send b&w tearsheets and promo pieces to Dennis Walston, Art Director, Senior Vice President. Reports back only if interested. Does not return materials. Keeps materials on file. Negotiates rights purchased. Pays by the project. Payment is based on skill of illustrator, turnaround and client's budget.

KARALIAS ADVERTISING, 9 South Main St., Ipswich MA 01938. (508)356-9665. Estab. 1986. Advertising agency and art/design studio that provides ads, packaging, direct mail pieces, computer graphics for games (Nintendo, Sega, PC) posters, brochures, logos and miscellaneous design for all types of clients. Current clients include Microsmiths, Parker Brothers, Pierce Furniture, Nynex, Charles River Apparel, First National Bank and Mass Eye & Ear. Needs humorous illustration and copywriting, animation, humor-oriented comprehensives, caricature, animatics and cartoons for print, videotape and radio. 50% of freelance humorous illustration is for print ads.

Illustration: Works with approximately 4 freelance humorous illustrators/year. For first contact send resume and client list to George Karalias, Creative Director. Reports back only if interested. Keeps materials on file. Negotiates rights purchased. Pays $20 minimum by the hour; $100 minimum by the project.

Writing: Works with approximately 2-3 humor-oriented writers/year. For first contact send cover letter, resume and client list to George Karalias. Reports back only if interested. Keeps materials on file. Negotiates rights purchased. Pays $20 minimum by the hour; $80 by the day; $250 by the project.

KRANZLER-KINGSLEY COMMUNICATIONS, 207 E. Broadway, Bismarck ND 58501. (701)255-3067. (701)222-2010. Estab. 1989. Advertising agency, art/design studio, communications/audiovisual company. Current clients include malls, hospitals and television. Needs humorous illustration and copywriting, animation for print, TV, radio, audiovisual, video tape.

Illustration: Looking for freelancers who "are easy to get in touch with and understandable about clients wants and needs." For first contact send resume to Scott Montgomery, Creative Director. Reports back in days. Returns materials only if requested. Negotiates rights purchased. Considers complexity of project, skill of illustrator, client's budget, usage when establishing payment.

Writing: Looking for freelancers who "are easy to get a hold of and are what we need." For first contact send cover letter, resume, audio tape to Scott Montgomery, Creative Director. Reports back within days. Returns materials only if interested. Negotiates rights purchased. Considers complexity of project, skill of writer, client's budget and date when establishing payment.

LARSEN COLBY, Suite 600, 4727 Wilshire, Los Angeles CA 90010. (213)931-0009. Estab. 1984. Advertising agency that provides print, TV, outdoor and radio ads to automotive, entertainment, healthcare, cosmetic and high tech clients. Current clients include VLSI, Subaru and Green Peace. Needs humorous illustration and copywriting and storyboards for print and radio. 99% of freelance humorous illustration is for print ads. Prefers to work with freelancers with fax capabilities.

Illustration: For first contact send b&w and color promo pieces to Bill Snitzer, Associate CD. Returns materials if accompanied by a SASE. Negotiates rights purchased. Pays $150-8,000 by the project.

Writing: For first contact send ½" or ¾" demo and audiotape to Judy Haruki, Producer. Does not return materials. Keeps materials on file.

LAVIN ASSOCIATES, 12 Promontory Dr., Cheshire CT 06410. (203)272-9121. Estab. 1947. Advertising agency that provides direct mail to industrial corporations. Needs humorous illustration and copywriting, humor-oriented comprehensives and cartoons for print and audiovisual. 10% of freelance humorous illustration is for print ads.

Illustration: Works with approximately 1 freelance humorous illustrator/year. Looking for local freelance humorous illustrators. For first contact send cover letter and b&w tearsheets to Dr. Henry Lavin, Senior Associate. Reports back only if interested. Keeps materials on file. Buys reprint rights. Payment is negotiable. Payment is based on client's budget.

Always include a self-addressed stamped envelope (SASE) or International Reply Coupon (IRC) with submissions.

Writing: Works with approximately 1 humor-oriented writer/year. For first contact send cover letter and writing samples to Dr. Henry Lavin. Reports back only if interested. Keeps materials on file. Buys reprint rights. Payment is negotiated according to client's budget.

*NORMA A. LEE COMPANY, 25 W. 39th St., New York NY 10018. (212)221-0410. FAX: (212)768-3746. Estab. 1972. PR firm that provides brochures and flyers for corporations, trade shows, non-profit foundations and entrepreneurs. Current clients include Advantar Communications, Happy Kids Productions, Active Media Services, Cosmetology Advancement Foundation. Needs humorous illustration and humor oriented comprehensives for print.
Illustration: Works with approximately 2 freelance humorous illustrators/year. Looking for freelancers "who can bring creative thinking to the table and keep within a budget." For first contact send resume, client list and b&w promo piece to Norma A. Lee, President. Reports back only if interested. Returns materials only if requested. Negotiates rights purchased. Pays $100-1,000, by the project. Payment is based on client's budget.

LIGGETT-STASHOWER, 1228 Euclid, Cleveland OH 44115. (216)348-8500. (216)861-1284. Estab. 1932. Advertising agency that provides full-service, advertising, public relations, yellow pages, media and studio for banks, utility companies, business-to-business consumer, retail, food. Clients include Ameritrust Bank, Babcock and Wilcox and Kenny Kings. Needs humorous illustration and copywriting, caricature, cartoons, animation, storyboards for print and radio. 20% of freelance humorous illustration is for print ads. Prefers to work with freelancers who have fax capabilities.
Illustration and Humor Writing: Looking for freelancers "who are reputable." For first contact send color tearsheets and promo piece to Linda Barberic, Creative Manager. Reports back within months only if interested. Returns materials only if requested. Keeps materials on file. Negotiates rights purchased. Pays $75-250, by the hour.

MACDANIELS, HENRY & SPROUL, Dept. HC, 930 Montgomery St., San Francisco CA 94133. (415)981-2250. FAX: (415)981-0164. Estab. 1989. Advertising agency that provides account, creative, marketing, broadcast production services and media planning for government departments, transportation, travel clients, newspapers, and sports clients. Current clients include California Department of Transportation, Caltrain and Cartrans—Amtrak San Joaquin and Amtrak San Diegan. Needs humorous illustration and copywriting, caricature, cartoons and storyboards for print, TV and radio. 24% of freelance humorous illustration is for print ads. Prefers to work with freelancers with fax capabilities.
Illustration: Works with approximately 2 freelance humorous illustrators/year. For first contact send cover letter, resume, client list, b&w and color promo pieces and "any special promo pieces to show style" to Cristina Gavin, Art Director/Copywriter. Reports back only if interested. Returns materials only if requested; keeps materials on file. Negotiates rights purchased. Pays $10,000 maximum by the project.
Writing: Works with approximately 2 humor-oriented writers/year. For first contact send cover letter, resume, client list, writing samples, demo tape, and audio tape to Cristina Gavin, Art Director. Reports back only if interested. Keeps materials on file. Negotiates rights purchased. Pays $10,000 maximum by the project.

MANN BUKVIC ASSOCIATES, Suite 1130, Dept. HC, 205 W. 4th St., Cincinnati OH 45202. (513)241-4444. Advertising agency that provides TV, radio, print, collateral, annual reports, but mostly ads. Current clients include Cincinnati Zoo, Tri-County Mall, Hudephol-Schoenling and Ryland Homes. Needs humorous illustration and animation for print, possible TV, newspaper and collateral. 100% of freelance humorous illustration is for print ads. Prefers to work with freelancers with fax capabilities.

Illustration: Works with approximately 1 freelance humorous illustrator/year. "Looking for freelance humorous illustrator who has printed pieces we can have for our files for reference." For first contact send b&w and color tearsheets, b&w and color promo piece to Teresa Newberry, Executive Art Director. Reports back within 3 days. Returns materials only if requested. Keeps materials on file. Negotiates rights purchased. Payment is based on complexity of project, business manner and professionalism of illustrator, ability of illustrator to work well under art direction, client's budget and skill of illustrator. *Inside Tips:* "I don't think we would use a humorous writer at this point. We have used humorous illustrators though—but not that often. Maybe once a year. That could increase though."

THE MARKET CONNECTION, Suite 203, Dept. HC, 4020 Birch St., Newport Beach CA 92660. (714)731-6273. FAX: (714)852-1819. Estab. 1986. PR firm that provides public relations/marketing services for packaged goods manufacturers, professional services, retailers and business-to-business. Current clients include All American Gourmet Company, Home Delivery Services, Inc., Active Sales, Chef America, Advanced Business Software, Baxter Healthcare and Kwikset. Needs humorous illustration, animation, caricature, cartoons and storyboards for print, videotape and radio. 5% of freelance humorous illustration is for print ads.
Illustration: Works with approximately 1-2 freelance humorous illustrators/month. For first contact send portfolio to Janie Roach, President. Reports back within 5 days. Does not return materials. Buys all rights. Pays $500-2500 by the project. Query for humor writing.

MARKETING ALTERNATIVE, INC., (formerly McKee Advertising), Suite 180, Dept. HC, 3721 Ventura Dr., Dept. HC, Arlington Hts. IL 60004. (708)253-1410. FAX: (708)523-2232. Advertising agency, PR firm and promotional company that provides ads, collateral, PR and promotional material to business-to-business. Current clients include Graber, Wasco and Novi American. Needs humorous illustration, cartoons and storyboards for print and audiovisual. 90% of freelance humorous illustration is for print ads. Prefers to work with freelancers with fax capabilities.
Illustration: Works with approximately 5-10 freelance humorous illustrators/year. For first contact send cover letter, resume, b&w and color tearsheets, b&w and color promo piece to Theresa Mronka, Sr. Art Director. Reports back only if interested or keeps on file. Returns materials only if requested and accompanied by a SASE. Buys all rights or negotiates rights purchased. Pays $20-100 by the hour; $20-500 by the project.

PIERSON & FLYNN, 405 N. Wabash, Chicago IL 60611. (312)644-6090. FAX: (312)644-3521. Estab. 1982. Advertising agency that provides TV and print ads to corporations, department stores and restaurants. Current clients include Ace Hardware, Ulta 3, Medical Management of America and Western Dressing. Uses humorous illustration and copywriting, animation, humor-oriented comprehensives and storyboards for print, TV and radio. 30% of freelance humorous illustration is for print ads. Prefers to work with freelancers with fax capabilities.
Writing: Send all writing materials to Art Pierson, Creative Director. Returns materials only if interested. Buys all rights or negotiates rights purchased. When establishing payment considers complexity of project, skill of writer, turnaround, ability of writer to work well under creative team, business manner and professionalism of writer, client's budget and usage.

PHILLIP ROSLER ASSOCIATES, INC., Box 2565, North Babylon NY 11703. (516)321-6273. Estab. 1981. Advertising agency and PR firm that provides full service. Needs cartoons and storyboards for print. 85% of freelance humorous illustration is for print ads.

*SHERRY WHEATLEY SACINO, INC., 235 Central Ave., St. Petersburg FL 33701. (813)894-7273. FAX: (813)823-3895. Estab. 1981. PR firm. "We are a marketing consulting firm. We do research, promotional planning, publicity and special event creation and execution. We create press kits and promotional materials for corporations and individuals. Current clients include Chef Tell, Paragon Cable and The Columbia Restaurant. Use humorous material for print, TV, radio and audiovisual.

Illustration: Works with approximately 2-3 freelance humorous illustrators/year. Looking for freelancers who "are willing to work on specific projects and have excellent examples of work displaying creativity and professionalism." For first contact send cover letter, resume, b&w and color promo pieces to Sherry W. Sacino, President. Reports back only if interested. Keeps materials on file. Pays $10 minimum, by the hour; $10 minimum, by the project. Payment is based on complexity of project, skill of illustrator, turnaround, business manner and professionalism of illustrator and ability of illustrator to work well under our art direction.

J. SPENCER & ASSOCIATES, (formerly Spencer Visuals), 134 Kings Hwy. E, Haddonfield NJ 08033. (609)354-9692. FAX: (609)354-6223. Advertising agency that provides advertising, marketing, graphic design and full service for business-to-business, consumer products, health care, retail and high technology companies. Current clients include Hella, Inc., USA-Video, Laser Track, Met Life and Ingram & Picker. Needs humorous illustration and copywriting, caricature and cartoons for print. 70% of freelance humorous illustration is for print ads. Prefers to work with freelancers with fax capabilities. Contact Joel Spencer, President.

TNT MARKETING, Suite 250, 10 East Cambridge Circle Dr., Kansas City KS 66103. (913)342-7785. FAX: (913)342-4778. Estab. 1986. Promotional marketing for packaging, premiums and promotional programs. Current clients include Wendy's, Burger King and McDonalds. Needs animation and cartoons for presentation and product. 5% of freelance humorous illustration is for print ads. Prefers to work with freelancers with fax capabilities.

Illustration: For first contact send cover letter, color tearsheets and promo piece to Tony Hoffman, President. Reports back only if interested. Returns materials only if requested. Keeps materials on file. Buys new designs only. Pays $25 minimum by the hour; $1,000 minimum by the project.

Writing: Works with approximately 2 humor oriented writers/month. Looking for freelance humorous writers who "can write for the children's market, age 3-12." For first contact send cover letter and writing samples to Tony Hoffman. Reports back only if interested. Keeps materials on file. Pays $25 minimum by the hour; $200 minimum by the project.

TRACY-LOCKE, Box 50129, Dallas TX 75250. (214)969-9000. FAX: (214)855-2480. Estab. 1914. Advertising agency that provides full service. Serving soft drink, oil and gas companies; banks; department stores; and snack foods clients. Current clients include Pepsi, Phillips Petroleum, Ben Hogan Co., Borden, Dillards, Frito-Lay and Texas Commerce Bank. Needs humorous illustration, animation, animatics and storyboards for print. 99% of freelance humorous illustration is for print ads. Prefers to work with freelancers who have fax capabilities.

Illustration: Works with approximately 3 freelance humorous illustrators/month. For first contact send cover letter, b&w and color tearsheets or b&w or color promo piece to Susan McGraner, Art Buyer. Reports back only if interested ("or if I have a job for them"). Returns materials only if requested; keeps materials. Negotiates rights purchased. Pay "absolutely depends on the job." Payment is based on complexity of project, turnaround, client's budget, skill of illustrator and usage.

*WEBER COHN & RILEY, 444 N. Michigan Ave., Chicago IL 60611. (312)527-4260. FAX:(312)527-4273. Full-service advertising and public relations firm that provides services for corporations, associations, business-to-business and consumers. Current clients include Van Kampen Merritt, Chicago Cable Marketing Council and Vein Clinics of America. Needs humorous illustration, cartoons and storyboards for print and TV. 30% of freelance humorous illustration work is for print ads. Prefers to work with freelancers who have FAX capabilities.

WILSON & WILSON ADVERTISING AND PUBLIC RELATIONS, INC., Dept. HC, 970 Arnold Way, San Jose CA 95128-3476. (408)271-7900. FAX: (408)292-9595. Estab. 1985. Advertising agency that provides services for business to business, trade publication ads, collateral and printed materials. Current clients include Mini Micro Supply Co., Inc., Ellenburg Capital Corporation, Anthem Electronics, Casey-Johnson Sales Inc. Needs humorous illustration and copywriting and slide shows for print, radio and audiovisual. 60% of freelance humorous illustration work is for print ads. Prefers to work with freelancers who have fax capabilities.

Illustration: Works with approximately 2-3 freelance humorous illustrators/year. Looking for freelance humorous illustrators who "are familiar with Macintosh systems." For first contact send cover letter, b&w tearsheets and b&w color promo piece to Erica Wilson, Art Director. Reports back. Returns materials only if requested and if accompanied by a SASE; otherwise keeps materials. Buys all rights or negotiates rights purchased. Pays by the hour $35-120; by the project $100-350.

Writing: Works with approximately 4-5 humor oriented writers/year. Looking for freelance humorous writers who "have Macintosh/modem capability." For first contact send cover letter, writing samples, audiotape, resume, client list, tearsheets to Rick Wilson,

Bark Like a Dog: *Tampa, Florida-based caricaturist Greg Williams uses his "smooth, 3-dimensional drawing style" to graphically capture Arsenio Hall. The caricature was created for a local advertising agency and shot as a transparent slide. "They wanted a lively caricature of Arsenio Hall," says Williams, "along with his 'let's get busy' phrase to close out a corporate slide presentation." Williams' original art was drawn with colored pencils on 14x10 toned paper.*

Creative Director. Reports back or returns material only if interested. Keeps materials on file. Buys all rights or negotiates rights purchased. Pays by the hour $35-100; by the project $100.

Advertising/Public Relations/Changes '91-'93

The following markets appeared in the last (1991) edition of *Humor and Cartoon Markets* but are absent from the 1993 edition. These companies failed to respond to our request for an update of their listing or for the reasons indicated in parentheses following the company name.

John Barnard (asked to be deleted)

Cahners Exposition Group (asked to be deleted)

Creative Mar/Comm (cannot be reached)

DDB Needham Advertising Inc. (out of business)

Ferrari Inc. (cannot be reached)

Guaramella Fitzgerald (overstocked)

Jerryend Communications Inc. (overstocked)

Howard Kahn & Associates, Inc. (asked to be deleted)

J.M. Kesslinger & Associates (asked to be deleted)

T.J. Lowenhaupt, Inc. (seldom uses freelancers)

Edward Lozzi & Associates (asked to be deleted)

Newmark's Advertising Agency, Inc. (cannot be reached)

Peartree Advertising (out of business)

Pihas, Schmidt, Westerdahl (cannot be reached)

Shark Communications

Tucker Associates Advertising (out of business)

Winfield Advertising Agency (asked to be deleted)

Animation

"I DON'T KNOW WHY THEY CALL IT ANIMATION. MY BUTT HASN'T MOVED FROM THIS CHAIR IN SIX DAYS!"

Did you ever think a person with bulging eyes, yellow skin and a bad attitude would ever become a TV star?

No, we're not talking about Cher. We're talking about Bart Simpson.

Forget the fact that "The Simpsons" is the best show on television, you'll never see one of the show's stars trying to slip the maître d´ at Spago a fifty for a table away from the kitchen. That's because "The Simpsons" are merely stuttered doodles on sheets of acetate. Nothing existential about it, "The Simpsons" just *don't exist*, and when you ponder the thought of *hugging* Homer, you're glad he's only made of ink and paint, not flesh and, well, flesh.

Indeed, "The Simpsons" have put animation back where it belongs—in *prime time*. It's also important to note that at the time of this writing, Nickelodeon has bought 40 new episodes of Spumco's "Ren and Stimpy Show," a wild, animated homage to everyone from Tex Avery to Hanna/Barbera. Undoubtedly these two retro-designed cartoon characters (Ren is the chihuahua, Stimpy is the cat) will be mega cult-stars-cum-commercial-stars by the time this book is in your hands. At least they *should* be.

And speaking of hands, do you know how many people it takes to *create* a second of animation? Like comic books, animation is an assembly line proposition. *Rarely* is a frame of commercial or theatrical animation created by a single individual. Rather, animated commercials, TV shows, spots and films are the byproduct of script writers, producers, directors, computer technicians, storyboarders, musicians, pencil artists, inkers, inbetweeners, cel painters and voice actors who make Beetlejuice sound like Beetlejuice and not Scooby Doo.

Animated writing

While advertising animation options for the humor writer remain somewhat limited (most scripts are handled by a client's advertising agency), this is usually not the case with animation companies that produce Saturday morning cartoon shows for kids. While most of the shows have (albeit small) writing staffs, scripts are frequently written by "outsiders" (another word for a freelancer). However, it is important to note that most story editors are accustomed to receiving freelance script submissions directly from a writer's agent.

If a script editor were to receive a bulky, unsolicited mailer, chances are he would assume it to be a script. Given potential conflict (your script might be identical to one already in production at the animation studio), you shouldn't be surprised if the mailer is returned to you, unopened, with "Non-solicited Material" stamped across it. If this happens to you, don't take it personally. The animation house is merely protecting its proverbial butt from a lawsuit. Agented submissions, however, are treated with a little more dignity.

Since script submission policies vary, you're best advised to study the individual listings in this chapter to determine how best to approach a given animation house.

"Frame" your art

Happily, most animation studios are always looking beyond their inhouse staff for humorous illustrators and cartoonists whose work is specialized or has a certain "look" which can be applied to animated segments. For example, I am occasionally called on by animation houses that need animation designed which incorporates one of my specialties—caricature.

If your work is distinct and you're interested in the possibility of designing an animated spot, you can assemble a package of your work for a given animation studio. Certainly the studio would like to see how your work "moves," but if you do not have a VHS demo tape showing animation that you have designed, then printed examples of your work will suffice. As usual, submit a color promo page, a black and white promo page, client list, resume, business card and a cover letter explaining that you're not interested in doing actual animation, rather you'd like to *design* it.

Character development sketches—of any kind—would also be important, as they can attest to your ability to effectively design model sheets to be used by the inhouse animators.

"Framers" for hire

When the work load gets too heavy, many animation studios will look beyond their four walls for animators who can handle cel-by-cel tasks ranging from storyboarding to pencilling, inbetweening to inking. To secure such assignments, it is almost essential that you have a ½" or ¾" demo tape to show to a director of animation. While it is relatively costly to mass-distribute your demo tape, the freelance animator can circulate 5-10 dubs to the various animation studios, which can then be returned with a SASE.

When circulating dubs, it's imperative that the freelancer create some method of tracking the costly tapes. I have stumbled across the work of a fine artist who uses a method that is *ideal* for animators who wish to circulate their demo tape: When you send out your demo tape (along with a SASE), enclose a pre-stamped, printed postcard similar to the one in the example.

Dear _____ :
    (Name of animator)

I have received your demo tape. Once I have viewed the tape, I will return
it to you in the SASE you have provided for me. Thank you.

_____   _____
Signature   Date

_____
Animation Studio

The postcard accomplishes two very important points. First, it is a tangible
record indicating where the demo tape is and, two, it's a tangible record that
a person on the other end did, in fact, receive it. If the tape isn't returned (and
yes, this happens all too often), you have proof that it was received and *someone*
has claimed responsibility for returning it. While you have better things to do
with your time than to badger a director of animation, the fact that you have
the postcard will greatly reduce the number of people who claim to have "lost"
your demo tape.

Payment

While every animation studio approaches payment differently, most projects
are handled on a job-by-job basis. A freelance animator can be paid an hourly
wage or can be assigned a budget for the delivery of the entire project. In the
latter case, the studio may advance the animator half of the contracted fee and
half upon completion of the project, or a third of the fee advanced, a third
midstream and a third upon completion.

Either way, it is highly recommended that the freelance animator negotiate
and hammer out a written contract and/or purchase order with the studio. The
freelancer will also want to determine if he will be allowed to use in his own
demo tape or self-promotions, work created for the animation studio or client.
Often this is a stipulation that is overlooked not only by the freelance animator,
but by the animation studio and the client as well.

ANIMART FX., Dept. HC, 505 North Weber, Colorado Springs CO 80903. (719)630-
7818. FAX: (719)473-2478. Estab. 1981. "We do cel and computer animation film and
video, full inhouse design, scripts, storyboards and promotion. We specialize in cel
animation and special effects." Clients are advertising agencies, PR firms and corporations, including State of Colorado, Hanna-Barbera, Warner Bros., Disney, U.S. Department of Education. Produces cel animation, special effects, computer animation, video
graphics and live action. Uses freelancers for assistant animators.
Illustration: 20% of work is done by freelance illustrators. Also subcontracts. "I men-
tion this only because our future needs may expand well beyond our now minimal
freelance requirements." For first contact send resume. "We'll ask if more is needed."
Send to Bob or Linn Trochim, Producers/Directors. Materials are filed and are returned
if accompanied by a SASE. Reports back only if interested. Negotiates rights purchased.
Pay is all negotiable by contract. *Inside Tips:* "If you're a qualified animator – go to L.A.
or New York for money. Otherwise it doesn't matter. It's a tough business."

Writing: "May need freelancers to help us with humor writing in the future." For first contact send resume to Bob or Linn Trochim, Producers. Materials are returned only if requested. Reports back only if interested. Negotiates rights purchased. Pay is negotiable by contract.

THE ANIMATION ATTIC, RR 1, Acton Ontario L752L7 Canada. (519)853-4767. Estab. 1988. Animation studio that provides classical animation. Clients are ad agencies, Hanna Barbera, and Warner Bros. Current clients include Old Hide House and Kennedy Cartoons. Produces cel animation. Uses freelancers for classical animation, character development and cel painting.
Illustration: 10% of work is done by freelance illustrators. Also subcontracts other animators or studios to help with overflow. Contact James Andrew Dawkins, Animation Director.
Writing: For first contact send resume to James Andrew Dawkins, Animation Director. Materials are filed and are not returned. Does not report back. Pays $10-20 by the hour.

ANIMATION COTTAGE, Suite 204, 4789 Vineland, N. Hollywood CA 91602. (818)763-0077. Estab. 1970. Animation studio that provides artistic rendering of traditional movement as well as avant-garde animation. A current client is ABC Network. Produces cel animation, special effects, video graphics and animation directly on cel with grease pencil. Uses freelancers for full animation, storyboarding, character development and layout. Prefers to work with freelancers who have fax capabilities.
Illustration: Materials are filed and are not returned. Pays $500-4,000 by the project; $12-50 by the foot for animation. *Inside Tips:* "Know your craft and don't try to bluff — it doesn't pay!"
Writing: 100% of work is done by freelance writers for series and specials. For first contact send cover letter, resume, writing samples and client list to Marija Miletic Dail, President. Materials are filed or are returned if requested. Buys all rights or negotiates rights purchased. Pays $1,000-5,000 by the project. *Inside Tips:* "We have a real need for animation writers who write visually rather than verbally."

ANIMATION STATION, LTD., Suite 1103, 633 S. Plymouth Court, Chicago IL 60605. (312)939-8003. FAX: (312)939-8041. Estab. 1987. Animation studio of computer/graphic designs. Clients are independent producers, ad agencies, television stations and corporations. Produces 3-D, computer animation and video graphics. Uses freelancers for animation, computer graphic design (ARTSTAR 3-D plus graphic systems). Experience preferred.
Illustration: 20% of work is done by freelance illustrators. For first contact send demo tape on VHS or ¾″ to Terry Choate, Executive Director. Materials are filed or are returned if accompanied by a SASE. Reports back only if interested. Pays $10-25 by the hour for computer animation, 3-D. *Inside Tips:* "Be willing to intern to learn new graphic systems."

ANIVISION, 981 Walnut St., Pittsburgh PA 15234. (412)563-2221. Animation studio that produces cel and clay animation and stop motion. "If it is a large project, we use in-betweeners and styling people" for animation, character development and pencil testing.

Market conditions are constantly changing! If you're still using this book and it is 1994 or later, buy the newest edition of **Humor and Cartoon Markets** *at your favorite bookstore or order directly from* **Writer's Digest Books.**

Close-up

Mark Baldo
Director
Broadcast Arts

"An artist must be willing to work incredibly fast and for long hours in the animation business," says Mark Baldo of Broadcast Arts. Baldo, who joined the busy staff in 1986 as a production artist, now serves as one of the studio's 25 directors responsible for organizing/coordinating the process of commercial animation. The work is complex, requiring approximately three months from start to finish for a 30-second spot. Since Baldo often handles three to four projects simultaneously, he hires freelancers to assist him. "We have had as many as 100 freelance animators and designers working for us at one time," he says.

Baldo says he calls upon freelancers from a pool of animators, designers and illustrators, sometimes as early as the design stage. Since these artists sometimes become very accomplished and leave the realm of freelancing for more permanent assignments elsewhere, Baldo is always looking for new talent. What is the best way for a freelancer to make himself known to Broadcast Arts? "I look for good organization," he says, "because there is so much art that must be generated. The illustrator must also show what he can do. I like to see a varied range—painting, drawing and sculpture."

A portfolio presented to Broadcast Arts will preferably be polished, slick and uncluttered, and the freelancer should be able to show how it relates to the studio's needs. In addition, he must demonstrate a thorough understanding of the animation process and be able to adapt to a look. "Show something relevant to animation, such as a completed cel or storyboard," says Baldo. Finally, he looks for design and color sensibility and consistency. "I like to see ink works on acetate, with lines consistent from cel to cel."

According to Baldo, "Our 'bread and butter' is commercials." Broadcast Arts has also done work for MTV, pilots for cable television, and the animation for the first season of "Pee Wee's Playhouse." Current clients include Foote, Cone & Belding (Chicago) and Grey Advertising (New York), and Baldo is currently working on a project for Kraft Foods. Although he prefers a flatter, more graphic style of animation, exemplified by cartoons such as "Mr. Magoo" and "Gerald McBoingboing," he says that clients generally like to see a "Roger Rabbit" look.

Regarding current trends, Baldo notes a rougher style of animation with grainier footage, and consumers tiring of the "shiny logo" in advertising. He suggests also that there may be a resurgence in the use of clay animation due to the success of the California Raisins© and Dominoes Pizza Noids© commercials. Regardless of trends, though, the appeal of the art of animation continues to grow. In fact, "A lot of illustrators become so interested in animation that they end up becoming animators," he says.

—Roseann Shaughnessy

A Boy and His Dog: The familiar Cracker-Jack kid, as animated by Broadcast Arts Studio for an ad campaign.

reprinted with permission of Broadcast Arts Studio

Illustration: 10% of work is done by freelance illustrators, mostly for ink and paint work. Send to Rick Catizone, Director.

Writing: 10% of work is done by freelance writers. Needs freelance writers for large projects and input on script writing. Send to Rick Catizone.

AVAILABLE LIGHT LTD., 3110 W. Burbank Blvd., Burbank CA 91505. (818)842-2109. Estab. 1983. Animation studio with "cutting-edge style" working in motion picture, special-effect animation and live action. Current clients include ILM, Paramount and Disney. Produces 3-D, motion control and special effects. Uses freelancers for special-effect animation.

Illustration: 70% of work is done by freelance animators. Also subcontracts. For first contact send VHS demo tape to J. Van Vliet. Materials are returned if accompanied by a SASE. Reports back only if interested. Pays $16 minimum by the hour for special-effects animation. *Inside Tips:* "Hang in there!"

BAJUS FILM CORPORATION, Dept. HC, 3414 Zenith Ave. S., Minneapolis MN 55416. (612)920-4173. Animation studio, cartoon illustration company that does TV commercials. Uses freelancers for storyboarding, character development and directing.

Illustration: 15-20% of work is done by freelance illustrators. Send all animation submissions to Don Bajus, President/Owner.

Writing: Needs freelance writers for animation, inking and painting. For first contact send demo tape (on VHS), tearsheets, client list and parts of film reel to Don Bajus, President/Owner. Materials are not filed and are returned.

BALL & CHAIN, 164 Fairfield Ave., Stamford CT 06902. (203)324-0018. Animation studio and production house. Produces cel and computer animation, some stop motion, 3-D, special effects, motion control and live action. Uses freelancers for model building, camera operatics, cel animation, storyboarding, character development, live action, comprehensives and pencil testing.

Illustration: Approximately 50% of work is done by freelance illustrators. For first contact send all animation submissions to Chuck Jepsen, Executive Producer.

Writing: 90% of work is done by freelance writers. For first contact send all writing submissions to Chuck Jepsen.

BANDELIER, INC., 3815 Osuna NE, Albuquerque NM 87109. (505)345-8021. FAX: (505)345-8023. Estab. 1953. Animation/production studio that provides "traditional" work. Clients are advertising agencies. Current clients include J. Walter Thompson; Grey West Indies; Wells, Rich, Greene; Saatchi & Saatchi; BBDO, Inc.; N.W. Ayer, etc. Produces cel animation and live action. Uses freelancers for all animation, storyboarding and character development. Prefers to work with freelancers who have fax capabilities.

Illustration: 100% of work is done by freelance illustrators. Also subcontracts. For first contact send demo tape on VHS or ¾" to Allan Stevens, President. Materials are filed. Reports back within weeks.

BIGMAN PICTURES CORP., 133 W. 19th St., New York NY 10011. (212)242-1411. Estab. 1983. Animation and special effects production house that provides avant-garde, traditional and cutting-edge style to advertising agencies, PR firms, music video companies and corporations. Produces cel and clay animation, stop motion, special effects, motion control, live action and time lapse. Uses freelancers for cel and montage animation, storyboarding, character development, live action, pencil testing, in-betweening, ink and paint work.

Writing: 25% of work is done by freelance writers. Needs freelance writers for promotional material, commercial spots, speculative projects. For first contact send cover letter, resume and demo tape (VHS or ¾") to John Donnelly, President. Materials are filed or are returned if requested. Negotiates rights purchased. Pays $200-5,000 by the project.

BROADCAST ARTS, Dept. HC, 632 Broadway, New York NY 10012. (212)254-5400. FAX (212)529-5506. Special effects production house. Produces cel and clay animation, stop motion, 3-D, special effects, video graphics, motion control and live action. Uses freelancers for cel animation, storyboarding, character development, live action and pencil testing. "We have our own directors but like to work with new directors."
Illustration: Approximately 80-90% of work is done by freelance illustrators. Send all animation submissions to Adele Solomon, Talent Cordinator.
Writing: 100% of work is done by freelance writers. "We deal mostly with an agency." Needs freelance writers for commercial spots, developing ideas for corporate ID's, writing for shows, original programing. Send all writing submissions to Adele Solomon. *Inside Tips:* "We are also interested in working with interns (young minds) and people who are interested in sales and marketing, art, etc."

BUZZCO ASSOCIATES INC., 110 W. 40th St., New York NY 10018. (212)840-0411. Animation studio and production house. Produces cel animation, stop motion and live action. Uses freelancers for character development, live action and comprehensives.
Illustration: Approximately 10% of work is done by freelance illustrators. Please send all animation submissions to Candy Kugel, Director/Producer.

THE CARTOON TYCOON, 311 Herr St., Dept. HC, Harrisburg PA 17102. (717)232-3200. Estab. 1974. Animation studio that Produces cel animation for traditional and non-traditional uses. Clients are ad agencies, corporations and trade shows. Current clients include MTV, MCI, various mid-sized ad agencies, Pennsylvania state agencies. Uses freelancers for animation (in-betweens) and character development.
Illustration: 25% of work is done by freelance illustrators. Send cover letter, resume and VHS demo tape to Fred Miles, Owner. Materials are filed. Pays $10 minimum by the hour for animation work. Pays $10 minimum by the hour for specialized animation work. *Inside Tips:* Looking for "good draftsmanship. I have to feel that a drawing style established for a project can be continued by the freelancer."
Writing: 10% of work is done by freelance writers. Needs freelance writers for commercial and corporate spots. For first contact send cover letter, resume, VHS demo tape to Fred Miles, Owner. Materials are filed. Reports back only if interested. Pays $10 minimum by the hour.

THE CEL PUNCH, 4311 Mary Ridge Dr., Baltimore MD 21133. (301)655-6537. Estab. 1989. Animation studio that provides "traditional cartoon cel animation, with a love for 40's animation design." Clients are advertising agencies and some corporations. Current clients include *USA Today*, Pennsylvania Blue Shield and local advertising agencies. Produces cel animation, special effects and motion control. Uses freelancers for in-betweening, storyboarding and ink/opaque. Prefers to work with freelancers who have fax capabilities.
Illustration: 30% of work is done by freelance illustrators. For first contact send cover letter, demo tape on VHS.
Writing: 100% of work is done by freelance writers. Needs freelance writers for scripts. For first contact send cover letter, resume, demo tape on VHS to Andrew Koelbl, Animation Director. Materials are filed or are returned if accompanied by a SASE. Reports back within weeks.

CELLULOID STUDIOS INC., 1422 Delgany St., Denver CO 80202. (303)595-3152. FAX: (303)595-4908. Produces animatic and live action TV commercials, cel animation, stop motion, special effects, motion control, live action. Uses freelancers for cel animation, animation storyboarding, character development and live action.
Illustration: Approximately 25% of work is done by freelance illustrators. Please send all animation submissions to Jeff Jurich, VP Head of Animation, James Wahlberg, Director or Maurice Konkler, Executive Producer.

*CINEMA CONCEPTS, 6720 Powers Ferry Rd., Atlanta GA 30339. (404)956-7460. FAX: (404)956-8358. Animation studio that produces cel, clay and computer animation, stop motion, 3-D, special effects and motion control. Uses freelancers for cel animation, storyboarding, character development, comprehensives and pencil testing.
Illustration: 25% of work is done by freelance illustrators. For first contact, send cover letter, resume, demo tape (VHS), color print samples, tearsheets, storyboard samples and client list to Jim Ogburn, General Manager

COLOSSAL PICTURES, 2800 3rd St., San Francisco CA 94107. (415)550-8772. FAX: (415)824-0389. Estab. 1976. Film design and production house. Produces cel, clay and computer animation; stop motion; 3-D; special effects; motion control and live action. Current clients include Nike, Charmin and MTV. "We use freelancers for everything from live action to animation production."
Illustration: "A small percentage of work is done by freelance artists. Send all animation submissions (photocopies **only**, please – NO original artwork) to Scott Tolmie, Animation."

CRAWFORD POST PRODUCTION, 535 Plasamour Dr., Atlanta GA 30324. (404)876-7149. FAX: (404)876-8956. Estab. 1980. Post production/animation studio that does work "ranging from traditional to cutting-edge." Clients are agencies and corporations. Current clients include Anheuser Busch, Southwestern Bell, Ralston Purina, D'Arcy. Produces cel, computer and clay animation; stop motion; 3-D; special effects; video graphics; motion control; live action; and rotoscope. Uses freelancers for cel animation, storyboarding, character development, live action, comprehensives, ink and paint.
Illustration: 30% of work is done by freelance illustrators. For first contact send resume and ¾" demo tape to John Ryan, designer/animator. Materials are filed or are returned if accompanied by a SASE. Reports back only if interested. Pays $12-15 by the hour for storyboarding/comp work; $15 minimum by the hour for animation work; $15 minimum by the hour for specialized animation work. *Inside Tips:* "Our clients seem to be wanting more animation that plays to character with warm expression and humor. Drawing skills cannot be overemphasized."
Writing: 60% of work is done by freelance writers. Needs freelance writers for commercial spots, promo material and industrial projects. For first contact send resume and writing samples to Nena Party, Assistant Manager. Materials are filed or are returned if accompanied by a SASE. Reports back only if interested. Pays $15 minimum by the hour. We have a real need for 30 second-spot and industrial people. Our clients seem to be wanting more humorous copy that motivates large groups of sales people."

*DIC ENTERPRISES, INC., 3601 W. Olive Ave., Burbank CA 91505. (818)955-5600. FAX: (818)955-5696. Cartoon production house with an emphasis on animation. Produces cel and computer animation, stop motion, 3-D, special effects, video graphics, motion control and live action. Uses freelancers for animation, storyboarding, character development, live action, comprehensives and pencil testing.
Illustration: 50% of work is done by freelance illustrators. For first contact send cover letter, resume, demo tape (3/4"), b&w and color print samples to Brian Miller, Vice President, Production.

Writing: "Writing accepted through agent only." Needs freelancers for entertainment only. For first contact send cover letter and resume to Robbie London, Sr. Vice President, Creative Affairs.

J. DYER, INC., Suite 900, 3340 Peachtree Rd., Dept. HC, Atlanta GA 30326. (404)266-8022. Estab. 1984. Animation studio that provides multi-design, traditional and mixed media cel animation, computer motion control, 3-D models and video compositing of film elements for advertising agencies, live action production companies, and sometimes corporate or retail clients. Current clients include McDonald's, Ford, Hardee's, Brach's Candy Company, CNN, WTBS, regional banks, hospitals, local card dealers and Delta Airlines. Produces cel animation, 3-D Logo treatments, special effects, motion control, live action, rotoscope and mixed media film graphics composited on tape. Uses freelancers for animation key and in-between drawing, storyboarding, character development, live action, pencil testing, stat camera operations, inkings, paintings, camera operators, matte prep, rotoscope art and model construction. "Prefer to work with freelancers who are willing to work in my studio."
Illustration: 20% of work is done by freelance illustrators, mostly background art for animation. For first contact send demo tape on ¼" to Illene Dyer, Studio Manager. "Normally, freelance animators don't have substantial demo reels or many copies. They usually make an appointment and come and show us a portfolio of art that may or may not relate to animation." Materials are filed and returned only if requested. Reports back only if interested. "If the work shows merit, we'll put you on the list and call as jobs come up." Buys all rights. "All part-time labor is paid a flat hour wage and waves ownership of art under 'Georgia Work for Hire' laws." Pays $12-20 by the hour for storyboarding; painters start at $6.50/hour; $12/hour for in-between, stat camera, paste up, rotoscope, matte cutting, key animation; $12/hour for specialized animation. *Inside Tips:* "Clients desire the secure feeling that they're not having to create anything that seems risky or original. They're all scared. We just try to keep a diverse, contemporary reel that we constantly update. It's an ever-changing animation menu. Be flexible."
Writing: "Very little work is done by freelance writers. Usually the agency supplies copy. Needs freelance writers for commercial spots. There are cases, however, when agencies are extremely weak in the copywriting department and they ask for our help." For first contact send demo tape ¼", but call first. Materials are returned only if requested. Reports back only if interested. Buys all rights. Negotiates fees. *Inside Tips:* "When it comes to freelance writing, we have a real need for humor and someone who can write copy for animation action."

FILM ROMAN, 12020 Chandler Blvd., Suite 200, North Hollywood CA 91607. (818)761-2544. FAX: (818)985-2973. Estab. 1984. Animation studio and production house. Produces cel animation. Uses freelancers for animation, layout and background. Current clients include CBS, Fox Television and General Foods.
Illustration: 50% of work is done by freelance illustrators. Send all animation submissions to Bill Schutz, VP Development and Production or Mike Wolf, Production Manager.
Writing: Needs series writers. For first contact send demo tape (on VHS or ¾"), writing samples, tearsheets and layout samples to Bill Schutz, VP Development and Production or Mike Wolf, Production Manager. Materials are filed or are returned if accompanied by a SASE.

FINE ARTS PRODUCTIONS INC., 4350 Tujunga Ave., Studio City CA 91604. (818)506-0095. Estab. 1970. Animation studio. Clients are cable and video companies. Current clients include NBC, CBS, ABC, Showtime, etc. Produces cel animation. Uses freelancers for character animation, storyboarding and character development. Prefers to work with freelancers who have fax capabilities.

Illustration: 50% of work is done by freelance illustrators. Also subcontracts. For first contact send resume and storyboard samples to John Wilson, Director.
Writing: 50% of work is done by freelance writers. Needs freelance writers for story-boarding, character and caricature and imaginative writing. For first contact send resume, tearsheets, sketches, Xeroxes and storyboards to John Wilson, Director. Materials are filed and are returned only if requested. Pays $25-2,500 maximum by the project. Looking for writing that contains "fantasy, folk, fun, frolic. Our clients seem to be wanting more humorous copy that is endearing, charming, imaginative (for sure, *not* amateur). We need sophistication!"

FLYING FOTO FACTORY INC., Box 1166, 107 Church St., Durham NC 27702. (919)682-3411. Animation studio and production house that produces cel animation, stop motion, special effects and motion control. Uses freelancers for animation (traditional character animation).
Illustration: "Percentage of work done by freelance illustrators depends on project at hand." Please send all animation submissions to Casey Herbert, Owner/President.

GALLERY IN MOTION, 415 East 71st Terrace, Kansas City MO 64131. (816)926-0444, outside Kansas City: (800)788-0445. FAX: (816)926-0444. Estab. 1989. Animation art gallery. "We present animation art exclusively! We stock a variety of production and limited edition cels, drawings, model-sheets, backgrounds and storyboards (when available): Walt Disney, Warner Bros., Hanna-Barbera, Walter Lantz, Fleischer Studios, Don Bluth, Bakski and more. We also will be happy to search for particular characters and scenes." Clients are collectors/investors of animation-oriented art. Private and corporate consultation. Buy, sell, trade, consignment and layaway. Free catalogs!

*GREENBERG ASSOC!ATES, 350 W. 39th St., New York NY 10018. (212)239-6767. FAX:(212)947-3769. Full-service production house that produces cel and computer animation, stop motion, 3-D, special effects, video graphics, motion control, live action and film opticals. Uses freelancers for animation (cel graphics), storyboarding, character development, comprehensives and pencil testing.
Illustration: For first contact send cover letter, resume, demo tape (VHS or 3/4"), b&w or color print samples, tearsheets, storyboard samples and client list to Rick Debbie, Animation Department Head.

HANNA-BARBERA PRODUCTIONS, INC., 3400 Cahuenga Blvd. W., Hollywood CA 90068. (213)851-5000. FAX (213)969-1201. Animation studio that produces cel animation, 3-D, computer animation and live action. Uses freelancers for animation, storyboarding, character development, live action, comprehensives and pencil testing.
Illustration: Please send all animation submissions to David Kirschner, President (CEO).
Writing: Need freelancers mostly for storyboarding. Please send all writing submissions to Paul Sabella, Director of Creative Projects.

THE INK TANK, 2 W. 47th St., New York NY 10036. (212)869-1630. FAX: (212)764-4169. Animation and graphic design studio. Produces cel and computer animation, stop motion, special effects and live action. Current clients include MTV, General Foods and CBS. Uses freelancers as ink and paint artists (to fill in colors) and opaquers, animation, storyboarding, live action and pencil testing.
Illustration: Approximately 50% of work is done by freelance illustrators. Send all animation submissions to Jim Romaine, Executive Producer.

KLASKY-CSUPO, 1258 N. Highland Ave., Hollywood CA 90038. (213)463-0145. FAX: (213)463-8709. Animation studio that produces character and graphic animation, TV commercials, TV shows, etc. Current clients include Columbia Pictures, Warner Broth-

ers Television and Capitol Records. Uses freelancers for design and directing.
Illustration: Send all animation submissions to Sherry Gunther, Supervising Producer.
Writing: For first contact send demo tape, tearsheets to Sherry Gunther, Supervising Producer. Materials are filed or are returned if accompanied by a SASE only if requested.

KOLIBA FILM STUDIOS – BRATISLAVA CZECHOSLOVAKIA, %IFEX, 201 W. 52 St., New York NY 10019. (212)582-4318. FAX: (212)956-2257. Estab. 1953. Animation studio and production house. Clients are film producers, advertising agencies and television stations. Current clients include Beta Films – Munich, International Film Exchange Ltd – New York, Today Home Entertainment – Los Angeles. Produces cel animation, claymation, stop motion, special effects and live action. Uses freelancers for character development and live action.
Illustration: Approximately 5% of work is done by freelance illustrators. Subcontracts animators to help with overflow. For first contact send cover letter, resume and demo tape (on VHS or ¾″) to Gerald Rappoport, President. Materials are returned only if requested. Reports back within 2 months. Buys first time rights, all rights or negotiates rights purchased.
Writing: Approximately 25% of work is done by freelance writers. Needs freelance writers for storyboarding for animated cartoon subjects. For first contact send cover letter, writing samples and ideas to Gerald Rappoport, President. Materials are returned. Reports back within 2 months. Buys first time rights, all rights or negotiates rights purchased. *Inside Tips:* "When it comes to freelance writing, we have a real need for good stories for 1-10 minute subjects animation."

KROYER FILMS, 7521 Woodman Ave., Van Nuys CA 91405. (818)778-2366. FAX: (818)787-8464. Estab. 1985. Animation Studio. "We use many cartoon styles from Tex Avery to Disney. We do have a computer system for 3-D effects." Clients are agencies, big film studios and corporations. Current clients include Warner Bros., Epcot, Disney Studio and Leo Burnett Advertising. Produces cel animation, 3-D, special effects, computer animation and live action. Uses freelancers for animation (all types), storyboarding and character development. Prefers to work with freelancers who have fax capabilities.
Illustration: 40% of work is done by freelance illustrators. Also subcontracts. For first contact send resume to Bill Kroyer, President. Materials are filed or are returned if accompanied by a SASE. Reports back only if interested. Negotiates rights purchased. "We pay union scale or more." *Inside Tips:* "Our clients seem to be wanting more animation that is funny! Do good work, be on time. Take direction well."
Writing: 20% of work is done by freelance writers. For first contact send cover letter and writing samples to Bill Kroyer. Materials are filed or are returned if accompanied by a SASE. Reports back only if interested.

JOHN LEMMON FILMS, 1216 Pinecrest Ave., Charlotte NC 28205. (704)532-1944. Estab. 1984. Animation studio that provides "high quality 'classic' clay animation for advertising agencies and corporations." Current clients include Sears, Tandy Corporation, Disney Channel and Coleman Company. Produces clay animation. Uses freelancers for clay animation and storyboarding.
Illustration: 10% of work is done by freelance illustrators. Also subcontracts. For first contact send demo tape on VHS to John Lemmon, President. Materials are filed. Reports back only if interested. Pays $10-50 by the frame for storyboarding; $15-30 by the hour for clay animation. *Inside Tips:* "Our clients seem to be wanting more animation that is expressive and appealing." To succeed "spend a lot of time producing one or two top-notch pieces of short animation."

BILL MELENDEZ PRODUCTIONS, 439 N. Larchmont, Los Angeles CA 90004. (213)463-4101. Animation studio and production house that produces cel animation, TV programs and commercials. Uses freelancers for animation, pencil testing, ink and paint.
Illustration: 25% of work is done by freelance illustrators. Send all animation submissions to Larry Leichliter, Animator, Al Pabiam, Animation Director or Nina Skahan, Office Manager.
Writing: For first contact send cover letter, demo tape to Al Pabiam, Animation Director or Nina Skahan, Office Manager. Materials are returned; "we will usually make a dub here to keep on file and return the originals."

MERGE FILMS, Suite 8, 4831 Myrtle St., Sacramento CA 95841. (916)332-4371 or 446-0769. FAX: (916)332-4371. Estab. 1965. "We are an animation studio that not only provides animation for businesses, but is also a studio where animators may 'merge' with other artists and musicians to produce films. Usually I provide the equipment and some material involvement; the artist provides the labor for his film with materials. Our design attitude is not set and is as varied as the animators associated with us." Clients are advertising agencies, producers and animator services. Produces cel and clay animation and stop motion. Uses freelancers for cel animation.
Illustration: 30% of work is done by freelance illustrator. Also subcontracts other animators or studios to help with overflow. For first contact send cover letter, resume, demo tape on VHS or ¾" to Paul Merta, Owner. Materials are returned if accompanied by a SASE. Payment varies.

THE MULTI-MEDIA PRODUCTION FELLOWSHIP, 6833 N. Haight Ave., Portland OR 97217-1719. (503)285-8814. Estab. 1988. Nonprofit organization, multi-media production house (sound, music, animation, special effects). "The MMPF is set up to gather funds for effects-oriented film production for inhouse productions in film and inhouse music production. It can also function as a parent company funneling entity for outside artists to secure funding from corporate foundations for outside projects." Clients are commercial, non-commercial, independent film and video producers, musicians, painters, avant-garde artists, theater arts, musicians, writers and any other form of creative artistry. Current clients include independent animators Joanna Priestly and Amy Bloomenstein, Tyee Productions, Volkswagon Hawaii dealership and independent film producer Tom Shaw. Produces cel and clay animation, stop motion, special effects, motion control, live action and "MultiMation" process combining all above techniques. Uses freelancers for object, model, cel and clay animation, storyboarding, character development, live action, comprehensives, pencil testing and experimental techniques.
Illustration: 50% of work is done by freelance illustrators. Also utilizes a resource list of other animators or studios to help with overflow. For first contact send cover letter, resume, demo tape on VHS, b&w print samples (only if original work is b&w), color print samples, storyboard samples, client list, "16mm film is OK also. For information on how you can apply for funding for your projects, send $5 and SASE with 52¢ postage to the MMPF. Checks should be made out to Daniel J. Fiebiger. Please include your phone number." Send all animation submissions to Daniel J. Fiebiger, President & CEO. Materials are filed and are not returned. Reports back only if interested. Pays $5-20 by the hour for storyboarding; $5-20 by the hour for animation work; $5-20 by the hour for motion control and live animation. *Inside Tips:* "Our clients seem to be wanting more animation that has a sense of humor and/or has quick, fast, slick eye-popping animation effects. Stay away from limited animation as demos. Study follow-through and stretch and squash techniques of Disney, Don Bluth, Warner Brothers cartoons; develop sense of humor (which clients like as a selling tool in commercials)."
Writing: Needs freelance writers for "gags for specific bits which still fit in the basic structure of the script and that won't disrupt the overall pacing of the story." For first contact send cover letter, resume, demo tape on VHS, writing samples, client list, Xe-

roxes of art and strips to Daniel J. Fiebiger, President & CEO. Materials are filed and are not returned. Does not report back "until funding for project that could use your talents is secured." Pays $5-20 by the hour. *Inside Tips:* Our clients seem to be wanting more humorous copy that avoids cheesy and cheap puns and emphasizes clever illiteration, malapropisms and parodies. Attempts at multilayered humor are encouraged. Short demo pieces are also encouraged." Buys one-time rights. Pays $15, b&w; on acceptance.

NOTE WORTHY GRAPHICS, 2562 Mid-Bellville, Mansfield OH 44904. (419)756-1988. FAX: (419)756-3088. Estab. 1988. Animation/graphics studio that provides "traditional but open-minded work. Quality and illustration capability respected. Concept important." Clients are ad agencies, TV stations, video production houses and Corporations. Produces 3-D, special effects, computer animation, video graphics, 2-D. Uses freelancers for animation, (computer/software knowledgeable), character development. Prefers freelancers who have fax capabilities.
Illustration: 50% of work is done by freelance illustrators. Also subcontracts. For first contact send cover letter to Larry Minor, Creative Director. Materials are filed and are returned if accompanied by a SASE. Reports back in days only if interested. Payment is negotiable and "depends on need and concept." *Inside Tips:* Don't give up if (we) first refused. Personal contact is better than a (sample) letter.
Writing: Send cover letter. Materials are filed and are not returned. Does not report back. The majority is done inhouse.

OLIVE JAR ANIMATION, 44 White Place, Brookline MA 02146. (617)566-6699. FAX: (617)566-0689. Estab. 1984. Animation studio that provides humor and attention grabbers for advertising agencies, PR firms, broadcast clients and corporations. Clients include MTV, Nickelodeon, CBS Television, McDonalds, Panasonic, Parker Brothers and Reebok. Produces cel and clay animation, stop motion, special effects and live action. Uses freelancers for animation, storyboarding, character development, live action, cel and clay animation, stop motion and special effects.
Illustration: 95% of work is done by freelance illustrators. Also subcontracts for live action and animation spots. For first contact send cover letter, resume, b&w print samples, storyboard samples and client list to Fred Macdonald, Executive Producer. Materials are filed. Reports back in weeks. Negotiates rights purchased. Sorry, policy is *not* to list pay scales. *Inside Tips:* "Show creative and imaginative artwork. Concepts are just as important as execution."
Writing: 50% of work is done by freelance writers. Needs freelance writers for commercial spots. For first contact send cover letter, resume, writing samples and client list to Fred Macdonald. Materials are filed. Reports back in weeks. Negotiates rights purchased.

PLAYHOUSE PICTURES, 1401 N. LaBrea, Hollywood CA 90028. (213)851-2112. FAX: (213)851-2117. Animation studio and production house. "We don't develop film. We do a lot of Disney commercials, Mattel commercials using Disney characters." Produces cel and clay animation, stop motion and live action. Uses freelancers for animation, storyboarding, character development, live action and comprehensives.
Illustration: 100% of work is done by freelance illustrators. Send all animation submissions to Gerry Woolery, Director.
Writing: 100% of work is done by freelance writers. Needs freelance writers for mostly storyboarding. Send all writing submissions to Gerry Woolery, Director.

PRODUCTION MASTERS, INC., 321 First Ave., Pittsburgh PA 15222. (412)281-8500. FAX: (412)391-7529. Estab. 1986. Computer animation company. "We produce what others imagine" for advertising agencies, PR firms, corporations, television stations and independent producers. Current clients include Ketchum Advertising, Della Famina Advertising, Burson Marstellar, PPG, Westinghouse and Heinz. Produces 3-D, special effects, computer animation and video graphics. Uses freelancers for animation and storyboarding.

Illustration: 10% of work is done by freelance illustrators. Also subcontracts. For first contact send cover letter and resume to Thomas Casey, Design Director. Materials are filed. Reports back within 2 weeks. Pays $100 minimum by the project for storyboarding/comp work; $500 minimum by the project for computer animation. *Inside Tips:* "Our clients seem to be wanting more animation that is design driven."

RHYTHM AND HUES, 910 N. Sycamore Ave., Hollywood CA 90038. (213)851-6500. Animation studio and production house. Produces computer animation. Uses freelancers for computer animation.

Illustration: 5% of work is done by freelance illustrators. Send all animation submissions to Charlie Gibson, Vice President.

Writing: For first contact send demo tape (on VHS or ¾") to Charlie Gibson, Vice President. Materials are filed or are returned.

*STARTOONS, 900 Ridge Rd., Homewood IL 60430. (708)335-3535. FAX: (708)335-3999. Animation studio. Current clients include Warner Brothers, Hanna-Barbera, Disney. Produces cel animation. Hires freelancers for cel animation.

Illustration: For first contact, send cover letter, demo tape (VHS) and resume to Chris McClenahan, Producer.

Writing: For first contact, send cover letter, resume and writing sample to Mark Lesser, Prod. Executive

1351 PRODUCTION, 1351 W. Grand, Chicago IL 60622. (312)421-0400. FAX: (312)421-1915. Animation studio that produces all types of animation.

Illustration: 50% of work is done by freelance illustrators. Also subcontracts. For first contact send demo tape (VHS or ¾") to Tom Kwilosz, Director. Materials are filed or are returned if accompanied by a SASE.

Writing: 50% of work is done by freelance writers. Needs freelance writers for all types of humor writing. For first contact send cover letter, demo tape (on ¾"), writing samples to Tom Kwilosz, Director. Materials are filed or are returned if accompanied by a SASE.

*VIDEO VENTURES PRODUCTIONS, 16505 NW 13th Ave., Miami FL 33169. (305)621-5266. FAX: (305)621-0803. Estab. 1979. Production company/facility agency. "We always look for a totally different approach to sometimes mundane commercial spot topics. Since we often create multiple spots per topic, a wide variety of concepts is also needed." Clients are corporations, government agencies, outside advertising agencies. Current clients include Armed Forces Radio & Television Service, Burger King Corp., American Express, U.S. Navy, U.S. Marine Corps., Bacardi Imports, Blockbuster Video, Baxter. Produces 3-D, special effects, computer animation, video graphics. Uses freelancers for concept development and scriptwriting.

Writing: 75% of work is done by freelance writers. Needs commercial spots and long format corporate presentations. For first contact send demo tape (VHS or ¾"), writing samples to Al Edick, Creative Producer. Materials are filed or returned if accompanied by SASE. Reports back only if interested. Pays by the spot, $150-200. *Inside Tips:* "We have a real need for people who can can take an unusual, off-beat look at everyday topics (i.e., physical fitness, diets, money problems, etc.) We want *unique* approaches and concepts. Our clients seem to be wanting more humorous copy that can poke fun at common, everyday problems and occurrences, without belittling or talking down to the audience. Our spots must *inform* people in a fun, light-hearted way."

PETER WALLACH ENTERPRISES, 17 West 17th St., New York NY 10011. (212)989-7892. Animation and special effects studio. Produces cel and clay animation, stop motion, special effects, live action. Uses freelancers for storyboarding, live action, pencil testing.

Illustration: 70% of work is done by freelance illustrators. Send all animation submissions to Frank Drucker, Producer.

Writing: For first contact send cover letter and resume to Frank Drucker, Producer. Materials are filed or are returned only if requested.

Animation/Changes '91-'93

The following markets appeared in the last (1991) edition of *Humor and Cartoon Markets* but are absent from the 1993 edition. These companies failed to respond to our request for an update of their listing or for the reasons indicated in parentheses following the company name.

Acme Animation & Design (overstocked)
Ambivision, Inc. (out of business)
The Big Picture (overstocked)
Danleyquest (overstocked)
Duck Soup (no longer uses freelancers)
KCMP Productions Inc. (cannot be reached)
Lester Pegues Jr. & Associates (overstocked)
Universal Images (no longer uses freelancers)
Mark Zander Productions

Art/Design Studios

Ever stop and wonder where all the art comes from?

It doesn't just "happen." It doesn't just sprout up. It doesn't even spontaneously generate from a pile of warm, steamy rags. Be nice if it did, but it doesn't.

Indeed, art is *created* by artists—even those rumored to be artists. Guys sitting in basement studios in Des Moines, and girls hunkered down in offices in Phoenix. And then there's art "created" by art and design studios.

Essentially, art/design studios are hired by advertising agencies, public relations firms, corporations and businesses to work in *tangent* with them by fully developing, administering and producing a myriad of communicative materials. They help create everything from print advertisements to posters, point-of-purchase displays to package design, signage to collateral pieces.

Most art/design studios either handle this work themselves or hire the appropriate (and usually specialized) copywriters, illustrators, designers and suppliers needed on a job-by-job basis. But don't assume that art/design studios merely "sub-contract" their assignments and mark-up their billings. *Good* art/design studios "flesh-out" each project before selecting the correct freelancer to finish it off.

Some art/design studios meticulously cultivate a certain image and are known for a particular "design attitude"—the general, overall look of their projects. Yet many studios are successful because they are able to bounce all over the drawing board by creating a stoic, corporate look for this account, and giving a maniacal, punk-inspired look to the next.

A freelance foot in the door for the humorous illustrator or cartoonist

When you approach an art/design studio with your work, professionalism cannot be over-stressed. You must bear in mind that it is easy for an art/design studio to hire an illustrator from any of the illustration directors (*American Showcase*, *Creative Illustration*, etc.), so any material you send must be just as polished—*more* so if you expect to snag an assignment!

If possible, submit material the art/design studio can keep on file, and if you're versatile, make sure your material adequately reveals this strength. Assemble a package of color promo pages, black and white promo pages, a client list and resume, tearsheets (to be returned in your SASE), business card and, of course, a cover letter.

A few weeks after sending your material, follow up with a quick phone call—just to touch base. If the individual expresses interest in your work, terrific—put them on your permanent mailing list and update them with new samples on a periodic basis.

The first step for a writer

Like a cartoonist or humorous illustrator, a freelance humor writer should approach art/design studios in a similar, always professional, manner. While you may think your dot matrix printer is the coolest thing since the 78rpm record, such antiquated submissions appear, well, "cheesy." The cost of letter quality printers, computers and word processors continues to drop, and by using one you improve your "visual appeal."

You'll also bolster a client's confidence when you show him tearsheets (or copies) of your published work. Simply stated, these tearsheets attest to the fact that you *are* professional, that you *have* done this type of work, and that hiring you won't be a risky proposition. Certainly you don't want to ask that copies of tearsheets be returned, but if you must submit original clips, you can request that they be returned in an accompanying SASE.

As always, include a copy of your resume, client list, business card and a cover letter. And remember, you're a *writer*—a single misspelling or typo on your cover letter and you should seriously start scouring the classifieds for jobs which involve wearing a hair net and a uniform!

Recession round-up!

As with advertising, art/design studios have also been hit severely by the recession. This is because most art/design studios do a majority of their work for wide advertising application. This has meant that many art/design studios have had no other recourse than to produce greater amounts of the work inhouse and cut back on freelance assignments. To succeed in this reduced market, a freelancer must ensure that his work is so unique, so highly specialized, that it cannot be created inhouse. This also means that when the freelancer *is* able to convince the art/design studio to hire his services, it is possible that he will be asked to work at "scaled-down" rates. Unfortunately, trimmed down budgets are the bitter pill of these bad economic times. Nevertheless, there are worse things than accepting a pay cut. If only Congress felt the same way.

A.T. ASSOCIATES, 63 Old Rutherford Ave., Charlestown MA 02120. (617)242-6004. FAX: (617)242-0697. Industrial and graphic design studio that provides P.O.P., annual reports, collateral, print advertising, brand identity, packaging and new product development for inventors, corporation and commercials. Needs caricature, animation, animatics, storyboards and slide shows for brochures, print ads, TV commercials, P.O.P., packaging, collateral, posters, slide shows, catalogs, annual reports, promotion and premiums. 5% of work done by freelance humorous illustrators is for print ads.

Illustration: Works with 0-2 freelance illustrators/month. For first contact send resume and small samples to Sarah Crissman, Administrative Assistant. Reports back only if interested. Keeps materials on file. Pays by the hour, $12-15. "Payment varies with budget."

MARK ALLEN DESIGN ASSOCIATES, 1601 Abbot Kinney Blvd., Venice CA 90291-3744. (310)396-6471. Estab. 1981. Art/design studio for real estate, museums and advertising agencies. Current clients include CBS, Buena Vista Television, Museum of Modern Art and Museum of Contemporary Art. Needs humorous illustration and copywriting for brochures, print ads, P.O.P., packaging, direct mail, posters, magazines, annual reports, promotions and premiums. 10% of work done by freelance humorous illustrators is for print. Prefers to work with freelancers who have fax capabilities.

Illustration: Is interested in nurturing an ongoing relationship with freelancers. For first contact send cover letter, resume, client list, b&w and color tearsheets and b&w and color promo pieces to Mark Allen, Creative Director. Reports back only if interested. Keeps materials on file. Buys all rights. Pays by the project, $100-2,500.

Writing: Works with 3 freelance writers/year. For first contact send cover letter, resume, client list and tearsheets to Mark Allen. Reports back only if interested. Keeps materials on file. Buys all rights. Pays by the project, $100 minimum.

APARTMENT 3-D, 726 South Ballas Rd., Saint Louis MO 63122. (314)961-2303. FAX: (314)961-6771. Estab. 1983. 3-D Studio. "Apartment 3-D is a full-service design studio specializing in the creation of 3-D imagery for advertising agencies, design groups, corporations and marketing clients. Publishes 3-D self-promotional posters for illustrators, manufactures custom 3-D glasses and produces 3-D television programming." Current clients include Ralston Purina, *Adweek*, Turner Broadcasting, Bazooka Bubble Gum, Hostess Cakes, Sunkist Fun Fruits, General Electric, Anheuser-Busch, Jim Henson Productions and Rockwell International. Needs line art for conversion into 3-D for packaging, collateral, promotions, TV commercials, direct mail, premiums and posters. 70% of work done by freelance humorous illustrators is for print. Works *only* with freelancers who have fax capabilities.

Illustration: Works with 2 freelance illustrators/month. Looks for "one who understands how to design for 3-D — able to grasp what works and what doesn't. We only work with top professional freelance illustrators! If you're just starting out or if illustration is your part-time 'hobby,' we highly recommend that you send your postage elsewhere. Be realistic when querying us." For first contact send cover letter, resume, client list, b&w tearsheets and promo pieces to Bob Staake, President. Reports back within 4 weeks only if interested. Returns material if accompanied by a SASE. Keeps material on file if interested. Negotiates rights purchased. Pays by the project, $100-10,000.

THE ART WORKS, 4409 Maple Ave., Dallas TX 75219. (214)521-2121. Art/design studio and design consortium that provides P.O.P., advertising and packaging for small businesses and large firms. Current clients include Jack in the Box and Meeting Planners International. Needs humorous illustration for print work. 10% of work done by freelance humorous illustrators is for print.

Illustration: Works with 1 freelance illustrator/month. For first contact send samples to Fred Henley, Illustrator. Payment varies.

BERSON, DEAN, STEVENS, 65 Twining Lane, Simi Valley CA 93065-6726. (818)713-0134. FAX: (818)713-0417. Estab. 1981. Art/design studio that provides P.O.P., annual reports, collateral, print and radio advertising and packaging for corporations, manufacturers and retailers. Current clients are Pepsi-Cola, Siemens and 3M National. Needs cartoons and humorous copywriting for brochures, print ads, collateral, direct mail, posters, magazine illustration, promotions and premiums. 20% of work done by free-lance humorous illustrators is for print. Prefers to work with freelancers who have fax capabilities.

Illustration: Works with 1-2 freelance illustrators/month. Is interested in nurturing an ongoing relationship with a humorous illustrator. For first contact send cover letter, resume, client list and b&w and color tearsheets to Lori Berson, Creative Director. Reports back only if interested. Returns materials only if requested. Keeps materials on file. Negotiates rights purchased. Pays by the hour, $40-80; by the project, $50-2,000.

Writing: Works with 1-2 freelance writers/month. For first contact send cover letter, resume, client list, tearsheets and photocopied writing samples to Lori Berson. Reports back only if interested. Returns materials only if requested. Keeps materials on file. Buys one-time rights. Pays by the hour, $40-80; by the project, $100-1,000.

BIG CITY GRAPHICS, 8270 SW 116 Terrace, Miami FL 33156. (305)235-4700. Estab. 1976. Art/design studio that provides graphic design, corporate graphics, print advertising, direct mail and publication design to ad agencies, corporations, hospitals, resorts and industries. Current clients include FPL, Radisson Hotel, Joe Robbie Stadium/Miami Dolphins, South Miami Hospital and Merchandise Mart. Needs humorous illustration, cartoons and humor-oriented comprehensives for brochures, print ads, collateral, direct mail, posters, magazines, slide shows and promotions. 30% of work done by freelance humorous illustrators is for print.

Illustration: Looks for freelancers with "a definite style to fit the assignment and ability to work with art director." Is interested in nurturing an ongoing relationship with free-lancers. For first contact send cover letter, b&w and color tearsheets to Joe Rodriguez, Owner. Reports back within 2 weeks only if interested. Keeps materials on file. Negotiates rights purchased. Considers complexity of project, skill of illustrator, ability of illustrator to work well under art direction, turnaround, client's budget, usage and possibility of long-term agency/illustrator relationship when establishing payment.

Writing: Works with 4-5 freelance writers/year. Looks for freelancers with "strong ability to identify assignment's needs, ability to work well with creative staff and willingness to make changes if needed." For first contact send cover letter, tearsheets and photocopied writing samples to Joe Rodriguez. Reports back within 2 weeks only if interested. Returns materials only if requested. Keeps materials on file. Negotiates rights purchased. Considers complexity of project, ability of writer to work well under direction of creative team, turnaround, client's budget, usage and possibility of long-term agency/writer relationship when establishing payment.

BOB BOEBERITZ DESIGN, 247 Charlotte St., Ashville NC 28801. (704)258-0316. Art/design studio that provides P.O.P., annual reports, collateral, print advertising, brand identity, packaging, etc. for advertising agencies and small businesses. Needs humorous illustration and copywriting, cartoons, storyboards and slide shows for brochures, print ads, TV commercials, P.O.P., collateral, magazine illustration and slide shows.

Illustration: Works with 1 freelance illustrator on occasion. For first contact send cover letter, color tearsheets, b&w promo piece and slides to Bob Boeberitz, Owner. Reports back only if interested. Keeps materials on file. Buys all rights. Pays by the project, $50 minimum.

LEONARD BRUCE DESIGNS, Suite 226, Box 2767, Jackson TN 38302. (901)668-1205. Estab. 1984. Art/design studio and syndicate that provides syndicate cartoons and strips, pushes cartoons to be syndicated and provides help for gag writers and cartoonists. Current clients include United States Space Education Association, Starlog and United Cartoonists Syndicate. Needs humorous illustration, caricature and cartoons for posters, magazines, catalogs and industrial film. 10% of work done by freelance humorous illustrators is for print.

Illustration: Works with 3 freelance illustrators/month. Looks for " 'off the wall' who dare to be different and good illustrators." For first contact send cover letter, resume, client list and b&w tearsheets to Leonard Bruce, Syndicator Cartoonist. Reports back within 3 weeks. Returns materials if accompanied by a SASE. Does not keep materials on file. Buys first time rights. Pays by the project, $15-30.

Writing: Works with 2 freelance writers/month. Looks for freelancers who "work well with my style of cartoons." For first contact send cover letter, resume, client list, tearsheets and photocopied writing samples to Leonard Bruce. Reports back within 2 weeks. Returns materials if accompanied by a SASE. Does not keep materials on file. Buys one-time rights. Pays by the project, $10-25.

CAREW DESIGN, 200 Gate 5 Rd., Sausalito CA 94965. (415)331-8222. (415)331-8222. Graphic design studio that provides P.O.P., collateral, advertising, brand identity and packaging for sporting good high-tech, software and cable TV clients. Current clients include Outdoor Products, Powder Line and Jandel. Needs direct mail pieces for brochures, print ads, P.O.P., direct mail, posters, magazine illustration, catalogs, industrial films and promotions. 5-10% of work done by freelance humorous illustrators is for print.

Illustration: Works with 6 freelance illustrators/year. For first contact send cover letter, b&w and color tearsheets. Reports back only if interested. Payment varies according to clients.

ROBERT COONEY GRAPHIC DESIGN, Box 684, Point Reyes Station CA 94956. (415)663-8230. Estab. 1977. Art/design studio. "We are a freelance design studio specializing in publications, magazines, newsletters, corporate identity and collateral." Serves small businesses, nonprofit institutions, political and humanitarian groups, publishers and individuals. Current clients are Strawberry Press, Feather River Co., Amnesty International and Marin Agricultural Land Trust. Needs humorous illustration, caricature and cartoons for brochures, magazine illustration, collateral and direct mail. 10% of work done by freelance humorous illustrators is for print.

Illustration: Works with 1-2 humorous illustrators/year. Looks for freelance illustrators who "share an irreverent and independent point of view and are funny and competent." Uses freelancers on one-time-only basis. For first contact send cover letter, b&w tearsheets and promo piece and examples to Robert Cooney. Reports back within 2 weeks only if interested. Returns materials only if requested and accompanied by a SASE. Keeps material on file. Negotiates rights purchased. Pays by the project or b&w work, $25-250. *Inside Tips:* "The kind of cartoons and humor I would be interested in seeing is that coming from an ecological and anti-war perspective, promoting health, global equality, social justice and nonviolence, or generally a more peaceful and honest world. Also interested in work about the sea and marine phenomena."

ANTHONY DIMARCO, 2948½ Grand Route St. John, New Orleans LA 70119. (504)948-3128. Art/design studio that provides packaging and fashion design for advertising agencies, corporations, banking institutions, churches and city and state government. Current clients include Louisiana Nature and Science Center and The Royal Courts of Mardi Gras. Need humorous and fashion illustration, caricature, cartoons, animation, storyboards for brochures, print ads, P.O.P., packing, posters, magazine illustration, catalogs, radio spots and promotions. 20% of freelance humorous illustration work is for print.

Illustration: Works with 6 humorous illustrators/year. For first contact send cover letter and samples, not originals to Anthony Di Marco, Owner. Reports back only if interested. Pays by the hour, $50 minimum.

Writing: Works with 6 freelance writers/year. For first contact send cover letter and writing samples to Anthony Di Marco, Owner. Reports back only if interested. Payment varies.

ERIKSON/DILLON ART SERVICES, 31 Meadow St., Kings Park NY 11754-3812. (516)544-9191. Art/design studio and ad agency that provides P.O.P., annual reports, collateral, print advertising, brand identity, packaging, etc., for small businesses and publishers. Current clients include Macmillan and Harcourt Brace Jovanovich. Needs humorous illustration, cartoons and humorous copywriting for brochures, print ads, packaging, direct mail, posters, magazine illustration, slide shows, catalogs, annual reports and promotions. 5% of work done by freelance humorous illustrators is for print.
Illustration: Works with 6-8 freelance illustrators/year. For first contact send cover letter, resume, b&w and color tearsheets and b&w promo piece, mail only to Toniann Dillon, Art Director. Reports back only if interested. Keeps materials on file. depends. Payment varies.

GILLIAN/CRAIG ASSOC. INC., Suite 301, 165 8th St., San Francisco CA 94103. (415)558-8988. FAX: (415)626-8266. Design studio that provides annual reports, collateral and corporate identity for corporations and small businesses. Needs humorous illustration, cartoons and slide shows for brochures, packaging, collateral, direct mail, annual reports and invitations.
Illustration: Works with 4 freelance illustrators/year. For first contact send cover letter and b&w and color tearsheets to Ms. Gillian Smith, President. Reports back only if interested.
Writing: "Clients haven't needed writing as of yet but there could be a time when we would have a need for humor writing."

ERIC GLUCKMAN COMMUNICATIONS, 24 East Parkway, Scarsdale NY 10583. (914)723-0088. FAX: (914)472-9854. Estab. 1973. Art/design studio that provides graphic design, brochures, magazines and corporate ads for a wide range of small to medium size clients. Current clients include *Decoy Magazine* — Peacock Publications and RJG Associates. Needs humorous illustration, caricature and cartoons for print ads, collateral, direct mail, posters, magazine, catalogs, annual reports and promotions. 50% of work done by freelance humorous illustrators is for print.
Illustration: Works with 10 freelance illustrators/year. Looks for freelancers "who will work on concept development with us." For first contact send b&w and color tearsheets and b&w and color promo pieces to Eric Gluckman, President. Reports back only if interested. Keeps materials on file. Negotiates rights purchased. Pays by the project, $50-3,500.

GRAPHIC ART RESOURCE ASSOCIATES, 257 W. 10th Street, New York NY 10014. (212)929-0017. Estab. 1969. Ad agency that provides humorous material for "whatever project seems appropriate for such an approach."
Illustration: Uses freelance illustrators infrequently. Looks for freelancers with a "likable style." For first contact send b&w and/or color promo pieces to Robert Lassen, Owner. Does not report back, but will call if services are desired. Does not return materials. Keeps materials on file. Buys all rights. Pays by the project, $150 minimum.
Writing: Uses freelance writers very infrequently. For first contact send photocopied writing samples and business card to Robert Lassen. Does not report back. Does not return materials. Keeps materials on file. Buys all rights. Pays by the project, $150 minimum.

*GREGORY & CLYBURNE, INC., 45 Church St., Stamford CT 06906. (203)327-6333. FAX: (203)353-8180. Ad agency that provides print and broadcast advertising and direct mail for corporate clients. Current clients include Reader's Digest, Chinet Paper Plates,

A Truck, A Guy, A Gal, and Some Ripped-off Art: *Well, in graphic design circles, it is referred to as "found" art. It's the legitimate practice of finding old, copyright-expired visual elements and incorporating them into a pleasing design. That's what Cincinnati, Ohio-based designer Kenneth Tompos did with this piece. "I just tried to keep the composition interesting," says Tompos, "and the overall idea light and silly." Tompos was paid $100 for one-time reproduction rights to the art.*

© 1991 Straight Face Studio

GE Capital. Needs humorous illustration, cartoons and humorous copywriting for brochures, print ads, TV commercials, collateral, direct mail, slide shows and radio spots. 70% of work done by freelance humorous illustrators is for print. Prefers to work with freelancers who have fax capabilities.

Illustration: Works with 3 freelance illustrators/month. Uses freelancers on a one-time only basis. Is interested in nurturing an ongoing relationship with a humorous illustrator. For first contact send b&w and color tearsheets to Creative Director. Reports back only if interested. Does not return materials. Negotiates rights purchased. Considers complexity of project, skill of illustrator, ability of illustrator to work well under art direction, turnaround, business manner and professionalism of illustrator, client's budget, usage, schedule of illustrator and possibility of long term agency/illustrator relationship when establishing payment.

Writing: For first contact send cover letter, resume and photocopied writing samples to Creative Director. Reports back only if interested. Does not return materials. Negotiates rights purchased. Considers complexity of project, skill of writer, ability of writer to work well under direction of creative team, turnaround, business manner and professionalism of writer, client's budget, usage, schedule of writer and possibility of long term agency/writer relationship when establishing payment.

IMPRESSIVE PRINTING COMPANY, (formerly Printing Today), 202-212 South 3rd St., Coopersburg PA 18036. (215)282-4561. FAX: (215)282-4561. Estab. 1980. Provides complete layout and full-service printing. Needs humorous illustration and copywriting, caricature and cartoons for brochures, print ads, packaging, direct mail, posters, magazine illustration, catalogs, annual reports, promotions and premiums. Prefers to work with freelancers who have fax capabilities.

The asterisk before a listing indicates that the listing is new in this edition. New markets are often more receptive to freelance submissions.

Illustration: Works with 1 freelance illustrators/month. Is interested in nurturing an ongoing relationship with a humorous illustrator. For first contact send cover letter and b&w promo piece; fax to Mike Zweifel, Owner. Reports back only if interested. Returns materials only if requested and accompanied by a SASE. Negotiates rights purchased. Pays by the hour, $5-100; by the day, $50-500; by the project, $5 minimum; by b&w work, $10 minimum; by color work, $25 minimum.

Writing: Works with 1 freelance writer/month. For first contact send cover letter and photocopied writing samples to Mike Zweifel. Reports back only if interested. Returns materials if requested and accompanied by SASE. Negotiates rights purchased. Pays by the hour, $5-100; by the day, $50-500; by the project, $10 minimum.

*INNOVATIVE DESIGN & GRAPHICS, 1234 Sherman Ave., #214, Evanston IL 60202. (708)475-7772. Estab. 1981. Art/design studio that provides publications, promotional material for institutions, associations and corporations. Needs humorous illustration and cartoons for brochures, magazine illustration and print ads. 50% of work done by freelance humorous illustrators is for print. Prefers to work with freelancers who have fax capabilities.

Illustration: Works with 3 freelance illustrators/year. Looks for freelancers "who are able to read a magazine story and develop an appropriate concept to illustrate the story." Is interested in nurturing an ongoing relationship with freelancers. For first contact send b&w tearsheets to Tim Sonder, Partner. Reports back only if interested. Does not return materials. Keeps materials on file. Buys one time rights or all rights. Pays by the project, $100; b&w work, $100; color work, $300. Considers complexity of project, skill of illustrator, client's budget and usage when establishing payment.

*KIPLING CARTOONS & CREATIVE DARE-DEVILS, P.O. Box 2546, Vista CA 92085. (619)727-1122. Estab. 1981. Opened to submissions 1983. Marketing of designs for licensing and business. We market cartoon characters and designs for licensing primarily for toys, clothing and food business (manufacturers' packaging and P.O.P.), snack food ideas for toy companies, food manufacturers and clothing manufacturers (ad agencies — sometimes). Current clients include Plaidberry Co., Ruggles Krumpet Cakes, Maui Monster Tee Shirts, Mirth Quakes (the comic strip), The Lak Agency. Needs humorous illustration, caricature, cartoons, humorous copywriting, creation of licensable ideas. We use such humorous material for print ads, P.O.P., packaging, posters, catalogs, promotions, premiums, licensing and toy design. (Toys for young girls — needed more.) 5% of work done by freelance humorous illustrators is for print.

Illustration: Must have "very" original work, fresh ideas. "Must be brave enough to submit insane thoughts, locked away in the back of your gray matter." (Creative Dare-Devils). Is interested in nurturing an ongoing relationship with a humorous illustrator. For first contact send cover letter, resume, client list, b&w tearsheets, color tearsheets, b&w promo piece or a clear idea and design to John Kipling, President/Owner. Reports back within 1 month. Returns materials only if requested. Negotiates rights purchased. Pays by the project, $200. Considers complexity of project, skill of illustrator, usage, possibility of long term agency/illustrator relationship when establishing payment. "When licensing a design and idea, we determine a royalty that is equal to both parties." (When working with third party only.)

Writing: Works with 4-6 freelance writers/year (want more). Looks for freelancers who "can write in the 'Bloom County' style and see themselves as an overweight dog, who shakes the ground and fools around." —(Send SASE for "Mirth Quakes" bio.) For first contact send cover letter, resume, client list, tearsheets, photocopied writing samples. "Send only your best work" to John Kipling "Mirth Quakes," President/Owner. Reports back within 1 month. Returns materials if accompanied by a SASE. Buys all rights. Pays by the project, $50-200. Considers possibility of long term agency/writer relationship and number of strips written when establishing payment.

*GENE KRACKEHL ASSOCIATES, 55 Lily Pond Ln., Katonah NY 10536. Estab. 1987. Art/design studio that provides corporate identity, packaging, advertising-print sales promotion, direct mail, publishing, motion picture advertising and title treatments, entertainment and real estate promo and catalogs for "Fortune 500 to small corporations-the most diverse clientele imaginable." Current clients include IBM, Ford Motor Co., Grolier, Planned Parenthood, Random House, General Foods, Walt Disney Co., Paramount Pictures, Readers Digest, TWA, New England Patriots, etc. Needs humorous illustration for brochures, print ads, P.O.P., packaging, collateral, direct mail, posters, magazine illustration, annual reports, promotions and premiums. Prefers to work with freelancers who have fax capabilities.
Illustration: Works with 2 freelance illustrators/year. Is interested in nurturing an ongoing relationship with a humorous illustrator. Does not report back. Returns materials if accompanied by a SASE. Keeps materials on file. Negotiates rights purchased. Payment "depends on job and client's budget." Considers complexity of project, skill of illustrator, ability of illustrator to work well under art direction, turnaround, business manner and professionalism of illustrator, client's budget and usage when establishing payment.
Writing: For first contact send cover letter, resume, photocopied writing samples. Does not report back. Returns materials if accompanied by SASE. Negotiates rights purchased. Considers complexity of project, skill of writer, ability of writer to work well under direction of creative team, turnaround, business manner and professionalism of writer, client's budget, usage, schedule of writer and possibility of long term agency/writer relationship when establishing payment.

*LOOK/FRONTIER GROUP, 100 Prospect St., Stamford CT 06901. (203)327-9003. FAX: (203)967-9559. Estab. 1988. Ad agency. Full service agency specializing in advertising, PR and interactive multimedia. All media such as print, broadcast, direct response, out-of-home, etc. Current clients include Mercedes Benz of North America, Sonitrol and Cahners Publishing Company. Needs caricature, cartoons, animation, animatics and storyboards for brochures, print ads, TV commercials, P.O.P., collateral, direct mail, posters, magazine illustration, radio spots (humor writing) and annual reports. 80% of work done by freelance humorous illustrators is for print. Prefers to work with freelancers who have fax capabilities.
Illustration: Uses freelancers on a one-time only basis. For first contact send cover letter, resume, client list and color tearsheets to Donald F. Torrey, SVP, Creative Director. Reports back only if interested. Returns materials only if requested. Buys first time rights or negotiates rights purchased. Considers complexity of project, skill of illustrator, turnaround and client's budget when establishing payment.
Writing: For first contact send cover letter, client list and photocopied writing samples to Jamison R. Davis, President, Executive Creative Director. Reports back only if interested. Returns materials only if interested. Buys one time rights or negotiates rights purchased. Considers complexity, skill of writer, ability of writer to work well under direction of creative team and client's budget when establishing payment.

*DONYA MELANSON ASSOCIATES, 437 Main St., Boston MA 02129. (617)241-7300. FAX: (617)241-5199. Estab. 1968. Art/design studio, ad agency that provides advertising and direct mail services, P.O.P., collateral, creative and design services, electronic de-

---

Always include a self-addressed stamped envelope (SASE) or International Reply Coupon (IRC) with submissions.

sign for corporations, associations, educational institutions, financial institutions and government agencies. Current clients include Cambridge College, The Seiler Corporation, American Psychological Association and U.S. Department of Agriculture. Needs humorous illustration and humorous copywriting for brochures, print ads, P.O.P., collateral and posters. Prefers to work with freelancers who have fax capabilities.

Illustration: Works with 4-5 freelance illustrators/year. Looks for freelancers who "fit the project." Uses freelancers on a one-time only basis. For first contact send cover letter, resume, client list, b&w tearsheets and color tearsheets (photocopies are acceptable) to Donya Melanson, Owner. Reports back only if interested. Does not return materials. Keeps materials on file. Negotiates rights purchased. Pays by the project, $150 minimum; b&w work, $150 minimum; color work, $150 minimum. Considers complexity of project, skill of illustrator, ability of illustrator to work well under art direction, turnaround, business manner and professionalism of illustrator, client's budget, usage and schedule of illustrator when establishing payment.

Writing: Works with 4-5 freelance writers/year. Looks for freelancers who "fit the project." For first contact send cover letter, resume, client list, tearsheets and photocopied writing samples to Donya Melanson, Owner. Reports back only if interested. Does not return materials. Keeps materials on file. Negotiates rights purchased. Pays by the hour, $50 minimum; by the day, $200 minimum; by the project, $100 minimum. Considers complexity of project, skill of writer, ability of writer to work well under direction of creative team, turnaround, business manner and professionalism of writer, client's budget, usage, schedule of writer and possibility of long term agency/writer relationship when establishing payment.

MOSER WHITE, 209 E. State St., Cherry Valley IL 61016. (815)332-2033. FAX: (815)332-2263. Estab. 1984. "We are an advertising design firm (9 people) with a wide variety of projects, such as package design, sales literature, display design, catalogs and annual reports." Serves industrial manufacturing in camping, beverage and food industries, publishing, medical, restaurants and retail. Current clients include Mobil Oil, Dean Foods, Duplex Products, Sundstrand Corp., Precision Twist Drill, Century Tool and Manucturing Co., Sears, Winnebago Camping Equipment, Random House, Kabel News Co., ABC Publishing and Harvestore. Needs humorous illustration, caricature, humor-oriented comprehensives and humorous copywriting for brochures, print ads, direct mail, P.O.P., direct mail, posters and promotions. 75% of work done by freelance humorous illustrators is for print. Prefers to work with freelancers who have fax capabilities.

Illustration: Works with 6 freelance illustrators/month. Looks for one "who has a portfolio he can leave or show a client." Uses freelance humorous illustrators on a one-time-only basis. For first contact send b&w tearsheets and b&w and color promo piece and portfolio to Carl White, Creative Director. Reports back within 3 days. Returns materials if accompanied by a SASE. Keeps materials on file. Buys all rights. Pays by the project, $100-1,100.

Writing: Works with 3 freelance writers/year. For first contact send tearsheets and photocopied writing samples to Rick Moser, Creative Director. Reports back within 2 days. Returns material if accompanied by a SASE or keeps materials on file. Buys all rights. Pays by the hour, $25-100.

LOUIS NELSON ASSOCIATES INC., 80 University Place, New York NY 10003. (212)620-9191. Art/design studio that provides packaging, brochures and corporate interior design for small and large companies. Current clients include AT&T, Grand Central Station and the National Endowment for the Arts.

Illustration: For first contact send cover letter and samples to Louis Nelson, Owner. Reports back only if interested. Payment varies.

PERSECHINI AND CO., Suite 202, 1501 Main St., Venice CA 90291. (310)314-8622. FAX: (310)314-8619. Design studio firm that provides P.O.P., annual reports, collateral, print advertising, brand identity, packaging, etc. for advertising agencies, corporations and small businesses. Needs humorous illustration for brochures, print ads, P.O.P., packaging, collateral, direct mail, posters, magazine illustration, catalogs, annual reports and promotions. 10% of work done by freelance humorous illustrators is for print.
Illustration: For first contact send cover letter and samples to Suzette Heiman, Art Director. Reports back only if interested. Buys one-time rights or all rights. Payment varies.

PINKHAUS DESIGN CORP., Suite 201, 2424 S. Dixie Hwy., Miami FL 33133. (305)854-1000. FAX: (305)854-7300. Estab. 1984. Graphic design studio. Clients are cruise lines, fashion, sunglass companies. Needs humorous illustration and copywriting, caricature, cartoons, animation and slide shows for brochures, print ads, P.O.P., packaging, collateral, direct mail, posters, slide shows, catalogs, industrial films, annual reports and promotions.
Illustration: For first contact send b&w and color tearsheets, b&w and color promo piece, slides and portfolio to Joel Fuller, Creative Director. Reports back within 2 weeks only if interested. Returns materials if accompanied by a SASE. Keeps materials on file. Negotiates rights purchased. Pays by the project, $200-15,000.
Writing: For first contact send tearsheets and photocopied writing samples to Joel Fuller, Creative Director. Reports back within 2 weeks. Returns materials if accompanied by a SASE. Negotiates rights purchased. Pays by the project, $200-15,000.

PRODUCTION INK, 2826 NE 19th Dr., Gainesville FL 32609. (904)377-8973. (904)373-1175. Art/design studio, ad agency and marketing firm that provides P.O.P., annual reports, collateral, print advertising, brand identity, packaging, etc. for advertising agencies, corporations and small businesses. Needs brochures and print ads.
Illustration: For first contact send cover letter and samples to Terry Van Nortwick, President. Reports back only if interested. Payment varies.

Take Midlantic's Capital Line Account and get relief as needed–up to $50,000 worth.

© 1987 American Showcase

Up in Smoke: *New York City-based humorous illustrator David Garner uses his elegantly-refined, exceedingly simple pen technique to create this sophisticated art.*

*QUALLY & COMPANY, INC., 30 E. Huron #2502, Chicago IL 60611. (312)944-0237. FAX: (312)642-1344. Estab. 1979. Art/design studio, design consortium, ad agency, marketing firm that provides integrated advertising and new product launches for corporations. Current clients include Nutra Sweet, U.S. Dept. of Labor, F&F Labs, Wilson Sporting Goods and Taito Software. Needs humorous illustration, caricature, cartoons, animation, animatics, slide shows and humorous copywriting for brochures, print ads, TV commericals, P.O.P. packaging, collateral, direct mail, posters, magazine illustration, catalogs, radio spots (humor writing), annual reports, promotions and premiums. 60% of work done by freelance humorous illustrators is for print. Prefers to work with freelancers who have fax capabilities.

Illustration: Works with 15 freelance illustrators/year. Looks for freelancers who are "talented/with the right attitude." Uses freelancers on a one-time only basis, nurturing an ongoing relationship with a humorous illustrator. For first contact send cover letter, resume, client list, b&w/color promo piece, slides and portfolio to Robert Qually, Creative Director. Reports back within 3-5 days only if interested. Returns material if accompanied by a SASE. Keeps materials on file. Negotiates rights purchased. Pays by the project. Payment depends on project budget. Considers complexity of project, client's budget and usage when establishing payment.

Writing: Works with 10-20 freelance writers/year. Looks for freelancers who are "talented/with the right attitude." For first contact send cover letter, resume, client list, photocopied writing samples and audio tape to Robert Qually, Creative Director. Reports back within 3-5 days only if interested. Returns materials if accompanied by a SASE. Keeps materials on file. Pays by the hour or by the project depending on project budget. Considers complexity of project, client's budget and usage when establishing payment.

PATRICK REDMOND DESIGN, Suite 300D, The Security Building, 2395 University, St. Paul MN 55114-1513. (612)646-4254. FAX: Available. Estab. 1966. Art/design studio that provides logo and trademark design; publication design—books, magazines, newsletters; packaging; posters; and brochures for retail. Clients are financial, food, arts, education, publishing, computer, manufacturing, ad agencies, government, nonprofit and community organizations. Clients include Soft-C Ltd., Irish Books & Media and Dos Tejedoras Fiber Arts Publications (over 90 clients have used graphic design and/or illustration by Patrick Redmond). Needs humorous illustration and copywriting and caricature for brochures, print ads, collateral, direct mail, posters, magazine illustration and promotions. 10% of freelance humorous illustration is for print ads. Prefers freelancers with fax capabilities.

Illustration: Works with 4 humorous illustrators/year. More apt to hire a humorous illustrator "who is fast, uses fax, has demonstrated track record—consistent quality and a look you can count on." Is interested in nurturing an ongoing relationship with a humorous illustrator. For first contact send cover letter, resume, client list, b&w tearsheets and promo pieces to Patrick Redmond, President. Reports back on submissions in 2 weeks if interested. Does not return materials. Keeps materials on file. Negotiates rights purchased. Pays $70-400 for b&w work; $250 minimum for color work.

Writing: Is more apt to hire a freelance humor writer "who has demonstrated ability to deliver what is needed." For first contact freelancer should send cover letter, resume, client list, tearsheets and photocopied writing samples to Patrick Redmond, Design/Owner/President. Reports in 2 weeks only if interested. Does not return materials. Keeps materials on file. Negotiates rights purchased. Pays $300 minimum by the project.

RITTER & RITTER, INC., 45 W. 10th St., New York NY 10011. (212)505-0241. FAX: (212)533-0743. Design studio that provides annual reports, print advertising and corporate identity for publishers and nonprofit organizations. Current clients include *Newsweek*, MacMillan and Cabrini Hospital. Needs humorous illustration for brochures,

Close-up

Kathie Thomas
Art Director
Fleishman-Hillard, Inc.

Any communicator, whether a writer, illustrator or designer, can't expect to find solutions without first properly evaluating the problems, says Kathie Thomas, art director at Fleishman-Hillard, Inc. "It's really easy for people to focus on executional aspects first. As a company we approach our work very strategically—we determine what we are trying to say and why. Those are really basic questions, but, I think any communicator has to answer those questions first. Then the execution becomes much clearer."

It was early in her career as a production artist that Thomas says she became interested in art direction. At the time, she had no design experience, but her skills in photography and fine art, combined with the portfolio she compiled while taking night classes at Washington University, secured her first position as a designer.

Art director at Fleishman-Hillard since 1984, Thomas says the company is involved in a wide range of corporate projects, including annual reports, corporate identity systems, package design, displays, self promotion and public relations support material. Some of the more prominent among the company's "huge" list of clients are Anheuser Busch, National Public Radio, Monsanto, Valvoline, Northwest Airlines and Ralston Purina.

According to Thomas, there really aren't any needs at Fleishman-Hillard for freelance writing due to the substantial number of writers employed by the company. However, there is a need for a wide variety of freelance illustrations and cartoons.

Thomas feels that estimating the demands for humorous illustration is difficult. "It's hard to define what humor really is. I think it's easier to define something that's serious. But I think many of our projects are graced with a lighthearted approach. Whether it's really classical humor I can't say." She points out using lighthearted tones has proven to be a good way to communicate serious messages and depict controversial issues. "We use this approach a lot in brochures, corporate messages, employee publications, posters and direct mail pieces. We also use it when we're talking to a younger audience."

Consistency in a portfolio is important, says Thomas. "Everyone does work they feel is not superior work. But then don't put it in your portfolio. That shows you don't really have an ability to discriminate between your own good and bad work." When reviewing interpretative work, she looks for conceptual ability and type of message communicated. "If I need art of a bowl of chocolate pudding, I don't literally look for whether an artist has illustrated pudding. I'm looking for the ability to visualize a wide range of subject matter."

Sometimes when presenting portfolio art, less means more, according to Thomas. "Six killer pieces with good stories and experience behind them are significantly more meaningful than 12 mediocre pieces." In addition, time and money limitations that existed while working on pieces should not be used as excuses for their lack of quality, she says. However, it is permissible to communicate the specific limitations when describing the pieces.

Thomas says there's a ton of work available for artists, but making a name for oneself involves not only working hard, but working smart. "In the very beginning an artist needs to find a balance between the profitable jobs and the jobs that stimulate and challenge creativity." As an example, she mentions worthwhile nonprofit organizations are always eager to receive creative donations, and appropriate pro-bono projects are perfect examples of challenging jobs. "Be willing to work pro-bono for a group with the understanding that you'll get something for your portfolio in return," says Thomas.

She says she considers two factors when considering working with an illustrator. "The first is the quality of work. But a close second is attitude. What kind of team player are you? Do you know how a job really transforms? Do you understand the necessary compromises at times with clients? How do you feel about alterations and changes?" Thomas says freelancers must be flexible and open to critiques and analyses of their work. "There are some illustrators who can't handle that. And if they're lucky, they're really popular and they don't have to. But, in general that's just not the case. It takes a long time to get to that point where you can be a prima donna."

—Lisa Carpenter

66 Everyone does work they feel is not superior work. But then don't put it in your portfolio. That shows you don't really have an ability to discriminate between your own good and bad work. 99

—Kathie Thomas

annual reports and promotions. 10% of work done by freelance humorous illustrators is for print.
Illustration: For first contact send cover letter and b&w and color tearsheets to Valerie Ritter, Art Director. Reports back only if interested. Rights purchased depend on clients. Payment varies.

*JACK SCHECTERSON ASSOCIATES, 5316 251 Place, Little Neck NY 11362. (718)225-3536. FAX: (718)423-3478. Estab. 1967. Art/design studio, ad agency that serves large and small corporations and consumer product companies. Uses humorous material for brochures, P.O.P., packaging, direct mail, catalogs, promotions and premiums as needed. 80% of work done by freelance humorous illustrators is for print. Prefers to work with freelancers who have fax capabilities.
Illustration: Looks for freelancer who "is local." Uses freelancers on a one-time-only basis. For first contact send resume, client list, b&w tearsheets, "SASE if work is be be returned." Reports back "ASAP" only if interested. Returns materials if accompanied by a SASE. Keeps materials on file. Buys all rights. Pays by the project "depending on job at hand." Considers skill of illustrator, ability of illustrator to work well under art direction, business manner and professionalism of illustrator, client's budget and possibility of long term agency/illustrator relationship when establishing payment.
Writing: Looks for freelancer who "is local." For first contact send resume, client list, tearsheets and/or photocopied writing samples. Reports back "ASAP" only if interested. Returns materials if accompanied by a SASE. Buys all rights. Payment "depends on work at hand." Considers ability of writer to work well under direction of creative team, business manner and professionalism of writer, client's budget and possibility of long term agency/writer relationship when establishing payment.

SMITH DESIGN ASSOCIATE, 205 Thomas St., Glen Ridge NJ 07028. (201)429-2177. FAX: (201)429-7119. Design studio that provides P.O.P., print, advertising, packaging and unusual merchandise design for corporations. Current clients include Popsicle, Good Humor, Tofutti Brands Inc. and Guardian Life Insurance. Needs humorous illustration and copywriting, caricature, cartoons, animation, storyboards and slide shows for brochures, print ads, P.O.P., packaging, direct mail, posters, magazine illustration, catalogs, radio spots (humor writing), promotions and premiums. 10% of work done by freelance humorous illustrators is for print.
Illustration: For first contact send cover letter and samples to Loraine Blauvelt, Account Executive. Payment varies according to client's budget.

SUPON DESIGN GROUP INC., Suite 415, 100 Connecticut Ave., Washington DC 20036. (202)822-6540. FAX: (202)822-6541. Art/design studio. Clients are corporations and associations. Needs humorous illustration, cartoons, storyboards and slide shows for brochures, print ads, packaging, direct mail, posters, magazine illustration, slide shows, catalogs, annual reports and promotions.
Illustration: For first contact send cover letter, resume, client list, b&w and color tearsheets, b&w and color promo piece and slides to Wayne Kurie, Art Director. Reports back only if interested. Returns materials only if requested if accompanied by a SASE. Keeps materials on file. Negotiates rights purchased. Payment varies per project.
Writing: For first contact send cover letter, resume client list, tearsheets and photocopied writing to Wayne Kurie, Art Director. Reports back only if interested. Returns materials only if requested if accompanied by a SASE. Negotiates rights purchased. Payment varies per project.

*TRIBOTTI DESIGNS, 22907 Bluebird Dr., Calabasas GA 91302. (818)591-7720. FAX: (818)591-7910. Estab. 1970. Art/design studio that provides advertising, catalogs and annual reports for corporations, nonprofit and educational institutions. Current clients include Northrop Corporation and South Western University. Needs humorous illustration, caricature and cartoons for brochures, print ads, collateral, direct mail and posters. 50% of work done by freelance humorous illustrators is for print. Prefers to work with freelancers who have fax capabilities.

Illustration: Uses freelancers on a one-time only basis. Is interested in nurturing an ongoing relationship with a humorous illustrator. For first contact send cover letter, b&w and color tearsheets, b&w and color promo pieces to Robert Tribotti. Reports back only if interested. Returns materials if accompanied by a SASE. Keeps materials on file. Negotiates rights purchased. Pays by the project, $75-2,000. Considers complexity of project, skill of illustrator, ability of illustrator to work well under art direction, turnaround, business manner and professionalism of illustrator, client's budget, usage and schedule of illustrator when establishing payment.

Writing: For first contact send cover letter, resume, client list, tearsheets and photocopied writing samples to Robert Tribotti. Reports back only if interested. Returns materials only if requested and accompanied by a SASE. Keeps materials on file. Negotiates rights purchased. Pays by the project, $100-2,000. Considers complexity of project, skill of writer, ability of writer to work well under direction of creative team, turnaround, business manner and professionalism of writer, client's budget, usage and schedule of writer when establishing payment.

Reptilian Rendering: *Marietta, Georgia-based humorous illustrator Robbie Short created this poster art. Short offers frank insight into his own self-promotional activities. "I have used American Showcase twice and not with good results," he laments. "I have also had a rep, who was not good either. I now call on clients sporadically and send out mailings when things are slow."*

© 1990 Robbie Short

VISUAL IDENTITY, INC., Suite L-5 & L-6, 6250 Mountain Vista, Henderson NV 89014. (702)454-7773. FAX: (702)454-6293. Estab. 1986. Art/design studio that provides P.O.P., annual reports, collateral, print advertising, brand identity and packaging to advertising agencies, corporations and the hotel and gaming industry. Current clients include Circus Circus, Colorado Belle, Edgewater, U.S. Mint, Geisha Lighting, Westward Ho various location movies and TV series. Needs humorous illustration, caricature, cartoons, storyboards and humorous copywriting for brochures, print ads, TV commercials, P.O.P., packaging, collateral, direct mail, posters, magazine illustration, catalogs, industrial films and radio spots (humor writing). 20% of work done by freelance humorous illustrators is for print. Prefers to work with freelancers who have fax capabilities.

Illustration: Works with 10 freelance illustrators/month. Looks for someone who "meets our needs." Uses freelance humorous illustrators on a one-time-only basis. For first contact send cover letter, resume, client list, b&w and color tearsheets, b&w and color promo piece to William Garbacz, Creative Designer. Reports back within 2 weeks. Returns materials only if requested. Keeps materials on file. Buys all rights. Pays by the hour, $25-100.

Writing: Works with 3 freelance writers/month. For first contact send cover letter, resume, client list, tearsheets and photocopied writing samples to William Garbacz. Reports back within 2 weeks. Returns materials only if requested. Keeps materials on file. Buys all rights. Pays by the hour, $25-100.

Art/Design Studios/Changes '91-'93

The following markets appeared in the last (1991) edition of *Humor and Cartoon Markets* but are absent from the 1993 edition. These companies failed to respond to our request for an update of their listing or for the reasons indicated in parentheses following the company name.

Antisdel Image Group Inc. (uses little humor)
Bare-Lemons Creative (cannot be reached)
Judy Barnett (asked to be deleted)
Butler Inc. (uses no humor)
Cheval Electronic Design

Studio (cannot be reached)
Dawson Design (uses no humor)
Gregory M. Flejtuch (overstocked)
Harrison Design Group (uses no humor)
Image Productions (over

stocked)
Manhattan Design (out of business)
Marketing Communications Services (overstocked)
Margaret Patterson Design Co. (doesn't use freelancers)

Book Publishers

"WHERE'S YOUR BATHROOM AND HUMOR SECTION? (NOT NECESSARILY IN THAT ORDER)."

If a mall didn't have a bookstore, would you go into it?

A rather existential question, but worth pondering. After all, what good would a mall be if it only sold polo shirts, running shoes and gift boxes of sausage 'n' cheese? It would be downright depressing if you asked me. Sure, everybody would be dressed well, but their breath would smell like pepperoni.

But happily, most malls boasting over 100 parking spaces also contain one, two or even three bookstores, and if it weren't for those bookstores, a shopping mall would be a wasteland devoid of any culture. You certainly wouldn't catch me dead, almost dead, or even clinging to life in one.

Most funny people enter a bookstore and ask the identical question: "Where's the humor section?" With that, a pimply-faced kid with a crooked name tag usually points to a corner of the store. Humor is big, and you can find no better proof of this than in a bookstore.

Indeed, collections of reprinted comic strips, original cartoon books, hilarious fact and fiction sell well enough to invade *The New York Times* Best-Seller List, a bastion once reserved for the dubious likes of Danielle Steele, Barbara Cartland and even pre-bust Donald Trump.

Sending the write stuff

Individual publishers have individual humor needs and tastes. However, if you've just written your humorous tome, most editors would prefer that you query them with a written outline of your book, your resume, bio and perhaps a sample chapter. The latter can serve you extremely well—providing, of course that it is well written and piques the interest of an editor. The best thing a sample chapter can do is give an editor a taste—which leaves them salivating for a closer look at your manuscript. The idea is to hook 'em like a barracuda.

You may, however, want to explore the possibility of having your manuscript represented by a literary agent (in fact, a number of publishers won't look at yours unless it's presented by an established literary representative). Indeed, an agent "legitimatizes" you and your work and the good ones are fully versed in the intricacies of the publishing biz. They know which publishers would have an interest in your manuscript (and which ones won't), but more importantly, they schmooze and "do lunch" with individual editors. Agents, to be sure, are known for getting their feet in the door and for wearing steel-capped shoes (though not necessarily in that order).

To find an appropriate literary agent, I suggest you snag a copy of *Guide to Literary Agents and Art/Photo Reps* (Writer's Digest Books, 1-800-289-0963). This is a tremendous resource, and the detailed listings give an agent's specific areas of interest. For example, you can find agents who handle everything from lesbian fiction to cartoon books.

Funny art for fun-minded publishers

Like a humorous manuscript, an original cartoon book can be submitted to a publisher by the cartoonist himself or via his agent. If you have a cartoon book in mind which would require a total of 120 cartoons, draw up 10 to 15 in finished form as examples. In submitting the material directly to a book publisher, include a written outline of the book's premise, perhaps a few rough drawings, a cover letter, a self-promotional page showing black and white examples of your finished cartoon work and, of course, a SASE. But be forewarned: With the advent of color Xerox technology, presentations are getting flashier and flashier. To stand out these days, it's important that your presentation be eye-catching if you want to have it considered.

A humorous illustrator or cartoonist who is interested in the *illustration* of books should send self-promotional material to the appropriate individual, usually an art director, although editors certainly do make art assignments. Color as well as black and white samples are essential ingredients in such a mailing, and a cover letter, resume, client list and business card are mandatory. Again, provide material that the book publisher can hang on to—if it has to snooze, let it snooze in *their* files rather than yours.

Pricing

Industry pricing varies drastically and is greatly determined by the size of the publisher. A publisher can pay an author royalties anywhere from 3-25 percent of the wholesale, retail or net price which are then paid quarterly, biannually or annually. Depending on their size, a publisher can also offer a healthy advance, set you up with an anemic stipend or offer no upfront money at all.

This is why it's so important to secure an agent. Many times it's not the writing or the illustration of the book that's so difficult, it's the negotiation of the contract itself. With every book I have written, illustrated or edited (the book in your hands included), there are countless pertinent contractual points that must be negotiated. With all the negotiation, it's almost *essential* for the cartoonist, illustrator or writer to have a qualified agent act essentially as his referee. Deals aren't done with a handshake any longer—they're done in *tripli-cate*.

It's also important to note a distressing overall trend in publishing these days. Due to the sorry state of the economy, few publishers have the confidence to go out on a limb. It's simply too risky. With sales down (not just in books, but with consumer goods as well), publishers seem reluctant to commit to less than sure-fire manuscripts written and/or illustrated by *established* talent. And when those books are given the green light, the guys in accounting insure that the advance looks more like an 8-year-old's allowance. This is not good.

However, it seems that publishers are doing nothing less than what the general public is doing. We're all holding our cash close to our chests as we watch (and hope) for an economic upturn. We don't spend money on a big screen TV, they don't bankroll a witty manuscript on the wacky czars of 19th century Russia. Both are pretty rational economic decisions.

All that said, the good news is that humor is alive and still valiantly kicking—even in these poor economic times. And as long as funny keeps selling, publishers will keep publishing it; people will keep buying it; and mall bookstores will keep stocking it.

Read the sidebar Take My Book . . . Please on page 100 for additional information on humor in book publishing.

*AEGINA PRESS, INC., 59 Oak Lane, Spring Valley, Huntington WV 25704. (304)429-7204. Estab. 1984. Book publisher. Publishes trade paperback originals, paperback originals and humor trade. Humor line includes cartoon books and written humor. Recently published *Freaks, Geeks, and Chicken Beaks*, by Pete Sanfacon and *An Explosion of Chemistry Jokes*, by Jon Nimitz.
Illustration: Works with approximately 5 freelance humorous illustrators/year. Needs full mss only primarily for author's own book projects. "Submit a full ms (photocopy is OK)." One thing considered when hiring a freelance humorous illustrator is skill of artist. Buys one time rights. For first contact send cover letter, b&w tearsheets, query or full ms to Ira Herman, Managing Editor. Reports back within 2 months. Returns materials if accompanied by a SASE. Pays $50-75, per book cover; $75 minimum, color cover; $40-negotiable, b&w inside illustration.
Writing: Published 3 humor titles in last year. Works with approximately 3 freelance humorous fiction writers/year and 3 humorous nonfiction writers/year. Uses freelancers primarily for their own book projects. Needs humorous fiction and nonfiction writing. Fiction mss needed on people, sports, business, family, etc. Will consider all subjects. Buys first time rights, negotiates each project separately. For first contact send query or entire ms to Ira Herman, Managing Editor. Reports back within 2 months. Returns materials if accompanied by a SASE. Pays on a royalty basis, 15%. "Some new projects will be subsidy published."

*AMERICAN ATHEIST PRESS, P.O. Box 140195, Austin TX 78714-0195. (512)458-1244. Estab. 1949. Book and magazine publisher. Publishes trade paperback originals. Humor line includes cartoon books and written humor. Recently published *Devilishness*, by Rius and *I Bought My First Six Pack When I Was 35*, by John Bryan.

The asterisk before a listing indicates that the listing is new in this edition. New markets are often more receptive to freelance submissions.

Illustration: Works with approximately 5 freelance humorous illustrators/year. Needs humorous illustration for fiction and nonfiction titles primarily for magazine illustration. Send samples. Some things considered when hiring a freelance humorous illustrator are skill of artist, ability of artist to take art direction well and compatibility of artist's drawing style with text. Buys one-time rights. For first contact send cover letter and b&w tearsheets to R. Murray-O'Hair, Editor. Reports back within 3 months. Returns materials if accompanied by a SASE. Keeps materials on file. Pays $50, b&w book cover; $100, color cover; $25, b&w inside illustration.

Writing: Published 1 humor title in last year. Works with 10 freelance humorous fiction and 10 freelance humorous nonfiction writers/year. Uses freelancers primarily for magazine. Needs humorous fiction and nonfiction writing. Fiction and nonfiction mss needed on religion and Atheism. Buys one time rights. For first contact send fiction and nonfiction sample chapter to R. Murray-O'Hair, Editor. Reports back in 3 months. Returns materials if accompanied by a SASE. Pays per project, $15-50; pays on royalty basis, 7-9% on retail price.

AMERICAN COUNCIL FOR THE ARTS, Dept. HC, #1 East 53rd St., New York NY 10022-4201. (212)245-4510. FAX: (212)245-4514. Estab. 1960. Arts advocate/publisher. Publishes works concerning arts policy, management and administration and education for arts policymakers, managers and educators. Needs humorous illustration for books and periodicals and humorous copywriting.

Illustration: For first contact send cover letter, resume and b&w promo piece to Doug Rose, Associate Director of Publishing. Reports back only if interested. Does not return materials. Keeps material on file. Buys one-time rights. Pays $50 minimum, by the project.

Writing: For first contact send cover letter, resume and writing sample to Doug Rose, Associate Director of Publishing. Reports only if interested. Does not return materials. Keeps material on file. Buys first or one-time rights. Pays $50 minimum, by the project.

*BALLANTINE-DEL RAY-FAWCETT-IVY BOOKS, 201 E. 50th St., New York NY 10022. (212)572-2372. FAX:(212)572-2200. Publishes original cartoon books, written humor.

Illustration: Needs humorous illustration for nonfiction titles, primarily for covers. For first contact send cover letter, resume, client list, b&w or color tearsheets, b&w or color promo piece, slides and portfolio to Ballantine Art Director.

Writing: Published "some" humor titles last year. Works with "several" freelance humorous fiction and nonfiction writers per year. For first contact send cover letter, resume, query, writing sample, published tearsheet, sample chapter and outline of manuscript to Ballantine Editorial.

BEHRMAN HOUSE, 235 Watchung Ave., West Orange NJ 07052. (201)669-0447. FAX: (201)669-9769. Estab. 1921. Publishes Jewish books for children and adults. Recently published *A Child's Bible*, *My Jewish World* and *The Ten Commandments*. Prefers working with freelancers who have fax capabilities.

Illustration: Works with approximately 4 freelance humorous illustrators/year. Needs humorous illustration for fiction and nonfiction titles, cartoons and caricature, primarily for illustrating texts. Buys reprint rights. For first contact send cover letter, resume, client list, b&w tearsheets and portfolio to Adam Siegel, Editor. Reports back in weeks. Keeps materials on file. Pays $200, b&w, $400, color, cover; $25, b&w, $15, color, inside.

Writing: Published 2 humor titles last year. Works with approximately 2 freelance humorous nonfiction writers/year. Uses freelancers primarily for children's books. Needs humorous nonfiction writing. Fiction mss needed on "family, religion, people, anything related to Judaism." Nonfiction mss needed on Judaism. Buys reprint rights. For first contact send cover letter, resume, writing sample, sample chapter and outline of manuscript to Adam Siegel, Editor. Returns materials "if we don't use them." Pays per project and on a royalty basis 2% minimum on retail price or makes outright purchase of $500 minimum. Average advance is $200.

CATBIRD PRESS, 44 N. Sixth Ave., Highland Park NJ 08904. (908)572-0816. Estab. 1987. Publishes hardcovers, trade paperback originals and humor trade. Humor line includes literary parody, humorous fiction, anthologies (in areas of travel and legal humor), legal humor (written) — upmarket humor; no joke or concept books. Recently published *Columbus à la Mode, Parodies of Contemporary American Writers, The Handbook of Law Firm Mismanagement* and *Here We Are: The Humorists' Guide to The United States*.

Illustration: Works with 2 freelance humorous illustrators/year. Needs humorous illustration for humor titles, primarily for cover illustrations. Buys all rights or negotiates rights purchased. For first contact send cover letter, resume, b&w and color tearsheets and "a small number of samples" to Robert Wechsler, Publisher. Reports back only if interested. Returns materials if accompanied by a SASE. Keeps materials on file. Pays $200-1,000, b&w; $500-2,000, color, cover.

Writing: Published 2 humor titles last year. Needs "books." Fiction mss needed on "quality literature with a comic vision, not subject-oriented or wild-and-crazy." Nonfiction mss needed on law and travel. Negotiates rights purchased. For first contact send cover letter, resume, writing sample and outline of manuscript (fiction and nonfiction) to Robert Wechsler, Publisher. Reports back in 1 month. Returns material if accompanied by a SASE; does not file materials. Pays on a royalty basis, 5-10% on retail price. Average advance is $1,000.

Inside Tips: "Catbird is interested only in humor that is well-written, breaks new ground and plays against stereotypes rather than exploiting them. It must be fresh — that is, not trendy, not simply running with an idea. It must not be simply wacky or going for every laugh, but rather tightly written, with laughs coming from the style and the characters."

CCC PUBLICATIONS, 20211 Prairie St., Suite F., Chatsworth CA 91311. (818)407-1661. FAX: (818)718-7651. Estab. 1983. Publishes trade paperback and paperback originals and mass market. Humor line includes written humor, "especially humorous how-to/self-help." Recently published *No Hang-Ups (Funny Answering Machine Messages), Hormones From Hell* and *The Absolute Last Chance Diet Book*.

Illustration: Works with approximately 10-15 freelance humorous illustrators/year. Needs humorous illustration for nonfiction titles, cartoons, caricature and cover art. One of the things considered when hiring a freelance humorous illustrator is "willingness to submit sample sketches prior to assignment." Buys all rights or negotiates rights purchased. For first contact send cover letter and b&w tearsheets ("samples of 'best' work") to Cliff Carle, Editorial Director. Reports back within 4-5 weeks *only* if SASE is enclosed!" Returns materials if accompanied by a SASE; keeps materials on file. Pays $350-1,000, color, cover; $50-125, b&w, inside.

Writing: Published 15 humor titles in last year. Works with approximately 20 freelance humorous nonfiction writers/year. Uses freelancers primarily for "original manuscripts (but *no* assignments)." Needs humorous nonfiction writing. Nonfiction mss needed on "all subjects appealing to a wide variety of people — we usually stay away from esoteric subjects. Avoid profanity." Buys all rights. For first contact send query to Cliff Carle, Editorial Director. Reports back within 3-4 weeks on queries, 1-2 months on mss. Returns materials if accompanied by a SASE; does not file materials. Pays on a royalty

---

For information on book publishers' and publications' areas of interest, see the Subject Index.

Take My Book . . . Please!

The following short clips are from an article which appeared in *Publishers Weekly*, the trade journal for the book publishing industry. They give you an inside-the-industry view of publishing humor.

More than any other genre, humor is a fragile contraption. Tricked out in cartoons, amusing essays or cheeky one-liners, what's funny to one person is stupid, offensive or utterly mystifying to another. None of this, however, has yet discouraged editors from grabbing at what they hope will be the next hilarious voice. Even in these difficult times, no one will admit to abandoning humor books.

"Humor is always dicey," concedes Mark Chimsky, Editor-in-Chief of Collier. "There is no sure bet unless you're Gary Larson, and there are very few Larsons out there. Luck has a lot to do with it. You need the right time and the right subject, as with our book Where's Dan Quayle?, *by Jim Becker and Andy Mayer" — which now exceeds 250,000 copies in print.*

Quayle? *was edited by Macmillan Senior Editor Rick Wolff, who is a humor author himself; his* Sports Illstated *magazine parody sold 79,000 copies for Andrews & McMeel. Even so, Wolff refers to Justice Potter Stewart's description of pornography when he remarks about humor, "I can't define it, but I know it when I see it."*

Sagely, Wolff avows that "there is no such thing as an expert in the humor field." When asked, editors don't cite agents who specialize in humor, and few major houses have one editor who is chiefly responsible for humor.

Susan Arnold, spokesperson for Waldenbooks, comments that the mix of fast-moving titles hasn't changed much there over the last year or so. "The list is still dominated by Larson, Watterson, Barry, Grizzard and Bombeck," she says. "You can also add Letterman and Leno."

Hardcover humor, where prose generally takes precedence over pictures, has been selling in uncommonly substantial numbers in recent years.

Morgan Entrekin, Publisher of Atlantic Monthly Press remarks, "Humor used to come from the Left, but now it's from the Right as well." Of the current crop of hardcover humor bestsellers, he adds, "There's a new substance to them. Molly Ivins is very funny, but she's also smart. The best humor today is smart humor." David Groff, Senior Editor at Crown, concurs on the quality aspect. "People are tired of cheap irony," he says. "The smarter the writer is today, the better."

So how do editors decide whom to pursue?

"I look for more than a quick idea," says Joelle Delbourgo, Editor-in-Chief of hardcovers and trade paperbacks at Ballantine and Fawcett, where Jim Davis' Garfield appears in titles that are approaching a grand total of 40 million in print.

"A proposal has to make me laugh," says Leslie Schnur, V-P and Editor-in-Chief at Dell. "It has to be funny with some kind of hook—a timely issue or an author with a following, somebody who's syndicated."

Syndication has been a major asset in building reader loyalty for Barry and Bombeck, Watterson and Larson. So is television stardom, perhaps even an author's television credits. Merrill Markoe, Emmy-winning writer for Late Night with David Letterman, has a book with Viking called What the Dogs Have Taught Me: And Other Amazing Things I've Learned.

In short, the author, more than the subject, sells humor.

"Timing is everything with humor," says Rick Horgan, senior editor at Warner, which published Earthtoons: The First Book of Eco-Humor, by Stan Eales. "I tend to avoid instant humor books, because they are quintessential ephemera. We have what we call the Warner Laugh Meter here—the number of people on the editorial board who think something is funny."

"It's harder and harder to find humor that's original and not derivative," says Editor-in-Chief Sally Kovalchick of Workman.

"The authentic comic voice will come as the 90s develop," says Crown's David Groff. "We don't really know what it is yet." Says Arnold Dolin, Senior V-P of Penguin USA and publisher of Plume Books, "We all want to be on the cutting edge, but who knows what that is?"

—by Robert Dahlin

Reprinted from *Publishers Weekly* March 9, 1992, pubilshed by Cahners Publishing Co., a division of Reed Properties U.S.A., ®1992 by Reed Properties U.S.A.

basis, 8-15% on wholesale price. Average advance offered "varies depending upon author's experience and/or notoriety."

COMPUTER TECHNOLOGY RESOURCE GUIDE, Crumb Elbow Publisher, Box 294, Rhodendron OR 97049. (503)622-4798. Estab. 1983. Publishes mass market books. Humor line includes books with original cartoons and written humor.
Illustration: Needs humorous illustration for fiction and nonfiction titles, cartoons and caricature. One of the things looks for in a freelance humorous illustrator is "patience. We get very busy and he or she may think that we've forgotten about them, but we won't." Buys first rights. For first contact send cover letter, resume, client list, b&w tearsheets and slides to Michael P. Jones, Editor. Reports on submissions within 2 months ("or sooner depending upon how busy we are.") Pays in published copies.
Writing: Published 4 humor titles last year through Crumb Elbow Publishing. "We're just starting to use humor-oriented computer books from freelancers." Needs humorous fiction and nonfiction writing. Fiction mss needed only on the subject of computers. Nonfiction mss needed on "computers and human interaction, problems with computers controlling our lives, computers fouling up our lives." Buys first rights. Send query to Michael P. Jones, Editor. Reports on submission within 2 months ("or a lot sooner, depending upon how busy we are—or later if we are very busy.") Returns materials if accompanied by a SASE. Pays in published copies.

*CONTEMPORARY BOOKS, 180 North Michigan, Chicago IL 60601. (312)782-9182. Publishes original comic strip collections, books on pop culture and satire humor books.
Illustration: Works with approximately 1 freelance humorous illustrator/year. Needs humorous illustration for fiction and nonfiction titles, cartoons and caricatures, primarily for covers. For first contact send resume and b&w tearsheets to Georgene Sainati, Art Director.
Writing: Published 2 humor titles last year. Works with approximately 1 freelance humorous nonfiction writer/year and 1 freelance humorous fiction writer/year for books on satire and pop culture satire. For first contact send query and outline of manuscript to Linda Gray, Editor.

*CROWN BOOKS, 201 E. 50th St., New York NY 10022. (212)572-6190. FAX:(212)572-6192. Publishes original cartoon books and written humor.
Illustration: Works with approximately 3 freelance humorous illustrators/year. Needs humorous illustration for fiction and nonfiction titles, and cartoons, primarily for humor books. For first contact send cover letter, resume and b&w tearsheets to Crown Editorial.
Writing: Published 10 humor titles last year. Works with approximately 3 freelance humorous nonfiction writers/year and 3 freelance humorous fiction writers/year. "Most submissions are made through an agent." For first contact send query to Crown Editorial.

CWW PUBLICATIONS, Box 223226, Carmel CA 93922. Estab. 1975. Publishes mass-market books, booklets and anthologies. Recently published *Spoofing!* (a series with folkloristic slant), *Slightly Naughty!* and "Tales" retold.
Illustration: Needs humorous illustration for fiction titles and cartoons, primarily for illustrating anthologies of specific themes. "We are looking for fairy tale material." Buys one-time rights. For first contact send cover letter, portfolio and sufficient postage to allow return. "Please query first." Send to Brigitta Geltrich, Publisher. Reports back within 2 months. Does not report back without SASE. Returns materials if accompanied by a SASE. Pays $20 minimum and one free copy, b&w book cover; $2-5, inside.

Writing: Works with approximately 1,000 freelance humorous fiction writers/year. Uses freelancers primarily for thematic anthologies. Needs 1 humorous nonfiction folkloristic writing. Fiction and nonfiction mss needed on "fairy tales retold." Buys first time rights. Query first with writing sample to Brigitta Geltrich, Publisher. Then send cover letter, query, writing sample, entire manuscript. "We do not publish anything longer than 1,000 words." Accepts submissions via disk ("Macintosh on Xerox 6085 or TRS-80 Model 3/4"). Reports back within 2 months if accompanied by a SASE. Pays: "We pay by reducing cost of issue by 20%."
Inside Tips: Please request guidelines that apply. "We provide an avenue for publishing one's thoughts and ideas. We consider ourselves a springboard to bigger and maybe better publishing opportunities down the road. To keep costs down, we do not respond to any correspondence without SASE."

DENLINGER PUBLISHERS LTD, Box 76, Fairfax VA 22020. (703)830-4646. FAX: (203)830-5303. Estab. 1926. Publishes hardcovers and trade paperback originals.
Illustration: Needs humorous illustration for fiction and nonfiction titles. Buys all rights. For first contact send cover letter, resume, b&w promo piece to W.W. Denlinger, Publisher. Reports back within 7 days. Returns materials if requested and accompanied by SASE. Pays $100-500, b&w and color, cover; $10-30, b&w and color, inside.
Writing: Uses freelance humor writers primarily for specialty books. Fiction mss needed on self help. Nonfiction mss needed on dogs. Buys all rights. For first contact send cover letter, resume, query to W.W. Denlinger. Reports back within 2 months. Returns materials if accompanied by SASE. Pays 10% royalty. Makes outright purchase of $100-5,000. Advance negotiable.

EDUCATIONAL INSIGHTS, 19560 S. Rancho Way, Dominguez Hills CA 90220. (213)637-2131. Estab. 1962. Publishes textbooks, teaching materials and produces educational toys and games. Humor line includes children's stories. Recently published *Brainboosters*, *Cliffhangers* and *Tuff Stuff Stories*.
Illustration: Works with 25 freelance humorous illustrators/year. Needs humorous illustration for fiction and nonfiction titles, cartoons and caricature. Uses freelance humorous illustrators primarily (80%). Send "excellent samples" and cover letter. Buys all rights. For first contact, send cover letter, color promo piece and tearsheets, slides and client list. Send to Laurie Fischer, Art Director. Reports back in 10 days. Returns materials only if requested and if accompanied by SASE. Keeps materials on file. Pays $50-350, b&w, $200-1,000, color, cover; $25-100, b&w, $50-600, color, inside.
Writing: Inhouse staff published 20 humor titles last year.

*GOLLEHON PRESS, INC., 6157 28th St. S.E., Grand Rapids MI 49546. (616)949-3515. FAX: (616)949-8674. Estab. 1983. Book publisher. Publishes trade paperback originals, mass market and humor trade books. Humor line includes cartoons, and all types of clean humor, including joke books. Recently published *Off The Strip*, by Mark Lewis.
Illustration: Works with approximately 2 freelance humorous illustators/year. Uses freelance humorous illustrators primarily for full mss (collection of jokes or cartoons). "Contact us and present proposal and a few samples of work. We make offers on either a fee or royalty basis." Negotiates rights purchased, or buys exclusive rights. For first contact send cover letter, resume and "small portion of work for our review. Do not send entire ms or complete work" to Becky Anderson, Editor. Reports back within 1-2 months only if interested. Returns materials only if requested and accompanied by a SASE.
Writing: "We do not look for an illustrator for other book projects. We seek cartoonists/illustrators/humor writers who can submit a full book-length mss or collection of cartoons/jokes." Published 2 humor titles last year. Works with approximately 2 freelance humorous nonfiction writers/year. Uses freelancers primarily for full book-length works.

"Crude" Drawing: *Having previously illustrated a Sports Illustrated book, Metuchen, New Jersey-based humorous illustrator Patrick McDonnell was approached by the same publisher to create this drawing. All told, McDonnell illustrated eight funny quotes for a Money magazine guide book. McDonnell describes his drawing style as "friendly" and uses pen, ink and watercolor to create his instantly-recognizable humorous illustrations. He was given an eight-week deadline on the book project.*

Get up early, work late—and strike oil.
– John D. Rockefeller, Jr. explaining the secret of his success.

© 1992 Patrick McDonnell

Needs humorous fiction and nonfiction writing and cartoons. Fiction and nonfiction mss needed on "any clean subject." Advance varies from $0-2,000.

Tips: "Gollehon Press is looking for gifted cartoonists and humor writers; first-time author/writers are fine. We are happy to work with unknown talent where we feel there is potential. We cannot be held responsible for unsolicited mailings of full manuscripts or other submissions of real value. A query should include a detailed cover letter, resume and a few samples of the materials that would make up the text of a book, be they cartoons, jokes or essays. If we are interested, we will contact the author/writer/illustrator and request the full work for our review. If SASE is included, the material will be returned if we are not interested. Our typical royalty is 7% of a book's cover price. Although our primary interest is adult humor, we are also interested in juvenile and children's books. We have absolutely no interest in off-color materials."

GRAPEVINE PUBLICATIONS, INC., Box 2449, Corvallis OR 97339. (503)754-0583. FAX: (503)754-6508. Estab. 1983. Publishes trade paperback originals, how-to and instructional softcover books. Recently published *House-training Your VCR*, *Lotus Be Brief* and *A Little Dos Will Do You*.

Illustration: Works with approximately 4 freelance humorous illustrators/year. Needs humorous illustration for nonfiction titles, primarily for illustrating instructional materials. "Looking primarily for b&w line drawings." Buys all rights. For first contact send cover letter, resume and b&w tearsheets to Mr. Chris Coffin, Editor-in-Chief. Reports back within 1 month if accompanied by SASE.

*GREAT QUOTATIONS, 825 E. Roosevelt Rd., Lombard IL 60148. (800)354-4889. FAX: (800)848-0118. Estab. 1982. Book publisher, gift items. Publishes hardcover and paperback originals, humor trade and gifts (humor, sports, inspirational). Humor line includes original cartoon, written humor. Recently published *Worms of Wisdom*, *Over the Hill Test* and *Smile Increases Your Face Value*.

Illustration: Works with approximately 6 freelance humorous illustrators/year. Needs humorous illustration for fiction titles, cartoons and caricature. Submit a few sample pieces. Some things considered when hiring a freelance humorous illustrator are drawing style of artist and compatibility of artist's drawing style with text. Buys one time rights and all rights. For first contact send cover letter, b&w tearsheets and color promo piece to Peggy Schaffer, Vice President. Returns materials only if requested and accompanied by a SASE. Keeps materials on file if interested. Pays $200-800, b&w book cover; $400-1,000, color cover; $50-75, b&w inside illustration; $100-300, color inside illustration.

Writing: Published 12 humor titles in last year. Works with approximately 4 freelance humorous nonfiction writers/year, 6 freelance humorous fiction writers/year. Uses freelancers primarily for new material—books. Needs humorous fiction and nonfiction writing. Fiction mss needed on politics, retirement, parenting, executive and sports. Nonfiction mss needed on parenting, women, men and economics. Buys one time rights, all rights or negotiates rights purchased. For first contact send cover letter, writing sample and sample chapter to Peggy Schaffer, Vice President. Reports back within days. Returns materials only if requested and accompanied by a SASE. Keeps materials on file (if interested). Pays on royalty basis, 3-5% on wholesale price; outright purchase, $800-1,000. Average advance $300-500.

HARVEST HOUSE PUBLISHERS, 1075 Arrowsmith, Eugene OR 97402. (503)343-0123. Publishes hardcovers, trade paperback originals and mass market paperbacks. Humor line includes written humor, joke books, trivia, puzzles/games—all with evangelical Christian theme. Recently published *All New Clean Joke Book* and *Love Lines*.

Illustration: Works with approximately 2 freelance humorous illustrators/year. Needs humorous illustration for fiction titles. For first contact send cover letter, resume, query and samples to Fred Renich, Production Manager. Reports back within 2 months if accompanied by a SASE.

Writing: Published 4 humor titles last year. Fiction and nonfiction mss needed with an evangelical Christian theme. For first contact send cover letter, resume, query, writing sample, sample chapter and outline of manuscript for fiction and nonfiction to Mary Conner, Manuscript Coordinator. Reports back within 2 months. Returns materials if accompanied by SASE.

INNER TRADITIONS INTERNATIONAL, Destiny Books, Park Street Press, 1 Park Street, Rochester VT 05767. (802)767-3174. FAX: (802)767-3726. Estab. 1976. Publishes humor trade, hardcovers, trade paperback originals, textbooks. Prefers working with freelancers who have fax capabilities.

Illustration: Works with approximately 2 freelance humorous illustrators/year. Needs humorous illustration for nonfiction titles. Uses freelance humorous illustrators primarily for humor books. When hiring a freelance humorous illustrator, considers skill, drawing style, compatibility of drawing style with text. Buys all rights. For first contact send cover letter, resume, b&w tearsheets and portfolio to Estella Arias, Art Director. Reports back within 2 weeks if requested and accompanied by a SASE. Pays $200-800, color, cover; $40-60, b&w, $50-80, color, inside.

Writing: Published 1 humor title last year. Works with approximately 1 freelance humorous nonfiction writer/year. Needs humorous fiction and nonfiction writing. Fiction mss needed on New Age topics, self-help. Nonfiction mss needed on religion, yuppies, New Age gurus, men's new roles, natural medicine, etc. Send a short letter with synopsis, table of contents and sample chapter. Buys all rights. For first contact, send query to Leslie Colket, Managing Editor. Accepts submissions via disk with hard copy. Reports back within 2 months if interested. Returns materials if accompanied by SASE. Pays per project, $1,000 for 30,000 words; royalty of 6% on retail price. Average advance of $2,000.

Inside Tips: "Look at other books. Is your subject topical? Does it add a new slant to the topic? Does your book make fun of New Age ideas, people, lifestyle, etc? Not interested in straight humor."

INTERVARSITY PRESS, Box 1400, Downers Grove IL 60515. (708)964-5700. FAX: (708)964-1251. Estab. 1940. Publishes hardcovers, trade paperback originals. Humor line includes cartoon books. Recently published *Way Off the Church Wall* and *Climbing the Church Walls.*
Writing: Send all humor fiction to Andrew T. LePeau, Managing Editor. Accepts submissions submitted via fax. Reports back within 10 weeks. Returns materials if accompanied by a SASE. Pays royalty of 5-15% on retail price or makes outright purchase of $600-2,500. Average advance of $3,000.

JSA PUBLICATIONS, INC., Box 37175, Oak Park MI 48237. (313)546-9661. FAX: (313)546-3010. Estab. 1982. Independent book packager of variety of humor contemporary, pop-culture titles. Recently published *The Ultimate Blonde Joke Book*, by Eva Rej and *Meet Mr. Bachelor*, by Jefferson Lanz. Packages 6-10 projects a year. Will publish 4-6 additional titles.
Illustration: "We will consider humorous illustrations if included within text."
Writing: For first contact query with cover letter and proposal to Lisa A. McDonald, Senior Editor. "Always include SASE."

*LAFFING COW PRESS, P.O. Box 7802, The Woodlands TX 77387. (713)363-3577. FAX: (713)292-9722. Estab. 1990. Publishes paperback originals, textbooks and humor trade. Humor line includes cartoon books and written humor.
Illustration: Needs humorous illustration for fiction and nonfiction titles and cartoons.
Writing: Nonfiction mss needed on rural-country living, farm-ranch, hunting, fishing and golfing. Negotiates rights purchased. For first contact send resume, query and sample chapter to Susannah Borg, Publisher. Reports back only if interested. Returns materials if accompanied by a SASE.

MEADOWBROOK PRESS, 18318 Minnetonka Blvd., Deephaven MN 55391. (612)473-5400. FAX: (612)475-0736. Estab. 1975. Publishes hardcovers, trade and paperback originals and humor trade. Humor line includes original cartoon and written humor books. Recently published *Dads Say The Dumbest Things* and *The Unofficial College Dictionary.*
Illustration: Works with approximately 5 freelance humorous illustrators/year. Needs cartoons and humorous illustration for nonfiction titles. Buys all rights. For first contact send cover letter and resume to Dan Verdick, Permissions. Reports back on submissions within 6 weeks. Returns materials if accompanied by a SASE. Keeps materials on file. Pays $100-500, color, cover; $25-100, b&w, color, inside.
Writing: Published 7 humor titles in last year. Works with approximately 5-10 freelance humorous nonfiction writers/year. Fiction mss needed on babies, dads, moms, grandparents, weddings, marriage, retirement, graduation and other gift-giving occasions. To sell fiction send an outline and sample chapters. To sell nonfiction send sample chapters and a proposal. Buys all rights. Send cover letter, query, sample chapter and outline of ms to Dan Verdick. Accepts fax submissions. Reports back in 6 weeks. Returns materials if accompanied by a SASE. Keeps materials on file. Pays per project, $1,000-5,000 or on a royalty basis, 5-7.5%. Average advance is $2,500.
Inside Tips: "Ignore what most 'How to Write' books say and start with a strong concept—for us, something pertaining to a gift occasion such as new baby, graduation, retirement, engagement, weddings, etc."

*MENASHA RIDGE PRESS, 3169 Cahaba Heights Rd., Birmingham AL 35243. (205)967-0566. FAX: (205)967-0580. Estab. 1983. Book publisher. Publishes trade paperback originals. Humor line includes original cartoon books—environmental or outdoor activities (hiking, camping, climbing, paddling). Recently published *Mountain Bike Way of Knowledge, Kayaks to Hell* and *Earth We Hardly Knew You.*

Illustration: "Interested only in ideas for original cartoon books." Send all humorous illustration submissions to Mike Jones, Associate Publisher. Reports back only if interested or if SASE is included. Returns materials if accompanied by a SASE.

NELSON-HALL PUBLISHERS, 111 N. Canal St., Chicago IL 60606. (312)930-9446. Estab. 1909. Publishes hardcovers, trade paperback originals, textbooks. Humor line includes scholarly and educational books.
Illustration: When hiring a freelance humorous illustrator, considers skill and compatibility of drawing style with text. Buys one-time rights. For first contact send cover letter, b&w tearsheets and promo piece to Richard O. Meade, General Manager. Reports back within 1 month if interested. Returns materials if requested and accompanied by SASE, or keeps materials on file. Pays $50-100, b&w, inside.
Writing: Rights purchased depends on author contract.

NEW VICTORIA PUBLISHERS, Box 27, Dept. HC, Norwich VT 05055. (802)649-5297. Estab. 1976. Publishes paperback and trade paperback originals. Humor line includes original cartoon books, written humor, mystery, romance and feminist titles. Recently published *Secrets*, *A Captive in Time* and *Mari*.
Illustration: Works with approximately 1 freelance humorous illustrator/year. Needs humorous illustration for fiction titles, covers and cartoons. Buys all rights; pays royalties on cartoon collections. For first contact send cover letter and b&w tearsheets to Claudia Lamperti, Editor. Reports back within 2 weeks. Returns materials if accompanied by a SASE. Pays $100, b&w, cover; $25, b&w, inside.
Writing: Published 2 humor titles last year. Works with approximately 2 freelance humorous fiction and nonfiction writers/year. Uses freelancers primarily for fiction. Needs humorous fiction writing. Fiction mss needed on lesbian-feminist issues, mysteries, cartoons, etc. Nonfiction mss needed on history of feminism. Negotiates rights purchased. For first contact send writing sample and outline of manuscript to Claudia Lamperti, Editor. Accepts submissions via disk. Reports back within 2 weeks. Returns materials if accompanied by a SASE. Pays 10% royalty on wholesale price or in copies. No advance.

NORTH LIGHT BOOKS, 1507 Dana Ave., Cincinnati OH 45207. (513)531-2222. FAX: (513)531-4744. Imprint of F&W Publications. Publishes trade paperback originals. Recently published *Clutter's Last Stand* and *Make Your House Do the Housework*. Prefers working with freelancers who have fax capabilities.
Illustration: Works with approximately 3 freelance humorous illustrators/year. Needs cartoons and humorous illustration for nonfiction titles. Send nonreturnable samples for file. For first contact send b&w tearsheets to Art Director. Reports back only if interested. Returns materials if accompanied by a SASE. Pays $50-200, b&w, color, cover; $15-75, b&w, $50-150, color, inside.

PACIFIC PRESS PUBLISHING ASSOCIATION, 1350 N. Kings Rd., Nampa ID 83687. (208)456-2500. FAX: (208)465-2531. Estab. 1874 by the Seventh-Day Adventist Church. Publishes hardcovers and paperback originals, textbooks and magazines for all age groups. Needs humorous illustration for nonfiction magazines and books. "Christian lifestyles and values are promoted." Recently published *Being Saved When You're Feeling Lost*, *The Pharasee's Guide to Perfect Holiness* and *Caught in Kuwait*. Prefers working with freelancers who have fax capabilities (or access to a fax machine in their town).
Illustration: Works with approximately 90 freelance humorous illustrators/year. Needs cartoons, humorous illustration and caricature, primarily for nonfiction titles and magazines. "Send slides or printed samples we can keep as reference of the artist's style." Buys first rights. Send cover letter, b&w and color tearsheets or slides to Merwin Stewart. Reports back only if interested. Returns materials if requested or keeps materials

on file. Payment is based on the size of use and complexity of artwork needed, and varies from $50 for a b&w spot illustration to $500 for a complex full-page color illustration.

*PAGE ONE PUBLISHERS & BOOKWORKS, INC., P.O. Box 6606, Eureka CA 95502. (707)443-2820. (707)445-0270. Estab. 1989. Book and periodical publisher. Publishes trade paperback originals, humor trade and periodicals. Humor line includes topical humor, humor columns, editorial cartoons, comic strip collections, graphic novels and original humor work. Recently published *Comic Relief*, *The Drawing Board* and *Blank Tapes Boots & Salads*.

Illustration: Works with approximately 25-30 freelance humorous illustrators/year. Needs humorous illustration for fiction and nonfiction titles, cartoons, caricature, humor columns, editorial cartoons, comic strips and panels, etc. Uses freelance humorous illustrators primarily for *Comic Relief*, *The Drawing Board* and graphic novels. Some things considered when hiring a freelance humorous illustrator are skill and drawing style of artist, ability of artist to take art direction well, compatability of artist's drawing style with text and professionalism and businesslike attitude of artist. Buys one time rights on editorial cartoons, reprint rights on longer works. For first contact send cover letter, b&w tearsheets and portfolio to Perry Bradford-Wilson or Michael Kunz, Editors. Reports back on submission within 3 months. Returns materials only if requested. Keeps materials on file. Payment depends on project—page rate for magazine use, royalties for book use.

Writing: Published 15 humor titles last year. Works with approximately 7 freelance humorous nonfiction writers/year. Uses freelancers primarily for humor columns in periodicals and book collections of humor columns. Needs humorous fiction and nonfiction writing. Fiction mss needed on "all topical subjects—if it's in the news, we make fun of it." Nonfiction mss needed on parenting, women, men and economics. "Send samples—sample chapters and summary on longer works—the more up-to-date and topical the better." Buys one time rights. For first contact send cover letter, writing sample, sample chapter and outline of manuscript. Send all humor fiction and nonfiction to: Perry Bradford-Wilson or Michael Kunz, Editors. Reports back on submissions within 3 months. Returns materials only if requested. Pays page rate for periodicals, royalty for book projects. Advance is offered "on book projects only—amount depends on nature of project. Periodicals pay upon publication."

Inside Tips: "Writers should be aware of the quickly changing world scene—for instance, jokes and cartoons about the Soviet Union were quickly dated during 1991. Keep in touch with the news, culture."

PELICAN PUBLISHING COMPANY, INC., 1101 Monroe St., Gretna LA 70053. (504)368-1175. Estab. 1926. Publishes hardcovers, paperback and trade paperback originals, textbooks, hard cover reprints and humor trade. Humor line includes editorial cartoon collections, cartoon reference books and original cartoon books. Recently published *Best Editorial Cartoons of the Year* series, *Flying Can Be Fun* and *The Armadillo Book*. Prefers working with freelancers who have fax capabilities.

Illustration: Buys all rights. For first contact send cover letter, resume, "a detailed query and maybe 2 samples (photocopies only). Send SASE" to Nina Kooij, Editor. Reports in 1 month, if query; 3 months, if long sample or full ms. Returns materials if accompanied by a SASE. Payment varies.

Writing: Published 1 humor title last year. Buys all rights. For first contact send cover letter, resume, detailed query letter, synopsis and no more than 2 chapters. Send SASE. Send all humor fiction and nonfiction to Nina Kooij, Editor. Reports back on submissions within 30 days, if query; 3 months, if long sample or full ms. Returns materials if accompanied by a SASE. Payment varies.

PICCADILLY BOOKS, Box 25203, Colorado Springs CO 80936. (719)548-1844. FAX: (719)548-1844. Estab. 1986. Publishes hardcovers and paperback and trade paperback originals. Humor line includes "humorous monologues, dialogues, plays and 'how-to' for children and adults. No blue humor." Recently published *Juggling Made Simple* and *How to Pick Pockets for Fun and Profit*.

Illustration: Works with approximately 3 freelance humorous illustrators/year. Needs humorous illustration for nonfiction titles and caricature, primarily for book illustration. Buys all rights. For first contact send cover letter, portfolio and "photocopies of work that we can keep on file" to Bruce Fife, Publisher. Reports back only if interested. Returns materials if accompanied by a SASE. Pays $100-500, color, cover; $5-20, b&w, inside.

Writing: Published 2 humor titles last year. Works with approximately 3 freelance humorous nonfiction writers/year for adult and children's books. Needs humorous non-fiction writing, how-to books on humor, comedy and fun activities. Nonfiction mss needed on how to be funny, comic technique and fun activities. Buys all rights. For first contact send query, sample chapter and outline of ms to Bruce Fife, Publisher. Reports back on submissions within 2 months. Returns materials if accompanied by a SASE. Pays on a royalty basis, 5-10%. Average advance "depends on material."

PLAYERS PRESS INC., Box 1132, Studio City CA 91614. (818)789-4980. Estab. 1965. Publishes hardcovers, trade paperback and paperback originals, mass market paperbacks, textbooks and hard cover reprints. Humor line includes written humor, theater specialty. Recently published *Late 4th Partner, A Matter of Degree* and *Humorous Monologues for Actors*.

Illustration: Works with approximately 1-3 freelance humorous illustrators/year. Needs humorous illustration for nonfiction titles, primarily for covers/plates. Buys all rights. For first contact send cover letter, resume and b&w tearsheets to Marjorie E. Clapper, Associate Editor. Reports back only if interested. Returns materials if requested; keeps materials on file. Pays $10-100, b&w, $25-500, color, cover; $5-50, b&w, inside.

Writing: Published 3 humor titles last year. Works with approximately 1-10 freelance humorous nonfiction writers/year. Uses freelancers primarily for plays, monologues and scenes. Needs humorous fiction, nonfiction and dramatic writing for theater material. Fiction mss needed on all subjects in theater format. Nonfiction mss needed on performing arts, theater, film and television. Buys all rights. For first contact send query to Robert W. Gordon, Vice President, Editorial. Accepts unagented submissions. Reports back within 4 months if interested. Returns materials if accompanied by a SASE. Pays per project, $50-250 for 1,000-10,000 words; royalty of 8-10% on wholesale price; or outright purchase of $50-5,000 for publishable work. Average advance varies depending on material.

Inside Tips: "We are interested only in theatrical works."

PRICE STERN SLOAN, 360 N. La Cienega Blvd., Los Angeles CA 90048. (213)657-6100. FAX: (310)445-3933. Estab. 1964. Publishes mass market paperbacks, humor trade, hardcovers, paperback originals and trade paperback originals. Humor line includes written humor, original humor books. Recently published *Murphy's Law Books, How to be a Jewish Mother, How to be an Italian, How to be a Celebrity*, and *Cheapskates Handbook*.

Illustration: Works with approximately 3 freelance humorous illustrators/year. Needs humorous illustration for fiction titles, primarily humor books. Submit query letter and sample illustrations (no original artwork). Buys all rights. For first contact send cover letter, color or b&w promo piece to Corrine Johnson, Associate Editor. Reports back within 6-8 weeks only if interested. Returns materials if accompanied by a SASE or keeps materials on file.

Writing: Published 4-6 humor titles last year. Works with approximately 4-6 freelance humorous fiction writers/year. Uses freelance humor writers primarily for humor books. Mss needed on society, people, business world, family, government, self-help, etc. Buys all rights. For first contact, send query, cover letter and outline of manuscript for nonfiction to Corrine Johnson. Reports back within 6-8 weeks. Returns materials if accompanied by a SASE; does not file materials.

Inside Tips: "Writers should keep on top of trends by visiting bookstores, screening bestseller lists, etc."

*RADIX PRESS, 2314 Cheshire Lane, Houston TX 77018. (713)683-9076. FAX: "Call for number." Estab. 1988. Book publisher. Publishes trade paperback originals. Humor line includes military and political books, bumper stickers, T-shirts and buttons. Recently published *Official Lite History of the Gulf War*.

Illustration: Works with approximately 10 freelance humorous illustrators/year. Needs cartoons, caricature and artwork drawn to spec. Send sample, name and P.O.C. and fee requirements. Some of the things considered when hiring a freelance humorous illustrator are ability of artist to take art direction well and cost. Negotiates rights purchased. Send all humorous illustration submissions to Steve Sherman, Director. Reports back only if interested. Returns materials if accompanied by a SASE. Pays $0-50, b&w inside illustration.

Writing: Published 2 humor titles in last year. Uses freelancers primarily for editorial copy. Negotiates rights purchased. Send writing sample. Reports back only if interested. Returns materials if accompanied by a SASE. Payment "to be negotiated on a project basis."

Tips: "We have occasion to look for freelance cartoonists, writers, editors, with a similar political persuasion, i.e. conservative, Vietnam veterans preferred. We are not financially successful as yet and are not offering significantly impressive fees. We might pay $25-50 for a cartoon drawn to spec or pay with copies of books."

READ'N RUN BOOKS, Box 294, Dept. HC, Rhododendron OR 97049. (503)622-4798. Estab. 1980. Book publisher that provides hardcovers, paperback originals, hard cover and mass market paperback reprints and humor trade. Humor line includes original cartoons, written humor. Recently published *The Dancing Chicken, The Dancing Chicken and Other Stories* and *The Wall*.

Illustration: Needs humorous illustration for fiction and nonfiction titles, cartoons and caricature. One of the things considers when hiring a freelance humorous illustrators is whether artist is "flexible and not pushy." Buys one-time rights. For first contact send cover letter, resume, client list, b&w tearsheets and portfolio to Michael P. Jones, Publisher. Reports back within 2 months. Returns materials if accompanied by a SASE. "We pay in published copies."

Writing: Published 5 humor titles last year. Works with approximately 20 freelance humorous nonfiction writers/year, 25 freelance humorous fiction writers/year. Needs humorous fiction and nonfiction writing. Fiction mss needed on "logging environment, Oregan Trout, wildlife, anti-hunting, anti-trapping, etc." Nonfiction mss needed on history, environment, wildlife, nature and logging. Buys one-time rights. For first contact send query and entire manuscript to Michael P. Jones, Publisher. Reports back within 2 months if accompanied by a SASE. Pays in published copies.

Inside Tips: "A creative person who isn't too rigid has an opportunity to break into new markets by listening, absorbing suggestions, and then plunging ahead with their own individual creativity intact."

RUTGERS UNIVERSITY PRESS, 109 Church St., New Brunswick NJ 08901. (908)932-7037. Estab. 1937. Publishes hardcovers, trade paperback originals, hardcover and trade paperback reprints. Humor line includes collection of Sidney Harris Science cartoons,

© St. Martin's Press

A Cover That Screams*: New York City-based comic artist Arlen Schumer designed this paperback book cover to "look like a miniature comic book cover. I wanted to evoke Roy Lichtenstein but not do an outright, slavish imitation with the 'dots,' like lesser illustrators have done." Given approximately two weeks to complete the art, Schumer was paid $1,500 for all rights to the illustration. On the left is Schumer's original pencil sketch, and on the right the final illustration. Note the subtle differences between the two pieces of art.*

comic novels, humorous essays. Recently published *Einstein Simplified*, by Sidney Harris (cartoons); *Tales of a Low Rent Birdie*, by Pete Dunne (essays); *The Cruz Chronicle* (humorous novel). "Harris book may have been a one-shot deal. His name recognition among scientists was crucial."

Illustration: Buys one-time or reprint rights. Send all humorous illustrations to Barbara Kopel, Production Manager.

Writing: Uses freelancers primarily for novels. Fiction mss needed on science, medicine, nature and women's studies. Nonfiction mss needed on science, medicine and natural history. Negotiates rights. For first contact, send cover letter, resume, query, writing sample, published tearsheet, entire manuscript, sample chapter, "as much as possible" for fiction and nonfiction to Kenneth Arnold, Director. Reports back within 3-4 weeks. Returns materials if requested and accompanied by a SASE. Pay is subject to negotiation.

Inside Tips: "We prefer gender-free, bias-free language and illustrations. Avoid generic 'he' for example. Avoid making all scientists male, all assistants female, all figures obviously white. We do not regularly publish humor, but obviously are open to it. Well-crafted comic novels have the best chance."

SHAPOLSKY PUBLISHERS, INC., 136 West 22nd St., New York NY 10011. (212)633-2022. FAX: (212)633-2123. Estab. 1986. Independent book producer/packager. Publishes hardcover reprints, humor trade, hardcover originals, paperback originals, trade paperback originals. Humor line includes "whatever has the potential to sell well." Recently published *The Joy of Depression, Guide to Being a Man in a Woman's World: How to be Macho without Offending Anyone*.

Illustration: Works with approximately 3 freelance humorous illustrators/year. Needs humorous illustration for fiction titles, nonfiction titles, cartoons and caricature. Send a few photocopies of best material for consideration. When hiring a freelance humorous illustrator, considers skill and drawing style. Buys all rights or reprint rights. For first contact send cover letter and b&w promo piece. Send submissions to Ian Shapolsky, Publisher. Reports back within 1 month. Returns materials if requested and accompanied by a SASE. Pays $100-500, b&w and color, cover; $20-250, b&w and color, inside. **Writing:** Published 4 humor titles last year. Works with approximately 3 freelance humorous fiction and nonfiction writers/year. Uses freelance humor writers primarily for new book projects. Needs humorous fiction and nonfiction writing. Fiction mss needed on relationships, parodies, self-help and spoofs. Interested in seeing nonfiction mss on relationships, cooking and religion. Negotiates rights purchased. Send cover letter and query to Ian Shapolsky. Accepts agented submissions only. Reports back within 1 month only if interested. Returns materials if requested and accompanied by a SASE. Pays $250-5,000 per project; royalty of 6-15% on retail price; outright purchase $350-7,000. Average advance $3,000.

Inside Tips: "Humor buyers are tough cookies, so try to be on the cutting edge of a new, unusual concept or genre of humor. Be different so we can awe the bookstore buyer with your book."

THE SPEECH BIN, INC., 1766 20th Ave., Vero Beach FL 32960. (407)770-0007. FAX: (407)770-0006. Estab. 1984. Publishes textbooks and books for speech-language pathology, audiology, and special education markets.

Illustration: Works with approximately 5-6 freelance humorous illustrators/year. Needs humorous illustration for nonfiction titles. Uses humorous/cartoon art for children's books, texts, diagnostic tests. Buys all rights "but will negotiate rights purchased." For first contact freelancer should send cover letter, resume, client list and b&w tearsheets to Jan J. Binney, Senior Editor. Reports back in 3 months. Returns materials only if requested and accompanied by SASE. Keeps materials on file. Pays $5-50, b&w, inside.

Writing: Submit query. "This is a specialized market. We generally consider art only, but are interested in looking at books and treatment materials for children with communication disorders and other handicaps. Send all humor nonfiction to Jan J. Binney. Accepts fax submissions. Reports back in 3 months. Returns materials only if requested and accompanied by SASE. Pays royalty of 8% minimum.

STERLING PUBLISHING CO., INC., 387 Park Ave. S., New York NY 10016. (212)532-7160. FAX: (212)213-2495. Estab. 1949. Publishes hardcovers and trade paperback originals and reprints. Humor line includes children's humor collections, humorous monologues and activity books. Recently published *Go Ahead—Make Me Laugh*, *What's the Verdict?* and *Comedy Writer's Workbook*.

Illustration: Works with approximately 10 freelance humorous illustrators/year. Needs humorous illustration for nonfiction titles, primarily for book illustration. "Send Xerox samples we can keep in our files." Buys all rights. For first contact send cover letter, resume if available and b&w and color tearsheets to Sheila Anne Barry, Acquisition Manager. Reports back only if interested. Returns materials if requested and accompanied by a SASE; keeps materials on file. "Payment determined by book budget."

Writing: Published 12 humor titles last year. Works with approximately 15 freelance humorous nonfiction writers/year, primarily for children's books (humor collections) and also for some general trade titles. Nonfiction mss needed of children's riddles, jokes, fun and science/nature activities. Buys all rights to work on royalty basis. For first contact send cover letter and resume if available to Sheila Anne Barry. Reports back within 2 months only if interested, unless SASE is enclosed. Returns materials if accompanied by SASE. Pays royalty of 5-10%. Advance "depends on material."

TAYLOR PUBLISHING COMPANY, 1550 W. Mockingbird Lane, Dallas TX 75235. (214)637-2800, ext. 220. Estab. 1980. Publishes hardcovers, trade paperback and paperback originals and humor trade. Humor line includes written humor. Recently published

What Sign is Your Pet?, *Waspleg and Other Mnemonics*, *Teed Off* and *P.S. My Bush Pig's Name Is Boris*.

Writing: Published 2 humor titles last year. Works with approximately 2 freelance humorous nonfiction writers/year. Needs humorous nonfiction writing. Negotiates rights purchased. For first contact send cover letter and sample chapter to Jim Donovan, Senior Editor. Accepts modem, fax and disk submissions. Reports back within 1 month. Returns materials if requested; does not file materials. Pays royalties of 7-10% on retail price. Average advance is $4,000.

Inside Tips: "Humor, of course, is highly subjective and thus, hard to pin down. But an attempted definition of the kind of humor we're looking for would include the following adjectives: fresh, topical, intelligent, original, and most importantly — funny."

TOPPER BOOKS, 200 Park Ave., New York NY 10166. (212)692-3700. Estab. 1985. Imprint of Pharos Books. Publishes trade paperback originals and humor trade books. Humor line includes reprint collections and original cartoon books. Recently published *Build a Better Life by Stealing Office Supplies*, *Dogbert's Big Book of Business* and *Mother Goose & Grimm's Night of Living Vacuum*.

Inside Tips: Looking for "original cartoon material with writing and drawing done by the same person." Also, "material with an up-to-date social conscience (and a jaundiced eye!)"

TRILLIUM PRESS, First Ave., Unionville NY 10988. (914)726-4444. Estab. 1978. Publishes trade paperback and paperback originals and textbooks.

Illustration: Needs humorous illustration for fiction and nonfiction titles, cartoons and caricature. Buys all rights. For first contact send cover letter and b&w tearsheets to William Neumann, Art Director. Reports back only if interested. Keeps material on file.

Writing: Published 20 humor titles last year.

Inside Tips: "We are interested in illustrators and cartoonists, but generally not in manuscripts."

*UNIVERSITY EDITIONS, INC., 59 Oak Lane, Spring Valley, Huntington WV 25704. (304)429-7204. Estab. 1984. Book publisher. Imprint of Aegina Press, Inc. Publishes trade paperback originals, mass market and humor trade. Humor line includes cartoons and written humor. Recently published *Freaks, Geeks and Chicken Beaks*, by Pete Sanfacon and *An Explosion of Chemistry Jokes*, by Jon Nimitz.

Illustration: "Uses freelancers only for their own book projects." Works with approximately 3 freelance humorous illustrators/year. Submit complete ms. One of the things considered when hiring a freelance humorous illustrator is skill of artist. Buys one time rights. For first contact send cover letter and b&w tearsheets to Ira Herman, Managing Editor. Reports back within 2 month. Returns materials if accompanied by a SASE. Pays $50 minimum, b&w book cover.

Writing: Published 3 humor titles in last year. Works with approximately 3 freelance humorous nonfiction writers/year. Uses freelancers primarily for their own books. Needs humorous fiction and nonfiction writing. Will consider all subjects. Submit complete ms. Buys first time rights. For first contact send query or entire ms to Ira Herman, Managing Editor. Reports back within 2 months. Returns materials if accompanied by a SASE. Pays on a royalty basis, 15%. Negotiates each project, some are subsidy published.

For information on book publishers' and publications' areas of interest, see the Subject Index.

VIKING/PENGUIN U.S.A., 375 Hudson St., New York NY 10014. (212)366-2000. FAX: (212)366-2920. Publishes comic strips such as "Doonesberry."
Writing: Published 3 humor titles last year. Do different styles of books. Needs humorous fiction and nonfiction writing. *Agented submissions only.*

WARNER BOOKS, Room 932, 1271 Ave. of the Americas, New York NY 10020. (212)522-2842. Publishes written humor: Jay Leno and Mad Books, for example.
Illustration: Works with very few freelance humorous illustrators/year. Needs humorous illustration for fiction and nonfiction cartoons. Send all humorous illustration submissions to Jackie Meyer, Art Director.
Writing: Uses freelancers primarily for adult market, "although we do have a children's department." Needs humorous fiction writing. Fiction mss needed on the business world, the family, self help, "anything." For first contact send query with short sample chapter and SASE to Mel Parker, Publisher, Paperback Division (fiction), Maureen Egen, Editor-in-Chief, Hardcover Division (nonfiction). Pays per outright purchase.

*WESCOTT COVE PUBLISHING CO., Box 130, Stamford CT 06904. (203)322-0998. Estab. 1968. Book publisher. Publishes trade paperback and paperback originals, cruising guides and nautical books, 2 of which are illustrated by cartoons. Humor line includes nautical books illustrated by cartoons. Recently published *I Don't Do Portholes!*, *Irma Quaterdeck Reports* and *Inside American Paradise*.
Illustration: Works with approximately 1 freelance humorous illustrator/year. (We commission the cartoonist.) Uses freelance humorous illustrators primarily for nautical books.
Writing: Nonfiction mss needed on nautical subjects. Submit an outline and 1 or 2 sample chapters. Buys all rights. For first contact send cover letter, resume, sample chapter and outline of manuscript to Jullus M. Wilensky, President. Reports back within 1 week. Returns materials if accompanied by a SASE. Pays in royalties. Average advance is up to $1,500.
Inside Tips: "We do not publish any books that do not have useful information. The humor is incidental."

WORD PUBLISHING, (Div. of Word, Inc.), Suite 1000, 5221 N. O'Connor, Irving TX 75039. Estab. 1951. Publishes hardcovers and trade and mass market paperback originals. Recently published *Stick a Geranium in Your Hat and Be Happy* and *Splashes of Joy in the Cesspools of Life*.
Illustration: Works with approximately 3 freelance humorous illustrators/year. Uses cartoons and humorous illustration for nonfiction titles, primarily for inside illustration. Buys all rights. For first contact send cover letter and b&w and color tearsheets to Tom Williams, Design Director. Reports back only if interested. "Please don't phone." Returns materials if accompanied by a SASE; keeps materials on file. Pays $250, b&w, $600, color, cover; $75-150, b&w, inside.

WORKMAN PUBLISHING, 708 Broadway, New York NY 10003. (212)254-5900. (212)254-8090. Publishes reprints of comic strips and original cartoon books.
Illustration: Works with approximately 12 or more freelance humorous illustrators/year. Needs humorous illustration for fiction and nonfiction titles, cartoons and caricature. Buys all rights. For first contact send cover letter and copies of artwork to Sally Kovalchick, Editor-in-Chief. Payment varies.

Writing: Published 10-15 humor titles last year, mostly nonfiction. Needs humorous fiction and nonfiction writing. Fiction mss needed on "society, people, the business world, the family, government, self help, etc." For first contact send query, writing sample fiction and nonfiction to Sally Kovalchick. Payment varies.

Book Publishers/Changes '91-'93

The following markets appeared in the last (1991) edition of *Humor and Cartoon Markets* but are absent from the 1993 edition. These companies failed to respond to our request for an update of their listing or for the reasons indicated in parentheses following the company name.

Avon (asked to be deleted)
Dolphin (out of business)
Fireside Books
Five Star Publications
Golden West Publications (overstocked)

Meriwether Publishing Ltd. (doesn't need freelancers)
Once Upon a Planet (may be closing)
Padre Productions (overstocked)

Rose Publishing Co., Inc. (no longer uses humor)
Wyrick & Company (asked to be deleted)

Comic Books

If you're looking for a laugh, you won't find it in most comic books.

Indeed, the comic book genre still seems to be firmly stuck in an intergalactic-space-warrior-snags-the-nubile-vixen-and-saves-the-world-from-tyranny mode. Sure, that stuff's awfully exciting for the first two pages, but after that, it's as appealing as cherry vanilla ice cream on SPAM.

No, funny characters don't seem to hang out in too many comic books. But while a number of comic book publishers express the desire to break away from hackneyed sci-fi themes and formula adventure story lines, few move beyond the cheap talk to pull out publishing contracts. And with the comic book industry intensely affected by the recession, publishers are proceeding very cautiously with new releases—humorous and nonhumorous.

"The problem," says Tony Caputo, publisher of NOW Comics, "is that it takes a very special genius to write humor for comic books. You have to get past the same, old tired stories told over and over again. It's very difficult to pull off humor within a comic book."

Recently, NOW has begun to publish comics (like *Ralph Snart* and *The Real Ghostbusters*) that may not be solely humorous, but contain more humor than you generally find in comic books. "Another good example," says Caputo, "is our *Married with Children* comic book line. While it's based on the TV show, in the comic book we have greater latitude to take the characters outside of their home and place them into different, humorous environments. Since comics are a highly visual medium, there's no limit to what you can do with them. To be successful, you have to stretch the traditional funny bone. The comic book industry is slowly learning that storylines based on space idiots who slash people just don't cut it anymore."

There's a lot of truth in what Caputo says. While the "Big Two," Marvel and DC, have come to epitomize the Super-Hero-Adventure-Comic-Genre, both have begun to dabble in humor (Marvel by optioning *Bill and Ted's Excellent Adventure*, and DC with *Tiny Toons*.) Harvey continues to crunch out "sweet" humor (both reprinted and new), and Archie Comics stubbornly cranks out 1963-era humor some 30 years later. After making a big humor push in 1990, Disney Comics drastically reduced their line by giving overtime to Donald Duck, Scrooge and the same, tired characters.

It's also important to note that the term "humor" in comic books may carry some negative connotations. I have always seen lots of "humor" in Fantagraphics' line, and find some of the Eclipse products hilariously sinister (remember their horridly tasteless "Famous Serial Killer" trading cards?), but both companies seem to avoid "the H-word" as if it were a killer virus. The reason may be as simple as terminology. "Traditionally, humor just doesn't sell in comic books," claims writer Raphael Nieves, "so if a comic book publisher *does* publish something that might be considered humorous, they're more apt to call it satire or parody—*anything* but humor."

Established as "a forum for anybody who has a pen and a piece of paper," St. Louis-based *Snicker* magazine is strongly devoted to humor. "The problem," says *Snicker* publisher Rich Balducci, "is that it's really hard for a funny comic book to take hold in the marketplace. That's because for every reader who finds your book funny, there are another 98 people who will be offended by it. They then complain to the retailer who carries the book, and all too often they pull it from their rack. It seems that it's only the safest, most bland forms of humor that find a way into your comic book stores. If it weren't for a strong underground following, it would be a totally hopeless situation for *Snicker*."

The dope on the dough

While pay for comic books fluctuates tremendously (from $20 to perhaps $250 per page for cartooning and generally less than that for writing), the profession *can* be lucrative if you come up with a hot property, the odds of which, needless to say, are regrettably slim. Indeed, *Teenage Mutant Ninja Turtles* don't mutate into cash-generating success stories every day of the week.

On the other hand, most comic book publishers extend an inordinate amount of creative freedom to both cartoonists and writers. Generally speaking, it is *expression*, not calculated commercialism, that guides most in this profession.

Nonetheless, it's always disheartening to hear of cartoonists or writers who simply refuse to *work* with a publisher. "Some artists," says Tony Caputo, "absolutely refuse to do anything to their work that might improve it. There are things an editor can point out to a comic book creator that can greatly improve the professionalism of the presentation. It's imperative that artists and writers understand how to work within the total process of comic book publishing."

General rules for cartoonists

If you've been interested in comic books for some time, you've surely either written and/or drawn a few pages of material (published or not) that you'd like to show around. Even if these pages are merely penciled and not inked, don't worry—a comic book publisher will still want to view this infrastructure, although they'll certainly be just as happy to review your inked work. This material gives a publisher a better sense of how you handle staging, character interaction, composition, framing and storytelling.

Do you have an idea for a comic book series? If so, query as you would any other book project. A couple of finished sample pages would be ideal, and you'll want to submit an outline detailing your story, plot, etc. Toss in a couple of Xeroxes of other examples of your comic art so that the publisher gets a better idea of what you do. Naturally, you'll want to include a cover letter, a business card if you have one, and a SASE if you ever expect to have your material returned.

If you're interested in *illustrating* someone else's stories, submit generally the same material, but make it very clear in your cover letter that you're looking to pencil and/or ink pages on a freelance/as needed basis. With more and more comic book covers being laser-separated, you'll want to toss in at least one example of how you handle color. A couple of weeks after you've sent this material, make a quick, courteous call to the publisher. Did they receive the material? Is it the type of stuff they're looking for? Are there any other examples they'd like to see? If the prognosis is positive, continue to update the publisher with a sample or two every three months or so and encourage them to keep your work on file.

General rules for writers

If there's any "rule," it's that the rules for writing submissions differ from one comic book publisher to the next. That's why you'll want to carefully study the individual submission policies of the publishers listed in this chapter. However, writers would be wise to follow some general guidelines. If you have an idea for a comic book, then it's time for an outline. Paint a general picture with the storyline, establish your characters, and whet the appetite of the editor who's reviewing your material (if you make him laugh at this early stage, he'll want to see more). If you can show him previous stories of yours that have been illustrated by a cartoonist, that's a *definite* plus. Xerox copies of these pages and include them with your cover letter, business card (if you have one) and a SASE.

Danger! Danger!

While our intent is not to impugn or malign the often misunderstood comic book industry as a whole, we would be remiss if we did not touch on the issue of payment. Many cartoonists, writers and artists have complained about the sluggish payment policies of certain publishers. Although you should negotiate payment terms (net 30, 60 or 90 days, upon acceptance or publication, royalty schedule, etc.), it is almost impossible to enforce terms even with a 390 pound sumo-wrestler named "Tito." Suffice to say, *professional* publishers will honestly and equitably abide by their negotiated terms. It simply takes time, experience and word of mouth to determine who's cool and who's to be avoided.

ARCHIE COMICS PUBLICATIONS INC., 325 Fayette Ave., Mamaroneck NY 10543. (914)381-8062. FAX: (914)381-2335. Audience is comprised of young readers age 8-15, approximately 60% female.

How to Contact: Humorous writers should send a cover letter to Fred Mauser, Editor. Cartoonist/humorous illustrators should send a cover letter to Fred Mauser, Editor.
Terms: Payment for writing is the outright purchase of manuscript. Varies on project. Pays upon invoice.

BAM PRODUCTIONS, Suite 211, 811 E. State St., Sharon PA 16146. (412)342-5300. Estab. 1980. Audience is comprised of "the general public, family-oriented." Circ. 5,000-10,000 internationally. Titles: *Adam and Eve* and *Sugar and Spike*. Approximately 90% of art and writing is humor-oriented. Approximately 100% of artwork and writing is done by freelancers.
Subject Needs: Needs general humor that is family-oriented. Doesn't want to see "vulgar or pornographic work."
How to Contact: Humorous writers should send a writing sample, a published tearsheet and a cover letter to Bill Murray, President. Cartoonists/humorous illustrators should send photocopied art samples, a published tearsheet and a cover letter to Bill Murray, President. Also interested in seeing samples from layout and inking artists and letterers. Prefers to work with freelancers with fax capabilities. For artist/writer guidelines, send $1 and a SASE. To query with ideas for a new humorous comic book title, send photocopied art and story outline. Reports back on unsolicited submissions/queries via letter in 3 weeks. Returns samples with SASE.
Terms: Payment for writing is per page, $25-1,000; for cartooning is $25-1,000, b&w, page. Pays on publication. Pays $50 kill fee for writing/cartooning.

BLUE COMET PRESS AND BLACK SKULL STUDIOS, 1708 Magnolia Ave., Manhattan Beach CA 90266. (213)545-6887. Estab. 1986. Audience is comprised of mostly adventure and fantasy with some super-heroes, but most sword and sorcery. Circ. 5,000. Titles: *Varmints Special #1*, *Rough Raiders Annual #1* and *Heavy Metal Monsters #1*. Approximately 20% of art and writing titles is humor-oriented.
Subject Needs: "We need talented sword & sorcery artists that want exposure and are willing to work for little until we build our sales and find a more secure place to sell our books than the 'direct market.' We want professional quality artists looking for exposure that want to help build a company and secure a future for themselves."
How to Contact: Humorous writers should send writing samples to C.A. Stormon, President/Owner. Cartoonists/humorous illustrators should send art samples, business card and cover letter to C.A. Stormon. Also interested in seeing samples from pencil, layout and inking artists; letterers; and painters. For artist/writer guidelines or sample copy, send $3 and #10 SASE. To query with ideas for a new humorous comic book title, send photocopied art and story outline. Reports back on unsolicited materials only if interested. Returns materials if requested.
Terms: Pays on percentage of profits basis. Pays after publication.
Inside Tips: "A good example of a 'dream comic book' is *Teenage Mutant Ninja Turtles*. Started with 3,000 copies, it now has a cartoon show, cereal and color and b&w comics that all sell well regardless of market swings. You must love to draw. If you don't love drawing more than sex or anything, then forget it. You have to draw and practice, day in and day out, every day! Until you lose all your friends, and you become a hermit; and you have to draw and practice from life—not comic books. To be a success in writing comics, you have to find a small company like mine that likes your work. Then you have to write for years on end for nothing to get the experience to know what must be done to get into the bigger publishers."

CAT-HEAD COMICS, Box 576, Hudson MA 01749. Estab. 1983. Circ. 2,000 to 3,500. Titles: *Buzzard, Bad, Death Warmed Over, Dangle, Bummer* and *Dog Boy*. Approximately 100% of art is humor-oriented. Approximately 100% of artwork is done by freelancers.

Subject Needs: Needs "funny, sardonic, satire. A personal vision is best." Doesn't want to see "super-heroes, genre fiction, anything like *Marvel* or D.C." Send all cartooning submissions to Steve Beaupre, Editor.

Inside Tips: The key to the success of a cartoonist in this market is "pandering to the lowest common denominator. It always makes a buck, but I recommend sticking to your own vision."

DARK HORSE COMICS, 2008 SE Monroe, Milwaukie OR 97222. (503)652-8815. Estab. 1986. "3rd biggest direct sales comics publisher in the country." Books targeted for a 18-25 year old market. Circ. 100,000 nationally. Titles: *Aliens, Predator, Aliens vs. Predator* and *Flaming Carrot*. Approximately 20% of art and writing is humor-oriented. 100% of artwork and writing is done by freelancers.

Subjects Needs: "Most of the humor material shows up in 8-page stories in *Dark Horse Presents.*"

How to Contact: Cartoonists/humorous illustrators should send published tearsheets, art samples and cover letter to Chris Warner. Also interested in seeing samples from pencil, layout and inking artists and letterers. For artist/writer guidelines, send #10 SASE. To query with ideas for a new humorous comic book title, send photocopied art and story outline. Reports back on unsolicited submissions/queries via letter in 2 months (at the most—quicker if interested). Returns samples with SASE.

Terms: Pay depends on art quality, etc. Pays upon invoice (net 30).

DC COMICS, 1325 Avenue of the Americas, New York NY 10019. (212)636-5400. Audience is comprised of young readers mostly, males, ages 3-25. Some comics are adult-oriented (college age).

Subject Needs: Needs "adventure strips, sci-fi, straightforward cartooning, no gags; be able to tell a story with pictures."

How to Contact: Send #10 SASE to Submissions Editor requesting artist or writer guidelines.

Terms: Payment for writing is per page basis. Sliding scale. Payment varies for cartooning.

ECLIPSE, Box 1099, Forestville CA 95436. (707)887-1521. Estab. 1978. Audience is comprised of adults and young adults for graphic albums and young adults and older adolescents for our periodical comic books. Circ. up to 400,000. Titles: *The Hobbit, James Bond, Miracleman, Appleseed, Tapping the Vein, Zot!* Approximately 8% of art or writing titles are humor oriented. 100% of artwork or writing titles are by freelancers.

How to Contact: "Humorous writers/cartoonist/humorous illustrators should send for our guidelines (SASE with request) and we'll tell you how to submit a portfolio to Submissions Editor." Also interested in seeing samples from pencil artists, inking artists and realistic renderers; humorous caricaturists who can *paint* their art. For artist/writer guidelines, send #10 SASE. To query with ideas for a new humorous comic book title, send photocopied art or story outline. Reports back on unsolicited submissions/queries via letter in 3 months, only if SASE is included.

Terms: Payment for writing is $35-50 per page against an 8% royalty split; artist and writer pay $100-150 per page against a total of 8% royalties split between writer and artist upon invoice (net 30). Pays full payment as per contract kill fee for writing/cartooning.

Inside Tips: "Better color technologies (laser scanning) has led to development of fully painted, slick 'art' comics. The trend now is toward fine art, realistic rendering and high quality printings." The 'dream comic book' for any publisher would be "one produced *on time* by a great artist, with good sales potential and fully painted in a style halfway between 'academic' and 'ad art'. Like, say a comic book by Norman Rockwell, N.C. Wyeth or Maxfield Parrish about the heroic adventures of a young woman who becomes a DEA agent, carries a gun and falls in love with the man she's been sent to set up for a drug bust by her crooked DEA boss who is actually in the pay of the medallion Cartel. And I want it next week! (The guy turns out to be okay, because he's a secret agent, so they blow away the crooked DEA guy and the whole thing ends with a nice clinch against a background of sunset—no, make that dawn—in the mountains.)"

*FANTACO ENTERPRISES INC., 21 Central Ave., Albany NY 12210. (518)463-1400. FAX: (518)463-0090. Estab. 1978. "We publish horror, suspense and science fiction comics." Target audience is age 16-50; international distribution. Circ. 40,000. Titles: *Shriek*. Approximately 10% of art and 30% of writing titles are humor oriented. 100% of artwork and writing titles are by freelancers.
Subject Needs: Abstract, surrealism photo-realism, dream imagery. Good humor material with horror or suspense setting. Doesn't want to see super heroes of *any* kind, "good girl" art, pre-pubescent sex fantasies, sex/violence stories, macho tales or X-rated material.
How to Contact: Cartoonist/humorous illustrators should send published tearsheets, business card, art samples and a cover letter explaining credits/background to Hank Jansen, Editor. Also interested in seeing samples from letterers. To query with ideas for a new humorous comic book title send photocopied art. Returns samples with SASE.
Terms: Payment for cartooning: b&w per page, $35-110; b&w cover, $125-200; 4-color cover, $200-500. Pays on publication. Pays full payment kill fee if material does not run.
Inside Tips: "The super hero market is bloated and sorely in need of a major fall from grace. Develop a unique concept, supply attractive art and be honest with your audience." A "dream" comic book would include "visually stunning art, completely inked and lettered; intriguing story; and a knockout painted and fully separated cover." The key to the success of a cartoonist or writer in this market is to "keep your ego in check; retain a sense of humor; remember you are in a highly competitive marketplace; remember that in the big scheme of things none of this really matters."

FANTAGRAPHICS BOOKS, 7563 Lake City Way NE, Seattle WA 98115. (206)524-1967. FAX: (206)524-2104. Estab. 1976. Audience is comprised of "normal, intelligent human beings who enjoy reading, among other things, comics." Circ. up to 25,000. Titles: *Eightball*, *Hate* and *Any Resemblance to Persons Living or Dead is Purely Coincidental*. Approximately 50% of writing and art is humor-oriented. 100% of humor-oriented titles is done by freelancers.
Subject Needs: "We don't have 'needs' per se; we publish what we like. No superheroes, no parodies of superheroes or genre crap; we don't dislike panels and short strips, but don't really have a lot of places to publish them."
How to Contact: Humorous writers should send published tearsheets and writing samples (but, "frankly, we tend to discourage writers; we're not set up to match up writers and artists at this point.") to Robert Boyd, Submissions Editor. Cartoonists/humorous illustrators should send published tearsheets and art samples to Robert Boyd, Submissions Editor. For artist/writer guidelines, send #10 SASE. To query with ideas for a new humorous comic book title, send photocopied art and story outline. Reports back on unsolicited submissions/queries via letter in 2 months. Returns samples with SASE.

The asterisk before a listing indicates that the listing is new in this edition. New markets are often more receptive to freelance submissions.

Terms: Payment for writing is percentage of gross; for cartooning is 6-8% of gross or $15 minimum, b&w, page. "Our terms for payment include contractually negotiated advances upon delivery and royalties 45 days after publication."

Inside Tips: "Market trends are too depressing to go into at the moment. There may be an upsurge in the 1990s, but humor is pretty well dead in the direct sales comic book market. (The fact that we publish 50% humor material can be attributed to utter mulishness on our part.) For just about any other publisher in the current marketplace, a dream comic book is a semi-pornographic, ultra-violent, full-color superhero mutant ninja movie tie-in. For us, a dream comic book is a deeply personal work by a cartoonist completely in command of his craft, regardless of format or subject matter."

FIRST PUBLISHING, 435 N. LaSalle St., Chicago IL 60610. (312)670-6770. FAX: (312)670-6793. Estab. 1982. Audience is predominantly male, 2 years of college, 22 years old. Circ. 500,000. Titles: *Classics Illustrated*, *Lone Wolf and Cub*, *Teenage Mutant Ninja Turtles* and *Beauty and the Beast*. Approximately 10% of writing is humor-oriented. 100% of writing is done by freelancers.

Subject Needs: "We are looking for action-adventure series in all genres. We are also looking for writers who are familiar with cartoon and daily comic strip characters. We are open to any submission geared to a 17-year-old and older audience."

How to Contact: Humorous writers should send complete manuscript, business card, writing samples and cover letter to Kurt Goldzung, Creative Director. For artist/writer guidelines, send #10 SASE. To query with ideas for a new humorous comic book title, send photocopied art, entire manuscript and story outline. Reports back on unsolicited submissions/queries only if interested. Returns samples with SASE.

Terms: Payment for writing is negotiable per page, $25-60. Pays upon approval. Pays 1/3 kill fee for writing.

Inside Tips: "Be aware that the comic book market is more demanding than ever. The characters you present have to be well-rounded and the situations well-examined. The audience is more sophisticated, and that means selling a new series to them is more difficult. People want to be entertained, and a new series needs to have a good balance between seriousness and comic relief. You have to be well-read inside of comics to avoid clichéd storylines, and well-read outside of comics, especially in the areas that your series covers. If you are writing a contemporary thriller, you must instill that comic with verisimilitude. You must also study people and their idiosyncracies; a good series character is multi-dimensional and should have unconscious mannerisms that add depth to his/her character, as well as a strong sense of self. People follow series characters who know who they are in an uncertain world."

HARVEY COMICS ENTERTAINMENT, Suite 500, 100 Wilshire Blvd., Santa Monica CA 90401. (213)451-3377. (213)458-6995. Estab. 1940. Audience is comprised of 7-13 year old boys and girls. Titles: *New Kids on the Block*, *Richie Rich*, *Casper the Friendly Ghost*, *Wendy*, and *Hot Stuff*. 100% of art and writing is humor oriented. 100% of artwork and writing is done by freelancers.

Subject Needs: Needs "primarily styles that accommodate our many characters and those we are presently trying to license — teenage and kiddie oriented."

How to Contact: Humorous writers should send published tearsheet, a cover letter to Sid Jacobson, Editor-in-Chief. Cartoonists/humorous illustrators should send photocopied art samples to Sid Jacobson, Editor-in-Chief. Also interested in seeing samples from pencil and inking artists. To query with ideas for new humorous comic book titles, send Xeroxed art and story outline. Returns samples with SASE.

Terms: Payment for writing is outright purchase of manuscript; per page, $40-70; for cartooning, $50-90, b&w, page. Pays upon invoice. Pays 1/2 kill fee for writing and cartooning.

BOB VERSANDI

"RATUS"

TRACY'S

UNNH!

32-14 213TH STREET BAYSIDE NY 11361   718-229-0041

© Robert Versandi

A Comical Approach to Self-Promotion:
To promote his different comic book styles, Bayside, New York-based comic strip artist Bob Versandi sends out postcards like these. Since they are printed two-up (each 5½ × 8½) in black ink only, they are very inexpensive to produce.

INNOVATION PUBLISHING, 3622 Jacob St., Wheeling WV 26003. (304)232-7701. FAX: (304)232-4010. Estab. 1988. Circ. 30,000. Titles: *The Vampire Lestat, Lost in Space, Hero Alliance, The Maze Agency*. Approximately 10% of art and writing titles is humor oriented. 100% of artwork and writing titles is by freelancers.

Subject Needs: "Anything fresh and innovative—comics that are marketable concepts, but which you wouldn't expect to see from one of the larger companies." Doesn't want to see anything "that resembles mainstream super-hero titles." Also looks for inventive b&w lines.

How to Contact: Humorous writers should send writing samples, a cover letter detailing credits/background and comic book scripts to Submissions Editor. Cartoonists/humorous illustrators should send art samples and a cover letter explaining credits/background to George Broderick. Never send originals. Also interested in seeing samples from pencil artists, inking artists, letterers, colorists and painters. For artist/writer guidelines, send #10 SASE. To query with ideas for a new humorous comic book title, send penciled pages, inked pages, photocopied art and story outline. Reports back on unsolicited submissions/queries via letter in 1 month with proper SASE only.

Terms: Payment for writing varies per book; for cartooning varies per book. Pays 10% kill fee for writing and 10% for cartooning.

Inside Tips: No phone calls. "This is one of the craziest, most unpredictable markets in human history. We just try to publish well-written, well-drawn comic books and cross our fingers. Licensed projects are currently doing very well, as in our project *The Vampire Lestat* and several others. If a publisher can get a movie or novel that will be a big hit, a comic book adaptation of same will almost certainly be a big seller as well. The key to the success of a cartoonist is MEETING DEADLINES! Also, a slick and consistent style derived from a close observation of real life. Originality and spontaneity in characterization, dialogue and situations within a commercial framework are essential for a writer."

JABBERWOCKY GRAPHIX, Box 165246, Irving TX 75016. Estab. 1975. Audience is comprised of a wide range, no specific single markets. Circ. 15,000. Titles: *Adventures of Olivia*, *Fever Pitch*, *Goodies*, *Stuff* and *Amused to No End*. Approximately 75% of art and writing is humor-oriented. Approximately 50% of artwork and writing is done by freelancers.
Subject Needs: Needs "sexually-oriented adult material, humorous stories but also serious. Artwork must be of attractive people, either cartoon or realistic styles. We are presently well-stocked on our non-sexual titles." Doesn't want to see "violent themes, rape, bondage, etc."
How to Contact: Cartoonists/humorous illustrators should send photocopied art samples of a sexual/erotic nature and SASE to Jabberwocky Graphix. Send $1.25 for copy of latest full catalog. "To query with ideas for a new sexual comic book title, send photocopied art, entire manuscript and story outline." Reports back on unsolicited submissions/queries via letter in 2-6 weeks. Must include a SASE.
Terms: Payment varies. "Usually a percentage of profits on issue work appears in. We buy one-time rights only. Copyrights are reassigned to the artist."

*KNOCKABOUT COMICS, 10 Acklam Road, London England W10 5QZ. (01)969-2945. FAX: (01)960-6865. Estab. 1975. Audience is comprised of teenage and adult readers. Circ. 15,000. Titles: *Ages of Woman*, *Rapid Reflexes* and *Freak Brothers #0*. 100% of art or writing titles are humor oriented. 100% of artwork or writing titles are by freelancers.
Subject Needs: Would like to find adult material (of an 'underground' style). "We want the most unusual strips, but only of professional quality. We don't want to see science fiction, super heroes, fantasy or toilet jokes."
How to Contact: Humorous writers should send writing samples, published tearsheets and a cover letter detailing credits/background to Carol Bennett, Editor. Send all cartooning submissions to Hunt Emerson, Editor. To query with ideas for a new humorous comic book title send penciled pages, photocopied art and story outline. Reports back on unsolicited submissions/queries only if interested. Returns samples with SASE if requested.
Terms: Payment for writing is $37-55/page. For cartooning $50-80 per b&w page; pays $100-300 advance upon publication. Pays $100 kill fee for writing/cartooning.

MAD, 485 MADison Ave., New York NY 10022. (212)752-7685. Estab. 1952. Audience is comprised of "everyone over six who likes to laugh." Circ. 1 million.
Subject Needs: "Funny stuff! Especially prized are articles on current hot trends. Send a paragraph or two explaining your premise and 3-4 examples of how you plan to carry it through, describing visual content. Rough sketches are welcomed but not necessary." No straight text pieces, poetry, song parodies, movie or TV satires ("unless they're entirely different in format or approach from what we're currently doing"), cartoon "characters" or rehashed MAD-like stuff.
How to Contact: Send all writing submissions to Nick Meglin or John Ficarra, Editors. Send all cartooning submissions to Leonard Brenner, Art Director.
Terms: Payment for writing, $400 for outright purchase of manuscript; for cartooning is $400, b&w, page. Pays upon approval.
Inside Tips: "MAKE US LAUGH! College students—send SASE for info on our summer intern program."

MALIBU GRAPHICS INC, 5321 Sterling Center Dr., Westlake Village CA 91361-7613. Estab. 1986. Audience is comprised of 18-30 year old males. Circ. 50,000. Titles: *Robotech*, *Ninja Highschool*, *Exiles*, *Ghastly the Dead Clown*, *Ex-Mutants* and *Dinosaurs for Hire*. Approximately 10% of art and writing titles are humor-oriented. 100% of artwork and writing titles are by freelancers.

Subject Needs: "Action titles with humorous elements work best for us. We like to add 4-6 titles a year in this direction."

How to Contact: Humorous writers should send proposal (no longer than 5 pages) to submissions editor. Cartoonists/humorous illustrators should send published tearsheets and multi-panel page samples to submissions editor. Also interested in seeing samples from pencil artists, inking artists, letterers, painters, any and all. For artist/writer guidelines, send #10 SASE. To query with ideas for a new humorous comic book title, send penciled pages, inked pages and story line. Reports back on unsolicited submissions and queries via letter in 3 months.

Terms: Payment for writing is on a royalty basis, 5-7% of net; for cartooning is 9-13% of net. Pays $100-500 advance, paid 15 days after acceptance; additional percentage paid 60 days after publication. Pays 10% of advance kill fee for writing and cartooning.

Inside Tips: "To have a successful comic book title, the artist/writer must be aware that the industry is crowded with talent and that a good portion of the buying public are collectors—not necessarily readers. Also, the average comic book buyer is now more than 20 years old. The 'dream comic book' for any publisher would be a brand new concept that would be able to generate both high per copy sales, but also various licensing possibilities . . . games, posters, T-shirts, etc."

*MANUSCRIPT PRESS, INC., Box 336, Mountain Home TN 37684. (615)926-7495. Estab. 1976. Audience is general. Circ. 4,000. Titles: *Comics Revue, Prince Valiant*. Approximately 50% of art/writing titles are humor oriented. No artwork or writing titles are by freelancers.

Subject Needs: "We do reprints of syndicated comic strips only, e.g. Bloom County, Steve Canyon. We are not looking for submissions at this time."

Terms: Payment for cartooning is $10 per b&w page upon publication.

*MARVEL COMICS, 387 Park Ave. South, New York NY 10016. (212)696-0808. Audience is comprised of 7-12 year olds. "Epic Comics are geared to an adult audience." Titles: *The X-Man*.

How to Contact: Humor writers should send one-page synopsis for a 22-page story only to Submissions Editor. Cartoonists/humorous illustrators should send published tearsheets to Submissions Editor. For artist/writer guidelines, send SASE. To query with ideas for a new humorous comic book title, send "either penciled or inked pages, photocopied. No originals. Call or write for guidelines."

NBM PUBLISHING CO., 185 Madison Ave., #1502, New York NY 10016-4325. (212)545-1223. Audience is comprised of well-educated 18-32 year olds. Titles: *Treasury of Victorian Murder, Penguins Behind Bars* and *Suburban Nightmares*. Approximately 20% of art and writing is humor-oriented. 100% of artwork and writing is done by freelancers.

Subject Needs: Needs humor graphic albums—"satire especially sought." Doesn't want to see "bad taste, sophomoric humor."

How to Contact: Humorous writers should send writing samples and cover letter to Terry Nantier, Publisher. Cartoonists/humorous illustrators should send art samples and cover letter to Terry Nantier. Also interested in seeing samples from letterers and layout artists. To query with ideas for a new humorous comic book title, send photocopied art and story outline. Reports back on unsolicited submissions/queries via letter in 1 month. Returns samples with SASE.

Terms: Payment for writing is on royalty basis, 2% of retail price; for cartooning on royalty basis, 8% of retail price. Pay negotiated in advance.

ON TARGET, (formerly E & M Comics), 18C Boyle Ave., Cumberland RI 02864. (401)658-3917. Estab. 1984. Audience is comprised of "self-publishers in the small press by way of a news magazine *E & M Comic News.*" Circ. 50-100 nationally.

Subject Needs: Needs pin-ups and posters for publication in *E and M Comic News.* Doesn't want to see " 'adults only' types of comics." Cartoonists/humorous illustrators should send art samples and cover letter. Also interested in seeing samples from pencil and inking artists. For artist/writer guidelines, send 75¢. To query with ideas for a new humorous comic book title, send photocopied art. Reports back on unsolicited submissions/queries via letter in 3 months.

Terms: Payment for cartooning is on royalty basis, 75% of net. Pays upon invoice.

RIP OFF PRESS, INC., Box 4686, Auburn CA 95604. (916)885-8183. FAX: (916)885-8219. Estab. 1969. Audience is comprised of 18-35 and older, ex-hippies, college educated iconoclastic types. Circ. 30,000 internationally. Titles: *Fabulous Furry Freak Brothers, Miami Mice, Doll.* Approximately 75% of art titles are humor-oriented. 100% of artwork is by freelancers.

Subject Needs: Would like to find "new comic creators with an offbeat, adult sense of humor and a sure hand with a pen." Doesn't want to see "full-length books from previously unpublished cartoonists, crude pencil sketches, children's comics, text stories, super-hero/sword and sorcery."

How to Contact: Cartoonist/humorous illustrators should send letter-size photocopies of finished comic book pages to Kathe Todd, Editor. Also interested in seeing samples from letterers. No dot matrix submissions. For artist/writer guidelines, send #10 SASE. To query with ideas for a new humorous comic book title, send photocopied art or story outline. Reports back on unsolicited submissions/queries only if interested. Returns samples with SASE if requested.

Terms: Payment for cartooning is $25-75 per b&w page, $50-150 per 4-color. Pays on publication.

Inside Tips: "Unquestionably the classic comic book genre represented by the publications of Marvel and DC is still the most popular. There is a trend for more adult-oriented plots, detailed characterizations and other concessions to the advancing average age of comic fans, however. In the non-mass market, mostly black-and-white comics published by Rip Off Press, the trend is for hardcore sex combined with humor and/or soap-opera-like plot lines to be the best selling type of material. The dream comic book for any publisher would be one such as *Freak Brothers #1*, which has continued to sell steadily in the many tens of thousands of copies over the entire 20 years since it was first published."

SNICKER, 1248 Oak Bark, St. Louis MO 63146. (314)993-1633. Estab. 1987. Quarterly tabloid. Circ. 5,000. Needs cartoon narratives, gag and spot cartoons. "*Snicker* is a forum for humor, truth and experimentation. Surprise us and your fellow artists. Invent new formats." Accepts previously published cartoons and humorous articles. Send $3 for sample issue.

Gag Cartoons: Uses numerous gag cartoons/issue. Doesn't want to see " 'Far Side' clones. For us, the 'dream' gag cartoon would be atomic cowboys." Preferred format is multi-panel narrative. Send submissions to Rich Balducci, Editor. Reports back in 2 weeks only if interested. Returns materials if accompanied by SASE. *Inside Tips:* A gag cartoonist should "use his or her soul as often as his or her pen, brush, rapidograph, pencil, crayon or marker."

Illustration: Uses approximately 2-3 humorous illustrations/issue for covers. Sometimes works on assignment. For first contact send "anything to Dillar, Creative Consultant." Reports back in 2 weeks. Samples are filed or are returned by SASE.
Writing: Uses approximately 1-2 humorous pieces/issue. Needs humorous nonfiction, interviews, fiction and cartoon stories. Subject matter includes experimental, underground, environmental, social, anarchist, predatory, contradictory, life and death. Length: 500-1,100 words. To query be familiar with magazine; study writer's guidelines, "then create your own rules." Send $2 for copy of *Snicker*. For first contact send anything to Kathleen Balducci, Co-publisher. Reports back in 3-4 weeks. Samples are filed or are returned with SASE.

STARLIGHT COMICS GROUP, Suite 4A, 1 David Lane, Yonkers NY 10701. (914)965-8717. Estab. 1988. Audience is comprised of "other self-publishers." Circ. 100-200 nationally. Titles: *Small Press Interview, Mercury Magazine, Captain Scorpion, The Protectors, Starlight Superheroes, Outland Warriors, Pop Cartoons* and *Rev. Ablack.* Approximately 75% of art and writing is humor-oriented. Approximately 100% of artwork and writing is done by freelancers.
Subject Needs: Needs "stories and art by amateurs and non-professionals, people who do this for fun or practice and not for profit." Doesn't want to see "hardcore pornography, senseless violence — unless it makes some kind of dramatic or humorous point."
How to Contact: Humorous writers should send query letter with brief synopsis to Lee Erwin, Senior Editor. Cartoonists/humorous illustrators should send art samples to Lee Erwin, Senior Editor. Also interested in seeing samples from pencil and inking artists and letterers. For artist/writer guidelines, send #10 SASE. To query with ideas for a new humorous comic book title, send story outline and sample art. Reports back on unsolicited submissions via letter in 2 weeks. Returns materials if requested.
Terms: Payment for writing is per page, $5 maximum; for cartooning is $5, b&w, page. "Artist/writer should understand the 'unprofit' nature of small presses. Write us for details. We pay all publishing costs and rarely 'buy.' " Pays upon publication.
Inside Tips: "In small presses we stress staying away from market trends entirely, opting for personal expression and fun as the driving force."

UNDERGROUND SURREALIST MAGAZINE, Box 2565, Cambridge MA 02238. (617)891-9569. Estab. 1986. Circ. 500. 90% of comics are humor-oriented and done by freelancers.
Subject Needs: Comic strips, panels and stories.
How to Contact: Humorous writers and cartoonists should send cartoons to Mick Cusimano, Editor. Prefer photocopies reduced to fit 8½ × 11. For sample copy send $3.
Terms: Pays in contributors copies.
Inside Tips: "Humor and satire on any subject. Looking for cartoons with a Monty Python, Saturday Night Live, Marx Brothers kind of feel to it."

Comic Books/Changes '91-'93

The following markets appeared in the last (1991) edition of *Humor and Cartoon Markets* but are absent from the 1993 edition. These companies failed to respond to our request for an update of their listing or for the reasons indicated in parentheses following the company name.

Acme Press Ltd. (asked to be deleted)
Blackbird Comics, Inc. (cannot be reached)
C&T Graphics/New Voice Productions (cannot be reached)
Comics Career (seldom publishes)
4 Winds Publishing Group (cannot be reached)
Now Comics
Sheldon Oppenberg Associates (asked to be deleted)
Pastime Productions (no longer using humor)
Piranha Press (cannot be reached)
Pure Imagination (overstocked)
Sword in Stone Productions (cannot be reached)

Gags/Entertainers

If it weren't for gag writers, 3×5 index cards would have little purpose other than to give nasty paper cuts.

After all, it's on these cards that gag writers type their pithy jokes, then stuff them into envelopes and hope that a comedian, cartoonist or entertainer finds them funny enough to buy.

Buy jokes? Comedians and cartoonists really *buy* jokes? Hey, before you go into cardiac arrest, think of Santa Claus and his elves. The elves actually make the toys for Santa, but Santa gets all the glory. Gag writers are sort of like the elves—only with better shoes.

Look, the truth of the matter is that cartoonists, comedians and other funny people rack their brains to come up with ideas, jokes and material. It may take eight minutes to draw the idea or eight seconds to utter the joke, but it may have taken eight hours for the humorist to coax the material from his skull. So to ensure that their strips, cartoons and acts include fresh, funny material, many humorists (more than you would ever realize) use the services of outside writers.

The practice is quite common, but you won't find comedians going out of their way to *advertise* their need for gags, jokes or one-liners, and rarely do you come across a cartoonist who publicly praises his brilliant gag writer. To be sure, gag writing is an "inside" business. Talking with other gag writers, networking with these funny folks, you soon learn which comedians seek one-liners about the "men's movement," which gag cartoonists need two-businessmen-in-bar-complaining-about-their-boss ideas, and which comic strip artists are looking for freelance balloon banter and blips to ensure that they make their syndicate deadlines.

Approaching comedians and cartoonists

The best way to approach gag writing is with a 29 cent stamp and a little *chutzpah*. Is there a comic strip that you have a symbiotic relationship with? Are you following the career of a comedian who makes you wonder if you were Siamese twins separated at birth? Then go ahead—introduce yourself!

Put together a succinct, business-like letter and inquire whether or not he is receptive to unsolicited writing submissions. If you're looking for a comic strip cartoonist not listed in the book, he can be reached through his syndicate which routinely forwards mail. Likewise, gag cartoonists not found within these pages can be contacted through the magazines in which their work appears, and you can get a hold of comedians by writing to their agents or managers.

If a comedian does seek writers, he'll most likely respond to your query by sending you a copy of his disclosure policy and a disclosure agreement that you will be required to sign and return. Generally, these disclosure agreements are simple documents which do not require the scrutiny of an attorney, but they certainly favor the comedian. But don't let this scare you off. I have come across many *gag writers* who steal from one another, but I have yet to encounter a comedian who blatantly stole material from a writer.

However, comedians who send you such disclosure agreements will not review your materials until the document has been signed, returned and retained in their files, and in most cases, this one signed disclosure agreement will cover all subsequent disclosures made to the comedian.

Generally speaking, a freelance gag writer submits individual jokes, gags, one-liners or ideas on white index cards, although some comedians and cartoonists prefer that the material be typed on 8½ × 11 paper. Either way, your name, address, phone number and Social Security number should be on *each* joke sheet or card and include a SASE if you want the material returned.

Methods for cataloging each gag vary drastically from one writer to the next—it depends on how much information you'd like to jam into a cryptic code. For example, you could code a gag 0992BUS529, which when broken down could mean that the gag was written in September of 1992 (09/92), the "slant" of the gag is "business" (BUS) and catalog number is 529. If you're submitting the same material to 10 different cartoonists and comedians, you'll want to come up with an additional "ABC" coding system.

Print the alphabet on the back of each joke and assign a letter to each cartoonist and comedian you submit material to. Only *you* know what letters are assigned to what cartoonists or comedians. When you submit the joke to cartoonist A, circle the letter A, when you submit to comedian B, circle the letter B, and so on. That way you know who has seen the joke, without divulging to others who those exact people are. Obviously, the purpose of such coding is to effectively track your material and ensure that you don't continue showing it to the same people over and over again.

Understand, of course, that a stigma is attached to index cards or joke sheets that show *many* circled code letters. When a cartoonist or comedian sees this, they realize that they are the 10th, 15th, even 20th person to be offered the joke. Even if they like the joke, they wonder why it never sold. They begin to second guess their own judgement and in the end pass on buying the joke. I know of few ways to avoid this situation. I suppose there's only one thing to do: Write better material so it's purchased by the second or third cartoonist or comedian.

Money talk

You'll find that payments vary dramatically and generally rise with a cartoonist's or comedian's relative success. Many comedians pay rates more laughable than their acts ($50 for a joke is considered a *good* rate), comic strip artists might pay $20, $40, even $100 for a strip idea, but gag cartoonists generally chop up their fee by retaining 75 percent of the check and giving 25 percent to their gag writer.

Terms jump all over the place as well. Most comedians pay upon acceptance or after the first initial usage of the material, comic strip artists generally pay 30 days from the date on which your joke was published, and gag cartoonists pay on publication—once they are paid by the magazine, they cut a check for you.

If a gag cartoonist elects to draw up your idea, prepare yourself for the long haul as they submit the cartoon to publication after publication. The submission process can be an excruciating one taking months (years?) until the drawing finds a home or unceremoniously ascends into cartoon Heaven.

Ideally, you want to establish an ongoing, collaborative relationship with select comedian(s) or cartoonist(s) and even be called on by them to "brainstorm" ideas or to add a new twist to their material. But the "chemistry" has to be there, needless to say, if the creative partnership between humorist and writer is to be a mutually rewarding one.

JEAN ADAMS, 6337 Droxford St., Lakewood CA 90713. (213)867-2954. Began selling cartoons in 1987. Cartoons have recently appeared in nonprofit organization/school newspapers. Currently selling *Jeans Jukebox*—custom made cartoons of favorite song titles.
How to Contact: Not using gag writers at this time—using own material. Will consider gags sent in the future.
Inside Tips: "The secret to a great gag/joke is that the gag must be set up for the viewer to expect a certain reaction and then you surprise him with a twist to his expectation. For custom cartoons—give the buyer what he wants, not necessarily what you want to draw."

EDOUARD BLAIS, 2704 Parkview Blvd., Robbinsdale MN 55422. (612)588-5249. Estab. 1982. 75% of cartoons are written by gag/joke writers or outside sources. Cartoons have recently appeared in *Gallery, Sun, Letters, Saturday Evening Post, Woman's World* and *Globe.*
How to Contact: Submit gags/jokes on 3 × 5 cards or slips. Looking for gags on general subjects, farm, rural, children's and adult humor. "General Rule: If you think it's funny, send it." Reports in 1 week. Returns materials only if provided with SASE. Pays writers 25% of total fee paid for cartoon.
Inside Tips: "Be persistent. Stay away from the obvious humor or humor that requires a very specialized knowledge."

ASHLEIGH BRILLIANT, 117 W. Valerio St., Santa Barbara CA 93101. (805)682-0531. Names of features: "Pot-shots" and "Brilliant Thoughts." Began selling cartoons in 1967. Number of cartoons written by gag/joke writers or outside sources varies. Cartoons have recently appeared in *Reader's Digest, Rocky Mountain News* and *American Way.*

How to Contact: "My work is so unconventional that freelancers will only be wasting their time unless they first study it carefully. A catalog and samples are available for $2 and a SASE." Submit 3½×5½ ready-to-print word and picture. Reports in 3 weeks. Returns materials only if provided with SASE. Pays $40 minimum outright purchase of gag/joke.

FRANCIS H. BRUMMER, 601 Arnold Ave., Council Bluffs IA 51503. Name of feature: "Rum." Began selling cartoons in 1954. 98% of cartoons are written by gag/joke writers or outside sources. Cartoons have recently appeared in *Good Housekeeping, VFW* and *American Machinist.*
How to Contact: Submit on 3×5 cards only. Looking for gags on working women, machine shops, insurance sales, teenagers and topics such as Valentine's Day, Easter, Thanksgiving and Christmas ("apply them to office, shops and sales, etc."). Doesn't want to see "vulgar material." Reports in 2 weeks. Returns materials only if provided with SASE. Pays "25% to top writers; 30% to those that furnish me with the type of gags I need."

JOE BURESCH, 6142 Carlton Ave., Sarasota FL 34231. (813)922-8833. Name of feature: "Dinah Mite" (weekly). Cartoons have recently appeared in *King Features*, *Good Housekeeping* and *National Enquirer.*
Inside Tips: "An aspiring cartoonist should lock the door and chain himself to the drawing table."

WILLIAM CANTY, Box 1053, S. Wellfleet MA 02663. (508)349-7549. Name of gag panel: "All About Town." Began selling cartoons in 1952. 10% of cartoons are written by gag/joke writers or outside sources. Cartoons have recently appeared in *Good Housekeeping* and *Saturday Evening Post.*
How to Contact: Submit 10-25 gags per batch on 3×5 cards. Looking for gags on general subjects. Doesn't want to see "adult material." Reports in 7 days. Returns materials only if provided with SASE. Pays writers 30% of total fee paid for cartoon.
Inside Tips: "The secret to a great gag/joke is that it must be *funny.* Be persistent and have a stomach for rejection. There are more markets, but they are specialized. Therefore, the cartoonist must spend more time marketing his/her work."

GRAHAM CARLTON CO., Box 5052, Evanston IL 60204. (708)328-0400. FAX: (708)328-1700. Act is primarily stand-up. Uses gag/joke writers for TV appearances and live act/routine. Buys 100 gags/jokes/one-liners per year.
How to Contact: Prefers working with gag/joke writers who have fax capabilities. For first contact send audiotape. Reports back only if interested. Returns materials if accompanied by a SASE. Does not file materials. Buys all rights or negotiates rights purchased. Pays $5-50.

DON COLE, 17 Lehigh St., Dover NJ 07801-2550. (201)328-9153. Began selling cartoons in 1954. Also cartoon animation, since 1984. 50% of cartoons are written by gag/joke writers or outside sources. Cartoons have recently appeared in *National Examiner, Fresh Start, Law Practice Management, Medical Aspects of Human Sexuality, Alive!, Made to Measure, Satellite Orbit Mag, The Sun* and *Home Life.*
How to Contact: Submit gags only; 6-12 gags per batch on 3×5 slips. Looking for "anything funny. The wholesome, positive or cute sell best." Doesn't want to see "off-color material." Reports in 1-5 days. Returns materials only if provided with SASE. Pays writers 25% of total fee paid for cartoon.
Inside Tips: "Do not duplicate and continue submitting any gag that is being "held" by a cartoonist. Magazine gag cartoons usually *must be funnier* (more competitive) than the daily syndicated newspaper stuff. Must be *outstanding.* In trade journals, getting the right technical slant is most important."

Close-up

Hester Mundis
Comedy Writer

With a name like Hester, she'd better be funny.

"My mother was a nut case," explains Hester Mundis, head writer for Joan Rivers. "She thought Hester was such a lovely name, and my full maiden name was 'Hester Nakamee.' It sounded like 'hysterectomy.' I got married just to get rid of my maiden name—literally."

With her thick Brooklyn accent and staccato delivery, Mundis could use a well-timed rimshot followed by an elephant tranquilizer. *Anything* to calm her down. Indeed, a chat with Mundis takes on a life of its own and quickly degenerates into a flurry of one-liners and quick-witted *shtick*. This woman is *on*.

It was back in 1978 when Mundis the novelist (she has written under various pseudonyms) received a phone call from Joan Rivers, who found Mundis' latest novel, *Jessica's Wife*, to be hysterical. Rivers asked Mundis to be her comedic collaborator. "I thought I was going to die," screams Mundis. The relationship developed over the years and now Mundis is head writer for "The Joan Rivers Show."

Like Rivers, Mundis has an essentially 'screw-'em-if-they-can't-take-a-joke' approach to humor. "A long time ago," she says, "I figured out that you have to be able to laugh at absolutely everything—everything has humor in it for me. There are no taboos. I do, however, believe your timing can be wrong. For example, I might not want to tell a really hysterical cancer joke in front of someone whose parent is at the moment dying from it, and I'm not going to tell a Challenger joke to Christie McAuliffe's husband. But it's the way I deal with things. Some people cry, I prefer to laugh. I don't like to run my mascara. It's shallow, but it works.

"Every time something happens to you and you feel like crying," says Mundis, "that's the time you start to laugh. If you're going to be a comedy writer, you literally have to wake up in the morning and try to *think* funny. You have to exercise your mind by looking at any situation to figure out how you can make it funny, or how you can get a joke or an anecdote out of it. I stockpile these things, tighten them, and turn them into really flip one-liners."

While Mundis was essentially "discovered" by Rivers, most who aspire to careers as comedy writers can take the usual approach. "You can send comedy material to any entertainer," explains Mundis. "They do buy jokes and pay anywhere from $10 to $50 per joke if they use it in their act. Sometimes you have to find out by making phone calls who you have to go through and what releases you have to sign. However, many of my friends have walked up to comedians at comedy clubs and asked, 'Are you buying material?'

"If a comedian likes your material," Mundis continues, "and uses more of your jokes, you are talked up. But most comedians won't tell other stand-up comedians who their writers are because they want to keep their little stable all to themselves."

While Mundis is well aware of the reasons for busy comedians depending on comedy material from writers, the general public is not. "People just don't realize," she says, "that it would be physically impossible for a comic to come up with brand new material for every performance. If a comic puts on the same show over and over again, people aren't going to pay money to hear the same old jokes."

If Mundis understands the funny side of comedy, she also insists that humor is a serious business. "People should approach comedy as a career," explains Mundis. "If you are serious about it, you approach it as you would any venture—you make a *commitment* to it. You take the same route you would with any job. First, you need to have the right background. You read or study humor, you know humorists and have some favorite comedians. Then you have to set a goal for yourself. If you want to write for 'The Tonight Show,' you find out if this is a way to make a living. You do the same thing if you want to write funny screenplays.

"There are plenty of humor markets out there," says Mundis. "Any comedy writer can get started by sending in little humorous anecdotes to *Reader's Digest*. The comedy writer feeds on recognition. Most of the time we hope it's laughs, but money helps. So if you send something in and it gets published or performed, it means you're *funny*."

—*Bob Staake*

Hilariously Hester

- *My parents hated me. My only bath toys were the radio and the toaster.*

- *Bo Derek is so dumb, she studies for a Pap Test.*

- *My husband is so young, I have to burp him after sex.*

- *I grew up in a tough neighborhood. The bloodmobile was a 57 Chevy and two guys with switchblades.*

- *Don't talk to me about "multiple orgasms." I'm lucky if both sides of my toaster pop.*

Wasting Away in the Waiting Room: *Gag cartoonist Charles Castleman of Spokane, Washington conveys in this cartoon "the never ending frustration we all experience in the doctor's office." Michele Cooke of the National Enquirer paid Castleman $300 for first time reproduction rights to the cartoon. Before sending batches of cartoons off to magazines he is not familiar with, Castleman will "send questionnaires to prospective markets. When the information they return to me is on the positive side, I send the cartoon editor a self-promotional sheet of my published work."*

"He must believe that time heals everything."

© Charles Castleman

*RON COLEMAN, Box 11147, Burbank CA 91510-1147. (812)883-2193. Began selling cartoons in 1958. 5% of cartoons are written by gag/joke writers or outside sources.
How to Contact: Submit sample gags and SASE; send gags/jokes on 3×5 cards or 3×5 slips of paper. Looking for gags on general, sex, farm, medical, trade journal, senior citizens, computers, etc. (any popular subject). Reports in 1 week. Returns material only if provided with SASE. Pays writers 25% of total fee paid for cartoon. Gags may be marketed to more than one publication, which would increase writer's commission.
Inside Tips: The single best tip to an aspiring gag writer is "remember—this is a numbers game. The more you write, the more you sell."

*ED DAVIS/SOUTHWEST HUMOR, Box 460327, Houston TX 77056-8327. (713)622-2590. FAX: (713)622-2992. Began selling cartoons in 1961. 25% of cartoons are written by gag/joke writers. Cartoons have recently appeared in *Hustler, National Enquirer* and *Genesis*.
How to Contact: "Am always interested in hearing from other gag writers and cartoonists."
Inside Tips: The secret to a great gag/joke is that it's "short or captionless. Develop a unique style, work discipline and marketing persistence."

ERIC DECETIS/DECETIS CARTOONS, 2717 Harkness St., Sacramento CA 95818. Began selling cartoons in 1983. 10% of cartoons are written by gag/joke writers or outside sources. Cartoons have recently appeared in *Penthouse, Omni, National Lampoon, Los Angeles Magazine* and *Campus Life*.
How to Contact: Submit sample gags; 10-20 gags/jokes per batch on 3×5 cards. Looking for quality gags on offbeat subjects, adult, sight gags. Reports in 2-4 weeks. Returns materials only if provided with SASE. Pays writers 25% of total fee paid for cartoon.

 The asterisk before a listing indicates that the listing is new in this edition. New markets are often more receptive to freelance submissions.

Inside Tips: "The secret to a great gag/joke is simple gags—sight gags or ones with short cut lines."

STEVE DELMONTE, 328 W. Delavan Ave., Buffalo NY 14213. (716)883-6086. FAX: (716)883-9182. Began selling cartoons in 1977. 30% of cartoons are written by joke writers or outside sources. Cartoons have recently appeared in *McCalls, Psychology Today, Woman's World, Diversion.*
How to Contact: Submit cover letter and sample jokes; 15-20 gags/jokes per batch on 3×5 cards. Looking for jokes on "everything." Reports in 1 month. Returns material only if provided with SASE. Pays writers 25% of total fee paid for cartoon one time.
Inside Tips: "The secret to a great joke is a surprise ending/twist. The single best tip to an aspiring cartoonist is don't give up."

STAN FINE, Suite A2, 125 Montgomery Ave., Bala Cynwyd PA 19004. (215)667-2045. 60% of cartoons are written by gag/joke writers or outside sources. Cartoons have recently appeared in *Saturday Evening Post, Woman's World, Good Housekeeping, National Enquirer, First, Medical Economics, King Features* and *McCall's.*
How to Contact: Submit cover letter, sample gags and resume; 12-15 gags/jokes per batch on 3×5 cards. Looking for gags on family, kids, school and working women. Doesn't want to see "far-out, implausible subject matter." Reports in 1 week. Returns materials only if provided with SASE. Pays writers 25% of total fee paid for cartoon.
Inside Tips: The secret to a great gag/joke is "anything that gives me an audible chuckle and relates to everyday happenings. If you are attaining positive results, work even harder to consolidate your toehold. Avoid any distractions, read, watch and observe the world around you. Know what is really funny and be able to slant material."

H. GLASSMAN, Box 46664, Los Angeles CA 90046. Uses gag/joke writers for stand-up. "I submit the subjects after I see your sample gags."
How to Contact: Submit 6-10 one-liners per batch on 8½×11 paper. For first contact send cover letter and sample material. Reports back within 3 weeks. Returns materials if accompanied by SASE. Pays $15.
Inside Tips: "Jokes must fit my style and be performable."

STUART GOLDMAN, 2318 Manning St., Philadelphia PA 19103. (215)732-5106. Name of strip: "Eavesdrawings." Began selling cartoons in 1975. 15-20% of cartoons are written by gag/joke writers or outside sources. Cartoons have recently appeared in newspapers (weekly features for lifestyle sections); also writes for performance comedy.
How to Contact: Submit sample gags and tearsheets (with first submission); no less than 5 gags/jokes per batch; presentation is unimportant. Prefers to work with gag/joke writers who have fax capabilities. Looking for gags on urban/suburban, working/family lives with the main concentration on yuppie lifestyle, business, dating and entertainment. "I also desire to look at scripts for comedy club—have need for sketch material and bits from 2-8 minutes duration, payment varies. Doesn't want to see any explicit bedroom material—talk about it yes, but not in it." Reports in 2 weeks. Returns materials only if provided with SASE. Pays writers $15 minimum, depending on where the material is used.
Inside Tips: "Study body language and develop an ear for conversation. We are getting away from classical humor and moving toward the esoteric"

BRIAN HANSEN/CARTOON SOURCE, P.O. Box 1197, Boulder CO 80306. (303)444-3660. Began selling cartoons in 1981. 5% of cartoons are written by gag/joke writers or outside sources. Cartoons have recently appeared in *Infoworld, Computerworld, Personal and Professional.*

How to Contact: Submit sample gags on 3×5 cards, 8½×11 paper, or any other form. Looking for gags on office, sophisticated, computer and "off-the-wall" subjects. Doesn't want to see "adult" material. Reports in 4 weeks. Returns material only if provided with SASE. Pays writers $25 flat fee for cartoon.
Inside Tips: "A gag should require both pictures and words—where neither words nor pictures alone can express the idea. If you can be clever enough to find out who might want to buy them you can sell your cartoons."

JONNY HAWKINS, Box 10329, Detroit MI 48210. (313)842-4129. Began selling cartoons in 1977. 5% of cartoons are written by gag/joke writers or outside sources. Cartoons have recently appeared in *Leadership*, *The Lutheran*, *Saturday Evening Post*, *The Rotarian*, *First*.
How to Contact: Submit short intro letter; 10-50 gags on 3×5 slips of paper. Looking for gags on general topics; "I do quite a few farm cartoons as well as church/pastor gags. I need captionless animal gags for a developing project, though." Doesn't want to see "girlie material or anything sick or offensive. I certainly welcome the strange and absurd, but nothing pornographic or blasphemous." Reports usually within a week. Returns material only if provided with SASE. Pays writers 25% of total fee paid for cartoon. After 5 sales with same writer it goes up to 30%; after 10 to 32%.
Inside Tips: The secret to a great gag/joke is "that irony is captured in the fewest possible words, or if the thought of it leaves your spleen hanging on the floor." The single best tip to an aspiring cartoonist or gag writer is "be persistent. Don't let a few rejections sink your ship. Learn from the ones who are successful, but be *yourself!* Do you! Do what *you* think is funny and work on developing it to perfection."

DAVID R. HOWELL, Box 170, Dept. HC, Porterville CA 93258. (209)781-5885. Began selling cartoons in 1973. 50% of cartoons are written by gag/joke writers or outside sources. Cartoons have recently appeared in *National Enquirer, TV Guide, Women's Enterprise, Judicature* and *True Detective*.
How to Contact: Submit sample gags and resume; at least 10 gags/jokes per batch on 3×5 cards. Looking for gags on law and crime, TV, electronics, computers, medicine and retail. Doesn't want to see "sex, politics or topical subjects." Reports in 2 weeks. Returns materials only if provided with SASE. Pays writers 25-30% of total fee paid for cartoon.
Inside Tips: "The secret to a great gag/joke is a combination of good, brief line with funny drawing. Don't ever give up. Watch humor trends closely."

DALE HUNT, 2414 Otto Dr., Stockton CA 95209. (209)957-6419. Began selling cartoons in 1982. Cartoons have recently appeared in *Stockton Record, Lincoln Chronicle, Delta Impact* and *Delta Digest Magazine*.
How to Contact: Submit "some kind of idea" on 8½×11 paper. Looking for gags on medicine and fishing. Doesn't want to see "kids' cartoons and cars." Reports in a few months "due to editors." Returns materials only if provided with SASE. Pays writers 25% of total fee paid for cartoon "only if they sell."
Inside Tips: "Draw all day, spend time studying other cartoonists and listen to your inner mind. Watch for situations around you and watch comedy shows. Sometimes you can get ideas from them; follow the example, but don't steal."

DIANA JORDAN, 4218 Whitsett Ave. #5, Studio City CA 91604-1676. Recently nominated as one of the top 5 female comics in the country. Act is stand-up. Uses gag/joke writers for TV appearances, live act/routine on subjects which include relationships, current events, "things that men and women do that drive each other crazy, sperm banks and surrogate mothers." Doesn't want to see material with four-letter words. Buys 40 gags/jokes/one-liners per year.

How to Contact: Gag/joke writers must request disclosure agreement before submitting gags/jokes. Submit 20 gags/jokes per batch on 8½" × 11" paper. For first contact send sample material. Reports back within 3 weeks only if interested. Returns materials if accompanied by a SASE. Keeps materials on file. Buys all rights. Pays $25 per joke, flat.

MILO KINN, 1413 SW Cambridge St., Seattle WA 98106. Began selling cartoons in 1942. 50% of cartoons are written by gag writers or outside sources. Cartoons have recently appeared in *Pet Health News, Legal Economics, American Machinist, Nebraska Farmer, Nutrition Health Review, Woman's World* and *Machinists Blue Book.*
How to Contact: Submit sample gags; 10-20 gags per batch on 3 × 5 cards or paper. Looking for gags on office situations, lawyers, farms, machine shops, family, general (of course), medicine and women. Doesn't want to see "girly" gags. Reports in 2 weeks. Returns materials only if provided with SASE. Pays writers 25% of total fee paid for cartoon.
Inside Tips: "The secret to a good gag is it makes a funny picture (even without a gagline). Cartoonists should keep drawings simple. Gag writers should write situations without too much description. Keep gag settings uncomplicated."

THOMAS L. LAIRD, 706 Scott St., Philipsburg PA 16866. (814)342-2935. Began selling cartoons in 1982. A small percentage of cartoons are written by gag/joke writers or outside sources. Cartoons have recently appeared in *State College, The Magazine* and *The Office.*
How to Contact: Submit cover letter; minimum of 6 gags/jokes per batch on 3 × 5 cards or 8½ × 11 paper. "I really need ideas dealing with holiday themes! Although I am wide open to subject and/or type of gag, I feel that ideas with broad appeal are easiest to move. Children, working, paying taxes/bills, eating, household budgets—etc." Reports in 4-6 weeks. Returns materials only if provided with SASE. Pays writers 25% of total fee received, up to $75.
Inside Tips: "Present yourself honestly. If you have never sold before, don't lie about it. There is nothing wrong with just getting started. Let a little of yourself show through in your gags and captions, as well as your characters. Also, don't concentrate on just the majors. Consistently selling to smaller publications often pays more in the long run. In trying to work with gag writers, I've found that writers often don't set up the situation or scene enough or the caption is not clear and concise. Correct that and you'll go far. A lot of the submissions I receive have misspelled words."

LEOLEEN-DURCK CREATIONS, LEONARD BRUCE DESIGNS, Suite 226, Box 2767, Jackson TN 38302. (901)668-1205. Contact Eileen Bruce. Names of strips: "Leotoons," "Fred," "Peggy and Sue," "The McNabs." Began selling cartoons in 1981. 25% of cartoons are written by gag/joke writers or outside sources. Cartoons have recently appeared in *Starlog, Space Age Times.*
How to Contact: Submit cover letter, sample gags, resume, tearsheets and cartoons; 18 gags/jokes per batch on 3 × 5 cards. Looking for gags on "off-the-wall, alien-type humor, senior citizen humor, sister to sister humor." Reports in 10 days. Returns material only if provided with SASE. Pays writers 10% of total fee paid for cartoon.
Inside Tips: "The secret to a great gag/joke is timely humor in a familiar setting."

LIEBE/PIPWYKK & CO., 2765 W. 5th St., Brooklyn NY 11224. (718)996-1480. Began selling cartoons in 1978. 75% of cartoons are written by gag/joke writers or outside sources. Cartoons have recently appeared in *National Enquirer, Good Housekeeping, First* and *Cosmopolitan.*

How to Contact: Submit sample gags; 15 gag/jokes per batch on 3×5 cards or paper. Looking for gags on general subjects, family, children, animals, romance, relationships and working women. Doesn't want to see "politics, science fiction, horror." Reports in 1 month. Returns materials only if provided with SASE. Pays writers 25% of total fee paid for cartoon."Keeps holds for own files."

Inside Tips: "In a great gag/joke there's a human or universal truth that we recognize. This is what can make a classic. Practice, practice, practice and mail out, mail out, mail out. As a matter of fact, instead of answering this questionnaire right now, I should be drawing."

HOW MANY CALORIES IN A MOUSE?

© Liebe Lamstein

And Do They Have a Lot of Cholesterol?*: When Brooklyn, New York-based gag cartoonist Liebe Lamstein created this cartoon, she wanted to "couple the humorous, almost human quality of cats with the age-old female concern and struggle with weight and body image." It worked. Lamstein sold first North American reproduction rights to the cartoon to a women's magazine for $250, and then it was reprinted in two other publications. Indeed, these kitties have seen quite a bit of ink.*

AL LIEDERMAN, 1700 St. Johns Ave., Merrick NY 11566. (516)379-6091. Name of strip: "Double Duty." Began selling cartoons in 1950. 80% of cartoons are written by gag/joke writers or outside sources. Cartoons have recently appeared in *King Features, Saturday Evening Post, National Enquirer* and *Journal of Commerce.*

How to Contact: Submit sample gags; 20 gags/jokes per batch on 3×5 cards. Looking for gags on office situations, politics and working women. Reports in 6 days. Returns materials only if provided with SASE. Pays writers 25% of total fee paid for cartoon.

Inside Tips: "Don't send (to the cartoonist) any old gag in hopes it'll go. 99 times it won't."

JEFFREY LOSEFF MANAGEMENT, Suite 205, 4521 Colfax Ave., North Hollywood CA 91602. (818)505-9468. Comedian has been in the business for 15 years and has performed on "The Tonight Show" and in most major comedy clubs in the US. Act is primarily stand-up and improv. Uses gag/joke writers for live act/routine, public appearances and developmental projects on all subjects. Doesn't want to see "blue material."
How to Contact: Gag/joke writers must request disclosure agreement before submitting gags/jokes. Please send $1 and a SASE for disclosure agreement. Submit 3-5 gags/jokes per batch on 8½ × 11" paper. For first contact send cover letter, credits, sample material and demo tape ½" or ¾". Reports back within 4-6 weeks. Returns materials if accompanied by a SASE. Does not file materials. Negotiates rights purchased. Pays $10 minimum.

ART McCOURT, Box 210346, Dallas TX 75211. (214)339-6865. Began selling cartoons in 1952. 90% of cartoons are written by gag/joke writers or outside sources. Cartoons have recently appeared in *National Enquirer, The Star, King Features, Reader's Digest* and *American International Syndicate.*
How to Contact: Submit sample gags; 15-20 gags/jokes per batch on 3 × 5 cards. Looking for gags on farms, medicine, hunting, fishing, office situations, working women, sophisticated subjects and computers. Doesn't want to see "male subjects, politics." Returns materials only if provided with SASE. Pays writers 25% of total fee paid for cartoon.
Inside Tips: "Make it simple, don't get complicated. Work at your craft, read a lot. See what others are doing. Be current, be aware and no puns."

THERESA McCRACKEN/McHUMOR, P.O. Box 299, Waldport OR 97394. Began selling cartoons in 1981. 15% of cartoons are written by gag/joke writers or outside sources. Cartoons have recently appeared in *American Medical Association News, American Bar Association, King Features, Ski, Adweek, California Computing, Chemtech* and *CEO.*
How to Contact: Submit sample gags; 15 gags/jokes per batch on 3 × 5 cards. "I use gag writers for trade journals I work with, and these range from computer to auto repair to refereeing magazines. *No general gags* please. I do all of my own generals." Reports in 1 month. Returns materials only if provided with SASE. Pays writers 25% of total fee paid for cartoon.
Inside Tips: "My favorite gags/jokes are captionless ones, ones that you get instantly, but then want to look at again carefully. Target material to a publication. Don't overwhelm a cartoonist with hundreds of gags at a time."

REX F. MAY, ("BALOO"), Box 9, Bellevue CO 80512. (303)482-2481. Began selling cartoons in 1975. 1% of cartoons are written by gag/joke writers or outside sources. Cartoons have recently appeared in *Wall Street Journal, Good Housekeeping, National Enquirer, Woman's World, National Review, Leadership, World Monitor, Cavalier, Parts Pups* and *Medical Economics.*
How to Contact: Submit cover letter and sample gags by mail; no limit on gags/jokes per batch on 3 × 5 slips of paper. Reports in 7 days. Returns materials only if provided with SASE. Pays writers 20% of total fee paid for cartoon.
Inside Tips: "I'm a gagwriter first, cartoonist second, so I use other writers sparingly, but I'm always in the market to work with other cartoonists. Humor has to *surprise* and therefore must be original. The fresher the better. Keep it simple, there should be nothing in the cartoon that doesn't contribute to getting the gag across. Get the spelling and punctuation right!"

*EARL T. MUSICK, P.O. Box 1215, Bucyrus OH 44820. (419)562-4778. Name of feature or strip "The P.O. Box." Estab. 1982. "I buy about 25-75 gags/jokes per year." Cartoons have recently appeared in artwork for the US Postal Service, the F.B.I., self-syndicated comic strip in over 50 publications.
How to Contact: Submit cover letter, sample gags, resume; 10-15 gags/jokes per batch on 3×5 cards. Looking for "good clean gags." Reports in 2-3 weeks. Returns material only if provided with SASE. Pays 25% of total fee paid for cartoon. "I am now buying many gag/jokes for my single panel magazine cartoons."

ANDRÉ NOEL, 161 Hilltop Acres, Yonkers NY 10704. (914)476-1263. Began selling cartoons in 1986. 75% of cartoons are written by gag/joke writers or outside sources. Cartoons have recently appeared in *Saturday Evening Post, National Enquirer, Woman's World* and *Cosmopolitan.*
How to Contact: Submit sample gags; 20 gags/jokes per batch on 3×5 cards. Looking for gags on office situations, working women, sophisticated, family type and off-the-wall types of gags. "Some may be spicy but not X-rated." Doesn't want to see "X-rated, ethnic and macho crap." Also looking for gag writers with experience in comic strips. Reports in 3-4 weeks. Returns materials only if provided with SASE. Pays writers 30% of total fee paid for cartoon.
Inside Tips: "Persist and keep good records on sales, holds, gags, etc. Keep your eyes and ears open, listen to people."

RICHARD ORLIN CARTOONS, 9147 Chesley Knoll Ct., Gaithersburg MD 20879. (301)921-0315. Name of strip: "TV Toons." Began selling cartoons in 1980. 5% of cartoons are written by gag/joke writers or outside sources.
How to Contact: Submit sample gags; 25 gags/jokes per batch on 3×5 cards. Looking for gags on family, sophisticated subjects, science, computers and television. Doesn't want to see "raunchy material." Reports in 5 days. Returns materials only if provided with SASE. Pays writers 25% of total fee paid for cartoon. For television gags makes outright purchase of $25.

*LADDIE L. PAYS, 5802 143rd St. S.E., Everett WA 98208. (206)337-7180. Estab. 1989. 10% of cartoons are written by gag/joke writers or outside sources. Cartoons have recently appeared in *Official Detective; Highlights For Children; Clubhouse; Solutions for Better Health; Bureau of Business Practice.*
How to Contact: Submit cover letter, sample gags and resume; 10 gags/joke per batch on 8½×11 paper. Looking for gags on office situations, working women, computers, general humor, family, travel. "No 'adult,' 'porn' or politics." Reports in 1 month. Returns material only if provided with SASE. Pays 25% of total fee paid for published cartoon.
Inside Tips: A gag/joke is successful "If reader can identify with a cartoon and it 'hits home' . . . it will be remembered and recommended. Delete the words 'rejection' and 'discouragement' from your vocabulary."

TOM PRISK, Nelson St., HCR-1 Box 741, Michigamme MI 49861. Began selling cartoons in 1977. 25% of cartoons are written by gag/joke writers or outside sources. Cartoons have recently appeared in *Woman's World, Writer's Digest, Byline, Sun, Globe, Saturday Evening Post, Yankee, The Lutheran, Good News* and *Wilson Library Bulletin.*
How to Contact: Submit cover letter and sample gags; 10-20 gags/jokes per batch on 3×5 cards. "I need gags about writers and the writing life. I will not consider pornography or racist material." Reports in 2 weeks. "Please *do not* submit material from June 1st through September 1st." Returns materials if SASE is included. Pays writers 25% of total fee paid for cartoon.

Inside Tips: "An aspiring cartoonist must *practice* and *never* quit! A gag writer should study published material, see what makes it funny and always strive for originality. There is a distinct lean toward the 'offbeat' in terms of humor content and the artist's drawing style."

Just Get Rid of the Kid and Forget the Rewrite!: *Using a "rather off-beat, contemporary drawing style," Michigamme, Michigan-based gag cartoonist Tom Prisk sold this cartoon to Johnene Granger, managing editor of Woman's World magazine. Granger paid Prisk $100 for first time reproduction rights to the cartoon. While Prisk does do mass self-promotion, he also sends "a promo sheet of published samples and/or business card to potential markets."*

"No hot dogs! No Twinkies! No pizza rolls! Mom, this grocery list needs a complete rewrite!"

© Tom Prisk

BRUCE ROBINSON, Box 22113, Fort Lauderdale FL 33335. Began selling cartoons in 1969. 50-70% of cartoons are written by gag/joke writers or outside sources. Cartoons have recently appeared in *Boy's Life*.
How to Contact: Submit cover letter, sample gags and tearsheets. Submit 20 gags/jokes per batch on 3×5 cards. Looking for gags on "religious themes, family, kids, general, sports, business, sophisticated, themes . . . keep it *clean*! No sex! No risque or girlies!" Reports in 2 weeks. Returns material only if provided with SASE. Pays 25% of total fee paid for cartoon.
Inside Tips: "Cartoon must work in unison with gag. If you can put your hand over the drawing and just read the gag, it won't work. Keep "wording" of the gag short and sweet!"

DAN ROSANDICH, Box 410, Chassell MI 49916. (906)482-6234. Name of strip: "The Golden Daze." Began selling cartoons in 1976. 50% of cartoons are written by gag/joke writers or outside sources. Cartoons have recently appeared in *National Enquirer, Saturday Evening Post, Star, King Features, Swank, Gallery, Sun, Examiner, Globe, Cavalier, Boy's Life, Diversion* and *Official Detective*.
How to Contact: Submit cover letter; 20-25 gags/jokes per batch on 3×5 cards or slips. Looking for "captionless gags relating to any subjects a person could conjure up." Reports in 2 weeks. Returns materials only if provided with SASE. Pays writers 25% of total fee paid for cartoon or makes outright purchase of $1 minimum.
Inside Tips: "The perfect gagwriter is also one who is able to supply the cartoonist with obscure trade journals or off-the-beaten path magazines which they know purchase cartoons. Any writers out there who might be aware of these types of journals, please let the artist know. This, in turn, increases both our chances of selling our collaborative efforts to a publisher."

BILL SCHORR, 1020 W. 56th St., Kansas City MO 64113. (816)333-8591. Name of strip: "Grizzwells." Began selling cartoons in 1973. 10% of cartoons are written by gag/joke writers or outside sources. NEA syndicates strip in 350 newspapers.
How to Contact: Submit sample gags, tearsheets; 15-20 gag/jokes per batch on 3×5" cards or 8½×11" paper. Looking for gags on "family situations, teen daughter and 3rd grade son; strip is based on family of bears." Reports in 3 weeks. Returns materials if provided with a SASE. Pays $30 minimum for outright purchase of gag/joke.

HARLEY SCHWADRON, Box 1347, Ann Arbor MI 48106. (313)475-3657. Name of syndicated panel: "Big Biz." Began selling cartoons in 1972. 20% of cartoons are written by gag/joke writers or outside sources. Cartoons have recently appeared in *Punch*, *Wall Street Journal*, *Woman's World*, *Phi Delta Kappan*, *Penthouse*, *Cosmopolitan* and *Good Housekeeping*.
How to Contact: Submit sample gags on 3×5 paper. Looking for gags on general, topical, automotive, education and business subjects. Reporting time varies. Returns materials only if provided with SASE. Pays writers 25% of total fee paid for cartoon.
Inside Tips: "Gags that have visual elements are best, or ones that tie into some current event or cultural phenomenon."

*BOB STAAKE, 726 South Ballas Rd., St. Louis MO 63122. (314)961-2303. FAX:(314)961-6771. Began selling cartoons in 1975. 10% of cartoons are written by gag/joke writers or outside sources. Cartoons have recently appeared in *Washington Post*, *USA Today*, King Features, Warner Books, *Parents* and *Los Angeles Times*.
How to Contact: Submit 10 gags/jokes per batch on 3×5 cards. Prefers to work with gag/joke writers who have fax capabilities. Looking for "any brilliant material on any subject." Does not want to see "anything on glass eyes." Reports in 2 weeks. Returns material only if provided with SASE. "Volume of mail does not allow me to answer non-SASE submissions." Pays writers 25% of total fee paid for cartoon.
Inside Tips: "Gag must work *symbiotically* with art. While I enjoy 'Talking Head' gags, they usually are not improved with the addition of a (gratuitous) drawing. A gag writer should understand not only how to write funny, but how to write *visually* funny."

SUZANNE STEINIGER, 9373 Whitcomb, Detroit MI 48228. (313)838-5204. Began selling cartoons in 1982. 80% of cartoons are written by gag/joke writers or outside sources. Cartoons have recently appeared in *Women*, *The Farmer*, *The Nebraska Farmer*, *The Chronicle of the Horse*, *Highlights for Children*.
How to Contact: Submit sample gags on 3×5 cards. Looking for animal gags with forest and farm animals for a variety of magazines. Also looking for writers to collaborate on strips for children. "Porno is a taboo with me." Reports in 6 weeks. Pays writers 25% of total fee paid for cartoon. Pays 30-35% for material sold to syndicates.
Inside Tips: "Simplicity in scene and saying is the secret to a great gag. Draw everything so you can be versatile. Read all kinds of material from a variety of magazines, especially from *The New Yorker*."

JOHN STINGER, Box 350, Stewartsville NJ 08886. (201)859-1150. Began selling cartoons in 1965. 10% of cartoons are written by gag/joke writers or outside sources. Cartoons have recently appeared in syndicated business features worldwide.

Always include a self-addressed stamped envelope (SASE) or International Reply Coupon (IRC) with submissions.

How to Contact: Submit sample gags; 10 gags/jokes per batch on 3×5 cards. Looking for gags on "office situations only." Doesn't want to see "off-color stuff." Reports in 1 week. Returns materials only if provided with SASE. Pays writers 20% of total fee paid for cartoon.

FRANK TABOR/CARTOON ART STUDIO, 2817 NE 292nd Ave., Camas WA 98607. (206)834-3355. Began selling cartoons in 1946. 98% of cartoons are written by gag/joke writers or outside sources. Cartoons have recently appeared in *First for Women, Cortlandt Forum-Letters* and *National Examiner.*
How to Contact: Submit sample gags; 10-20 gags/jokes per batch on file slips. Looking for gags on home and family. "Also want medical gags and ideas for editorial workup with a senior citizen theme. Writers should keep in touch for my current needs." Doesn't want to see "raw sex." Reports 1 day after receiving material. Returns materials only if provided with SASE. Pays "steady" writers 33% of total fee paid for cartoon; 25% to occasional submitters.
Inside Tips: "Draw and submit, draw and submit, draw and submit. Write in volume. I sell the most for those who send me the most."

"I'm moving your copy of *The Joy of Sex* to the fiction shelf."

© Frank Tabor

Just Don't Ban It*: Camas, Washington-based cartoonist F.C. Tabor uses a "bold slapstick" drawing style when creating his uncluttered gag cartoons. Tabor was paid $125 for first time reproduction rights to the cartoon.*

BOB THAVES, Box 67, Manhattan Beach CA 90266. Name of feature: "Frank and Ernest." Began selling cartoons in the early 1950's. ". . . nothing would make me happier than to have a brilliant gagwriter writing everything for me!"

Close-up

Doug Gamble
Humor Writer

If it weren't for Doug Gamble, there would be nothing funny for us to read on George Bush's lips.

While Bush may stand at a podium and mouth pre-digested sound bite after pithy one-liner, those witticisms are hardly crafted spontaneously by the President himself. Instead, many of those quotable quips are crafted by Doug Gamble, a 47-year-old transplanted Canadian who now works from the fax machine in his Manhattan Beach, California home. Indeed, it's Gamble's job to make Bush come off as a little less presidential, and a little more Rodney Dangerfield.

A former newspaper humor columnist/radio personality from Toronto, Gamble's career as a presidential pundit began completely by chance. "I wrote a little piece of political satire," says Gamble, "that Paul Harvey read on the radio. Much to my surprise, it happened to be heard by somebody at the (Reagan) White House who asked if I would like to try submitting some lines to the President. It never occurred to me in a million years to send jokes to anyone in Washington, much less President Reagan."

After writing material for Reagan, Gamble started penning for President Bush. In fact, during a recent State of the Union address, Bush opened his speech with two jokes written by Gamble. "With the big build up that this speech has had," said the President, "I wanted to make sure that it would be a big hit. Unfortunately, I couldn't get Barbara to deliver it for me." With guffaws rising from the Senate floor, Bush launched into his second punch. "I noticed," continued the President, "that Vice President Quayle and Speaker (Tom) Foley are laughing. After what happened to me in Tokyo, they're just glad they're sitting *behind* me," a self-deprecating reference, of course, to Bush's inopportune "regurgitation" at a state dinner in Japan.

And while these days Gamble writes material for politicos such as Bush and even Dan Quayle, he comes from a background of writing for some of the top stand-ups in the business. Rodney Dangerfield, Joan Rivers, Tom Dreesen, Byron Allen, Jimmy Walker and even Bob Hope have snagged laughs by performing Gamble's material.

"I started going to the Los Angeles comedy clubs," says Gamble, "and hung around to hear exactly what kind of material certain comedians were doing. After their sets, I'd physically approach them and hand them a batch of material. You really can't make a living at it because comedians pay on a per-joke basis, but what you want to do is establish credit for yourself. You can then go on to another comedian and say, 'I've sold to Joan Rivers'."

Gamble also suggests that anyone can get in touch with any comedian by simply contacting The American Federation of Television and Radio Artists (AFTRA—see Organizations on page 311). "If you call AFTRA," Gamble points out, "they will give you the name and phone number of the agent who represents a specific comedian. It's then easy to write to the agent and ask 'Does your client look at new material?' I started writing for Tom Dreesen this way after I saw him on "The Tonight Show." I submitted material that he liked, and he asked me to meet him at the Improv a week later. Writing a letter is something that anyone in the country can do."

Since 1992 was an election year, most of the material Gamble wrote last year was for politicians and not comedians, although the distinction can at times become blurred. Happily, he was paid by the Republican National Committee and not the American taxpayer to write *schtick* for the President, although he was not obliged to crunch out a regimented number of jokes of one-liners each week.

"The President's speech-writing staff," says Gamble, "looked to me not only for humor, but for what the media has come to call 'sound bites.' For example, a line I wrote for Bush in New Hampshire talked about anti-isolationism and protectionism and how America cannot ignore the rest of the world. The line I wrote was 'Let's remember that the symbol for the United States isn't the ostrich, it's the eagle.' That's not humor, but it's a highly symbolic line that the press picked up on."

Even if Gamble writes for the nation's Chief Executive, he still has no reservations about writing comedy material for smaller corporate titans who must speak before groups. "I do a fair amount of corporate humor writing for CEOs and company executives," says Gamble, "but I think the days of Kiwanis-Club-luncheon-humor are gone where a speaker gets up and tells a joke or two. Today that approach is passe for speakers who want to effectively communicate in a humorous way with their audiences. There's no reason why the president or the CEO of a small company can't stand at a podium and be almost as funny as Jay Leno or Johnny Carson."

And while Gamble appears firmly established as a White House court jester with a word processor and a fax machine, he recalls the advice given him years ago by radio/TV personality Gary Owens. "He told me," Gamble remembers, "that the big mistake a lot of writers make is that they give up too soon when they get discouraged. He told me to remember that talent will always win out in the end. If a writer starts to make a few sales here and there, then he knows he's got it. Eventually he will win out. I used that advice to help me get through a lot of discouraging times."

—Bob Staake

66 I started going to the Los Angeles comedy clubs and hung around to hear exactly what kind of material certain comedians were doing. After their sets, I'd physically approach them and hand them a batch of material. **99**

—Doug Gamble

How to Contact: Submit any number of gag/jokes per batch in any form. Looking for gags on offbeat subjects. Reports in 2 weeks. "Will return [materials] once without SASE, but not a second time. Why should I pay the costs to return materials people are trying to sell to me?" Variable pay—depends on frequency and quality of submission, and varies by use (that is, syndicated feature, licensed product, etc.).

Inside Tips: "The point of the gag should be something unexpected. Be yourself—don't try to mimic what's 'hot' today. 1) Don't plagiarize; 2) avoid 'talking heads' gags; 3) avoid the same old, tried, stock situations. Try to do something different and distinctive."

FRED H. THOMAS, P.O. Box 2039, Edgartown MA 02539. (508)627-7973. FAX: (508)627-3339. Name of feature: "Long Shots." Began selling cartoons in 1958. 50% of cartoons are written by gag/joke writers or outside sources. Cartoons have recently appeared in *Better Homes & Gardens, Good Housekeeping, Family Circle, National Enquirer* and *Conde Nast Traveler.*

How to Contact: Submit sample gags; 12-20 gags/jokes per batch on 3×5 cards. Reports in 1 week. Prefers material be provided with a SASE. Pays 25% of total fee paid for cartoon.

Inside Tips: "The secret to a great gag/joke is talent and a sense of the market and what's going on in the world." To succeed "draw, draw, draw—submit, submit and be funny."

CHUCK VADUN, 14814 Priscilla St., San Diego CA 92129. (619)672-0212. Began selling cartoons in 1965. 50% of cartoons are written by gag/joke writers or outside sources. Cartoons have recently appeared in *Kiwanis, Good Housekeeping* and *Wall Street Journal.*

How to Contact: Submit sample gags; 10-20 gags/jokes per batch on 3×5 cards. Looking for gags on "anything except smut." Reports in 1 week. Returns materials only if provided with SASE. Pays writers 25% of total fee paid for cartoon.

Inside Tips: "There is no best use for a rejection slip unless, of course, you save them up until you have enough to wallow in self-pity."

MOM, DID YOU AND DAD EVER TWIST AND SHOUT?

© Charles Vadun

Quizzical Kid: *When creating this cartoon, San Diego, California-based gag cartoonist Charles Vadun didn't want to "get too cerebral—I just wanted to show how kids think about their parents' history."* **Woman's World** *paid Vadun $100 for the right to print the cartoon, which was submitted on speculation.*

KAREN WEST, Rt. 2, Box 224, Seneca MO 64865. Began selling cartoons in 1978. 30-40% of cartoons are written by gag/joke writers or outside sources. Cartoons have recently appeared in *Saturday Evening Post, Easyriders, Family Circle, Complete Woman, The Mirror* and many minor markets.

How to Contact: Submit sample gags; 12 gags/jokes per batch on 3×5 cards. Looking for gags on mostly family, work and general subjects. Doesn't want to see "girlies" or politics. Reports in 10-14 days. Returns materials only if provided with SASE. Pays writers 25% of total fee paid for cartoon. "If I'm overloaded with gags from time to time I'll advise writers of this."

Inside Tips: "Please, no long, drawn out gags that would take 3 panels to explain—I like pungent, off-the-wall, immediate humor! Fresh, potent situations—simple is best—gags that are three sentences long are rarely funny. Forced gags just don't get it. Be yourself in your gags."

KEVIN WEST, Suite 354, 13601 Ventura Blvd., Sherman Oaks CA 91423. (818)775-0044. Estab. 1986. Management: Kathy Lymberopoulos/Lymberopoulos, Inc. Kevin West has performed in clubs all over the country, lots of talk shows and comedy shows, movies, TV series and commercials (big commercial star). Act is primarily stand-up, improvisation. Uses gag/joke writers for TV appearances and live act/routine on everything except politics (mostly on himself and things that happen to him.)

How to Contact: Submit up to 20 gags/jokes per batch on 8½×11 paper. For first contact send cover letter, resume and credits. Reports back in 2 weeks. Must provide SASE and will return material. Does not file materials. Buys all rights.

Inside Tips: The benefit of working with gag/joke writers is that there is "someone to bounce off of."

Gags/Entertainers/Changes '91-'93

The following markets appeared in the last (1991) edition of *Humor and Cartoon Markets* but are absent from the 1993 edition. These companies failed to respond to our request for an update of their listing or for the reasons indicated in parentheses following the company name.

Fran Capo (overstocked)
Dave Carpenter (doesn't use freelancers)
Charles T. Castleman
Thomas W. Davie (overstocked)
Frank (overstocked)
Futzie Nutzel (overstocked)
George Haessler/Concept Re

alization (cannot be reached)
Bruce Higdon (asked to be deleted)
Frank Johnson (doesn't use freelancers)
Gene Machamer Cartooning
Dr. Bill Miller (cannot be reached)

Precision Productions (overstocked)
Dan Riley (doesn't use freelancers)
Morrie Turner (overstocked)
Joseph F. Whitaker (asked to be deleted)

Greeting Cards

To find a greeting card company that *doesn't* use humor is like finding a beach that doesn't have sand.

Indeed, greeting cards continue to be rife with humor ranging from convulsion-provoking "slam" sentiments to harmlessly cynical snipes. There are even entire women-to-women card lines that bash men with acidic, yet clever, jabs (guys, we have to change this!).

No matter if you want to wish your sister a happy birthday, urge your lingering uncle to have a speedy recovery, or congratulate your cousin for breezing through med school, you'll be able to find the perfect (and funny) card to express your thought. And with greeting card companies continually creating new "holidays," card categories continue to expand (perhaps "Pet Day" is on the way).

While some greeting cards are nauseatingly banal and match overly-sweet messages with watercolor paintings of tulips, others sport big-eyed critters intent on staring you down until you shed tears, while other cards bear cover motifs of sunsets, hand-holding couples and seagulls.

But happily, there are also the *funny* cards—and there are tons of these! And because humor *thrives* in the greeting card industry, the market remains terrific for the freelance writer, humorous illustrator and cartoonist.

While highly competitive, each greeting card company tries to put its own distinctive "spin" on its humor line. While one publisher may be receptive to "put down" (or slam) greetings, another may not. Company XYZ may prefer simple humorous illustration styles that do not compete with copy, while Company ABC might seek wacked-out art that looks busier than a mall on Christmas Eve.

When you approach greeting card companies, understand that when you work for them on a freelance basis, you'll need to satisfy their specific *needs* — not your *whims*. Therefore, study their various lines to determine what *type* of art and writing they're looking for, and then submit appropriate examples to demonstrate stylistic compatibility.

Don't lose sight of the fact that humor is a funny, but serious, business. A professional presentation attests to a card editor, art director or line designer that you care enough to put some effort behind your submission. It's important to understand that it is easier for an editor or art director to work with an inhouse writer or illustrator, so you should do everything in your power to convince them that you can work with them on a *professional* freelance basis.

Getting your art in front of their eyes

Generally speaking, a greeting card art director or line designer will be more interested in seeing your color, rather than black and white, work. With this in mind, it would be ideal if you could send them a color self-promotional sheet which they could keep on file. Assuming, however, that you don't have such a color collateral piece to freely distribute, you'll probably want to show color tearsheets, and even color Xeroxes are fine these days.

However, there's a major problem with tearsheets and color Xeroxes — they become dog-eared, worn and damaged after they've made two or three rounds. You can end the problem (or significantly minimize it) by laminating your tearsheets and color Xeroxes as soon as they are made available to you. You can also type your name, address and phone number on the back of the tearsheet or color Xerox prior to lamination, but be forewarned: some color Xeroxes are created in such a way that their colors actually *smear* when heat laminated. Before having a number of color Xeroxes ruined, have one test-laminated.

Most stationery or school supply stores offer lamination services, and the entire process is quite inexpensive. Better yet, it ensures that your tearsheets and color Xeroxes survive repeated mailings.

Certainly you'll want to include a SASE so the tearsheets and color Xeroxes can be returned to you, but you'll also want to provide some material that the art director will hopefully keep on file. A black and white promo page would be nice, and a resume, client list and cover letter should fill out your package.

While greeting card art directors live crazy, hectic business lives, you may be able to chat with them for a minute or two on the phone. A couple of weeks after sending your package, give the art director a quick call just to touch base and to make sure that he received your material. Ask him if he had a chance to take a look and if he liked what he saw. If the answer is "yes" on both counts, continue to update him with tearsheets and/or promotional pieces every three or four months.

Presenting your writing

Assuming you understand a greeting card company's various humor lines and have a good idea of what written material it will be receptive to, you'll want to disclose some copy to it. However, most greeting card companies (and certainly all the large ones) won't even consider reviewing your writing submissions until you've signed and returned their disclosure contract or submission agreement.

Typically, the agreement is very straightforward and doesn't require the expensive scrutiny of an attorney—in fact, the document protects *you* as much as it does the greeting card company. Once the agreement has been signed, returned and filed, you're clear to send in your material.

There are a number of ways to submit written greeting card material. You can write each individual card idea on a 3 × 5 card, or you can present a number of complete card ideas (good for thematic material) on 8½ × 11 bond paper. If you have artistic talents or can at least sketch out your greeting card ideas, you have a distinct advantage over those writers who can't (or simply won't *try*). But if you can do this, simply take a piece of 8½ × 11 paper and fold it in half. Place your "page 1" copy on the cover and render your rough sketch, then add your "page 3" copy to the interior of the card. Since most inhouse writers submit their material to their editors in this fashion, it's a good idea for the freelancer to get into the same habit.

A strong cover letter is a must, and you'll also want to include a resume, client list and business card (if you have one). A SASE also ensures that your card ideas will be returned.

Cultivating a relationship

While most greeting card companies have big inhouse art and writing departments, they still understand the importance of being able to call on talented freelancers. Because freelancers aren't part of a greeting card company's internal political infrastructure, many times they have wonderfully fresh approaches to the writing and drawing of cards.

If a greeting card company likes the type of material you submit (either art or copy or both), they may "officially" sanction you as an "approved" freelancer. You don't get a medal or plaque or anything like that, but it does mean that the greeting card company *really* likes you.

It also means that when the greeting card company needs *special* help, you'll be one of the chosen few to receive a "Needs" or "Hot" list. A Writing Needs List usually lets the freelance writer know what the greeting card company's current card needs are. For example, a freelance writer may receive a Need List calling for humorous birthday card sentiments for a grandfather, generally sarcastic get well card sentiments, and lighthearted Halloween card ideas. The Needs List is almost always accompanied with Xeroxes of present, top-selling cards in the current line.

The freelancer can then write greeting cards addressing these specific themes. If a writer cares to respond to the Needs List by returning his written ideas by the deadline date, he does so voluntarily and usually is *only* paid when his written ideas are purchased by the greeting card company. The advantage to the greeting card writer is that he is writing material *that the greeting card company is expressly looking for*. Therefore, he is able to sell a greater amount of material to the company because he is privy to the company's *specific* greeting card needs. At least that's the theory.

Greeting card companies also send Needs Lists to special freelance cartoonists, humorous illustrators and designers. Generally, these are sent out when the various card and line designers are looking for new graphic "stylings." For example, a greeting card company may send a Christmas Needs List to freelancers during the holiday season while everybody is being bombarded with Christmas motifs, designs and images.

While I draw numerous cards for Hallmark, I have never written any for them. Conversely, with American Greetings, I write cards for them, but I have never illustrated one. I suppose Hallmark is very content with its inhouse writers, and American Greetings feels the same about its art staff. However, the medium-size greeting card companies simply die to be able to call on freelance talent that can draw and write. It's therefore important to understand your specific (or broad) talents so you can make your work known to the right greeting card companies. If your stuff is what they're looking for, they'll let you know almost immediately.

AMBERLEY GREETING CARD CO., 11510 Goldcoast Dr., Cincinnati OH 45249-1695. (513)489-2775. FAX: (513)489-2857. Estab. 1966. Publishes humorous greeting cards for birthday, friendship, get well and anniversary.
Illustration: *Uses local artists only.* Buys all rights. Pays $75. Also assigns local freelance humorous illustration duties. Assigns approximately 10 jobs/month. One of the things considers when hiring a freelance humorous illustrator is dependability.
Writing: Looking for humorous greeting card writing that is "short and to the point, not subtle." For first contact send in editorials (ideas) to Ned Stern, Editor. Reports back within 1 month. Returns materials if accompanied by SASE. Buys all rights. Pays $50. *Inside Tips:* If a humorous writer wants to sell his work, he should "see what's in the stores."

AMERICAN GREETINGS CORPORATION, 10500 American Rd., Cleveland OH 44144. (216)252-7300. Estab. 1906. Publishes greeting cards, calendars, books/booklets, paper plates/partyware, gifts and gift wrap for all occasions. Occasionally purchases humorous illustration for all product categories. Most interested in humor writing for greeting cards.
Illustration: For first contact send cover letter and resume to Lynne Shlonsky, Director of Creative Recruitment. "We do not accept unsolicited ideas." Reports back within 1-2 months.
Writing: For first contact send cover letter and resume to Lynne Shlonsky, Director of Creative Recruitment. "We do not accept unsolicited ideas." Considers skill, ability, effective use of humor and experience when assigning freelance humorous writing. Do not send samples. Buys all rights. Request writer's waiver submission form.

*ARGUS COMMUNICATIONS, One DLM Park, Allen TX 75002. (214)248-6300. FAX:(214)727-2175. Publisher of posters, postcards, greeting cards and calendars. "We publish posters for kids ages 10-18, and posters for the education market (primarily teachers of grades 4-12)." Needs humorous illustration for posters, postcards and calendars and humor writing for posters and postcards.
Illustration: For first contact send cover letter, client list, b&w or color tearsheets, b&w or color promo piece and slides to Susan Smith, Product Manager. To query with specific greeting card ideas, submit in format to Susan Smith. Reports back only if interested. Returns materials only if requested and accompanied by a SASE. Negotiates rights purchased.

 The asterisk before a listing indicates that the listing is new in this edition. New markets are often more receptive to freelance submissions.

Close-up

Mark Stringer
Creative Director
American Greetings

As creative director at American Greetings, Mark Stringer serves both a creative and business role. He is involved in long-term directional development, seeks out new areas for the company and directs most of the creative aspects of the alternative humor line. And as a result of looking for the best writers or illustrators for particular projects, he often utilizes the work of freelancers.

"When I became creative director," says Stringer, "there was a list of 75-100 freelancers. I have gradually scaled that down to a hot list of a workable size: about 30 currently for the alternative line." These are the freelancers he calls on regularly, but he says he is always on the lookout for new talent. In fact, freelance copy is reviewed daily by a team seeking "copy we can't write easily ourselves; copy which breaks the common formulas (i.e., copy which handles the standard setup/punch in a unique way); new sending situations which might appeal to today's card buyer; and finally, that indefinable quality we call 'alternative.'" For the alternative humor line specifically, freelance writers are needed more than illustrators, since most illustration is done in-house. "Unless you have gags that are very visual in nature," he advises, "just send concepts.

"Writers/illustrators may rough up art to help sell their copy ideas," says Stringer. "A finished quality of art is not required to sell copy ideas, although freelancers may wish to submit a few pieces close to finish to demonstrate their ability in both areas." In the actual development of an alternative humor card at American Greetings, the concept is almost always considered first, followed by interpretation by an illustrator. Printed samples of completed greeting cards undergo a rigorous testing process on the market before actual production. "Because of this built-in check point," says Stringer, "we are willing to take some risks."

Aside from the obvious importance of submitting concepts that are original, he stresses, "Don't send anything you don't know the status of." In other words, simultaneous submissions are a definite *no*. He admits that, while it is a rare occurrence, American Greetings must avoid the possibility of publishing ideas that have been or are currently being published elsewhere. Beyond abiding by this common courtesy, freelancers must "be patient. We do the best we can to get back to people as quickly as possible."

According to Stringer, the alternative attitude in greeting cards, which represents 25 percent of the market, is here to stay and will continue to grow.

"American Greetings is working harder than ever in this area. We aim toward producing more designs more often." With its broad base of resources, including merchandising services, the company has historically been on the cutting edge of the greeting card industry. "From a product standpoint," he says, "we have a willingness and mentality to look at new ideas."

—*Roseann Shaughnessy*

© Carlton Cards

That's What Tweezers Are For: This humorous card designed by American Greetings reflects the unique approach of alternative greeting cards.

Writing: For first contact send cover letter, resume, client list, clips and writing sample to Lori Potter, Editorial Coordinator. To query with specific greeting card ideas, submit material to Lori Potter, Editorial Coordinator. Reports back only if interested. Returns materials if accompanied by a SASE. Buys all rights.

*BLACKMAIL GREETINGS, INC., P.O. Box 871261, 3737 Timberglen Rd. #2403, Dallas TX 75287. (214)306-4663. FAX: (214)306-4766. Estab. 1990. Greeting card publisher that "publishes African-American greeting cards for Christmas, Kwanzaa and everyday occasions." Needs humorous illustration for greeting cards, spot cartoons for promotional and merchandising needs, editorial coverage, humorous greeting cards series (illustrations and writing), humor writing for greeting cards and promotional pieces.
Illustration: Looks for humorous greeting cards/illustration that "depicts a true, but humorous, portrayal of African-American life in the 90s." Doesn't want to see ideas that "stereotype and generalize and are out of date." For first contact send coverletter, color tearsheets and color sample of original work (sketches OK) to Lisa C. Cooper, President. To query with specific greeting card ideas, submit to Lisa C. Cooper, President. Reports back within 2 weeks only if interested. Does not return materials. Buys all rights. Pays $25-250 outright purchase, 1-1.5% royalty (optional) for life of card. Also assigns freelance humorous illustration/cartooning duties. Assigns 12 jobs/year for promotional and display materials. Some of the things considers when hiring a freelancer are skill of artist, ability of artist to take art direction well, "marketability" of artist's drawing style and work habits of artist (punctuality, neatness, etc.) Pays by the hour, $10-25; by the project, $100-250. Pays 1% for life of card. If a cartoonist/humorous illustrator wants to sell his work, he should submit cover letter with description of work and/or sample of actual work (color reproduction OK). *Inside Tips:* "Within the Black community, the trend is moving more and more toward Afrocentric pride; illustrations emphasize and highlight those features unique to African-Americans."
Writing: Looking for humorous greeting card writing that "appeals to today's modern young African-American adult without sounding derogatory or stereotypical; "Black English" is acceptable and sometimes preferred." Doesn't want to see greeting card writing that shows Black faces but use White sentiment/language. For first contact send cover letter and writing sample to Lisa C. Cooper, President. To query with specific greeting card ideas, submit material to Lisa C. Cooper, President. Reports back within 2 weeks only if interested. Returns material if accompanied by a SASE. Buys all rights. Pays $10-25 outright purchase. Also assigns approximately 3 other freelance writing jobs/year for promotional pieces and display materials. Some of the things considers when hiring a freelance humorous writer are skill of writer, writer's effective use of humor and writer's innate knowledge of Black life and situations. Pays by the project, $100-250. *Inside Tips:* If a humorous writer wants to sell his work, he should submit a cover letter with brief description of the work and possibly an excerpt/sample. "The vernacular of the street has invaded music and will move into the greeting card industry soon; rap is here to stay."

BRILLIANT ENTERPRISES, 117 W. Valerio St., Santa Barbara CA 93101. (805)682-0531. Estab. 1967. Provides publishing, licensing and syndication. Publishes greeting cards and books/booklets for non-occasion. Needs humorous illustration and humor writing for postcards and greeting card series.
Illustration: Looking for humorous greeting cards/illustration that "conform to our established line and combine words with illustration." For first contact send $2 and SASE for catalog of samples to Ashleigh Brilliant, Humor Editor. Reports back within 2 weeks. Returns materials if accompanied by SASE. Buys all rights. Pays $40 minimum.
Writing: Looking for humorous greeting card writing that "conforms to our established line and is submitted camera-ready with illustration." For first contact send $2 and SASE for catalog and samples to Ashleigh Brilliant, Humor Editor. Reports back within

2 weeks. Returns materials if accompanied by SASE. Buys all rights. Pays $40 minimum. *Inside Tips:* "We strive to make our line different from anything else on the market. Freelancers will only be wasting their time and ours unless they study it carefully first."

*CITY MERCHANDISE INC., 750 8th Ave., New York NY 10036. (212)944-6592. FAX: (212)944-6621. Estab. 1984. Postcard publisher that provides NY postcards, maps/calendars, gifts, greeting cards, posters, novelties, books/booklets and promotional products. Needs humorous illustration for calendars, postcards, books, gifts; caricatures for political postcards.
Illustration: Looking for humorous greeting cards/illustration that are New York-oriented. For first contact send cover letter and tearsheets to Jack Gindi, President. Reports back within 10 days. Returns materials only if requested. Negotiates rights purchased. Pays $100 outright purchase. Also assigns freelance humorous illustration/cartooning duties. Assigns approximately 5 jobs/year. Most of these jobs are new designs for postcards. One of the things considers when hiring a freelance illustrator is "marketability" of artist's drawing style. Pays by the project, $50-400. Pays 5% royalty for one year. *Inside Tips:* Send color copy and letter.

CLASS POSTERS, (formerly Class Publication), 71 Bartholomew Ave., Hartford CT 06106. (203)951-9200. FAX: (203)951-4084. Estab. 1983. Publishes posters for college market. Needs humorous illustration for posters.
Illustration: Looking for humorous illustrations that "have a lot going on in the picture." For first contact send cover letter, color tearsheets and slides (dupe) with SASE for return to Leo Smith, Art Director. Reports back within 10 days only if interested. Returns materials if accompanied by SASE. Buys one-time or reprint rights. Pays $500-800 or 7% royalty for three years.

COMSTOCK CARDS, INC., Suite 15, 600 S. Rock Blvd., Reno NV 89502. (702)333-9400. FAX: (702)333-9406. Estab. 1986. Publishes/manufactures greeting cards, gifts, promotional products, notepads, invitations and postcards for Christmas, anniversary, get well, Hanukkah, Halloween, congratulatory, non-occasion, birthday, Valentine's Day and retirement. Has "the sophisticated buyer in mind." Needs humorous greeting card series and humor writing for notepads and invitations.
Illustration: For first contact send cover letter to David Delacroix, Art Director. Reports back within 3 weeks. Returns materials if accompanied by SASE. Buys all rights. Pays $50-60, by the cartoon. Also assigns freelance humorous illustration/cartooning duties. Assigns approximately 50 jobs/year for greeting cards and notepad designs. Pays $50-60, by the project; per line or image.
Writing: Looking for humorous greeting card writing that contains "outrageous humor, double entendres and sexual connotations (although not too blatant)." Doesn't want to see "rhymes or ho-hum writing." For first contact send cover letter with SASE to David Delacroix, Art Director. To query with specific greeting card ideas, submit idea on 3 × 5" card. Reports back within 3 weeks. Returns materials if accompanied by SASE. Keeps copies of materials on file. Buys all rights. Pays $50-60 for outright purchase. *Inside Tips:* "Keep away from blatant sexuality and from using animals in people situations."

CONTEMPORARY DESIGNS, 213 Main St., Gilbert IA 50105. (515)232-5188. FAX: (515)232-3380. Estab. 1977. Paper products company that publishes memo pads and invitations and manufactures totes, novelties, mugs and pillowcases for everyday, Christmas, Valentine's Day, Mother's Day, Hanukkah, Passover, Halloween, Father's Day and Grandparent's Day. Needs short messages and one-liners for humorous greeting card series for kids who go to camp, Hanukkah, Jewish New Year and everyday Jewish, professions (teachers, secretaries), special people (Mom, Dad, Grandma, etc.) and seasonal merchandise. Also needs humor writing for memo pads and gift items.

Writing: For first contact send cover letter, resume, client list and writing samples to Sallie Abelson, President. Reports back only if interested. Returns materials if accompanied by SASE. Pays for outright purchase. "Unique ideas only." Pays $25-50, depending on usage.

CONTENOVA GIFTS INC., Box 69130 Station K, Vancouver BC V5K 4W4 Canada. (604)253-4444. FAX: (604)253-4014. Estab. 1965. Wholesale, manufacturer and distributor of impulse novelty products including mugs, plaques, greeting cards, gifts and magnets for Christmas, anniversary, get well, Mother's Day, congratulatory, Father's Day, birthday, retirement, Grandparent's Day and Valentine's Day. Needs humorous illustration for greeting cards; humorous greeting card series (illustration and writing); and humor writing for mugs, buttons and bumper stickers.
Illustration: For first contact send cover letter, resume, client list, tearsheets and color promo pieces to Jeff Sinclair, Creative Director. Reports back in 1 week. Returns materials if accompanied by SASE. Buys all rights. Pays $75 minimum. Also assigns freelance humorous illustration/cartooning duties. Assigns approximately 2 jobs/month for greeting cards. "Freelancers must be fax capable."
Writing: Looking for humorous greeting card writing that is "short and humorous but not too risqué." Doesn't want to see "outdated material or writing that is too wordy." For first contact send writing samples to Jeff Sinclair, Creative Director. To query with specific greeting card ideas, submit idea on 3×5" card. Reports back within 1 week. Returns materials if accompanied by SASE. Buys all rights. Pays $50 minimum.

*CREATE-A-CRAFT, P.O. Box 330008, Fort Worth TX 76163-0008. (817)292-1855. Estab. 1967. Greeting card publisher, paper products company that provides greeting cards, calendars, posters, novelties, puzzles, gifts, paper plates/partyware, T-shirts, etc. for nonoccasion, Christmas, birthday, anniversary, Halloween, get well, congratulatory, New Year's, Mother's Day, Father's Day, Hanukkah. Needs humorous illustration for T-shirts, products, cards; caricatures for cards, calendars; humorous greeting card series (illustrations and writing).
Illustration: Looking for humorous greeting cards/illustration that convey "family-oriented humor." Doesn't want to see cards which "deal with overt sex, racism, religion, condoms, foul language." For first contact send tearsheets, color tearsheets, "submit through agent only." To query with specific greeting card ideas, "submit through agent only" to the editors. Reports back within 3 months only if interested. Does not return materials. Buys all rights. Pays royalty (depends upon project). Also assigns freelance humorous illustration/cartooning duties. Assigns approximately 3 jobs/year for preparation art. Some of the things considers when hiring a freelance illustrator are skill of artist, ability of artist to take art direction well, humor of artist, "marketability" of artist's drawing style and experience of artist. Pays "by project and complexity of project." Pays royalty for one year "if work warrants it." "Contact through agent—show finished art only."

DESIGNER GREETINGS, Box 140729, Staten Island NY 10314. (718)981-7700. Publishes greeting cards for all occasions and all seasons. Needs humorous illustration for cards and humorous greeting card series *only*.
Illustration: Looking for humorous greeting cards/illustration that "depicts the verse well." For first contact send tearsheets to Fern Gimbelman, Art Director. Reports back within 1 month only if interested. Returns materials if accompanied by SASE. Buys all rights. Pays $40 minimum for outright purchase. Also assigns freelance humorous illustration/cartooning duties. One of the things considers when hiring a freelance illustrator is "adaption of verse." Pays by the project, $40 minimum.

*DIEBOLD DESIGNS, Box 236, High Bridge Rd., Lyme NH 03768. (603)795-4592. FAX: (603)795-4222. Estab. 1978. Greeting card publisher. "We produce special cards for special interests and greeting cards for businesses, primarily Christmas." Needs humorous illustration for cards, calligraphy and mechanicals.

Illustration: Looking for humorous greeting cards/illustration that "appeal to individual's specific interests—golf, tennis, etc. Looking for an upscale look." For first contact send cover letter, tearsheets and portfolio to Peter Diebold. Reports back only if interested. Returns materials if accompanied by a SASE. Keeps materials on file. Negotiates rights purchased. Negotiates payment based on extent/complexity of job.

EARTH CARE PAPER INC., Box 14140, Madison WI 53714. (608)277-2920. FAX: (608)277-2990. Estab. 1983. Greeting card publisher and paper products company that manufactures note cards, posters, gift wrap, stationery and greeting cards for Christmas, non-occasion and birthday on recycled paper "for people who support environmental protection and appreciate nature." Needs humorous illustration for cards and humorous greeting card series (illustration and writing): nature, environmental protection, peace and justice themes.

Illustration: Looking for humorous greeting cards/illustration that "fit one of these themes: nature, environmental protection, peace and justice." For first contact send tearsheets and slides to Cynde Quinn, Art Director. To query with specific greeting card ideas, submit slides or reproductions to keep on file. Reports back within 2 months. Does not return materials; keeps materials on file. Negotiates rights purchased. Pays 5% royalty for life of card. Also assigns freelance humorous illustration/cartooning duties. Assigns approximately 20 jobs/year for greeting cards. Offers a royalty basis of 5% for life of the product; $100 minimum advance on royalties.

Writing: Looking for humorous greeting card writing that "fits one of these themes: nature, environmental protection, peace and justice." For first contact send writing samples to Cynde Quinn, Art Director. To query with specific greeting card ideas, submit on 3×5" card. Reports back within 2 months. Does not return materials; keeps materials on file. Negotiates rights purchased. Pays $30 minimum, negotiable for outright purchase. Also assigns approximately 20 other freelance writing jobs/year. These include greeting cards with environmental humor theme. Pays $30 minimum.

EASY ACES, INC., 387 Charles St., Providence RI 02504. (401)272-1500. FAX: (401)272-1503. Estab. 1977. Produces giftware, stationery, original children's items, seasonal novelties, party goods, birthday items. Needs humor writing for miscellaneous items and humorous product concepts.

Writing: Looking for humorous greeting card writing that "embodies original product concepts." Doesn't want to see writing "which depends on puns!" For first contact send cover letter and writing sample to Fred Roses, President. Reports back only if interested. Returns materials only if requested. Negotiates rights purchased. Pays 5% for life of card or by negotiation. Also assigns approximately 6 other freelance writing jobs/year. When assigning freelance humorous writing, considers writer's effective use of humor.

EPHEMERA BUTTONS, P.O. Box 490, Phoenix OR 97535. (503)535-4195. Estab. 1979. Novelty-button producer. "Produces outrageous, provocative and irreverent buttons for all markets from the 'hip' and trendy to the convenience store crowd." Need humorous original slogans for novelty buttons.

Writing: "90% of our slogans come from freelance humor writers." Looking for humorous button writing which is "bold, shocking, concise, high impact, weird, rude, funny, outrageous." Doesn't want to see writing consisting of "tired old clichés." For first contact send list of slogans and SASE to Ephemera Editor. Reports back within 3-6 weeks. Returns materials if accompanied by SASE. Buys all rights. Pays by the slogan, $25 for outright purchase. Paid when produced (3 times a year). *Inside Tips:* "Send a SASE for our guidelines. Send 3 first-class stamps for our complete retail catalog."

*EVERGREEN PRESS, 3380 Vincent Rd., Pleasant Hill CA 94523. (510)933-9700. Greeting card publisher. Needs humorous illustration and writing for cards and humorous greeting card series.
Illustration: For first contact send cover letter, resume, client list and tearsheets to Malcom Nielson, President. To query with specific greeting card ideas, submit in format to Malcom Nielson.
Writing: For first contact, send cover letter, resume and writing samples to Malcom Nielson, Publisher. To query with specific greeting card ideas, submit in format to Malcom Nielson.

*GIBSON GREETINGS, INC., 2100 Section Rd., Box 371804, Cincinnati OH 45237. (513)841-6600. Greeting card and paper products company that publishes greeting cards and calendars and produces paper products, novelties and gift wrap. Needs humorous illustration and writing for greeting cards.
Illustration: For first contact send cover letter, resume and portfolio to Editorial Department. Returns materials if accompanied by a SASE.
Writing: For first contact, send cover letter and resume to Editorial Department. To query with specific writing ideas, request disclosure form first. Returns materials if accompanied by a SASE.

GRAPHIC CREATIONS, 94-02 148 St., Jamaica NY 11435. (718)657-5050. FAX: (718)688-8009. Estab. 1979. Paper products company. Publishes bookcovers for back to school, elementary to high school. Needs humorous illustration, caricatures, spot cartoons and humor writing—all for bookcovers.
Illustration: For first contact send promo piece. Does not return materials. Negotiable payment.

HALLMARK CARDS, INC., Box 419580, Mail Drop 216, Kansas City MO 64141-6580. Estab. 1910. "Contact Carol King for submission agreement and guidelines; include SASE, no samples. Not currently soliciting designs or sentiments. Work is on an assignment basis only. Buys all rights. Most needs are met by large creative staff; freelancers must show exceptional strength with conceptual ideas, originality and stylings not available from in-house employees. Previous design and/or sentiment writing experience preferred."

INNOVISIONS, INC., 445 West Erie St., Chicago IL 60610. (312)642-4871. FAX: (312)642-4209. Estab. 1980. Greeting card publisher that manufactures risque/adult greeting cards for Christmas, anniversary, get well, Hanukkah, congratulatory, non-occasion and birthday. Needs humorous illustration and humor writing for greeting cards.
Writing: Looking for humorous greeting card writing and general ideas. They must contain, however, some biting humor without being trite. Doesn't want to see " 'puns' and trite humorous anecdotes." For first contact ask for guidelines, then send cover letter and writing samples. Send all humor writing and specific greeting card ideas to Jay Blumenfeld, President. Reports back within 1 month. Returns materials if accompanied by a SASE. Buys first rights. Pays $75 for outright purchase. Assigns approximately

10 jobs/month. One of the things considers when hiring a freelance humorous writer is writer's effective use of humor.

It's Alive!: *While this design was never published as a Hallmark card, it is a good example of the increasing trend in greeting cards of bolder, high-impact art. Drawn in ink, watercolor and colored pencil, Larry Bowser's art was part of a "humorous styling project" at Hallmark.*

© Larry Bowser

INTERCONTINENTAL GREETINGS LTD., 176 Madison Ave., New York NY 10016. (212)683-5830. FAX: (212)779-8564. Estab. 1967. Sells design and reproduction rights to card, paper and giftware industries and provides design, artwork and humorous illustration with text to publishers and manufacturers. Publishes/manufactures greeting cards, calendars, posters, puzzles, gifts and gift wrap for Christmas, get well, non-occasion and birthday. Needs humorous illustration for cards, illustrations and writing for humorous greeting card series and humor writing for licensing series.
Illustration: Looking for humorous greeting cards/illustrations that "can be used for a card series that might lead to a licensing character." Doesn't want to see cards which are "done badly, not funny, too 'cartoon-y' and without color." For first contact send cover letter, resume, client list, color tearsheets, promo piece and slides to Robin Lipner, Art Director. To query with specific greeting card ideas submit to Robin Lipner. Reports back within 4 weeks. Returns materials if accompanied by a SASE. Keeps materials on file. Buys all rights for contract period or negotiates rights purchased. Pays royalty, 20% for life of card. Pays for reproduction rights, $35-500 per project. *Inside Tips:* "If a cartoonist/humorous illustrator wants to sell his work, he should have a clear, concise and thoughtful presentation. Explore all available avenues to market it. Insults and racial/ethnic/sexist humor are *out*."
Writing: For first contact send cover letter, resume, client list, clips and writing and artwork samples to Robin Lipner. To query with specific greeting card ideas, submit idea in format to Robin Lipner. Reports back within 3 weeks only if interested. Returns material if accompanied by a SASE. Keeps materials on file. Buys all rights or negotiates rights purchased during the 2 year contract period. Pays for outright purchase $30-500, 20% royalty for life of card. Assigns approximately 10 jobs per year. Payment for assignments is $10-500 per project. Royalties: 5-20% for life of product.

*INTERMARKETING GROUP, 29 Holt Rd., Amherst NH 03031. (603)672-0499. Estab. 1985. "Licensing agency representing a wide range of illustrators, cartoonists and designers for application to paper products, books, gifts, toys, comic strips and consumer products." Licenses/manufactures greeting cards, calendars, posters, books/booklets, puzzles, gifts, gift wrap, paper plates/partyware, giftbags and consumer products for nonoccasion, Christmas, Easter, birthday, anniversary, Halloween, retirement, get well, congratulatory, New Year's, Mother's Day, Father's Day and Hanukkah. Needs humorous illustration for all categories of merchandise, spot cartoons for all categories of merchandise and humorous greeting card series.

Illustration: Looking for humorous greeting cards/illustration that "have a theme approach." Doesn't want to see cards which "have been done before." For first contact send cover letter, resume, client list, tearsheets, color tearsheets, promo piece, color promo piece and slides to Linda L. Gerson, President. To query with specific greeting card ideas, submit to Linda L. Gerson, President. Reports in 1 month. Returns materials only if requested and accompanied by a SASE. Does not file materials. Buys all rights. Pays outright purchase, royalty. Also assigns freelance humorous illustration/cartooning. Assigns jobs "based on assignments I get from manufacturers." Some of the things considers when hiring a freelance illustrator are skill of artist, ability of artist to take art direction, humor of artist, "marketability" of artist's drawing style and ability to meet deadlines and request from manufacturer. Pays 7% royalty for term of license. *Inside Tips:* "Innovate and follow market trends in fads, fashions and themes." Some trends in the greeting card market include "more traditional themes—moving away from biting, sarcastic and rude themes."

*KALAN, INC., 97 S. Union Ave., Lansdowne PA 19050. Estab. 1971. Greeting card and novelty products company that publishes "hip, humorous greeting cards, key rings, etc." for Christmas, birthday and Valentine's Day. Needs humorous greeting card series (writing) and humor writing for key rings ("funny one-liners that don't carry a personal me-to-you message"). "We will review ideas for innovative new lines or series of greeting cards. They must be different from anything out there. You must enclose a SASE with appropriate postage."

Writing: Looking for humorous greeting card writing that is "hip and humorous and trendy. We like double entendré and clever lists. We also produce cartoon x-rated cards with funny copy." Doesn't want to see greeting card writing that "looks too much like the other 49 submissions reviewed that week." For first contact send cover letter, client list (if available) and writing samples to Editor. (Guidelines should be requested with SASE before submissions are sent.) To query with specific greeting card ideas, submit in format (3×5 cards or mock-ups for cards; type several funny jokes and one-liners on 8½×11 paper for key rings). Reports back within 1 month. Returns materials if accompanied by a SASE. Purchases all rights. Pays $75 for outright purchase. Also assigns 8 other freelance writing jobs/year "in response to our specific needs at that time, e.g., x-rated birthday and general cards, Christmas, etc." Considers writer's effective use of humor and "ability to write in Kalan's style, while being outrageous enough to make us burst out laughing" when hiring a freelance humorous writer.

MAINE LINE COMPANY, Box 947, Rockland ME 04841. (207)594-9418. FAX: (207)594-9420. Estab. 1979. Publishes/manufactures greeting cards, gifts, mugs, buttons, key rings, magnets, gift bags, postcards, bookmarks, pocketcards, impulse gifts, social-expression items, etc. for anniversary, get well, non-occasion and birthdays. *No seasonal cards.* Needs humorous greeting card series and other novelty items (illustrations and writing) and humor writing for buttons, mugs, magnets, keyrings.

Illustration: Looking for humorous greeting cards/illustrations that "are attractive, well-drawn with good characters—also good writing with non-cliché messages." Doesn't want to see greeting cards which are "unoriginal, old hat." For first contact send cover letter, resume, color tearsheets and promo piece and slides to Perri Ardman, President. To query with specific greeting card ideas, submit in format either 5×7 vertical or 6⅛×4½ horizontal (not both) to Perri Ardman. Reports back within 3 months. Returns materials if accompanied by a SASE. Keeps materials on file if there might be interest in the future. Buys all rights. Pays $25-200 for outright purchase. Also assigns freelance humorous illustration/cartooning duties. Assigns approximately 10-25 jobs/year. Pays $25 minimum for assigned humorous illustrations. Greeting cards are put out in series of 24-32 cards.

Writing: Looking for humorous greeting card writing "that is not nasty or rude. Cute double entendres OK." Doesn't want to see writing "that is vulgar and crude." For first contact send writing sample. Best to send specific ideas for cards or other products to Perri Ardman. Reports back within 3 months. Returns materials if accompanied by a SASE. Keeps materials on file if there might be interest in the future. Buys all rights. Pays $25-100. Also assigns other freelance writing jobs, approximately 25 jobs/year. Pays by the project. *Inside Tips:* "Good communication and writing that sounds like what a person would actually say are important in humor writing."

*DAVID MEKELBURG & FRIENDS, 1222 N. Fair Oaks, Pasadena CA 91103. (818)798-3633. FAX: (818)798-7385. Estab. 1988. Greeting card publisher, paper products company. Publishes/manufactures greeting cards, calendars, posters and gifts for friendship, encouragement, Christmas, Easter, birthday, anniversary, Halloween, get well, congratulatory, New Year's, Mother's Day, Father's Day and Hanukkah. Needs humorous illustration for greeting cards (all occasions) and humorous greeting card series (illustration and writing).

Writing: "I would like 'something' whimsically humorous and gentle—not harsh or vulgar. (Cheerful, clever—more of a *New Yorker* magazine feel)." For first contact send cover letter, resume, client list to Richard Crawford, Sales Manager. Reports within 1 week. Returns materials if accompanied by a SASE. Does not file materials (generally). Rights purchased "depend upon art." Pays 5% royalty for life of card. Some of the things considers when hiring a freelance humorous writer are skill of writer, ability of writer to work well with our editors and writer's effective use of humor.

OATMEAL STUDIOS, Box 138H, Rochester VT 05767. (802)767-3171. FAX: (802)767-9890. Estab. 1979. "We publish humorous greeting cards, magnetic notepads, and post-it notes for all occasions and holidays." Needs humorous illustration for cards, humorous greeting card series (illustrations and writing) and humor writing for cards.

Illustration: Looking for humorous greeting cards/illustrations that are "fresh looking, fun and original." Doesn't want to see "a repeat of lines in the industry." For first contact send color tearsheets, promo piece or slides to Helene Lehrer, Creative Director. Reports back within 1-2 months. Returns materials if requested and accompanied by a SASE. Keeps materials on file. Negotiates rights purchased. Also assigns freelance humorous illustration/cartooning duties.

Writing: For first contact send writing samples and request guidelines. To query with specific greeting card ideas, submit in 3 × 5 index card format with name and address on back to Helene Lehrer, Creative Director. Reports back within 6-8 weeks. Returns materials if accompanied by a SASE. Does not file materials. *Inside Tips:* "The writing must be fresh and original. We see lots of ideas that have been on the market for years. I don't feel there are any trends—a well-written card can be on the market for years."

*P.S. GREETINGS, 4459 W. Division St., Chicago IL 60651. (312)384-0909. Greeting card publisher that specializes in greeting cards. Needs humorous illustration, humorous greeting card series (illustration and writing) and humor writing for cards.

Illustration: Looking for humorous greeting cards/illustration that "deal with Christmas. Seasonal art is what we are most interested in." For first contact send cover letter, color tearsheets and slides to Art Department. "An appropriate sized SASE is required for the return of any material." To query with specific greeting card ideas, submit to Art Department.

Writing: For first contact, send greeting card verses only to Art Department. To query with specific greeting card ideas, submit in format to Art Department.

PAPER MOON GRAPHICS, Dept. HC, Box 34672, Los Angeles CA 90034. (213)645-8700. FAX: (213)645-4238. Estab. 1976. Specializes in greeting cards and stationery products. Publishes greeting cards for Christmas, anniversary, get well, Valentine's Day, congratulatory, non-occasion and birthday. Needs humorous illustration for greeting cards and humorous greeting card series (illustration and writing).
Illustration: Looking for humorous greeting cards/illustration that "appeal to a contemporary market and also adhere to a specific card sending situation or occasion." Doesn't want to see "predictable, insulting or offensive material that is unprintable." For first contact send cover letter, tearsheets, b&w and color promo pieces and slides to Robert Fitch, Art Director. To query with specific greeting card ideas, submit on 4⅝ × 6¾″ folded card mock-up. Reports back within 2 months only if interested. Returns materials if requested and accompanied by SASE. Buys reprint rights. Pays $100-150 for outright purchase. Also assigns freelance humorous illustration/cartooning duties. Pays $100-150, by the project. *Inside Tips:* "Trends are friendly, off-the-wall, female-oriented, dealing with contemporary issues that are shared by all women both working and non."
Writing: Looking for humorous greeting card writing that "embraces receiver, in a humorous and friendly way, not too saccharin or heavy." Doesn't want to see "predictable writing that looks like it was done 6 years ago." For first contact send cover letter and writing samples to Brenda Wyse. To query with specific greeting card ideas, submit on 4⅝ × 6¾″ folded card mock-up. Reports back within 2 months. Returns materials only if requested and accompanied by SASE. Buys reprint rights. Pays $100-150 for outright purchase. *Inside Tips:* "Submit work often and be sure that the writing speaks directly to someone, as opposed to stand-up comedy one-liners."

PARAMOUNT CARDS, INC., Box 6546, Providence RI 02940-6546. Estab. 1906. Full-line greeting card company offering cards, gift wrap, candles and buttons for everyday, Christmas, anniversary, get well, Mother's Day, Hanukkah, Easter, Halloween, congratulatory, Father's Day, non-occasion, birthday, retirement, New Year's, Grandparent's Day, graduation, Thanksgiving, Valentine's Day and St. Patrick's Day. Needs humorous illustration and humor writing for greeting cards for all occasions.
Illustration: Looking for humorous greeting cards/illustration that "set or follow trends in an alternative style; new looks, funny and cute-looking characters can sell a card." Doesn't want to see "emulation of studio-card art." For first contact send cover letter and portfolio to Susan Pagnozzi, Freelance Coordinator. To query with specific greeting card ideas, submit sketch and copy on index or other card with very little inside art to Susan Pagnozzi, Freelance Coordinator. Returns materials if accompanied by SASE. Keeps materials of interest on file. Buys all rights. Also assigns freelance humorous illustration/cartooning duties. Assigns approximately 30 jobs/year for page-one designs, all captions/seasons, deadlined. *Inside Tips:* "Send samples demonstrating diversity, or typical 'look,' and apply it to greeting cards of any kind; understand that we do most work inhouse, so be patient. Receptive and cooperative artists with flair work best for us. We want new and interesting approaches."

Always include a self-addressed stamped envelope (SASE) or International Reply Coupon (IRC) with submissions.

Writing: Looking for humorous greeting card writing that is "fresh, clever, intelligent, and sendable; which lends itself to visual interpretation; and which indicates that the writer is up-to-date on current humor themes, trends, and treatments." Doesn't want to see "the obviously derivative, which merely rehashes outdated formulas; and which is illegible, ungrammatical, and rife with misspellings." For first contact or to query with specific greeting card ideas, submit on 3×5″ card with name, address, social security number and SASE to Elizabeth Gordon. Returns materials if accompanied by SASE. Buys all rights. Also assigns approximately 10 other freelance writing jobs/year. "These include rush jobs where we need to fill certain captions by a deadline." *Inside Tips:* "Don't waste time trying to impress us with a fancy cover letter, but simply send us 10-15 of your best humorous card ideas. The best cards are attuned to the unique relationship between the sender and recipient. Topicality is important. Cards that are gross or lewd may garner lots of laughs, but are often poor sellers."

PEACHTREE COMMUNICATIONS, INC., Box 3146, Pompano Beach FL 33072. (305)941-2926. FAX: (305)491-6290. Estab. 1988. Publishes booklets and calendars for the mass market. Publishes greeting cards for Christmas, anniversary, get well, Mother's Day, Hanukkah, Easter, Halloween, congratulatory, Father's Day, non-occasion, birthday, retirement, New Year's and Grandparent's Day. "Cartoon comic strips considered for possible syndication (humorous or adventure.) Single panel cartoons also considered."

Illustration: Looks for greeting cards/illustration which "appeal to the whole family." Doesn't want to see greeting cards which "are Blah! Needs humorous greeting cards which are really funny without being X-rated or offensive." For first contact send cover letter, resume, client list and tearsheets to Fred Chapin, Art Director. To query with specific greeting card ideas, request disclosure agreement first. Reports back only if interested. Returns materials if accompanied by SASE; keeps materials on file. Pays $50-250 for outright purchase or royalty for life of card. Assigns freelance humorous illustration/cartooning duties. Assigns approximately 32 jobs/year. Pays $50-250, by the project.

Writing: For first contact send cover letter, resume, client list, clips and writing samples to Fred Chapin, Editor. To query with specific greeting card ideas, request disclosure form first. Reports back only if interested. Returns materials if accompanied by SASE; keeps materials on file. Negotiates rights purchased. Pays $50-250 for outright purchase or royalty for life of card. Also assigns other freelance writing jobs for greeting cards in specific category.

PEACOCK PAPERS, INC., 273 Summer St., Boston MA 02210. (617)423-2868. FAX: (617)423-9033. Estab. 1982. Gift and party manufacturer that produces and distributes contemporary typographically designed paper and party and apparel products. Manufactures greeting cards, partyware, gifts, gift bags, T-shirts, sweatshirts, boxers, coverups, mugs, buttons and keytags for most holidays and occasions. Needs humorous work for all occasions.

Writing: Looking for humor in short messages and one-liners. Needs fresh, current-trend as well as special occasion subject matter. Subjects also include golf, aging, boating and birthdays. Doesn't want to see "mundane or unoriginal material." For first contact send cover letter and writing samples to Mia Miranda, New Product Manager. Reports back within 3-4 weeks. Returns materials only if requested. Keeps materials on file. Buys outright purchase. Pays $25-50 for selected lines depending on product usage. Negotiates payment. Most jobs are an ongoing process. When assigning freelance humorous writing, considers originality, appeal of line and application to product.

PICTURA, INC., 4 Andrews Dr., West Paterson NJ 07424. (201)890-1070. FAX: (201)890-1292. Estab. 1969. Greeting card publisher that produces greeting cards, books/booklets, gift wrap and gifts for gift and stationery-store market. Publishes greeting cards for Christmas, anniversary, get well, Mother's Day, Easter, Halloween, congratulatory, Father's Day, non-occasion, birthday, retirement and New Year's. Needs humorous greeting card series (illustrations).
Illustration: Looking for humorous greeting cards/illustration that "appeal to female market — ages 18-35 years." Doesn't want to see "greeting cards which are not fresh and new." For first contact send cover letter, promo piece and specific greeting card ideas to Ramona J. Coughlin, Vice President. Reports back within 1 month only if interested. Returns materials only if requested. Does not file materials. Negotiates rights purchased. Pays 5-10% royalty for life of card.

PLUM GRAPHICS INC., Box 136, Prince Station, New York NY 10012. (212)966-2573. Estab. 1983. Publishes greeting cards primarily for birthdays.
Writing: Looking for humorous greeting card writing that is "easily understood and doesn't limit the market." For first contact send SASE with request for guidelines to Yvette Cohen, President. Sends guidelines 3 times a year. Returns materials if accompanied by SASE. Pays $40-50.

PRICE STERN SLOAN, 11150 Olympic Blvd., 6th Fl., Los Angeles CA 90064. (310)477-6100. FAX: (310)445-3933. Book and calendar publisher "known for its Murphy's Law books and Mad Libs. Funny golf books." Needs humorous illustration for books and calendars and humor writing for books. "Please submit manuscripts for joke books, humorous books, etc."
Illustration: For first contact send cover letter, tearsheets and promo pieces to Rick Penn-Kraus, Art Department Supervisor/Senior Design. Reports back within 1 month. Returns materials if accompanied by SASE; keeps materials on file. Pays $50 minimum for outright purchase. Also assigns freelance humorous illustration/cartooning duties. Assigns approximately 5 jobs/year. Pays $50 minimum, by the project. *Inside Tips:* The cartoonist/humorous illustrator "might try illustrating 2-3 examples from preexisting humor books and calendars."
Writing: Send book ideas to Rick Penn-Kraus. Reports back within 2 months. Returns materials if accompanied by SASE. *Inside Tips:* "Be very funny. It's a tough field, and 99% of manuscripts are rejected. We are not looking for anything too 'cute.' New ideas are always welcome."

RECYCLED PAPER PRODUCTS, INC., 3636 N. Broadway, Chicago IL 60613. (312)348-6410. Estab. 1971. Paper products company that provides everyday and seasonal cards, buttons, keychains and mugs. Needs humorous illustration for cards and humorous greeting card series (illustrations and writing).
Illustration: Looking for humorous greeting cards/illustrations that "are not like what we already have. We want to be surprised by an artist's unique slant on life." For first contact send a SASE for guidelines. Send all submissions to Melinda Gordon, Art Director. Reports back within 1 month. Returns materials if accompanied by a SASE. Does not file materials. Pays $250 minimum for outright purchase. "We do offer royalty contracts when an artist has enough work with us." *Inside Tips:* "We want art that will catch the customer's attention, coupled with messages that one would really like to send to a friend, lover or relative."
Writing: Looking for humorous greeting card writing that "is coupled with illustration, photos, etc." Doesn't want to see "work which is overly risque, not really a sendable message, or boring." Write for guidelines. Send all humor writing submissions to Melinda Gordon, Art Director. Reports back on submissions within 1 month. Returns

materials if accompanied by a SASE. *Inside Tips:* "We only want writing accompanied by art."

Did the U.S. Postal Service Have Anything To Do with the Delay?*: While she would like to do a syndicated comic strip, in the meantime, Long Beach, California-based cartoonist Anne Gibbons is "concentrating on greeting cards." This illustration, done for Recycled Paper Products, is typical of the style Gibbons works in. When this card sells, Recycled Paper Products pays Gibbons a royalty." Recycled Paper Products generally accepts my card sketches as submitted," says Gibbons, "but occasionally I'm asked to do something special with the card design (i.e., add a valentine heart, use lots of red, etc.), but this is rare." Oh, in case you haven't already figured it out, the copy inside the card says "I prefer to call it 'fashionable.' Happy Belated Birthday."*

Some people would say this card is late . . .

© 1989 Recycled Paper Products, Inc.

*RED FARM STUDIO, 1135 Roosevelt Ave., Pawtucket RI 02861. (401)728-9300. FAX: (401)728-0350. Estab. 1955. Paper products company that "publishes greeting cards, only 5% of which are humorous. No hard core humor—just enough to give a smile." Publishes/manufactures greeting cards and gift wrap for nonoccasion, Christmas, birthday, anniversary, get well and congratulatory. Needs humorous greeting card series (writing). "This is the only category and only a few ideas are accepted for the entire year."

Writing: Looking for humorous greeting card writing that "will just give a smile to someone—no hard core humor, no humor that is distasteful or improper." Doesn't want to see greeting card writing that is too "cute." For first contact request guidelines with #10 SASE to Production Coordinator. Reports back within 4-6 weeks. Returns materials if accompanied by a #10 SASE. Buys all rights. Pays $3 per line for outright purchase. "Does not assign work." One of the things considers when hiring a freelance humorous writer is experience of writer. Pays $3 per line, by the project. *Inside Tips:* "Request guidelines with #10 SASE and follow them!"

*RENAISSANCE GREETING CARDS, P.O. Box 845, Springvale ME 04083. (207)324-4153. FAX: (207)324-9564. Estab. 1977. Greeting card publisher. "We are an alternative card company with an extensive line that covers a wide variety of occasions with a wide variety of styles. We also produce Christmas Advent Calendars." Publishes greeting cards, gift tags, boxed notes for nonoccasion, Christmas, Easter, birthday, anniversary, Halloween, retirement, get well, congratulatory, New Year's, Mother's Day, Father's Day, Hanukkah, cards for relatives, thank you, belated birthday, friendship, Valentine's Day and Thanksgiving. Needs humorous illustration for greeting cards, Advent calendars, humorous greeting card series (illustrations and writing).

Illustration: Looking for humorous greeting cards/illustration that "are positive, upbeat, colorful, with strong punch lines or jokes." Doesn't want to see greeting cards which "are insulting or too offensive." For first contact send cover letter, tearsheets, color tearsheets, promo piece, color promo piece or slides to Janice Keefe, Art Director.

To query with specific greeting card ideas submit to Janice Keefe, Art Director. Reports back within 6 weeks. Returns materials if accompanied by a SASE. Keeps materials on file (only if interested). Negotiates rights purchased. Pays $200 minimum outright purchase, or royalty percentage with advance—negotiable. Also assigns freelance humorous illustration/cartooning duties. Assigns approximately 25-50 jobs/year for individual card designs. Some of the things considers when hiring a freelance illustrator are skill of artist, ability of artist to take art direction well, humor of artist and "marketability" of artist's drawing style. *Inside Tips:* "Start by sending for our guidelines, then submit samples."

Writing: Looking for humorous greeting card writing that "is positive, upbeat, with strong punchlines or jokes." Doesn't want to see card writing which "is too insulting." For first contact send cover letter and writing sample(s) to Melody Martin, Verse Editor. To query with specific greeting card ideas, submit idea in format: 3×5 cards to Melody Martin, Verse Editor. Reports back within 2 weeks. Keeps materials on file. Returns materials if accompanied by a SASE (only if interested). Negotiates rights purchased. Pays $25-50 for outright purchase. *Inside Tips:* Humorous writer should send for guidelines. "We are primarily interested in seeing complete concepts that include the illustration and writing. We'd like to see fresh, original ideas and styles that are appropriate to various card sending situations."

*ROCKSHOTS, INC., 632 Broadway, New York NY 10012. (212)420-1400. Estab. 1979. Paper products company that publishes greeting cards, humorous and sexy calendars, invitations, post cards and giftwrap for Christmas, get well, non-occasion and birthday. Needs humor writing for birthday, Christmas and all occasion.

Illustration: For first contact send promo piece to Bob Vesce, Editor. "Do not send original art work; samples and photocopies only." Reports back within 1 month. Returns materials if accompanied by a SASE. Buys all rights. When considering freelance humorous illustrators, considers skill and originality. Payment negotiable.

Writing: Looking for humorous greeting card writing that is risque, sexy, geared to younger set. Doesn't want to see messy submissions. For more information, send SASE requesting writer's guidelines. Lines should be submitted on index cards. Reports back within 1 month. Returns materials if accompanied by a SASE. Buys all rights. Pays $50 for outright purchase. When assigning freelance humorous writing, considers writer's effective use of humor. *Inside Tips:* "Sexy, sarcastic humor sells here."

*SANGAMON, Box 410, Taylorville IL 62568. (217)824-2261. FAX: (217)824-2300. Estab. 1981. Greeting card publisher, paper products company. Publishes/manufactures full service line—mass market greeting cards, calendars and gift wrap for nonoccasion, Christmas, Easter, birthday, anniversary, Halloween, retirement, get well, congratulatory, New Year's, Mother's Day, Father's Day, Grandparent's Day and Hanukkah. Needs humorous illustration, humorous greeting card series (illustrations and writing) and work on assignment.

Illustration: For first contact send cover letter to Editorial Dept. To query specific greeting card ideas, submit to Editorial Dept. Reports back within 6 weeks. Returns materials if accompanied by a SASE. Buys all rights. Pays $100 minimum for outright purchase. One of the things considers when hiring a freelance illustrator is experience of artist.

Writing: Looking for humorous greeting card writing that "shows experienced greeting card background and contemporary approach." For first contact send cover letter and writing samples to Editorial Dept. Reports in 6 weeks. Returns materials if accompanied by a SASE. Buys all rights. Pays $100 miminum for outright purchase. Some of the things considers when hiring a freelance humorous writer are writer's effective use of humor and experience of writer in greeting card humor. *Inside Tips:* "Know the market, keep sending situations in mind. Alternative style humor is still very big. We are always looking for good, strong visual ideas that work in greeting card sending situations."

SILVER VISIONS, Box 49, Newton MA 02161. (617)244-9504. Estab. 1981. Greeting card and paper products company that publishes photographic cards, calendars and posters for Christmas, anniversary, get well, Mother's Day, Hanukkah, Easter, Halloween, congratulatory, Father's Day, non-occasion, birthday, retirement, New Year's, Grandparent's Day and Judaic. Needs humorous greeting card series (writing).
Writing: Looking for humorous greeting card that "works well with a photograph, and also Jewish cards." Doesn't want to see "put-downs, bad puns, smut, studio cards or crass material." For first contact send cover letter, writing samples and assurance of ownership and right to submissions to B. Kaufman, President. To query with specific greeting card ideas, submit in 3 × 5 index card format to B. Kaufman. Reports back only if interested. Returns materials if accompanied by a SASE. Negotiates rights purchased. Pays $35. *Inside Tips:* "Current trends are reality humor, difficulty of life situations and relationships."

SUNRISE PUBLICATIONS, INC., P.O. Box 4699, 1145 Sunrise Greetings Ct., Bloomington IN 47401. (812)336-9900. FAX (812)336-8712. Estab. 1974. Greeting card publisher geared toward the alternative card market for Christmas, anniversary, get well, Mother's Day, Hanukkah, Easter, Halloween, congratulatory, Father's Day, non-occasion, birthday, New Year's, baby, wedding, thank-you, Thanksgiving, graduation, St. Patrick's Day and Valentine's Day. Needs humorous illustration, caricature and spot cartoons for cards and humorous greeting card series (illustration and writing).
Illustration: Looking for humorous greeting cards/illustration that "tie in very well to an editorial message and to a specific sending occasion." Doesn't want to see greeting cards which are "risque." For first contact or to query with specific greeting card ideas, send color tearsheets and/or slides to Nancy Jacobus, Product Design Coordinator. Reports back within 1 month. Always returns materials. Negotiates rights purchased. Pays $350 per card. Also assigns freelance humorous illustration/cartooning duties. Assigns approximately 150 jobs/year. *Inside Tips:* "Submit art, slides or transparencies. We are interested in artistic humor."
Writing: Looking for humorous greeting card writing that is "good-natured." Doesn't want to see greeting card writing which is "risque." For first contact or to query with specific greeting card ideas, send writing samples and SASE to Sheila Gerber, Editorial Coordinator. Reports back within 10 weeks. Returns materials if accompanied by SASE. Keeps materials on file. Buys all rights. Pays $35-125. Also assigns various amounts of other freelance writing jobs. Pays $35-125. *Inside Tips:* "Send editorial, one idea per 3 × 5" card. Group cards in 20's and enclose a SASE. We may be somewhat interested in cynical humor."

TLC GREETINGS, 615 McCall Rd., Manhattan KS 66502. (913)776-4041. FAX: (913)776-4041 Ext. 232. Estab. 1986. "We publish and design humorous greeting cards directed to women from 18-70 years of age. Could use positive humor." Publishes/manufactures greeting cards for anniversary, get well, congratulatory, non-occasion and birthday. Needs humorous illustration for greeting cards, caricatures for greeting cards, humorous greeting card series (illustrations and writing) and humor writing for greeting cards.
Illustration: Looking for humorous greeting cards/illustrations that "are pleasing, that apply to women." For first contact, send cover letter, resume and tearsheets to Michele Johnson, Creative Director. To query with specific greeting card ideas, request disclosure agreement first. Reports back on submissions within 3 weeks. Returns materials if accompanied by SASE. Keeps materials on file if interested. Negotiates rights purchased. Pays $50-200 for outright purchase. Also assigns freelance humorous illustration/cartooning duties. Pays $10-12, by the hour and $50-200, by the project for humor-

ous illustration. *Inside Tips:* "Prepare an original, unique tearsheet of your work. Show both color and b&w design. Our success is with fun illustrations. Keep your ideas simple, yet clever."

Writing: Looking for humorous greeting card writers who "can look at what we've published and produce ideas which reflect our style." For first contact, send cover letter, resume and writing sample to Michele Johnson. To query with specific greeting card ideas, request disclosure form first and submit material to Michele Johnson. Reports back within 3 weeks. Returns material if accompanied by SASE. Pays for ideas upfront. Buys all rights. Pays $30-100, outright purchase. Pays $10-15 by the hour; $50-200 by the project. *Inside Tips:* "Send humorous ideas which fit the company's product line. We publish no risque work. Unique ideas only. First impressions are very important. Send your best ideas or illustrations. Be confident."

U.S. ALLEGIANCE INC., P.O. Box 12000, Eugene OR 97440. (503)484-7250. FAX: (503)484-7279. Estab. 1980. Greeting card publisher of "greeting cards for military personnel. Also publishes postcards and occasionally posters for the same." Publishes greeting cards and posters for nonoccasion, Christmas, birthday, congratulatory, Mother's Day, "mainly 'Miss You, Love You'." Needs humorous illustration for greeting cards, postcards and humorous greeting card series (illustrations).

Illustration: Looking for humorous greeting cards/illustration that "Are well drawn, well thought out—can be off-color but not tasteless or offensive." Doesn't want to see greeting cards which "are poorly thought out and poorly drawn." For first contact send cover letter and photocopies of work (8½×11) to Denise Fagliano, Creative Director. Reports back within 2 weeks only if interested. Returns materials if accompanied by a SASE. Keeps materials on file. Buys publication rights. Pays $50-200 for outright purchase (will negotiate). Also assigns freelance humorous illustration/cartooning duties. Assigns approximately 20 jobs/month; 200 jobs/year. Some of the things considered when hiring a freelance illustrator is skill of artist, ability of artist to take art direction well, humor of artist, "marketability" of artist's drawing style and professional appearance of work. *Inside Tips:* "Have a professional presentation. Show what you can and have done. Be explicit—the person reviewing your idea can't read your mind! The buyer has to feel like he/she wrote the card!"

VAGABOND CREATIONS, INC., 2560 Lance Dr., Dayton OH 45409. (513)298-1124. FAX: (513)298-1124. Estab. 1957. Publishes illustrated stationery, calendars (small size) and greeting cards for Christmas, anniversary, get well, Mother's Day, congratulatory, Father's Day, non-occasion, Valentine's Day, graduation and birthday.

Illustration: For first contact send cover letter only. Returns materials if accompanied by SASE. "**Only** accepts materials for greeting cards that feature illustrations only on the cover with a short tie-in punch line on the inside page." Buys all rights. Pays $15-30 for outright purchase.

*VINTAGE IMAGES, Box 228, Lorton VA 22199. (703)550-1881. FAX: (703)550-7992. Estab. 1986. Greeting card publisher and manufacturer of other gift products for "sophisticated humor in numerous formats, stationery and gift." Publishes greeting cards, posters, novelties and postcards for nonoccasion, Christmas, birthday, anniversary, get well, congratulatory, romance, fun. Needs humorous illustration for postcards, humorous greeting card series (illustrations), postcards and other formats.

Illustration: Looking for humorous greeting cards/illustration that "are sophisticated, clever and have a *unique* style." Doesn't want to see greeting cards which are "cutesy." For first contact send tearsheets, color tearsheets and slides to Brian Smolens, Art Director. To query with specific greeting card ideas, submit in non-returnable format to Brian Smolens, Art Director. Reports back only if interested. Returns materials if accompanied by a SASE. Keeps materials on file. Buys all rights. Pays $75-200 for outright purchase, royalty. Also assigns freelance humorous illustration/cartooning duties. Assigns approximately 3 jobs/year for postcards and posters. Some of the things considers when hiring a freelance illustrator are skill of artist, humor of artist, and "marketability" of artist's drawing style. Pays $25-50, by the hour. Pays 5% royalty for life of the product. *Inside Tips:* "Submit a range of work or a series, in non-returnable format."

Writing: Looking for humorous greeting card writing that "is sharp, hip, sophisticated." Doesn't want to see greeting card writing which "isn't submitted with quality images, either our photos or freelance drawing/cartoons." For first contact send SASE for guidelines to Brian Smolens, Art Director. To query with specific greeting card ideas, submit idea in "our format only." Reports back only if interested. Keeps materials on file. Buys all rights. Pays $40-100 for outright purchase. Also assigns approximately 2 jobs/year. These jobs vary with the project. Some of the things considers when hiring a freelance humorous writer is writer's effective use of humor and use of our style. Pays $40-100, by the project. Pays royalty 5% for life of the product. *Inside Tips:* "Use our images or link up with illustrator/cartoonist." Current trends reflect "more hard-hitting, explicit" material.

WEST GRAPHICS, 238 Capp St., San Francisco CA 94110. (415)621-4641. FAX: (415)621-8613. Estab. 1980. Publishes/manufactures greeting cards, calendars, gift bags and books. Publishes cards for birthday, rude birthday, adult humor, Valentine's Day, Thanksgiving, Christmas, anniversary, get well, Mother's Day, Hanukkah, Easter, Halloween, congratulatory, Father's Day and friendship from a woman's point of view. Needs humorous and satirical illustration and concepts for cards.
Illustration: Doesn't want to see cards which are "cute or cliché." For first contact send cover letter, tearsheets and slides to Tom Drew, Art Director. Reports back within 1 month. Returns materials if accompanied by SASE. Also assigns freelance humorous illustration/cartooning duties. Pays $200 minimum, by the project.
Writing: For first contact send cover letter requesting submission guidelines and SASE to Editorial Department. To query with specific greeting card ideas, submit each idea on 3×5″ index cards (with name, address and phone number on each) to Editorial Department. Reports back within 1 month. Returns materials if accompanied by SASE. Pays $100 for outright purchase.

CAROL WILSON FINE ARTS, INC., Box 17394, Portland OR 97217. (503)281-0780. Estab. 1982. Greeting card publisher. Publishes humorous cards and fine arts cards for the contemporary card market. Publishes/manufactures greeting cards and postcards for Christmas, anniversary, get well, Mother's Day, Hanukkah, Easter, Halloween, congratulatory, Father's Day, non-occasion, birthday, retirement, Valentine's, friendship, "love" and most everyday occasions. Needs humorous greeting card series (illustrations and writing) and humor writing for greeting cards and postcards.
Illustration: Looking for humorous greeting cards/illustrations that "are clever but upbeat and positive, humor which is not only funny but conveys a 'sendable' sentiment." Doesn't want to see cards which "rely on trite puns, old age jokes, or are funny but not 'sendable' as a greeting card from one person to another." For first contact send slides or photocopies of artwork and writing on small cards to Gary Spector, President/Art Director. Reports back within 3-4 weeks. Returns material if accompanied by SASE. Negotiates rights purchased. Pays $50-150 outright purchase; negotiable. *Inside Tips:* "I think humorous illustrations for greeting cards are going to be more positive, less 'raunchy.'"
Writing: Looking for humorous greeting card writing that is "clever, funny, positive in attitude and very 'sendable.' It is a card that is 'from me to you.' Imagine the buyer purchasing the card to send to someone the buyer knows." Doesn't want to see cards that "are trite or that don't relate to the situation of actually buying and sending cards."

For first contact or to query on specific greeting card ideas, send writing samples to Gary Spector. Reports back within 2-4 weeks. Returns materials if accompanied by SASE. Negotiates rights purchased. Pays $50-80 outright purchase. *Inside Tips:* Trends in the market are "more positive, less 'wordy.' "

*ZTC INC., Suite B-28, 6065 N.W. 167th St., Hialeah FL 33015-4329. (305)827-8036. FAX: (305)827-8472. Estab. 1978. Sticker company that provides Fotocomic Talking Stickers for photographs and greeting cards. Needs humor writing for stickers.
Illustration: Send all cartoon/humorous illustration samples to Edward Zaret, President. To query with specific greeting card ideas, request disclosure agreement first. Reports back within 1 month. Returns materials only if requested. Buys first time, all rights. Pays outright purchase. Also assigns freelance humorous illustration/cartooning duties. Assigns approximately 1 job/month. Some of the things considers when hiring a freelance illustrator are ability of artist to take art direction well and "marketability" of artist's drawing style. Pays by the project. *Inside Tips:* "Include cost with first contact."
Writing: Send all humor writing submissions to Edward Zaret, President. To query with specific greeting card ideas, request disclosure form first. Returns materials only if requested. Buys all rights.

Greeting Cards/Changes '91-'93

The following markets appeared in the last (1991) edition of *Humor and Cartoon Markets* but are absent from the 1993 edition. These companies failed to respond to our request for an update of their listing or for the reasons indicated in parentheses following the company name.

Freedom Greetings (over-
  stocked)
Maid in the Shade (doesn't
  use freelancers)

Merlyn Graphics Corporation
  (out of business)
New Heights (now photography oriented)

Open End Studios (cannot be
  reached)

Playwriting

Before developing this edition of *Humor and Cartoon Markets*, we invited some funny people (including 2 cartoonists, 1 humorous illustrator and 1 humor writer) into our Cincinnati headquarters for a free dinner and tour of the building (yeah, right). In return, we asked that they give us all of their brilliant ideas on how we could improve the book. We hope they enjoyed the food, 'cause the ideas they gave us were superb.

One of the more significant suggestions, and one that we have decided to implement, is that we list more markets for writers of funny material, including humorous scripts. While in the past we provided listings of buyers of funny TV and radio scripts, we now will also feature markets for humorous plays.

Thus marks the inception of the Playwriting section. Here you will find both publishers and producers of humorous plays, as well as sponsors of play contests. Each listing contains important information such as numbers of plays published/produced per year; recent publications/productions; genre, length and subject matter preferred; and rights and payment policies. Although we have provided basic submission guidelines for each listing, we recommend that you write to the publishers and producers you intend to submit work to for more specific guidelines.

*ACTORS THEATRE OF LOUISVILLE, 316 W. Main St., Louisville KY 40202-4218. (502)584-1265. FAX: (502)583-9922. Producing Director: Jon Jory. Estab. 1964. "Actors Theatre of Louisville is a professional resident nonprofit theater that produces plays annually from September through June in its two theater complex in Louisville KY." Produces 20 ten-minute plays, selected from submissions to the National Ten-Minute Play Contest. Recent productions include *American Welcome*, by Brian Friel; *Eukiah*,

by Lanford Wilson and *Marred Bliss,* by Mark O'Donnell. For first contact submit complete ms to National Ten-Minute Play Contest. Scripts must be postmarked by Dec. 1, 1992. "There is a limit of two scripts per author, and each script must be no more than 10 pages long. Previously submitted plays, plays that have received an Equity production, musicals, children's shows and any unsolicited one-act or full-length plays are not accepted and will be returned." Reports back within 9 months. Buys production rights. Pays "standard Dramatists Guild Contract royalty." Submissions returned with SASE.
Tips: "In addition to all the concerns regarding subject and style, we pay close attention to scripts that have particularly good roles for young actors."

*ALLEYWAY THEATRE, 1 Curtain Up Alley, Buffalo NY 14202-1911. (716)852-2266. Artistic Director: Neal Radice. Estab. 1980. Plays are professional productions for the general public. Number of play produced/year varies. Recent productions include *Modern Maturity,* by Edna Pelonero (world premiere 6/91.) For first contact submit complete ms to Joyce Stilson, Dramaturg. Deadline for play competition, September 1 each year. Finalists announced January 1. If script is submitted directly, response is in 6-8 weeks. Alleyway must be cited as premiere producer of accepted plays. Competition winners receive prize award plus royalties. Submissions returned with SASE.
Needs: "Scripts of any style are accepted, but special attention will be given to those scripts that take place in unconventional settings and explore the boundaries of theatricality." Two categories: full-length and one-act. Prefers cast size of no more than 10 performers for full lengthplays, no more than 6 performers for one-acts. Plays must accommodate a unit or simple set.

*ARAN PRESS, 1320 S. Third St., Louisville KY 40208. (502)636-0115. Editor/Publisher: Tom Eagan. Estab. 1983. Plays are professional, community, college, university, summer stock and dinner theater. "*No* children's plays." Publishes 20 plays/year. Recent publications include *House that Ate Their Brains,* by Rolando Perez; *Disenchantment,* by Barbara Blum; *Feast of the Dancing Monkey,* by Tom Eagan; *May I Borrow Your Bed Pan,* by Francis Hoffmann. For first contact send query and synopsis to Tom Eagan. Reports back within 2 weeks. Buys stage production rights. Pays 50% royalty (on a production; 10% on book sales.) Submissions returned with SASE.
Needs: "Looking for marketable scripts. Humor and good taste are not necessarily contradictory."

*ARKANSAS REPERTORY THEATRE, P.O. Box 110, Little Rock AR 72203-0110. (501)378-0445. Artistic Director: Cliff Fannin Baker. Estab. 1976. Plays are professional productions for a general audience. Produces 11 plays/year. Recent productions include *Lend Me a Tenor; Laughing Wild* and *Little Lulu in a Tight Orange Dress.* For first contact send query and synopsis to Brad Mooy, Literary Manager. Reports back within 6 months. Buys 5% rights on future productions. Pays 5-10% royalty or $50-70/performance on second stage. Submissions returned with SASE "if patient."
Needs: Produce comedies, dramas, musicals, premieres; *all* mainly full-length. "We prefer small cast shows."
Tips: "Continue to submit—keep us posted on all progress."

The asterisk before a listing indicates that the listing is new in this edition. New markets are often more receptive to freelance submissions.

*BAKER'S PLAYS, 100 Chauncy St., Boston MA 02111. (617)482-1280. FAX: (617)482-7613. Managing Director: John Welch. Estab. 1845. Publishes plays for 80% high school theater, 20% religious organizations, regional theater and community theater. 40% of plays published each year are humoruos. Recent publications include *First Night*, by Jack Neary; *Faith Country*, by Mark Landon Smith; *Good Help Is So Hard to Murder*, by Pat Cook; and *Icarus All Over Again*, by Gordon and Rucker. For first contact submit complete ms ("include resume, script history, reviews, etc.) to Raymond Pape, Associate Editor. Reports back within 3-4 months. Obtains rights to publish and promote exclusively. Pays 50% royalty, $40-60/performance (for full-length play), book royalty of 10%. Submissions returned with SASE.
Needs: "Full-length or one-act plays, comedy or drama, that can be produced on the high school stage, church chancel or community theater stage."
Tips: "Know which market you are writing for before you submit your work. I reject countless plays that are simply 'not for us.' Know your market. Although we rarely commission work, we will do so with an established author."

*J. LARKING BROWN, P.O. Box 27032, Richmond VA 23273. (804)672-5100. FAX: (804)672-5284. Artistic Director: J. Larkin Brown. Plays are amateur productions for community theater. Produces 4 plays/year. Recent production include *Old Flames*, *The Gift of Life* and *Old Friends*. For first contact send complete ms to J.L. Brown. Reports back within a matter of months. Buys production rights. Pays award of $250 for (5) productions. Submissions returned with SASE.
Needs: One-acts with small cast and simple set requirements—plays and musicals considered.

*CHARLOTTE REPERTORY THEATRE, 345 N. College St., Suite 211, Charlotte NC 28202. (704)375-4796. Artistic Director: Mark Woods. Estab. 1976. Plays are professional productions and workshop readings. Produces 9-10 plays/year. Recent productions include *Lend Me A Tenor*, *Other People's Money* and *Widow's Best Friend*. For first contact send query and synopsis to Carol Bellamy, Literary Manager. Reports back within 3 months. Pays royalty. Submissions returned with SASE.
Needs: Unproduced full-length plays. "We traditionally do not do musicals."

*COLLAGES & BRICOLAGES, P.O. Box 86, Clarion PA 16214. (814)226-5799. Editor: Marie-José Fortis. Estab. 1986. Publishes plays for writers, college educated people who read *Collages & Bricolages*. Has published short one-act plays. For first contact submit complete ms to Marie-José Fortis. Reports back within 1-3 months. Rights revert to author after publication. Payment in copies of the magazine. Submissions returned with SASE.
Needs: One-act plays, 15 pgs. or less; literary, philosophical, existentialist.
Tips: "Send excellent, carefully thought-out, carefully 'worded' material."

*THE CREAM CITY REVIEW, University of Wisconsin-Milwaukee, Box 413, Milwaukee WI 53201. (414)299-4708. Estab. 1975. For first contact submit complete ms to Fiction Editors. Reports back within 2 months. Buys first rights; rights revert to author upon publication. "Pay varies, plus 2 copies of the issue." Submissions returned with SASE.
Needs: "Literary in nature. About 30 pages maximum. All topics."
Tips: "Read literature and send us literary plays."

*ENCORE PERFORMANCE PUBLISHING, P.O. Box 692, Orem UT 84057. (801)225-0605. Editor: Michael C. Perry. Estab. 1978. Publishes plays for family and youth audiences. Publishes 6-10 plays/year. Recent publications include *The Visitor*, by Ev Miller; *The Perils of Pusher*, by James Witherell; *Shakespeare's Clowns*, by Lane Riosley and Rebecca Byars. For first contact send query and synopsis or complete manuscript,

Close-up

Tom Eagan
Editor/Publisher
Aran Press

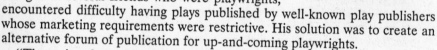

Named after the desolate islands located off the
west coast of Ireland, Aran Press was established
in 1983 by Tom Eagan, a veteran of the theater
who has been involved in all aspects of play production. It was his experience as a playwright that
sparked the impetus for founding the press. He,
along with several friends who were playwrights,
encountered difficulty having plays published by well-known play publishers
whose marketing requirements were restrictive. His solution was to create an
alternative forum of publication for up-and-coming playwrights.

"The major play publishers have narrow requirements — such as a play must
be done in New York or in national theater, or it has to have a string of
reviews," he says. "I'm giving an opportunity to playwrights who don't meet
this high criteria. I am able to do this by having the playwright kick in some
money toward the publication. So, the playwright is sort of putting his money
on the line to say, 'I believe in this play.' " Eagan says that, while he does not
publish everything that crosses his desk, he will accept plays that he doesn't
necessarily have a taste for himself. "There are a lot of plays in the catalog that
I call 'exotic flowers.' They're weird, sort of 'back porch' plays that Samuel
French would never look at because of economics. But I encourage these playwrights and they develop."

Eagan publishes approximately 20-25 humorous plays each year, and says
that his preferences lean toward "straight dinner theater comedy." In reviewing
manuscripts, he looks for a play's producibility and a small cast. Professionalism
in manuscript submission is a must. "I get an impression right off whether the
writer knows anything about theater. If he doesn't know theater he is wasting
my time and probably his own because, to be frank, I don't read those types of
plays. I get enough material from writers who know theater and know the
proper format for submission of a script."

Humor and good taste are not necessarily contradictory, according to Eagan.
"It saddens me that you have to use foul language to get a laugh. Sometimes
foul language does make a laugh. But there is a lot of good humor that contains
language that you would not be ashamed to have your grandmother hear." He
admits that truly funny writers are rare. "There are very few people who write
funny stuff. I don't have as many good comedy writers in the catalog as I would
like. Unfortunately, most people see the dark side of life, I think, and they
write to that. Comedy is the way you look at it. I have plays that could be done
serious but are done funny."

Play producers and directors seeking scripts for production make up the audience of Aran Press. Eagan says he has of late been concentrating on promoting the catalog to directors of school and university theater departments. "We are just starting to catch on with producers," he says. "They are starting to look at this as an alternative catalog to Samuel French and Dramatist's." Two plays published by Aran Press, *Movin' On* and *Bullets are a Girl's Best Friend*, were recently produced in Hollywood, the latter as a showcase for Cinemax and Home Box Office.

To be successful, says Eagan, the playwright must write for a specific audience. "There must be a match between the audience and the play," he says. "You need to capture the uniqueness of your own little community. Humor is like lettuce—it wilts. It is temporary and has one time and place." He also stresses the importance of getting a play produced. "A playwright without a production is like a plumber without a toilet bowl or an architect with plans but no buildings," he says. He acknowledges, however, that it is difficult for a new playwright to get a production. "Too many theaters are not using their own taste buds, but are going by someone else's. They are still afraid to present something that is untried or untested. And if they are given something they haven't heard of, they don't know how to react to it."

Eagan offers aspiring playwrights the following advice: "I would recommend to anyone who wants to write plays to not do it—to write novels instead. But if they are insane enough to say, 'No, I've got to write plays, it's the only way I can express myself,' then I would say get connected with a little theater group in your area, because the real high you get out of writing a play is writing for specific people. When you know the audience, their strengths and weaknesses, you get immediate gratification."

—Roseann Shaughnessy

❝There must be a match between the audience and the play. You need to capture the uniqueness of your own little community. Humor is like lettuce—it wilts. It is temporary and has one time and place.❞

—Tom Eagan

(agented submissions only) to Editor. Reports back within 2 weeks (query), 3 months (ms). Buys publishing, performance and option on ancillary rights. Pays royalty, 50% performance, 10% book sales. Submissions returned with SASE.

Needs: "Encore is dedicated to wholesome, thought-provoking, experimental, issue-oriented theater, as well as to the adaptation of classics from literature and fairy tale. We prefer a close to even ratio of male/female roles."

Tips: "Plays should always be produced twice before submitting to a publisher. The writers should make himself/herself available for rewrites. Staged readings do not count as a production."

*FERNDALE REPERTORY THEATRE, Box 892, Ferndale CA 95536. (707)725-4636. Artistic Director: Clinton Rebik. Estab. 1972. Plays are "semi-professional community theater; theater serves mainly residents (100,000) of Humboldt County CA." Produces 3-4 plays/year. Recent productions include *Nunsense*; *Return Engagements*; *Noises Off*; *The Nerd*; *Wilde West* and *Brighton Beach Memoirs*. For first contact send query and synopsis or submit complete ms (for "new works competition") to above address, attn: New Works Competition. Reports back within months—depending on script arrival; submission deadline is Oct. 15; entrants are notified Jan. 15-June 1. Buys production rights for world premiere; all subsequent rights revert to author. Pays royalty—$250 for 8 performances; writer also receives copy of all press, publicity and photo materials. Submissions returned with SASE.

Needs: "Comedies with a twist; dramas with uplifting endings; new theatrical ideas. Cast limit of 10; simple technical requirements; length: approx. 1.5 hrs. to 3 hrs.

Tips: "*Always* include synopsis of script; send cover letter if idea is *unique* and merits special attention."

*FLORIDA STUDIO THEATRE, 1241 N. Palm Ave., Sarasota FL 34236. (813)366-9017. Artistic Director: Richard Hopkins. Estab. 1973. Plays are professional productions. Produces "as many good plays as we can find." Recent productions include *Hi-Hat Hattie*, *Dynamic Products* and *One Foot in Scarsdale* (all world premieres). For first contact send query and synopsis to Steve Ramay. Reports back within 6 months. Negotiates rights purchased. Pay is negotiable. Submissions returned with SASE.

Needs: "All genres, styles—also seeking short, short plays of 5 pp. or less."

*GREAT AMERICAN HISTORY THEATRE, 30 East 10 St., St. Paul MN 55101. (612)292-4323. Artistic Directors: Lynn Lohr/Lance Belville. Estab. 1978. Plays are professional productions for mainstream audiences. Produces 0-3 plays/year. Recent productions include *A Couple of Blaguards* and *Last Hooch at the Hollyhocks*. For first contact send query and synopsis to Lance Belville, Co-Artistic Director. Reports back within 2 weeks (synopsis), 6 months (after we ask to see a script). Pays royalty (subject to negotiation). Submissions returned with SASE. Query with synopsis first.

Needs: Plays based on historical people, places, events and ideas. "We prefer casts of no larger than 10 actors and simple sets."

Tips: "We're interested in plays in which *history* plays some part. **Nothing else, please.** Query with synopsis first is a must."

*KALLIOPE, a journal of women's art, 3939 Roosevelt Blvd., Jacksonville FL 32205. (904)381-3511. Artistic Director: Aimee Young Jackson. Estab. 1978. Publishes plays for readers of literary magazines/art journals. Publishes 1-3 plays/year. Recent publications include *17A*, by A. Michele Leslie (winner of national one-act play competition sponsored by *Kalliope*). For first contact submit complete ms to Mary Sue Koeppel. Reports back within a matter of months. Buys first publishing rights. Pays in free copies of issue in which the play was published or one free year's subscription to *Kalliope*. Submissions returned with SASE.

Needs: "Only one act plays or those shorter than 15 typed pages (we are limited by space); any theme is interesting to us as long as it is in a well made, experimental format."
Tips: "Send us a short, experimental, fascinating piece. Show us that the author has insight into the human condition and the work is therefore worth reading and publishing. We reject much that fits only the musical or mainstream market."

*LOS ANGELES DESIGNERS' THEATRE, P.O. Box 1883, Studio City CA 91614-0883. (213)650-9600. FAX: (818)985-9200. Artistic Director: Richard Niederberg. Estab. 1970. "All performances are at nonprofit, professional stage theaters. Audience is primarily entertainment industry, TV, film, music, theater executives who have 'seen it all' and are very jaded." Produces plays for local use and for sale to film and TV industry. Produces 20 plays/year. Recently produced *Is Nudity Required?*; *Casting Agency!* and *Let's Blow This Popstand!* For first contact send complete ms to Richard Niederberg. Reports back within 3 + months. Buys performance rights only (and publishing by separate contract with separate criteria). Pays royalty, outright purchase, per performance "as negotiated." Submissions returned with SASE "but we prefer to keep submissions for several seasons, on occasion, waiting for the right mix of shows to produce."
Needs: "All genres, prefer 80-100 minute length, controversy preferred. Street language, nudity, etc., OK; religious themes, political themes, satiric themes, OK. The larger the better. No helicopters, please."
Tips: "Send me a highly commercial, easy to produce, play. Also, state in cover letter what the writer's involvement would be, other than as the writer, i.e., director, designer, actor, publicist, etc."

*MAGIC THEATRE, Fort Mason Center, Bldg. D, San Francisco CA 94123. (415)441-8001. General Director: Harvey Seifter. Estab. 1967. Plays are "professional (Equity theater) productions for a sophisticated audience." Number of plays "varies—nine new plays per season of all varieties; current season: five could be considered comedies." Recent productions include *Hunger*, by Peter Mattei; *Fat Men in Skirts*, by Nicky Silver; *Oscar and Bertha*, by Maria Irene Fornes and *Angel of Death*, by Charlie Schulman. For first contact send query and synopsis. No unsolicited plays. Submit *first* 10-20 pp. of script, short synopsis, resume or artistic bio and SASE to Mary DeDanan, Literary Manager. Reports back on queries within 1-3 months; scripts 2-7 months. All rights revert to playwright. Pays 6-8% of gross ticket receipts plus small stipend up front. Submissions returned with SASE. "Plays without SASE will be recycled."
Needs: "Looking for full-length plays; one-acts only if capable of filling an evening (about 90 minutes). Innovative, unusual comedies, often absurd, understated or exagerated, non-realistic. Tragi-comedies common." Prefer small cast (6 or less), simple sets.
Tips: "Always send SASE. Be patient, we're usually swamped. Don't call and pester (see above). Read and/or see our previously produced plays—they are *not Charley's Aunt* (Listings of past seasons can be found in TCG's *Theatre Profiles*."

*MIDWEST RADIO THEATRE WORKSHOP, 915 E. Broadway, Columbia MO 65201. (314)874-5676. Artistic Director: Diane Huneke. Estab. 1979. Plays are live radio plays produced each fall. Publishes plays primarily for radio directors and radio producers. Publishes 2-6 plays/year; produces 1-2 plays/year. Recent productions/publications include *A Night's Work*, *Vince Washburn: New Age Detective* and *The Odyssey of Runyan Jones*. For first contact send submissions (to radio script contest only) to Diane Huneke. Reports back within 6 months. Buys "the right to produce play within a 3-year period." Pays $150-500 per radio production plus prizes to contest winners.
Needs: Radio plays 15-60 minutes in length; "interested in social satire, contemporary issues and work by women and people of color. *Radio plays only*—follow contest guidelines."

Tips: "Attend a workshop and learn to write for radio—radio plays are not stage plays, screen plays or monologues. Write for our script contest guidelines, send SASE."

*MISSISSIPPI STATE UNIVERSITY THEATRE, P.O. Drawer PF, Mississippi State MS 39762. (601)325-7952. Artistic Director: Jeffrey Scott Elwell. Estab. 1963. Plays are university theater (477-seat house) productions for the university and rural southern communities. Produces "2-3 plays per calendar year; full productions and staged reading." Recent productions include *The Debutante Ball*, by Beth Henley; *Beyond Therapy*, by Christopher Durang and *Pippin* (musical). For first contact send query and synopsis to Jeffrey Scott Elwell. Reports back within 2 months. Buys first performance rights. Pays $25-50 per performance; $200, $100 as prizes in MSU Festival of New Plays. Submissions returned with SASE.
Needs: Comedies, dramas, musicals, full-length for mainstage season; short plays for MSU Festival of New Plays. "We prefer (for Festival) to produce works about the south or by southern writers."
Tips: "We are seeking tight, well-written comedies with interesting characters, good plots and roles for 18-23 year-olds."

*MIXED BLOOD THEATRE CO., 1501 S. 4th S., Minneapolis MN 55454. Artistic Director: Jack Reuler. Estab. 1977. Plays are professional productions for a broad range audience. Produces 2-3 plays/year. Recent productions include *I'm Not Rappaport* and *How to Improve Your Golf Game*. For first contact send query and synopsis to David Kunz, Script Czar. Reports back within 3 months. Buys production rights. Submissions returned with SASE.
Needs: "We're wide open."
Tips: "*Always* send a query letter and synopsis for any produced play. *Never* send an unsolicited script. For unproduced plays send an SASE for a copy of our annual playwriting contest guidelines."

*OLD GLOBE THEATRE, P.O. Box 2171, San Diego CA 92112-2171. (619)231-1941. FAX: (619)231-5879. Artistic Director: Jack O'Brien. Estab. 1935. Plays are professional regional theater productions (LORT B+, B, and C stages) for largely subscription audience. "We produce 12 plays/year; their content, i.e., humorous, tragic, etc., varies." Recent productions include *Rumors*, by Neil Simon; *The School for Husbands*, by Moliere (translated by Richard Wilbur); *Bargains*, by Jack Heifner and *Breaking Legs*, by Tom Dulack. For first contact send query and synopsis to Mark Hofflund, Director, Play Discovery Program. "Two week response time for queries; ten month response time for scripts." Pays 5% royalty. Submissions returned with SASE.
Needs: Productions subject to normal budgetary considerations/limitations.

*ROCKFORD WRITERS' GUILD, P.O. Box 858, Rockford IL 61105. Editor: David Ross. Estab. 1940. Publishes annual *Rockford Review* (national lit magazine) and quarterly *Tributary* (supplement to Review). Publishes 5-6 plays/year. Recent publications include *Give and Take*; *Black Widows Invade Coney Island* and *William Shakespeare Goes to Hollywood*. Submit complete ms to David Ross, Editor. Reports back within a matter of weeks. Buys first North American serial rights. Pays copy of magazine and eligibility for $25 readers' poll and $50 editor's choice prizes. Submissions returned with SASE.
Needs: One-acts up to 15 pages for *Review*—2 to 4 pages for *Tributary*; wide open to genre and style. Prefers small casts and minimal props and stage direction. "We like to think of our magazines as 'lean and mean' in terms of readability."
Tips: "Send for guidelines (SASE). Order sample lit mags: $6 *Rockford Review*; $2.50 *Tributary*. We publish 5-6 plays a year, selected from hundreds of plays submitted—so the shorter one-acts with few characters stand the best chance. Writers who get pub-

lished are invited to a 'party' in October each year and may perform their plays at that time. There are always eager readers ready to play a role."

*SLIDELL LITTLE THEATRE, P.O. Box 969, Slidell LA 70459. (504)641-0324. Artistic Directors: Amateurs (6 or 7 per season). Estab. 1964. Plays are amateur productions for a general audience. Publishes for general public. Produces 4 or 5 plays/year. Recent productions include *Brighton Beach; Importance of Being Ernest; Steel Magnolias* and *I'm Not Rappaport* and *Social Security.* "Submissions are accepted during playwright competition. Dates to be announced. Send to above address. Reports back within 3 months. "Contest winner receives staged reading and theater receives right to negotiate with winnings, which will be royalties for said production." Pays royalty, $500 plus room and board—not to exceed $400.
Needs: "Plays must be suitable for our stage."
Tips: "Enter our competition contest for 1992-1993."

*TACOMA ACTORS GUILD, 1323 S. Yakima Ave., Tacoma WA 98405. (206)272-3107. Artistic Director: Bruce K. Sevy. Estab. 1978. Plays are professional productions for subscription/single ticket audience in the South Puget Sound area. Produces 6 plays/year. Recent productions include *Lend Me a Tenor, Rumors, Broadway Bound* and *First Night.* For first contact send query and synopsis to Nancy Hoadley, Literary Manager. Reports back within a matter of weeks on synopses; months on scripts. Buys "negotiable" rights. Pays royalty, outright purchase. Submissions returned with SASE.
Needs: "We prefer single set and smaller cast. Our audience is conservative. Nudity is a no go. Language (depends!) For new work, cast under 8-10. Staging must currently be modest due to space and budget considerations."
Tips: "Our slots for new work are rare!! Be patient, funny and good!!"

*BEVERLY VOLDSETH, Box 12, Goodhue MN 55027. Estab. 1982. Publishes for "small literary magazine audience." Publishes 1 play/year. For first contact submit complete ms to Beverly Voldseth. Reports back within 3 months. Buys first rights only. Pays copy of magazine. Submissions returned with SASE.
Needs: Publishes short plays. "We also use cartoons."

*WEST COAST ENSEMBLE, 6240 Hollywood Blvd., Hollywood CA 90028. (213)871-8673. FAX: (213)462-6741. Artistic Director: Les Hanson. Estab. 1982. "Plays are produced in one of our two theaters operating under the Equity 99-seat theater plan for Los Angeles. The audience is a variety of theater-goers from Southern California." Produces 6 plays/year. Recent productions include *Your Life Is A Feature Film; Another Man's Shoes; The Man Who Came to Dinner* and *SSexx Rangers of Venus.* For first contact submit complete ms to West Coast Ensemble, P.O. Box 38728, Los Angeles CA 90038. Reports back within 6 months. "If published—playwright receives a credit for having been produced at the West Coast Ensemble." Pays $15-50 per performance. Submission returned with SASE.
Needs: A variety of styles and topics: comedy, drama, musicals, classics. "We prefer a cast size of no more than 10 for full-lengths; 6 for one-acts; simple sets."

*WOOLLY MAMMOTH THEATRE COMPANY, 1401 Church St., Washington DC 20005. (202)234-6130. Artistic Director: Howard Shelwitz. Estab. 1980. "A small, 136 seat Washington DC theater. Our audience is typically theatrically sophisticated and discerning and very politically suave." Produces/publishes 2-5 plays/year. Recent productions/publications include *Fat Men in Skirts,* by Nicky Silver; *The Day Room,* by Don Delillo and *The Dead Monkey,* by Nick Derke. For first contact send query and synopsis to Greg

Tillman, Literary Manager. Reports back within 1-2 months. Submissions returned with SASE.

Needs: "We produce full-length off-beat plays, often premieres. We look for unusual styles, use of language, structure and character development. Minimal settings and casts of 6 or less are preferred."

Tips: "Use of humor to explore an issue of importance/social relevance."

Publications

How many trees does it take to print *The New York Times Sunday Magazine*? And how much pulp goes into the *Sports Illustrated* swimsuit edition? Must we sacrifice an entire forest to print this week's issue of *TIME*?

Well, being that the batteries in my calculator have run down, I guess we'll never know the answers to those questions. But if a tree has to die for something, it might as well die in the interest of publishing.

Magazines

If it weren't for magazines, waiting to see your doctor would be an incredibly boring experience. While most doctors' offices come equipped with a token oil panting of outer Cape Cod and a potted, plastic philodendron, you can also find a fistful of magazines to help take your mind off of the touching and probing that is soon to come.

But unfortunately, many doctors' offices are stocked with the wrong *kind* of magazines, and to make matters worse, they were printed in the previous decade. Don't doctors know that there are some really good, funny magazines out there? Imagine if they supplied their waiting rooms with such magazines as *SPY*, *National Lampoon*, *MAD* and even *Cracked*! Patients might *laugh* themselves into wellness. Aha! *That's* why doctors don't subscribe to funny magazines!

Indeed, magazines remain one of the most receptive markets for freelance humor. These publications seek everything—from humorous fiction to humorous nonfiction, gag cartoons to humorous illustration, even caricature to editorial cartoons.

Nonetheless, it is extremely important to understand a particular magazine's editorial format, slant or philosophy before submitting material. You wouldn't, for example, submit risque gag cartoons to *Family Circle*. On the other hand, gentle cartoons about gardening probably won't stand a chance at *High Society* (unless, of course, you draw the gardener doing something really weird with a rake). There's no better way to waste postage than to blindly submit inappropriate material to a nonreceptive market.

Humor writing

When it comes to written humor, both fiction and nonfiction, it is almost always best for the writer to query a potential market with his story idea first rather than submit his completed manuscript. Remember that editors must read through stacks of unsolicited material, so the writer best serves himself if he keeps his presentation succinct while ensuring that it piques the editor's interest. The writer should also send along a cover letter explaining his background, past publishing achievements and professional experience, but must bear in mind that an editor isn't interested in learning his life story. When it comes to his cover letter, less is definitely more. After all, the writer wants the editor to read his query, not his resume.

Provided you're querying an editor with a good proposal for an article, you have a chance of placing the article if it's appropriate for the magazine. Even if the slant of the proposed article is a little off the mark, a good editor can suggest ways to modify the manuscript so that it *will* fit in with the magazine's editorial philosophy. If an editor suggests minor changes in your proposal, this is a good sign—it means he wants to buy the article. Therefore, listen to what he says. Editors are more willing to work with freelance humor writers who work with *them*.

Humorous illustration

When submitting examples of your humorous illustration to a magazine, put together a package of your work (self-promotional color page, black and white page, client list, tearsheets, etc.) and send it off to the appropriate art buyer. You also want to tell the buyer to keep the materials on file. The *last* thing you want is to have the material returned. Let the art director *keep* these materials (hopefully on file), so he can reacquaint himself with your work when and if the appropriate assignment comes up.

It's also important to point out that, while your illustration attests to your artistic talent, a well-written, professional cover letter convinces the art director of your intelligence. Humorous illustration, after all, is much more than the physical pushing around of a pen on paper. In your cover letter, tell the art director about your ability to conceptualize, your knack for solving tough graphic problems and your other, nonartistic skills. Remember, freelance humorous illustration is *extremely competitive*, and you want to do everything you can to assure an art director that you are not only talented, but *competent*.

Like the rest of the world around us, magazine publishing is fast moving and extremely mutable by nature. Magazines that may have used lots of humorous illustration in February may be using almost none by June. Things also shake up graphically when an art director leaves a magazine and is replaced by a new art director. Suddenly, the magazine can take on an entirely new look.

Magazines can even set illustration trends by using certain illustrators. When high-profile consumer magazines such as *Rolling Stone, TIME, Newsweek* and *Esquire* use humorous illustration styles that make graphic reference to "retro" illustration styles of the 1940s, smart illustrators pick up on this subtlety. For example, as sophisticated as their work is, humorous illustrators such as Elwood Smith, Lou Brooks and Gary Hallgren work in styles that pay homage to popular art styles of the mid 20th century. Indeed, everything old is new again.

It's also good to see top magazine art directors continuing to put stock in humorous illustration as *design*, not just pounded-out, low-brow art. Smaller consumer magazines and trade publications may have no problem using humorous illustrators who "draw funny pictures," but that simply isn't enough for art directors who are the vanguards of their profession. For these art directors, it's important to work with humorous illustrators who understand how to create sublime art that *complements* an article, rather than overshadowing it with a slapstick, coarse visual treatment.

If you've studied the visual difference between the top consumer magazines and the smaller trade publications, you certainly can recognize the work of humorous illustrators who understand how to design, and those who merely create an uneventful drawing to go alongside an article. To succeed in magazines, it's important for the freelancer to understand that there is indeed an *Art* (with a capitol A) to humorous illustration.

Gag cartooning

Whether a magazine has mass-audience appeal or caters to a specialized readership, the gag cartoons they publish must be of a particular "slant." For example, a trade magazine for dog groomers may only be interested in seeing gag cartoons dealing with schnauzers and shampoo, while general "women's" magazines will look for gag cartoons on pertinent subjects like relationships, parenting, cooking, children, the workplace, etc. Happily, most of the following listings adequately reveal a given magazine's particular slant.

Cartoonists employ a number of methods for submitting gag cartoons. One cartoonist may draw his cartoons in finished form and then submit the drawing for purchase, while others may briskly render rough sketches which, when approved, are drawn in final form for publication. Generally speaking, either way is acceptable to most magazines unless otherwise indicated.

Likewise, the system of cataloging each gag cartoon can vary. For example, you could code a gag cartoon 1092REL747 which when deciphered could mean that the gag cartoon was drawn in October of 1992 (10/29), the subject matter of the gag cartoon is "relationships" (REL) and the catalog number of the cartoon itself is 747. If you're submitting the same cartoon to 10 different magazines, you'll want to come up with an additional "ABC" coding system.

ABC coding is as simple as, well, ABC. The cartoonist merely prints the alphabet on the back of each cartoon (either finished or rough drawing) and assigns a letter to each magazine he submits material to. When he submits the cartoon to magazine A (perhaps *The New Yorker*, he circles letter A on the cartoon, when he submits the cartoon to magazine B (which might be *National Lampoon*), he circles letter B, and so on. That way only the cartoonist knows who has seen the cartoon, without divulging to others what those exact magazines are.

Obviously, the purpose of such coding is to effectively track your cartoons and ensure that you don't continue showing it to the same people over and over again. There is, however a certain stigma attached to cartoons that exhibit a profusion of circled code numbers. I have seen some cartoonists solve that problem in this admittedly cumbersome way: They submit their cartoons in "rounds" by modifying their coding system. Round One would be the above mentioned ABC system, but Round Two would be a double ABC system (i.e., AA, BB, CC, etc.). Round Three would be AAA, BBB, CCC, etc. In the event that ten letters (A-J) are filled up on Round One, the cartoonist then moves on to Round Two and begins submitting cartoons to magazine AA, then BB, etc. By doing this, no magazine is assigned a letter lower than J, so the modified system gives the *illusion* that the cartoon is relatively fresh and hasn't passed through many hands.

Again, it may be a rather ingenious system, but it can be troublesome. Additionally, the Round System is difficult to use for cartoonists who submit finished, original cartoons. But for those cartoonists who circulate Xerox copies of rough cartoons, the system is ideal. If the cartoon does not sell during Round One, a brand-new Xerox is made of the rough and the crisp Round Two code numbers are added to the backside of the drawing.

I have even heard of a computer program designed by a hacker to make the process of submitting gag cartoons a little less taxing, though I have not seen the software. Indeed, the nature of freelance gag cartooning necessitates that the cartoonist spend far too much time and energy *submitting* his cartoons. This is why gag cartoonists are always searching for new, simpler ways of submitting their work so they can spend more time actually *cartooning*.

Payment and terms

The recession has hit virtually every area of American business, and because publications depend heavily on advertising for their very survival, they have taken quite a hit. Indeed, these days magazines are watching their budgets very closely. When they spend money, you can rest assured they've justified the expenditure a number of times.

Naturally, payment fluctuates greatly from magazine to magazine. Major consumer magazines continue to pay top dollar for humorous writing and art, while the dinkiest of trade magazines may pay a small stipend and a fistful of frayed tearsheets (try paying your rent with a tearsheet). But these small publications are banking on your need for tearsheets and, if you're just starting out, these printed pieces *are* important as they attest to your status as a *published* humorist.

Still, smaller consumer and trade magazines can pay reasonably well for freelance art and writing, and if a freelancer can establish ongoing working relationships with some of these publications, he can make in three or four jobs what he makes in a single job for one of the giant consumer magazines.

This is the same for gag cartooning, and more and more gag cartoonists are concentrating their efforts on trade magazines who may only pay $75 per cartoon, but are less difficult to get into than *The New Yorker*, *Playboy*, *Cosmopoli-*

tan, etc. Given the above mentioned, time-consuming process of submitting gag cartoons to publications, you can see why some gag cartoonists are willing to work for smaller rates and try to make up the difference in sales volume.

Like rates, rights and usages will vary drastically as well. With art, first time reproduction rights or a one time usage fee are usually bought, but the rights purchased for writing tend to be broader. First North American serial rights seem to be the most commonly negotiated terms for magazine humor writing, though all rights, reprint rights, etc. may be contracted.

If you look at magazines in general terms, there are far more magazines with rates at the low end of the pay scale than those that can afford to pay top dollar. But happily, it's magazine publishing's editorial diversity that presents freelancers with unlimited opportunities. Just written a hilarious fiction piece from a depression-era dinner plate's point of view? Thanks to magazine publishing's eclectic sense of humor, chances are good that someone will want to publish it.

Newspapers

Because of their sheer numbers, you would consider newspapers to be a relatively easy market to break into. But when it comes to humor, newspapers seem to be locked firmly into their own unusual predicament. When their regular staff can't comply, newspapers buy their humorous articles, columns, comic strips, editorial cartoons and graphics from the major syndicates. While a Dave Barry, Bill Watterson or Jeff MacNelly wouldn't complain about such an arrangement, a freelance humorist certainly could. However, one can break into the market with reasonable success if he understands the realities which face the editor or art director of the daily newspaper.

Take a look at this hypothetical scenario: The syndicates service the average daily newspaper with 75 percent of its total humorous art/writing. An additional 20 percent of exclusive humorous art/writing is handled by the newspaper's fulltime staff. That leaves 5 percent of the pie for the freelancer to claw, scratch and bite at. Sound discouraging? It need not be.

For a freelancer to be successful in the newspaper market, he would be well-advised to approach newspapers with humorous material that is exceptionally uncommon or has strong local, state or regional appeal. The Op-Ed editor in Albuquerque, New Mexico may be inundated with clever editorial cartoons about Richard Nixon's threat to make a political comeback, when he'd *really* like cartoons of a more local, parochial nature. Of course, the same holds true for written humor.

Newspapers have a little more latitude when it comes to humorous illustration. While they all have fulltime art staffs, many newspapers, especially the larger ones, see benefit in giving assignments to freelance humorous illustrators. And with the advent of the fax machine, they're doing it more and more.

For example, I am called often and on short notice by *The Washington Post* to create humorous illustrations to augment various articles or news stories. I am usually given a couple hours to draw up a few roughs and fax them in. The art director and editor then select one of the roughs and I take the drawing to finish. Once I have completed the final drawing, I fax it to Washington whereupon the fax is reduced as a stat and pasted-up. Because of fax technology, I am able to work this way with many newspapers literally around the world.

Newspapers are by no means known for their blockbuster freelance budgets. Even big newspapers that boast mega-circulations pay mini-money to freelance writers, illustrators and cartoonists. The main reason that newspapers have such low freelance rates is because they publish on a *daily* basis rather than weekly or monthly.

But if most newspapers don't pay freelancers stellar sums, they do tend to pay very quickly—usually within two weeks. It is this prompt payment that can help relieve the sting of the relatively low rate.

AARDVARK ENTERPRISES, Division of Speers Investments Ltd., 204 Millbank Dr. SW, Calgary, Alberta T2Y 2H9 Canada. (403)256-4639. Estab. 1962. "General interest, quarterly international magazine; something for all ages, upbeat theme." Circ. 150-250. Approximately 50% of art and writing is humor-oriented. Approximately 100% of artwork and writing is done by freelancers.
Subject Needs: Needs "cartoons with upbeat theme; no porno or uncouth material wanted." Doesn't want to see "black and white line drawings whose style is not readily adaptable to photocopy process."
How to Contact: Humorous writers should send complete manuscript, writing samples and cover letter and cartoonists/humorous illustrators should send art samples and cover letter to J. Alvin Speers, Editor. Also interested in seeing samples from pencil and inking artists. For artists/writers guidelines send #10 SASE. Query with ideas for a humorous comic book title. Returns samples with SASE.
Terms: Payment for writing and cartooning is $5-8. "Paid by readers' vote for best 3 items overall per issue."
Tips: "Artist/writer must be acquainted with our magazine theme. This is a 'subscribers only' market, due to economic reality of survival needs. Watch ongoing reports of 'ceased publication' for proof. Nevertheless, our participants are happily supportive of what we are doing—'showcasing' their work to a wide audience."

ABOARD, Suite 220, 100 Almeria Ave., Miami FL 33134. (305)441-9744. FAX: (305)441-9739. Estab. 1976. Bimonthly inflight magazine. Circ. 100,000. Needs humorous illustration and writing and gag cartoons for Latin American audience. Accepts previously published cartoons and humorous articles.
Gag Cartoons: Prefers gag cartoons on travel and related themes. "No political jokes or play on words." Doesn't want to see gag cartoons on planes. Preferred format is with gagline, color wash. Send submissions to Editorial Department. Reports back within 2 months. Returns materials only if requested. Negotiates rights purchased. Pays $20, b&w, $20, color. Pays on publication.
Illustration: Buys approximately 3 humorous illustrations/year for articles. When hiring a freelance humorous illustrator, these abilities are considered: a truly unique drawing style; effective use of humor; ability to "fun up" an otherwise "flat" manuscript. For first contact send cover letter, resume, slides, portfolio and "price and rights" to Editorial Department. Looks for "good quality for printing; bright, humorous and not controversial." Reports back if interested. Samples are filed; returned if requested with SASE. Negotiates rights purchased. Pays $20, b&w, $25, color, page.
Writing: Buys approximately 2 humorous pieces/year. Needs humorous fiction and anecdotes, "fillers." Length: 1,500 words; 800 for filler. To query make sure article is appropriate and study writer's guidelines. Send SASE for copy. For first contact send

For information on book publishers' and publications' areas of interest, see the Subject Index.

cover letter, outline of proposed story and writing sample to Editorial Department. Reports back within 2 months. Samples are filed; returned if requested. Negotiates rights purchased. Pays $100 for 1,500 words. *Inside Tips:* "Use clear language, go to the point, describe the situation. We need humor for Latin American readers—ours is a bilingual magazine."

ABYSS MAGAZINE, Box 140333, Austin TX 78714. (512)472-6535. Estab. 1979. Bimonthly topical magazine. Circ. 2,200. Needs comic strips, spot cartoons and humorous writing.
Illustration: Buys 2 humorous illustrations/issue for articles and spots. For first contact send cover letter, b&w tearsheets and promo piece to D. Nalle, Editor. Reports back within 6 weeks. Samples are filed or are returned if requested by SASE. Buys one-time rights. Pays $2-8, b&w, page; $20-30, b&w, cover. Pays on publication.
Writing: Buys approximately 1 humorous piece/issue. Needs humorous nonfiction, fiction and cartoon stories. Subject matter includes fantasy, science fiction, horror, gaming and dark humor. Length: 1,000-2,000 words. To query be familiar with magazine; make sure article is appropriate; and study writer's guidelines first. Send $3 and SASE for copy of guide and latest issue. For first contact send cover letter, query, outline of proposed story and manuscript to D. Nalle, Editor. Reports back within 1½ months. Samples are returned with SASE only if requested. Buys one-time rights. Pays 1-3¢/word. *Inside Tips:* "Be funny, not just silly."

ACCENT ON LIVING, Box 700, Bloomington IL 61702. (309)378-2961. FAX: (309)378-4420. Estab. 1956. Quarterly consumer magazine. Circ. 20,000. Needs humorous writing and gag cartoons. Prefers to buy first rights on cartoons and humorous articles.
Gag Cartoons: Buys 10-15 gag cartoons/issue. Prefers gag cartoons on disability issues. Preferred format is b&w line art, 5×7". Send submissions to Betty Garee, Editor. Reports back in 2 weeks. Returns materials if accompanied by SASE. Buys first rights. Pays $20, b&w. Pays on acceptance.
Writing: Buys approximately 1 humorous piece/issue. Needs humorous nonfiction, "slice-of-life" and fiction on disability. Length: 500-1,000 words. Study writer's guidelines first; send $2.50 and SASE for copy of magazine. For first contact send query and outline of proposed story to Betty Garee, Editor. Reports back in 2 weeks. Samples returned with SASE. Buys first rights. Pays 10¢/word.

AIM, Box 20554, Chicago IL 60620. (312)874-6184. Estab. 1974. Quarterly consumer magazine. Circ. 7,000. Needs material "showing stupidity of racism." Accepts previously published cartoons and humorous articles.
Gag Cartoons: Buys 3 gag cartoons/issue. Prefers gag cartoons on "the stupidity of bigotry." Preferred format is with gagline. Send submissions to Bill Jackson, Art Director. Reports back in 1 month. Returns materials only if requested. Buys first rights. Pays $5, b&w. Pays on publication. *Inside Tips:* Cartoonist should "have some feeling on the unequal opportunities for members of minorities."
Illustration: Buys approximately 2 humorous illustrations/issue. One of the things considers when hiring a freelance humorous illustrator is a bold, powerful, attention-getting drawing style. For first contact send finished b&w drawing to Bill Jackson, Art Director. Looks for "clear illustration." Reports back in 1 month. Samples are returned if requested. Buys first rights. Pays $5, b&w, page.
Writing: Buys approximately 2 humorous pieces/issue. For first contact send manuscript to Bill Jackson, Art Director. Reports back in 1 month. Samples are returned only if requested. Buys first rights. Pays $5 minimum.

ALIVE! A MAGAZINE FOR CHRISTIAN SENIOR ADULTS, Box 46464, Cincinnati OH 45246. (513)825-3681. Estab. 1988. Quarterly newsletter. Publishes news and features of interest to Christian Seniors—55 and up. Humorous articles and stories acceptable. Circ. 5,000. Accepts previously published cartoons and humorous articles.

Gag Cartoons: Prefers gag and spot cartoons on retirement. Preferred format is single panel, of national appeal. Looks for "the ability to read a manuscript and come up with a strong visual idea as opposed to our supplying illustration idea." For first contact send b&w tearsheets and portfolio to A. June Lang, Office Editor. Reports back in 6 weeks. Returns materials if accompanied by SASE. Buys first or reprint rights. Pays $25 for spot cartoons.

Writing: Needs humorous fiction, anecdotes and "fillers" for "Heart Medicine" section. Subject matter includes "subjects of interest to over-55 age group and retirees." Length: 200-1,200 words. For first contact send manuscript and published tearsheets to A. June Lang, Office Editor. Unsolicited material is returned with SASE. Buys first rights or reprint rights. Pays 3¢/word for 200-1,200 words.

AMAZING HEROES, 7563 Lake City Way NE, Seattle WA 98115. (206)524-1967. FAX: (206)524-2104. Estab. 1981. Monthly trade journal and comics fan magazine. Circ. 10,000. Needs humorous illustration and writing, spot illustration and gag and spot cartoons.

Gag Cartoons: Buys up to 3 gag cartoons/issue. Uses, almost exclusively, gag cartoons on adventure comic book themes. Doesn't want to see gag cartoons on "*Batman*. We get lots of super-hero jokes. It's refreshing to see takeoffs on other comic book genres (science fiction, Western, fantasy, etc.)." Preferred format is single panel without gagline, b&w line art or wash. Query with 3-5 camera ready drawings/batch to Mark Thompson, Art Director. Reports back within months. Returns materials if accompanied by SASE. Buys first rights. Pays $5 minimum, b&w. Pays on publication. *Inside Tips:* A gag cartoonist should "know adventure comic books but have broader art skills than can be obtained just from reading comics. Also present submissions in a neat, reproducible way."

Illustration: Buys approximately 10 humorous illustrations/issue for spots. For first contact send b&w tearsheets to Mark Thompson, Art Director. Reports back within months. Samples are not filed; returned with SASE. Buys first rights. Pays $5 minimum, b&w, page. Pays on publication. *Inside Tips:* "We also accept non-humorous comic book character studies. Be original, be satirical; explore other comic book genres besides super-heroes."

Writing: Buys approximately 1 humorous piece/issue. Needs humorous nonfiction on comic book related material. Length: 2,000-10,000 words. To query be familiar with magazine and make sure article is appropriate. For first contact send cover letter and query to Thomas Harrington, Editor. Reports back in weeks. Samples are filed; returned only if requested. Pays 1.5¢/word. *Inside Tips:* "Our best humor pieces come from work where the writer discovers some obscure but intriguing facet of the comic book hobby (real or made up) and lets the topic speak for itself."

AMELIA MAGAZINE, 329 E St., Bakersfield CA 93304. (805)323-4064. Estab. 1983. Quarterly literary magazine. Circ. 1,250. Needs humorous illustration and writing, gag and spot cartoons and 3-5 panel cartoon spreads. Accepts previously published cartoons.

Gag Cartoons: Buys 3-8 gag cartoons/issue. Prefers gag cartoons on "virtually any theme pertinent to a literate audience." Doesn't want to see gag cartoons on "wishing wells and anthropomorphic 'doodads.' For us the 'dream' gag cartoon would be one that draws an immediate laugh out loud." Preferred formats are single, double or multi-panel, with or without gagline, b&w line art or wash. Query with 3-6 rough drawings/batch to Frederick A. Raborg, Jr., Editor. Reports back within 2 weeks. Returns materials if accompanied by SASE. Buys first or one-time rights. Pays $5-25, b&w.

On the magazine cover:

ACADEME

BULLETIN OF THE AMERICAN ASSOCIATION OF UNIVERSITY PROFESSORS

SEPTEMBER-OCTOBER 1991

"Just a few years ago we academics were dismissed as silly and irrelevant. Suddenly, like Godzilla rising from the muck, we are threatening the very existence of Western civilization."

—PH STANDS FOR POLITICAL HYPOCRISY
by Cathy Davidson

SAVING THE SENATE: A SYMPOSIUM

© Richard Thompson

Professor or Godzilla?: *To illustrate "everyone's worst fear of the politically-correct professor on the rampage," Richard Thompson of Gaithersburg, Maryland came up with this monstrous art. Thompson was paid $1,000 for first reproduction rights to the art. The cartoonist describes his marketing plan as "practically nonexistent. I've got enough repeat customers to make me fat and happy (or lazy). This particular job was the first I had done for this client, and I think they had seen my stuff in a newspaper, which seems sufficient PR in itself."*

Illustration: Buys approximately 2 humorous illustrations/issue for spots and articles. For first contact send cover letter, b&w tearsheets and promo pieces, resume and samples of offered work to Frederick A. Raborg, Jr., Editor. Looks for "uniqueness and effect on attention span." Reports back within 2 weeks. Samples are filed; returned with SASE. Buys first or one-time rights. Pays $15 minimum, b&w, page; $50 minimum, b&w, $100 minimum, color, cover. Pays on acceptance for cover; on publication for inside spots. *Inside Tips:* "We like wit in addition to humor; we like to know the illustrator has some knowledge of what we tend to use."

Writing: Buys approximately 2 humorous pieces/issue. Subject matter includes all types—including science fiction, Gothic romance and mainstream. Length: 1,000-2,500 words. To query be familiar with magazine; make sure article is appropriate; study writer's guidelines. Send SASE for copy. For first contact send cover letter and manuscript to Frederick A. Raborg, Jr., Editor. Reports back within 2 weeks. Samples are not filed; returned with SASE. Buys first rights. Pays $10-35 for 1,000-2,500 words. Offers 50% kill fee. *Inside Tips:* "Try out the material on responsive listeners or readers before submitting. Humor writing should sound humorous as well as read so, just as good dialogue must sound true. A good humor writer must think in universal terms. So much humor is regionally slanted and is lost on the majority of the readers. Be catholic in your approaches, more liberal than conservative."

AMERICAN ATHEIST, Box 140195, Austin TX 78714-0195. (512)458-1244. FAX: (512)467-9525. Estab. 1958. Monthly cause magazine. Circ. 30,000. Needs comic strips, humorous illustration, caricature and spot cartoons. Accepts previously published cartoons and humorous articles.

Gag Cartoons: Buys 2-5 gag cartoons/issue. Prefers gag cartoons on "the difficulties of being an atheist in a religious culture; what's wrong with religion." Doesn't want to see gag cartoons on "Noah's ark." Preferred format is single panel, b&w line art. Query with 5-10 rough drawings/batch to R. Murray-O'Hair, Editor. Reports back in 2 months only if interested. Returns materials if accompanied by SASE. Buys first rights. Pays $15, b&w. Pays on acceptance. *Inside Tips:* A gag cartoonist should "have an understanding of the atheist position."

Illustration: Buys approximately 10 humorous illustrations/year for articles and spots. For first contact send cover letter, b&w tearsheets, and "samples of work that apply to our special needs" to R. Murray-O'Hair, Editor. Reports back in 2 months only if interested. Samples are filed; returned with SASE. Buys first rights. Pays $25, b&w, page. Pays on acceptance.

Writing: Buys approximately 10 humorous pieces/year. Needs humorous nonfiction, fiction, anecdotes and "fillers." Humorous material must be "pertinent to atheism or state/church separation." Length: 1,000-3,000 words. To query be familiar with magazine; make sure article is appropriate; study writer's guidelines. For first contact send cover letter to R. Murray-O'Hair, Editor. Reports in 2 months. Samples are filed; returned with SASE. Buys first rights. Pays $15 for 1,000 words.

THE AMERICAN BAPTIST, Box 851, Valley Forge PA 19482-0851. (215)768-2000. FAX: (215)768-2275. Estab. 1803. Bimonthly consumer and company magazine. Circ. 65,000. Needs comic strips, humorous illustration and writing, cartoon narratives, caricature and spot cartoons. Accepts previously published cartoons and humorous articles. Prefers working with freelancers who have fax capabilities.

Gag Cartoons: Buys 6-8 gag cartoons/year. Prefers gag cartoons with religious themes. Preferred format is single panel, with gagline, color wash. Query with 8-10 rough drawings/batch to Ronald J. Arena, Managing Editor. Reports back in 2 weeks. Returns materials only if requested. Negotiates rights purchased. Pays up to $50, b&w, $75, color. Pays on acceptance. *Inside Tips:* A gag cartoonist should "meet deadlines, make me laugh, submit material suitable for a church-related magazine."

Illustration: Buys approximately 4-6 humorous illustrations/year for articles and spots. Works on assignment only. For first contact send cover letter and color promo pieces and tearsheets to Ronald J. Arena, Managing Editor. Looks for "refined illustrations that are humorous and appropriate to a church-related publication. Most church humor/cartoons are clichéd and not funny—give us something fresh and contemporary." Reports back in 2 weeks. Samples returned if requested. Negotiates rights purchased. Pays $150, b&w, $200, color, page; $300, b&w, $400, color, cover. Pays on acceptance.

AMERICAN FITNESS, Suite 310, 15250 Ventura Blvd., Sherman Oaks CA 91403. (818)905-0040. FAX: (818)990-5468. Estab. 1983. Bimonthly trade journal. Circ. 25,000. Needs humorous cartoons. Accepts previously published cartoons. Prefers working with freelancers who have fax capabilities.
Gag Cartoons: Doesn't want to see gag cartoons on "fat people." Preferred format is single panel. Query with rough drawings per batch to Rhonda Wilson, Managing Editor. Returns material. Buys first rights. Pays $35 for b&w cartoons. *Inside Tips:* "Be very funny and flexible."
Illustration: Buys approximately 12 humorous illustrations/issue for articles. When hiring a freelance humorous illustrator, considers whether artist uses humor effectively. For first contact send b&w tearsheets.

AMERICAN LEGION MAGAZINE, Box 1055, Indianapolis IN 46206. (317)635-8411. Needs gag cartoons.
Gag Cartoons: Buys 1-2 cartoons/issue. "Avoid slam cartoons or insult humor. We want American traditional, good-value cartoons." Preferred format is single panel. Query with finished drawings to Doug Donaldson, Editor.

*AMERICAN WOMAN, 1700 Broadway, 34th Fl., New York NY 10019. (212)541-7100. FAX: (212)246-0820. Estab. 1991. Bimonthly consumer magazine. Circ. 150,000. Needs gag cartoons and humorous illustration. Accepts previously published cartoons.
Gag Cartoons: Buys 1 cartoon/issue; 6 cartoons/year. Prefers gag cartoons on relationships, sex, diets, female entrepreneurial. Doesn't want to see gag cartoons on male bashing. Preferred format is b&w line art. Query with "as many rough drawings as you like" to Debi Turek, Assistant Editor. Reports back within 4-6 weeks. Returns material if accompanied by a SASE. Buys first time rights, reprint rights. Pays $100 minimum, b&w; $100 minimum, color. Pays on publication.
Illustration: Buys 3 humorous illustrations/year for articles. More apt to hire a humorous illustrator if he or she uses humor effectively. For first contact send client list, b&w tearsheets and samples to Debi Turek, Assistant Editor. Looks for "humor with a new angle—it has to make me laugh—or at least smile!" Reports back within 4-6 weeks. Buys first time rights, reprint rights. Pays $100, b&w; $100, color, page. *Tips:* "Be different—I'm sick of PMS cartoons!"

*ATLANTIC CITY MAGAZINE, P.O. Box 2100, Pleasantville NJ 08232. (609)272-7900. FAX: (609)272-7910. Estab. 1978. Monthly consumer magazine. Circ. 50,000. Needs humorous illustration.
Illustration: Buys 1-2 humorous illustrations/issue; 20 humorous illustrations/year. "Depends on our need." When hiring a freelance humorous illustrator, these abilities are considered: truly unique drawing style, conceptualizes well and has clever ideas—

The asterisk before a listing indicates that the listing is new in this edition. New markets are often more receptive to freelance submissions.

good use of metaphors and shows flexibility, broad potential in drawing style. For first contact send cover letter to Michael Lacy, Art Director. Looks for "Someone who is not afraid to be different." Reports back within 6 weeks. Samples are returned by SASE. Buys one-time rights. Pays $150, b&w; $250, color page; $400, color cover. Pays on publication. "Be capable of solving our problems. We want to hear your concept; don't just follow our direction."

Writing: Needs local subjects only. Subject matter includes local subjects only. To query, familiarize yourself with our magazine; make sure article is appropriate; study writer's guidelines. Send $4 and SASE for copy. For first contact send cover letter, query, outline of proposed story, published tearsheets and writing sample to Ken Weatherford, Editor. Samples not filed are returned with SASE. Buys one-time rights. Pays $150 minimum. Offers 20% kill fee. *Inside Tips:* "Humor must be local; it must be interesting and funny to our readers, not just to you. Avoid 'I remember growing up at the shore' pieces."

*AUTO RACING DIGEST, 990 Grove St., Evanston IL 60201. (708)491-6440. Estab. 1972. Monthly consumer magazine. Circ. 40,000-200,000. Needs gag cartoons. Accepts previously published cartoons.

Gag Cartoons: Buys 1-2 gag cartoons/issue; 60 gag cartoons/year. Prefers gag cartoons on sports. Doesn't want to see gag cartoons on golf, tennis or jogging. Preferred format is b&w line art with gagline. Send to Cartoon Editor. Reports back in 1 month. Returns material if accompanied by a SASE. Buys first time rights. Pays $20, b&w. Pays on publication.

*AUTOMUNDO MAGAZINE, 525 NW 27 Ave. #204, Miami FL 33135. (305)541-4198. FAX: (305)541-5138. Estab. 1982. Monthly consumer magazine. Circ. 54,000. Needs comic strips and spot cartoons. Accepts previously published cartoons and humorous articles.

Gag Cartoons: Prefers gag cartoons on cars, automobiles and motorcycles. Preferred format is single panel, without gagline, b&w line art. Send to Jorge Koechlin, Vice President. Returns material only if requested and if accompanied by a SASE. Buys all rights. Pays $5, b&w. Pays on publication.

Illustration: Buys 1 humorous illustration/issue for spots. When hiring a freelance humorous illustrator, these abilities are considered: clean, graphically-pleasing drawing style, not too much exaggeration or distortion and is businesslike, meets deadlines and is responsive to my needs. For first contact send cover letter, b&w tearsheets and b&w promo piece. *Inside Tips:* "We are a Spanish language automobile publication."

BALLOON LIFE, 2145 Dale Ave., Sacramento CA 95815. (916)922-9648. Estab. 1985. Monthly consumer magazine. Circ. 4,500. Needs humorous illustration and writing, and caricature. Accepts previously published cartoons and humorous articles.

Illustration: Buys approximately 3 humorous illustrations/year for articles. Works on assignment only. For first contact send cover letter and b&w tearsheets to Glen Moyer, Editor. Looks for "clean graphic style, clever captions—not interested in the obvious, technically correct illustrations." Reports back only if interested. Samples are filed or are returned by SASE. Buys one-time rights. Pays $25, b&w and color, page; $50, color, cover. Pays on publication. *Inside Tips:* "Know our subject 1) hot air balloons and 2) gas balloons and their differences, i.e.—sand bags hanging off a hot air balloon are erroneous. Despite humorous content, cartoons should be technically correct. Don't mix hot air and gas!"

Writing: Buys approximately 6 humorous pieces/year. Needs humorous nonfiction, "slice-of-life," fiction and anecdotes, "fillers." Subject matter includes "humorous first-time flights, humorous happenings at balloon events or during a chase." Length: 800-1,600 words. To query study writer's guidelines first. Send $1.65 and SASE for copy.

For first contact send query and manuscript to Glen Moyer, Editor. Reports back within 2 weeks only if interested. Samples are filed or are returned with SASE. Buys one-time rights. Pays $50 for 800-1,600 words. Offers 50-100% kill fee. *Inside Tips:* "Balloonists have great senses of humor—just look at what they fly! Spend some time with them and you'll find lots of material to work with."

WE HAVE SEEN THE FUTURE &ND IT IS FUNNY

© Bob Staake

A Cover That Screams: *St. Louis, Missouri-based* Snicker *magazine recently commissioned Apartment 3-D (an art studio, not a studio apartment) to design the cover of its special edition on "Conspiracy Theories." While* Snicker *is by no means rolling in cash, they are typical of humor magazines or "fanzines" that pay in copies of their publication. And because* Snicker *is printed in an oversized newspaper tabloid format, the resulting tearsheets can be pretty impressive.*

BARTENDER, Box 158, Liberty Corner NJ 07938. (201)766-6006. FAX: (201)766-6607. Estab. 1979. Bimonthly trade journal. Circ. 140,000. Needs comic strips, humorous illustration and writing, cartoon narratives, caricature and gag cartoons. Accepts previously published cartoons and humorous articles. Prefers working with freelancers who have fax capabilities.
Gag Cartoons: Buys 3 gag cartoons/issue.

*BASKETBALL DIGEST, 990 Grove St., Evanston IL 60201. (708)491-6440. Estab. 1972. Monthly consumer magazine. Circ. 40,000-200,000. Needs gag cartoons. Accepts previously published cartoons.
Gag Cartoons: Buys 1-2 gag cartoons/issue; 16 gag cartoons/year. Prefers gag cartoons on sports. Doesn't want to see gag cartoons on golf, tennis or jogging. Preferred format is b&w line art with gagline. Send to Cartoon Editor. Reports back in 1 month. Returns material if accompanied by a SASE. Buys first time rights and reprint rights. Pays $20, b&w. Pays on publication.

*BASSIN', 15115 S. 76th E. Ave. Bixby OK 74008. (918)366-4441. FAX: (918)366-4439. Estab. 1972. Consumer magazine published 8 times/year. Circ. 220,000. Needs spot cartoons and humorous writing.
Gag Cartoons: Buys 1+ gag cartoons/issue; 10 gag cartoons/year. Prefers gag cartoons on crappie and bass fishing subjects (no flyfishing please). Doesn't want to see gag cartoons on flyfishing. Preferred format is single panel and b&w line art with gagline. Query with 3-6 rough drawings per batch to Gordon Sprouse, Managing Editor. Reports back within 3 weeks if interested. Returns material. Buys first time rights. Pays $50, b&w. "Be aware of the latest trends in the fishing industry."

Illustration: Buys 8 humorous illustrations/year for articles. Works on assignment only. When hiring a freelance humorous illustrator, these abilities are considered: conceptualizes well and has clever ideas—good use of metaphors, clean graphically-pleasing drawing style, not too much exaggeration or distortion. For first contact send cover letter and b&w tearsheets to Gordon Sprouse, Managing Editor.
Writing: Buys approximately 1 humorous piece/issue; 8 humorous pieces/year. Needs humorous nonfiction, interviews and slice-of-life. Subject matter includes fishing, boating, camping, etc. Length: 1,000 words. To query, familiarize yourself with our magazine; make sure article is appropriate for us; study writer's guidelines. For first contact send cover letter, query and writing sample to Gordon Sprouse, Managing Editor. Reports back within 3 weeks. Samples are returned only if requested. Buys first time rights. Pays $275-350. Offers 33% kill fee.

BETTER HOMES & GARDENS, 1716 Locust St., Des Moines IA 50336 (515)284-3000. FAX: (515)284-3684. Needs comic strips, humorous illustration, caricatures and spot cartoons.
Cartoons: Buys 1 spot cartoon/issue. Prefers spot cartoons appropriate for feature articles. All cartoon formats acceptable. Query with 5-10 rough drawings/batch to Paul Krantz, Feature Editor. Buys all rights. Pays on publication.
Illustration: Buys 3-5 humorous illustrations for inside spots. For first contact send b&w and color tearsheets or b&w or color promo piece to Paul Krantz, Feature Editor. Buys all rights. Payment varies.
Writing: Buys approximately 3-5 humorous pieces/issue. Needs humorous nonfiction and interviews. Subject matter includes "home, auto, family, travel—all areas." For first contact send cover letter and query to Paul Krantz, Feature Editor. Buys all rights.

*BICYCLE GUIDE, 545 Boylston St., 12th Fl., Boston MA 02116. (617)236-1885. FAX: (617)267-1849. Estab. 1984. Consumer magazine published 9 times/year. Circ. 165,000. Needs comic strips, cartoon narratives, humorous illustration and spot cartoons. Accepts previously published cartoons.
Gag Cartoons: Preferred format is single panel without gagline, double panel with gagline, multi-panel with balloons and b&w line art. Please send all gag cartoon submissions to Christopher Koch, Editor. Reports back within 2 weeks. Returns material if accompanied by a SASE. Buys one-time rights. Pays $200, b&w, $300, color. Pays on publication. *Inside Tips:* "Know cycling."
Illustration: Buys 1-2 humorous illustrations/issue for articles and spots. When hiring a freelance humorous illustrator, these abilities are considered: conceptualizes well and has clever ideas—good use of metaphors, know cycling. For first contact send cover letter, resume, client list and b&w tearsheets to Christopher Koch, Editor. Reports back within 2 weeks. Samples are filed. Buys one-time rights. Pays $800, b&w, $800, cover. Pays on publication.

BIRD TALK, Box 6050, Mission Viejo CA 92690. (714)855-8822. FAX: (714)855-3045. Estab. 1983. Monthly consumer magazine. Circ. 175,000. Needs gag cartoons and humorous writing.
Gag Cartoons: Buys 4-7 gag cartoons/issue. Prefers gag cartoons on pet birds. Doesn't want to see gag cartoons on "Polly want a cracker." Preferred format is single panel with/without gagline, b&w line art. Query with 3-10 good line drawings/batch to Kathleen Etchepare, Art Editor. Reports back within 1 month. Returns material if accompanied by a SASE. Buys one-time rights. Pays $35 minimum, b&w. Pays on publication. *Inside Tips:* "Understand the personalities of pet birds."
Writing: Buys approximately 1 humorous piece/issue. Needs humorous nonfiction, "slice-of-life" and anecdotes. Subject matter includes "personal experiences detailing humorous and unusual things pet birds do." Length: 500-2,500 words. To query be familiar

with magazine; make sure article is appropriate; and study writer's guidelines. Send $3.50 and SASE for copy. For first contact send cover letter, manuscript and query to Julie Rach, Managing Editor. Reports back within 1 month. Samples are not filed and are returned with SASE. Buys one-time rights. Pays 5-15¢/word. *Inside Tips:* "Please make the humor in the actions of the bird, not in exaggeration. No pseudo-Erma Bombeck pieces."

BIRD WATCHER'S DIGEST, P.O. Box 110, Marietta OH 45750. (614)373-5285. FAX: (614)373-8443. Estab. 1978. Bimonthly consumer magazine. Circ. 75,000. Needs gag cartoons. Accepts previously published cartoons.
Gag Cartoons: Buys 1-3 gag cartoons/issue. Wants gag cartoons *only* on wild birds/wild bird watching. Preferred format is single panel, b&w line art. Query with 2-7 rough drawings/batch to Mary Bowers, Editor. Reports back in 6-8 weeks. Returns material if accompanied by SASE. Buys one-time rights. Pays $15, b&w. Pays on publication.

BOSTONIA, 10 Lenox St., Brookline MA 02146. (617)353-9711. Estab. 1900. Quarterly consumer magazine. Circ. 140,000. Needs humorous illustration and writing. Prefers working with freelancers who have fax capabilities.
Gag Cartoons: Send copies—do not send originals—will request originals if accepted. Buys first rights. Pays minimum $150, b&w, $250, color.
Illustration: Buys approximately 6 humorous illustrations/issue for covers, articles and spots. Works on assignment only. For first contact send cover letter, b&w or color tearsheets, b&w or color promo pieces and slides to Douglas Parker, Art Director. Looks for "originality and communication skills." Reports back if interested. Samples are filed. Buys first rights. Pays minimum $300, b&w, $500, color, page. Pays on publication. *Inside Tips:* "Illustration should be an aid to reading comprehension."
Writing: Buys approximately 1-2 humorous pieces/issue. Needs humorous nonfiction, fiction and "slice-of-life." Length: 500-1,000 words. To query be familiar with magazine. For first contact send cover letter and manuscript to Janice Friedman, Managing Editor. Reports back within 6 months if interested. Samples are filed or returned with SASE. Buys first rights. Pays $200-400 for 500-1,000 words. Offers 25% kill fee.

BOY'S LIFE, 1325 W. Walnut Hill Lane, Irving TX 75015-2079. (214)580-2373. FAX: (214)580-2079. Needs comic strips, gag and humorous illustration and writing and spot cartoons.
Gag Cartoons: Buys 1-5 cartoons/issue. Prefers gag cartoons on "kids, pets, school, parent relationship." Preferred format is single or double panel, with or without gagline or balloons, b&w line art or wash. Send all gag cartoon submissions to Joe Connally, Director of Design. Buys all rights. Payment varies. Pays on acceptance.
Illustration: Buys 1-5 humorous illustrations/issue for spots, "filler mostly." For first contact send cover letter and b&w tearsheets or appropriate samples to Joe Connolly, Director of Design. Buys all rights. Payment varies.
Writing: Buys 1-2 pieces a year. Needs humorous nonfiction, fiction and anecdotes, "fillers." Subject matter includes "appeals to boys ages 8-13. Length: 350-500 words. For first contact send cover letter and samples to Jeff Csatari, Nonfiction Special Editor. Kathy DaGroomes, Fiction Editor. Buys all rights. Pays $750 and up for a fiction piece of 500-1,200 words.

BUREAU OF BUSINESS PRACTICE, 24 Rope Ferry Rd., Waterford CT 06386. (800)243-0876. FAX: (203)434-3078. Monthly and bimonthly newsletters. "Has over 30 publications that deal with training and education for the work force. Our informational and educational products are targeted to a broad spectrum of professional audiences—from the production floor to the front office, from the line employee to the manager."

Cartoons & Illustrations: Needs spot cartoons on business, safety and health. Considers whether artist follows cartoon guidelines. For first contact send cover letter for cartoonist packet and guidelines. For editorial cartoons contact Florence Kaplan, Administrative Assistant. Reports back within months. Returns materials if accompanied by SASE. Buys all rights. Pays for spot cartoons, $15 minimum. *Inside Tips:* "Follow guidelines. Stick to subject area of particular newsletter. Cartoons should be nonsexist and nonoffensive."

THE CALIFORNIA HIGHWAY PATROLMAN, 2030 V St., Sacramento CA 95818. (916)452-6751. Estab. 1937. Monthly consumer magazine. Circ. 19,000. Needs humorous writing and spot cartoons. Accepts previously published cartoons, "if we are told when and where they were printed."
Gag Cartoons: Buys 5-6 gag cartoons/issue. Gag cartoons must be California Highway Patrol-related. Preferred format is single panel, b&w line art, with gagline or balloons. Query with finished cartoons to Carol Perri, Editor. Returns materials if accompanied by SASE. Buys one-time rights. Pays $15, b&w. Pays on publication. *Inside Tips:* "Keep our audience in mind."
Writing: Buys approximately 6-10 humorous pieces/year. Needs humorous nonfiction and "slice-of-life." Length: under 1,000 words. Be familiar with magazine; make sure article is appropriate and CHP related; study writer's guidelines. Send manuscript to Carol Perri, Editor. Reports back in 3-6 months. Samples are not filed; returned with SASE. Buys one-time rights. Pays 2½¢/word. *Inside Tips:* "Send complete manuscript. Can't tell humorous writing quality from a query."

CALIFORNIA JOURNAL, 1714 Capitol Ave., Sacramento CA 95814. (916)444-2840. Estab. 1980. Monthly consumer magazine. Circ. 18,000. Needs humorous illustration and caricatures.
Illustration: Buys approximately 4 humorous illustrations/issue for articles. Works on assignment only. For first contact send cover letter, resume, b&w or color tearsheets and b&w or color promo piece to Richard Zeiger, Editor. "In reviewing humorous illustrations we look for illustrations that have political content." Samples are filed. Buys all rights. Pays $100 minimum, b&w, page; $300, color, cover. Pays on publication.

CAMPUS LIFE, 465 Gundersen Dr., Carol Stream IL 60188. (708)260-6200. FAX: (708)260-0114. Estab. 1942. Monthly consumer magazine (published 10 times/year, combined issues—July-Aug., May-June). Circ. 130,000. Needs humorous writing, gag and spot cartoons. Accepts previously published humorous articles.
Gag Cartoons: Buys 5-10 gag cartoons/issue. Prefers gag cartoons on "teen themes that laugh with teens—not at them." Doesn't want to see gag cartoons on "silly puns or worn clichés. For us, the 'dream' gag cartoon would be funny, bizarre, something kids will laugh at and hang up in their lockers." Preferred format is single panel, b&w line art. Submit 5-10 rough drawings/batch to Chris Lutes, Cartoon Editor. Reports back in 5-6 weeks. Returns materials if accompanied by SASE. Buys first rights. Pays $50, b&w. Pays on acceptance. *Inside Tips:* A gag cartoonist should "understand current youth contemporary style; avoid sounding like a parent. Don't send cartoons that look like they were drawn in the 50s."
Illustration: Buys approximately 3 humorous illustrations/issue for articles, spots and departments. Works on assignment only. For first contact send b&w and color tearsheets and promo pieces to Doug Johnson, Art Director. *Inside Tips:* "I enjoy trying out new artists and tend to look for more original styles."
Writing: Buys approximately 3-5 humorous pieces/year. Needs humorous nonfiction, teen "slice-of-life," fiction, cartoon stories—*Mad* style—on anything that covers the high-school experience. Length: 500-1,000 words. To query be familiar with magazine; make sure article is appropriate; study our "Guidelines for Writing Campus Life Hu-

© Beata Szpura

"The Lawyers Are Falling," Cried Chicken Little: *Beata Szpura of Woodside, New York uses acrylic paint and watercolor crayons to achieve her "loose, free, humorous style." While this piece was originally created by Szpura as self-promotional art, it was later used in a trade publication. The magazine paid Szpura $500 for reprint rights to the illustration.*

mor." Send $2 and SASE for copy of the magazine. For first contact send writing sample, query, outline of proposed story and published tearsheets to Chris Lutes. Reports back in 60 days. Include SASE with query. Buys first rights. Pays $100-150. *Inside Tips:* "Must be carefully targeted to high-school students, should attempt to reflect current humor trends. For style, think the "clean side" of David Letterman, also a Dave Barry style for high school students would work."

CAPITOL COMEDY, 5800 Inman Park Circle #140, Rockville MD 20852. Estab. 1989. Newsletter of "quotable quips with political emphasis on the national and regional level." Circ. 750/month.
Cartoons & Illustrations: Needs single panels and spot cartoons of national appeal and Washington DC subjects. Considers whether artist can turn around art on short deadline, has ability to read a manuscript and come up with a strong visual idea, uses humor effectively. For first contact send cover letter, b&w tearsheets and promo piece to Elaine Bole. Returns materials if accompanied by SASE. All rights purchased. Pays for all cartoons/humorous illustrations, $10-25.
Writing: "We seek in-the-news humor, topical timely humor and humor a professional speaker could use." Accepts humorous material that has a regional, national or international slant. Also sports, business and current events. Length: one-liners. For first contact send writing sample. Unsolicited material is returned with SASE. Buys all rights. Pays $2 per joke.

A month before the April 7 primary here, Jerry Brown's New York campaign organization is "an elaborate phone tree." To judge from a few of those perched at the top, Brown is indeed drawing from the disenchanted and the "apolitical."

JERRY BROWN

© Bill Plympton

Earth to Jerry: *Once an editorial cartoonist, displaced Oregonian now New Yorker Bill Plympton spends most of his time these days creating cultish animated shorts. Nevertheless, he does find the time to bang out occasional doodles like this one. He was paid $10 (that's no typo) for first time reproduction rights to the drawing.*

CARTOON MARKETS, Suite 1, 90 W. Winnipeg Ave., St. Paul MN 55117-5428. Estab. 1963. Monthly newsletter, offset, 22 pp. Circ. 600. Needs gag cartoons.
Gag Cartoons: Buys 1 gag cartoon/issue. Prefers gag cartoons on "the humor of creating humor." Doesn't want to see gag cartoons "unrelated to our theme. For us the 'dream' gag cartoon would be muse to frowning cartoonist at art table: 'You can't get the right slant because your table is at the wrong angle.' " Preferred format is single panel, b&w line art with gagline. Query with 1-15 rough drawings/batch to Loanne Engen, Art Director. Reports back within 1 month. Returns materials if accompanied by SASE. Buys first rights. Pays $5 minimum, b&w. Pays on acceptance. *Inside Tips:* "Read and understand the needs of our publication, which goes to professional cartoon-

ists and gagwriters. Subscription rates: $40/year, $4/sample copy."

CARTOON WORLD, Box 30367, Lincoln NE 68503. (402)435-3191. Estab. 1936. Monthly newsletter. Circ. 300. Needs only articles on cartooning and gagwriting. *Inside Tips:* This publication is only published to find new markets for cartoonists and has articles on "How to Cartoon," and "How to Write Gag Ideas" only. For sample send $5.

THE CARTOONIST MAGAZINE, (formerly Canadian Cartoonist Magazine), Box 725, New Westminster, British Columbia V3L-4Z3 Canada. (604)524-5585. P.O. Box 31122, Seattle WA 98103. Estab. 1989. Quarterly trade journal. Circ. 500. Needs profiles on cartoonists and "how to" cartoon information. Accepts previously published humorous articles.
Writing: Buys approximately 4 humorous pieces/issue. Needs humorous interviews. Subject matter includes profiles, "how to," and organizational updates. Length: 500-1,000 words. To query be familiar with magazine, make sure article is appropriate and study writer's guidelines. Send $5.00 and SASE for copy. For first contact send cover letter and outline of proposed story to Charles B. Walker, Editor. Reports back within 2 months. Samples are returned with SASE. Buys first rights. Pays $50 for 500-1,000 words. *Inside Tips:* "I need articles about American and Canadian cartoonists and cartooning in general."

CASINO DIGEST, Suite 123, 1901-G Ashwood Ct., Greensboro NC 27408. (919)375-6358. Estab. 1984. Monthly consumer tabloid newsletter. Circ. 40,000. Needs humorous illustration, cartoon narratives, caricature, gag, spot and political/editorial cartoons. Accepts previously published cartoons and humorous articles.
Gag Cartoons: Buys 1 gag cartoon/issue. Prefers gag cartoons on "casino gambling, political (for news purposes) plus editorial." Doesn't want to see "gag cartoons on gambling games. For us the 'dream' gag cartoon would be one that reflects the consumer's, and the casino's, feelings toward given situations . . . from both in and out of the casino." Preferred formats are single or double multi-panel, with or without gagline or balloons, b&w line art or wash. Query with 2-4 rough drawings/batch to Joe Lawless, Publisher/Editor. Reports back within 1 month. Returns materials if accompanied by SASE. Negotiates rights purchased. Pays minimum $50, b&w; on publication. *Inside Tips:* "Have a keen sense of the casino gambling world, not a stereotype, and be aware of what motivates casino patrons both in thought and in action. Should also be well-informed on the viewpoints of the casino operators and express them in articulate form both in drawing and captions."
Illustration: Buys approximately 1 humorous illustration/issue for articles, spots and editorials. Works on assignment only. One of the things considers when hiring a freelance humorous illustrator is ability to draw serious editorial cartoons for news. For first contact send cover letter, b&w tearsheets and promo piece, if available, client list and examples of serious and humorous cartoons to Joe Lawless, Publisher/Editor. Looks for "sophistication of the drawing, how well the idea is presented and communicated." Reports back within 1 month. Samples are filed or returned by SASE. Negotiates rights purchased. Pays $50 minimum, b&w, page. *Inside Tips:* "Realistic people and situations are the key. A person standing in front of a slot machine or at a gambling table is old hat . . . unless it makes a unique point."
Writing: Buys approximately 1 humorous piece/issue. Needs humorous nonfiction, fiction, interviews, "slice-of-life," editorial and/or political. Subject matter must be in direct relation to casino gambling in some way; other forms of gambling do not apply. Length: 500-1,000 words. To query be familiar with magazine and make sure article is appropriate. For first contact send cover letter, outline of proposed story and published tearsheets to Joe Lawless, Publisher/Editor. Absolutely no phone calls. Reports back

within 1 month. Samples are filed or returned with SASE. Negotiates rights purchased. Pays 10¢/word for 500-1,000 words. Offers 50% kill fee. *Inside Tips:* "The more you know about casino gambling (not stereotype) from both the patrons' and casino operators' viewpoints, the more successful you will be. Cartoons should have one of two characteristics: (1) drawn and presented in the fashion of the *Saturday Evening Post* and *New Yorker* or (2) to suit the serious nature of the editorial sections of any major daily newspaper. *Example of the latter:* a patron is sitting at a non-smoking blackjack table in a casino. He shows a *large bankroll* while lighting a cigarette. The Pit Boss says 'You can't play here. The smoking blackjack tables are across the room.' In the second panel the patron picks up his bankroll and says 'No thank you, I'll go across the street.' "

*CASINO PLAYER, 2524 Arctic Ave., Atlantic City NJ 08401. (609)344-9000. FAX: (609)345-3469. Estab. 1985. Monthly consumer magazine. Circ. 150,000. Needs gag cartoons, caricatures and spot cartoons. Prefers working with freelancers who have fax capabilities.
Gag Cartoons: Buys 4 cag cartoons/year. Prefers gag cartoons on gambling. Preferred format is single panel with gagline.
Illustration: Send humorous illustration material to Roger Gros, Editor. Looks for "Clean drawing, good gag." Reports only if interested. Samples not filed are returned by SASE if requested. Buys all rights. Pays $25, b&w page; $100, color page; $200, color cover.

CAT FANCY, Box 6050, Mission Viejo CA 92690. (714)855-8822. Estab. 1965. Monthly consumer magazine. Circ. 332,000. Needs humorous illustration and writing, gag and spot cartoons.
Gag Cartoons: Buys 12-15 gag cartoons/year on cats. Doesn't want to see gag cartoons that "are hostile about or negative toward cats." Preferred format is single panel, with or without gagline, b&w line art. Send submissions to K.E. Segnar, Editor. Returns materials if accompanied by SASE. Buys first rights. Pays $35, b&w. Pays on publication. *Inside Tips:* "Understand the audience. This means that the cartoonist should love cats as much as we do."
Illustration: Buys 5-7 humorous illustrations/year for articles. Works on assignment only. When hiring a freelance humorous illustrator, these abilities are considered: a clean, graphically-pleasing drawing style; effective use of humor; businesslike attitude — meets deadlines and is responsive to editor's needs and direction. For first contact send cover letter, resume and photocopied samples that can be kept on file to K.E. Segnar, Editor. Looks for "someone who can draw both cats and people effectively." Reports back only if interested. Samples are filed or returned by SASE. Buys first rights. Usually pays $50-100, sometimes more for b&w, page. Pays on publication. *Inside Tips:* "We are not interested in satire. We are looking for gentle, upbeat humorous styles."
Writing: Buys approximately 2-4 humorous pieces/year and would like to buy more. Needs humorous nonfiction, "slice-of-life," anecdotes, fiction and "fillers." Subject matter includes "cat care or life with cats." Length: 500-2,500 words. To query be familiar with magazine; make sure article is appropriate; study writer's guidelines. Send SASE for copy. For first contact send cover letter, manuscript (if story is shorter than 1,000 words) and query to K.E. Segnar, Editor. Reports back in 6 weeks. Samples are not filed; returned with SASE. Buys first rights. Pays according to quality of the writing, usually $50-250 for 500-2,500 words. *Inside Tips:* "We look for humorous pieces that reflect a love for and appreciation of cats. The first contact, and all subsequent contacts, should be professional in every way. This includes the cover letter (typed and with no misspellings or typos), clean samples (pen-and-ink, no pencil) or a manuscript that adheres to the requirements in our writer's guidelines, even an SASE with your name and address neatly written or typed in the appropriate space. We look at your entire submission as a package. Don't shortchange yourself."

CATHOLIC DIGEST, Box 64090, St. Paul MN 55164. (612)647-5298. Estab. 1936. Monthly consumer magazine. Circ. 620,000. Needs humorous writing. Accepts previously published humorous articles.
Writing: Buys approximately 20 humorous pieces/issue. Needs humorous nonfiction, "slice-of-life" and anecdotes, "fillers." Subject matter includes religion, family, science, health, human relationships, nostalgia and good works. Length: 1-liners to 500 words for fillers, 1,000 to 3,000 words on articles. To query be familiar with magazine and make sure article is appropriate. For first contact send manuscript to Susan Schaefer, Filler Editor. Reports back only if interested. Samples are not filed and are returned with SASE. Buys one-time rights. Pays $4-50 for 1-line to 500 word filler. "Our rates vary for articles: usually $100 for reprints and $200 for originals."

CHESSLIFE, 186 Route 9W, Dept. HC, New Wendsor NY 12553. (914)562-8350. FAX: (914)561-1869. Estab. 1962. Monthly consumer magazine. Circ. 60,000. Needs caricatures, gag cartoons and spot cartoons.
Gag Cartoons: Buys 2 gag cartoons/issue. Prefers gag cartoons on chess and chess players. Doesn't want to see cartoons on how weird chess players are. Preferred gag cartoon formats are single panel, with/without gagline and b&w line art. Send submissions to Jami Anson, Art Director. Reports back if interested. Returns material if accompanied by a SASE. Buys first time rights. Pays $25 minimum for b&w. Pays on publication. *Inside Tips:* "Understand chess."
Illustration: Buys approximately 1 humorous illustration/year for articles.
Writing: Buys approximately 1 humorous piece/year. Needs humorous nonfiction. Central subject matter must be chess. Length: 250 words. To query be familiar with magazine, make sure article is appropriate and study writer's guidelines. For first contact send cover letter, query and manuscript to Glenn Petersen, Editor. Reports back within 3 months. Samples are returned only if requested. Buys first time rights. Pays $10-100 for 100-750 words. Offers 50% kill fee.

*CHILDSPLAY, 401 Dickenson St., Springfield MA 01108. (413)567-1631. FAX: (413)567-5805. Estab. 1984. Bimonthly consumer magazine. Circ. 5,000. Needs spot cartoons. Accepts previously published cartoons and humorous articles.
Gag Cartoons: Prefers gag cartoons on general parenting. Preferred format is single panel with gagline, b&w line art. Query with 3-4 rough drawings per batch to Barbara Cohen, Publisher. Reports only if interested. Does not return material. Buys one-time rights. Pays $25, b&w. Pays on publication.
Illustration: Buys humorous illustrations for spots. More apt to hire a humorous illustrator is he has a clean, graphically-pleasing drawing style; uses humor effectively; can "fun up" an otherwise "flat" manuscript; is businesslike, meets deadlines and is responsive to my needs. For first contact send cover letter, resume, client list and b&w tearsheets to Barbara M. Cohen, Publisher. Looks for "succintness." Reports only if interested. Samples are filed; not returned. Buys one-time rights. Pays $25, b&w. "Parenting is a skill not taught in school. Parents always make mistakes. The idea is to make parents fee OK when poor skills were used in a judgment call."
Writing: Buys approximately 3 humorous pieces/issue; 18 humorous pieces/year. Length: 500-750 words. To query we advise that you familiarize yourself with our magazine; that your article be appropriate for us. For first contact send cover letter, published tearsheets, writing sample, "whatever is deemed worthwhile" to Barbara Cohen, Publisher. Reports only if interested. Samples are filed; not returned. Buys one-time rights. Pays $25 total.

THE CHRONICLE OF THE HORSE, Box 46, Middleburg VA 22117. (703)687-6341. FAX: (703)687-3937. Estab. 1937. Weekly equestrian consumer magazine. Circ. 24,000. Needs humorous writing and spot cartoons.

© Jeff Shelly

Confused Ref: *New York City-based humorous illustrator Jeff Shelly created this nifty illustration for a children's magazine. Shelly works in goauche and describes his style as "animated, fun and bright."*

Gag Cartoons: Buys 1-3 gag cartoons/issue. Prefers gag cartoons on horses or English horse sports. Doesn't want to see gag cartoons on cowboys. The "dream" gag cartoon would be "foxhunting or dressage or combined training." Preferred format is single panel. Query with 1-20 rough drawings/batch to Cynthia Foley, Assistant Editor. Reports back within 2 weeks. Returns material unpublished. Buys first rights. Pays $20, b&w. Pays on publication.

Writing: Buys approximately 50 humorous pieces/year. Needs humorous nonfiction, "slice-of-life" and anecdotes, "fillers." Subject matter includes horses and horse people. Length: 300-1,200 words. To query, be familiar with magazine. Make sure that article is appropriate and study writer's guidelines. Send $1.50 and SASE for copy. For first contact send cover letter, query, outline of proposed story and published tearsheets (if available) to Cynthia Foley. Reports back within 1 month. Samples are returned. Buys first rights. Pays $25-200, article. *Inside Tips:* "Know horses and horse people. You must be involved in the sport to understand these people. We love good humor and are very picky."

CLEANING BUSINESS, 1512 Western Ave., Box 1273, Seattle WA 98111. (206)622-4241. FAX: (206)622-4221. Estab. 1982. Quarterly digest. Circ. 5,000+. Needs comic strips, cartoon narratives, gag and spot cartoons, humorous illustration and writing.

Gag Cartoons: Buys 2-3 gag cartoons/issue. Prefers gag cartoons on "cleaning and self-employment only—janitorial, maids, house cleaners, window washers, carpetcleaners. The 'dream' gag cartoon would be something funny with educational, social, moral value for janitors or self-employed cleaning contractors." Preferred formats are single, double or multi-panel with or without gagline or balloons, b&w line art or b&w or color wash. Query with 2-5 rough drawings/batch to Wm. R. Griffin, Publisher or Gerri LaMarche, Editor. Reports back within 6-12 weeks. Returns materials if accompanied by SASE. Buys all rights. Pays $3-20, b&w, $3-30, color. Pays on publication. *Inside Tips:* "Deal specifically with our subject matter. Don't depict janitors as dumb."

Illustration: Buys approximately 2-3 humorous illustrations/issue for articles and spots. When hiring a freelance humorous illustrator, these abilities are considered: good conceptualization and clever ideas—good use of metaphors; bold, powerful, attention-getting drawing style; effective use of humor. For first contact send cover letter and b&w tearsheets to Gerri LaMarche, Editor. Looks for "subject of cleaning and self-employment." Reports back within 6-12 weeks. Samples are filed or are returned by SASE. Buys all rights. Pays $5-20, b&w, $50, color, page; $100, b&w, $100, color, cover.

Writing: Buys approximately 1 humorous piece/issue. Needs humorous nonfiction, interviews, "slice-of-life," fiction, anecdotes, "fillers" and cartoon stories. Length: 1-3 pages. To query be familiar with magazine; make sure article is appropriate; study writer's guidelines. Send $3 and SASE for copy. For first contact send cover letter, query and outline of proposed story to Gerri LaMarche, Editor. Reports back with 6-12 weeks. Samples are filed or are returned with SASE. Buys all rights. Pays $5-75 for ¼-3 pages. *Inside Tips:* "Review our publication, it has a very specific target audience."

THE CLERGY JOURNAL, Box 162527, Austin TX 78716. (512)327-8501. Estab. 1924. Monthly trade journal. Circ. 16,000. Needs gag and spot cartoons.

Gag Cartoons: Buys 5 gag cartoons/issue. Prefers gag cartoons on religion. The "dream" gag cartoon would be "about preaching." Preferred format is single panel with gagline, b&w line art. Query with 5-10 rough drawings/batch to Manfred Holck Jr., Editor. Reports back in 2 weeks. Returns material if accompanied by SASE. Buys first rights. Pays $10, b&w. Pays on acceptance. *Inside Tips:* "Remember that ministers are our primary audience."

*COLLEGIATE INSIDER, 20695 S. Western Ave., #140, Torrance CA 90501. (310)533-8722. FAX: (310)533-8748. Estab. 1983. Consumer magazine published 10 times/year. Circ. 1.1 million. Needs gag cartoons, humorous illustration and writing.
Gag Cartoons: Buys 5-12 cartoons/year. Prefers gag cartoons on anything pertaining to the college student. Preferred format is single panel with gagline or with balloons, b&w line art. Query with 2-8 rough drawings/batch to Elizabeth Loprest, Editor-in-Chief. Reports back within 1 month. Returns material if accompanied by a SASE. Buys first time rights. Pays $10, b&w; $10, color. Pays on publication.
Illustration: Buys approximately 1-10 humorous illustrations/year for articles. Works on assignment only. More apt to hire a humorous illustrator if he or she conceptualizes well and has clever ideas—good use of metaphors; has a clean, graphically-pleasing drawing style; uses humor effectively; can "fun up" an otherwise "flat" manuscript; is businesslike, meets deadlines and is responsive to my needs. For first contact send cover letter, b&w and color tearsheets to Elizabeth Loprest, Editor-in-Chief. Looks for quality. Reports back within 1 month. Samples are filed. Samples not filed are returned by SASE. Buys first time rights. Pays $10, b&w; $10, color, page. Pays on publication. *Inside Tips:* "Be able to conceptualize article idea."
Writing: Buys approximately 1-2 humorous pieces/issue. Needs humorous nonfiction, interviews and "slice-of-life." Subject matter includes "campus life—1st person narrative about life on campus/as a student; relationships—1st person narrative about love, lust, jealousy, sex and college students." Length: 550-900 words. To query be familiar with magazine; make sure article is appropriate; study writer's guidelines. Send 95¢ and SASE for copy. For first contact send cover letter, manuscript to Elizabeth Loprest, Editor-in-Chief. Reports back within 1 month. Samples are filed. Samples not filed are returned with SASE. Buys first time rights. Pays 1¢/word or $9 maximum for a piece of 550-900 words. *Inside Tips:* "Our readership is solely college students, primarily female ages 18-26."

COLLEGIATE MICROCOMPUTER, Rose-Hulman Institute Technology, Terre Haute IN 47803. Estab. 1983. Quarterly scholarly journal. Circ. 1,500. Needs gag and spot cartoons.
Gag Cartoons: Buys 5 gag cartoons/issue. Prefers gag cartoons on uses of microcomputers at college level. Preferred format is single panel, b&w line art. Send submissions to Brian J. Winkel, Editor. Reports back within days. Returns materials if accompanied by SASE. Buys one-time rights. Pays $25, b&w, on acceptance.

COMEDY WRITERS ASSOCIATION NEWSLETTER, Box 023304, Brooklyn NY 11202-0066. Estab. 1989. Quarterly newsletter.
Writing: Needs short "how-to" articles on writing and selling jokes, comedy scripts and humorous stories. Short original jokes also wanted. For first contact send article or jokes to Robert Makinson, Editor. Unsolicited material is returned with SASE. Buys all rights. Pays 3¢/word for articles, $1-3 for jokes. Send SASE for guidelines. Sample issue $4.

COMPLETE WOMAN, 1165 N. Clark, Chicago IL 60610. (312)266-8680. Estab. 1980. Bimonthly consumer magazine. Circ. 100,000. Needs humorous illustration, gag and spot cartoons.
Gag Cartoons: Buys 12 gag cartoons/issue. Prefers gag cartoons on women/men, work, etc. Preferred format is with gagline, b&w wash. Query with 10-12 rough drawings/batch to Bonnie Krueger, Editor. Reports back within 3 weeks. Returns materials if accompanied by SASE. Buys one-time rights. Pays $20 minimum, b&w, on publication. *Inside Tips:* "Know about women and don't stereotype them."
Illustration: Buys approximately 10 humorous illustrations/issue for articles. Works on assignment only. For first contact send cover letter and b&w tearsheets to Evy Lui, Art Director. Looks for "style and appeal to women." Reports back within 3 weeks. Samples

are returned by SASE. Buys one-time rights. Pays $50 minimum, b&w, page. *Inside Tips:* "Review our magazine prior to sending in."

Writing: Buys approximately 1 humorous piece/issue. Needs humorous nonfiction, interviews and "slice-of-life." Subject matter includes information geared toward women. Length: 800 words. To query be familiar with magazine and make sure that article is appropriate. For first contact send cover letter, writing sample, query and published tearsheets to Susan Handy, Managing Editor. Reports back within 3 weeks. Samples are returned with SASE. Buys one-time rights. Pays approximately 10¢/word. *Inside Tips:* "Research our magazine and position story to appeal to our market."

*COMPUTER SHOPPER, 1 Park Ave. 11th Fl., New York NY 10016. (212)503-3900. FAX: (212)503-3995. Estab. 1981. Monthly consumer magazine. Circ. 350,000. Needs spot cartoons.

Gag Cartoons: Buys 5 gag cartoons/issue; 60 gag cartoons/year. Prefers gag cartoons on "computer users in an office environment, at home, etc." Doesn't want to see gag cartoons on "robots, aliens, flying saucers, outdated computer models, please — no sexist submissions!" Preferred format is single panel with gagline, b&w line art or wash. Query with 5-20 rough drawings/batch to Nadine G. Messier, Art Assistant. Reports back in 2 months. Returns material. Buys first time rights. Pays $200, b&w. Pays on acceptance. *Inside Tips:* "Have a nice, clean style of illustration; should not focus on 'nerdy' aspects of computer users, technology, etc.; should focus on users in the computer industry that is not necessarily only humorous to them specifically; aim towards the lighthearted, personal 'run-ins' with computers that users deal with in a work environment."

© Michael Moran

Making Off with the Merchandise*: Madison, New Jersey-based humorous illustrator Michael Moran wanted to give a "sneaky, soft feeling" to his spot illustration of convention center employees who steal from exhibitors. Given a week by the trade journal's art director to complete the drawing, Moran netted the assignment after dropping off his portfolio at the magazine.*

CONSTRUCTION PUBLICATIONS, Box 1689, Cedar Rapids IA 52406. (319)366-1597. FAX (319)364-4853. Estab. 1948. Bimonthly trade journal. Circ. 70,000. Needs gag cartoons and spot cartoons.

Gag Cartoons: Buys 10 gag cartoons/issue on heavy construction industry. "For us, the 'dream' gag cartoon makes construction people feel good about themselves." Preferred format is single panel with gagline, b&w line art or wash. Reports back within 3 weeks.

Returns materials if accompanied by SASE. Buys all rights. Pays $15, b&w; on acceptance. *Inside Tips:* "Relate to the industries served by the publication."

CRACKED, 441 Lexington Ave., New York NY 10017. (212)490-0172. Estab. 1958. Consumer magazine published 9 times/year. Circ. 700,000. Needs humorous writing.
Writing: Needs humorous fiction. Subject matter includes "that which is most familiar to the most people!" Wants to see "a premise with some examples; no finished script initially." To query be familiar with magazine. Send all humorous writing to Lou Silverstone, Editor. Kill fee is 25% of contracted fee. *Inside Tips:* "We're interested in new formats—not more of the same. Movie and TV parodies are done in house as we attend advance screenings. Writers need not be able to draw (even roughs), though they should *try* to think visually!"

CURRENT, 1319 18th St., Washington DC 20036-1802. (202)296-6267. FAX: (202)296-5149. Estab. 1960. Monthly public-commentary journal. Circ. 5,000. Needs gag and spot cartoons and caricature. Accepts previously published cartoons.
Gag Cartoons: Buys 3 gag cartoons/issue on current events/political subjects. Preferred format is single panel with or without gagline, b&w line art. Query with 5-10 rough sketches, "plus enough finished examples to give us an idea of the appearance of the finished work. We *really prefer finished* gag cartoons, though, to cut down on correspondence." Send all submissions to Joyce Horn, Production Editor. Reports back only if interested. Returns materials if accompanied by SASE. Buys reprint rights or negotiates rights purchased. Pays $50, b&w.

CURRENTS, 314 N. 20th St., Colorado Springs CO 80904. (719)473-2466. FAX: (719)475-1752. Estab. 1979. Quarterly magazine for whitewater river enthusiasts. Circ. 10,000. Needs humorous illustration and writing and spot cartoons.
Illustration: Buys approximately 2-4 humorous illustrations/year for articles and spots. For first contact send cover letter and b&w tearsheets or query letter with roughs of proposed illustrations to Greg Moore, Editor. Looks for "illustrations pertaining to whitewater rivers/river running. We need people who have done their 'homework' on what is going on in the sport of river running and who are readers of past issues of *Currents* and have professional artistic skills." Reports back in 2 weeks. Samples are returned by SASE. Buys first rights. Pays $15 plus, b&w; does not publish color.
Writing: Buys approximately 1 humorous piece/year. Needs humorous fiction, nonfiction and interviews. Subject matter must pertain to whitewater rivers/river running. Length: 600-1,200 words. To query be familiar with magazine; make sure article is appropriate; study writer's guidelines. Send $1 for sample copy and guidelines. For first contact send cover letter, manuscript, query, published tearsheets and outline of proposed story to Greg Moore, Editor. Reports back in 2-4 weeks. Samples are returned with SASE. Buys first rights. Pays $30 and up. *Inside Tips:* "It is very difficult to be published in *Currents*. You must know subject matter well. Our readers are experienced paddlers and politically knowledgeable. Be sure to read a copy of *Currents* to get a feel for what we and our readers care about."

DAKOTA COUNTRY, Box 2714, Bismark ND 58502. (701)255-3031. Estab. 1979. Monthly hunting and fishing magazine. Circ. 10,350. Needs comic strips and spot cartoons. Accepts previously published cartoons.
Gag Cartoons: Buys 2-4 gag cartoons/issue on hunting and fishing. Preferred format is single panel, b&w line art. Query with 10-30 rough drawings/batch to Bill Mitzel, Publisher. Reports back in 2 weeks. Returns materials if accompanied by SASE. Prefers to buy 5-10 cartoons at a time. Buys reprint rights. Pays $10, b&w, on acceptance.

DIVERSION MAGAZINE, Suite 2424, 60 E. 42nd St., New York NY 10165. (212)297-9600. FAX: (212)808-9079. Magazine for doctors. Needs humorous illustration and writing and cartoons.

Gag Cartoons: Buys 10 gag cartoons/issue. Prefers gag cartoons on "travel, sports, wine, food, lifestyle, family and animals. "Although the magazine goes to doctors, we do not want anything related to medicine." Preferred format is single panel with gagline, b&w line art or wash. Query with 1-15 rough drawings/batch to Cartoon Dept. Buys first rights. Pays $100 b&w. Pays on acceptance.

Illustration: Buys 15 humorous illustrations/issue. For first contact send query with letter, samples and SASE to Cartoon Dept. Buys first rights. Payment negotiable. Pays on acceptance.

DOG FANCY, Box 6050, Mission Viejo CA 92690. Estab. 1969. Monthly consumer magazine. Needs gag and spot cartoons. Accepts previously published cartoons and humorous articles.

Gag Cartoons: Buys 2 gag cartoons/issue. Prefers gag cartoons on dogs. Preferred format is single panel with gagline, b&w line art. Query with 5-10 rough drawings/batch to Kim Thornton, Editor. Reports back within 6 weeks. Returns materials if accompanied by SASE. Buys one-time rights. Pays $35 minimum, b&w. Pays on publication. *Inside Tips:* "Truly know dogs. A lot of people think they know about dogs, but unless they are really familiar with dog breeds, activities, actions and personalities, their cartoons aren't very funny at all."

Illustration: Buys approximately 1 humorous illustration/year for articles. When hiring a freelance humorous illustrator, these abilities are considered: good conceptualization and clever ideas—good use of metaphors; lack of exaggeration or distortion; ability to "fun up" an otherwise "flat" manuscript; businesslike attitude—meets deadlines and is responsive to editor's needs. Samples are filed or returned by SASE. Buys one-time rights.

Writing: Buys approximately 1 humorous piece/year. Needs humorous nonfiction. To query be familiar with magazine; make sure article is appropriate; study writer's guidelines. Send $3.50 and SASE for copy. For first contact send query to Kim Thornton, Editor. Reports back within 6 weeks. Samples are filed or returned with SASE. Buys one-time rights. Pays $50-150 for 500-1,500 words.

*DRAGON MAGAZINE, P.O. Box 111, Lake Geneva WI 53147. (414)248-3625. FAX: (414)248-0389. Estab. 1975. Monthly consumer hobby magazine. Circ. 100,000. Needs gag cartoons. Accepts previously published cartoons.

Gag Cartoons: Buys 6 gag cartoons/issue; 72 gag cartoons/year. Prefers gag cartoons on role playing game situations, D&D and AD&D preferred. Doesn't want to see gag cartoons on "beholders at the optometrist." For us the 'dream' gag cartoon would be "fast and universally funny, well-drawn." Preferred format is single panel with, without captions, with ballons, b&w line art or wash. Query to Larry Smith, Art Director. Reports back in 2 weeks. Returns material if accompanied by a SASE. Buys first time rights, reprint rights. Pays $40-90, b&w. Pays on publication. *Inside Tips:* A gag cartoonist should "have a good style, an appropriate sense of humor and knowledge of game mechanics, but not be so involved as to produce arcane gags."

Illustration: Works on assignment only. More apt to hire a humorous illustrator if he is businesslike, meets deadlines and is responsive to our needs and "has understanding of our market (RPG systems)." For first contact send b&w tearsheets and promo piece to Larry Smith, Art Director. Looks for "appropriate, intelligent humor, not violent or sexist or insulting." Reports back in 2 weeks. Samples are filed; returned by SASE. Buys first time rights. Pays $225, full page b&w; $900, color cover. *Tips:* "Not too stylized—we are looking for graphic storytellers—not decorative illustrators."

EAP DIGEST (EMPLOYEE ASSISTANCE PROGRAM), Performance Resource Press, 1863 Technology Dr., Troy MI 48083-4244. (313)588-7733. FAX: (313)643-4435. Estab. 1980. Bimonthly trade journal. Circ. 20,000. Accepts gag cartoons. Accepts previously published cartoons.
Gag Cartoons: Prefers gag cartoons "on employees' personal problems, primarily substance abuse, and other problems an employee might seek help for from an employee assistance counselor. Preferred formats are single or double panel with gagline, with or without balloons. Query with any number of rough drawings/batch to Brent Chartire, Managing Editor. Reports back in 4 weeks. Returns material only if requested with SASE. Buys first or one-time rights. Pays $15-30, b&w, on publication.

ELECTRICAL APPARATUS, Barks Publications, Inc., Suite 1016, 400 N. Michigan Ave., Chicago IL 60611-4198. Estab. 1948. Monthly trade journal. Circ. 16,000. Needs spot cartoons.
Gag Cartoons: Prefers gag cartoons on industrial, electrical and managerial subjects. Preferred format is single panel, b&w line art. Send all submissions to Elsie Dickson, Associate Publisher. Reports back within 2-3 weeks. Returns materials if accompanied by SASE. Buys all rights. Pays $15, b&w. Pays on acceptance.

ENVIRONMENT, 1319 18th St., NW, Washington DC 20036. (202)296-6267 ext. 236. Estab. 1958. Monthly consumer magazine and trade journal. Circ. 16,000. Needs spot cartoons. Accepts previously published cartoons.
Gag Cartoons: Buys 1-2 gag cartoons/issue. Prefers cartoons that comment on human interaction with the environment. Current or topical environmental subjects are welcomed—ozone depletion, deforestation, pollution, etc.; however, we do not publish political cartoons. Preferred format is single panel without gagline, b&w line art or wash. Query with 10-20 finished drawings to Production/Graphics Manager. Reports back in 2 months. Returns materials if accompanied by SASE. Buys first time rights. Pays $35, b&w. Pays on publication. *Inside Tips:* "We only publish witty cartoons on environmental subjects. Stay away from anything too judgemental or negative."

FAIRFIELD COUNTY WOMAN, 15 Bank St., Stanford CT 06901. (203)323-3105. Estab. 1982. Monthly consumer magazine (tabloid). Circ. 50,000. Needs comic strips (possibly), humorous illustration and writing and spot cartoons. Accepts previously published cartoons and humorous articles.
Illustration: Buys approximately 2 humorous illustrations/issue for articles and spots. Works on assignment only. When hiring a freelance humorous illustrator one of the things considers is a non-sexist attitude. For first contact send cover letter, b&w and color tearsheets and slides to Joan Honig, Editor. Reports only if interested. Samples are returned by SASE. Buys first rights. Pays $25, b&w, page.
Writing: Buys approximately 1 humorous piece/issue. Needs humorous nonfiction and "slice-of-life." Subject matter includes women's issues, monthly column on man's point of view, family, children, relationships and career. Length: 1,000 words. To query be familiar with magazine and study writer's guidelines. Send $1.50 and SASE for copy. For first contact send cover letter, writing samples and published tearsheets to Joan Honig, Editor. Reports back only if interested. Samples returned with SASE. Buys first rights. Pays $35-65 for 600-1,200 words.

FAMILY MOTOR COACHING, 8291 Clough Pike, Cincinnati OH 45244. (513)474-3622. FAX: (513)474-2332. Estab. 1963. Monthly association publication. Circ. 85,000. Needs humorous writing, spot cartoons. Accepts previously published cartoons.
Gag Cartoons: Buys 1-2 gag cartoons/issue. Prefers gag cartoons on "outdoors, motorcoach travel and camping. For us, the 'dream gag cartoon' would be drawn by a cartoonist who travels by RV and thus has a first-hand understanding of the lifestyle." Preferred

format is single panel, b&w line art. Send all gag cartoon submissions to Pamela Wisby Kay, Editor. Reports back within 6 weeks. Returns material. Buys one-time rights. Pays $20, b&w. Pays on publication. *Inside Tips:* "For our publication, we need cartoons that depict self-contained motor homes rather than travel trailers, tents and other types of RVs. Also, it helps if the cartoonist is familiar with the motor-home lifestyle."
Writing: Buys approximately 6 humorous pieces/year. Subject matter includes motor-home-related themes. Length: 1,000 words. To query be familiar with magazine; make sure article is appropriate; study writer's guidelines first. Send SASE for copy. For first contact send query, writing sample to Pamela W. Kay, Editor. Samples are filed or are returned with SASE only if requested. Buys first time rights. Pays $70 minimum.

FARM & RANCH LIVING, 5400 S. 60th St., Greendale WI 53129. (414)423-0100. FAX: (414)423-0138. Estab. 1978. Bimonthly consumer magazine. Circ. 350,000. Needs gag cartoons. Accepts previously published cartoons.
Gag Cartoons: Buys 6-7 gag cartoons/issue on farm and ranch situations. Preferred format is single panel with gagline or balloons, b&w line art or wash. Send submissions to Bob Ottum, Editor. Reports back within approximately 3 weeks. Returns materials if accompanied by SASE. Buys one-time rights. Pays $35 minimum, b&w, on acceptance.

FFA NEW HORIZONS, Box 15160, Alexandria VA 22309. (703)360-3600. FAX (703)360-5524. Estab. 1952. Bimonthly association magazine. Circ. 420,000. Needs humorous illustration, gag and spot cartoons. Accepts previously published cartoons.
Gag Cartoons: Buys 2 gag cartoons/issue on teenagers, agriculture, school, dating and teachers. Doesn't want to see gag cartoons on "stereotypical farm kids/farmers. For us, the 'dream' gag cartoon would be youthful, hip and very funny." Preferred format is single panel with gagline, b&w line art. Query with 8 rough drawings/batch to Lawinna McGary, Associate Editor. Reports back within weeks. Buys one-time rights. Pays $20, b&w, on acceptance.
Illustration: Buys approximately 2 humorous illustrations/issue for articles. Works on assignment only. When hiring a freelance humorous illustrator, these abilities are considered: good conceptualization and clever ideas—good use of metaphors; effective use of humor; flexibility, broad potential in drawing style. For first contact send cover letter and b&w tearsheets to Lawinna McGary, Associate Editor. Reports back within weeks. Samples are filed. Buys all rights. Pays minimum $50, b&w, page; on acceptance. *Inside Tips:* "Many of our cartoonists have been around awhile, so we're ready for some fresh ideas and styles!"

FIELD & STREAM, 2 Park Ave., New York NY 10016. (212)779-5000. FAX: (212)725-3836. Estab. 1895. Monthly consumer magazine. Circ. 2 million. Needs humorous illustration, writing and gag cartoons.
Gag Cartoons: Prefers gag cartoons on "hunting and fishing." Doesn't want to see gag cartoons on "talking animals." Preferred format is single panel with gagline, b&w line art. "We prefer that cartoons be finished, b&w line drawings 8×10″ in size." Send submissions to Duncan Barnes, Editor. Reports back in 6-8 weeks. Returns material. Buys first time rights. Pays $100, b&w. *Inside Tips:* "Be familiar with the magazine and its subject matter."
Writing: Buys approximately 12 humorous pieces/issue. Needs humorous nonfiction. Subject matter must be humor that relates to fishing or hunting. "See our magazine." Length: 1,000-1,500 words. To query be familiar with magazine (most important) and make sure article is appropriate. For first contact send cover letter and manuscript to Duncan Barnes. Reports back in 6-8 weeks. Samples are not returned. Buys first time rights. Pays $800 for 1,000-1,500 words. *Inside Tips:* "Study past humor columns in *Field & Stream*. See if submitted material is in the same vein."

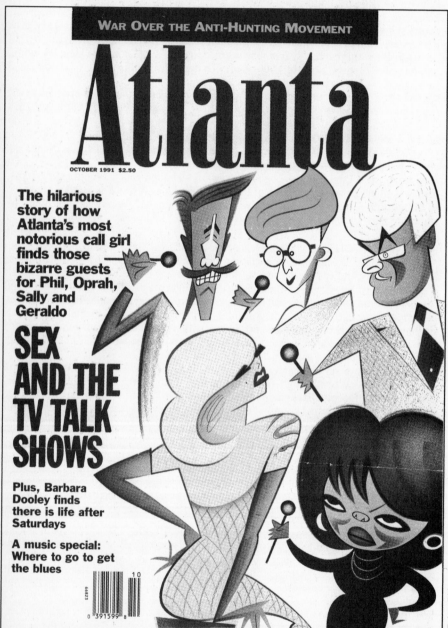

Can We Talk?: *The incomparable New York-based Robert Risko caricatures Geraldo, Sally, Phil and Oprah on the cover of Atlanta magazine. While Risko occasionally advertises in such directories as RSVP or American Showcase, he finds that having his work published "in high profile magazines is the best publicity."*

FILLERS FOR PUBLICATIONS, Box 14733, Albuquerque NM 87191-4733. (505)884-7636. Estab. 1956. Monthly newsletter that focuses on business-related cartoons ("nothing pertaining to sex, politics or religion").

Cartoons & Illustrations: Needs gag and spot cartoons, single panels of national appeal and humorous illustration. Must be line drawings. For first contact send samples. For humorous illustration/spots contact Lucie Dubovik, Manager. Reports back within 2 weeks. Returns materials if accompanied by SASE. Buys first or one-time rights. Pays $5-10.

THE FINAL EDITION, Box 294, Rhododendron OR 97049. (503)622-4798. Estab. 1982. Monthly company magazine. Circ. 8,000. Needs comic strips, humorous illustration and writing, cartoon narratives, caricature, gag and spot cartoons and portfolios. "We can feature one artist per month. It is something new that we are trying out." Accepts previously published cartoons and humorous articles.

Gag Cartoons: Preferred format is single, double or multi-panel with or without gagline or balloons, b&w line art. Query with 10-15 rough drawings/batch to Michael P. Jones, Editor. Trys to report back within 2 months. Returns materials if accompanied by SASE. Buys first rights. Pays in published copies.

Illustration: When hiring a freelance humorous illustrator, these abilities are considered: a truly unique drawing style; good conceptualization and clever ideas—good use of metaphors; a bold, powerful, attention-getting drawing style; a subtle, understated drawing style; effective use of humor; lack of exaggeration or distortion; flexibility, broad potential in drawing style; ability to "fun up" an otherwise "flat" manuscript; businesslike attitude—meets deadlines and is responsive to editor's needs. For first contact send cover letter, resume, client list, b&w tearsheets and portfolio to Michael P. Jones, Editor. "Just starting to incorporate into publication, but we'll be looking for new and interesting ways of dealing with real life issues." Reports back within 2 months ("generally, depending upon workload.") Samples are returned by SASE. Buys first rights. Pays in published copies. *Inside Tips:* "Give us enough samples of your work so that we can see the real artist within you."

Writing: Needs humorous nonfiction, fiction, interviews, cartoon stories, "slice-of-life" and anecdotes, "fillers." Subject matter includes anti-racism, anti-pollution, anti-hunting, anti-logging and other environmental and social issues. For first contact send cover letter, published tearsheets and writing samples to Michael P. Jones, Editor. Reports back within 2 months depending upon workload. Samples are returned with SASE. Buys first rights. *Inside Tips:* "Be yourself! Don't copy someone else's style. Develop your own individualized style. And, stay away from what's in 'vogue' today—your work should be timeless, just like fine art."

FLORIDA LEADER, Box 14081, Gainesville FL 32604-2081. (904)373-6907. Estab. 1982. Quarterly magazine for college students. Circ. 27,000. Needs humorous illustration.

Illustration: Buys approximately 5 humorous illustrations/issue for articles. Works on assignment only. When hiring a freelance humorous illustrator, these abilities are considered: a truly unique drawing style; good conceptualization; effective use of humor; ability to "fun up" an otherwise "flat" manuscript; businesslike attitude—meets deadlines and is responsive to art director's needs. For first contact send cover letter and portfolio to Jeffrey Riemersma, Art Director. Looks for "ability to work with college-related subject matter." Reports back in 2 weeks. Samples are returned by SASE. Negotiates rights purchased. Pays $25, b&w, $35, color, page. Pays upon printing of magazine.

FLOWER & GARDEN MAGAZINE, 4251 Pennsylvania Ave., Kansas City MO 64111. (816)531-5730. FAX: (816)531-3873. Estab. 1957. Bimonthly consumer magazine. Circ. 600,000.

Illustration: Buys approximately 2-3 humorous illustrations/year for spots. Looks for gardening humor. Reports back in 6 weeks. Samples not filed are returned. Buys first rights. Pays $20+, page; on acceptance. *Inside Tips:* "We are looking for straightforward humor that would be appreciated by gardeners. Too many cartoons submitted to us depict gardening as a frustrating experience — a view not shared by readers."

*FOOTBALL DIGEST, 990 Grove St., Evanston IL 60201. (708)491-6440. Estab. 1972. Monthly consumer magazine. Circ. 40,000-200,000. Needs gag cartoons. Accepts previously published cartoons.

Gag Cartoons: Buys 1-2 gag cartoons/issue; 16 gag cartoons/year. Prefers gag cartoons on sports. Doesn't want to see gag cartoons on golf, tennis, jogging. Preferred format is b&w line art with gagline. Send query to Cartoon Editor. Reports back in 1 month. Returns material if accompanied by a SASE. Buys first time rights, reprint rights. Pays $20, b&w. Pays on publication.

*FORUM, 118 N. Monroe St., Tallahassee FL 32399-1700. (904)224-1161. FAX: (904)681-2905. Estab. 1886. Quarterly trade journal. Circ. 53,000. Needs humorous writing, gag cartoons and spot cartoons. Accepts previously published cartoons and humorous articles.

Gag Cartoons: Prefers gag cartoons on educational, political or generic topics. For us, the "dream" gag cartoon would be pro-education, pro-union. Preferred gag cartoon format is single panel b&w line art, or double panel with gagline b&w wash. Query with 3 rough drawings/batch to Carey McNamara, Art Director. Reports back if interested. Returns material if accompanied by a SASE. Buys one-time rights. Pays $10 minimum for b&w. Pays on publication.

Illustration: Buys humorous illustrations for spots. When hiring a freelance humorous illustrator, these abilities are considered: a truly unique drawing style; ability to conceptualize well and clever ideas — good use of metaphors; businesslike attitude — meets deadlines and responsive to editor's needs. For first contact send cover letter, b&w tearsheets and client list to Carey McNamara. In reviewing humorous illustrations "we look for distinct style — tight concept." Reports back if interested. Samples are filed or returned by SASE. Buys one-time rights. Pays $100 minimum for b&w page.

Writing: Buys approximately 6 humorous pieces/year. Needs humorous nonfiction/fiction, humorous interviews, humorous "slice-of-life," cartoon stories, humorous anecdotes and fillers. Subject matter is education-related. Length: under 200 words. To query: make sure article is appropriate and study writer's guidelines. For first contact send cover letter, writing sample and published tearsheets to April Herrie, Editor. Reports back within 3 weeks. Samples are filed. Negotiates rights purchased. Pays $5-20 for a piece.

THE FREEDONIA GAZETTE, Darien 28, New Hope PA 18938-1224. (215)862-9734. Estab. 1978. Semi-annual fanzine. Circ. 400. Needs comic strips, humorous illustration and writing, caricature, gag and spot cartoons. Accepts previously published cartoons and humorous articles.

Gag Cartoons: Buys 1-2 gag cartoons/issue on the Marx Brothers and their films; use of "Groucho glasses" as a disguise. "For us, the 'dream' gag cartoon would be funny and relevant to the effect of Marx films on the world at large." Preferred formats are single, double or multi-panel with or without gagline or balloons, b&w line art only. Query with 1-2 rough drawings/batch to Neal Gorman, Cartoon Editor. Reports back in 10 days. Returns materials if accompanied by SASE. Negotiates rights purchased. Pays $5, b&w, on publication. *Inside Tips:* "Be original, be funny, have a real sense of appreciation for the humor of the Marx Brothers."

Illustration: Buys approximately 1-2 humorous illustrations/issue for covers, articles and spots. For first contact send cover letter, b&w tearsheets and promo pieces to Neal Gorman, Art Director. Looks for "originality, not just a copy from a photograph; creativity, unique drawing style that stands out from other artists; unusual shapes which can have text filled in around them." Reports back in 10 days. Samples are filed or are returned by SASE. Negotiates rights purchased. Pays $5, b&w, page; $10, b&w, cover; on publication. *Inside Tips:* "Don't copy from a photograph; chances are most of our readers also own that photo. Be sure artwork is camera-ready so we can do it justice."
Writing: Buys approximately 1-2 humorous pieces/issue. Needs humorous fiction, non-fiction and anecdotes, fillers. "As you've guessed by now, we're very narrow-minded. Humorous writing must relate to the Marx Brothers and their effect on the writer." Length: 100-1,000 words. To query "make sure that your article is appropriate and be a fan of the Marx Brothers." For first contact send cover letter and outline of proposed story to Paul Wesolowski, Editor-in-Chief. Reports back in 10 days. Samples are filed or are returned with SASE. Negotiates rights purchased. Pays $5-10 for 500-1,000 words.

Freezing Their (Hamburger) Buns Off:
To illustrate a story on winter barbecuing, Brooklyn, New York-based humorous illustrator Gary Baseman whipped up this shiver-provoking art. Baseman uses pastels and acrylic paint to create his art, and refrains from using the word "style" when asked to describe his work." I don't call it a style," he says, "it is an approach."

© Gary Baseman

THE FUNNY TIMES, 3108 Scarborough Rd., Cleveland Heights OH 44118. (216)371-8600. Estab. 1985. Monthly newspaper and tabloid. Circ. 30,000. Needs cartoon narratives, gag and editorial cartoons, humorous writing and "interviews with funny people." Accepts previously published cartoons. and humorous articles.
Gag Cartoons: Buys 25 gag cartoons/issue. Prefers single, double and multi-panel. Submit 10-15 rough drawings/batch to Editors. Reports back in months only if interested. Returns materials only if requested if accompanied by a SASE. Buys reprint or one-time rights. Pays $5-20, b&w; on publication.

Writing: Buys approximately 2-3 humorous pieces/issue. Needs humorous nonfiction, fiction, interviews, "slice-of-life," anecdotes, "fillers." Subject matter includes "political, modern life, human nature, realistic." Length: 500-2,500 words. To query be familiar with magazine; make sure article is appropriate; study writer's guidelines first. Send $2 and SASE for copy. For first contact send cover letter, manuscript to Editors. Reports back in months only if interested. Samples returned with SASE only if requested. Buys reprint rights or one-time rights. Pays $20-75 for 500-2,500 words.

*GALLERY, 3rd Fl., 401 Park Ave. South, New York NY 10016. (212)779-8900. Needs humorous writing and cartoon narratives.
Gag Cartoons: Buys 3-5 gag cartoons/issue. Prefers gag cartoons on any subject. Preferred formats are single, double or multi-panels with or without gaglines or balloons, b&w line art or b&w wash, "all but color." Query with 10-12 rough drawings/batch to Judy Linden, Cartoon Editor.
Illustration: Buys approximately 10 humorous illustrations/issue for covers and articles. For first contact send cover letter and b&w or color tearsheets to Judy Linden, Cartoon Editor.
Writing: Buys approximately 5-10 humorous pieces/issue. Needs humorous fiction and nonfiction. Subject matter varies. Length: 1,000-2,500 words. For first contact send query and published tearsheets to Articles Editor.

*GALLERY/FOX, 401 Park Ave. S., New York NY 10016. (212)779-8900. Estab. 1975. Monthly men's magazine. Circ. 450,000. Needs gag and spot cartoons.
Gag Cartoons: Prefers gag cartoons on sex. Preferred format is single panel, b&w line art, b&w wash. Query to Judy Linden, Senior Editor. Reports back within 1 month. Returns material if accompanied by a SASE. Buys first time rights. Pays $75, b&w.
Illustration: Buys 60 humorous illustrations/year for spots. For first contact send cover letter. Samples not filed are returned by SASE. Buys first time rights.
Writing: Buys approximately 5-10 humorous pieces/issue. Needs humorous fiction and nonfiction. Subject matter varies. Length: 1,000-2,500 words. For first contact, send query with published tearsheets to Articles Editor.

GEM SHOW NEWS, Rt. 2, Box 78, Blue Ridge TX 75424. (214)752-5192. FAX: (214)752-5205. Estab. 1977. Trade journal published 10 times/year. Circ. 12,000-30,000. Needs humorous writing, gag and spot cartoons that are gem, jewelry and mineral related. Accepts previously published cartoons and humorous articles.
Gag Cartoons: Buys 1-2 gag cartoons/issue on gemstones, jewelry, mineral collecting, security (security related must be positive theme). "The 'dream' gag cartoon would be a crook not getting away with an attempted hold-up." Preferred format is b&w line art with gagline. Send submissions to Stacy Hobbs, Managing Editor. Reports back in 2 months. Returns material if accompanied by SASE. Buys first time rights, reprint rights or one-time rights. Pays $8, b&w simple one panel; on acceptance; 5¢ per word on articles.
Illustration: Buys approximately 1 humorous illustration/issue for spots. When hiring a freelance humorous illustrator, considers whether artist has businesslike attitude—meets deadlines and is responsive to editor's needs. For first contact send finished items only for acceptance/rejection to Stacy Hobbs, Managing Editor. Reports back in 2 months only if interested. Samples are returned by SASE if requested. Pays $8, b&w, page. *Inside Tips:* "Try your best. Don't be discouraged; keep up the good work. Don't take a rejection too seriously, you may get another some day."
Writing: Buys approximately 5 humorous pieces/year. Needs humorous nonfiction, interviews, "slice-of-life," anecdotes and "fillers." Subject matter includes gem jewelry, mineral collecting. Length: most are 1,000 words; annual issue, 3,000 words. To query study writer's guidelines. Send 90¢ and SASE (9×12) for copy. For first contact send

finished pieces ready for acceptance/rejection to Edward J. Tripp. Reports back in 2 months. Samples are returned with SASE. Pays 5¢/word for 1,000-3,000 words.

GENESIS, 20th floor, 1776 Broadway, New York NY 10019-2002. (212)265-3500. FAX: (212)265-8087. Estab. 1973. Monthly consumer magazine. Circ. 500,000. Needs gag cartoons.
Gag Cartoons: Buys 3-4 gag cartoons/issue. Prefers gag cartoons on "risque subjects, sex gags—no gross gags." Doesn't want to see gag cartoons "of people at a bar or people in bed with the generic gagline. For us the 'dream' gag cartoon would be well-drawn, humorous and off-the-wall." Preferred format is single panel with or without gagline, b&w line art or wash or color wash. Query (no roughs) to Don Lewis, Art Director. Reports back within 1 month. Returns materials if accompanied by SASE. Buys first rights. Pays $75 minimum, b&w; $200 minimum, color. *Inside Tips:* "I'm always looking for someone new and funny! Black-and-white cartoons should fill a 4½ × 4½" box nicely; 4-color cartoons should fill a 9½ × 7" box.

GLASS FACTORY DIRECTORY, Box 2267, Hempstead NY 11550. (516)481-2188. Estab. 1912. Annual book. Circ. 1,500. Needs gag and spot cartoons. Accepts previously published cartoons.
Gag Cartoons: Buys 3-4 gag cartoons/issue on making glass. Doesn't want to see gag cartoons on "breaking glass of any kind. For us, the 'dream' gag cartoon would be one that takes the improbable (not the impossible) and makes it visually real." Preferred format is single panel with or without gagline, b&w line art. Query with any number of rough drawings/batch to Liz Scott, Managing Editor. Reports back in 2-4 months. Returns materials if accompanied by SASE. Buys all rights. Pays $25, b&w; on acceptance (or on publication, depending on situation). *Inside Tips:* A gag cartoonist should "learn about making glass—read, visit plants, etc."

*GOLF DIGEST, 5520 Park Ave., Trumbull CT 06880. (203)373-7000. FAX:(203)373-7033. Estab. 1950. Monthly consumer magazine. Circ. 1.4 million. Needs comic strips, humorous illustration and writing, caricatures, gag and spot cartoons.
Gag Cartoons: Prefers gag cartoons on golf. Preferred format is single panel, b&w line art. To query, send all gag cartoon submissions to Lois Hains, Assistant Editor. Returns materials only if requested. Buys first time, one-time and all rights. Pays on publication.
Illustration: Buys approximately 8 humorous illustrations/year for spots. For first contact send cover letter and portfolio to Lois Hains, Assistant Editor. Looks for "pertinence and originality." Samples are returned if requested. Buys first time, one-time and all rights. Pays on publication. *Inside Tips:* "We are interested primarily in cartoons."
Writing: Needs "golf-related" writing. To query, be familiar with magazine; make sure article is appropriate; study writer's guidelines. For first contact, send cover letter and manuscript to Lisa Sweet, Submissions Editor. Samples are returned with SASE. Buys first time, one-time and all rights.

*GOLF FOR WOMEN MAGAZINE, All American Plaza, 2130 Jackson Ave. W., Oxford MS 38655. (601)234-7570. FAX: (601)236-3949. Estab. 1988. Bimonthly consumer magazine. Circ. 275,000. Needs comic strips, gag and spot cartoons, humorous illustration, caricatures and humorous writing. Accepts previously published cartoons. Prefers working with freelancers who have fax capabilities.
Gag Cartoons: Buys 1-2 gag cartoons/issue; 8 gag cartoons/year. Prefers gag cartoons on women and golf situations. Doesn't want to see gag cartoons on "women golfers being belittled. For us the 'dream' gag cartoon would be very funny, intelligent and not offensive." Preferred format is single panel, with or without gagline, b&w line art, b&w and color wash. Query with 3-5 rough drawings/batch to John Roquet, Art Director. Reports only if interested. Returns material only if requested. Buys one-time rights, all

rights. Pays $50, b&w, $75, color. *Inside Tips:* "Present women, especially women golfers, in a positive light."

Illustration: Buys 6 humorous illustrations/issue; 36 humorous illustrations/year for articles and spots. Works on assignment only. More apt to hire a humorous illustrator if he conceptualizes well and has clever ideas—good use of metaphors, has a clean, graphically-pleasing drawing style, is businesslike, meets deadlines and is responsive to my needs. For first contact send cover letter, client list, b&w and color tearsheets to John Roquet, Art Director. Looks for "a clean, effective style that draws the reader into the article." Reports back if interested. Samples are filed; returned by SASE. Buys one-time rights. Pays $200, b&w; $300, color page. *Inside Tips:* "Use bright, rich colors (no pastels!) stay away from dark, moody colors."

Writing: Buys approximately 1 humorous piece/issue; 6 humorous pieces/year. Needs humorous nonfiction, "slice-of-life," anecdotes and fillers. "We'd like articles and pro-files about and with famous and amateur female golfers which are humorous but not derogatory—funny golf stories, etc." Length: 150-2,000 words. To query, familiarize yourself with our magazine and make article appropriate for us. For first contact send cover letter, query, outline of proposed story, ms, published tearsheets and writing sample to Debra Brumitt, Editorial Director. Reports back only if interested. Samples are filed. Samples not filed are returned with SASE only if requested. Buys one-time rights, all rights. Pays 35¢/word. Offers 20% kill fee.

GOLF JOURNAL, Golf House, Box 708, Far Hills NJ 07931. (201)234-2300. FAX: (201)234-2179. Estab. 1894. Nonprofit governing magazine for members/golfers. Needs humorous illustration and spot cartoons.

Illustration/Cartoons: For first contact send cover letter, slides, b&w and color tear-sheets and color promo piece to David Earl, Editor. Reports back within 1 month. Returns material only if requested and accompanied by a SASE. Buys one-time rights. Pays by the project, $50-200. *Inside Tips:* "Cartoonists/humorous illustrators should know golf, be funny and draw well."

Writing: For first contact send cover letter, writing samples and ms to David Earl, Editor. Reports back within 1 month. Returns material only if requested if accompanied by a SASE. Buys one-time rights. Pays by the project, $25-1,000. *Inside Tips:* "Write well; be funny, original and know golf. No articles about 'my first round,' or 'the time I played a famous course,' or 'teaching my spouse to play,' or 'my career round/hole in one.' Familiarize yourself with our format!"

GOOD HOUSEKEEPING, 959 8th Ave., Dept. HC, New York NY 10019. (212)649-2000. FAX: (212)265-3307. Needs humorous illustration and writing and gag and spot cartoons.

Gag Cartoons: Buys 9 cartoons/issue. Prefers gag cartoons on "family, women, house-wives." Preferred format is single panel with gagline, b&w line art or wash. Query with up to 12 rough drawings/batch to Ann Elkins, Cartoon Editor. Buys all rights. Pays $250. Pays on acceptance.

Illustration: Buys 9 humorous illustrations/issue for articles, spots and fillers. For first contact send cover letter and samples and SASE to Ann Elkins, Cartoon Editor. Buys all rights. Pays $250 b&w page. Pays on acceptance.

Writing: Buys approximately 5 humorous pieces/issue. Needs humorous nonfiction, poems and quips—2 liners. Subject matter includes homemaking, witty, cute, short, family and women. Length: 8 lines. For first contact send writing sample and SASE to Rosemary Leonard, Assistant Editor. Buys all rights. Pays $25 for 4 lines, $50 for 6-8 lines.

*GOOD OLD DAYS, 306 E. Parr Rd., Berne IN 46711. (219)589-8741. FAX: (219)589-8093. Estab. 1964. Monthly consumer general interest magazine. Circ. 120,000. Needs humorous illustration and writing. Accepts previously published cartoons (must indicate when and where used).

Gag Cartoons: Buys 1 or less cartoon/issue. Prefers gag cartoons on "true stories and poems about anything to do with growing up and life between the years 1900-1950." Doesn't want to see gag cartoons on "tipping over the outhouse on Halloween (unless a surprise slant was added.)" Preferred format is single panel, b&w line art. Query with 1-5 rough drawings/batch (photocopies of previous work OK) to Bettina Miller, Editor. Reports back in 3 weeks. Returns material if accompanied by a SASE. Negotiates rights purchased. Pays $35-60, b&w. Pays on acceptance. *Inside Tips:* "Study the publication and ideally have lived (grown up) for a period of the 'good old days' — (1900-1949.)"

Illustration: Buys humorous illustration for articles. More apt to hire a humorous illustrator if he conceptualizes well and has clever ideas — good use of metaphors, has a clean, graphically-pleasing drawing style, uses humor effectively, does not exaggerate or distort too much, can "fun up" an otherwise "flat" manuscript, illustrate one of our many "Mother's Washday Rigamorale" stories with a humorous sketch, which would ease the drudgery aspect. For first contact send b&w tearsheets (photocopies OK) to Bettina Miller, Editor. Looks for "good detail, authentic-to-the-time format; not too goofy; a more realistic look or else a pleasing original look; an understanding of the subject. We look for more of an old-time comic drawing style rather than the bold and bare nouveau style." Reports back in 3 weeks. Samples are filed. Samples not filed are returned by SASE. Negotiates rights purchased. Pays $35-60, b&w page. Pays on acceptance. *Inside Tips:* "We are looking for real-life-experience humor. Embarrassing experiences are always fun, or things that "get" the universal goat."

Writing: Buys approximately 2 humorous pieces/issue. Needs humorous nonfiction, "slice-of-life," anecdotes, "fillers." Subject matter includes "Anything humorous (and true!) pertaining to life in the small stown, country or city, and how it was affected by the everyday or world events (Pearl Harbor, Depression, etc.) Keep some sort of focus to the piece. Topics are limitless as long as they keep to our time format." Length: 50-800 words. To query be familiar with our magazine, study our writer's guidelines first: Send $2 and SASE for copy. For first contact send ms to Bettina Miller, Editor. Reports back in 3 weeks. Samples not filed are returned with SASE. Negotiates rights purchased. Pays $25-75 for 50-1,500 words. "We rarely assign articles to be written." *Inside Tips:* "Your humility, empathy, delight or disgust for a topic (particularly old time), clearly written and incorporated into an amusing true story, are most appreciated."

GOOD READING FOR EVERYONE, Box 40, Sunshine Park, Dept. HC, Litchfield IL 62056. (217)324-3425. Estab. 1964. Monthly consumer magazine. Circ. 5,000. Needs spot cartoons.

Gag Cartoons: Buys 1 gag cartoon/issue on family, business, weather, sports and seasons. Preferred format is single panel with gagline, b&w line art. Send finished art. Reports back in 3 months. Returns materials if accompanied by SASE. Buys first rights. Pays $15, b&w; on acceptance.

Writing: Buys approximately 1 humorous piece/issue. Needs humorous nonfiction, "slice-of-life" and anecdotes, "fillers." Length: 200 words. To query study writer's guidelines. Send 50¢ and SASE for copy. For first contact, send cover letter and manuscript to Editor. Reports back in 3 months. Samples returned with SASE. Buys first rights. Pays $20 for 200 words.

*GOVERNMENT EXECUTIVE, 1730 M St. N.W., Washington DC 20036. (202)862-0638. FAX:(202)857-0452. Estab. 1982. Monthly trade journal. Circ. 40,000. Needs gag and spot cartoons, humorous illustration and caricatures. Accepts previously published cartoons. Prefers working with freelancers who have fax capabilities.

© Slug Signorino

A Little of this, a Little of That, and Suddenly You Have SPAM! *: To illustrate a newspaper article on "neighborhood composting," LaPorte, Indiana-based humorous illustrator Slug Signorino created this hip art. Signorino first showed his portfolio to the client in 1975, and has "done at least one drawing for them a week since." Describing his illustration style as "funny and original," Signorio was paid $300 for first reproduction rights to the artwork.*

Gag Cartoons: Buys 6 cartoons/year. Prefers gag cartoons on "government, politics, Washington. For us, the 'dream' gag cartoon would relate to federal government workers." Preferred formats are single, double or muti-panel, with or without gagline or with balloons, b&w line art or wash. Query with 6-12 rough drawings/batch to Tessa Tilden-Smith, Art Director. Reports back within 1 month only if interested. Returns material only if requested. Buys first time and one-time rights. Pays $75, b&w; $125, color. Pays on publication.

Illustration: Buys approximately 2 humorous illustrations/issue, 24/year for articles and spots. Works on assignment only. When hiring a freelance humorous illustrator, these abilities are considered: good conceptualization and clever ideas—good use of metaphors; clean, graphically-pleasing drawing style; effective use of humor; ability to 'fun up' an otherwise 'flat' manuscript; businesslike attitude—ability to meet deadlines. For first contact, send cover letter, client list, b&w or color tearsheets, and b&w or color promo piece to Tessa Tilden-Smith, Art Director. One of the things considered when hiring a freelance humorous illustrator is "clear, easy to understand art that makes me laugh." Reports back within 1 month only if interested. Samples are filed or are returned with SASE. Buys first time and one-time rights. Pays $200, b&w page; $300, color cover; on publication.

*GRAND RAPIDS PARENT MAGAZINE, 549 Ottawa NW, Grand Rapids MI 49503. (616)459-4545. FAX: (616)459-4800. Estab. 1989. Monthly consumer magazine. Needs comic strips, humorous illustration and spot cartoons.

Gag Cartoons: Prefers gag cartoons on parenting topics/children. Preferred format is single, double or multi-panel; with, without gagline, with balloons; b&w line art, wash. Query to Carole Valade Smith, Editor. Reports in a matter of months only if interested. Returns material only if requested and accompanied by a SASE. Negotiates rights purchased. Pays $25 minimum, b&w. Pays on publication.

Illustration: Buys a minimum of 12 humorous illustrations/issue; a minimum of 12 humorous illustrations/year. Buys humorous illustrations for articles. More apt to hire a humorous illustrator if he conceptualizes well and has clever ideas. For first contact send b&w promo pieces to Carole Valade Smith, Editor. Reports back in months only if interested. Samples not filed are returned if requested. Negotiates rights purchased. Pays $35 minimum, b&w, $75 minimum color, page.

HEALTH, (formerly In Health), 301 Howard St., 18th Fl., San Francisco CA 94105. (415)512-9100. FAX: (415)512-9660. Estab. 1987. Bimonthly consumer magazine. Circ. 800,000. Needs "cartoons only."

Cartoons: Buys 3 cartoons/issue. Prefers gag cartoons on "health, nutrition *only!*" Photocopies acceptable. Send all submissions to Cassandra Writsen, Editorial Assistant. Reports back within 2 months. Returns materials. Buys first rights. Pays $350, b&w, $350, color. Pays on acceptance.

*HEALTH JOURNAL AND DIGEST, Madison Publishing Corp., 347 Congress St., Boston MA 02210. (617)451-1155. FAX: (617)451-3320. Estab. 1988. Quarterly consumer magazines. Circ. 1 million. Uses occasional humorous illustration and writing and spot cartoons. Accepts previously published cartoons and humorous articles.

Gag Cartoons: Prefers gag cartoons on health. Doesn't want to see gag cartoons on "operations (appendectomy, e.g.)" "For us the 'dream' gag cartoon would be someone trying to stay/get healthy by eating right and exercising." Preferred format is single panel. Query with any number of rough drawings/batch to Steven Krauss, Editor, Madison Publishing. Reports back within 1 month. Returns material if accompanied by a SASE. Buys first time rights, one-time rights. Pays $150, color. Pays on acceptance.

Illustration: Buys 4-8 humorous illustrations/year for articles. Works on assignment only. More apt to hire a humorous illustrator if he has a truly unique drawing style; conceptualizes well and has clever ideas—good use of metaphors; is businesslike, meets deadlines and is responsive to my needs. For first contact send cover letter and client list to Dianne Barrett, Design Director. Reports back if interested. Samples not filed are returned by SASE. Negotiates rights purchased. Pays $200, b&w (¼ page), $250, color (¼ page).

Writing: Needs humorous nonfiction. Subject matter includes "health from a self-help point of view—i.e., through proper nutrition and exercise program." Length: 500-1,000. To query be familiar with magazine; make sure article is appropriate. Send SASE for copy. For first contact send cover letter, query, published tearsheets to Steven Krauss, Editor, Madison Publishing. Reports back within 1 month. Samples are filed. Samples not filed are returned with SASE. Buys first time rights, one-time rights. Pays $250-400 for 500-1,000 words. "Our kill fee for solicited yet unaccepted articles is 20% of the contracted fee."

HEAVEN BONE MAGAZINE, Box 486, Chester NY 10918. (914)469-9018. Estab. 1986. Semiannual literary magazine. Circ. 1,000. Needs comic strips and humorous illustration. Accepts previously published cartoons.

Gag Cartoons: Query with 3-10 rough drawings/batch to Steve Hirsch. Reports in 6 months. Returns materials if acompanied by SASE. Buys one-time rights. Pays in copies of publication. Occasionally pays $3-5 for cartoon strips.

Illustration: Uses 1-3 illustrations/issue. A freelance humorous illustrator must "understand our needs before submitting." For first contact send cover letter and b&w tearsheets to Steve Hirsch. Reports back in 6 months. Samples are filed or are returned by SASE. Buys one-time rights. Pays in copies of publication.

Tips "We like esoteric, literary and spiritual humor. We recommend buying a sample issue before submitting ($5)."

*HIGH PERFORMANCE PONTIAC, 11503 N. Poema Pl. #204, Chatsworth CA 91311. (818)709-4005. FAX: (818)718-8608. Estab. 1979. Bimonthly consumer magazine. Circ. 45,000. Needs humorous illustration, spot cartoons. Previously published cartoons OK.

Illustration: Buys 2 humorous illustrations/year for articles. Works on assignment only. More apt to hire a humorous illustrator is he has a truly unique drawing style, uses humor effectively, is businesslike, meets deadlines and is responsive to my needs. For first contact send cover letter, b&w and color tearsheets to Sue Elliott, Editor. Looks for "Understanding of the subject, style, humor value, price." Reports back within 1 month. Samples are filed. Samples not filed are returned. Buys first time rights. Pays $100, b&w, $150, color, page. *Tips:* "Appeal to a very knowledgeable reader—one who knows the car hobby, and particularly Pontiacs, very well."

HIGH SOCIETY MAGAZINE, 10th floor, 801 Second Ave., New York NY 10017. (212)661-7878. FAX: (212)883-1244. Estab. 1976. Monthly sophisticated men's consumer magazine. Circ. 230,000. Needs comic strips, humorous illustration, caricature, gag and spot cartoons.

Gag Cartoons: Buys 5 gag cartoons/issue on sex and sex-related topics. Preferred format is multi-panel with balloons, b&w line art. Query with 10-20 rough drawings/batch to Steve Loshiavo, Cartoon Editor. Reports back within 3 weeks if interested. Returns materials if accompanied by SASE. Buys first rights. Pays $200 minimum, color, $150 minimum, b&w; on acceptance.

Illustration: Buys approximately 5 humorous illustrations/year for articles. When hiring a freelance humorous illustrator, these abilities are considered: a clean, graphically-pleasing drawing style; businesslike attitude—meets deadlines and is responsive to editor's needs. For first contact send cover letter and color tearsheets to Stephen Loshiavo. Reports back within 2 weeks. Samples are returned by SASE. Buys first rights. Pays $1,000 for 2 page color spread.

Writing: Buys approximately 5 humorous pieces/issue. Needs humorous interviews and anecdotes, "fillers." To query be familiar with magazine. For first contact send cover letter, writing sample and published tearsheets to Stephen Loshiavo. Reports back within 2 weeks. Samples are returned with SASE. Buys first rights. Pays $400 for 6-8 pages. Offers 10% kill fee.

HIGHLIGHTS FOR CHILDREN, 803 Church St., Honesdale PA 18431. (717)253-1080. FAX: (717)253-0179. Estab. 1946. Monthly children's magazine (11 issues a year, July/August is combined). Circ. 3,000,000. Needs humorous illustration and writing, gag and spot cartoons.

Market conditions are constantly changing! If you're still using this book and it is 1994 or later, buy the newest edition of Humor and Cartoon Markets *at your favorite bookstore or order directly from Writer's Digest Books.*

Gag Cartoons: Buys 1-2 gag cartoons/issue for *Highlights*, approximately 250/year total for all publications. Doesn't want gag cartoons on flying carpets, snake charmers or kangaroo pouches. Preferred formats are single, double or multi-panel with or without gagline, b&w line art or color wash. Send submissions to Kent L. Brown Jr., Editor. "No queries." Reports back in 30 days. Returns materials. Buys all rights. Pays $20, b&w; on acceptance. *Inside Tips:* "Capture humor that will apply to youngsters. Mostly we get adult cartoons."

Illustration: Buys approximately 3-5 humorous illustrations/issue for covers, articles and spots. Works on assignment only. For first contact send cover letter, b&w or color tearsheets and resume to Roseanne Guararra, Art Director. Reports in 30 days. Samples are filed. Buys all rights. Pays $100 minimum, color, page; $425 minimum, color, cover; on acceptance.

Writing: Buys approximately 2 humorous pieces/issue. Needs humorous fiction, nonfiction, quizzes, games, puzzles and cartoon stories. No derogatory, violent or anti-authority humor. Length: very short—to 800 words. No query necessary. For first contact send cover letter (optional) and manuscript to Rich Wallace, Assistant Editor. Reports back in 30 days. Samples are not filed; returned with SASE. Buys all rights. Pays 14¢/word and up. *Inside Tips:* "Humor at the expense of the child is not acceptable. We are looking for tasteful humor which makes children laugh. Humorous writing need not exclude warmth, realism and emotion."

*HOCKEY DIGEST, 990 Grove St., Evanston IL 60201. (708)491-6440. Estab. 1972. Bimonthly consumer magazine. Circ. 40,000-200,000. Needs gag cartoons. Accepts previously published cartoons.

Gag Cartoons: Buys 1-2 gag cartoons/issue; 16 gag cartoons/year. Prefers gag cartoons on sports. Doesn't want to see gag cartoons on golf, tennis, jogging. Preferred format is b&w line art with gagline. Query to Cartoon Editor. Reports back within 1 month. Returns material if accompanied by a SASE. Buys reprint rights. Pays $20, b&w. Pays on publication.

HOME, 2176 Jog Rd., West Palm Beach FL 33415. (407)434-1114. FAX: (407)434-0667. Estab. 1948. Bimonthly consumer/controlled publication. Circ. 90,000-100,000. Needs humorous writing and spot cartoons. Simultaneous submissions OK.

Gag Cartoons: Buys 8-10 cartoons/year; "sometimes uses 2/issue, sometimes none." *Inside Tips:* "The humour we look for is the kind that makes the reader smile and recall being in a similar situation, not the kind that evokes guffaws; a different and improbable way of doing something most people take seriously, and laughing at yourself when it goes wrong."

Writing: Buys approximately 1-2 humorous pieces/issue. Humorous and/or light nostalgic nonfiction, vignettes, anecdotes. No fiction, no fillers. "As a general interest publication, just about any subject is okay if it is in good taste and aimed at family audience." Length: 300-1,500 words. To query be familiar with magazine and study writer's guidelines. Send SASE for guidelines, $1 for sample copy and guidelines. For first contact send query or manuscript to Karl H. Meyer, Associate Editor. Samples are filed; returned only if requested. Buys first, reprint or one-time rights. Pays 30¢/line, $25 maximum. *Inside Tips:* "Don't use 'sophisticated' words as a basis of humor. A smooth, friendly tone must be maintained as if you were relating a humorous occurrence that actually happened. We welcome new writers."

*HOME OFFICE OPPORTUNITIES, P.O. Box 780, Lyman WY 82937. (307)786-4513. Estab. 1990. Bimonthly newsletter. Circ. 500. Needs gag and spot cartoons. Accepts previously published cartoons.

Gag Cartoons: Buys 1-2 cartoons/issue. Prefers gag cartoons on "the funny things that happen to those of us who operate home businesses." Preferred format is single panel, with or without gagline, with balloons, b&w line art. Query to Diane Wolverton, Editor. Reports back within 2-3 months. Buys first time rights. Pays $2, b&w. Pays on acceptance.

HOUSEWIFE-WRITER'S FORUM, P.O. Box 780, Lyman WY 82937. (307)786-4513. Estab. 1987. Bimonthly magazine. Circ. 1,000 (printed). Needs humorous illustration and writing, caricature, gag and spot cartoons. Accepts some previously published cartoons and articles.
Gag Cartoons: Buys 2-3 gag cartoons/issue on children, spouses and writing. Preferred formats are single, double or multi-panel with or without gagline or balloons, b&w line art. Query with 1-5 rough drawings/batch to Diane Wolverton, Editor/Publisher. Reports back in 2-3 months. Returns materials if accompanied by SASE. Buys one-time rights. Pays $2, b&w; on acceptance. *Inside Tips:* A gag cartoonist should "have strong artistic and humor writing skills. We don't match artists with writers due to time constraints."
Illustration: Buys approximately 1-3 humorous illustrations/issue for spots. "I like to publish a variety of artistic and humorous styles." For first contact send cover letter and b&w tearsheets to Diane Wolverton, Editor. "I prefer to see submissions sent directly." Looks for "clean, understandable and reproducible art." Reports back in 2-3 months. Samples are not filed; returned by SASE. Buys first rights. Pays $2, b&w, page or cover; on acceptance. *Inside Tips:* "Humorous illustrations must stand on their own since I don't (at this point) match artists with writers. I may incorporate your artwork into a humorous article or short story, so keep it generic."
Writing: Buys approximately 3-5 humorous pieces/issue. Needs humorous fiction, non-fiction, "slice-of-life," anecdotes and "fillers." Subject matter includes women's lives at home or work, children, spouses, family relationships, pet peeves, personal experiences. "All types presented vividly, wryly, perhaps sardonically." Length: 25-1,500 words, average of 500-750 words. To query be familiar with magazine; make sure article is appropriate; study writer's guidelines. Send $4 and SASE for copy. For first contact send cover letter, manuscript and published tearsheets to Diane Wolverton, Editor. "I don't assign humorous stories on the basis of a proposal or query since humor is so difficult to predict." Reports back in 2-3 months. Samples are not filed; returned with SASE. Buys first rights. Pays 1¢/word. *Inside Tips:* "The most important thing to recognize is the difference between what's funny to you and what's funny to the majority of readers. *Housewives' Writer's Forum* is a good beginner's market because our goal is to introduce the reading audience to new humorists on an ongoing basis."

HOUSTON METROPOLITAN, Box 25386, Houston TX 77265. (713)524-3000. FAX: (713)524-8213. Estab. 1974. Monthly consumer magazine. Circ. 90,000. Needs humorous illustration.
Illustration: Buys approximately 10 humorous illustrations/issue for articles, spots. Works on assignment only. For first contact send cover letter, resume, client list, b&w and color tearsheets to Fernande Bondarenko, Art Director. Looks for "style and ability to interpret story." Reports back within 2 weeks. Samples returned by SASE. Buys first time rights. Pays minimum $300, b&w, $450, color, page; $600 color, cover. Pays on acceptance.

THE INSTRUMENTALIST, 200 Northfield Rd., Northfield IL 60093. (708)446-5000. Estab. 1944. Monthly trade journal. Circ. 20,000. Needs gag cartoons.
Gag Cartoons: Buys 5 gag cartoons/issue. Prefers "positive cartoons on music (especially classical)." Doesn't want to see gag cartoons on "how nerdy musicians are or what a trial it is to have a child who plays an instrument." Preferred formats are single or

double panel with or without gagline, b&w line art or wash. Query with 1-10 rough drawings/batch to Cathy Sell, Assistant Editor. Reports back in 1 month. Returns materials. Buys all rights. Pays $20, b&w; on publication. *Inside Tips:* A gag cartoonist should "enjoy music so he can be funny and not insult those in the profession."

INTENSIVE CARING UNLIMITED, 910 Bent Lane, Philadelphia PA 19118. (215)233-4723. FAX: (215)233-5795. (Call first.) Estab. 1978. Bimonthly newsletter that focuses on information and support for families of children with medical or developmental problems. Circ. 3,000. Accepts previously published humorous articles.
Writing: Needs humorous nonfiction, interviews and "slice-of-life" on "how families deal with crises and children in general." Length: approx. 1,000 words. "Query editor for upcoming topics." For first contact send cover letter and writing sample to Lenette S. Moses, Editor. Unsolicited material is filed if applicable or returned with SASE. Author retains all rights. "Ours is a nonprofit newsletter. We offer no pay, just national publication exposure."

INTERNATIONAL BOWHUNTER MAGAZINE, Box 67, Rt. 1, Box 41E, Pillager MN 56473-0067. (218)746-3333. Estab. 1983. Seven times/year consumer magazine. Circ. 57,000. Needs comic strips, humorous illustration and writing.
Gag Cartoons: Buys 20 gag cartoons/year on bowhunting. Preferred formats are single, double or multi-panel with gagline, b&w line art. Send submissions to Johnny E. Boatner, Editor. Reports back within 6 weeks. Returns material if accompanied by SASE. Buys first rights. Pays $10 minimum, b&w; on publication.
Illustration: Buys approximately 20 humorous illustrations/year for spots.
Writing: Needs humorous "slice-of-life," fiction and anecdotes, "fillers." Subject matter includes bowhunting. Length: 600-900 words. To query make sure article is appropriate. For first contact send manuscript to Johnny E. Boatner, Editor. Reports back within 6 weeks. Samples are returned with SASE. Buys reprint rights. Pays $50-100 for 600-900 words. *Inside Tips: "Think* bowhunting; use dry humor."

JAPANOPHILE, Box 223, Okemos MI 48864. (517)349-1795. Estab. 1974. Quarterly literary magazine. Circ. 800. Needs humorous writing and gag cartoons. Accepts previously published humorous articles. Sample copy $4.
Gag Cartoons: Buys 1 gag cartoon/issue on Japan and Japanese culture. Preferred format is single panel with gagline, b&w line art. Query with 1-2 rough drawings/batch to editor. Reports back in 2 months. Returns materials if accompanied by SASE. Buys one-time rights. Pays $5, b&w; on publication.
Illustration: Buys approximately 1 humorous illustration/issue. When hiring a freelance humorous illustrator, these abilities are considered: a clean, graphically-pleasing drawing style; effective use of humor. For first contact send cover letter and b&w tearsheets.

JOURNAL OF READING, Box 8139, Newark DE 19714. (302)731-1600. Estab. 1948. Monthly (September through May with combined Dec./Jan. issue) professional membership journal. Circ. 20,000. Needs cartoons about reading, language, libraries and literacy among high schoolers and adults. Accepts previously published cartoons.
Gag Cartoons: Preferred format is double panel, b&w line art. "Horizontal drawings are preferred (wider than high). We're 8½"×11" format with two columns 20 picas wide, total 42 pica width/page. Cartoons are fit in at the end of articles, centered on page." Query with 1-10 rough drawings/batch to editor. Reports back in 2 weeks. Returns materials. Buys one-time rights. Pays $25, b&w; on acceptance. *Inside Tips:* "Stick to our topic, do not put down teachers or kids."

JUDICATURE, Suite 1600, 25 E. Washington, Chicago IL 60602. (312)558-6900. Estab. 1917. Bimonthly scholarly journal. Circ. 20,000. Needs humorous illustration and gag cartoons. Accepts previously published cartoons.

Gag Cartoons: Buys 4 gag cartoons/year on law, judges and especially court-related themes. Preferred format is single panel with gagline, b&w line art. Query with 5-6 rough drawings/batch to David Richert, Editor. Reports back in 1 week. Returns materials if accompanied by SASE. Buys one-time rights. Pays $35, b&w; on publication.

Illustration: Buys approximately 4 humorous illustrations/year for covers and articles. Works on assignment only. For first contact send cover letter and b&w tearsheets to David Richert, Editor. Reports back in 2 weeks. Samples are filed or are returned by SASE. Buys one-time rights. Pays $175, b&w, page; $250, b&w, cover; on publication.

JUGGLER'S WORLD, Box 443, Davidson NC 28036. (704)892-1296. FAX: (704)892-2625. Estab. 1947. Quarterly consumer magazine. Circ. 3,500. Needs comic strips, humorous illustration, cartoon narratives, caricature, gag and spot cartoons. Accepts previously published cartoons and humorous articles.

Gag Cartoons: Buys 4 gag cartoons/year on juggling. Doesn't want to see gag cartoons on chain saw juggling. Preferred formats are single or multi-panel with gagline, b&w line art. Query with 1-3 rough drawings/batch to Bill Giduz, Editor. Reports back in 1 week. Returns materials. Buys first or reprint rights; will negotiate. Pays $15, b&w; on acceptance.

Illustration: Buys approximately 2 humorous illustrations/issue for articles and spots. When hiring a freelance humorous illustrator, these abilities are considered: a truly unique drawing style; good conceptualization and clever ideas—good use of metaphors; a clean, graphically-pleasing drawing style; businesslike attitude—meets deadlines and is responsive to editor's needs. For first contact send cover letter and b&w tearsheets to Bill Giduz, Editor. Reports back in 1 week. Samples are filed or returned. Buys first or reprint rights; will negotiate. Pays $15, b&w, page; on acceptance.

Writing: Buys approximately 2 humorous pieces/issue. Needs humorous fiction, nonfiction, interviews, anecdotes, and "fillers." Subject matter includes juggling. Length: 250-750 words. To query make sure article is appropriate; study writer's guidelines. Send $2 and SASE for copy. For first contact send cover letter and writing sample to Bill Giduz, Editor. Reports back in 1 week. Samples are filed or returned. Buys first or reprint rights; will negotiate. Pays $25-75 for 250-750 words. Offers 100% kill fee.

*JUST FOR LAUGHS, 22 Miller Ave., Mill Valley CA 94941. (415)383-4746. FAX: (415)383-0142. Estab. 1982. Monthly newspaper, tabloid, trade journal. Circ. 50,000. Needs humorous illustration, caricatures, spot cartoons. Accepts previously published cartoons.

Gag Cartoons: Buys 6 cartoons/year. Prefers gag cartoons on comedy themes. Preferred format is single panel with gagline, b&w line art, b&w wash. Query with 2-4 rough drawings/batch to Jon Fox, Editor/Publisher. Reports back within 3-4 weeks if interested. Returns material if accompanied by a SASE. Buys one-time rights. Pays $15-25, b&w. Pays on publication.

Illustration: Buys 10-12 humorous illustration/year for articles. Works on assignment only. More apt to hire a humorous illustrator if he conceptualizes well and has clever ideas—good use of metaphors; has a clean, graphically-pleasing drawing style; uses humor effectively; is businesslike, meets deadlines and is responsive to my needs. For first contact send cover letter, b&w tearsheets to Jon Fox, Editor/Publisher. Reports back within 3-4 weeks. Samples not filed are returned by SASE. Buys one-time rights. Pays $15-25 b&w, page.

Writing: "We are a comedy newspaper specializing in stand-up comics. We do interviews, profiles, reviews of stage, TV, movies, etc. and columns on the industry. Any illustrations to that end are welcomed."

KASHRUS MAGAZINE, Box 204, Parkville Station, Brooklyn NY 11204. (718)336-8544. Estab. 1980. Bimonthly consumer magazine. Circ. 10,000. Needs humorous writing, cartoon narratives, gag and spot cartoons.

Gag Cartoons: Prefers gag cartoons on kosher food and other Jewish themes. Preferred formats are single panel, double panel or multi-panel with gagline, b&w line art. Query with 2 rough drawings/batch to Rabbi Wikler, Editor. Reports in 2 weeks only if interested. Returns materials if accompanied by SASE. Buys first or all rights; negotiates rights purchased. Pays $75, b&w. Pays on publication. *Inside Tips:* "Read our magazine, understand the market, call us to discuss the matter."

Illustration: Buys humorous illustration for articles and spots. Works on assignment only. One of the things considers when hiring a freelance humorous illustrator is "an understanding of our concept and audience." For first contact send $2 for a copy of *KASHRUS* (no SASE necessary); "then call if it interests you."

Writing: Buys humorous articles on assignment only. For first contact send query and published tearsheets to Rabbi Wikler. Reports back only if interested. Samples are filed or are returned with SASE. Negotiates rights purchased. Pays $100-150 for 750-1,200 words. Offers 50% kill fee. *Inside Tips:* "Writer must understand our readers—kosher, observant Jews—and our subject—kosher food, food production and technology. If you can adapt your humor to kosher food, you have a market."

KENTUCKY AFIELD, THE MAGAZINE, (formerly Kentucky Happy Hunting Ground), Department of Fish and Wildlife Resources, 1 Game Farm Rd., Frankfort KY 40601. (502)564-4336. FAX: (502)564-6508. Estab. 1945. Bimonthly state government conservation magazine. Circ. 35,000. Needs humorous writing and gag cartoons. Accepts previously published cartoons and humorous articles.

Gag Cartoons: Buys up to 6 cartoons/year. "Cartoons must be related to wildlife, conservation and nature." Doesn't want to see gag cartoons on a man and woman in a boat. "For us, the 'dream' gag cartoon would be something that, while humorous, at the same time makes a serious point about wildlife conservation." Preferred format is single panel, b&w or color wash. Send submissions to Editor. Reports back in 2 months only if interested. Returns materials if accompanied by SASE. Buys one-time rights. Pays $30, b&w; $50, color; on publication. *Inside Tips:* A gag cartoonist should "make a point about conservation using humor."

Writing: Buys approximately 2-3 humorous pieces/year. Needs humorous fiction, non-fiction, "slice-of-life," anecdotes and "fillers." "Subject matter must relate to wildlife, natural resources conservation, the out-of-doors." Length: 1,500 words. To query be familiar with magazine; make sure article is appropriate. For first contact send query and manuscript to Editor. Reports back in 2 months. Samples are not filed; returned with SASE. Buys one-time rights. Pays $50-250 (maximum pay only if accompanied by illustrations) for 800-2,000 words. *Inside Tips:* "My publication—a state wildlife conservation magazine—is basically serious. Often I think it's serious to the point of being dull. There's a great potential for the use of humor to enliven publications with basically serious concerns."

KIWANIS, 3636 Woodview Trace, Indianapolis IN 46268. (317)875-8755. Monthly association magazine. Circ. 300,000. Needs spot cartoons.

Gag Cartoons: Buys 4 gag cartoons/year. Send all submissions to Jack Brockley, Associate Editor. Reports in weeks. Returns materials only if requested and accompanied by SASE. Buys first rights. Pays $25, b&w.

*LAF!, P.O. Box 313, Avilla IN 46710. Estab. 1991. Monthly newspaper tabloid. Needs comic strips, gag cartoons, spot cartoons, humorous writing. Accepts previously published cartoons and articles.

Gag Cartoons: Buys 5 cartoons/issue; 60 cartoons/year. Prefers gag cartoons on family, modern life for a general audience, small towns, work, singles, etc. Doesn't want to see gag cartoons on religion, politics and sex. Preferred format is single panel, double panel, multi-panel with gagline, b&w line art, b&w wash. Query with 1-10 rough drawings per batch to Julie Scher, Editor. Reports back within 6 weeks. Returns material if accompanied by a SASE. Buys one-time rights. Pays $5-10, b&w. Pays on publication. *Inside Tips:* "Remember that ours is a general audience of newspaper readers, but our publication is aimed at baby boomers and younger."

Writing: Buys approximately 8 humorous pieces/issues; 96 humorous pieces/year. Needs humorous nonfiction, fiction, interviews, "slice-of-life," anecdotes, "fillers" and cartoon stories. Subject matter includes family, small towns, suburbs, work, singles, modern life — for a general audience. Length: 250-500 words. To query make sure article is appropriate, study our writer's guidelines. For first contact send query, ms and writing sample to Julie Scher, Editor. Reports back within 6 weeks. Samples are not filed and are returned with SASE. Buys one-time rights. Pays $5-15 for 250-500 words. "We are looking for writing that surprises, twists and turns; odd slants on familiar subjects; well-written pieces with smooth transitions; writing that is easily understood by a wide audience."

LATEST JOKES, Box 023304, Brooklyn NY 11202-0066. (718)855-5057. Estab. 1974. Monthly newsletter that focuses on short, up-to-date jokes.
Writing: Needs "short, original jokes satirizing modern trends." Send jokes to Robert Makinson, Editor. Pays $1-3 for jokes. Send SASE for guidelines. Sample issue $3.

*LEADERSHIP, 465 Gundersen Dr., Carol Stream IL 60188. (708)260-6200. FAX: (708)260-0114. Estab. 1980. Quarterly professional journal. Circ. 80,000. Needs gag cartoons, humorous illustration and writing, caricatures and spot cartoons. Accepts previously published cartoons and articles.
Gag Cartoons: Buys 25 cartoons/issue; 110 cartoons/year. Prefers gag cartoons on inside humor of the professional ministry and the church. Doesn't want to see gag cartoons on Noah's Ark and Moses. "For us, the 'dream' gag cartoon would poke gentle fun at the foibles of people in the church milieu." Preferred format is single panel, b&w line art. Query with 5-10 rough drawings/batch to Marshall Shelley, Editor. Reports back within 1 month. Returns material if accompanied by SASE. Buys first time rights, reprint rights. Pays $125, b&w. Pays on acceptance. *Inside Tips:* "Know the Protestant Church very well and be able to lampoon its weaknesses and foibles."
Illustration: Buys 1 humorous illustration/issue; 2 humorous illustrations/year (other than cartoons) for articles. Works on assignment only (humorous illustrations). More apt to hire a humorous illustrator if he has a truly unique drawing style, conceptualizes well and has clever ideas — good use of metaphors, has a bold, powerful, attention-getting drawing style, uses humor effectively. For first contact send cover letter, b&w tearsheets and one panel cartoons to Marshall Shelley, Editor. Reports back within 1 month if interested, otherwise returned with SASE. Samples are not filed. Buys first time rights. Pays from $125 for a one panel cartoon to $250 for illustrations. Pays on acceptance.
Writing: "Most pieces are written by ministers from their own experiences, but work of other writers will be considered." Buys approximately 2 humorous pieces per issue; 8-10 humorous pieces/year. Needs humorous nonfiction. Length: 1,000 words. To query be familiar with our magazine, study writer's guidelines. "Cartoonists' guidelines are available with SASE but we'd like to consider a submission first. Writers' guidelines are available upon request." For first contact send query, outline of proposed story to Marshall Shelley, Editor. Reports back within 6 weeks. Samples not filed are returned. Buys first time rights. Pays $50-300 for 50-3,000 words. Offers 50% kill fee. *Inside Tips:*

"The writer must know our magazine and our audience very well. A particular slant is required."

LIGHT & LIFE PRESS, Box 535002, Indianapolis IN 46253. (317)244-3660. Estab. 1897. Sunday school take-home quarterly in weekly parts. Circ. 30,000. Needs gag and spot cartoons. Accepts previously published cartoons and humorous articles.
Gag Cartoons: Buys 10 gag cartoons/year. Preferred format is single panel b&w line art, with gagline. Query with 10-20 rough drawings/batch to Vera Bethel, Editor. Reports back in 1 month. Returns material if accompanied by SASE. Buys one-time rights or reprint rights. Pays $10, b&w; on publication.

*LIGHT QUARTERLY, Box 7500, Chicago IL 60680. (312)271-2432. Estab. 1992. Quarterly consumer magazine. Circ. 600 (now), 2,000-6,000 (projected). Needs gag cartoons, humorous illustration and writing, line drawings.
Gag Cartoons: Buys 3-8 cartoons/issue. Prefers gag cartoons on "off-beat, avant-garde themes (see *New Yorker, National Lampoon*)." Doesn't want to see "anything obvious, trite, clichéd." Preferred format is single, double, multi-panel with or without gagline, b&w line art. Query with 4-12 rough drawings/batch to John Mella, Editor. Reports back within 2 months. Returns material if accompanied by a SASE. Buys first time rights. Pays 2 copies.
Illustration: Buys approximately 4-8 humorous illustrations/issue for covers, articles and spots. More apt to hire a humorous illustrator if he or she has a truly unique drawing style; conceptualizes well and has clever ideas—good use of metaphors, has a clean, graphically-pleasing drawing style; has a subtle, understated drawing style; uses humor effectively; does not exaggerate or distort too much; is businesslike, meets deadlines and is responsible to my needs. For first contact send cover letter and b&w tearsheets to John Mella, Editor. Reports back within 2 months. Samples not filed are returned by SASE. Buys first time rights. Pays 2 copies. *Tips:* "Nothing obvious, trite."
Writing: Buys approximately 2-4 humorous pieces/issue. Needs humorous nonfiction, fiction and anecdotes, "fillers." Length: 100-1,200 words. To query be familiar with magazine; make sure article is appropriate. Send SASE for copy. For first contact send cover letter and manuscript to John Mella, Editor. Reports back within 2 months. Samples not filed are returned with SASE. Buys first time rights. Pays 2 copies.

*LINK-UP, 143 Old Marlton Pike, Medford NJ 08055. (609)654-4888. FAX: (609)654-4309. Estab. 1985. Bimonthly consumer magazine, tabloid. Circ. 10,000. Needs comic strips, gag cartoons, spot cartoons.
Gag Cartoons: Buys 2 cartoons/issue; 9 cartoons/year. Prefers gag cartoons "that deal with using a modem." Doesn't want to see gag cartoons on general computer topics. Preferred format is b&w line art with gagline. Query with 5-15 rough drawings/batch to Joe Webb, Editor. Reports back in 1 month. Returns material if accompanied by a SASE. Buys first time rights. Pays $25, b&w. Pays on publication. *Inside Tips:* "Know what is funny."
Writing: Buys approximately 2 humorous pieces/year. Needs humorous nonfiction. Subject matter includes going online with a modem. Length: 700 words. To query be familiar with magazine; make sure article is appropriate; study writer's guidelines. For first contact send cover letter, ms to Joe Webb, Editor. Reports back within 2 months. Samples are not filed. Samples not filed are returned with SASE. Buys all rights. Pays $90-220 for 500-1,500 words. *Inside Tips:* "The freelance writer should be just as knowledgeable about going online as regular writers."

THE LION MAGAZINE, 300 22nd St., Oak Brook IL 60521-8842. (708)571-5466. FAX: (708)571-8890. Estab. 1917. Needs gag and spot cartoons.
Gag Cartoons: Buys 1-2 gag cartoons/issue. Prefers gag cartoons on "wholesome families, no sex. Avoid politics, violence and religion." Preferred format is single panel with gagline, b&w line art. Query with 5-10 rough drawings/batch to Robert Kleinfelder, Senior Editor. Buys first rights. Pays $50 b&w.

*LISTEN, 1350 North Kings Road, Nampa ID 83687. (208)465-2592. FAX: (208)465-2531. Estab. 1948. Monthly consumer magazine. Circ. 70,000. Needs humorous illustration, caricatures and spot cartoons. Accepts previously published cartoons if they illustrate one of the articles directly.
Illustration: Buys approximately 3 humorous illustrations/issue; 36/year for articles. When hiring a freelance humorous illustrator, these abilities are considered: a truly unique drawing style; a bold, powerful, attention-getting drawing style (our magazine is marketed to a teen audience); businesslike attitude—meets deadlines and responsive to editor's needs. For first contact send b&w or color tearsheets, b&w or color promo piece and slides to Robert Mason, Art Director. In reviewing humorous illustration we look for a drawing style which is "different than anything I'm already buying." Reports back only if interested. Samples are filed or returned by SASE if requested. Buys first time rights and one-time rights. Pays $150 minimum/b&w page; $300+/color. Pays on acceptance. *Inside Tips:* "Being able to work within a two-week time frame, long-distance and meeting the deadline are essential to receiving on-going projects for *Listen* magazine. *Listen* is marketed to a teen audience."

LIVING AMONG NATURE DARINGLY, 4466 Ike Mooney Rd., Silverton OR 97381. (503)873-8829 or 873-6585. Estab. 1986. Five times/year consumer magazine. Circ. 1,000. Needs comic strips, caricature and political satire. Accepts previously published cartoons.
Gag Cartoons: Query with 1-3 rough drawings/batch. Reports back within 3 weeks with SASE required. Returns materials if accompanied by SASE. Negotiates rights purchased. Pays $10 minimum, b&w; on publication.
Illustration: Buys approximately 5 humorous illustrations/year for articles and spots. For first contact send cover letter and b&w promo pieces to Bill Anderson, Editor/Publisher. Note: "Material is published from paid subscribers only, although we will review submissions from non-subscribers. Subscriptions cost $9 for 1 year, $15 for 2 years." In reviewing humorous illustrations "we look for a good chuckle and wholesomeness." Reports back within 3 weeks with SASE required. Samples are not filed; returned by SASE. *Inside Tips:* "Probably the best cartoonist of a sort we're looking for is Trudeau of *Doonesbury* fame. He reminds us of what we can make America—make the reader want to think socially for a better America."
Writing: Buys approximately 5 humorous pieces/year. Needs humorous nonfiction. Subject matter includes current national and international events, from a slightly liberal, strongly populist viewpoint. Length: 150-500 words. To query be familiar with magazine; make sure article is appropriate; study writer's guidelines. Send $2.50 and SASE for copy. For first contact send cover letter and outline of proposed story to Bill Anderson, Editor/Publisher. Reports back within 3 weeks with SASE required. Samples are returned with SASE. Negotiates rights purchased. Pays $7.50-20 for 150-500 words. *Inside Tips:* "Study Mike Royko or Art Buchwald, but tone it down two decibels. No anti-religious material of any sort, (Jewish, Moslem, Christian, etc.). *LAND* magazine specializes in showing people how to farm the old-fashioned way to break loose from dependence on a system which enslaves people to make ever-more money and ever-rising debts. This bourgeois mode can be depicted with caricatures of any visible politician or financier or. . . . only when we stop keeping up with the Jones' can enough pressure be taken off that drug abuse can stop."

*LONG ISLAND UPDATE MAGAZINE, 770-10 Grand Blvd., Deer Park NY 11729. (516)242-7722. FAX: (516)242-7387. Estab. 1981. Monthly consumer magazine. Circ. 53,000. Needs spot cartoons and humorous writing. Prefers working with freelancers who have fax capabilities.

Gag Cartoons: Query with 5-10 rough drawings/batch. Reports only if interested. Returns materials if accompanied by a SASE. Buys all rights. Pays $25, color.

Writing: Buys approximately 1 humorous piece/issue; 12 humorous pieces/year. Needs humorous nonfiction, fiction and "slice-of-life." Length: 700 words. For first contact send cover letter, ms and published tearsheets to Allison A. Whitney, Managing Editor. Samples not filed are returned with SASE. Buys all rights.

THE LUTHERAN, 8765 W. Higgins Rd., Chicago IL 60631-4183. (312)380-2540. FAX: (312)380-1465. Estab. 1968. Triweekly denominational magazine. Circ. 1,000,000 +. Needs gag cartoons and humorous writing "tailored to Lutherans." Accepts previously published cartoons and humorous articles.

Gag Cartoons: Buys 20-25 gag cartoons/year. Prefers gag cartoons with religious theme. Preferred format is single panel with or without gagline, b&w line art or wash. Query with 6-12 rough drawings/batch to Roger Kahle, Managing Editor. Reports back within 1 month. Returns materials if accompanied by SASE. Buys one-time rights. Pays $35 +, b&w. Pays on acceptance.

Illustration: Buys approximately 3 humorous illustrations/year for articles. Works on assignment only. When hiring a freelance humorous illustrator, these abilities are considered: good conceptualization and clever ideas — good use of metaphors; clean, graphically-pleasing drawing style; effective use of humor; lack of exaggeration or distortion; ability to "fun up" an otherwise "flat" manuscript; businesslike attitude — meets deadlines and is responsive to needs. For first contact send b&w and color tearsheets and promo pieces to Jack Lund, Art Director. Reports in 1 month. Samples are filed. Buys first rights. Pays $300, b&w, $400, color, page; $500, color, cover. Pays on publication.

Writing: Buys approximately 3 humorous pieces/year. Needs humorous nonfiction and "slice-of-life" relating to Lutheran Church. Length: 500-1,500 words. To query be familiar with magazine; make sure article is appropriate. Send 75¢ and SASE for copy and writer's guidelines. For first contact send cover letter, query, outline of proposed story and writing sample to David L. Miller, Features Editor. Reports back in 1 month. Samples are filed or are returned with SASE. Buys one-time rights. Pays $150-500. Offers 50% kill fee.

MCINTOSH PUBLISHING LTD., Box 430, North Battleford, Saskatchewan S9A-245 Canada. (306)445-4401. FAX: (306)445-1977. Estab. 1906. Newsletter, weekly newspaper, "alternative" weekly, trade journal. Circ. 42 million; 20 million for community newspaper. Previously published cartoons/humorous illustrations and articles are accepted. Prefers working with freelancers who have fax capabilities.

Cartoons & Illustrations: Needs comic strips and editorial cartoons on wildlife, hunting, skiing and fishing subjects. Considers whether artist uses humor effectively. For first contact send b&w promo piece. For editorial cartoons, op-ed or caricatures, contact Rod McDonald, Marketing and Sales. Reports back within 4 weeks. Returns material only if requested. Buys reprint rights. Pays for editorial cartoon/humorous illustration, $10-25.

Writing: Needs humorous "slice-of-life" and material for hunting, fishing and skiing section. Accepts humorous writing that has a regional slant. For first contact send cover letter and writing samples to Bill McIntosh, Publisher. Unsolicited material is filed. Buys reprint rights.

MANAGEMENT ACCOUNTING, 10 Paragon Dr., Montvale NJ 07645. (201)573-6269. FAX: (201)573-8185. Estab. 1919. Monthly trade journal. Circ. 85,000. Needs gag cartoons. Accepts previously published cartoons.
Gag Cartoons: Buys 1 gag cartoon/issue. Prefers gag cartoons on business, finance and accounting. Doesn't want to see gag cartoons on "dumb secretaries or sexist themes. The 'dream' gag cartoon would be *New Yorker* style with high level satire or *Wall Street Journal* style." Preferred format is single panel with gagline. Query with 1-10 rough drawings/batch to Robert F. Randall, Editor. Reports back within 1 week. Returns material if accompanied by a SASE. Buys first time rights. Pays $25 minimum, b&w. Pays on acceptance.

MANAGEMENT REVIEW MAGAZINE, American Management Association, 135 W. 50th St., New York NY 10020. (212)903-8393. FAX: (212)903-8168. Monthly magazine. Circ. 70,000. Needs humorous illustration and spot cartoons. Prefers working with freelancers who have fax capabilities. Send samples to Seval Newton.

*MANGAJIN, P.O. Box 49543, Atlanta GA 30359. (404)634-3874. FAX: (404)634-1799. Estab. 1990. Consumer magazine published 10 times/year. Circ. 18,000. Needs humorous illustration and caricatures. Prefers working with freelancers who have fax capabilities.
Illustration: Buys 3 humorous illustrations/issue; 30 humorous illustrations/year for covers and articles. Works on assignment only. More apt to hire a humorous illustrator if he conceptualizes well and has clever ideas—good use of metaphors, uses humor effectively, is businesslike, meets deadlines and is responsive to my needs, and can incorporate Japanese "flavor" effectively. For first contact send cover letter and b&w tearsheets to Vaughan P. Simmons, Editor and Publisher. Reports back within 1 month. Samples not filed are returned by SASE. Negotiates rights purchased. Pays $50, b&w, page; $350, color, cover. *Inside Tips:* "This is a magazine for people interested in Japanese language and pop culture. All of our illustrations are Japan-related."

*MANHATTAN MAGAZINE/NEW WORLD JOURNAL, 330 West 56th St. #3G, New York NY 10019. (212)265-7970. Estab. 1983/1992. Quarterly consumer magazine. Circ. 50,000/100,000. Needs comic strips, cartoon narratives, humorous illustration. Prefers working with freelancers who have fax capabilities.
Illustration: Buys 5 humorous illustrations/issue for articles, spots and departments. Works on assignment only. More apt to hire a humorous illustrator if he conceptualizes well and has clever ideas—good use of metaphors, has a clean, graphically-pleasing drawing style, has a subtle, understated drawing style. For first contact send cover letter, resume, b&w promo piece to Rick Bard, Editor and Publisher. Looks for "What strikes me—topics for *New World Journal* on environment, in terms of business, arts, politics, male-female relationships—illustrating issues here . . . with an insight (warm or caustic) into human aspects." Reports back if interested. Samples are filed. Samples not filed are returned if requested with SASE. Negotiates rights purchased. Pays $50, b&w; $100, color, page. Pays on publication. *Inside Tips:* "We are looking for humorous illustrators who are able to offer graphic perspective on pieces to be illustrated."

*MATURE YEARS, Box 801, 201 8th Ave. S., Nashville TN 37202. (615)749-6292. Estab. 1967. Quarterly church-related magazine. Circ. 80,000. Needs humorous writing (brief), cartoon narratives and gag cartoons.
Gag Cartoons: Buys 1-2 gag cartoons/issue, 4-6/year. Prefers gag cartoons on older persons and the church. Preferred gag cartoon format is single panel b&w line art, with gagline. Send submissions to Marvin W. Cropsey, Editor. Returns material if accompanied by SASE. Buys all rights. Pays $15-25/b&w on acceptance.

Illustration: Buys approximately 5 humorous illustrations/issue, 20/year for articles. Works on assignment only. When hiring a freelance humorous illustrator, these abilities are considered: not too much exaggeration or distortion. For first contact, send b&w tearsheets to Dave Dawson, Art Procurement Director. Pays $50/b&w page on acceptance.

Writing: Buys approximately 5 humorous pieces/year. Needs humorous fiction/nonfiction, humorous interviews, humorous "slice-of-life," humorous anecdotes and humorous "fillers." Length: 1,000-2,000 words. To query: be familiar with magazine; make sure article is appropriate; study writer's guidelines. Send $3 and SASE for copy. For first contact send query and outline of proposed story to Marvin W. Cropsey, Editor. Reports back in 6 weeks. Buys all rights and negotiates rights purchased. Pays 4¢/word.

MEDICAL ECONOMICS, 5 Paragon Dr., Montvale NJ 07645. (201)358-7200. Needs gag cartoons.

Gag Cartoons: Buys 6-10 cartoons/issue. Prefers gag cartoons on "no particular theme—stay away from religion and sex." Preferred format is single panel with gagline, b&w line are or wash. Query with 1-50 rough drawings/batch to Cartoon Editor. Buys all rights. Pays $100, b&w, $100, color. Pays on acceptance.

Illustration: Buys 20 humorous illustrations/year for articles and editorials. For first contact send color tearsheets and promo piece. "We do not accept unsolicited material." Make appointment to send all humorous illustration material to Donna DeAngelis, Art Administrator. Buys one-time rights. Payment varies.

*MESSENGER, 1852 Century Pl., Atlanta GA 30345. (404)320-3388. FAX: (404)320-7964. Estab. 1974. Monthly Christian denominational magazine. Circ. 13,000. Needs humorous illustration, spot cartoons. Accepts previously published cartoons and articles. Prefers working with freelancers who have fax capabilities.

Gag Cartoons: Buys 6-10 cartoons/year. Prefers gag cartoons on church life, Christian experience. Doesn't want to see gag cartoons on "father as dummy." "For us the 'dream' gag cartoon would be family in situation easily identified by everyone." Preferred format is single panel, b&w line art. Query with 10-12 rough drawings/batch to G. Blaylock, Coordinator. Reports back within 2 weeks. Returns material only if requested. Buys one-time rights. Pays $25, b&w. Pays on publication. *Inside Tips:* "Understand conservative church-going Christians."

Illustration: Send humorous illustration material to G. Blaylock, Coordinator. Reports within 2 weeks if interested. Samples are filed. Buys one-time rights. Pays $25, b&w, page.

METRO, 410 S. First St., San Jose CA 95113. (408)298-8000. Weekly newspaper. Circ. 70,000. Needs comic strips, humorous illustration, gag and spot cartoons. Accepts previously published cartoons and humorous articles. Prefers working with freelancers who have fax capabilities.

Gag Cartoons: Buys 10-20 gag cartoons/year. Preferred format is b&w line art. Query with 5-10 rough drawings/batch to Michael S. Gant, Arts Editor. Reports back only if interested. Does not return material. Buys one-time rights. Pays $10, b&w; on publication.

Illustration: Buys approximately 5-10 humorous illustrations/year for articles. Works on assignment only. When hiring a freelance humorous illustrator, these abilities are considered: ability to conceptualize well and have clever ideas—good use of metaphors; a bold, powerful, attention-getting drawing style; businesslike attitude—meets deadlines and responsive to editor's needs. For first contact, send cover letter, b&w tearsheets and resume to Michael S. Gant. Looks for originality and graphic design. Reports back only if interested. Samples are not returned. Buys one-time rights. Pays $15, b&w, page; $50, b&w, cover; on publication.

MAGIC JOHNSON ,
*All-time leader in
playoff assists,*
kidsports

© Marcia Staimer

Magical Caricature: *Washington, DC-based caricaturist Marcia Staimer created this terrific caricature of Magic Johnson. Paid $900 for one-time reproduction rights to the drawing, Staimer had to "work with an extremely tight layout for the caricature. That was the only restriction given to me, as the art director works with me often and wants my style."*

Writing: Buys approximately 5 humorous pieces/year. Needs humorous nonfiction and "slice-of-life." Subject matter includes "political satire, but not heavy-handed propaganda." Length: 750 words. To query be familiar with magazine. For first contact send cover letter, query, published tearsheets, resume and writing sample to Michael S. Gant, Arts Editor. Reports back only if interested. Samples are not returned. Buys one-time rights. Pays 5¢/word. Offers 50% kill fee.

MILITARY MARKET, 6883 Commercial Dr., Springfield VA 22159. Estab. 1950. Monthly trade journal. Circ. 10,000. Needs gag cartoons.

Gag Cartoons: Buys 4 gag cartoons/issue on department store and supermarket situations from point of view of managers, suppliers and in-store workers. Doesn't want to see gag cartoons on "bimbos." Preferred format is single panel with or without gagline, b&w line art. Query with 5-20 rough drawings/batch to Nancy Tucker, Editor. Reports back in 4-6 months. Returns materials if accompanied by SASE. Buys one-time rights. Pays $25, b&w; on acceptance.

MINNE HA! HA!, "THE TWIN CITIES' SORELY NEEDED HUMOR MAGAZINE", Box 14009, Minneapolis MN 55414. (612)729-7687. Estab. 1978. Bimonthly tabloid. Circ. 20,000. Needs comic strips; humorous photos, illustration and writing; cartoon narratives; caricature; gag and spot cartoons. Accepts previously published cartoons and humorous articles.

Gag Cartoons: Buys 5-10 gag cartoons/issue. Prefers avant garde, artsy, politically incorrect gag cartoons on "the arts, skateboarders, street gangs, Scandinavians, new age, politics, environment, media and yuppies. For us the 'dream' gag cartoon would be lampooning the politically correct (right or left), and/or gangs and crime — anything urban." Preferred formats are single or multi-panel without gagline, b&w line art. Query with 10-25 rough drawings/batch to Lance Anger, Editor. Reports back only if interested. Does not return materials. Buys one-time rights. Pays $5 minimum, b&w; $20 minimum, color. *Inside Tips:* "Be sarcastic and satirical about modern cities, especially crime and street gangs — also a plus to know Minnesotan Scandinavian culture."

Illustration: Buys approximately 2 humorous illustrations/issue for covers and articles. When hiring a freelance humorous illustrator, these abilities are considered: unique drawing style; bold, powerful, attention-getting drawing style; effective use of humor; businesslike attitude — meets deadlines and is responsive to needs. For first contact send b&w or color tearsheets and promo pieces, resume and client list to Lance Anger, Editor. Reports back if interested. Samples are filed and not returned. Buys one-time rights. Pays $10 minimum, b&w, $25 minimum, color, page; $20 minimum, b&w, $45 minimum, color, cover. Pays on publication. Co-op payment schedule; "we pay more if advertising is up in that issue."

Writing: Buys approximately 2 humorous pieces/issue. Needs humorous fiction, nonfiction, interviews, "slice-of-life" and anecdotes; cartoon stories; and "fillers." Length: up to 2,000 words. Short pieces more likely to be used. "In querying our magazine, we advise that your article be appropriate for us." For first contact send manuscript, writing sample, published tearsheets and outline of proposed story to Lance Anger, Editor. Reports back if interested. Samples are filed and not returned. Buys one-time rights. Pays $0-50 for 100-2,000 words. *Inside Tips:* "We take risks! Our advertisers are alternative, progressive, hip and therefore few in number. So we can't pay a lot but you will find a very special readership and an opportunity to get away with more than in most any other publication. Our favorite target this year is the politically correct crowd. We are definitely left of center, but see those who would suppress artistic freedom in the name of "progress" as most worthy of pointed sarcastic attack."

MODERN DRUMMER, 870 Pompton Ave., Cedar Grove NJ 07009. (201)239-4140. FAX: (201)239-7139. Estab. 1977. Monthly consumer magazine. Circ. 95,000. Needs humorous illustration and writing, gag and spot cartoons. Accepts previously published cartoons.

Gag Cartoons: Buys 4 gag cartoons/year on drummer-oriented gags. Preferred format is single panel, b&w line art. Query with 6-12 rough drawings/batch to R. Spagnardi, Editor, or S. Bienstock, Art Director. Reports back within 2 weeks. Returns materials if accompanied by SASE. Buys all rights. Pays $25 minimum, b&w; on publication.

Writing: Buys approximately 2 humorous pieces/year. Needs humorous nonfiction and interviews. Subject matter includes music industry, specifically from a drummer's point of view. "Write magazine editor to see what editorial needs are."

Illustration: Buys approximately 3 humorous illustrations/year for articles. Works on assignment only. When hiring a freelance humorous illustrator, these abilities are considered: good conceptualization and clear ideas — good use of metaphors; a clean, graphically-pleasing drawing style; effective use of humor; lack of exaggeration or distortion. For first contact send cover letter, b&w tearsheets and promo pieces to R. Spagnardi, Editor. Reports back within 2 weeks. Buys all rights. Pays $25 minimum, b&w, page; on publication.

*THE MONTHLY, 1301 59th St., Emeryville CA 94608. (510)658-9811. FAX: (510)658-9902. Estab. 1970. Monthly consumer magazine. Circ. 75,000. Needs gag cartoons.

Gag Cartoons: Buys 3 cartoons/issue; 36 cartoons/year. Prefers gag cartoons on "anything." Preferred format is single panel, double panel (if vertical in format), multi-panel (if vertical in format), with or without gagline, with or without balloons, b&w line art, b&w wash (prefer line art). Query to Andreas Jones, Kartoon Editor. Reports back within 1 month. Returns material if accompanied by a SASE. Buys one-time rights (no reprint if previously published in the San Francisco area). Pays $35 b&w. Pays 30 days after publication.

*THE MONTHLY INDEPENDENT TRIBUNE TIMES JOURNAL POST GAZETTE NEWS CHRONICLE BULLETIN, 1630 Allston Way, Berkeley CA 94703. Estab. 1983. Irregularly published consumer magazine. Circ. 500. Needs gag cartoons, humorous illustration and writing, spot cartoons and "humorous graphic concoctions."

Gag Cartoons: Buys 1 cartoon/issue. Prefers gag cartoons on any subject. "For us the 'dream' gag cartoon would be funny, bizarre, cryptic." Preferred format is single, double or multi-panel, with or without gagline, with balloons, b&w line art, b&w wash. Send completed cartoons to Denver Tucson, Assistant Editor. Reports back within weeks. Returns material if accompanied by a SASE. Buys one-time rights.

Illustration: Buys humorous illustrations mainly for spots. More apt to hire a humorous illustrator if he or she has a truly unique drawing style, uses humor effectively, "makes little sense." For first contact send cover letter, finished illustrations to Denver Tucson, Assistant Editor. Looks for "Something that's funny and/or horrible." Reports back within weeks. Samples are not filed and are returned by SASE. Buys one-time rights. *Inside Tips:* "Don't be imitative."

Writing: Buys approximately 2 humorous pieces/issue. Needs humorous nonfiction and fiction, cartoon stories, humorous anecdotes, "fillers." Subject matter includes any topic. Length: 1,200 words or less. To query be familiar with magazine; make sure article is appropriate. For first contact send cover letter and ms to T.S. Child, Editor. Reports back within weeks. Samples are not filed. Samples not filed are returned with SASE. Buys one-time rights.

MONTREAL MIRROR, 400 McGill, Montreal, Quebec Canada. (514)393-1010. "Alternative" weekly that focuses on local news and culture. Circ. 50,000. Accepts previously published cartoons/humorous illustrations.

Cartoons & Illustrations: Needs comic strips of regional appeal, editorial cartoons of local appeal, gag and spot cartoons, especially on food. For first contact send cover letter, b&w tearsheets and promo piece to Ava Chisling, News Editor. Reports back if interested. Returns materials if accompanied by SASE. Keeps materials on file. Buys one-time rights. Pays for editorial cartoon, $15 minimum.

© Tim Walker

One Size Doesn't Fit All: How do you draw on the subject of condoms? Veeeeerrrry carefully. Tim Walker of Madison Heights, Michigan did just that when he created a whimsical "condom-oriented" humorous illustration for a women's magazine. Paid $225 for usage of the illustration, Walker rendered the art in watercolor and colored pencils.

MOTHER EARTH NEWS, 24 E. 23 St., New York NY 10010. (212)260-7210. Estab. 1970. Bimonthly consumer magazine. Circ. 400,000. Needs humorous writing. Accepts previously published humorous articles.

Writing: Buys approximately 6 humorous pieces/year. Needs humorous "slice-of-life" and reflective anecdotes. Subject matter includes "how-to," country life, environmental issues, regional, folksy and rural humor. Length: 800 words. To query be familiar with magazine; "make sure article is appropriate for our 'Last Laugh' column." For first contact send manuscript, query and outline of proposed story to Submissions Editor. Reports back within a matter of weeks. Samples are returned. Buys all or first rights. *Inside Tips:* "It can be first person, a well-strung collection of jokes, 'how I screwed up' — whatever, as long as it's appropriate to our subject areas and is really funny (not just cute)."

MOUNTAIN FAMILY CALENDAR, Box 294, Rhododendron OR 97049. (503)622-4798. Estab. 1982. Monthly general interest magazine. Circ. 7,000. Needs comic strips, humorous illustration and writing, cartoon narratives, caricature, gag and spot cartoons. Accepts previously published cartoons and humorous articles.
Gag Cartoons: Buys 4 gag cartoons/issue on Oregon Trail, outdoor recreation, wildlife and fisheries, nature and logging. Doesn't want to see gag cartoons on sex. "For us, the 'dream' gag cartoon would be pioneers crossing over the Oregon Trail." Preferred formats are single, double or multi-panel with or without gagline or balloons, b&w line art. Query with 5-12 rough drawings/batch to Michael P. Jones, Editor. Reports back in 2 months (hopefully). Returns materials only if requested and accompanied by SASE. Buys first rights. Pays in copies, upon publication. *Inside Tips:* "Be flexible and willing to try new things. If work has merit and if we are interested, then we will ask the illustrator to work on a book project with us."
Illustration: Buys approximately 3 humorous illustrations/issue for spots. "Be patient and flexible. If you're a demanding prima donna, don't bother us." For first contact send cover letter, b&w or color tearsheets and promo pieces, resume, slides, client list and portfolio to Michael P. Jones, Editor. Looks for "the potential to do new things with talent." Reports back in 2 months. Samples not filed are returned if requested by SASE. Buys first rights. Pays in copies, on publication. *Inside Tips:* "Be flexible and try new things."
Writing: Buys approximately 1 humorous piece/issue. Needs humorous fiction, nonfiction, interviews, "slice-of-life," cartoon stories, anecdotes and "fillers." Subject matter includes anti-logging, nature, fish and wildlife, outdoor recreation and travel. Length: open. To query study writer's guidelines. Send 45¢ and SASE for copy. For first contact send cover letter, manuscript, writing sample, query, outline of proposed story, published tearsheets and resume to Michael P. Jones, Editor. Reports back in 2 months, depending upon workload. Samples are returned with SASE only if requested. Buys first rights. Pays in copies, on publication. *Inside Tips:* "Keep it clean! We are a family-oriented publication."

MUSCLE MAG INTERNATIONAL, Unit 2, 52 Bramsteele Rd., Brampton ON L6W3M5 Canada. (416)457-3030. FAX: (416)791-4292. Estab. 1974. Monthly consumer magazine. Circ. 220,000. Needs comic strips, humorous writing, caricatures and gag cartoons.
Gag Cartoons: Buys 25 gag cartoons/year. Prefers gag cartoons on bodybuilding. Doesn't want to see gag cartoons "that are poorly drawn." The "dream" gag cartoon would be "a strong drawing with a strong caption." Preferred formats are full page color, now needed. Query with 6-10 rough drawings/batch to Robert Kennedy, President. Reports back in 30 days. Returns material with postage. "We are Canadian, so Canadian stamp only or $3 cash for return postage." Buys first time rights. Pays $50, b&w, $100, color; payment varies according to quality. Pays on acceptance. *Inside Tips:* "Be professional. Don't ever submit work that is shakily drawn, dirty, folded or poorly executed. No cartoonist should submit work unless he or she is properly trained or diligently self-taught."
Illustration: Buys approximately 6 humorous illustrations/year for articles. For first contact send cover letter and b&w tearsheets to Robert Kennedy. Reports back in 10 days only if interested. Samples are not filed; returned if requested. Buys first time rights.
Writing: Buys approximately 6 humorous pieces/year. Needs humorous fiction, anecdotes and "fillers." Subject matter includes "body builders or editors and publishers of bodybuilding publications." Length: 1,000-8,000 words. To query be familiar with magazine; make sure article is appropriate. For first contact, send cover letter and manuscript to Robert Kennedy. Reports back in 10 days only if interested. Samples are not filed; returned with Canadian postage or $3 cash. Buys first time rights. Pays $150-400. *Inside Tips:* "Humor writing should enable readers to relate to the quirks relative

to bodybuilders. Humor work must be honed and reworked more than regular fiction or nonfiction because balance is most important to make the humor stand out as humor."

NATIONAL ENQUIRER, 600 SE Coast Ave., Lantana FL 33464. Newspaper.
Cartoons & Illustrations: Needs gag cartoons. For first contact send cover letter with social security and phone numbers. Send all cartooning submissions to Michele Cooke, Assistant Editor. Reports back within weeks only if interested. Returns materials only if accompanied by SASE; does not file materials. Buys first rights. Pays by the cartoon, $300 ($40 for each extra panel). *Inside Tips:* "Be original, neat and funny. We are a top cartoon market and buy 8-10 of the 2,000 we receive weekly. No photocopies, no half-sheets."
Writing: For first contact send cover letter and writing samples to Michele L. Cooke, Assistant Editor. Reports only if interested and if accompanied by SASE. Buys first rights. Pays $25 per filler. *Inside Tips:* "We are looking for short humorous poetry, jokes, etc. All should be original. No 'arty' stuff. Very important that contributor study several issues to see what we do buy. We are *not* a market for humorous illustrations; I can't stress enough that freelancers should *know their market*. Each publication is different and what will work at one won't necessarily work at the other. Learn to behave in a professional manner. Not every cartoon or item of writing you create will be bought and it does you no good professionally to bemoan your lack of a sale to an editor. Freelancing is not for the thin-skinned."

NATIONAL REVIEW, 150 E. 35th St., New York NY 10016. (212)679-7330. FAX: (212)696-0309. Needs humorous illustration and writing, caricatures, gag and spot cartoons. Accepts previously publiched cartoons and articles.
Gag Cartoons: Buys 10 gag cartoons/issue. Prefers gag cartoons on any "politics, off-the-wall humor." Preferred format is single panel with or without gagline or balloons, b&w line art or wash. Query with 5-6 rough drawings/batch to Geoffrey Morris, Cartoon Director. Buys first rights. Pays $50, b&w. Pays on publication.
Illustration: Buys 10 hujmorous illustrations/issue for spots. For first contact send cover letter and b&w promo piece to Geoffrey Morris. Buys first rights. Pays $50 b&w page.
Writing: Buys 10 humorous pieces/issue. Needs humorous nonfiction, fiction, "slice-of-life" and anecdotes, "fillers." Subject matter includes "conservative politics, day-to-day situations." Length: 20 words. For first contact send cover letter, query and writing samples to Geoffrey Morris. Buys first rights. Payment varies.

NEW BLOOD MAGAZINE, Suite 3730, 540 W. Foothill Blvd., Glendora CA 91740. Estab. 1986. Quarterly magazine. Circ. 15,000. Needs comic strips, humorous illustration, gag and spot cartoons. Accepts previously published cartoons and humorous articles.
Gag Cartoons: Buys 10-20 gag cartoons/issue. Gag cartoons on any subject accepted. "The more controversial, the better." Preferred formats are single, double and multi-panel with gagline or balloons, b&w line art or b&w or color wash. Submit 5-10 drawings/batch to Chris Lacher, Editor. Reports back in 3 weeks. Returns material if accompanied by SASE. Buys first time rights. Pays $25 minimum, b&w; sometimes negotiates payment for color. Pays half on acceptance, half on publication; mostly publication.
Illustration: Buys approximately 1-2 humorous illustrations/issue for articles. When hiring a freelance humorous illustrator, these abilities are considered: a clean, graphical-ly-pleasing drawing style; effective use of humor; businesslike attitude—meets deadlines and responsive to editor's needs. For first contact send cover letter and b&w tearsheets to Chris Lacher. "Especially interested in new talents—hence the title." Reports back in 3 weeks. Samples are filed; samples not filed are returned by SASE if requested. Buys first time rights. Pays $10-100, b&w, page. Pays half on acceptance, half on publica-

"I need your medical history. Have you ever sued a doctor?"

NATIONAL ENQUIRER

© Stan Fine

No, But There's Always a First Time: *Bala Cynwyd, Pennsylvania-based gag cartoonist Stan Fine draws on the proverbial doctor/patient relationship in this cartoon. Originally published in the* National Enquirer, *Fine was paid $300 by the weekly supermarket tabloid. "I've been mailing my cartoons to the National Enquirer for 15 years," says Fine. "They like my work and buy 10-14 cartoons a year from me."*

tion. *Inside Tips:* "Follow our guidelines, don't be averse to a few suggestions for changes and you'll do well at NB."

*NEW LIVING, P.O. Box 1519, Stony Brook NY 11790. (516)981-7232. FAX: (516)585-4606. Estab. 1991. Monthly guides and special publications. Circ. 20,000. Needs comic strips, humorous illustration and writing, spot cartoons.
Gag Cartoons: Buys 2-3 cartoons/issue. Prefers gag cartoons on health and fitness. Preferred format is b&w line art. Query with 2-5 rough drawings/batch to Christine Harvey, Publisher. Reports back if interested. Does not return material. Buys all rights, Pays $75, b&w. Pays on publication. *Inside Tips:* "Send samples pertaining to health and fitness subject matter along with clips."
Illustration: Buys 2 humorous illustrations/issue for articles, spots. More apt to hire a humorous illustrator if he has a truly unique drawing style; conceptualizes well and has clever ideas—good use of metaphors; has a subtle, understated drawing style; does not exaggerate or distort too much; is businesslike, meets deadlines and is responsive to my needs. For first contact send cover letter, resume, b&w tearsheets and b&w promo piece to Christine Harvey, Publisher. Looks for "Unique but simple style fitting in with the demos of our publication's readers." Reports back if interested. Samples not filed are not returned. Buys all rights. Pays $150, b&w, page. Pays on publication. *Tips:* "Know

the trends, fads and demographics of the health and fitness market."
Writing: Buys approximately 1 humorous piece/issue. Needs humorous nonfiction, "slice-of-life" pertaining to health and fitness. "We accept material only dealing with health and fitness." Length: 500 words. To query, be familiar with publication; make sure article is appropriate; "Send SASE for copy of our editorial guidelines." For first contact send query, outline of proposed story, writing sample to Christine Harvey, Publisher. Reports back if interested. Samples not filed are not returned. Buys all rights. Pays $25-150 for 500 words.

NEW TIMES, INC., 1201 E. Jefferson, Phoenix AZ 85034. (602)271-0040. FAX: (602)340-8806. Estab. 1970. Weekly news and arts journal focusing on local interest stories. Also extensive listings of restaurants, clubs, events (separate adult and children's sections), and entertainment. Includes music, theater, restaurant, movie and art reviews. Circ. 140,000.
Cartoons & Illustrations: Will accept humorous illustrations and caricature for review. "Ability to turn around on very short deadlines, b&w style, effective use of humor and artist's creative input are consideration priorities." For first contact, include cover letter, resume and b&w tearsheets or slides. Color work is welcome but rarely contracted. Publishes occasional color covers. Send to: Editorial Art Director. Response will accompany *only* SASE. Returns material *only* if requested. Keeps material on file otherwise. Buys all rights. Pays $75 for interior illustration, $125 for covers (negotiable based on artist's input, difficulty of assignment and turnaround time).

NEW WOMAN MAGAZINE, 215 Lexington Ave., New York NY 10016. (212)251-1601. FAX: (212)251-1590. Needs cartoon narratives, gag and spot cartoons. Accepts previously published cartoons and articles.
Gag Cartoons: Buys 1 gag cartoon/issue for *Pin-Ups* section (a group of quotes on a different topic chosen each month.). Prefers gag cartoons on "womanhood, being a woman." Preferred format is single panel with gagline or balloons, b&w line art or wash. Query with 5-10 rough drawings/batch to Anne Marie Dunatov, Cartoon Editor. Buys one-time rights. Pays on publication.
Writing: Needs humorous nonfiction, interviews (short items) and cartoon stories. Subject matter includes "psychology, self discovery, profiles, updates, male points of view, relationships, love/sex, finding romance." Length: 1,000-300 words. For first contact send cover letter, query and manuscript to Susan Kane, Executive Editor. Buys one-time rights. Pays $50 per word.

*NEW YORK UPDATE MAGAZINE, 770-10 Grand Blvd. Deer Park NY 11729. (516)242-7722. FAX: (516)242-7387. Estab. 1981. Monthly consumer magazine. Circ. 53,000. Needs spot cartoons, humorous writing. Prefers working with freelancers who have fax capabilities. Query with 5-10 rough drawings/batch. Reports only if interested. Returns material if accompanied by a SASE. Buys all rights. Pays $25 minimum, color. Pays on publication.
Writing: Buys 1 humorous piece/issue; 12 humorous pieces/year. Needs humorous nonfiction, fiction and "slice-of-life." Length: 700 words. For first contact send cover letter, ms and published tearsheets to Allison R. Whitney, Managing Editor. Samples not filed are returned with SASE. Buys all rights.

THE NEW YORKER, 25 W. 43rd St., New York NY 10036. (212)840-3800. Estab. 1925. Weekly consumer magazine. Circ. 650,000. Needs gag cartoons.
Gag Cartoons: Buys 25 gag cartoons/issue, 780/year. Prefers gag cartoons on "anything fresh, original and graphically distinguished." Doesn't want to see gag cartoons on "husbands and wives. For us, the 'dream' gag cartoon would be 'a complete surprise.' " Preferred format is single panel. Query with 8-20 rough drawings/batch to Art Editor.

Close-up

Roz Chast
Cartoonist

Tell Roz Chast what an influence she's been on magazine gag cartooning, and she'll immediately try to change the subject.

Before she sold her first cartoon to *The New Yorker* in 1978, the gag cartoon was essentially a square box in which either men in bars would commiserate about their short-sheeted lives, or suburban women would sip afternoon tea and snip at their lazy husbands. Male-dominated gag cartoons *certainly* weren't the place for quirky, neurotic drawings and sardonic ideas. Today, the art form enjoys less boundaries than ever, due greatly to Chast's emergence in the late 1970s as a cartoonist with a decidedly different and fresh approach.

Indeed, the most compelling aspect of Chast's earliest published gag cartoons was that they didn't *look* like gag cartoons. Her drawing style looked almost calculatedly sophomoric, and her "gags" (a very inappropriate term for Chast's work), seemed to celebrate the insignificant trials, tribulations and feats of those people who *didn't* experience their own Warholian 15 minutes.

While she never acknowledges her rejuvenating impact on the evolution of the gag cartoon, Chast is delighted that the art form *did* change. "I think," says 37-year-old Chast, "that (gag) cartooning is less rigid than it used to be. It's much looser and less standardized now. Today you don't have to draw a guy at a desk with his secretary, or cocktail parties, or cannibal jokes. In the 50s and 60s there were also gag cartoons about hold-up men or bums and winos—stuff like that. It's not that you don't see things like that today, but you have to draw about them in a different context. There are a lot of things that used to be standard (in gag cartoons) that just aren't funny anymore."

Ironically, Chast never set out to be a cartoonist. A 1977 graduate of The Rhode Island School of Design, Chast left the prestigious art school with a degree in painting, and after graduation began to take her "dreadful" illustration portfolio around to magazine at directors in New York, only to find few assignments. After "a lot of rejection," Chast started to show her cartoons to the magazines.

"I thought of those drawings as cartoons," she recalls, "because they were drawings and they were funny so they must have been cartoons, but I didn't see any other magazine cartoons that looked like what I was doing. I started to show my cartoons around because I realized, 'what do I have to lose?'" Once she decided to push her cartoons, she began almost immediately to sell

FROM THE TOURNAMENT OF NEUROSES PARADE

The "I Never Really Broke Away From My Parents" Float

The "In My Mind's Eye, I Will Always Be a Fat, Short, Frizzy-Haired, Glasses-and-Braces-Wearing Sixth Grader" Float

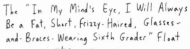

The "People Who Have Difficulty Forming Bonds of Intimacy with Other People" Float

The "I Only Want What Is Unattainable" Float

The "Hypochondria" Float

The "Fear of Chickens" Float

© 1989 Roz Chast

r. Chst

Not the Tournament of Roses: There's a neurosis for everyone in this cartoon by Roz Chast.

them and saw her work published in *National Lampoon*, *The Village Voice* and, of course, *The New Yorker*.

Now under contract to *The New Yorker*, Chast spends each Monday and Tuesday preparing a portfolio of eight to ten proposed, rough cartoons for her Wednesday morning meeting with *New Yorker* cartoon editor Lee Lorenz. "It's not that I don't draw up cartoon ideas on *other* days," says Chast, "it's just that my Mondays and Tuesdays are very serious and focused." When she *is* inspired during the week, she jots down a cartoon idea on a small slip of paper and stuffs it into a box on her desk.

Chast admits that if she were to randomly pull a slip of paper from the box, chances are good that it would make absolutely no sense to anyone but herself. She demonstrates this by unraveling slips of paper that read "movable feast," "go ballistic" and "life is a fluid sitution" — hardly quotes that conjure up immediate visual images, but then this is the woman who created a classic cartoon showing various floats from "The Tournament of Neuroses Parade."

"The notes are just little sayings that drift through my mind," says Chast. "Maybe a note in the box will spark an idea, and maybe it won't. I could write down anything. It could be a phrase I remember as a kid, or something I hear on the TV news. When I'm coming up with ideas, I'll leaf through the notes and perhaps get an idea or it might set me off on a train of thought."

To be sure, Chast's thought process is mildly eccentric, but she explains that "everyone has their own way of working." She recalls how she came up with last year's Thanksgiving cover of *The New Yorker*, which depicts various canned holiday items like *By-Golly Stuffing*, *Mor-Pleeze Gravy* and *Yippee-Yi-Yay Fruit Cocktail*. "I started to think about cranberry sauce," she remembers, "and how it comes in a can. It's so peculiar that the cranberry sauce then has the marks of the can when you serve it. That's very weird for an edible thing." By the end of the cartoon, Chast had canned *every* Thanksgiving dinner tradition including *Komfort King Extra Chairs*, *Company's Favorite Linen Napkins* and a *Nev-R Fail Extra Table Leaf*.

Chast strongly believes in the symbiotic relationship between a gag cartoon's art and its writing. "I like to write, but I like to draw too," she points out. "I find it really difficult to write *without* also drawing. While some of my cartoons can be heavy on the writing, I prefer to have them more artistically balanced."

But if Chast lauds gag cartooning's healthy evolution, she laments the fact that each year there are fewer markets for it. "It's not the golden age of (gag) cartooning any more," she says, "because the number of markets is shrinking and their variety is more limited. A cartoonist can't really make a living from just selling cartoons to *The New Yorker*. I don't know if that ever was the case, but it certainly isn't true now."

—Bob Staake

Does not accept material by fax. Reports back in 3 weeks. Returns material if accompanied by SASE. Buys all rights. Pays $75, b&w. Pays on acceptance.

NORTH AMERICAN HUNTER, Box 3401, Minnetonka MN 55343. (612)936-9333. FAX: (612)936-9333. Estab. 1979. Bimonthly North American Hunting Club official publication. Circ. 420,000. Needs gag cartoons. Accepts previously published humorous articles.
Gag Cartoons: Prefers hunting related cartoons. Doesn't want to see gag cartoons on "dumb wives who don't hunt or understand hunting." The "dream" gag cartoon would be "a humorous hunting experience that all hunters can relate to." Preferred format is single panel, with gagline. Query with 6-12 rough drawings/batch to Debra Morem, Senior Editorial Assistant. Reports back in 10 days. Returns material if accompanied by SASE. Buys all rights. Pays $15, b&w; on acceptance.
Writing: Buys approximately 6 humorous pieces/year. Needs humorous hunting related stories from NAHC members only. For first contact send cover letter and query to Bill Miller, Editor. Reports back in 2 weeks. Samples are returned with SASE. Buys all rights.

NORTHEAST OUTDOORS, Box 2180, Waterbury CT 06722. Estab. 1968. Monthly newspaper that focuses on upbeat, first-person experiences and advice about the "where-to's and how-to's" of camping in the Northeast. Circ. 14,000. Accepts previously published cartoons/humorous illustrations.
Cartoons & Illustrations: Needs editorial and gag cartoons of regional appeal, especially about camping. Considers whether artist uses humor effectively. For first contact send cover letter to John Florian, Editorial Director. Reports back within 4 weeks. Returns materials. Buys one-time rights. Pays for op-ed humor illustration, $20. *Inside Tips:* "Target campers (especially RVers) in Northeast."
Writing: Needs humorous nonfiction and "slice-of-life" on camping. Accepts humorous material that has a regional slant. Length: 1,000 words. For first contact send cover letter and query for proposed article to John Florian, Editorial Director. Unsolicited material is returned. Buys first or one-time rights.

THE NORTHERN LOGGER, Box 69, Old Forge NY 13420. (315)369-3078. FAX: (315)369-3736. Estab. 1952. Monthly trade journal. Circ. 14,000. Needs humorous illustration, gag and spot cartoons. Accepts previously published cartoons.
Gag Cartoons: Buys 1 gag cartoon/issue. Doesn't want to see gag cartoons on "beavers." Preferred format is with gagline, b&w line art. Query with 1 rough drawing/batch to Eric Johnson, Editor. Reports back in 1 month. Returns material if accompanied by SASE. Buys one-time rights. Pays $15, b&w; on acceptance.

NOW AND THEN (East Tennessee State University), Box 70556 A, ETSU, Johnson City TN 37614. (615)929-5348. Estab. 1984. Published 3 times a year. Circ. 2,000. Needs comic strips, humorous illustration and writing, cartoon narratives, caricature, gag and spot cartoons.
Gag Cartoons: Buys 3 gag cartoons/year. "We only take gag cartoons on life in Appalachia or other related themes." Preferred format is single, double or multi-panel with or without gagline or balloons, b&w line art or wash. Query with 1-8 rough drawings/batch to Pat Arnow, Editor. Reports back in 4 months. Returns materials if accompanied by SASE. Buys one-time rights. Pays $25, b&w; on publication.

For information on book publishers' and publications' areas of interest, see the Subject Index.

Illustration: "Never have bought humorous illustration, but we would, if something comes up we like." Works on assignment only. When hiring a freelance humorous illustrator, these abilities are considered: businesslike attitude—meets deadlines and is responsive to editor's needs; familiarity with Appalachian region. For first contact send cover letter, client list and samples to Pat Arnow, Editor. Looks for "appropriateness to our publication; no mindless stereotypes." Reports back in 4 months. Samples are filed or are returned by SASE. Buys one-time rights. Pays $25, b&w, page or cover; on publication. *Inside Tips:* "Would be nice if illustrator were familiar with our publication and interested in what we are trying to do, which is to show a full range of life in Appalachia, not just the poverty."

Writing: Buys approximately 1 humorous piece/issue. Needs humorous fiction and cartoon stories. Subject matter is Appalachian-oriented. Length: less than 2,000 words. To query be familiar with magazine; make sure article is appropriate. Writer's guidelines free. Sample issue $3.50. For first contact send cover letter, manuscript and list of credits to Pat Arnow, Editor. Reports back in 4 months. Samples are returned with SASE. Buys one-time rights. Pays $50, any length. *Inside Tips:* "We are not interested in humor that insults the region; stereotypes are entirely unwelcome. Irony about the stereotypes, yes; making fun of hillbillies, no, no, no."

NUTRITION HEALTH REVIEW, 27 Tunbridge Rd., Haverford PA 19041. (212)679-3590. Estab. 1976. Quarterly consumer magazine, tabloid and newsletter. Circ. over 100,000. Needs comic strips, humorous illustration, caricatures, gag and spot cartoons.

Gag Cartoons: Buys 15 gag cartoons/issue. Prefers gag cartoons on medicine, food psychology, domestic relations, nutrition, mental health. Doesn't want to see gag cartoons on weight loss/gain or fractures. Preferred format is single panel with gagline. Send to Frank Ray Rifkin. Reports back within 30 days. Returns material only if requested. Buys first time rights. Pays $15 minimum, b&w. Pays on acceptance.

*NW KITCHEN & BATH QUARTERLY, P.O. Box 58866, Seattle WA 98138. (206)248-2064. FAX: (206)852-4854. Estab. 1988. Consumer magazine, tabloid published 3 times/year. Circ. 135,000. Needs humorous illustration and caricatures. Accepts previously published cartoons and humorous articles. Prefers working with freelancers who have fax capabilities.

Gag Cartoons: Prefers gag cartoons on anything relating to kitchen or bath remodeling. Send query to Dave Cockrill, Publisher. "Haven't bought cartoons yet—but interested." Somehow relate to kitchen and bath remodeling.

Illustration: Buys humorous illustrations for articles. More apt to hire a humorous illustrator if he uses humor effectively. Send all humorous illustration to Dave Cockrill, Publisher. Samples not filed are returned.

Writing: Needs humorous nonfiction, interviews, "slice-of-life" and anecdotes, "fillers." Subject matter includes anything related to kitchen or bath remodeling. Length: 500 words or less. To query make sure article is appropriate. For first contact send outline of proposed story to Dave Cockrill, Publisher. Samples not filed are returned. Negotiates rights purchased.

OMNI, 1965 Broadway, New York NY 10023. (212)496-6100. FAX: (212)580-3693. Needs humorous illustration, cartoon narratives, gag and spot cartoons.

Gag Cartoons: Buys 5-6 gag cartoons/issue. Preferred gag cartoons on "science, fiction, most anything." No preferred gag cartoon format. Query for submission. No limit to number of rough drawings/batch. Send all gag cartoon submissions to Bill Lee, Cartoon Editor. Buys all rights. Pays $300, color, $250, b&w, full page; $200, color, $150, b&w, spot.

Writing: Buys 1 humorous piece/issue. Needs humorous nonfiction, fiction and anecdotes, "fillers." Subject matter includes "technology, the future and change." Length: 800 words maximum. For first contact send query, writing sample and writer's credit to Keith Ferrell, Editor. Buys all rights. Pays $1/word for 800 word story, depends on section of mag; $75 for a short, short piece.

THE ONION, Suite 270, 33 University Square, Madison WI 53715. (608)256-1372. Estab. 1988. Humor-entertainment tabloid that "serves the college student population of Madison. Smart, hip and irreverent humor, not afraid of the shocking or disturbing." Circ. 25,000. Accepts previously published cartoons/humorous illustrations and humorous writing, "though we prefer unpublished."
Cartoons & Illustrations: Needs comic strips or panels of college and national appeal on college life, adult single life and life in general. "We consider buying cartoons/humorous illustrations if we roll over laughing while reading them." For first contact send work, submitted for potential publication to Richard Dahm, Submissions Editor. Returns materials only if requested and accompanied by SASE. Buys one-time rights. Pays for regular cartoon feature, $10-20. "We always pay if we print your work."
Writing: Needs humorous pieces geared toward a college audience. Length: 200-2,000 words. For first contact send typed, double-spaced writing samples (computer printout is fine too, but please double space) to Richard Dahm, Submissions Editor. Unsolicited material is returned only with SASE. Buys one-time rights. Pays $10-60 for 200-2,000 words. "We don't assign articles." *Inside Tips:* "Blow us away with your humor. We're looking for cutting-edge stuff that will turn our office into a gigglefest. Don't waste your time with elaborate queries, cover letters, designer envelopes or scented full-color submissions. Send for our writer's guidelines or an issue of *The Onion* (with $1.25 postage) if you'd like, then send us camera-ready column-friendly cartoons or aptly-lengthed written pieces that will make us laugh. Madison is a tremendously ripe market for humor, and yours could gain a large following if you can keep it coming."

*ONLINE ACCESS, 920 N. Franklin, Chicago IL 60610. (312)573-1300. Estab. 1986. Quarterly consumer magazine. Circ. 50,000. Needs humorous illustration and writing. Accepts previously published cartoons and humorous articles.
Gag Cartoons: Prefers gag cartoons on "online computer-related subjects—must have modem!" Doesn't want to see gag cartoons on non-online subjects. "For us the 'dream' gag cartoon would be hilarious and applicable to online industry." Query with 2-6 rought drawings/batch to Tracy Weisman, Managing Editor. Reports back only if interested. Returns material if accompanied by a SASE. Pays $50, b&w, $50, color. *Inside Tips:* "Understand our business—know what it's like to use an online service to appreciate potential for funny situations!"
Illustration: Buys 2 humorous illustrations/issue; 8 humorous illustrations/year for articles and sports. Works on assignment only. More apt to hire a humorous illustrator if he conceptualizes well and has clever ideas—good use of metaphors, has a clean, graphically-pleasing drawing style, uses humor effectively, is businesslike, meets deadlines and is responsive to my needs. For first contact send cover letter, b&w tearsheets to Tracy Weisman, Managing Editor. Looks for a "quick read" and relevance to online industry. Reports only if interested. Samples not filed are returned by SASE. Buys first time rights. Pays $50, b&w, $50, color, page. Pays on acceptance.
Writing: Buys 1 humorous piece/issue; 4 humorous pieces/year. Needs humorous nonfiction, "slice-of-life." Subject matter must relate to online industry, modems. Length: 750-2,000 words. To query be familiar with magazine; make sure article is appropriate. For first contact send cover letter, outline of proposed story and published tearsheets to Tracy Weisman, Managing Editor. Reports back only if interested. Samples not filed are returned with SASE. Buys first time rights. Pays $100-350 for 750-2,000 words. Offers 50% kill fee. *Inside Tips:* "The best humor writer for Online Access is him/herself

a user of online services. For this kind of writing, having been there yourself is essential!"

*OPTOMETRIC ECONOMICS MAGAZINE, American Optometric Assoc., 243 N. Lindbergh Blvd., St. Louis MO 63141. (314)991-4100. FAX: (314)991-4101. Estab. 1991. Monthly trade journal. Circ. 28,000. Needs humorous illustration and writing, spot cartoons. Accepts previously published cartoons and humorous articles.
Illustration: For first contact send cover letter, resume, b&w and color tearsheets to Gene Mitchell, Managing Editor. Reports back within 2 weeks. Reports back only if interested. Samples are filed or are returned by SASE. Buys first time rights, all rights. *Inside Tips:* "Understand optometry and the interests of our readers."
Writing: "Only materials relating directly to optometry and vision care are relevant to *Optometric Economics*." For first contact send cover letter, resume and writing sample to Gene Mitchell, Managing Editor. Reports back within 2 weeks. Reports back only if interested. Samples are not filed and are returned with SASE. Buys all rights, negotiates rights purchased. Pays $50-400.

OUR FAMILY, Box 249, Battleford ST S0M-0E0 Canada. (306)927-7771. FAX: (306)937-7644. Estab. 1949. Monthly consumer magazine. Circ. 13,000. Needs humorous illustration and writing. Accepts previously published cartoons and articles.
Gag Cartoons: Buys 30 gag cartoons/year. Prefers gag cartoons on family, marriage and religion. Preferred format is single panel with gagline, b&w line art. Query with 5 rough drawings/batch to Nestor Gregoire, Editor. Reports back in 1 month. Returns materials if accompanied by SASE. Buys first rights. Pays $15, b&w; on acceptance.
Illustration: Works on assignment only.
Writing: Buys approximately 6 humorous pieces/year. Needs humorous nonfiction, "slice-of-life" and anecdotes, "fillers." Subject matter includes family and church. Length: 100-500 words. To query make sure article is appropriate. Send SASE for copy. For first contact send manuscript to Nestor Gregoire, Editor. Reports back in 1 month. Samples not filed are returned with SASE. Buys first and reprint rights. Pays 7¢/word.

OUTDOOR AMERICA, Level B, 1401 Wilson Blvd., Arlington VA 22209. (703)528-1818. FAX: (703)528-1836. Estab. 1922. Quarterly association magazine. Circ. 58,000. Needs humorous writing. Accepts previously published cartoons and humorous articles.
Illustration: Buys varying number of humorous illustrations/issue; 8-10/year for articles and spots. For first contact send cover letter, resume, b&w and color tearsheets to Kristin Merriman, Editor. Looks for "something that makes me smile, such as a humorous way of looking at something ordinary." Reports back in 3 weeks, often sooner. Samples are filed or are returned by SASE. Buys one-time rights. Pays $50-150, b&w, $75-150, color, page. *Inside Tips:* "Introduce yourself to me. Let me know if you are an outdoor lover, what your hobbies are and what your specialty is."
Writing: Buys approximately 1 humorous piece/issue. Needs humorous nonfiction and outdoor articles. Subject matter includes hunting, fishing, camping, the senior citizen outdoor lover, conservation and outdoor ethics. Length: 750-1,000 words. To query be familiar with magazine; make sure article is appropriate; study writers' guidelines. Send SASE for free copy of guidelines; $1.50 for sample magazine. For first contact send cover letter, manuscript, published tearsheets, resume and writing sample to Kristin Merriman, Editor. Reports back within 3 weeks. Samples are filed; returned with SASE. Buys one-time rights. Pays 20¢/word.

OVERSEAS, Kolping St. 1, 6906 Leimen, West Germany. (011)49-6224-7060. FAX: (011)49-6224-70616. Estab. 1971. Monthly consumer magazine. Circ. 80,000. Needs comic strips, humorous illustration and writing, cartoon narratives, gag and spot cartoons. Accepts previously published cartoons and humorous articles.

Gag Cartoons: Buys only gag cartoons on "living in Europe, being a tourist in Europe and working in U.S. military." Preferred formats are single, double or multi-panel with or without gagline or balloons, b&w line art. Query with finished photocopied cartoon to Greg Ballinger. Reports back in 2-3 weeks. Returns materials only if requested and accompanied by SASE. Buys first rights. Pays $20, b&w. Pays on publication.

*PACIFIC BOATING ALMANAC, P.O. Box 341668, Los Angeles CA 90034. (310)287-2830. FAX:(310)287-2834. Annual almanac. Circ. 10,000. Needs humorous illustration and spot cartoons. Accepts previously published cartoons.
Gag Cartoons: Preferred format is b&w line art with gagline. Send all gag cartoon submissions to Art Director. Reports back in 2 weeks. Returns material. Pays $10, b&w; on publication.
Illustration: Buys humorous illustration for spots. When hiring a freelance humorous illustrator, these abilities are considered: a clean, graphically-pleasing drawing style; effective use of humor; a businesslike attitude—ability to meet deadlines. For first contact, send cover letter, b&w tearsheets and b&w promo piece to Peter L. Griffer, Production. Reports back within 3 weeks. Samples are filed or are returned if requested. Buys first time, reprint, one-time or all rights, or negotiates rights purchased. Pays $10, b&w; on publication. *Inside Tips*: "We are looking for nautical subjects—boating, fishing, etc."
Writing: Buys approximately 10 humorous pieces/year.

*PAINTBALL, 4201 Vanowen Pl., Burbank CA 91505. (818)845-2656. FAX: (818)845-7761. Estab. 1988. Monthly consumer magazine. Needs comic strips, gag cartoons, humorous illustration and writing and spot cartoons. Accepts previously published cartoons and humorous articles *with clearances*.
Gag Cartoons: Prefers gag cartoons on paintball only. "For us the 'dream' gag cartoon would be about paintball." Preferred format is single, double or multi-panel with or without gagline, with balloons, b&w line art, b&w wash. Query with 1 rough drawing/batch to Jessica Sparks, Editor. Reports back within 3 weeks. Returns material. Negotiates rights purchased. Pays $25, b&w, $25, color. Pays on publication. *Inside Tips:* "Understand paintball thoroughly before submitting items."
Illustration: Buys humorous illustrations for articles and spots. More apt to hire a humorous illustrator if he or she conceptualizes well and has clever ideas—good use of metaphors; has a clean, graphically-pleasing drawing style; has a bold, powerful, attention-getting drawing style; has a subtle, understated drawing style; uses humor effectively; is businesslike, meets deadlines and is responsive to my needs. For first contact send cover letter, resume, "just send on spec" to Jessica Sparks, Editor. Reports back within 3 weeks. Samples not filed are returned. Negotiates rights purchased. Pays $25, b&w, $25, color, page; $75, b&w, $75, color, cover. *Inside Tips:* "Only those who understand the sport of paintball should send materials."
Writing: Needs humorous nonfiction, fiction, interviews, "slice-of-life" and anecdotes, "filler." Subject matter includes paintball—all aspects. Length: 250-5,000 words. To query be familiar with magazine; make sure article is appropriate; study writer's guidelines. Inquire for copy of writer's guidelines and sample magazine. For first contact send cover letter, manuscript, resume and photo of self to Jessica Sparks, Editor. Reports back within 3 weeks. Samples not filed are returned. Negotiates rights purchased. Pays $25-150 for 250-5,000 words. *Inside Tips:* "You must understand the sport of paintball or at *least* visit a field or interview players. This magazine is for the corporate and recreational paintball player. Themes must reflect paintball humor."

PARENTGUIDE NEWS, 2 Park Ave., New York NY 10021. (212)213-8840. Estab. 1983. Monthly newspaper. Circ. 205,000. Needs comic strips, humorous illustration and writing and spot cartoons.

Gag Cartoons: Send submissions to Leslie Elgort, Editor. Returns material if accompanied by SASE.

PARISH FAMILY DIGEST, 200 Noll Plaza, Huntington IN 46750. (219)356-8400. FAX: (219)356-8472. Estab. 1945. Bimonthly, Roman Catholic, family oriented. Circ. 150,000. Needs humorous writing, gag and spot cartoons.
Gag Cartoons: Buys 3-5 gag cartoons per issue on family life, religious life ("all in good taste, please"). Preferred format is single panel with gagline, b&w line art. Send submissions to Corine B. Erlandson, Editor. Reports back within 3-4 weeks. Returns materials if accompanied by SASE. Buys first rights. Pays $10 per cartoon, b&w; on acceptance.
Writing: Buys approximately 1 humorous piece per issue. Needs humorous nonfiction, "slice-of-life" and anecdotes, "fillers." Subject matter includes family or religious life from a Catholic perspective. Length: 500-1,000 words for articles; 100-word maximum for fillers. To query be familiar with magazine; make sure article is appropriate; study writer's guidelines. Send 6 × 9″ SASE and 52¢ stamps for writer's guidelines and sample copy. For first contact send manuscript to Corine B. Erlandson. Reports back within 3-4 weeks. Samples are not filed; returned with SASE. Buys first rights. Pays $25-50 for 500-1,000 words.

PEACE NEWSLETTER, 924 Burnet Ave., Dept. HC, Syracuse NY 13203. (315)472-5478. Estab. 1936. "Alternative" monthly newsletter. "The PNL is the internal organ of the Syracuse Peace Council and a forum for articles which discuss issues of concern to the peace movement." Circ. 4,500. Previously published cartoons/humorous illustrations and articles are accepted.
Cartoons & Illustrations: Needs comics strips of regional or national appeal; editorial cartoons of local, regional or national appeal; gag cartoons; single panels of regional or national appeal, especially about peace issues (nuclear war, etc.); humorous illustration; op-ed humorous illustrations; caricatures; spot cartoons. Considers whether artist can draw on localized news, turn around art on short deadline, has ability to read a manuscript and come up with strong visual ideas and uses humor effectively. For first contact send cover letter and b&w tearsheet to PNL Coordinator. Reports back within 2 months only if interested. Returns material if accompanied by SASE (if requested); keeps material on file. "We do not (cannot) pay."
Writing: Needs humorous interviews, op-ed pieces. "All humorous writing should have a peace movement slant." Accepts humorous material that has a regional, national and international angle. Length: 500-800 words. For first contact, send cover letter, resume, outline of proposed article and writing sample to PNL Coordinator. Unsolicited material is filed or returned with SASE if requested. "We cannot pay."

PENNSYLVANIA MAGAZINE, Box 576, Camp Hill PA 17001-0576. (717)761-6620. Estab. 1981. Bimonthly consumer magazine. Circ. 40,000. Needs humorous writing and spot cartoons. Accepts previously published cartoons and humorous articles.
Gag Cartoons: Just starting to buy gag cartoons. Preferred format is single panel, b&w line art. Topics must be related to or based within the state of Pennsylvania. Query with 5-10 rough drawings/batch to Editor. Reports back within 2 weeks. Returns materials if accompanied by SASE. Buys one-time rights. Pays $10-25, b&w; on acceptance. *Inside Tips:* "Deal with a subject in or unique to Pennsylvania."
Illustration: Just starting to buy humorous illustration for spots. Looks for art skill and ideas pertaining to Pennsylvania. Reports back within 2 weeks. Buys one-time rights. Pays $10-25, b&w, page; on acceptance.
Writing: New. Needs humorous nonfiction and anecdotes, "fillers." Subject matter includes anything based in Pennsylvania. Length: 50-200 words. To query be familiar with magazine; make sure article is appropriate; study writer's guidelines. Send $3 for

Plasticine President: *Providence, Rhode Island-based illustrator Bob Selby executed this acrylic paint on plasticine sculpture of George Bush for his local newspaper. While Selby is a staff illustrator at the newspaper, freelance sculpture assignments do "find their way" to him. Selby also teaches caricature and 3-D illustration at the prestigious Rhode Island School of Design.*

copy of magazine; SASE for writer's guidelines. Reports back within 2 weeks. Buys one-time rights. Pays 15¢/word or $10-35 for 50-200 words. *Inside Tips:* "We are interested in items we can use in a 'life in Pennsylvania' department, and in cartoons for spot use. All materials must pertain to our state."

*PENNSYLVANIA SPORTSMAN, 430 N. Front St., P.O. Box 90, Lemoyne PA 17043. (717)761-1400. FAX: (717)761-4579. Estab. 1959. Consumer magazine published 8 times/year. Circ. 67,000. Needs gag and spot cartoons.
Gag Cartoons: Buys 5 cartoons/year. Prefers gag cartoons on fishing and hunting. Preferred format is single panel. Query with 5-10 rough drawings/batch to Sherry Ritchey, Managing Editor. Reports back within 2 weeks. Returns material if accompanied by a SASE. Buys first time rights. Pays $10, b&w. Pays on acceptance.

I'll Have the Mystery Meat: *Defining his drawing style as "primitive, regressive, yet efficient," Dumont, New Jersey-based satirist Mark Marek uses a nifty word shift to create this maliciously funny cartoon. Published in a magazine which Marek has had an "ongoing relationship with for a number of years," he was paid $200.*

PENTHOUSE, 1965 Broadway, New York NY 10023. (212)496-6100. FAX: (212)580-3693. Needs comic strips, humorous illustration and writing, caricatures and gag and spot cartoons.
Gag Cartoons: Buys 10-12 gag cartoons/issue. Prefers gag cartoons on "sex, politics, general adult humor." No preferred gag cartoon format. Query with 1-50 rough drawings/batch to Bill Lee, Humor Editor. Pays $500, color, $400, b&w, full page; $350, color, $300, b&w, spot.

Illustration: Buys 10-12 humorous illustrations/issue for spots. For first contact send cover letter and samples to Bill Lee, Humor Editor. Buys all rights. Pays on publication.

PHENOMENEWS, Suite 105, 18444 W. 10 Mile, Southfield MI 48075. (313)569-3888. Estab. 1978. Monthly tabloid. Circ. 46,000. Needs comic strips and gag cartoons. Accepts previously published cartoons.
Gag Cartoons: Buys 1-2 gag cartoons/issue. Prefers gag cartoons on "New Age (astrology, crystals, past lives, palmistry, etc.), holistic health, human potential movement. For us, the 'dream' gag cartoon would be cute, well-drawn characters not putting down New Age philosophies but can poke fun, also with a positive message." Preferred formats are single or double panel with balloons, b&w line art. Query with 2-5 rough drawings/batch to Cindy Saul, Editor. Does not report back. Returns materials if accompanied by SASE. Pays $5-10, b&w. Pays on publication. *Inside Tips:* A gag cartoonist should "have a good working knowledge of the New Age and what's 'hot' at the moment. Have a positive, non-sexist outlook on life and be able to convey it in their work."

PHI DELTA KAPPAN, Box 789, Eighth & Union, Bloomington IN 47402-0789. (812)339-1156. Estab. 1915. Professional education journal published 10 times/year (Sept.-June). Circ. 150,000. Needs humorous illustration and gag cartoons. Accepts previously published cartoons.
Gag Cartoons: Buys 20 cartoons/issue. Prefers well-drawn cartoons on education. "For us, the 'dream' cartoon would be of *New Yorker* quality." Preferred format is single panel with gagline or balloons, b&w line art or wash. Query with 10-15 finished cartoons, "no more," to Terri Hampton, Permissions. Reports back in 3 weeks. Returns materials if accompanied by SASE. Buys one-time rights. Pays $25, b&w; on acceptance. *Inside Tips:* "Be original; draw well and understand education issues and themes; develop a recognizable, personal style. We review as many as 300 cartoons a week. Please send only your very best. Keep track of your submissions and don't resubmit work. Don't take rejection personally—it's a competitive field. We'll let you know clearly if we find your work unsuitable for our publication, otherwise keep trying."
Illustration: Buys approximately 1-5 humorous illustrations/issue for articles and spots. Works on assignment only. For first contact send cover letter, b&w or color tearsheets, client list and b&w promo piece to Carol Bucheri, Design Director. "Ballpark your fee range or indicate willingness to work within our fees. Send some samples for me to keep on file and send examples of the kind of work you like to do (what you feel comfortable with) in your preferred media. Looks "for editorial experience, personal style, good drawing, intelligent humor and technical knowledge (i.e., what will reproduce)." Reports back only if interested. Samples are filed or are returned by SASE. Buys first or one-time rights. Pays $150, b&w, page; on acceptance. *Inside Tips:* "Students and educators at all levels—from preschool children to classroom teachers to administrators and professors—are people of a variety of races and ethnic backgrounds and both sexes. We will give special consideration to cartoons that depict our multiracial/multicultural society and that show sensitivity to gender issues. We will *not* consider cartoons that denigrate children or that depict or imply approval of corporal punishment or abuse."

THE PLAIN DEALER, 1801 Superior Ave., Cleveland OH 44114. (216)344-4800. FAX: (216)694-6370. Estab. 1842. Daily newspaper. Circ. 450,000. Previously published cartoons/humorous illustrations and humorous writing accepted.
Cartoons & Illustrations: Needs editorial cartoons of local, regional and national appeal; humorous and op-ed humorous illustrations; and caricatures. Considers whether artist has ability to read a manuscript and come up with a strong visual idea. For first contact send cover letter, b&w tearsheets and slides. For editorial cartoons contact Jim Strang, Deputy Editorial Director or Gloria Millner, Associate Editor; for humorous illustration/spots contact Christine Jindra, Features Editor. Reports back

within 2 weeks. Returns material only if requested and accompanied by a SASE. Does not file material. Buys first or reprint rights. Pays for editorial cartoons, $25 minimum; for humorous illustration, $25 minimum; for spot cartoons, $25 minimum; for op-ed humor illustration, $25 minimum.

Writing: Needs humorous op-ed pieces, "slice-of-life" and humor for Sunday magazine. Accepts humorous material that has a local, regional, national or international angle. Length: 700-900 words. For first contact send cover letter, query for proposed article and writing sample. For humorous op-ed piece contact Jim Strang; for humorous feature/article contact Christine Jindra; for humorous piece for Sunday magazine contact Clint O'Connor, Sunday Magazine Editor. Unsolicited material is not filed and returned only if requested with SASE. Buys first rights or negotiates rights purchased. For inside feature page pays $75; for op-ed pieces daily $50, for op-ed pieces Sunday, $150.

PREVENTION MAGAZINE, 33 E. Minor St., Emmaus PA 18098. (215)967-5171. FAX: (215)967-3044. Estab. 1940. Monthly consumer magazine. Circ. 3.5 million. Needs humorous illustration, caricature and spot cartoons. Accepts previously published cartoons.

Gag Cartoons: Buys 12-15 gag cartoons/year on health and fitness and losing weight. Preferred format is single panel with gagline, b&w line art or wash. Query with 5-25 rough drawings/batch to Wendy Ronga, Executive Art Director. Reports back in 1 month only if interested. Returns materials. Buys first rights. Pays $250, b&w; on acceptance.

Illustration: Buys approximately 4 humorous illustrations/issue for articles and spots. Works on assignment only. For first contact send cover letter, client list, b&w or color tearsheets and b&w promo pieces to Wendy Ronga, Executive Art Director. Looks for concepts and style. Reports back in 2 weeks if interested. Samples are filed or returned. Buys first rights. Pays $500, b&w, $1,000, color, page; on acceptance.

*THE PUNDIT, P.O. Box 5040, Station A, Toronto, Ontario M5W 1N4 Canada. (416)922-1100. FAX: (416)922-1100. Estab. 1981. Monthly newsletter. Needs brief "punecdotes." Accepts previously published humorous articles.

Writing: Needs humorous fiction, anecdotes, "fillers." For first contact send ms to John S. Crosbie, Editor. Does not report back. Samples are filed. Samples not filed are not returned.

*RACQUETBALL MAGAZINE, 815 N. Weber, Colorado Springs CO 80903. (719)635-5396. FAX: (719)635-0685. Estab. 1990. Bimonthly consumer magazine, membership publication. Circ. 35,000. Needs, comic strips, humorous illustration and writing, caricatures, spot cartoons. Accepts previously published cartoons and humorous articles.

Gag Cartoons: "We have not purchased to date." Prefers gag cartoons on racquetball. Preferred format is double panel, multi-panel, with gagline, with balloon, b&w line art. Query with 6-10 rough drawings to Linda Mojer, Director, Media/PR. Reports only if interested. Returns material only if interested. Buys one-time rights. Pays $25-50, b&w. Pays on publication. *Inside Tips:* "Have a good background on the sport."

Illustration: "Have not purchased to date." Will consider humorous illustration for articles, spots. More apt to hire a humorous illustrator if he conceptualizes well and has clever ideas—good use of metaphors and has a clean, graphically-pleasing drawing style. For first contact send cover letter, resume, b&w tearsheets and b&w promo piece to Linda Mojer, Director, Media/PR. Looks for specific humor applicable to specialized readership. Reports only if interested. Samples not filed are returned if requested. Buys one-time rights. Pays $25-50, b&w, page; $25-50, b&w, cover. Pays on publication.

Writing: Needs humorous nonfiction, fiction, interviews, "slice-of-life," anecdotes, "fillers." Subject matter includes racquetball. Length: 500-1,000 words. To query be familiar with magazine; make sure article is appropriate. For first contact send cover letter,

outline of proposed story, resume and writing sample to Linda Mojer, Director, Media/
PR. Reports only if interested. Samples are filed. Samples not filed are returned only
if requested. Buys one-time rights. "Anyone submitting material should have a good
background in racquetball, as our publication is targeted to a specialized reading audience . . . members of the American Amateur Racquetball Association."

RADIANCE, The Magazine for Large Women, Box 30246, Oakland CA 94604.
(510)482-0680. Estab. 1984. Quarterly consumer magazine. Circ. 25,000. Needs comic
strips, humorous illustration and writing, cartoon narratives, caricature and spot cartoons. Accepts previously published cartoons and humorous articles.
Gag Cartoons: Query with 2-6 rough drawings/batch to Alice Ansfield, Editor. Reports
back in 6-8 weeks. Returns materials if accompanied by SASE. Buys one-time rights.
Pays $25-100; on publication. *Inside Tips:* A gag cartoonist should "know the magazine
philosophy and read the article she/he is drawing for."
Illustration: Buys approximately 1 humorous illustration/issue for articles and spots.
One of the things considers when hiring a freelance humorous illustrator is whether
artist "listens well to what we are trying to get across and comes up with good ideas."
For first contact send cover letter, b&w tearsheets and promo pieces to Alice Ansfield,
Editor. Looks for "style, design, clarity." Reports back in 6-8 weeks. Samples are filed
or are returned by SASE. Buys one-time rights. Pays $25-100.
Writing: Buys approximately 1 humorous piece/issue. Needs humorous nonfiction, interviews, "slice-of-life," fiction and cartoon stories. Subject matter includes stories
about being a large woman in today's society; anecdotes about daily life events, shopping, relationships, etc.; fantasy/fiction with large-sized heroines and characters.
Length: 800-2,000 words. To query be familiar with magazine; make sure article is
appropriate; study writer's guidelines. Send $3.50 and SASE for copy. For first contact
send cover letter, query, outline of proposed story, manuscript, published tearsheets
and writing sample to Alice Ansfield, Editor. Reports back in 6-8 weeks. Samples are
filed; returned with SASE. Buys one-time rights. Pays $50-75 for 800-2,000 words. Offers
50% kill fee. *Inside Tips:* "The writer should be familiar with the large woman—have
sensitivity, compassion, insight into her before writing for us. Humor is a good vehicle
for us to give our readers greater perspective on what is often a hard life to live as a fat
person."

*RANDOM LENGTHS, P.O. Box 731, San Pedro CA 90733. (310)519-1442. FAX:
(310)832-1000. Estab. 1979. Biweekly newspaper. Circ. 30,000. Needs comic strips, cartoon narratives, humorous illustration, caricatures and gag and spot cartoons. Accepts
previously published cartoons and humorous articles.
Gag Cartoons: Buys 2-3 cartoons/issue. Prefers gag cartoons on political satire and
current events. Doesn't want to see gag cartoons "that just aren't funny." Preferred
format is single panel, double panel, with gagline or balloons, b&w line art. Query to
Carol Tice, Editor. Reports back in 2 weeks only if interested. Returns material if
accompanied by a SASE. Buys first time rights, reprint rights, one-time rights. Pays $10,
b&w. Pays 60 days after publication. *Inside Tips:* "Be sharp, funny, politically aware and
draw well."

*THE REALIST, Box 1230, Venice CA 90294. (310)392-5848. FAX: (310)392-5848. Estab.
1958. Quarterly newsletter. Circ. 3,000. Needs gag cartoons, caricatures, humorous writing.
Gag Cartoons: Buys 2 cartoons/issue; 8 cartoons/year. Prefers gag cartoons on controversial social and political issues. Doesn't want to see gag cartoons on "obvious targets."
"For us the 'dream' gag cartoon would be laughter with a strong point of view." Query
with 1-12 rough drawings/batch to Paul Krassner, Editor. Reports back within weeks.
Returns material if accompanied by a SASE. Buys first time rights. Pays $50, b&w. Pays

on acceptance. *Inside Tips:* "Be original, and not indulge in self-censorship."

Illustration: Buys 2 humorous illustrations/issue; 8 humorous illustrations/year for covers, articles and spots. More apt to hire a humorous illustrator if he has a truly unique drawing style, conceptualizes well and has clever ideas—good use of metaphors and has a clean, graphically-pleasing drawing style. For first contact send b&w tearsheets to Paul Krassner, Editor. Looks for satirical approach. Reports back within weeks. Samples not filed are returned by SASE. Buys first time rights. Pays $100, b&w, page; $100, b&w, cover. Pays on acceptance. *Tips:* "Make me squirm with delightful surprise."

Writing: Buys approximately 4 humorous pieces/issue; 16 humorous pieces/year. Needs humorous nonfiction. Subject matter includes controversial social and political satire. Length: 500 words. To query make sure article is appropriate; send $2 and SASE for copy. For first contact send ms to Paul Krassner, Editor. Reports back within weeks. Samples not filed are returned with SASE. Buys first time rights. Pays $1/word for a piece 300-1,000 words. Offers 25% kill fee. *Inside Tips:* "In keeping with tradition of Mort Sahl and Lenny Bruce."

REPORTER/WOMEN'S AMERICAN ORT, (formerly Women's American ORT Reporter), 17th floor, 315 Park Ave. S., New York NY 10010. (212)505-7700. Estab. 1966. Quarterly magazine. Circ. 104,000. Needs humorous illustration and writing, caricature and spot cartoons. Accepts previously published cartoons and humorous articles. Prefers working with freelancers who have fax capabilities.

Gag Cartoons: Buys occasional gag illustrations. Prefers gag illustrations on the Jewish culture and women. Preferred format is single panel, b&w or color line art. Query with 2-4 rough drawings/batch to Eve Jacobson, Editor. Reports back in 3 months. Returns material if accompanied by SASE. Buys first or reprint rights.

Illustration: Buys approximately 2 humorous illustrations/year for articles and spots. Works on assignment only. For first contact send cover letter, resume and b&w or color tearsheets to Eve Jacobson, Editor. Reports back within 3 months. Samples are filed; returned by SASE. Buys first or reprint rights. Pays $75, b&w, page; $150, b&w, cover; on publication.

Writing: Buys approximately 1 humorous piece/issue. Needs humorous nonfiction and interviews. Subject matter includes the Jewish culture and women. Length: 1,000 words. For first contact send cover letter, manuscript, published tearsheets and resume to Eve Jacobson, Editor. Reports back within 3 months. Samples are returned with SASE only if requested. Buys first or reprint rights.

REPORTER–YOUR EDITORIAL ASSISTANT, 7015 Prospect Place NE, Albuquerque NM 87110-4311. (505)884-7636. Estab. 1956. Monthly newsletter that focuses on teen-related cartoons.

Cartoons & Illustrations: Needs gag cartoons of national appeal and humorous illustration; "nothing pertaining to sex, politics or religion." Considers whether artist uses humor effectively. Must be line drawings. For first contact send samples to Lucie Dubovik, Manager. Reports back within 2 weeks. Returns materials if accompanied by SASE. Buys first or one-time rights. Pays $5-10.

*RIO GRANDE PRESS/SE LA VIE WRITER'S JOURNAL, EDITOR'S DIGEST, Box 371371, El Paso TX 79937. (915)595-2625. Estab. 1987. Quarterlies. "*Se La Vie* is for poets and writers; *RGP* also publishes poetry anthologies."

Cartoons & Illustrations: "Needs cartoons about poets, writers and small poem illustrations (all subjects). Will consider cover designs, but send postcard inquiry first for current cover subject." For first contact send 4-5 photocopies and brief bio to Rosalie Avara, Editor/Publisher. Buys first rights. "Payment is one copy of issue in which published."

ROAD KING MAGAZINE, Box 250, Park Forest IL 60466. (708)481-9240. FAX: (708)481-1063. Estab. 1963. Bimonthly consumer magazine. Circ. 210,000. Needs humorous writing about trucking and spot cartoons.
Gag Cartoons: Buys 1 gag cartoon/issue. Wants to see gag cartoons on trucking over-the-road. Preferred format is b&w line art with gagline. Query with 4-6 rough drawings/batch to Kevin Warren, Associate Editor. Reports back within 3-6 months if interested. Returns material if accompanied by a SASE. Buys all rights. Pays $25 minimum, b&w. Pays on publication.
Writing: Buys approximately 1-2 humorous pieces/year. Needs humorous fiction on trucking. Length: 1,200 maximum. To query be familiar with magazine and make sure article is appropriate. For first contact send copy of manuscript to Kevin Warren. Reports back within 3 months if interested. Samples are returned with SASE. Buys all rights. Pays $200-400 for 1,000-1,200 words. *Inside Tips:* "Have an understanding of the long-haul trucker market. No sex or violence."

THE ROTARIAN, 1560 Sherman Ave., Evanston IL 60201. (708)866-3000. FAX: (708)328-8554. Estab. 1911. Monthly service club magazine. Circ. 535,000. Needs gag cartoons.
Gag Cartoons: Buys 7-8 cartoons/issue. Prefers gag cartoons on "business, sports, environment, animals." Doesn't want to see "women drivers, desert islands, kids." Preferred format is single panel with or without gagline, b&w line art. Query with 10-20 rough drawings/batch to Charles Pratt, Managing Editor. Reports back within 2 weeks. Returns material if accompanied by a SASE. Buys all rights. Pays $75, b&w. Pays on acceptance. *Inside Tips:* "Draw well; be funny; have an international outlook."
Writing: Buys approximately 2 humorous pieces/year. Needs humorous "slice-of-life." Length: 700-850 words. To query be familiar with magazine; make sure article is appropriate; study writer's guidelines. Send $1 and SASE for copy. For first contact send cover letter, query, writing sample to Charles Pratt, Managing Editor. Reports back within 2 weeks. Samples are not filed. Buys all rights or negotiates rights purchased. Pays $300-400 for 700-1,000 words. *Inside Tips:* "No ethnic humor, no sexist humor. Be inoffensive; sports/business/gardening are good situations."

*SATELLITE RETAILER, 1300 S. DeKalb St., Shelby NC 28150. (704)482-9673. FAX: (704)484-8558. Estab. 1985. Monthly trade journal. Circ. 15,000. Needs gag and spot cartoons, caricatures. Accepts previously published cartoons.
Gag Cartoons: Buys 2 cartoons/issue; 24 cartoons/year. Prefers gag cartoons on satellite TV and TV related subjects. Doesn't want to see gag cartoons on "satellite dishes as bird baths." Preferred format is single panel, with gagline, b&w line art, b&w wash, color wash. Query with 5-10 rough drawings/batch to David B. Melton, Editor. Reports back within 2 weeks. Returns material. Negotiates rights purchased. Pays $20, b&w, $50, color. Pays on publication. *Inside Tips:* "Understand how satellite TV works and be at least technically inclined enough to lace your own sneakers."
Illustration: Buys 4 humorous illustrations/year for articles and spots. Works on assignment only. More apt to hire a humorous illustrator if he has a clean, graphically-pleasing drawing style and shows flexibility and broad potential in drawing style. For first contact send cover letter, b&w and color tearsheets, b&w and color promo pieces to David B. Melton, Editor. Looks for "the ability to convey the ideas put forth in the story or to brainstorm with writer or editor." Reports back within 1 month. Samples are not filed and are returned if requested. Buys first time rights. Pays $100, b&w, $200, color page. Pays on publication. *Tips:* "Understand satellite TV and be able to convey a mechanical piece of equipment."

THE SATURDAY EVENING POST, Box 567, Indianapolis IN 46202. (317)636-8881. Consumer magazine published 6 times/year. Circ. 700,000. Needs gag and spot cartoons.
Gag Cartoons: Buys 30 gag cartoons/issue. Prefers gag cartoons on kids, family, pets and jobs. Doesn't want to see gag cartoons on "overweight people or the homeless." Preferred format is single panel. Query with 10-15 rough drawings/batch to Steven Pettinga, Cartoon Editor. Reports in 6 weeks. Returns material if accompanied by SASE. Buys all rights. Pays $125; on publication. *Inside Tips:* A gag cartoonist should "have patience."
Illustration: Buys approximately 30 humorous illustrations/issue for spots. Works on assignment only. When hiring a freelance humorous illustrator, these abilities are considered: a truly unique drawing style; a clean, graphically-pleasing drawing style; effective use of humor.

SCHOOL MATES, 186 Route 9W, New Windsor NY 12553. (914)562-8350. FAX: (914)561-2437. Estab. 1987. Bimonthly juvenile magazine. Circ. 10,850. Needs gag and spot cartoons.
Gag Cartoons: Prefers gag cartoons on chess. "For us the 'dream' gag cartoon would be one that also offered chess instruction." Preferred format is single panel with or without gagline, b&w line art. Send submissions to Jennie L. Simon, Editor. Returns material if accompanied by a SASE. Buys first time rights. Pays $25 minimum for b&w. Pays on publication. *Inside Tips:* "Be a chess player."
Illustration: Buys approximately 2 humorous illustrations/year for articles. For first contact send cover letter and b&w tearsheets to Jennie L. Simon. Samples are returned by SASE. Buys first time rights. Pays $25 minimum, b&w page. Pays on publication. *Inside Tips:* Looking for "whimsical" drawings, not *Mad* magazine type.
Writing: "In querying our magazine, we advise that you familiarize yourself with our magazine, so that the article is appropriate for us; study writer's guidelines."

THE SCIENCES, 622 Broadway, New York NY 10012. (212)838-0230. FAX: (212)260-1356. Bimonthly company magazine. Circ. 70,000. Needs comic strips, cartoon narratives and gag cartoons.
Gag Cartoons: Buys 1 gag cartoon/issue. Prefers gag cartoons on science. Preferred formats are single or multi-panel with balloons, b&w line art, b&w or color wash. Send submissions to Elizabeth Meryman, Picture Editor. Reports back within weeks. Returns material only if requested. Buys one-time rights. Pays $3-500, color.

*SCUBA TIMES MAGAZINE, 14110 Perdido Key Dr., Pensacola FL 32507. (904)492-7805. FAX: (904)492-7807. Estab. 1978. Bimonthly consumer magazine. Circ. 37,000 (with pass-on readership of 100,000.) Needs humorous illustration and writing and spot cartoons.
Writing: Buys "less than 1 humorous piece per issue, would like 1 per issue." Needs humorous nonfiction, "slice-of-life" and anecdotes, "fillers." Subject matter includes "scuba diving—it would be difficult for a non-diver to write for us." Length: 300-900 words. To query be familiar with magazine, make sure article is appropriate and study writer's guidelines. Send SASE for copy. For first contact send cover letter, query, outline, ms, published tearsheets and writing sample to Gwen Roland, Copy Editor. Reports back within 6 weeks. Buys first time rights. Pays $75/page. Offers no kill fee. *Inside Tips:* "We desperately need sophisticated humor for our 'Free Flowing' column. Our readers are mainly upper income well-educated. They are avid divers who take an average of 2 international dive vacations per year. They are not armchair divers—they make an average of 30 dives per year."

*THE SECRETARY, 2800 Shirlington Rd., Suite 706, Arlington VA 22206. (703)998-2534. FAX: (703)379-4561. Estab. 1942. Trade journal published 9 times/year. Circ. 45,000. Needs humorous illustration and spot cartoons. Accepts previously published cartoons. Prefers working with freelancers who have fax capabilities.

Gag Cartoons: Preferred format is single panel, without gagline, b&w line art.

Illustration: Buys 2 humorous illustrations/issue; 20 humorous illustrations/year for articles. More apt to hire a humorous illustrator if he has a clean, graphically-pleasing drawing style; uses humor effectively; "is sensitive to women's issues, avoids stereotypes." For first contact send cover letter, client list and b&w tearsheets to Tracy Fellin Savidge, Managing Editor. Looks for "non-stereotypical portrayals of women, clean style — not too outrageous." Reports only if interested. Samples are filed or are returned by SASE. Buys first time rights. Pays $150, b&w, page, $400, color page; $200, b&w, cover, $500, color, cover. *Inside Tips:* "Samples that specifically address current workplace issues topics are most likely to receive our attention."

SENIOR, 3565 S. Higuera, San Luis Obispo CA 93401. (805)544-8711. FAX: (805)544-4450. Estab. 1981. Monthly tabloid. Circ. 140,000. Needs humorous illustration and writing and caricature. Accepts previously published cartoons and humorous articles.

Gag Cartoons: Preferred format is single panel, b&w line art. Query with 3-10 rough drawings/batch to George Brand, Editor. Returns materials if accompanied by SASE. Buys one-time rights. Pays $10, b&w; on publication.

Illustration: Buys humorous illustration mainly for covers and articles. For first contact send cover letter and b&w promo piece to George Brand, Editor. Reports back in 2 weeks. Samples returned by SASE. Buys one-time rights. Pays $50, b&w, page; $100, b&w, cover.

Writing: Buys approximately 3-4 humorous pieces/issue. Needs humorous nonfiction, interviews and "slice-of-life." Length: 600-900 words. To query be familiar with magazine; study writer's guidelines. Send $1.50 and SASE for copy. For first contact send cover letter and manuscript to George Brand, Editor. Reports back in 2 weeks. Samples returned with SASE. Buys one-time rights. Pays $1.50/inch.

SENIOR EDITION USA, Suite 218, 1385 S. Colorado Blvd., Denver CO 80222-3312. (303)758-4040. FAX: (303)758-2728. Estab. 1972. Monthly newspaper. Circ. 50,000. Needs humorous writing.

Writing: Buys approximately 1-2 humorous pieces/issue. Needs humorous nonfiction, "slice-of-life," anecdotes, "fillers." Subject matter includes "anything of interest or relevance to senior citizens, not stereotypical or condescending to senior citizens." Length: 150-300 words. To query make sure article is appropriate; study writer's guidelines. Send $1 and SASE for copy. For first contact send manuscript or writing sample to Rose Beetem, Managing Editor. Reports back. Samples returned with SASE. Buys first time rights. Pays $5-25 for 150-800 words. *Inside Tips:* "We look for true experience — many articles are rejected because they are cliché, denigrate age or seniors, or are irrelevent to our market age group. We also syndicate through Senior Wire."

SKYDIVING, Box 1520, DeLand FL 32721. (904)736-9779. Estab. 1979. Monthly magazine. Publishes news about the techniques, events, equipment, people and places of sport parachuting. Circ. 8,300. Accepts previously published cartoons/humorous illustrations.

Gag Cartoons/Humorous Illustrations: Subjects include skydiving. For first contact send cover letter and b&w tearsheets to Sue Clifton, Editor. Reports back in weeks. Returns materials. Buys first rights. Pays $15-25. *Inside Tips:* "Know the sport of parachuting."

*SMALL BUSINESS OPPORTUNITIES, 1515 Broadway, 8th Fl., New York NY 10010. (212)807-7100. FAX: (212)627-4678. Estab. 1988. Monthly consumer magazine. Circ. 80,000. Needs humorous illustration. Accepts previously published cartoons. Prefers working with freelancers who have fax capabilities.
Gag Cartoons: Prefers gag cartoons on "Running your own business, self-employment, dumb bosses." Preferred format is single panel, with gagline, b&w line art. Query to Patrick Calkins, Art Director. Reports back within 1 month. Reports only if interested. Returns material if accompanied by SASE. Buys first time rights. Pays $50, b&w. Pays on acceptance.
Illustration: Buys 40 humorous illustrations/year for articles, columns. More apt to hire a humorous illustrator if he conceptualizes well and has clever ideas—good use of metaphors, has a clean, graphically-pleasing drawing style, does not exaggerate or distort too much, "has a style like Roy Doty, Walt McGougen, Guy Billout." For first contact send b&w tearsheets, b&w promo piece, "faxes or photocopies OK" to Patrick Calkins, Art Director. Looks "to see if it will be understood and appreciated by our audience." Reports back within 1 month. Samples not filed are returned by SASE. Pays $50, b&w, page; $300, color, cover.

SNOW COUNTRY, 5520 Park Ave., Trumbull CT 06611. (203)373-7029. FAX: (203)373-7033. Estab. 1988. Consumer magazine published 8 times/year. Circ. 300,000. Needs humorous illustration and writing, caricature, gag and spot cartoons. Accepts previously published cartoons.
Gag Cartoons: Buys 5-7 gag cartoons/issue. Prefers gag cartoons on "skiing, biking, climbing, skating, fishing, tennis, golf, hiking, hot air ballooning, real estate. For us, the 'dream' gag cartoon would be funny situations on the slopes." Preferred format is single panel with or without gagline, b&w line art or wash. Send all submissions to Douglas Wheeler, Assistant Art Director. Reports in 1 month. Returns materials if accompanied by SASE. Buys one-time rights. Pays $125, b&w. Pays on publication. *Inside Tips:* "Have a sense of humor and be familiar with skiing."
Illustration: Buys 1 humorous illustration/issue for articles. Works on assignment only. For first contact send color tearsheets and promo piece and portfolio to Julie Curtis, Art Director. Looks for "art that supports the story in a humorous way." Reports back within 1 month. Samples are filed. Buys one-time rights. Pays $350-500, color, page. Pays on acceptance.
Writing: Buys approximately 1 humorous piece/issue. Needs humorous interviews, fiction and anecdotes, "fillers." Length: 500-750 words. To query be familiar with magazine; make sure article is appropriate; study writer's guidelines. For first contact send cover letter, outline of proposed story, published tearsheets, resume and writing sample to John Fry, Editor. Reports back within 1 month. Samples are not filed, are returned. Buys one-time rights.

*SOCCER DIGEST, 990 Grove St., Evanston IL 60201. (708)491-6440. Estab. 1972. Monthly consumer magazine. Circ. 40,000-200,000. Needs gag cartoons. Accepts previously published cartoons.
Gag Cartoons: Buys 1-2 cartoons/issue; 12 cartoons/year. Prefers gag cartoons on sports. Doesn't want to see gag cartoons on golf, tennis, jogging. Preferred format is b&w line art, with gagline. Query to Cartoon Editor. Reports back within 1 month. Returns material if accompanied by a SASE. Buys first time rights, reprint rights. Pays $20, b&w. Pays on publication.

SPY, 5 Union Square W., New York NY 10003. (212)633-6550. FAX: (212)633-8848. Estab. 1986. Monthly consumer magazine. Needs humorous illustration and writing, caricatures, gag and spot cartoons.

Gag Cartoons: Buys 5 gag cartoons/issue. Prefers gag cartoons on general interest and satire. Preferred format is single panel with or without gagline, b&w line art or wash. Query with 5-6 rough drawings/batch to Gina Duclayan, Cartoon Editor. Buys all rights. Payment varies.
Illustration: Buys 5 humorous illustrations/issue for articles and spots. For first contact send cover letter, resume and samples to Gina Duclayan, Cartoon Editor. Buys all rights. Payment varies.
Writing: Buys approximately 5 humorous pieces/issue. Needs humorous nonfiction and anecdotes, "fillers." Subject matter includes general topics. Check out Spy to see what we are looking for. For first contact send cover letter, query and writing sample to Gina Duclayan, Cartoon Editor. Buys all rights. Payment varies.

STUDENT ASSISTANCE JOURNAL, Performance Resource Press, 1863 Technology Dr., Troy MI 48083-4244. (313)588-7733. FAX: (313)643-4435. Estab. 1988. Trade journal published 5 times/year. Circ. 50,000. Needs gag and spot cartoons. Accepts previously published cartoons.
Gag Cartoons: Prefers gag cartoons "on students' personal problems, for which they might seek the help of a counselor, especially substance abuse issues." Preferred formats are single or double panel, with or without gagline or balloons. Query with any number of rough drawings/batch to Jerri Andrews, Editor. Reports back in 4 weeks. Returns material only if interested. Buys first time rights or one-time rights. Pays $15-30, b&w; on publication.

STUDENT PRESS LAW CENTER REPORT, Suite 504, 1735 Eye Street NW, Washington DC 20006. (202)466-5242. Estab. 1974. Triannual magazine that focuses on cases and controversies involving free-press rights of student journalists. Illustrations used to advocate student press freedom and condemn censorship. Circ. 7,000. Previously published cartoons/humorous illustrations accepted.
Cartoons & Illustrations: Needs comic strips, editorial and gag cartoons and single panels of regional and national appeal, op-ed humorous illustration, caricatures and spot cartoons. Considers whether artist can turn around art on short deadline and is a high school or college student. For first contact send cover letter and b&w tearsheets. Reports back within 1 month. Returns material only if requested. All illustrations/cartoons are contributed by volunteer students with an interest in press freedom issues.

*SUDS 'N STUFF, 4764 Galicia Way, Oceanside CA 92056. (619)724-4447. Estab. 1979. Bimonthly 16 pg. mini-magazine. Circ. 20,000. Needs spot cartoons and humorous writing.
Gag Cartoons: Buys 1 cartoon/issue; 6 cartoons/year. Prefers gag cartoons on beer. Preferred format is single panel, with gagline, b&w line art. Query with 2-3 rough drawings/batch to Sandra Powers, Editor. Reports back within 2 weeks if interested. Returns material if accompanied by SASE. Negotiates rights purchased. Pays $10-20, b&w. Pays on publication. *Inside Tips:* "Have a humorously interesting angle on some subject related directly to beer."
Writing: Buys approximately 2 humorous pieces/issue; 12 humorous pieces/year. Needs humorous nonfiction, fiction, interviews, "slice-of-life," anecdotes, fillers (must all relate to beer). Length: 1,000 words. To query make sure article is appropriate; study writer's guidelines: send SASE for copy. For first contact send cover letter, ms to Sandra Powers, Editor. Reports back within 2 weeks if interested. Samples not filed are returned with SASE. Negotiates rights purchased. Pays $10-20 for 800-1,000 words.

SUNRISE, Box 6767, Seeger Square Station, St. Paul MN 55106-0767. (612)774-4971. Estab. 1977. Monthly tabloid that focuses on neighborhood news. Circ. 16,000. Accepts previously published cartoons/humorous illustrations and humorous articles.

Close-up

David Sheldon
Humorous Illustrator

David Sheldon has one heck of a commute to work each morning.

You see, Sheldon lives in Cincinnati, but works most Mondays through Fridays in New York. Relax. As long as Sheldon has a fax machine and a well-tipped Fed–Ex man, he can do business in New York without having to zoom into JFK. It's the humorous *illustrations* that do the flying, not the humorous *illustrator*.

Sheldon is one of a growing breed of humorous illustrators who is based in illogical metropolitan or suburban neighborhoods but still churns out high profile work for the top Manhattan-based consumer magazines.

To be sure, Sheldon's work is seen all over the place—in *SPY*, *Sports Illustrated*, *Entertainment Weekly* and even on Nickelodeon's retro-inspired "Ren and Stimpy Show"—and because Sheldon's graphic style borrows heavily from animation design of the 1950s and 60s, he was called on by "Ren and Stimpy" creator John Kricflausi to design the "fake commercials" which were meant to look like actual toy commercials from the Eisenhower to Kennedy era. *No one in illustration could have pulled off the feat better than Sheldon.*

"My stuff," says Sheldon, "looks a little like early Hanna-Barbera. I grew up watching that stuff. You know, "Huckleberry Hound," "Quick Draw McGraw," "Yogi Bear" and "Topcat." I was also influenced by Disney animation of the 1950s which had a hipper kind of look. "Rocky and Bullwinkle," "Mr. Magoo" and "Gerald McBoingboing" were other cartoons that I was a big fan of." And while Sheldon has been able to apply his hip, retro style to animation projects, it's particularly interesting that 99 percent of his work is for editorial clients.

But while Sheldon's work exudes an appealing level of self-confidence, it didn't always. "I look at my early work," he says, "and I wonder how I was able to get work and survive. I also look back on the early work and see how far I've come. A freelance humorous illustrator is pretty self-critical. You have to be your own CEO and the mail clerk at the same time. You therefore have to be concerned with 'quality control' in your work."

Sheldon surmises that, while there are advantages to working outside of New York City as a humorous illustrator, there are disadvantages as well and he admits that being in Cincinnati may have slowed his success. "I remember," he says, "the first year I began freelancing and got a call from an art director in New York. She asked me when I was moving to New York City. I informed her that I was going to stay in Cincinnati. She then said, 'when you move to

New York, I'll give you work.' I know illustrators who live in New York and they tell me they get work many times because they go to a party and come in contact with the right art director.

"I get enough work most of the time," Sheldon continues, "to keep me busy and I realize I would make more money if I lived in New York, but I don't know if I could live as well there as I do in Cincinnati. Besides, there are still plenty of art directors who prefer to use illustrators outside of New York City."

To market his work, Sheldon uses the traditional self-promotional vehicles. "I should be in more of the illustration directories," he admits, "but it's probably due to my lack of planning that I'm not. Anyway, each of the directories claims to be the best. I was in the *Adweek Illustration Annual* while it was being published, and I didn't get a single job from that. I was in *American Showcase* for two years when I was with (a rep) and I didn't get any work the second year from that."

But the kind of self-promotion that works best for Sheldon is the postcard. "The good thing," he says, "about doing a self-promotional postcard is that you can target it to specific art directors—postcards aren't lost in a big book of illustration that sits up on someone's shelf."

To find the appropriate art directors to which to send the postcards, Sheldon often rents labels from certain mailing list services. "But I don't waste money," he says, "by sending my stuff to magazines that simply don't use illustration, although this isn't always a safe bet. For example, I sent a postcard of my stuff to *SPY*, but I almost didn't do it because they simply weren't using illustration. Alex Eisley (then *SPY* art director) called and I got this huge assignment of five illustrations, which was the biggest thing I had done at that time. I was tickled to get that. So you learn that you just don't know.

"You have to remind your clients that you're out there," advises Sheldon. "If you *don't* promote, people forget about you. When I send out a postcard, I'm not necessarily trying to get work right then. But I hope an art director likes my work well enough to put the postcard up on his bulletin board."

Apparently, David Sheldon's work is up on a lot of bulletin boards.

—Bob Staake

What Insects Do When We're Not Around: David Sheldon's animation-influenced style shines in this magazine illustration.

© Konald Coddington

Ten Chief Execs: *Washington, DC-based caricaturist Ron Coddington skewers every President from Hoover to Reagan in this gorgeous black and white spread. Coddington, whose caricature style is highly influenced by Bill Plympton, has promoted his work in the last three editions of RSVP, but this year plans to "work with my wife as a representative/agent. We plan to circulate several mailers."*

Cartoons & Illustrations: Needs comic strips, single panels and editorial cartoons of local appeal; gag and spot cartoons; humorous and op-ed humorous illustration; and caricature. Considers whether artist can draw on localized news and turn around art on short deadline. For first contact send cover letter, b&w tearsheets and promo pieces and resume to editor. Enclose SASE. Reports back only if interested. Does not return or file materials. Buys all rights. Pays for editorial cartoon, humorous illustration, spot cartoons and op-ed humor illustration, $10-15.
Writing: Needs all types of humorous writing. Accepts humorous material that has a local or regional slant. Length: 500-700 words. For first contact send cover letter, resume, query and outline for proposed article to editor. Enclose SASE. Unsolicited material is not filed or returned. Buys all rights. *Inside Tips:* "Be very local."

*SWANK MAGAZINE, 1700 Broadway, New York NY 10019. (212)541-7100. FAX: (212)245-1241. Men's sophisticated consumer magazine published 13 times/year. Circ. 125,000. Needs gag and spot cartoons and humorous illustration.
Gag Cartoons: Buys 8-10 cartoons/issue; varied number of cartoons/year. Prefers gag cartoons on sex and relationships, bad taste jokes. Doesn't want to see "guys walking in on their wives with another guy. For us the 'dream' gag cartoon would be very funny, very colorful—sex-oriented." Preferred format is single panel, double panel, multi-panel, without gagline, with gagline, with balloons, color wash. Query to Brian J. English, Editor. Reports back within 2 weeks. Returns material if accompanied by a SASE. Buys first time rights. Pays $125, color. Pays on publication. "Be original, outrageous and very, very visual."
Illustration: Number of humourous illustrations used/issue varies. Buys humorous illustration for spots. More apt to hire a humorous illustrator if he has a truly unique drawing style, conceptualizes well and has clever ideas—good use of metaphors, has a bold, powerful, attention-getting drawing style, uses humor effectively, "different and outrageous sex angles and jokes." For first contact send cover letter, art available to sell for sample and usable examples of work done for *Swank* to Brian J. English, Editor. Reports back within 2 weeks. Samples not filed are returned. Buys first time rights. Pays $125,

color, page. *Inside Tips:* "We follow certain censorship guidelines."
Writing: Number of humorous pieces/issue varies. Needs humorous nonfiction, interviews, "slice-of-life," all sex-oriented. "All must have sexual slant. Accompanying photos a huge plus." Length: 2,500-3,500 words. To query be familiar with magazine, make sure article is appropriate, study writer's guidelines: Send $5.95 and SASE for copy. For first contact send cover letter, ms and published tearsheets to Brian J. English, Editor. Reports back within 2 weeks. Samples are filed or are returned with SASE. Buys first time rights. Pays $350-800 for 1,500-3,500 words. Offers 25% kill fee. *Inside Tips:* "Be familiar with men's market trends and our readers' standpoint. i.e., nothing too esoteric."

TECH DIRECTIONS, (formerly School Shop/Tech Directions), Box 8623, Dept. HC, Ann Arbor MI 48107. (313)769-1211. FAX: (313)769-8383. Estab. 1940. Monthly (Aug.-May) trade journal. Circ. 45,000. Needs gag cartoons.
Gag Cartoons: Buys approximately 2 gag cartoons/issue. Accepts only gag cartoons on vocational, technical and technology education. Must be a school, not industrial setting. Preferred format is single panel with or without gagline, b&w line art. Query with 1-10 rough drawings/batch to Susanne Peckham, Managing Editor. Reports back in 1 month. Buys first rights. Pays $20; on publication. *Inside Tips:* "Send us a few examples of cartoons which deal with the industrial education field, with special emphasis on classroom situations."

TENNIS MAGAZINE, 5520 Park Ave., Trumbull CT 06611. Monthly consumer magazine. Circ. 750,000. Needs tennis-related gag cartoons.
Gag Cartoons: Buys 9-12 gag cartoons/year. Preferred format is single panel, b&w line art. Query with any number of rough drawings/batch to Kathleen Burke, Art Director. Reports back in 1 month only if interested. Returns materials if accompanied by SASE. Buys first or reprint rights. Pays $75, color; on publication. *Inside Tips:* A gag cartoonist should "understand the subject; have original concepts; execute concepts professionally; and make us all laugh."

THRASHER MAGAZINE & THRASHER COMICS, Box 884570, San Francisco CA 94188-4570. (415)822-3083. FAX: (415)822-8359. Estab. 1981. Monthly skateboarding and rock 'n roll consumer magazine. Circ. 400,000. Needs comic strips, humorous illustration and writing, cartoon narratives and illustration.
Gag Cartoons: Buys 4-6 gag cartoons/year on skateboarding, punk rock and youth. Send submissions to Kevin Ancell, Cartoon/Comics Editor. Reports back if interested. Returns materials if accompanied by SASE. Buys all rights. Pays $50 minimum, b&w; on publication.
Illustration: Buys approximately 1-2 humorous illustrations/year for articles. Works on assignment only. One of the things considers when hiring a freelance humorous illustrator is a truly unique drawing style. For first contact send b&w or color tearsheets to Enrico Chandoha, Art Director. Looks for "boldness, guts, raw humor and reality." Reports back if interested. Samples are filed or are returned if requested. Buys all rights. Pays $100 minimum, b&w, page. *Inside Tips:* "We don't want anything 'cute.' "
Writing: Buys approximately 6-8 humorous pieces/year. Needs humorous nonfiction, fiction, interviews and cartoon stories. Subject matter includes skateboarding and rock 'n roll. Length: 500-1,500 words. To query be familiar with magazine and make sure article is appropriate. For first contact send outline of proposed story and writing sample

---

Always include a self-addressed stamped envelope (SASE) or International Reply Coupon (IRC) with submissions.

to Kurt Carlson, Copy Editor. Reports back if interested. Samples are filed or are returned if requested. Buys all rights. Pays 15¢ per word. Offers 50% kill fee. *Inside Tips:* "We print pieces that have attitude, sarcasm, satire and wit. We're not above 'strengthening' it a bit. Our magazine is about youth and the street."

*TODAY'S CHRISTIAN WOMAN, 465 Gundersen Dr., Carol Stream IL 60188. (708)260-6200. FAX: (708)260-0114. Bimonthly consumer magazine. Needs gag cartoons. Accepts previously published cartoons.
Gag Cartoons: Buys 5 cartoons/issue; 30 cartoons/year. Prefers gag cartoons on women, family, relationships, parenting, marriage, work, church life, seasonal. Doesn't want to see gag cartoons "that portray women negatively. For us the 'dream' gag cartoon would be one that takes a positive, light, humorous approach to day-to-day events." Preferred format is b&w line art with gagline. Query with 5-10 rough drawings/batch to Jan Senn, Assistant Editor. Reports back within 1 month. Returns material if accompanied by a SASE. Buys first time rights. Pays $50, b&w. Pays on acceptance.
Illustration: Buys 5 humorous illustrations/year for articles. Works on assignment only. More apt to hire a humorous illustrator if he or she conceptualizes well and has clever ideas — good use of metaphors; uses humor effectively; can "fun up" an otherwise "flat" manuscript; is businesslike, meets deadlines and is responsive to my needs. For first contact send cover letter, b&w and color tearsheets to Christa Jordan, Designer. Reports only if interested. Samples are filed or are returned if requested. Buys first time rights. Pays $350-400, color, page; $150 minimum for spot.

TOLE WORLD, Box 5986, Concord CA 94524. (510)671-9852. FAX: (510)671-0692. Estab. 1977. Bimonthly consumer magazine. Circ. 40,000. Needs topical cartoons with illustration and caption.
Gag Cartoons: Prefers gag cartoons on tole painting, classroom situations and goof-ups. Doesn't want to see "plays on the word 'tole.' For us, the 'dream' gag cartoon would be harmless, evocative, hilarious and timeless." Preferred format is single panel with gagline, b&w line art or wash. Query with 2-10 rough drawings/batch to Zach Shatz, Editor. Reports back in 4 weeks. Returns materials if accompanied by SASE. Buys all rights. Pays $25, b&w; on acceptance. *Inside Tips:* A gag cartoonist should "understand the readership, the specifics of the magazine focus and the necessity for lightness in humor."
Illustration: Buys approximately 1 humorous illustration/issue for spots. When hiring a freelance humorous illustrator, these abilties are considered: good conceptualization and clever ideas — good use of metaphors; a clean, graphically-pleasing drawing style; flexibility, broad potential in drawing style. For first contact send query of possible ideas.

*TOURING AMERICA, Box 6050, Mission Viejo CA 92690. (714)855-8822. FAX: (714)855-1850. Estab. 1991. Bimonthly consumer magazine. Circ. 95,000. Needs gag cartoons and humorous illustration.
Gag Cartoons: Buys 6-8 cartoons/year. Prefers gag cartoons on travel — in North America only (no overseas). "For us, the 'dream' gag cartoon would be knee-slapping funny." Preferred format is single panel, b&w line art. Query with 6-12 rough drawings/batch to Gene Booth, Editor. Reports back within 2 weeks. Returns material if accompanied by a SASE. Buys first time rights. Pays $25-50, b&w.
Illustration: Buys 6-12 humorous illustrations/year for articles. Works on assignment only. More apt to hire a humorous illustrator if he has a truly unique drawing style; conceptualizes well and has clever ideas — good use of metaphors; has a bold, powerful, attention-getting drawing style; uses humor effectively; can "fun up" an otherwise "flat" ms; is businesslike, meets deadlines and is responsive to my needs. For first contact send resume and b&w tearsheets to Gene Booth, Editor. Looks for "style and ability

to conceptualize points of the article." Reports back within 2 weeks. Samples are filed. Buys first time rights. Pays $50-75, b&w (spot).

TREASURE CHEST, Suite 211A, 253 W. 72nd St., New York NY 10023. (212)496-2234. Estab. 1988. Monthly tabloid focusing on antiques and collectibles. Provides information source and marketplace for collectors and dealers. Circ. 50,000. Accepts previously published cartoons/humorous illustrations and humorous articles.
Cartoons & Illustrations: Needs humorous illustration, caricature and spot cartoons that are "positive and upbeat and focus on antiques and collectibles." Considers whether artist has ability to read a manuscript and come up with a strong visual idea and use humor effectively. For first contact send b&w tearsheets and sketches to Howard Fischer, Editor. Reports back in 1 month. Returns materials if accompanied by SASE. Negotiates rights purchased. Pays for humorous illustration and spot cartoons, $10-25.
Writing: Needs humor writing relating to antiques and collectibles. Subject matter includes auction scenes, antique shop buyers and sellers, collectors and his/her collections—"all upbeat and positive." Length: 500-1,000 words. For first contact send manuscript to Howard Fischer, Editor. Unsolicited material is returned with SASE. Negotiates rights purchased. Pays $15-25 for 500-1,000 words. *Inside Tips:* "Those interested in working with *Treasure Chest* should send $1 for sample copy and writers' and artists' guidelines in order to better understand what we seek."

*TRUCKIN, 2145 W. La Palma, Anaheim CA 92801. (714)778-6091. FAX: (714)533-9979. Estab. 1975. Monthly consumer magazine. Circ. 240,000. Needs humorous illustration and spot cartoons. Prefers working with freelancers who have fax capabilities.
Gag Cartoons: Buys 5-6 cartoons/issue; 70 cartoons/year. Prefers gag cartoons on custom and classic trucks. "For us, the 'dream' gag cartoon would be good spot cartoons." Preferred format is single panel with gagline, b&w line art. Query with 4-8 rough drawings/batch to Steve Stillwell, Editor. Reports back within 1 month. Buys first time rights. Pays $25+ b&w. Pays on publication. *Inside Tips:* "Deliver batches of line art spot cartoons which will reproduce whether used large or small."
Illustration: Buys 12-14 humorous illustrations/issue for articles. For first contact send cover letter and b&w promo piece to Steve Stillwell, Editor. Looks for reproducible b&w line art. Reports back within 1 month. Samples not filed are returned by SASE. Buys first time rights. Pays $25+, b&w, page, four spots. Pays on publication.
Writing: Buys approximately 5-6 humorous pieces/issue; 70 humorous pieces/year. Needs humorous anecdotes, "fillers." "Spots should have custom truck or truck owner type humor." Length: 1,500 words. To query be familiar with magazine; make sure article is appropriate. Send $3.25 and SASE for copy. For first contact send cover letter and writing sample to Steve Stillwell, Editor. Reports back within 1 month. Samples not filed are returned with SASE. Buys first time rights. *Inside Tips:* "Material must apply to custom trucking, i.e., pickups, mini-trucks—not semis."

*TV TIME MAGAZINE, 415 5th Ave. #1207, New York NY 10017. (212)683-6116. FAX: (212)683-8051. Estab. 1990. Weekly consumer magazine. Circ. 500,000. Needs gag cartoons, humorous illustration and writing, caricatures.
Gag Cartoons: "We buy 1 cartoon per quarter." Prefers gag cartoons that relate to the TV themes. Preferred format is single panel, b&w line art. Query to Ronnie Brandwein, Assistant Art Director. Reports back within 2 days. Returns material. Buys first time rights. Pays $50, b&w. Pays on publication. *Inside Tips:* "Catch a reader's eye and make them laugh. It must be new material and be interesting."
Illustration: Buys approximately 12 humorous illustrations/year for articles, spots. More apt to hire a humorous illustrator if he has a truly unique drawing style; conceptualizes well and has clever ideas—good use of metaphors; uses humor effectively. For

THE TOURIST H

In honor of National Tourism Week (May 5 to 11), *Travel Life*

MR. BIG

Demands that all his hotel rooms come equipped with five phones, four fax machines, three computer terminals, two secretaries, and a regulation putting surface; expects flights to arrive *ahead* of schedule; will power-lunch only at restaurants where the tab exceeds the price of his suit; despite having traveled throughout the world, cannot name one distinctive landmark or historic site in any domestic or foreign city.

MR. AND MRS. BY-THE-BOOK

Never venture more than 100 yards from the tour bus; give wake-up calls to hotel staffs each morning and greet tardy tour mates with dramatic glances at their stopwatches; can recite entire chapters of Baedeker, Birnbaum, and Berlitz from memory; buy souvenirs—usually prepackaged slides—only from "official" gift shops; refuse to accept "an act of God" as a justifiable reason for alteration of their tour schedule.

MR. INDECISION

Really wants to travel but isn't sure when and where to go, how much he'd like to spend, or whether to fly, drive, or sail; seeks so much advice while formulating an itinerary that he often ends up canceling the trip, feeling as though he's already been there; once circled the Epcot Center's World Showcase for three days because he couldn't pick which country's pavilion to visit first.

MS. BLAH-BLAH

Spends the majority of each flight informing aisle mates of the intimate details of her sister's divorce and her husband's hiatal hernia; explains the historical significance (read: whether a miniseries was filmed there) of every place of interest on her tour; will converse with a local for 15 minutes before asking, "You *do* speak English, right?"; upon return, delays the customs line when she voluntarily divulges the place of purchase and chemical composition of each gift in her suitcases.

ALL ⚬ᶠ FAME

Illustrations by
Robert de Michiell

salutes the classic client types that make agents' lives such a joy.

MR. "IS-THAT-THE-BEST-YOU-CAN-DO?"

Asks to be booked on crowded flights in order to get bumped and add to his stash of free tickets; skips restaurants during the first week of his trip, eating instead the peanuts and crackers he has collected on planes; tries to obtain a refund of his tours' land costs by claiming that he was traumatized by noise from the bus engine; was once arrested in Rome when caught snorkeling for coins that had been tossed into fountains.

THE PRINCESS OF WAILS

Howls nonstop during overseas flights while slinging her bottle, pacifier, and assorted plush toys at fellow passengers; once made headlines by cracking stained glass in three cathedrals with her reverberating screams and by shouting "Mine, mine, mine" upon viewing the Crown Jewels; because of her button nose and big eyes, has been granted a sort of diplomatic immunity and is never held accountable by anyone (least of all, her parents) for her misbehavior.

MR. AND MRS. GROUSE

"The weather's Siberian, the coffee tastes like transmission fluid and the breakfast rolls are harder than croquet balls, the waiter's a Neanderthal, the tour guide's English sounds like Serbo-Croatian, the exchange rate's a ripoff, the cabbie thinks he's Mario Andretti, there's no place to get a decent steak and potato around here, the locals keep staring at us like we're from Mars, the hotel's a chicken coop compared with the one across the street, the countryside looked 10 times better in the movies, the prices are ungodly . . . " but other than that, they're having a wonderful time.

HAROLD AND MARGE

Always travel in tour buses with double-wide seats and enjoy at least one meal daily at an all-you-can-eat buffet; wardrobes are composed entirely of polyester/rayon blends and matching T-shirts emblazoned with such slogans as WE'RE SPENDING OUR CHILDREN'S INHERITANCE and 39 AND HOLDING; have accumulated an extensive collection of miniature shampoo bottles; can spend an entire week's vacation shuttling between outlet malls.

TRAVEL LIFE MAY/JUNE 1991 **19**

Well-Traveled Art: *New York City-based humorous illustrator Robert de Michiell creates a number of ultra-cool spot illustrations depicting various types of tourists for a two-page spread in a travel magazine. Describing his style as contemporary, de Michiell promotes his work in American Showcase, and sends out "promo mailers frequently to 150 regular clients."*

first contact send portfolio to Jill Armus, Art Director. Looks for eye catching work; unique styles. Reports back within 1 week. Samples are filed. Samples not filed are returned. Buys first time rights. Pays $200, b&w, page, $350, color page. Pays on publication.
Writing: Buys approximately 12 humorous pieces/year. Needs humorous nonfiction, interviews, "slice-of-life." "Subject matter must be about TV." Length: 500 words. For first contact send query to Katrina Brown, Editorial Assistant. Samples are not filed. Samples not filed are returned with SASE. Buys first time rights. Pays 50¢/word. Offers 25% kill fee.

U. THE NATIONAL COLLEGE NEWSPAPER, 1900 Century Park East #820, Los Angeles CA 90067. (310)551-1381. FAX: (310)551-1679. Estab. 1987. Monthly newspaper. Circ. 1,425,000. Needs comic strips, humorous illustration and writing, caricature and spot cartoons. Accepts previously published cartoons and humorous articles.
Cartoons & Illustrations: Buys 8 gag cartoons/year, 16 humorous illustrations/year. Prefers cartoons and illustrations on "college-related issues." For cartoons "any format is OK"; for illustrations send b&w or color tearsheets. Send all cartoon and illustration submissions to Jacki Hampton, Managing Editor. Reports back within 2 weeks only if interested. Returns materials only if requested. Buys reprint rights. Pays $25, b&w, $25, color. Pays on publication. "Material accepted from college students only."
Writing: Buys approximately 20 humorous pieces/year. Needs humorous interviews, "slice-of-life," anecdotes. "Must be of interest to college audience." Length: 200-500 words. For first contact send published tearsheets to Jacki Hampton, Managing Editor. Reports back within 2 weeks only if interested. Samples are filed; returned only if requested. Buys reprint rights. Pays $25-50 for 200-500 words. "Material accepted from college students only." *Inside Tips:* "We reprint articles and artwork written by college students, previously published in their student newspaper. All submissions are paid—$25 to the artist/writer and $25 to the student newspaper."

*VETTE, 299 Market St., Saddle Brook NJ 07662. (201)712-9300. FAX: (201)712-9899. Estab. 1976. Monthly consumer magazine. Circ. 60,000. Needs spot cartoons.
Gag Cartoons: Buys 1 cartoons/issue; 14 cartoons/year. Preferred format is single panel, multi-panel with gagline, b&w line art. Query with 1-2 rough drawings/batch to Matt Blitz, Art Director. Reports back within 2 weeks. Returns material only if requested. Buys first time rights. Pays $50, b&w. Pays on publication. *Inside Tips:* "Know the subject (Corvettes) extremely well."

VIRTUE, Box 850, 548 Sisters Parkway, Sisters OR 97759. (503)549-8261. FAX: (503)549-0153. Estab. 1978. Bimonthly consumer magazine. Circ. 150,000. Needs humorous illustration and writing, cartoon narratives, gag spot cartoons and continual feature character. Accepts previously published cartoons.
Gag Cartoons: Buys 2-3 gag cartoons/issue. Prefers gag and spot cartoons on woman's relationships, family, animal humor, holidays and seasons. Doesn't want to see gag cartoons on religion, domestic conflict. Preferred formats are single or double panel with or without gagline, b&w line art or wash. Query with 5-10 rough drawings/batch to David Uttley, Art Director. Reports back in 2 months. Returns material if accompanied by SASE. Buys one-time rights or negotiates rights purchased. Pays $25, b&w; on publication. *Inside Tips:* "Develop a clean, consistent drawing style and work with funny, positive situations. Do not contrive gags. Relate to everyone's experiences. Avoid duplicating Gary Larson."
Illustration: Buys approximately 1 humorous illustration/issue for articles and spots. For first contact send cover letter, resume, client list, b&w or color tearsheets, b&w or color promo pieces, slides and portfolio to David Uttley. Looks for "clean style, strong potential for finished art look. Handle human form in a believable way. Be capable of

© David Milgrim

On Your Mark, Get Set, Crawl: *Originally created as a self-promotional piece, this illustration by David Milgrim of New York City was reprinted for an article in a parenting magazine. "When I created the drawing," says Milgrim, "I had in mind the whole super-baby thing and how parents push their kids to excel at a young age. The drawing was then used to illustrate an article on the very same subject."*

a broad range of expression and emotion." Reports back only if interested. Samples are filed or returned by SASE. Buys first time rights. Pays $150, b&w, $250, color, page. *Inside Tips:* "Develop a clean style. Be willing to work FAST. Make use of fax machines for sending roughs."

Writing: Buys approximately 1 humorous piece/issue. Needs humorous nonfiction, "slice-of-life" and fiction. Subject matter includes family life. Avoid satire and sarcasm. Length: 1,000-1,500 words. To query be familiar with magazine; make sure article is appropriate; study writer's guidelines. Send SASE for copy of guidelines, $3 (no SASE) for magazine sample. For first contact, send query, outline or proposed story and writing sample to Marlee Alex, Editor. Reports back in 4-6 weeks. Samples are not filed; returned if requested. Buys first time rights. Pays 15-25¢/word for 1,000-1,500 words.

WEIGHT WATCHERS MAGAZINE, 360 Lexington Ave., New York NY 10017. (212)370-0644. FAX: (212)687-4398. Estab. 1968. Monthly consumer magazine. Circ. 4,000,000. Needs humorous illustration and writing and spot cartoons.

Gag Cartoons: Prefers gag cartoons on "weight loss." Preferred format is single panel with gagline, b&w line art. Send all submissions to Stephanie Graziadio, Assistant Editor. Reports back within days. Returns materials if accompanied by SASE. Buys first rights. Pays on acceptance.

Illustration: Buys humorous illustration mainly for articles. When hiring a freelance humorous illustrator, these abilities are considered: good conceptualization and clever ideas—good use of metaphors; effective use of humor; a clear, graphically-pleasing drawing style; lack of exaggeration or distortion. For first contact send cover letter and color tearsheets to Jennifer Simpson, Art Assistant. Reports back in weeks only if interested. Samples are filed. Buys first rights. Pays $350, color, page. Pays on acceptance.

Writing: Buys 1 humorous piece/issue. Needs humorous nonfiction, fiction and "slice-of-life." Subject matter includes "weight loss." To query be familiar with magazine; make sure article is appropriate; study writer's guidelines. For first contact send query and manuscript to Mary Novitsky, Managing Editor. Reports back within weeks. Samples are returned with SASE. Buys first rights.

*THE WESTERN HORSE, 321 Kalili Pl., Kapa'a HI 96746. FAX: (808)822-7713. Estab. 1977. Monthly consumer magazine. Needs gag cartoons.

Gag Cartoons: Buys 12 cartoons/issue. Prefers gag cartoons on horses. Preferred format is single panel with gagline, b&w line art. Query to R. Gibson. Does not report back. Returns material if accompanied by a SASE. Buys one-time rights. Pays $12-15. Pays on acceptance.

WINNING, 15115 S. 76th East Ave., Bixby OK 74008. (918)366-4441. FAX: (918)366-6250. Estab. 1977. Monthly consumer magazine. Circ. 160,000. Needs humorous illustration and writing. Prefers working with freelancers who have fax capabilities.

Gag Cartoons: Buys 1 gag cartoon/issue. Prefers gag cartoons on "any aspect of gaming-contests, sweepstakes, lottery, casinos. For us, the 'dream' gag cartoon would be very humorous, yet not actively insulting to readers." Preferred format is single panel with gagline, b&w line art. "Don't use excessive film screening!" Query with 1-5 rough drawings/batch to Simon P. McCaffery, Managing Editor. Reports back within 2 months. Returns material if accompanied by a SASE. Buys first time or reprint rights. Pays $50 b&w. Pays on acceptance.

Illustration: Buys approximately 1 humorous illustration/issue for articles. Works on assignment only. For first contact send cover letter, b&w tearsheets to Simon P. McCaffery, Managing Editor. Looks for "artistic skill, strong concept and visualization, appropriate subject." Reports back within 2 months. Samples are filed or are returned by SASE if requested. Buys first time or reprint rights. Pays $100 b&w, page. Pays on acceptance. *Inside Tips:* "Know your subject, keep it graphically simple and strong, and read at least one issue of the magazine."

Writing: Buys approximately 1 humorous piece/issue. Needs humorous nonfiction, "slice-of-life" and anecdotes, "fillers." Subject matter includes "anything related to gaming and travel." Length: 500-2,000 words. "Some short-shorts are used." To query be familiar with magazine; make sure article is appropriate; study writer's guidelines. Send $1.50 and SASE for copy. For first contact send cover letter, query, manuscript ("would rather see query first, but will read mss)" to Simon P. McCaffery, Managing Editor. Reports back within 2 months. Samples are returned with SASE. Buys first time rights. Pays $50-250 for 560 to 2,000 words. Offers 30% kill fee. *Inside Tips:* "Avoid clichés (bad luck in Las Vegas, etc) Come up with a unique premise or situation. Don't 'over write.' "

WISCONSIN, THE MILWAUKEE JOURNAL MAGAZINE, Box 661, Milwaukee WI 53201. (414)224-2341. Estab. 1969. Weekly Sunday newspaper magazine. Circ. 500,000. Needs humorous writing and gag cartoons. Accepts previously published cartoons and humorous articles.

Gag Cartoons: Buys 2 gag cartoons/issue. Prefers gag cartoons on contemporary subjects. Doesn't want to see gag cartoons on wife/mother-in-law themes. The "dream" gag cartoon would be "something that made an interesting comment on people while being

funny." Preferred format is single panel b&w line art. Send submissions to Alan Borsuk, Editor. Reports back within 2 months. Returns material if accompanied by a SASE. Buys one-time rights. Pays $17 minimum, b&w. Pays on acceptance.
Writing: Buys approximately 1 humorous piece/issue. Needs humorous nonfiction and "slice-of-life." Subject matter includes "women's personal essays that, below the surface, contain substantial commentary. Wisconsin angle is a strong plus." Length: 750-1,000 words. Send for free copy. For first contact send manuscript to Alan Borsuk. Reports back within 2 months. Buys one-time rights. Pays $125-175 for 750-1,250 words. Offers a negotiated kill fee.

WOMAN'S WORLD MAGAZINE, 270 Sylvan Ave., Englewood Cliffs NJ 07631. (201)569-6699. FAX: (201)569-3584. Needs humorous illustration and writing, gag and spot cartoons.
Gag Cartoons: Buys 5-6 gag cartoons/issue. Prefers gag cartoons on "domestic humor—children, school, husbands and wives and life in general." Preferred format is single panel with or without gagline, b&w line art or wash. Query with 1-10 rough drawings/batch to Johnene Granger, Managing Editor. Buys first rights. Pays $125 b&w. Pays on acceptance.
Illustration: Buys 1 humorous illustration/issue for spots. For first contact send cover and b&w promo piece to Jean Gissubel, Associate Art Director. Buys first rights.

*WOMEN'S GLIB™, P.O. Box 259, Bala Cynwyd PA 19004. (215)668-4252. Estab. 1991. Quarterly book format (trade paperback). Circ. 20,000. Needs comic strips, cartoon narratives, gag cartoons, humorous illustration, caricatures, spot cartoons, humorous writing, amusing photos and photo essays. Accepts previously published cartoons and humorous articles.
Gag Cartoons: Buys 300-500 gag cartoons/year. Prefers gag cartoons on "material about women by women with a feminist outlook." Doesn't want to see gag cartoons on dieting/weight loss. Preferred format is single, double, multi-panel with or without gagline, b&w line art, b&w or color wash. Query with 1-100 rough drawings/batch to Roz Warren, Editor. Reports back within "one week but only if SASE is provided." Returns material if accompanied by a SASE. Buys one-time rights. Pays $20, b&w. Pays on publication (plus 2 copies). *Inside Tips:* "Be a woman addressing issues of interest to women with a feminist outlook—try to come up with a new angle—be political—keep trying—hate the status quo. Love Nicole Hollander's 'Sylvia.' "
Illustration: Buys 100 humorous illustrations/year for spots. More apt to hire a humorous illustrator if she has a unique drawing style; has clever ideas—good use of metaphors; has a graphically-pleasing drawing style; has a bold, powerful, attention-getting drawing style; uses humor effectively, meets deadlines and "is an uppity feminist illustrator." For first contact send cover letter and b&w tearsheets to Roz Warren, Editor. "Work should be eye catching, feminist and funny." Reports back within "one week only if SASE included." Samples are filed or are returned by SASE. Buys one-time rights. Pays $20, b&w, page (plus 2 copies). Pays on publication. *Tips:* "Just give me a good idea of what you're up to and if I like your style I'll work with you."
Writing: Buys approximately 100 humorous pieces/year. Needs humorous nonfiction, fiction, interviews, "slice-of-life," anecdotes, fillers and cartoon stories. "I need funny material by women about a female protagonist with a feminist outlook on any topic of interest to women—sex, politics, romance—you name it!" Length: from a funny "quote" or one-liner to a funny paragraph or story—maximum length 10 manuscript pages. To query be familiar with *Women's Glib*; make sure submission is appropriate. For first contact send cover letter, manuscript, published tearsheets and SASE to Roz Warren, Editor. Reports back within 1 week only if accompanied by a SASE. Samples are filed or are returned with SASE. Buys one-time rights. Pays a minimum of $5 per page plus 2 copies.

WOMEN'S SPORTS & FITNESS, Suite 421, 1919 14th St., Boulder CO 80302. (303)440-5111. FAX: (303)440-3313. Estab. 1974. 8/year consumer magazine. Circ. 134,000. Needs humorous illustration. Prefers working with freelancers who have fax capabilities.
Gag Cartoons: Currently buys no gag cartoons "but will consider the possibility." Doesn't want to see "diet, anything trivializing pursuit of health and fitness or demeaning to women. For us, the 'dream' gag cartoon would be athletic women as hero, humor would provide sharp insight but be simple." Preferred format is single panel, b&w line art. Buys all rights.
Illustration: Buys approximately 6 humorous illustrations/issue for spots. For first contact send cover letter, b&w tearsheets, color promo piece, "anything that shows what you do" to Mark Tuchman, Art Director. Reports back "if interested." Samples are filed or are returned by SASE if requested. Negotiates rights purchased. Pays $75, b&w and color, page. Pays $25/spot illustration. Pays on publication. *Inside Tips:* "Familiarize yourself with magazine so submission can be appropriate. Professionalism counts."

WOODMEN OF THE WORLD MAGAZINE, 1700 Farnam St., Dept. HC, Omaha NE 68102. (402)342-1890. Estab. 1890. Monthly membership magazine. Circ. 475,000. Needs humorous writing, gag and spot cartoons. Accepts previously published cartoons and humorous articles.
Gag Cartoons: Buys 1-2 gag cartoons/issue of interest to the American family. Preferred format is single panel with or without gagline, b&w line art or b&w or color wash. Send submissions to Billie Jo Foust, Assistant Editor. Reports back in 2 weeks. Returns materials. Buys one-time rights. Pays $15, b&w, $20, color; on acceptance.
Writing: Needs humorous nonfiction and "slice-of-life." Subject matter includes material of interest to families. Length: 500-1,500 words. To query make sure article is appropriate. For first contact send manuscript to Billie Jo Foust, Assistant Editor. Reports back in 2 weeks. Buys one-time rights. Pays $50-150 for 500-1,500 words.

WORKBENCH, 4251 Pennsylvania, Kansas City MO 64111. (816)531-5730. Estab. 1957. Bimonthly consumer magazine for do-it-yourselfers. Circ. 800,000. Needs humorous illustration, gag and spot cartoons.
Gag Cartoons: Buys 2 gag cartoons/issue.

THE WORLD & I, 2800 New York Ave. NE, Washington DC 20002. (202)635-4000. FAX: (202)269-9353. Estab. 1986. Monthly academic magazine. Circ. 30,000. Needs humorous writing.
Writing: Buys approximately 1 humorous piece/issue. Needs humorous nonfiction, interviews, "slice-of-life" and anecdotes, "fillers." Length: 2,000 words. To query be familiar with magazine; make sure article is appropriate; and study writer's guidelines. For first contact send cover letter and manuscript to Rick Pearcey, "Life" Section Editor. Reports back within 1 month. Samples are not filed and are returned with SASE. Buys first time rights, one-time rights or all rights. Pays $300-700 for 1,500-2,000 words. Offers 20% kill fee.

WRITER'S DIGEST, 1507 Dana Ave., Cincinnati OH 45207. (513)531-2222. Estab. 1920. Monthly consumer magazine. Circ. 215,000. Needs humorous illustration and writing, gag cartoons and light verse. Accepts previously published cartoons and humorous articles. Prefers working with freelancers who have fax capabilities for illustration.
Gag Cartoons: Buys 2 gag cartoons/issue on writing and literary topics. Doesn't want to see gag cartoons on writer's block. "For us the 'dream' gag cartoon would be captionless line drawings; horizontals often fill page layout needs most immediately." Send submissions to Peter Blocksom, Managing Editor. Reports back within 2 weeks. Returns materials if accompanied by SASE. Buys first North American serial rights for one-time use. Pays $50 minimum, b&w; on acceptance. *Inside Tips:* "Keep up-to-date with trends

Toothy Predicament: *It's ironic that New York City-based humorous illustrator David Neubecker was paid $3,000 to create this cover illustrating how the recession has adversely affected the middle class, but then this is a crazy world. Certainly Neubecker's hip and sophisticated cover illustration was worth every penny of that tidy fee. To actively promote his work, Neubecker uses his illustration agents, and runs "a spread in* American Showcase, *in addition to sending out mailers throughout the year."*

in humor, use an expressive drawing style and always realize that cartooning is an art form in which the illustration is about 55% of the final product."

Illustration: Buys approximately 3 humorous illustrations/year for articles. Works on assignment only. For first contact send color or b&w promo piece to Clare Finney, Design Director. Reports back only if interested. Samples are not filed and not returned. Buys first North American serial rights for one-time use. Pays $150 minimum, b&w, page; on acceptance.

Writing: Buys approximately 24 short and 3 long humorous pieces/year. Needs nonfiction, "slice-of-life" and anecdotes, "fillers" for Writing Life and Chronicle sections. Subject matter includes writing and the problems and joys thereof. Avoid the subject rejection. Length: 50-750 words for Writing Life, 2,000 words maximum for Chronicle. To query be familiar with magazine; make sure article is appropriate; study writer's guidelines. For first contact send manuscript to Peter Blocksom, Managing Editor. Reports back within 2 weeks. Samples are not filed; returned only if requested. Buys first North American serial rights for one-time use. Pays 10¢/word. Offers 20% kill fee. *Inside Tips:* "Humor is tough to shape and mold. Let it flow and find its own shape."

WRITER'S FORUM, (formerly Book Author's Newsletter), 1507 Dana Ave., Cincinnati OH 45207. (513)531-2222. Estab. 1988. Periodic publication that focuses on news items and articles on writing/marketing novels, articles, stories and nonfiction books. Circ. 3,000. Accepts previously published cartoons/humorous illustrations.
Cartoons & Illustrations: Needs spot cartoons. Considers whether "artist aims content at the freelance writer." For first contact send cartoons to Bruce Woods, Editor. Reports back within 3 weeks. Returns materials if accompanied by SASE. Buys one-time rights. Pays for spot cartoons, $10.

WRITER'S GUIDELINES MAGAZINE: A ROUNDTABLE FOR WRITERS AND EDITORS, (formerly Guidelines Magazine), Box 608, Pittsburg MO 65724. (417)993-5544. Estab. 1988. 4 newsletters and 4 consumer magazines. Circ. 700. Needs comic strips, humorous illustration and writing, cartoon narratives, caricature, gag and spot cartoons.

Gag Cartoons: Buys 2-3 gag cartoons/issue; 20/year. Prefers gag cartoons on writing and/or editing. Preferred format is single panel with gagline, b&w line art. Query with 2-4 rough drawings/batch to Susan Salaki, Editor. Reports back within 1 month. Returns materials if SASE. Buys first or one-time rights. Pays $2-5 on acceptance.
Illustration: Buys approximately 2 humorous illustrations/issue; 20/year for articles and spots. For first contact send cover letter and b&w promo piece to Susan Salaki, Editor. Looks for material appropriate to the magazine's writing and editing topics. Reports back within 1 month. Samples are returned by SASE. Buys first or one-time rights. Pays $2-5, b&w, page. Pays on publication.
Writing: Buys approximately 1 humorous piece/issue; 10/year. Needs humorous nonfiction, "slice-of-life," anecdotes, "fillers" but the #1 need is humorous interviews. Subject matter includes "writers and the potential creativity derived from dreams, writers of the 19th century and romance from the writer's perspective." Length: 400-800 words. Send $4 for copy. For first contact send cover letter and manuscript to Susan Salaki, Editor. Reports back within 1 month. Samples are returned with SASE. Buys first or one-time rights. Pays $5-30 for 400-800 words. Offers 25% kill fee.

YANKEE MAGAZINE/THE OLD FARMERS ALMANAC, P.O. Box 520, Main St., Dublin NH 03444. (603)563-8111. FAX: (603)563-8252. Needs humorous illustration and writing, caricatures, gag and spot cartoons.
Gag Cartoons: Buys 4-5 gag cartoons/issue. Prefers gag cartoons on New England for *Yankee*. Preferred format is single panel with gagline, b&w line art or wash. Query with 4-5 rough drawings/batch to Judson D. Hale, Editor. Buys one-time rights. Pays $100 b&w. Pays on publication.
Illustration: Buys 5-8 humorous illustrations/issue for spots. For first contact send cover letter and b&w samples to Judson D. Hale, Editor. Buys one-time rights. Pays $100 b&w spot. Pays on publication.
Writing: Buys approximately 5-8 humorous pieces/issue. Needs humorous nonfiction, fiction for stories, anecdotes, "fillers" for *Old Farmer's*. Subject matter includes New England for *Yankee*. For first contact send query and writing samples to Judson D. Hale, Editor. Buys one-time rights. Pays $600 and up for features.

Publications/Changes '91-'93

The following markets appeared in the last (1991) edition of *Humor and Cartoon Markets* but are absent from the 1993 edition.

Alaska Outdoors (asked to be deleted)
All About Beer (no longer using humor)
American Retailer
Arete Magazine
Isaac Asimov's Science Fiction Magazine
Baja Times
Believers (asked to be deleted)
Cavalier (out of business)
Chicago Reader (asked to be deleted)
Clubhouse (doesn't use freelancers)
Cosmopolitan (overstocked)
Creating Excellence (out of business)
Current Comedy (cannot be reached)
Forest City Review (cannot

be reached)
Golf Illustrated (publication sold)
Group Magazine
Hippocrates (asked to be deleted)
Humor Magazine (cannot be reached)
Hustler (overstocked)
Living Among Nature Daringly
The Mayberry Gazette (cannot be reached)
Mother Earth News
National Lampoon (overstocked)
New York Habitat (not currently using cartoons)
North Myrtle Beach Times
Parents of Teenagers Magazine (out of business)

Picture Perfect Magazine
Pig Iron
The Player-America's Gaming Guide
Prime Time Sports & Fitness
Read Me (cannot be reached)
Rolling Stone (staff only)
Ruralite (overstocked)
Sagebrush Journal/Carolina Veterans News (out of business)
The Single Parent (asked to be deleted)
Ski Magazine
Solutions for Better Health
Thoughts for All Seasons (out of business)
The Wisconsin Restauranteur
Women Wise (cannot be reached)

Syndicates

"I THINK IT ONLY FAIR TO WARN YOU THAT I DESPISE CAT STRIPS."

George Bush and Gary Larson have a lot in common.

When Bush says something, it's printed in thousands of newspapers. And when Larson draws something, it's printed in *kabillions* of newspapers.

Bush, of course, has the power of the Presidency, but Larson has an even stronger syndicate behind him.

Indeed, newspaper syndicates have the power to turn drawn cartoon characters into full-fledged symbols of popular culture. Once the characters have penetrated every major and minor newspaper in the industrialized world, they're then plastered on a plethora of ephemera—from lunch boxes to pillow cases, note pads to calendars (have you seen the new *Cathy* condoms?).

The merchandising objectives of syndicates do anything but dissuade aspiring cartoonists from creating strips and panels, their heads spinning with dreams of becoming the next Jim Davis or Charles Schultz. In seeking the dream, grocery store clerks, housewives and auto mechanics concoct strips in the off-hours, which are then submitted to the top ten syndicates for the thumb up or thumb down. The latter being the more common outcome, "don't quit the day job" should be the credo tattooed into the aspiring syndicate's drawing hand.

To be sure, you stand a better chance of being struck by lightning twice than of becoming syndicated. Of course this doesn't mean you should not pursue syndication, but you are best advised to understand the harsh realities of this business. Sheer numbers are your worse enemy. Hundreds, make that *thousands* of cartoonists, humor writers and humorous illustrators would *love* to do a single cartoon or column a day and get paid enough to choke an S&L. And even if the majority of those people can't draw or write themselves out of a paper bag, a healthy number of them *can*.

Now add to the equation the fact that only one out of every 1,500 or more submissions becomes syndicated, and you see how dismal the odds really are. Once the feature is taken into syndication, industry insiders say the feature has a maximum of three months in which it must take hold or it will die. Yes, syndication is quite the ruthless business.

Syndicated humor writing

For the writer hoping to make his mark in syndication, he may first want to make his mark as a newspaper staffer. With rare exceptions, syndicates tend to distribute regular humor columns written by established writers. There are, of course, exceptions to the rule, but for the most part it is the staffed writer who first makes a name for himself with his localized humor column and then attracts the attention of one of the big syndicates. His column may then become broadened for a national audience and taken into syndication.

While most syndicates are interested in syndicating regular, ongoing written features and columns, some of the smaller syndicates have an occasional need for short features, articles and other humorous writing (sometimes called "special" features). If you're interested in doing special feature work, it would be best to inquire about a specific syndicate's freelance writing needs with a cover letter, resume, client list and writing sample before submitting your article/feature outline. Once you are apprised of the syndicate's expectations, you can better tailor your outline to its needs.

Many syndicates also distribute highly specialized columns written on particular topics or areas of interest. For example, you can find syndicated columns about everything from bass fishing to antique collecting. And while many of these columns are written in a more serious, dry tone, this doesn't mean that you couldn't write such columns from a more humorous perspective. In fact, doing so would probably be enthusiastically *encouraged* by the syndicates, and in turn by newspaper editors and readers.

Syndicated editorial cartoons

When it comes to editorial and political cartoons, it is extremely rare for a syndicate to distribute the work of an editorial cartoonist who is not already staffed by a daily newspaper. Since cartoonists have somewhat deserved reputations for conveniently missing deadlines, the syndicates prefer to distribute the graphic commentary of cartoonists who essentially work under the thumb of an editor. The syndicate may then distribute three, four, five or even six of their editorial cartoons per week to subscribing newspapers/publications.

However, syndicates have been known to help place young, talented editorial cartoonists at newspapers. The newspaper then has its own editorial cartoonist who is staffed in a structured working environment, and the syndicate can feel comfortable about distributing his work.

To give the syndicates a solid look at your editorial cartoons, let them see 10-12 examples to mull over. The subject matter of the cartoons should be of a national or international nature, but toss in two or three examples which tackle strictly local issues. A cartoon on a regional, state or local concern will demonstrate your ability to handle more parochial matters. Naturally, you'll also want to enclose a cover letter and resume which outlines your schooling as well as journalistic and print experience.

The problem these days with syndicated editorial cartoons is that too many editorial cartoonists are syndicated. This situation first arose in the late 1970s and has yet to subside. With a plethora of editorial cartoonists competing for placement in the same newspapers and small slivers of the pie are cut up and doled out. Only a handful of editorial cartoonists can boast 80 or more client newspapers, and the rest can perhaps claim a mere handful of subscribing newspapers. This means that the latter editorial cartoonists cannot rely on syndication royalties as their chief form of income; rather, these monies are viewed as supplemental.

Syndicated comic strips

I've never met a cartoonist who didn't have a desire (either blatant or secret) to draw a comic strip. Although desire alone doesn't create comic strips, it's a good place to start.

Therefore, after you've created the next "Shoe," "Fox Trot" or "Herman," you'll need to submit it to the syndicates to find out if it sinks, swims or perhaps treads water. Generally speaking, most syndicates like to see at least 14 daily examples of your proposed strip, but some cartoonists feel that sending three weeks worth of work (or 21 examples) will give the syndicate a better, more representative view of the strip. When initially submitting your daily strip, don't worry about drawing up a special "Sunday Funny" color version of your strip. As a rule of thumb, the only time you should concern yourself with showing a Sunday strip is when what you propose is *exclusively* for the Sunday comics page.

You also don't want to make the mistake of sending only pencilled, yet uncompleted, copies of your strip for syndicate consideration. Print reproduction is of paramount importance in the distribution process and the syndicates will want to see your inked work in finished form to determine how well it will reduce and appear in newsprint. However, this is not to say that you can't submit roughed-up drawings in *conjunction* with copies of your finished strips just to show the syndicate where you plan to go with the strip idea.

It's also important to understand that a syndicate is looking for quality comic strips—*not* necessarily quality *presentations* of those comic strips. Therefore, you're best advised to avoid loading your presentation with glitz (color cover, glorified outline of your strip and biographical info on each regular character, pictures of you at the drawing board, etc.), and merely stuff your envelope with incredibly funny examples of your comic strip.

While it would be wonderful if the syndicate Powers-That-Be had the time (or interest) to read paragraph after paragraph of undoubtedly fascinating insights into the likes, dislikes and favorite snack foods of your lead characters, they simply can't. If you understand that the syndicates must cull from *hundreds* of comic strip submissions each week, you'll realize how pressed for time they really are. What they really care about is *funny*. How *funny* are your strips? How well are the strips *drawn*? How well are they *written*? Would editors drop "The Far Side" and run your strip instead?

This is not to say that you shouldn't give the syndicates some smattering of info on yourself. You'll want to include a brief cover letter telling the syndicate a little more about your background, a *short* blip about the storyline of the strip and, of course, a large SASE if you expect to have the material returned. You also have no reason to submit your strip to only one syndicate at a time. Simultaneous submissions to 10, 15 or even 20 syndicates at a time is a standard, accepted practice.

Prepare yourself for rejection. If you receive enough impersonal rejection slips to wallpaper a small bathroom, you'll have a lot in common with established cartoonists who have also received their fair share of downed thumbs. In fact it's very common for a number of syndicates to turn down strips that have been picked up by a rival syndicate and then gone on to be hugely successful. You also should not expect any sort of feedback (other than the rejection slip) from an uninterested syndicate. Again, because of the tremendous amount of material the syndicates must filter, it simply isn't possible for them to write back explaining what aspects of your strip they like, and what aspects they don't.

However, if a syndicate *does* like what they see, they may respond with a short, typewritten note. Surely, the personalized note should be taken as encouraging, but that's about it. The note merely means that compared to all the garbage the syndicate has to look at, the quality of your work is good. But remember, it takes just as many *personal* rejection slips as impersonal rejection slips to cover any wall.

How syndication works

Syndication is a very simple concept. Syndicates essentially buy regular features (strips, columns, panels, etc.) on a contractual basis and then offer those features to newspapers. If a newspaper wants to "pick up" the feature and publish it on a territorially exclusive basis, it will do so. The rate that the newspaper pays for the feature is primarily determined by its circulation. A newspaper with a 543,000 home circulation will pay more for the right to carry the feature than a newspaper with a 54,300 home circulation.

Ideally, the syndicate salespeople who shop the features around have one objective in mind: to get your feature into as many newspapers as possible. A top strip with mass appeal could be in 2,000 papers internationally, a 3-time-a-week humor column might be in 600 newspapers in North America alone. In the end, the syndicate and the creator of the syndicated feature split the profits made from the distribution of the feature, and the creator's share of this money can be well into six figures. Add advances and royalties for the licensing of the feature, and accrued revenues can quite literally go into the millions.

But as one can imagine, syndicates are extremely picky when it comes to signing on new properties. Although a syndicate may be queried with over 5,000 new comic strip ideas a year, it may only elect to syndicate two or three. And with the present recession, syndicates are more cautious then ever when committing to new features.

Yet when syndicates do elect to pick up new features, they tend to offer contracts that lean too heavily in their favor, especially when cartoonists are not established. For example, a syndicate may pick up your comic strip, but in doing so require that you sign a binding ten-year contract, essentially transferring the strip's copyright to the syndicate. These contracts can also prevent the cartoonist from going to a competing syndicate for as long as ten years. Such contracts can enable the syndicate to "own" the creator as well as the feature.

Like all contracts, syndicate contracts are negotiable, and the more established you are, the more leverage you have to negotiate. There are also attorneys and agents who specialize in negotiating intellectual property contracts, and I would seriously advise *anyone* presented with a syndication contract to have it studied by a qualified attorney or an agent with a strong background in law. Of course this will cost you money, but you shouldn't be penny wise and pound foolish when a syndicate is seriously interested in picking up your work.

So as you sit at the word processor or drawing board, try to resist the urge to second guess the syndicates. It is absolutely pointless to attempt to coldly calculate a comic strip or feature which will appeal to a syndicate (a strip on the "men's movement," a column written from a zany fetus' point-of-view?). By the time you recognize a "trend" or "fad," it is already rotting on the vine and is about to take a chair next to the Pet Rock.

Be yourself. Write and draw about what interests *you* — then see what happens. Channel your energy into creating a *better* comic strip or feature — not into the calculation of characters which you think will make a syndicate snicker. After all, the best, most long-lasting syndicated features are the ones not based on mutable trends, short-lived fads or gimmicky story lines. If you make yourself laugh, I guarantee there's someone else out there to laugh along with you. And if you can find a syndicate to join in the laughter, you've got the inside track.

*THE AGENCY, P.O. Box 139, Kings Park NY 11754. (516)544-0703. Estab. 1985. Syndicates 20 comic strips/panels ("Zen Again," "Garden Tips"); 8 editorial cartoons ("Wilson's World," "Cook's View"); 12 written columns ("The Natural World," "Cook's Books," "Music Review"); 10 illustrated columns ("Gardening," "Video Review," "Consumer's Review.") Considers comic strips, editorial cartoons, humorous illustration, columns/articles and columns (features) on all subjects for syndication in newspapers and magazines. Reports back in 4-6 weeks. Will only return submissions if accompanied by SASE. Payment varies. Rights purchased vary.
Comic Strip/Panels: Buys a variable number of new comic strips or panels/year. "We are open to all ideas." Comic strip artists work between 6-52 weeks in advance. Submit 6-18 cartoons for proposed strip or panel to Joel Cook, Editor. "It takes us a great deal of time and expense to shop around a new strip or panel (6 months on average); sometimes we ask for the creator to send us a one time payment for our time ($500-1,000)."
Editorial Cartoons: For first contact send cover letter and cartoons to Joel Cook, Editor. Uses freelance writers for fiction, fillers, jokes/one liners, magazine columns, newspaper columns, newspaper features, news items, promotion and one-shot humorous material. For first contact submit query with clips or tearsheets of published work "whatever contributor has available (a sample of your work is useful)" to Joel Cook, Editor.
Clip Art: Needs natural history, video, music, gardening, consumer products. For first contact send cover letter and copies.

 The asterisk before a listing indicates that the listing is new in this edition. New markets are often more receptive to freelance submissions.

*ARGONAUT ENTERTAINMENT, INC., 455 Delta Ave. #204, Cincinnati OH 45226 (513)871-2746. FAX: (513)871-0793. Estab. 1989. Publishes comic strips/panels and editorial cartoons. Considers comic strips, editorial cartoons, gag cartoons, humorous columns/articles, games and puzzles. "Distributed to high volume, targeted audiences." Reports back within 1 month. Will return submissions if requested and accompanied by SASE. Looking for comic strip/panel that is truly unique in the marketplace; has merchandising/marketing potential; is very well drawn and written. Comic strip artists work between 1-2 months in advance. Submit 15-30 cartoons for proposed strip or panel to Lenny Dave, Creative Director.

CARTOON COLLEGE, Box 3008, Carlsbad CA 92009. (619)942-7487. FAX: (619)942-8575. Estab. 1990. Purchases one gag cartoon/week for syndication as a Sunday comic feature. Will only return submissions if accompanied by SASE. Payment is $25 for cartoon. "Cartoon College" is syndicated by United Features Syndicate. "Cartoon College reaches millions of households every week in USA and Canada."
Comic Strips/Panels: Buys 52 new panels/year. Editors and readers want strips/panels about general interest appropriate for Sunday newspaper/family readership.

CHRONICLE FEATURES, Suite 1011, 870 Market St., San Francisco CA 94102. (415)777-7212. Estab. 1960. Syndicates 4 comic strips/panels ("Bizarro," "Quality Time"); 16 written columns ("no humor-only columns"). Considers comic strips and editorial and gag cartoons, as well as columns. "We don't syndicate one-shots of anything, only ongoing features," in newspapers primarily, some magazines. Reports back in 5-6 weeks. "Prefers to receive all inquiries—submissions and questions regarding previously sent submissions—by mail, not by telephone." Will only return submissions if accompanied by SASE. Payment is 50% of the gross sales. Buys all rights.
Comic Strips/Panels: Buys 1-2 new comic strips or panels/year. "All we want is great material; we don't care about the logistics as long as newspapers can accommodate the format." Looking for comic strip/panel that "has spark." Comic strip artists work between 4-6 weeks in advance. Submit 24-35 cartoons for proposed strip or panel to Jean B. Arnold. *Inside Tips:* "It is an incredibly competitive market. Only the stellar survive. We would like to see more submissions from the underrepresented portions of the population."
Humor Writing/Columns: Uses freelance writers for newspaper features (600-750 words) "that are fresh to us (not previously seen in print). We would be willing to syndicate writers who aren't currently affiliated with a publication, but only if they are willing to produce weekly columns over an indefinite period. We don't use one-shots, fillers, puzzles, games, jokes, news items, gag writers or promotional material." For first contact send complete manuscript to Jean B. Arnold. *Inside Tips:* The humor writer should be aware that it's extremely competitive "due to all the free material (general interest and humor) available over the wire services. Even so, we would like to hear from contributors with unusual backgrounds and viewpoints."

CONTINENTAL FEATURES/CONTINENTAL NEWS SERVICE, Suite 265, 341 W. Broadway, San Diego CA 92101. (619)492-8696. Estab. 1981. Syndicates 1 comic strip/panel ("Portfolio," by William F. Pike); 9 written columns ("Travelers Checks √√√" and "Freedom Watch.") Considers comic strips for syndication in newspapers and magazines. Reports back in 1 month. Will only return submissions if accompanied by SASE. Payment is 70% of gross sales. Contributor retains rights; "we publicize, promote and distribute."
Comic Strips/Panels: Buys a variable number of new comic strips or panels/year. Prefers syndicating strips in which regular characters appear and which do not have continuing storylines. Editors and readers want strips/panels about "contemporary life prob-

lems and situations." Submit 10-15 cartoons for proposed strip or panel to Gary P. Salamone, Director.

COPLEY NEWS SERVICE, Box 190, San Diego CA 92112. (619)293-1818. Weekly panel comics and graphics accepted. Send 10 photocopied samples, resume, query and SASE to Nanette Wiser, Editorial Director. Allow six weeks for response. "No phone calls please."

COWLES SYNDICATE, (see King Features Syndicate Inc.)

"...and that concludes 'Luigi's Kitchen'. Stay tuned for 'Rescue 911'. Tonight: a studio crew is poisoned by a TV cook."

© Richard Orlin

Cooking Up Death*: Gaithersburg, Maryland-based gag cartoonist Richard Orlin regularly lampoons the television industry with his weekly "TV Toons" panel. Syndicated by Copley News Service since 1989, Orlin's deadline is five weeks.*

CREATORS SYNDICATE, Suite 700, 5777 W. Century Blvd., Los Angeles CA 90045. (310)337-7003. Estab. 1987. Syndicates: 3 comic strips/panels ("B.C.," "Baby Blues" and "Kudzu.") Considers comic strips and panel, editorial and gag cartoons, humorous illustration, caricatures and humorous columns. For contributor's guidelines send SASE.

Comic Strips/Panels: Buys 4-5 new comic strips or panels/year, "and growing fast." Submit cartoons for proposed strip or panel to Editorial Review Board; "specify cartoon or column."

Editorial Cartoons: Political point of view does not matter. Send editorial cartoons to Editorial Review Board.

Humor Writing/Columns: Considers humorous columns for syndication. Send humorous material to Editorial Review Board.

*DISTRIBUTORS SYNDICATE, 5141 Arbor Glen Circle, Lake Worth FL 33463. Estab. 1990. Considers gag cartoons and single panel cartoons for syndication in magazines. "Company is half syndicate, half magazine. We publish a directory of single panel cartoons from various cartoonists and distribute to approximately 100 magazines." Will only return submissions if accompanied by a SASE. Contributor receives 100%. Editors and readers want strips/panels about all subjects. Submit strip/panels to Panel Editor.

EXTRA NEWSPAPER FEATURES, 18 First Ave. SE, Rochester MN 55903-6118. (507)285-7671. FAX: (507)285-7666. Estab. 1985. Syndicates: 3 comic strips/panels ("Country Things" and "Memories of a Former Kid," by B. Artley and "Stampede," by J. Palen); 3 editorial cartoons (Fischer, Plante, Jorgensen); 3 written columns ("Career Strategies," by Dr. Reed Belt, "This & That," by B. Hall and "Commentary," by L. Soth.) Considers editorial cartoons, caricatures and humorous columns/articles for syndication in newspapers and magazines. Reports back in 3-4 months. Will only return submissions if accompanied by a SASE. Payment and purchase of rights are negotiated.
Comic Strips/Panels: Prefers single panels in which regular characters appear, which do not have continuing storylines. Panel artists work between 2-3 weeks in advance. Submit 12-36 panels to Kelly Boldon, Director.
Editorial Cartoons: Editorial cartoonist's political viewpoint does not matter. When hiring an editorial cartoonist these abilities are considered: a unique drawing style and good use of dialogue. For first contact send cover letter, resume and 12 cartoons to Kelly Boldon, Director.
Humor Writing/Columns: Uses freelance writers for fillers—500-750 words per column, 1 per week. For first contact send query with clips or tearsheets of published work to Kelly Boldon, Director.

HARRIS AND ASSOCIATES, 12084 Caminito Campana, San Diego CA 92128. (619)487-1789. Estab. 1970. Syndicated features: "How to Take the Fun Out of Golf," "How to Take the Fun Out of Tennis," "How to Take the Fun Out of Jogging" and "How to Take the Fun Out of Skiing." Considers editorial and gag cartoons, humorous illustrations and caricatures for syndication in newspapers and magazines. Reports back in 2 weeks. Will only return submissions if accompanied by a SASE. Pay is negotiated. Buys first North American serial rights.
Comic Strips/Panels: Buys 1 new comic strip or panel/year. Submit editorial cartoons to Dick Harris, Owner/Editor. *Inside Tips:* "Trends in editorial cartooning include more sports, fitness and health."

*JODI FILL FEATURE, 2888 Bluff St. Suite 143, Boulder CO 80301. Estab. 1986. Syndicates 2 comic strips/panels; 2 written columns; 5 puzzles. Considers comic strips, gag cartoons, humorous columns/articles, visuals or humorous puzzles for syndication in newspapers, magazines and publications. Reports back within 1 month. Will only return submissions if accompanied by SASE. Payment is 40% of net sales. "Must be worked out individually." Buys all rights.
Comic Strips/Panels: Buys 1-10 new comic strips or panels/year. Prefers syndicating strips/panels in which regular characters appear; which do not have continuing storylines. Editors and readers want strips/panels about people-puzzles-America. Looking for comic strip/panel that is truly unique in the marketplace and is controversial. Comic strip artists work between 4-6 weeks in advance. Submit 6-40 cartoons for proposed strip of panel to Carol Hands, Art Editor.
Writing/Columns: Uses freelance writers for fillers ("We always consider different kinds of fillers to 500 words"); Jokes/one liners, ("Especially agriculture/ranch/country living/'Western' funny-funny-funny"); Newspaper columns ("Will consider well written humor newspaper columns, 500-750 words"); News items ("We use these sometimes to 500 words"); One-shot humorous material ("must be agriculture, ranch country living/

Western-500 words"). For first contact submit complete ms to Jarmin Heckle, Editor. Tips: "People are coming home to read short funny, simplistic stories. Remember, if a person can't read it, it isn't funny."

Clip Art: Works with approximately 10 freelance illustrators/year. Needs all subjects with emphasis on happiness. Looking for humorous clip art that is cute, pleasing to the eye and non-offensive; is stylistic and unique to the market; has generic appeal and each illustration can be used for a number of applications. For first contact send cover letter and SASE to Carol Hands, Art Editor. *Inside Tips:* "You need to find a smile in every piece of work published or you won't find our name on it."

KING FEATURES SYNDICATE INC., 235 E. 45th St., New York NY 10017. (212)455-4000. "World's longest established syndicate, founded in 1915" ("Blondie," "Beetle Bailey," "Hagar the Horrible," "Family Circus," "Popeye," "Zippy the Pinhead," "Ernie" and "The New Breed"). Considers comic strips, cartoon panels, editorial cartoons and humorous text columns for syndication in newspapers, product licensing and broadcast media. Reports back in 6 weeks, "but only if the work is accompanied by SASE." Will not consider faxed submissions. "Write for guidelines on how to prepare a proper submission for full consideration."

Comic Strips/Panels: Buys 3 new features/year and hundreds of individual panels for "The New Breed" (see separate listing). "We have found that humorous strips with regular characters do best, but we're also very open-minded to innovative cartoon ideas that break standard preconceived notions of what cartoons should be." Comic strips and panels should be sent to Jay Kennedy, Comics Editor.

Editorial Cartoons: "The editorial cartoon market is tighter than ever. Nonetheless, we're interested in seeing insightful and incisive work. Compellingly strong work may lead to syndication or spur other opportunities." Editorial cartoons should be sent to Jay Kennedy, Comics Editor.

Humor Writing/Columns: Would like to see clips of published humor columns and/or review ideas for new humor columns. Send 6 samples with SASE. Column ideas should be sent to Tom Pritchard, Executive Director. *Inside Tips:* "Be funny, contemporary, write well and all in 650 words or less!"

LEOLEEN-DURCK CREATIONS—LEONARD BRUCE DESIGNS, Box 2767 #226, Jackson TN 38302. (901)668-1205. Estab. 1981. Syndicates 4 comic strips/panels ("The McNabs"). Considers comic strips, editorial and gag cartoons for syndication. Reports back in 3 weeks. Will only return submissions if accompanied by SASE. Payment is 30% of net sales. Buys all rights.

Comic Strips/Panels: Buys 3 new comic strips or panels/year. Editors and readers want strips/panels about "family and today's ideas." Comic strip artists work between 8-12 weeks in advance. Submit 15-21 cartoons for proposed strip or panel to Leonard Bruce, Cartoonist/Syndicator. *Inside Tips:* "Tough competition. Trend is toward using well-known established cartoonists, so your comic strip must be almost perfect to break in."

Editorial Cartoons: Political point of view does not matter. Looking for editorial cartoonist with a unique drawing style, humorous comment on the news of the day and little use of dialogue. For first contact send cover letter, resume, tearsheets and a number of cartoons to Leonard Bruce, Cartoonist/Syndicator. *Inside Tips:* "Trends are on topics more than people."

Humor Writing/Columns: Uses gag writers for comic strips/panels and one-shot humorous material. Looking for "off-the-wall humor and humor with respect to the elderly and single parents." For first contact send query with clips or tearsheets of published work to Leonard Bruce, Cartoonist/Syndicator. *Inside Tips:* "Everyone should get the humor, not just a certain few."

Close-up

Glenn McCoy
Comic Strip Cartoonist

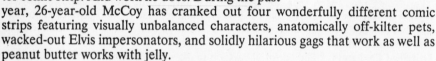

If you don't count the time in the morning when
he disrobes to take a shower, Glenn McCoy doesn't
do a regular strip.

From nine to five McCoy works as art director/
editorial cartoonist for the *Belleville* (IL) *News-
Democrat*, but in the evenings works to build a better comic strip. And work he does. During the past
year, 26-year-old McCoy has cranked out four wonderfully different comic
strips featuring visually unbalanced characters, anatomically off-kilter pets,
wacked-out Elvis impersonators, and solidly hilarious gags that work as well as
peanut butter works with jelly.

First there was McCoy's strip about the backstage bustle of a TV news show
called "The Nupe Network," then came "Percy," a strip about a single guy in
his mid-20s who could best be described as an under-achieving geek. The third
strip remained untitled, but was a family strip with a mom, dad, and the unusual
twist of two teenage sons and zero pets. Finally, McCoy's strip about two cheesy
late–20ish guys who live next door to two hip 20ish women was called, appropri-
ately enough, "The Duplex."

Only one problem: None of the McCoy's strips has been picked up for syndication (yet), and the fact illustrates just how difficult it is for a cartoonist to get
a strip off the ground. McCoy may be enormously talented, but that and a
quarter will get him a cup of coffee in the syndicate lounge.

To be sure, McCoy's strip presentations were able to engender interest at
the syndicates in part because they were so *good*, and because McCoy received
first place honors in a contest sponsored by King Features called "Create the
Comics of the 90s." "You had to enter a week's worth of strips," says McCoy,
"and the winner won a trip to New York. After I won the contest, I had to
contend with all these syndicates taking an interest in me."

With "Percy," four syndicates showed interest, but none were "overly enthu-
siastic," according to McCoy. When this strip died, McCoy submitted the family
strip and things looked quite promising. "With that strip," he says, "I had
three syndicates that were very interested, with two saying they were possibly
considering offering me a contract." King Features did, in fact, offer McCoy a
contract on this strip.

"The offer from King," says McCoy, "wasn't really made with a specific strip
in mind. At that point, King had realized that I had some writing and drawing
ability that they could capitalize on. They just wanted to sign me with a nine-
month developmental period attached to the initial term, which would give me

time to develop a strip. After the nine months, I would hopefully have a strip for them to launch, and the terms of the actual contract would then take effect. They offered an initial sum of a few thousand dollars. I would then receive 50 percent of whatever the strip took in, in addition to a monetary basement figure."

Tempting as the contract may have been, McCoy wisely passed on it because it would have essentially locked him into King for 10 years. At this writing, however, King says it will again offer McCoy a contract—this time for "The Duplex."

Because a number of syndicates showed active interest in McCoy, he felt pressured to come up with new strip ideas. Was he rushing a parade of strips before the eyes of the syndicate Powers-That-Be? "Sure," he admits. "I was trying to hold the interest of the syndicates and I thought that unless I bombarded them with material, I could easily be forgotten. But I'm sure I was seen as a cartoonist who was totally all over the board by sending a strip each week. That could have worked against me."

But McCoy understands that he shouldn't be catering to a syndicate's vision of what a comic strip should be. "When the syndicates showed interest in one of my strips during the development," says McCoy, "one syndicate would want one thing and another would want something else. The first strip I worked on came to an impasse when I realized I couldn't please everyone and had to find a way to back out because I wasn't pleased with the strip. Essentially, I felt as if the strip was being taken away from me. I couldn't keep working that way, so I gradually backed out of the strip and said I'd send them something else in a couple of weeks. Now I write for myself, and if the syndicate appreciates that, then I know that's the syndicate I want to be working with.

"I've realized," says McCoy confidently, "that to launch a successful comic strip, I have to please myself instead of eight different people with eight different points of view, even though that might narrow the field as far as how many syndicates will be interested in my work. I know my sense of humor is akin to other people's and that's who I'm writing for."

—Bob Staake

The Duplex by Glenn McCoy

Scenario at the Beach: Glenn McCoy captures a battle of the sexes in "The Duplex."

LEW LITTLE ENTERPRISES, INC., Box 850, Borrego Springs CA 92004. (619)767-3148. Estab. 1986. Syndicates 5 comic strips ("The Fusco Brothers," "Sibling Revelry," "The Free Wheelers," "Hasty Pudding" and "Brainstormers"). Considers comic strips, editorial and gag cartoons and humorous columns/articles for syndication in newspapers. "We also develop and broker comics to the major syndicates." Reports back in 6 weeks. Will only return submissions if accompanied by SASE. Payment is negotiable. Buys all rights. For contributor guidelines send SASE and two first-class stamps.
Comic Strips/Panels: Buys 1-2 new comic strips or panels/year. Prefers syndicating strips/panels in which regular characters appear. Comic strip artists work between 6-12 weeks in advance. Submit 12 cartoons for proposed strip or panel to Lewis A. Little, Editor. *Inside Tips:* "New children's comics are needed, but they must appeal to adults as well as children like 'Calvin & Hobbes' and 'Sibling Revelry.' "
Editorial Cartoons: Political point of view does not matter. For first contact send cover letter, resume, 12 cartoons and a brief description of feature proposed to Lewis A. Little, Editor.
Humor Writing/Columns: Uses freelance writers for newspaper features; gag writers for comic strips/panels. "We buy gags for some well-known syndicated cartoonists. We occasionally add new writers to a small group of regular contributors." For first contact send query with clips or tearsheets of published work to Mary Ellen Corbett, Managing Editor. *Inside Tips:* "The market is very hard to crack; editors are looking for a truly fresh approach."

LOS ANGELES TIMES SYNDICATE, Times Mirror Square, Los Angeles CA 90053. (213)237-3213. Considers comic strips, editorial and gag cartoons, humorous illustration, caricatures, spot drawings, humorous and politics columns/articles. For contributor's guidelines send SASE.
Comic Strips/Panels: Buys 3-4 new comic strips or panels/year. Strips/panels should be submitted to Steven Christensen, Executive Editor.
Editorial Cartoons: It is essential that an editorial cartoonist be on staff at a daily newspaper. "We prefer that an editorial cartoonist have 'like-minded politics.' " Editorial cartoons should be sent to Steven Christensen, Executive Editor.
Humor Writing/Columns: Uses freelance writers for newspaper columns and one-shot humorous material. Humor writing should be submitted to Don Michel, Vice President/ Editor.

MINORITY FEATURES SYNDICATE, Box 421, Farrell PA 16121. (412)342-5300. Estab. 1980. Syndicates 20 comic strips/panels, 25 editorial cartoons, 20 written columns. Considers comic strips, editorial and gag cartoons and humorous columns/articles for syndication in newspapers, magazines and newsletters. Reports back in 1 month. Will return submissions if requested and accompanied by a SASE. Payment is 20% of the gross sales or by contract. Buys all rights. For contributor guidelines send $2 and a SASE.
Comic Strips/Panels: Buys 100 new comic strips or panels/year. Prefers syndicating panels in which regular characters appear and which have continuing storylines or are serials. "Editors and readers want strips/panels about family-oriented material." When buying a comic strip/panel, considers if it is truly unique in the marketplace, has merchandising/marketing potential, is consistently funny or clever, is nonoffensive, harmless and noncontroversial. Comic strip artists work between 2 and 6 weeks in advance. Submit 2-10 cartoons for proposed strip or panel to Merry Frable, Editor.

Always include a self-addressed stamped envelope (SASE) or International Reply Coupon (IRC) with submissions.

Editorial Cartoons: "We prefer that an editorial cartoonist have a conservative point of view." When hiring an editorial cartoonist these abilities are considered: a unique drawing style, humorous comment on the news of the day, little use of dialogue and ability to draw more on national rather than international politics/events. For first contact send cover letter, resume, tearsheets and 2-10 cartoons to Merry L. Frable.

Humor Writing/Columns: Uses freelance writers for short stories—500 words or less; fillers—50 words, general interest; jokes/one-liners—clean, 10 minimum; magazine columns—200 words, general interest; newspaper columns/features—150 words, general interest pertaining to today's news; news items—200 words general interest nationally, pertaining to today's news; promotion general interest; one-shot humorous material—clean, 100 words, general interest. For first contact send query with clips or tearsheets of published work to Merry L. Frable.

Clip Art: Works with approximately 50 freelance illustrators/year. Needs general interest. Considers work that is bold, graphic and dynamic; stylistic and unique to the market; reflecting a broad style capable of effectively rendering a variety of subject matter; with generic appeal/versatility. For first contact send cover letter, 5 copies, b&w work only, and resume to Merry L. Frable.

THE NEW BREED, King Features Syndicate, 235 E. 45th St., New York NY 10017. Estab. 1915. Considers single panel cartoons for syndication in newspapers. Reports back in 3-5 weeks. Will only return submissions if accompanied by SASE. Payment is $50 flat fee. Buys first world-wide serial rights. For contributor's guidelines send SASE.

Comic Strips/Panels: Buys 468 single panel cartoons (no strips)/year. "As the title implies, the New Breed editors are looking for cartoons from cartoonists who are working on the cutting edge—wacky, innovative, and clever contemporary cartoons. When buying a panel, editors also consider whether the cartoonist's overall body of work demonstrates consistent humor and talent. The feature is intended as a means for King Features to encourage and stay in touch with cartoonists who show potential for one day developing their own successful syndicate comic feature." Submit 10-20 cartoons at a time to the New Breed editors.

NORTH AMERICA SYNDICATE, (see King Features Syndicate Inc.)

*OCEANIC PRESS, 1030 Calle Cordillera, Suite 105, San Clemente CA 92672. (714)498-7227. FAX: (714)498-2162. Syndicates comic strips/panels, ("Howie, Li'll Ones"); written columns ("Dr. P. Carbone's Medical") and ("Sheila Cluff-Fitness.") Considers comic strips, gag cartoons, caricatures and humor dealing with celebrities in newspaper, magazines, book publishers, greeting cards, video, world wide. Reports back in 3 weeks. Will only return submissions if accompanied by a SASE. Payment 50% of gross sales. Distributes all rights and foreign rights. For contributor guidelines send $2 and #10 SASE.

Comic Strips/Panels: Distributes new comic strips or panels. Prefers syndicating single panels. Prefers syndicating strips in which regular characters appear, "well drawn, not just 2 characters talking. Prefer background drawings as well." Editors and readers want strips/panels about business management, golf, credit cards, fax, ecology, seasonal and travel. Looking for comic strip/panel that is truly unique in the marketplace, has merchandising/marketing potential, is very well drawn, is timeless, with specialized mass market target. Submit 6-12 cartoons for proposed strip or panel to Scott Thompson, Associate Editor. "Comic strips must be of worldwide interest and not only for U.S. distribution."

MARGULIES
©1992 NORTH AMERICA
SYNDICATE

MIKE TYSON

I'd Know That Face Anywhere. It's 553982861!: But before he had his name changed to a prison number, you knew him as Mike Tyson. Here he's caricatured rather well by Hackensack, New Jersey-based Jimmy Margulies, whose newsmaker caricatures are syndicated by North American Syndicate. In creating this caricature, Margulies wanted to "make Tyson look like a slightly sub-human creature, with a small, almost pinhead forehead, a dopey grin, and tree-trunk neck." Hey, Jimmy—lucky for you this guy's locked up!

Editorial Cartoons: For first contact send cover letter, tearsheets and 10 cartoons.
Writing/Columns: Uses freelance writers for magazine columns dealing with celebrities, newspaper columns, newspaper features, one-shot humorous material interviews with celebrities, "interested in cartoon books on special subjects." For first contact send complete ms and query with clips to Peter Carbone, Editor.

ROTHCO CARTOONS, 1463 44th St., Brooklyn NY 11219. (718)853-5435. Considers editorial cartoons and single panel general cartoons in newspapers, magazines. Reports back in 6 weeks. Will only return if accompanied by a SASE. Payment varies. Buys all rights or first North American serial rights. Interested in single panel cartoons only. Submit 2-10 cartoons to Editorial Dept.
Editorial Cartoons: For first contact send cover letter, resume and tearsheets to Editorial Dept. For first contact send query with clips or tearsheets of published work to Editorial Dept.

Parenting the Fascist Way: Creating drawings that have "a humorous side and a point," Merrick, New York-based editorial cartoonist Al Liederman's work is distributed by Rothco Syndicate. "I use a simple drawing style," says Liederman, "and work more on getting the idea across than the style."

SINGER MEDIA CORP., Seaview Business Park, 1030 Calle Cordillera, Unit #106, San Clemente CA 92672. (714)498-7227. FAX: (714)498-2162. Estab. 1940. Syndicates comic strips/panels, cartoons and written columns. Considers comic strips for newspapers, magazines, book publishers, ad agencies and greeting cards. Reports back in 3 weeks. Will only return submissions if accompanied by SASE. Payment is 50% for worldwide syndication. *Inside Tips:* "We see a need for the following cartoon material in the 1990s: computers, medicine, fax, credit cards, senior management, corporate takeovers, Japanese investment, golf and baseball."

TRIBUNE MEDIA SERVICES, INC., 64 E. Concord St., Orlando FL 32801. (407)839-5600. FAX: (407)839-5794. Estab. 1933. Syndicates 28 comic strips/panels ("Shoe," "Mother Goose and Grimm"); 10 editorial cartoonists (MacNelly, Don Wright); 50+ columnists (Royko, Dave Barry, Andy Rooney, Bob Greene). Considers comic strips, editorial cartoons and columns for syndication in newspapers. Reports back within 6 weeks. Will return submissions if accompanied by SASE. Negotiated contract.

Comic Strips/Panels: Syndicates several new comic strips or panels/year. Looking for strips/panels that are truly unique in the marketplace, consistently funny or clever, timely and relevant. Comic strip artists work between 6-10 weeks in advance. Submit 18-30 cartoons for proposed strip or panel to Evelyn Smith, Managing Editor.

Editorial Cartoons: Editorial cartoonists seeking syndication should possess a unique drawing style; a proclivity for scathing, biting cartoons; humorous comment on the news of the day; moderate use of dialogue. For first contact send cover letter, resume, tear-sheets and 18 cartoons to Evelyn Smith, Managing Editor.

Humor Writing/Columns: Writers seeking syndication should have solid credentials, preferably with books, magazine articles or newspaper columns to writer's credit. For first contact send query with clips or tearsheets of published work to Evelyn Smith, Managing Editor.

UNITED FEATURE SYNDICATE, Newspaper Enterprise Association, 200 Park Ave., New York NY 10166. (212)692-3700. Syndicates comic strips/panels ("Peanuts," "Garfield," "Born Loser," "Frank & Ernest"); editorial cartoons (Mike Peters, Ed Stein); written columns (Jack Anderson, "Miss Manners"). Considers comic strips, editorial cartoons and humorous columns/articles for syndication in newspapers and reprint in magazines and books. Reports back in 10-12 weeks. Will only return submissions if accompanied by SASE. Payment is 50% of the net sales. Buys all rights.

Comic Strips/Panels: Buys 2-4 new comic strips or panels/year. Prefers syndicating cartoon strips/panels which do not have continuing storylines but likes to see anything. Comic strip artists work between 6-10 weeks in advance. Submit 18-40 cartoons for a proposed strip or panel to Sarah Gillespie, V.P. and Director of Comic Art. *Inside Tips:* "It's a tougher market than ever and rejection should not be taken as a sign that the work is particularly bad—we just can't use it."

Editorial Cartoons: It is essential that an editorial cartoonist be on staff at a daily newspaper. Political point of view does not matter. Looking for editorial cartoonist with a unique drawing style and humorous comment on the news of the day. For first contact send cover letter and 12 cartoons to Robert Levy, Managing Editor.

Humor Writing/Columns: Uses freelance writers for weekly newspaper columns and features. No one-shots. Send query with clips or tearsheets of published work and at least 6 samples to Robert Levy, Managing Editor. "The market for editorial cartoons is extremely tough; for humor columns it's even tougher. By all means send samples of your best work, but realize that we start maybe 1-2 cartoonists each year and have not launched a humor column in quite some time."

UNIVERSAL PRESS SYNDICATE, 4900 Main St., Kansas City MO 64112. (816)932-6600. Estab. 1970. Syndicates 15 comic strips/panels ("Calvin & Hobbes," "Doonesbury," "The Far Side"); 6 editorial cartoons (Oliphant, Auth); 50 written columns ("Dear Abby," Erma Bombeck). Considers comic strips, editorial and gag cartoons for syndication in newspapers. Reports back in 1 month. Will only return submissions if accompanied by SASE.

Comic Strip/Panels: Buys 2 new comic strips or panels/year. Looking for comic strip/panel that is truly unique in the marketplace, consistently funny or clever, controversial or groundbreaking. Comic strip artists work between 1-2 months in advance. Submit 24 cartoons for proposed strip or panel to Lee Salem, Editorial Director.

Editorial Cartoons: It is essential that an editorial cartoonist be on staff at a daily newspaper. Political point of view does not matter. Looking for editorial cartoonist with a unique drawing style and proclivity for scathing, biting cartoons. For first contact send cover letter and 24 cartoons to Lee Salem, Editorial Director.

WASHINGTON POST WRITERS GROUP, 1150 15th St. NW, Dept. HC, Washington DC 20071-9200. (202)334-6375. Estab. 1974. Syndicates comic strips ("Outland," "Pickles," "Safe Havens"); editorial cartoons (Dana Summers). Considers comic strips, editorial cartoons and humorous columns/articles for syndication in daily, Sunday and college newspapers throughout the United States, Canada and abroad. Reports back in 2 weeks. Will return all submissions. Payment is not disclosed until contract agreement is made. Buys all rights.

Comic Strips/Panels: Syndicates 1-2 new comic strips or panels/year. Comic strip artists work between 3-5 weeks in advance. Submit 10-25 cartoons for proposed strip or panel to Alan Shearer, General Manager/Editorial Director. *Inside Tips:* "It's a very competitive market!"

Editorial Cartoons: "A cartoonist's political viewpoint does not matter to us." Looking for editorial cartoonist with a unique drawing style and humorous comment on the news of the day. For first contact send cover letter, tearsheets and 10-20 cartoons to Alan Shearer, General Manager/Editorial Director.

Humor Writing/Columns: For first contact send query with clips or tearsheets of published work to Alan Shearer, General Manager/Editorial Director.

WHITEGATE FEATURES SYNDICATE, 71 Faunce Dr., Providence RI 02906. Estab. 1988. Syndicates comic strips/panels (Jane Adler; Dave Berg "Citizen Senior"; Malcom Hancock, "Malfunction Junction";); 15 written columns ("Indoor Gardening" by Jane Adler; Gloria Linterman's "Beauty, Health & Fashion"). Considers comic strips, editorial and gag cartoons, humorous illustration, spot drawings and humorous columns/articles for syndication in newspapers and magazines. "We like to keep material on file if we like it for future reviews (no promises). Plese send photostats we can keep. No returns. We will call you if we'd like to see more. Send SASE postcard if you'd like an answer." Payment is 50% of the net sales. Buys all rights.

Comic Strips/Panels: "We will be buying a number of new comic strips or panels this year. We're looking for the same quality as the bigger syndicates." Comic strip artists work between 4-8 weeks in advance. Submit 12 (minimum) cartoons for proposed strip or panel to Eve Green, Talent Manager.

Editorial Cartoons: It is essential that an editorial cartoonist be on staff at a daily newspaper. Political point of view does not matter. For first contact send cover letter, resume, tearsheets, a number of cartoons and "anything to tell us who you are and what you've done "to Eve Green, Talent Manager." Do not ask us if we'd like to see work unless you include a SASE."

Humor Writing/Columns: Uses freelance writers for fiction (sometimes); fillers (very little); jokes/one-liners; magazine and newspaper columns; newspaper features (sometimes); promotion (occasionally); gag writers for comic strip/panels ("to pair with cartoonists"); one-shot humorous material. For first contact send complete manuscript and query with clips or tearsheets of published work to Eve Green, Talent Manager. *Inside Tips:* "Trends lean toward lots of humor. We're actively looking for good material but try us before the big syndicates. We don't want the 'rejects'; we're looking for the new stars!"

THE WORDTREE, 10876 Bradshaw W117, Overland Park KS 66210-1148. (913)469-1010. Estab. 1984. Publishes columns serialized in technical periodicals. Sporadically publishes a linguistic newsletter, parts of which are reprinted by others as a column "New Times, New Verbs."

Illustration: Works with approximately 2 freelance humorous illustrators/year. Needs cartoons or caricature. Uses freelance humorous illustrators primarily for illustrating the part of the "New Times, New Verbs" column that is called "A Needed Verb." "Submit one nonreturnable specimen of each of two cartoons illustrating the far ranges of your ability, whether or not they have already been published." Buys all rights. For first contact send portfolio of two items to Dr. Henry G. Burger, Editor. Reports back only if interested. Returns materials if accompanied by SASE. Pays $15-100, b&w, inside illustration. *Inside Tips:* "We need ability to draw very precise lines in small space, to illustrate complex ideas."

Syndicates/Changes '91-'93

The following markets appeared in the last (1991) edition of *Humor and Cartoon Markets* but are absent from the 1993 edition. These companies failed to respond to our request for an update of their listing or for the reasons indicated in parentheses following the company name.

Artists and Writers Syndicate
   (doesn't use freelancers)
Cartoon-Caricature-Contor
College Press Service (being
   sold)

Television/Radio

Most people merely want to watch TV and listen to the radio, but then there are those people who want to work *in* TV and radio. The next question, of course, should be obvious: How the heck does one fit inside a Sony?

Fortunately, a person doesn't have to be the size of an electronic tube to get into TV or radio. All one needs is motivation, a little luck, and the inability to take "no" for an answer. And it's a *real* plus if you have talent.

Of course, everyone realizes that the television industry employs producers, directors, editors, sound engineers, lighting technicians, make-up artists, hair stylists and even animal trainers; but writers, animators and humorous illustrators also play significant roles in TV. Radio, however, is an entirely different situation. Writers are regularly hired, but Marconi never discovered a way to transmit humorous illustration and animation over radio waves.

Within this chapter, you'll find detailed listings of independent television producers, film/video production companies, and radio comedy services. If they have a common thread, it's that they need *funny people*: the kind of people who can produce hilarious doodles, laugh-inducing copy and zany comedy material.

Radio

One of the best ways for a comedy writer to get a taste for radio is to write for one of the many radio "comedy services." Most radio comedy services publish weekly, biweekly or monthly newsletters featuring jokes, topical one-liners, anecdotes and pithy patter. Some of these services feature fairly daring material that most FCC censors would nonetheless let slide, but there are also services that specialize in the cleanest, most innocent material this side of Fred Rogers.

Disc jockeys, entertainers, on-air personalities and even public speakers can cull and use this material when they subscribe to the comedy service (services that specialize in *topical* comedy material even fax their material to eager subscribers). When the subscriber recites the material in public, they come across as possessing lightning-fast improvisational talents sure to make Jay Leno worry about job security.

Still other radio comedy services produce full-scale auditory material that is distributed via audio cassette tape to subscribing radio stations. These radio services develop comedy scripts which are then performed and embellished with music, sound effects, impersonations and aural sound bites. They produce everything from song parodies to fake commercials, phone celebrity interviews to fictitious news reports—all which must begin with a funny, written concept.

Again, every radio comedy service has its own particular brand of comedy and likes to see writing that addresses its needs. Therefore, it's best to request a sample newsletter (provide a SASE) from a comedy service before submitting material. Of course, this benefits you greatly since you're then able to determine what material to submit and what material to sit on. For example, I know some radio comedy services that specialize in toastmaster "slams," while others seek one-liners on Washington politics.

After you have studied the sample newsletter, send samples of your written material for review and offer specific material for sale. Copy some representative samples of your writing, an example of a radio script if you have one, include a brief cover letter along with your resume/client list and ship with a SASE.

And while there are a handful of radio comedy services that pay good rates for scripts, most remit fees almost as funny as their jokes. One radio service may pay $25 for a joke, while the guy next door pays $10, and the guy next door to him could pay as little as $1 (it would cost *you* money to write for that guy).

It's also important to point out that many writers never think of tapping the radio market within their own city. Listen to the disc jockeys in your town. Pretty funny guys, huh? Well, they may write a lot of their material themselves (or better yet, they simply blurt it out), or they may be subscribers to a couple of the above mentioned radio comedy services, or they *could* be getting some of their material from freelance writers.

What could a freelance comedy writer give a disc jockey that he couldn't already get from one of the comedy services? It's simple. Material with *local* appeal. Why, here in St. Louis, our zealous, anti-pornography County Prosecutor was arrested for soliciting a prostitute. When this happened, I know a couple of local writers who supplied two top area disc jockeys with hilarious, marginally off-color material on the incident. They simply seized a terrific opportunity and wrote jokes on a topic that *none* of the national comedy services would even get wind of.

Approaching a disc jockey in your local area is a very easy thing to do. Simply put together the same sort of package you would assemble for a comedy radio service and ship it off to the disc jockey. You'll want to be sure to explain to the disc jockey that you wish to write locally-oriented material for his review. If you can include a few examples of local material along with your general comedy material, this would be ideal.

The problem with writing local, topical material and trying to place it is that you can only submit to one disc jockey at a time (pretty embarrassing if two *competing* disc jockeys rattled off your material within a few hours of one another). Therefore, if you're able to establish a relationship with a disc jockey, you want to make sure he understands the he must promptly accept or reject material so you have a chance to place it elsewhere. Tell him to buy the material before his *competition* does!

Television

Like advertising, television lures freelancers with promises of Porsches, Armani suits and Valentino sunglasses. And with the advent of cable, opportunities for independent television production companies have increased dramatically. Once only able to sell their properties to the big three commercial networks, producers now have greatly expanded options. Subsequently, increased opportunities trickle down to writers.

However, TV production companies produce far more corporate or industrial films than they do commercials or theatrical programming. Company XYZ may have to explain its new method for squeezing positive ions from palm fronds to a technologically naive public—consequently, a corporate film may be produced to explain the process in friendly, humorous or layman's terms.

Television production companies can also offer terrific opportunities for freelance writers, especially those who can adapt their writing style from project to project and make technical information more accessible.

To pique the interest of a TV production company, a writer should assemble a strong self-promotional kit and send it off to the appropriate contact (usually a producer). Include a couple of examples of your writing, particularly material that has obviously been written for a decision-making client (ad copy, advertising script, etc.). You'll also want to include a short but professional cover letter, client list, and resume that lists your professional writing experience.

However, theatrical programming (movies, sitcoms, etc.) is a considerably tougher nut to crack. Production companies involved in the creation of everything from game shows to sitcoms, variety shows to made-for-TV movies have their own specific agendas—therefore, it is difficult to generalize on this industry as a whole.

Nevertheless, most comedy writers who have a desire to write for a specific sitcom will simply locate the production company that produces the show and then provide them with samples of their work. Understand, however, that almost all production companies prefer that scripts, show ideas, etc. be submitted to them through the writer's agent (see *Guide to Literary Agents and Art/Photo Reps* (Writer's Digest Books).

If you send an unsolicited, bulging envelope to the producers of *The Golden Girls*, chances are very good that the envelope will be unceremoniously returned to you—unopened. The reason is quite simple: Producers just cannot expose themselves to potential legal conflicts arising from the material submitted to them by an outside writer. For example, you could submit a script on Bea Arthur's hip surgery just as *The Golden Girls* writing staff is booking Arthur's character for surgery. You tune into the show, see Arthur under anesthetic (and the knife), and immediately phone your lawyer screaming that the bastards (and bastardettes) at *The Golden Girls* stole your script. A producer *needs* this? It has therefore become standard practice for producers to avoid large, unsolicited manila envelopes as if they contained killer viruses (hey, now *there's* a *Golden Girls* script idea!).

But if you do have a wild hair and still wish to submit a script or treatment to a sitcom, it's best if you outline your desires in a simple letter to the producers. Tell them that you have this dynamite storyline and you'd like them to take a look at it. Explain to them that you're "between agents" now, so you'd like to submit the script *directly* to them. Depending on the producer, they'll probably respond in writing and inform you that before they even cast eyes on your script, they'll require you to sign and return their Disclosure Agreement.

These Disclosure Agreements usually do one thing: they protect the producer, not you. But if you're just starting out in this business, you'll probably want to sign the agreement and get on with the disclosure. As my attorney always tells me, "having your material in your own files does you no good. Sign their agreement and take a chance. If they screw it up, we'll sue 'em." My attorney. Very nasty guy.

Additionally, this chapter will also give more freelance opportunities for writers. When you read the *individual* listings, you'll be able to easily determine the individual needs of the various companies. One company may produce nothing but made-for-TV movies, the next may only concentrate on industrial/corporate films. By studying the listings, you'll be able to direct your material only to those companies that will be most receptive to it.

Funny pictures for TV

Television production companies have a need, though not a constant one, for humorous illustration and animation. Since you (nor they) never know when such services will be needed, it's best to send them material which they can keep in their resource files.

If you're an animator, you should send a demo tape (VHS is fine), a cover letter, resume, client list, perhaps a storyboard example and business card. A humorous illustrator should assemble a color self-promotional page, perhaps past character design or storyboard work, a cover letter, resume, client list and business card. I don't, however, suggest that humorous illustrators or cartoonists send *mass* self-promotional mailings to hundreds of TV production companies. Since this is not a huge market, study the various TV production companies and pick out those that would *likely* be interested in your work.

ALL GOD'S CREATURES, Division of Mirimar Entertainment, Box 4621, N. Hollywood CA 91617. (818)784-4177. Estab. 1965. TV and film production company that provides print advertising, TV and film production and slide shows for ad agencies, TV production companies and film studios. Clients include Mirimar Entertainment, Margery Productions, PBS, independent production companies in LA and NYC and ad agencies (subcontracting). Needs storyboards, humorous copywriting, animation, animatics, slide shows and theatrical-based humor for industrial films, print ads, radio spots, promotions, TV commercials, slide shows and TV and film production. 30% of work done by freelance humorous illustrators is for print ads.
Illustration: Works with 1 freelance illustrator/year. Looking for "someone who fits our limited needs." Uses freelancers on a one-time-only basis. For first contact send slides to Mirk Mirkin, CEO. Reports back within 1 month. Returns materials only if

requested and accompanied by SASE. Negotiates rights purchased. Pays by the project, $100-300.

Writing: Works with 3 freelance writers/year. Looking for professionally oriented, (though a novice) in style and quality. Must be highly original. For first contact send cover letter, resume, tearsheets, photocopied writing samples, ½" demo tape and audiotape (film is OK, but prefer tape) to Mirk Mirkin, CEO. Reports back within 1 month only if interested. Returns materials only if requested and accompanied by SASE. Negotiates rights purchased. Pays by the project, $100-1,000. *Inside Tips:* "We are only interested in completely new and fresh ideas, not reworked formulae, especially for TV and other video-based media (but also for print)."

AMERICAN COMEDY NETWORK, Park City Plaza, Bridgeport CT 06604. (203)384-9443. FAX: (203)367-9346. Estab. 1983. Radio syndication company that "provides radio morning shows with short-form topical comedy features." Recent productions/projects: 2-hour national radio network comedy specials, including "The 1980's: This is a Test," "The History of Rock: The Real Story" and "The American Comedy Network Awards." Clients include 270 radio stations in the U.S. and Canada, Unistar Radio Network. Needs humorous scriptwriting for radio spots. Uses freelancers for 5-10% of all humor writing.

Scriptwriting: Works with approximately 3 humorous scriptwriters/month. Looking for comedy scripts or concepts on "topical news events and people: the stuff you'd see in USA Today, People Magazine, National Enquirer." Doesn't want to see comedy scripts on "any subject that every comedy writer in the world would think of (e.g. Roseanne Barr singing anything)." For first contact send photocopied writing samples and scripts to Freelance WDB, Maggie Dugan, General Manager. "Due to the volume of freelance submissions, scripts will not be returned and you may not receive a personal reply." Buys syndication rights. Pays $25-250.

LEE CAPLIN PRODUCTIONS, INC., 8274 Grand View Trail, Los Angeles CA 90046. (213)650-1882. Estab. 1980. TV and feature film production and comic publishing (books/graphic novels) company that provides development and production of feature films and TV programs. Recent productions/projects: the original "Pee Wee," "Nervous Rex" and "Crow of Bear Clan" (animation). Needs humorous scriptwriting and cartoon characters/stories for developmental projects, programming and comic books. Uses freelancers for 100% of illustrations, humor writing and animation.

Writing: Uses freelance humor writers for developmental projects and screenplays. Needs reality-based, contemporary action/humor for live action feature films; reality-based, contemporary humor for TV sitcoms. For first contact send cover letter, resume, signed standard release form and completed screenplay for feature, treatment for TV *only*, to Sonia Mintz, Director of Development. Reports back within 2 months if interested. Keeps materials on file; does not return. Negotiates rights purchased.

Animation: Works on approximately 3 animation projects/year. Uses animation for programming. Looks for contemporary, traditional and stylish animation styles. For first contact send cover letter, resume and demo tape (½") to Sonia Mintz, Director of Development. Reports back in 2 months if interested. Does not return materials. Negotiates rights purchased.

CLASSIC ANIMATION, 1800 S. 35th St., Galesburg MI 49053. (616)665-4800. Estab. 1986. Video production house that provides traditional and computer animation—2-D, 3-D—cartoon illustration services. Recent productions/projects: Amway video report (graphics), Upjohn employee communication videos and anti-drug abuse video for children (in progress). Clients include Amway, Upjohn and Allen Testproducts. Needs humorous illustration and scriptwriting, cartoons, animatics, animations and storyboards for developmental projects, programming, promotion and TV commercials. Uses

freelancers for 50% of all illustrations; 100% of all humor writing; 25% of all animation.
Illustration: Works with approximately 10 humorous illustrators/month. Needs corporate illustrations for newsletter articles. For first contact send cover letter, resume and video tape (job reel) to David B. Baker, President. Reports back within weeks only if interested. Returns materials if accompanied by a SASE. Keeps materials on file. Buys all rights. Pays by the hour, $5-35; by the day, $50-200; by the project, $100-5,000.
Scriptwriting: Works with approximately 1 humor scriptwriter/month. Looking for comedy scripts or concepts on school programs and corporate communications. Doesn't want to see comedy scripts "on sex, drugs and rock and roll." For first contact send cover letter, resume, demo tape (½″). Concept submissions should be submitted with query detailing premise of concept and outline. Send scripts to David Baker. Reports back within weeks only if interested. Returns materials if accompanied by SASE. Keeps materials on file. Buys all rights. Pays $100 minimum.
Writing: Works with approximately 1 freelancer/month. Uses freelance humor writers for advertising/promotion, writing for specific shows and developmental projects. Needs corporate communications and commercials. For first contact send cover letter, resume, and demo tape (½″) to David Baker. Reports back within weeks only if interested. Returns materials if accompanied by a SASE. Keeps materials on file. Buys all rights. Pays by the hour, $20-35.
Animation: Works on approximately 3 animation projects/month. Uses animation for programming, commercial advertising and promotional purposes. Looks for avant-garde, contemporary, traditional, stylish ("and we're open to suggestions") animation style. For first contact send cover letter, resume, and demo tape (½″) to David Baker. Reports back within weeks only if interested. Returns materials if accompanied by a SASE. Keeps materials on file. Buys all rights. Pays by the frame, $5-15; by the hour, $5-20; by the project, $200-5,000.

CONTEMPORARY COMEDY, Box 271043, 5804 Twineing, Dallas TX 75227-1043. (214)381-4779. Estab. 1974. "We are a comedy service that supplies topical and seasonal comedy material (jokes) on a subscription basis." Clients include NBC, BBC and 800 local radio stations in the U.S., Canada, Europe and Australia. Needs one-line jokes for programming by local disc jockeys. Uses freelancers for 50% of all humor writing.
Writing: Works with approximately 7-8 freelancers/month. "Uses regular contributors, but always looking for new ones." Uses freelance humor writers for topical and seasonal one-liners: weather, fads, fashions, sports, movie/television. "We purchase approximately 100 one-line jokes per month." For first contact send cover letter and writing samples to Joe Hickman, Editor. Reports back within 3 weeks. Returns materials if accompanied by SASE. Does not file materials. Buys all rights. Pays by the one-liner, $3; on acceptance; regular contributors may receive more.

DELTA MAX PRODUCTIONS, Paramount Pictures Corp., 5555 Melrose Ave., Hollywood CA 90038. (714)760-9638. Estab. 1983. Film production company that provides feature film productions and computer graphics. Recent productions/projects: Due Process, Klone, Father Figure. Needs humorous illustration, caricatures, "on scene" illustrations, animations and storyboards for developmental projects, posters, advertising and promotion. Uses freelancers for 100% of illustrations, humor writing and animation. Prefers working with freelancers with fax capabilities.
Illustration: Works with approximately 5 humorous illustrators/year. For first contact send cover letter, resume, client list and portfolio to Robert Swanson, President. Reports back only if interested. Returns materials if accompanied by a SASE. Keeps materials on file. Buys all rights or negotiates rights purchased. Pays by the project, $1,000 minimum.

Scriptwriting: Works with approximately 7 humor scriptwriters/year. For first contact send cover letter, resume, client list and demo tape (½″). Concept submissions should be submitted with script to Robert Swanson. Reports back only if interested. Returns materials only if requested and accompanied by a SASE. Buys all rights. Pays $1,000 minimum.

Writing: Uses freelance humor writers for developmental projects. For first contact send cover letter, resume, client list and demo tape (½″) to Robert Swanson. Reports back only if interested. Returns materials if requested and accompanied by a SASE. Buys all rights. Pays by the project, $1,000 minimum.

Animation: Works on approximately 12 animation projects/year. Uses animation for films. Looks for avant-garde animation style. For first contact send cover letter, resume, client list, demo tape (½″). Reports back only if interested. Returns materials if accompanied by a SASE. Buys all rights. Pays by the project, $1,000 minimum.

THE ELECTRIC WEENIE, INC., Box 2715, Quincy MA 02269. (617)749-6900. FAX: (617)749-3691. Estab. 1970. Humor publication servicing radio industry that provides a monthly publication of 160 topical gags, one-liners and jokes. Currently working on humor publication for speakers. "We service 1,400 subscribers in U.S., Canada, New Zealand and England." Needs short humor writing (one or two lines), topical gags, jokes and observations for radio spots and by disc jockeys. Uses freelancers for 80% of humor writing.

Writing: Works with approximately 10-15 freelancers/month. Uses freelance humor writers for brochures, on-air announcements, writing for specific shows and brainstorming. Needs "topical, witty, short (2-3 line) gags, jokes, observations—95% clean humor—we use 10 'off-color' jokes per issue." For first contact send cover letter, writing samples and other available samples to K. Adam Renbud, Managing Editor. Reports back within 5 weeks. Returns materials if accompanied by a SASE. Buys all rights and reprint rights. Pays by the project, $2-5 per joke/gag to start.

ENTERTAINMENT PRODUCTIONS, INC., Suite 744, 2210 Wilshire Blvd., Santa Monica CA 90403. (310)456-3143. Estab. 1971. TV and motion picture production company that provides feature film and television productions. Recent productions/projects: "The Inventor," "Here Comes Trouble," "Las Vegas Shows" and "The Hawks & The Doves." Clients include various worldwide distributors, cable and syndicators. Uses humorous illustration and storyboards for developmental projects and posters. Uses freelancers.

Illustration: Works with approximately 5 humorous illustrators/year. Needs "illustrations that need no words of explanation." For first contact send best sample(s) of work to Edward Coe, Producer. Reports back within 1 month only if accompanied by SASE. Negotiates rights purchased. Pays by the project for buy-out of rights.

HEDQUIST PRODUCTIONS INC., Box 1475, Fairfield IA 52550. (515)472-6708. FAX: (515)472-7400. Estab. 1984. Audio production company that provides radio spots; original music; audio for TV, film and video; audiovisual; animation; and audio cassette programs. Recent productions/projects: national radio commercials for Hardee's, Lennox and Konica and regional commercials for clients in 26 states. Clients include Aetna, Farmer's State Bank and regional Oldsmobile dealers in 6 states. Needs humor writing and humorous scriptwriting for radio spots. Uses freelancers for 10% of all humor writing. Prefers working with freelancers with fax capabilities.

Scriptwriting: Works with approximately 1 humorous scriptwriter/month. For first contact send cover letter, resume, audiotape and photocopied writing samples to Jeffrey P. Hedquist, President. Returns materials if accompanied by SASE. Negotiates rights purchased. Pays $50-300.

Writing: Works with approximately 1 freelancer/month. Uses freelance humor writers for creative consulting, developmental projects, brainstorming and radio spots. Needs freelance humor writers with the ability to "integrate the humorous, entertainment value of a commercial with marketing and selling value." For first contact send cover letter, resume, client list, audiotape and writing samples to Jeffrey P. Hedquist, President. Returns materials if accompanied by SASE. Negotiates rights purchased. Pays by the project, $50-300.

*KEZE-FM, P.O. Box 8007, Spokane WA 99203. (509)448-1000. FAX: (509)448-4549. Radio station that provides AOR "rock radio"—morning show and afternoon comedy. Recent productions/projects: "Several 'on air' characters for comedy bits and sports features, one on-going 'five o'clock funnies' project—features 30- and 60-second standup type bits." Needs humor writing and scriptwriting, caricatures, radio spoofs, comedy commercials, stand up bits for developmental projects and radio spots. Uses freelancers for 30% of all humor writing.
Scriptwriting: For first contact send cover letter and audio tape. For a concept for a comedy series or programming, submit script and synopsis of concept /programming to Jeff Horton, Comedy Producer. Reports back within 2 weeks only if interested. Returns materials if accompanied by SASE. Keeps materials on file. Negotiates rights purchased. Pays by the project/property, $25-100.
Writing: Works with approximately 1-2 freelancers/month. Uses freelance humor writers for advertising/promotion, direct mail, writing for specific shows, creative consulting, developmental projects and brainstorming. For first contact send cover letter and writing samples to Jeff Horton, Comedy Producer. Reports back within 2 weeks only if interested. Returns materials if accompanied by SASE or keeps materials on file. Negotiates rights purchased. Pays by the project, $50-200.

*LINEAR CYCLE PRODUCTIONS, Box 2608, Sepulveda CA 91393. (818)895-8921. Estab. 1980. TV/audio production company that provides "programming for both audio and video outlets." Recent productions/projects: "The Laff Hour" and "Cheap Rotten Mallet." Clients include Katz Systems. Needs humor writing and scriptwriting, animatics and storyboards for developmental projects, radio spots, programming, promotion and TV commercials. Uses freelancers for 75% of all illustrations.
Illustration: For first contact send cover letter, resume, client list, tearsheets, slides and portfolio and complete sample scripts to R. Borowy, Programming. Reports back within 1-2 months only if interested. Returns material if accompanied by SASE. Keeps materials on file. Negotiates rights purchased. Payment negotiable.
Scriptwriting: Works with approximately 5 humorous scriptwriters/month; 30 humorous scriptwriters/year. Looking for comedy scripts or concepts on all elements suitable for broadcast. For first contact send cover letter, resume, client list, tearsheets, demo tape (½", ¾"), photocopied writing sample, complete script material. For a concept for a comedy series or programming, submit query detailing premise of concept, script, outline and synopsis of concept/programming to R. Borowy, Programming. Reports back within 1-2 months only if interested. Returns materials if accompanied by SASE. Keeps materials on file. Negotiates rights purchased.
Writing: Works with approximately 5 freelancers/month; 35 freelancers/year. Uses freelance humor writers for advertising/promotion, programming guides, on-air announcements, writing for specific shows, developmental projects and scripts. Needs any mate-

The asterisk before a listing indicates that the listing is new in this edition. New markets are often more receptive to freelance submissions.

rial for broadcast. For first contact send cover letter, resume, client list, tearsheets, demo tape (½", ¾"), audio tape, writing samples and complete scripts to R. Borowy, Programming. Reports back within 1-2 months. Returns materials if accompanied by a SASE. Keeps materials on file. Negotiates rights purchased. Payment negotiable.

Animation: Works on approximately 1 animation project/month. Uses animation for programming and promotional purposes. Looks for avant garde, contemporary, traditional, stylish style. For first contact send cover letter, resume, client list, demo tape, (½", ¾"), storyboards, slides, complete scripts to R. Borowy, Programming. Reports back within 1-2 months only if interested. Returns materials if accompanied by a SASE. Negotiates rights purchased. Payment negotiable.

NEAL MARSHAD PRODUCTIONS, 76 Laight St., New York NY 10013. (212)925-5285. FAX: (212)925-5681. Estab. 1983. TV production company and video production house providing creative production of TV programming. Recent productions/projects: Johnnie Walker Comedy Search, short films for NBC Saturday Night Live and segments for HBO comedy channel. Clients include NBC. Needs humorous scriptwriting, humor writing and storyboards for developmental projects, programming and promotion. Uses freelancers for 50% of all humor writing. Prefers working with freelancers with fax capabilities.

Illustration: For first contact send cover letter to Neal Marshad, Producer. Reports back in days only if interested. Returns materials only if requested and accompanied by SASE. Keeps materials on file. Buys all rights. Pays, by the day, $150-250.

Scriptwriting: Works with approximately 1 humorous scriptwriter/month. Looking for comedy scripts or concepts on adult humor. Doesn't want to see comedy scripts on "14-year-olds and sex." For first contact send cover letter, resume, client list, tearsheets and demo tape. For a concept for a comedy series or programming, submit query detailing premise of concept, script, and synopsis of concept/programming. Send scripts to Neal Marshad, Producer. Reports back in 2 weeks. Buys all rights. Pays by the project, $500.

Animation: Works on approximately 2 animation projects/year. Uses animation for programming. Looks for avant-garde, contemporary, stylish animation. For first contact send cover letter and demo tape to Neal Marshad, Producer. Reports back in 2 weeks. Returns materials if accompanied by SASE. Buys first rights. Pays by the project, $250.

PDK PICTURES, INC., Suite C-203, 3712 Barham Blvd., Los Angeles CA 90068. (213)851-0572. Estab. 1976. Film production company. Clients include Universal, MGM, Warner Brothers, ABC, CBS and NBC. Needs humor writing and humorous scriptwriting for developmental projects and programming. Uses freelancers for 100% of all humor writing.

Illustration: For first contact send cover letter and resume to Wilbur Stark, President. Reports back within weeks if interested. Returns materials if accompanied by SASE. Buys all rights or negotiates rights purchased. Pays by project, $500-5,000.

Scriptwriting: Works with approximately 6 humorous scriptwriters/year. For first contact send cover letter, resume and photocopied writing samples. For a concept for a comedy series or programming, submit script and outline. Send scripts to Wilbur Stark, President. Reports back within 2 months. Buys all rights or negotiates rights purchased. Pays $500-5,000.

Writing: Works with approximately 10 freelancers/year. Uses freelance humor writers for writing for specific shows and developmental projects. For first contact send cover letter and resume to Wilbur Stark, President. Reports back within 2 months only if interested. Returns materials only if accompanied by SASE. Buys all rights or negotiates rights purchased. Pays by the project, $500-5,000.

SINNOTT AND ASSOCIATES, INC., 676 N. LaSalle, Chicago IL 60610. (312)440-1875. Estab. 1975. TV commercial production company that does animation and special effects. Recent productions/products: Cap'n Crunch, McDonald's, Amoco, Spots & Long Animated Projects. Clients include Hallmark, McDonald's, Quaker Oats, Amoco and major advertising agencies. Needs humorous illustration, animation and storyboards for development projects and TV commercials. Uses freelancers for 75% of illustrations and 25% of animation. Prefers freelancers with fax capabilities.
Animation: Works on approximately 20 animation projects/year. Uses animation for commercial advertising and promotional purposes. Looks for avant-garde, contemporary and traditional animation style. For first contact send cover letter and (½" or ¾") demo tape to Tom Sinnott, Director. Reports back if interested. Keeps materials on file.

EDGAR S. SPIZEL PRODUCTIONS, 1782 Pacific Ave., San Francisco CA 94109. (415)474-5735. Estab. 1950. TV/video production company that provides TV, video, audio-creative work with celebrities from sports, entertainment, TV and motion pictures. Recent productions/projects: Bay Area Rapid Transit, Henny Youngman, San Francisco Office of Economic Development, City of Oakland, Oakland A's Jose Canseco.
Illustration: Send cover letter, resume, client list and tearsheets to Edgar S. Spizel, President. Reports back only if interested. Returns materials if accompanied by SASE. Keeps materials on file.
Scriptwriting: For first contact send cover letter, resume, client list and audiotape. Reports back only if interested. Returns materials if accompanied by SASE.

TALCO PRODUCTIONS, 279 E. 44th St., New York NY 10014. (212)697-4015. Estab. 1968. TV/video/radio production company providing TV documentaries, industrials, PR and radio series. Produces trade newsletter. Recent productions/projects: "Can You Name the Year?", "A Funny Thing Happened. . . . " Needs humor writing and humorous scriptwriting for radio spots and programming. Uses freelancers for 30% of all humor writing.
Illustration: For first contact send cover letter and resume. Reports back within weeks. Returns materials if accompanied by SASE. Buys all rights. Pays by project, $200-5,000.
Scriptwriting: Works with approximately 1 humorous scriptwriter/month. Will not read unsolicited scripts. For first contact send cover letter and resume to Alan Lawrence, President. Reports back within 2 weeks. Returns materials if accompanied by SASE. Buys all rights. Pays by the project, $100-10,000.
Writing: Works with approximately 1 freelancer/month. Uses freelance humor writers for on-air announcements and writing for specific shows. Gag writers needed for one liners used in trade newsletter. For first contact send cover letter and resume to Alan Lawrence, President. Reports back within weeks. Returns materials if accompanied by SASE. Buys all rights. Pays by the project, $100-10,000.

TEEMAN/SLEPPIN ENTERTAINMENT, 147 W. 26th St., New York NY 10004. (212)243-7836. FAX: (212)206-7457. Estab. 1978. TV production and entertainment and video products house that produces films, home videos and television shows. Producers of short and feature length films. Recent productions/projects: many for Proctor & Gamble, Warner-Lambert, Kraft General Foods, Quaker Oats, Kenner-Parker Toys. Needs

---

Always include a self-addressed stamped envelope (SASE) or International Reply Coupon (IRC) with submissions.

humorous illustration, humor writing, "on scene" illustrations and cartoons for developmental projects, programming, promotion. Uses freelancers for 80% of illustration, 60% of humor writing and 25% of animation.

Illustration: Works with approximately 6 humorous illustrators/year. For first contact, send cover letter, resume, tearsheets, slides to Stu Sleppin, Director. Reports back only if interested. Returns materials if accompanied by a SASE. Keeps materials on file. Negotiates rights purchased. Pays by the day, $250.

Scriptwriting: Works with approximately 5 humorous scriptwriters/year. Doesn't want to see comedy scripts on "just plain bad comedy." For first contact send cover letter, resume, demo tape (½ or ¾") and photocopied writing sample. For a concept for a comedy series or programming, submit script, outline, synopsis of concept/programming, "whatever gets the idea across" to Stu Sleppin, Director. Reports back only if interested. Returns materials if accompanied by SASE. Keeps materials on file. Negotiates rights purchased. Pays $2,500 minimum.

Writing: Works with approximately 6 freelancers/year. Uses freelance humor writers for advertising/promotion, developmental projects, brainstorming. Needs funny material "that would attract youth." For first contact send cover letter, resume, demo tape (½ or ¾"), writing samples to Stu Steppin, Director. Reports back only if interested. Returns materials if accompanied by a SASE. Keeps materials on file. Negotiates rights purchased. Pays by the project, $500 minimum.

Animation: Works on approximately 3 animation projects/year. Uses animation for programming, promotional purposes. Looks for avant-garde. For first contact send demo tape (½ or ¾") to Stu Sleppin, Director. Reports back only if interested. Returns materials if accompanied by a SASE. Keeps materials on file. Negotiates rights purchased. Pays by the project, $2,000 minimum.

TELESTAR MEDIA, 11101 Aqua Vista, Suite 103, Studio City CA 91602. Estab. 1982. Syndication/publishing company that syndicates and publishes cartoons and humorous gags. Clients include Paramount Pictures. Needs humorous illustration, caricatures, cartoons, storyboards, ("cute, Disney-ish style") for advertising, TV commercials and publishing. Uses freelancers for 100% of all illustrations; 5% of all humor writing. Prefers to work with freelancers who have fax capabilities.

Illustration: Varies. Needs "cute Disney-ish style." For first contact send tearsheets, portfolio to Brian Starr, President. Reports back within 2 weeks. Reports back only if interested, accompanied by a SASE. Keeps materials on file. Buys all rights. Pays by the hour, $50-150.

Writing: Works with approximately 3 freelancers/month. Uses freelance humor writers for advertising/promotion, writing for specific shows. Needs sight gags, clever humor. For first contact send writing samples to Brian Starr, President. Reports back within 3 weeks only if interested. Returns materials if accompanied by a SASE. Keeps materials on file. Buys all rights. Pays by the hour, $25 minimum.

RIC TOWER CREATIONS, 401 South 1st St., Suite 1316, Minneapolis MN 55401. Estab. 1985. "We write 400-500 gags/month for radio personalities on over 800 stations coast to coast." Clients include KIIS/LA, WHTZ/NYC, WBBM-Chicago and Armed Forces Radio. Needs humor writing and topical one-liners for programming and broadcast. Uses freelancers for 10% of gags.

Writing: Works with approximately 15 freelancers/month. Uses freelance writers to write for radio broadcasters. Needs topical one-liners about people, places and topics in today's news. For first contact send writing samples to Steve Mitchell, Asst. Editor. "We don't have specific writers' guidelines. If it's funny, send it however you want." Reports back in 5 days. Returns materials if accompanied by SASE. Does not file materials. Buys all rights. Pays by the project, $2-10/min per gag.

*WORKING BOY PRODUCTIONS, 3575 Cahuenga Blvd. West, Suite 600, Los Angeles CA 90068. (213)850-1600. FAX: (213)850-6709. Estab. 1991. TV production company that provides animated and live action children's television. Recent productions/projects: "Wake, Rattle & Roll" (Fender Bender 500/Monster Tales) and "Don Coyote." Clients include Hanna-Barbera, Television Networks. Needs humor writing, animations, storyboards for developmental projects and programming. Uses freelancers for 100% of all illustrations, 100% of animation. Prefers to work with freelancers who have fax capabilities.

Scriptwriting: For first contact send cover letter, resume and photocopied writing sample. For a concept for a comedy series or programming, submit synopsis of concept/programming to Sam Ewing, Producer. Reports back within weeks. Returns materials if accompanied by SASE. Keeps materials on file. Buys all rights. Pays by the project/property, $2,000 minimum.

Writing: Works with approximately 3-5 freelancers/month. Uses freelance humor writers for writing for specific shows and developmental projects. Needs animation writers who can write *character* comedy. For first contact send cover letter, resume and writing samples to Sam Ewing, Producer. Reports back within weeks. Returns materials if accompanied by a SASE. Buys all rights. Pays by the project, $500 minimum.

Animation: Works on approximately 2 animation projects/year. Uses animation for programming. Looks for contemporary, stylish style. For first contact send cover letter, resume, client list and storyboards to Sam Ewing, Producer. Reports back within weeks. Returns materials if accompanied by a SASE. Buys all rights or negotiates rights purchased. Payment negotiable.

*WWRX-FM, 55 Access Rd., Warwick RI 02886. (401)732-5690. FAX: (401)738-9329. Estab. 1972. Radio station that provides classic rock radio. Needs humor writing for developmental projects, advertising, radio sports and promotion. Uses freelancers for 25% of humor writing. Prefers to work with freelancers who have fax cababilities.

Illustration: Works with approximately 1 humorous illustrator/month. Needs "Reality in the real world." For first contact send cover letter, resume, tearsheets and portfolio to Dave Richards, Program Director. Reports back within months. Returns materials *only if requested.* Negotiates rights purchased. Pays by the project, $10 minimum.

Scriptwriting: Works with approximately 2 humorous scriptwriters/month; 10 humorous scriptwriters/year. Looking for comedy scripts or concepts on "anything topical." Doesn't want to see comedy scripts on "Same old stuff—what everyone else is doing." For first contact send cover letter, resume, client list, demo tape and audio tape. For a concept for a comedy series or programming, submit script and outline to Dave Richards, Program Director. Reports back within weeks. Keeps materials on file. Negotiates rights purchased. Pays by the project/property, $50 minimum.

Writing: Works with approximately 2 freelancers/month; 10 freelancers/year. Uses freelance humor writers for advertising/promotion, brochures, direct mail, programming guides, writing for specific shows and developmental projects. For first contact send cover letter, resume, client list, demo tape, audio tape and writing samples to Dave Richards, Program Director. Reports back within weeks only if interested. Keeps materials on file. Negotiates rights purchased. Pays by the project, $50 minimum.

Television/Radio/Changes '91-'93

The following markets appeared in the last (1991) edition of *Humor and Cartoon Markets* but are absent from the 1993 edition.

Bear Creek Recording
Continental Film Productions
(asked to be deleted)
Bert Elliot (overstocked)
G Nine (overstocked)

Hadden Manganello
Handsome Brothers (doesn't use humor)
Deborah Hutchison Productions (asked to be deleted)

KDOC-TV
Le Duc Video Productions
Verne Pershing Productions
(asked to be deleted)
Proimage (cannot be reached)

Contests

Is this too cool, or what? We've finally found a bunch of contests that don't involve playing an accordion, wearing an evening gown or singing "You Light Up My Life."

Of course, beauty contests will always have a place (in the 1950s), and Pillsbury will always stage its annual Send-Us-Your-Favorite-Way-To-Use-Yeast competition, but there are *other* contests that matter in the big scheme of things. Humor, of course, is a very serious matter, and a number of organizations want to *support* it by holding these nifty competitions.

Happily, to win one of these contests, you'll have to either draw or write funnier than anyone else who enters. And while we have not personally checked out each and every contest, none appear to involve wearing a revealing swimsuit or getting intimate with any of the judges as they do in those Miss Junior Texas deals. They may also do that kind of stuff to win an Emmy, but we've got morals here.

Seriously, there are some pretty interesting contests here—more than we thought even existed. We list the basic facts (type of contest, open to professionals/amateurs, deadline, etc.), but we highly recommend that you request the *complete* entry information from those contests that interest you.

We did our best to translate the information provided by foreign contest officials. For example, we *thought* we had received information on a Romanian humor writing contest, but it really turned out to be a competition calling for the best stir-fried yak recipes in Bucharest. Tasty, we're sure, but not very funny.

Prizes range from cash to a handshake, publication of your winning entry to bronzed, plasticized trophies. On your mark. Get set. Make that judge laugh!

ANN ARBOR FILM FESTIVAL, Box 8232, Ann Arbor MI 48107. (313)995-5356. Estab. 1963. Contest is for a 16mm independent and experimental film and animation festival. Open to all. Deadline is February.
How to Enter: Write or call for details. Entries are returned. Receives 250 entries/year. Fee is $25 per film entry. Judged by 3 filmmakers; award is $7,000 cash distributed according to judges. Winners notified by mail. Call for contest rules and forms.

BAY GUARDIAN CARTOON CONTEST, 520 Hampshire St., San Francisco CA 94110. (415)255-3100. Contest is "for cartooning—single panel, single strip, ongoing strip, silent cartoon, political cartoon, comic strip parody, single cartoon with San Francisco Bay area focus, computer generated cartoon and cartoon drawn by children 14 years and under." Open to all. Deadline varies.
How to Enter: "For contest rules and forms must enclose SASE. Available in May."

BEST EDITORIAL CARTOONS, Pelican Publishing Company, Box 189, Gretna LA 70054. (504)368-1175. FAX: (504)368-1195. Estab. 1926. Publishes "Best Editorial Cartoons of the Year" series. "Cartoons must have appeared in printed form in magazines or newspapers."
Humorous Illustrations: Needs editorial cartoons only. "There is no cash payment for cartoons used. Each cartoonist receives 2 copies of the edition he/she is in. Cartoonists send in what they consider their top 5 cartoons. These are sent to Chuck Brooks, who puts them into categories and then chooses the best of each category. The categories are determined by what has happened in the previous year." Cartoonists interested in being included should send a letter to Pelican requesting to be put on mailing list for next edition. "Letters with information of where to send cartoons go out in November."

CA "93", Box 10330, Palo Alto CA 94303. (415)326-6040. Contest is for all areas of humorous illustration. Open to all. Must be a published piece. Deadline is June 22.
How to Enter: Call or write for entry form.

COVER DESIGN CONTEST, Snicker Magazine, 1248 Oak Bark Dr., St. Louis MO 63146. (314)993-1633. Estab. October 1990. Contest is "to expose new artists on one of the largest cover spotlights in publishing!"; for cartooning and humorous illustration. Open to all. Deadlines are May, September and January.
How to Enter: Send 10 × 16″ illustrations in any media. "Remember to leave room for our logo at top. Illustrations may be in either b&w or full color." Entries judged on "imagination, design and charm." Entries are not returned. Receives 100-200 entries/year. "There is no entry fee, but sample issues with past winning artists are available for $3 (includes postage.)" Judged by editors; award is "worldwide cartooning fame plus whatever cool prize we're giving away at the moment!" Winners notified by mail or phone. Winning entries are published on *Snicker Magazine*'s current front cover. "A back issue should clarify contest to interested artist. Iraqi presidents are not eligible to enter."

CREATIVITY "93", 6th floor, 10 E. 39th St., New York NY 10016. (212)889-6500. FAX: (212)889-6504. Contest is for cartooning, humorous nonfiction and fiction writing, humorous illustration and advertising. Deadline is May.
How to Enter: For contest rules and forms call or write. Send SASE. Send entry to Mae Wills.

Always include a self-addressed stamped envelope (SASE) or International Reply Coupon (IRC) with submissions.

DELACORTE PRESS PRIZE FOR A FIRST YOUNG ADULT NOVEL, 666 Fifth Ave., New York NY 10103. (212)765-6500. FAX: (212)492-9698. Contact: Delacorte Press, Dept. BFYR, Attn: L. Oldenburg. Estab. 1983. Contest is "to encourage the writing of contemporary young adult fiction." Open to all, providing that the entrant has not previously published a young adult novel. Entries must be *postmarked* after Labor Day and before the first day of the next year.

How to Enter: Send a book length manuscript of 100-224 pages suitable for ages 12-18, and include a short summary. Entries judged on merit. Entries are returned if accompanied by SASE. Receives 250 entries/year. Judged by editors; award is $1,500 cash prize, $6,000 advance against royalties and publication of novel. "Honorable Mentions may also be published, terms to be negotiated, if we find such a manuscript." Winning entries are published as soon as possible, depending on how much work they need. Write and request contest rules and forms. "We do like entrants to comply with the rules. Approximately 10% of entrants are rejected every year for, say, sending us a historical novel. Our contest is not exclusively for humorous fiction, but humor goes a long way with us."

EASY READER WRITING, PHOTO AND CARTOON CONTEST, Easy Reader, Box 427, Hermosa Beach CA 90254. (213)372-4611. FAX: (213)318-6292. Estab. 1970. Contest is "to encourage local cartoonists, writers and photographers and to bring them recognition" for cartooning, humorous nonfiction and fiction writing. Open to South Bay Los Angeles residents. Past recipient: Keith Robinson. Deadline is September 30.

How to Enter: "Writers and cartoonists should send copies of work. Stories not to exceed 3,000 words." Entries judged on "humor and quality." Entries returned with SASE. Receives 100 entries/year. No fee. Judged by editors; award is $100-500. Winner(s) notified by mail. Winning entries are published in *Easy Reader*'s annual anniversary issue. For contest rules and forms send SASE.

EUROPEAN CARTOON CONTEST, 9770 Kruishoutem, Belgium. (091)83-66-96. Contact: Rudy Gheysens. Contest is "to promote the cartoon as a form of art—offer people the possibility to see the real thing (and not just as a publication in a magazine) by organizing exhibitions of selected cartoons." Open to all. Contest is organized every two years. Deadline 1993 Contest: November 15, 1992.

How to Enter: Send unpublished cartoons on a given theme (for 1993: Magic). Entries will be judged on originality of the idea, artistic merit and style. Entries are not returned, they become property of the organization. Receives over 2,000 entries every two years. Judged by art professors, artists, officials of ministry of culture and journalists; awards are 1st, 20,000 BF & Trophy (golden egg); 2nd, 15,000 BF and silver egg; 3rd, 10,000 BF and bronze egg and free stay in the village hotel. Winners are notified by mail or telegram. Winning entries and selected cartoons are published in cartoon book edited by the organization and in newspapers. For contest rules and forms, send a letter. Contest is organized every two years. Free catalogue is sent to each participant. Selected cartoons are shown during Easter exhibition in Kruishoutem. Afterwards, at exhibitions all over Belgium. "The Eurokartoenale is an organization of a Flemish cultural association called Willemsfonds."

JOHN FISCHETTI EDITORIAL CARTOON COMPETITION, 600 S. Michigan Ave., Chicago IL 60605. (312)663-1600. Contact: Columbia College Chicago. Estab. 1982. Contest is to "help raise funds for journalism scholarship endowment;" for cartooning. Open to professionals. Past recipients: Lee Judge, Bill DeOre, Tom Toles, Scott Willis, Doug Marlette, Dich Locher, Arthur "Chip" Bok, Lambert Der. Deadline is August.

How to Enter: Submit 1 published editorial cartoon in a size that fits a 9 × 12 envelope. All entries must include letter of nomination or endorsement from editor, publisher or employer. Entries judged on style, humor and political and social relevance. Entries are not returned. Receives 125-150 entries/year. Judged by editors, professors, newspeople. Awards are 1st, $3,000; 2nd, $1,500; plaques to other winners, including Honorable Mentions. Winners notified by mail. "Winning entries are displayed at annual dinner which first prize winner is invited to attend."

HARVEY AWARDS, % Bulldog Productions, Inc., Box 820388, Dallas TX 75382. (214)739-5123. Contact: Larry Lankford. Contest is for work done in comic book market. Open to professionals. Nominating is done in March and April. Selection is by ballot.

HIGHLIGHTS FOR CHILDREN FICTION CONTEST, 803 Church St., Honesdale PA 18431. (717)253-1080. Estab. 1978. "Send SASE for guidelines and rules because category changes each year." Open to all. Deadline is Jan. 1 to Feb. 28.
How to Enter: Send stories "no longer than 900 words, considerably shorter for younger readers. No use of derogatory humor, war or violence. Mark ms 'Fiction Contest.' No entry fee." Entries are returned with SASE. Receives 1,000 entries/year Award is 3 $1,000 prizes. Winning entries are announced in June edition of *Highlights*. Contest rules and entry forms available with SASE.

ILLUSTRATION WEST 31, The Society of Illustrators of Los Angeles, Suite 300, 5000 Van Nuys Blvd., Sherman Oaks CA 91403-1717. FAX: (818)995-0878. Estab. 1961. Contest is for illustration. Open to all. "Please call for deadline info; it is around April/May/June."
How to Enter: Send 35mm slide with completed entry form and entry fee. The way entries are judged depends on category: advertising, entertainment, editorial, institutional, technical, student, unpublished, black and white. Entries are not returned. Receives 600-700 entries/year. Fee is $15-23 per entry; hanging fee is $40-55. Judged by illustrators and art directors; award is plaque and certificates. Winners notified by mail and/or phone. "We hold an exhibition for winning entries." For contest rules and entry forms please contact Alyce Heath.

ILLUSTRATORS 35, 128 E. 63rd St., New York NY 10021. (212)838-2560. Contact: Society of Illustrators. Contest is "to recognize illustrators, cartoonists, artists and graphics professionals for communication arts achievement." Open to professionals. Deadline is October 1, annually.
How to Enter: Request complete rules from the Society. Entries are not returned. Fee is $17 per entry. Judged by professionals from the graphics industry; awards are gold medal, silver medal, award certificate and certificate of merit. Winners notified by mail. Winning entries are published in *Illustrators 35*.

INTERNATIONAL SPORTING CARTOON EXHIBITION, Centro Sportivo "Riviera Del Conero," Via Panoramica, 40 60123 Ancona, Italy. (071)201344. Estab. 1972. Contest is "to popularize sport ideals"; for cartooning. Open to all. Deadline is October 31, 1992.
How to Enter: Send original cartoons. Entries judged on "style, artistic merit and content. The prizewinning works remain the Organizing Committee's property." Receives 6,000-7,000 entries/year, from about 80 countries. Judged by professors and critics; awards are cash, plaques and medals. Winners notified by mail. Winning entries are sometimes published. "Buys the rights to reproduce the works in order to popularize the exhibition." Contest rules are sent by mail to anyone who asks for them.

STEPHEN LEACOCK AWARD FOR HUMOR, Box 854, Orillia, Ontario, L3V 6K8 Canada. (705)325-6546. Estab. 1947. Contest is "to promote *Canadian* authors' humorous writing;" for cartooning, humorous fiction and nonfiction writing. Open to all. Past recipients: Eric Nicol, Donald Jack and Pierre Berton. Deadline is Dec. 31st.

How to Enter: Send published works—10 copies, photo and bio. Entries judged on humor and writing. Entries are not returned. Receives 40 entries/year. Fee is $25 per entry. Judged by "persons of all different backgrounds;" award is $3,500 J.P. Wiser cash award and silver medal. Winner notified by phone. Awards presented at special dinner in Orillia, Ontario. Winning entries are published in book form. Contest rules and entry forms available with SASE.

THE MOBIUS ADVERTISING AWARDS, 841 N. Addison Ave., Elmhurst IL 60126-1291. (708)834-7773. FAX: (708)834-5565. Estab. 1970. Contest is "yearly selection and recognition of the world's most outstanding TV and radio commercials as well as print advertising and package design. Includes category in humor and illustration" for humorous illustration and humorous fiction and nonfiction writing. Open to professionals. Past recipients: Chiat Day Mojo, Cliff Freeman and Partners, NY and radio/TV rentals, London, etc. Deadline is October 1st.
How to Enter: Send "videotape or audiotape of broadcast commercials or tearsheets of ads or illustration mounted on crescent board." Entries judged on use of humor in medium. Entries are returned if requested. Receives 3,000-4,000 entries/year. Fee is $60-90, "depending on medium." Judged by industry peers, writers, illustrators, creative directors, producers, etc.; award is Mobius statuette. Winners notified by mail. Winning entries are published in yearly award booklet and displayed at public showing. For contest rules and forms send SASE.

NATIONAL 10-MINUTE PLAY CONTEST, Actors Theatre of Louisville, 316 W. Main St., Louisville KY 40202-2916. (502)584-1265. Estab. 1989. Contest is "to discover the best new 10-minute play by an unknown or established playwright." Open to all U.S. residents. Deadline is December 1.
How to Enter: Send typed, secured manuscript with manuscript-size SASE. Limit 10 pages per script, 2 scripts per author. "Unsolicited full-lengths and one-acts will be returned unread." Entries judged on literary and dramatic merit. Entries are returned if accompanied by SASE. Receives 2,000 entries/year. Judged by theater staff; award is $1,000 with possible production. Winner(s) are notified by mail. For contest rules and forms send SASE.

OVERSEAS PRESS CLUB AWARD, Suite 2116, 310 Madison Ave., Dept. HC, New York NY 10017. (212)983-4655. Estab. 1939. Contest is "to find the best editorial cartoon in foreign affairs." Open to professionals. Past recipients: Herblock, Paul Conrad, Tony Auth. Deadline is January 30.
How to Enter: Send 4-10 different cartoons per entry. Contact: Mary Novick. Entries are returned if accompanied by SASE. Fee is $50 per entry. Judged by journalism professionals; award is $500. For contest rules and forms send SASE.

PREMIO SATIRA POLITICA, % Comune di Forte dei Marmi, 55042 Forte dei Marmi, Lucca Italy. (584)82966. FAX: (584)83843. Estab. 1973. Contest is for cartooning; humorous nonfiction writing, illustration and fiction writing; movies; cabaret; radio; and TV. Open to all. Past recipients: David Levine, Jules Feiffer, Gary Trudeau, Ralph Steadman. Deadline is April, annually.

How to Enter: "Cartoonists should send copies of their work. Then cartoonists are invited to have an exhibition here in Forte dei Marmi. Another possibility is to make a show with all the different cartoons which arrive from the States." Entries judged on wit and artistic merit. Entries are not returned. Judged by editors, professors and journalists; award is plaque and sculpture. Winning entries are published in catalog.

THE CHARLES M. SCHULZ FOR COLLEGE CARTOONIST, The Charles M. Schulz Award, % United Media, 200 Park Ave., New York, NY 10166-0079. (212)692-3700. FAX: (212)867-1620. Estab. 1980. Contest is "to honor outstanding college cartoonists and to encourage them to launch post-graduate professional careers in cartooning and editorial illustration." Open to students (cartoonists). Past recipients: Nick Anderson, Ohio State University; Chris Kalb, Yale University; Michael Thompson, University of Wisconsin/Milwaukee. Deadline is January 5 (approximately the same time each year).
How to Enter: Send portfolio of 5-15 representative samples (one per page) on 8½×11″ paper. Entry must include a written statement (250 words or less) by the cartoonist outlining his or her goals in cartooning. Do not submit original artwork. Entry blank must accompany entry. Entries judged on "style, originality and artistic ability." Entries are not returned. Receives 200 entries/year. Judged by Charles M. Schulz, professor of journalism and managing editor of newspaper; award is $2,000 and bronze plaque. Winner(s) notified by mail or phone. Send request for fact sheet and entry blank to Scripps Howard Foundation, 1100 Central Trust Tower, Cincinnati OH 45202.

SE LA VIE WRITER'S JOURNAL, Box 371371, El Paso TX 79937. (915)595-2625. Contact: Rio Grande Press. Estab. 1987. Contest is "to give new or experienced artists/cartoonists a place to show their work and be published." Open to all. Deadline is quarterly, March 31, June 30, Sept. 30 and Dec. 31.
How to Enter: Send humorous cartoons and illustrations about poets, writers, etc. For cover designs send postcard query for subject. Entries judged on originality, humor, appropriateness for publication in which entered and professionalism. Entries are not returned. Receives 15 cartoons/year; 8-10 designs/year. Judged by managing editor; award is publication plus copy of issue in which work appears. Winner(s) notified by mail. Winning entries are published in *Se La Vie Writer's Journal.* Purchases first North American serial rights; after publication all rights return to artist. For contest rules and forms send SASE. "The contest organizers want material that reflects 'life' theme (La Vie), be it poem, essay, story, cartoon, column or article."

SNICKER'S ENVELOPE CONTEST, Snicker Magazine, 1248 Oak Bark Dr., St. Louis MO 63146. (314)993-1633. Estab. since "the beginning of the pony express." Contest is to "drive the post office crazy and for us to show our readers and neighbors that we get the wildest mail in the country!" Contest is for cartooning, humorous illustration and oragami. Open to all "and to U.S. Postmaster General." Sample issues available for $3 (includes postage.)
How to Enter: "Send us a decorated, painted, airbrushed, cartooned, homespun or otherwise artful envelope (any size) that you've created especially for lil' ol' us. It can even be empty inside (but we hope it isn't!). Entries judged on imagination, invention, color, design, humor, cleverness and the fact that the post office could actually figure out where to send it!" Entries are not returned. Judged by editors; award is publication of "coolest" envelopes and letters; "we'll mail you back a free Snicker poster (while they last) or some other hip item." Winners notified by mail. Winning entries are published in *Snicker Magazine.* Buys no rights. Contest rules and forms not available.

Resources

Organizations

Okay, so now that you're selling your humor, you'll want to look at the possibility of joining an appropriate professional organization or two. Many of these organizations hold annual conventions and events, and I don't think any of them requires its members to wear a fez and drive small cars in parades. Since most of these organizations function on very small operating budgets, it's highly advisable that you include a SASE when you write to them.

NCS Reaches Out

In an effort to expand its membership, the venerable National Cartoonist Society (NCS) invites gag cartoonists, comic strip creators, editorial cartoonists, humorous illustrators, comic book artists, advertising cartoonists and animators to apply for membership in the organization. Because NCS is getting so big, regional chapters have started to spring up. Therefore, you're best advised to request a membership application from your regional chapter. If your area does not have a NCS chapter, direct your inquiry to NCS headquarters in New York. Again, send a SASE when requesting information.

THE ADVERTISING COUNCIL, 825 Third Ave., New York NY 10022.

AMERICAN ASSOCIATION OF ADVERTISING AGENCIES, 13th Floor, 666 Third Ave., New York NY 10017.

*AMERICAN FEDERATION OF TELEVISION AND RADIO ARTISTS (AFTRA), 6922 Hollywood Blvd., 8th Fl., Hollywood CA 90028.

AMERICAN SOCIETY OF JOURNALISTS AND AUTHORS (ASJA), Suite 1907, 1501 Broadway, New York NY 10036.

THE ART DIRECTORS CLUB, INC., 250 Park Ave. S., New York NY 10003.

ASIFA-EAST (ANIMATION), % Dick Rauh, 11 Admiral Lane, Norwalk CT 06851.

ASSOCIATION OF AMERICAN EDITORIAL CARTOONISTS (AAEC), Suite 201, 4101 Lake Boone Trail, Raleigh NC 27607. (919)787-5181.

THE AUTHOR'S LEAGUE OF AMERICA, INC., 234 W. 44th St., New York NY 10036.

CARTOONISTS ASSOCIATION, Box 4203, Grand Central Station, New York NY 10163-4203.

COMEDY WRITERS/PERFORMERS ASSOCIATION, Box 023304, Brooklyn NY 11202-0066. Estab. 1984. "With membership you receive 1 year subscription to *Latest Joke*, the booklet *Being a Comedian* and current issue of *Comedy Writer's Newsletter*. All questions answered relative to comedy writing and performing. Annual membership $24."

COMIC ART PROFESSIONAL SOCIETY (CAPS), 139 S. Carr Dr. #7, Glendale CA 91205.

FREELANCE EDITORIAL ASSOCIATION, Box 835, Cambridge MA 02238.

GRAPHIC ARTIST'S GUILD OF NEW YORK, 11 W. 20th St., New York NY 10011. (212)463-7759.

*THE LOONIES, P.O. Box 20443, Oakland CA 94620.

MEDIA ALLIANCE, 2nd Floor, Fort Mason Bldg. D, San Francisco CA 94123.

NATIONAL CARTOONIST SOCIETY HEADQUARTERS (NCS), Suite 904, 157 W. 57th St., New York NY 10019.

NCS Northern California Chapter
79 Highmeadow Lane,
Carmel CA 93923

NCS Long Island Chapter
102 Bay Dr.,
Huntington NY 11743

NCS Southern California Chapter
P.O. Box 696,
Ojai CA 93023

NCS New Jersey Chapter
443 Hillside Ave.,
Mountainside NJ 07092

NCS Florida Chapter
344 Brown Pelican Dr.,
Daytona Beach FL 32119

NCS North Central Chapter
1608 South Dakota Ave.,
Sioux Falls SD 57105

NCS Southeastern Chapter
1800 Progress Lane,
Charlotte NC 28205

NCS District of Columbia Chapter
7109 Pebble Lane West,
Spotsylvania VA 22553

NCS South Central Chapter
6342 Southwood,
Studio 3 East,
St. Louis MO 63105

NCS Philadelphia Chapter
214 School St.,
North Wales PA 19454

NATIONAL SOCIETY OF NEWSPAPER COLUMNISTS (NSNC), Box 8318, Fremont CA 94537.

NATIONAL WRITERS UNION, 13 Astor Place, New York NY 10003.

PROFESSIONAL COMEDIANS ASSOCIATION, Suite 3C, 581 9th Ave., New York NY 10036.

SOCIETY OF ILLUSTRATORS, 128 E. 63rd St., New York NY 10021.

WRITERS ALLIANCE, Box 2014, Setauket NY 11733.

WRITER'S GUILD OF AMERICA (WGA), East: 555 W. 57th St., New York NY 10019; West: 8955 Beverly Blvd., W. Hollywood CA 90048.

Recommended Publications

There's so much to learn about the business of humor. We've compiled this nifty list of reading material which will enable you to keep on top of this wacky biz (and hey—subscriptions are tax-deductible!).

Magazines
Advertising Age, 740 Rush St., Chicago IL 60611
Adweek, A/S/M Publications, 49 E. 21st St., New York NY 10010
Airbrush Action, 317 Cross St., Lakewood NJ 08701.
Animation Magazine, Box 25547, Los Angeles CA 90025
Art Direction, 6th floor, 10 E. 39th St., New York NY 10016-0199
The Artist's Magazine, 1507 Dana Ave., Cincinnati OH 45207
Cartoonist Profiles, 281 Bayberry Lane, Westport CT 06880
Comedy USA Newswire, 915 Broadway, New York NY 10010
Comic Buyer's Guide, 700 E. State St., Iola WI 54990
Comics Career, 601 Clinkscales, Columbia MO 65203
Communications Arts, 410 Sherman Ave., Box 10300, Palo Alto CA 94303
Editor and Publisher, 11 W. 19th St., New York NY 10011
Factsheet Five, 6 Arizona Ave., Rensselaer NY 12144-4502
Gag Recap Publications, Box 86, East Meadow NY 11554
Get Animated!, Box 1458, Burbank CA 91507
Greetings Magazine, MacKay Publishing, 309 Fifth Ave., New York NY 10016
HOW Magazine, 1507 Dana Ave., Cincinnati OH 45207
Modern Cartooning and Gagwriting, Box 1142, Novato CA 94947
Political Pix, Box 804C, Norwich VT 05055
Print, 9th Floor, 104 Fifth Ave., New York NY 10017
Publisher's Weekly, 205 W. 42nd St., New York NY 10017
Publishing News, Box 4049, Stamford CT 06907-0949
Step-by-Step Graphics, 6000 N. Forest Park Dr., Peoria IL 61614-3597
Witty World, Box 1458, North Wales PA 19454
Writer's Digest, 1507 Dana Ave., Cincinnati OH 45207

Illustration directories
Adweek Portfolios, A/S/M Communications, 49 E. 21st St., New York NY 10010
American Showcase, 724 Fifth Ave., New York NY 10019
Chicago Creative Directory, 333 N. Michigan Ave., Chicago IL 60601
Creative Black Book, Friendly Press, 401 Park Ave. S., New York NY 10016
The Creative Illustration Book, 115 Fifth Ave., New York NY 10003

Madison Avenue Handbook, Peter Glenn Publication, 17 E. 48th St., New York NY 10017

RSVP, Box 314, Brooklyn NY 11205

The Work Book, Scott and Daughters Publishing, Suite 204 1545 Wilcox Ave., Los Angeles CA 90028

Books

Amazing Heroes, (Annual Comics Preview Special) by Fantagraphics Books, 7563 Lake City Way, Seattle WA 98115

Animation: From Script to Screen, by Shamus Culhane, St. Martin's Press, 175 Fifth Ave., New York NY 10010

The Animator's Workbook, by Tony White, Watson-Guptill Publications, P.O. Box 2013, Lakewood NJ 08701.

Art Director's Annual, 250 Park Ave. S., New York NY 10003

The Art of Humorous Illustration, by Nick Meglin, Watson-Guptill Publications, Box 2013, Lakewood NJ 08701

Artist's Market, Writer's Digest Books, 1507 Dana Ave., Cincinnati OH 45207

Best Editorial Cartoons of the Year (annual), edited by Charles Brooks, Pelican Publishing, Box 189, 1101 Monroe St., Gretna LA 70053

Cartoon Animation: Introduction to a Career, Milton Gray, The Whole Toon Catalog, P.O. Box 369, Issaquah WA 98027

Comedy Writing Secrets, by Melvin Helitzer, Writer's Digest Books, 1507 Dana Ave., Cincinnati OH 45207

The Complete Book of Caricature, by Bob Staake, North Light Books, 1507 Dana Ave., Cincinnati OH 45207

The Craft of Comedy Writing, by Sol Saks, Writer's Digest Books, 1507 Dana Ave., Cincinnati OH 45207

Directories in Print, Gale Research Co., Penobscot Bldg., Detroit MI 48226

Gale Directory of Publications, Penobscot Bldg., Detroit MI 48226

Graphic Artist's Guild Handbook: Pricing and Ethical Guidelines, F&W Publications, 1507 Dana Ave., Cincinnati OH 45207

A Guide to Greeting Card Writing, edited by Larry Sandman, Writer's Digest Books, 1507 Dana Ave., Cincinnati OH 45207

Handbook of Magazine Article Writing, by Lisa Collier Cool, Writer's Digest Books, 1507 Dana Ave., Cincinnati OH 45207

How to Draw and Sell Cartoons, Ross Thompson and Bill Hewison, North Light Books, 1507 Dana Ave., Cincinnati OH 45207

How to Draw and Sell Comic Strips, by Alan McKenzie, North Light Books, 1507 Dana Ave., Cincinnati OH 45207

How to Draw Cartoons Editors Will Buy, George Crenshaw, Paramount Press, 703 Ridgemark Dr., Hollister CA 95023.

Humor, edited by The Society of Illustrators, Madison Square Press, Suite 510, 10 E. 23rd St., New York NY 10010

Literary Market Place, R.R. Bowker Company, 245 W. 17th St., New York NY 10011

Standard Directory of Advertising Agencies, National Register Publishing, 3004 Glenview Rd., Wilmette IL 60091

Working Press of the Nation, National Research Bureau, Suite 1150, 310 S. Michigan Ave., Chicago IL 60604

Writer's Market, Writer's Digest Books, 1507 Dana Ave., Cincinnati OH 45207

Mail order catalogs

Rhino Records Catalog, (animation videotapes, comedy performances) 2225 Colorado Ave., Santa Monica CA 90404-3555

The Whole Toon Catalog, (cartoon-oriented books, incredible collection of animation videotapes) Box 369, 1460 19th Ave. NW, Issaquah WA 98027

Bud Plant's Comic Art Update, (comic/cartoon-oriented books/posters) Box 1689, Grass Valley CA 95945

Glossary

Acceptance (payment on). Payment is made as soon as the buyer decides to use your work.

All rights. If a buyer or publisher purchases all rights to material, they have the exclusive owner-ship of the material and can publish, republish or sell rights at any time without further compensation to the creator.

Animatics. Simple, low-cost animation showing limited motion or none at all.

Balloon. A floating orb in which comic strip character dialogue or thoughts are placed.

Benday. A mechanically produced film comprised of various densities of dots used by cartoonists to create halftone areas in their line art.

Camera-ready. Art that is completely prepared for copy camera platemaking.

Cel animation. Hand-drawn animation inked and painted on a clear acetate "cel."

Collateral. Any printed material distributed to promote or market one's services (e.g., a printed, self-promotional flyer is a piece of collateral).

Comprehensive (comps). Rough, yet fairly detailed drawing which shows client what proposed, finished art will look like.

Copy. Usually refers to the written text a writer has typed or generated.

Copyright. The exclusive legal right to reproduce, publish and sell the matter and form of a literary or artistic work.

Direct mail package. Sales or promotional material that is distributed by mail. Usually consists of an outside envelope, a cover letter, brochure or flyer, SASE or reply postcard, or an order form and business reply envelope.

Editorial. Usually describes writing or illustration work done for magazines or newspapers.

Editorial cartoon. A cartoon cointaining the cartoonist's editorialized opinion about a socio/political event or issue. Same as a "political cartoon."

First North American serial rights. The right to publish material in a periodical for the first time in North America.

First rights. The right to publish material for the first time, one time. The artist or writer agrees not to publish the material anywhere else for a limited amount of time.

Gagline. The words printed, usually directly beneath a cartoon; also called a caption.

Halftone. Reproduction of a continuous tone illustration with the image formed by dots produced by a camera lens screen.

Inbetweening. If a second of animation requires 12 drawings, the animation studio may draw the first, sixth and twelfth frames. An "inbetweener" draws all the cels inbetween those done by the studio.

IRC. International Reply Coupon. A coupon purchased at the post office which can be turned in for stamps in any country. IRCs should be sent instead of stamps when you want a foreign buyer to return mail.

Keyline. Identification, through signs and symbols, of the positions of illustrations and copy for the printer.

Kill fee. Portion of the agreed-upon price received for the job that was assigned and started, but then canceled.

Layout. Arrangement of photographs, illustrations, text and headlines for printed material.

License. An arrangement wherein the owner of the copyright grants permission allowing another person (or company) to exercise one or more of the owner's exclusive rights.

Light table. A table utilizing a glass top with light source underneath. Used for tracing or animation work.

Mechanicals. Paste-up or preparation of work for printing.

Monologue. A routine, skit, series of jokes or act performed by a solitary comedian (e.g., Johnny Carson performs a "monologue" at the beginning of "The Tonight Show").

Ms,mss. Abbreviation for manuscript, manuscripts.

One-time rights. The right to publish material for one time only.

Overlay. Transparent cover over copy, where instruction, corrections or color location directions are given.

Panel. In cartooning, a boxed-in illustration; can be single panel, double panel or multiple panel.

Paste-up. Procedure involving coating of the backside of art, type, photostats, etc., with rubber cement or wax and adhering them in their proper positions to the mechanical board. The boards are then used as finished art by the printer.

Pencil test. A rough test (video or film) used to make sure that pencilled, animated scenes move correctly before they are inked.

Photostat. Black-and-white copies produced by an inexpensive photographic process using paper negatives; only line values are held with accuracy. Also called stats.

PMT. Photomechanical transfer; photostat produced without a negative, somewhat like the Polaroid process.

P.O.P. Point-of-purchase; display device, signage or structure located at retail outlets to attract attention to a product.

P.O.S. (Point-of-sale) see P.O.P.

Portfolio. A group of samples assembled to demonstrate an artist's or writer's talent and abilities, often presented to buyers.

Publication (payment on). Payment for work made when it is published.

Query. Letter of inquiry to an editor or buyer eliciting interest in a work you want to illustrate or write.

Reprint rights. The right to publish material that has been previously published.

Roughs. Preliminary sketches of drawings.

Royalty. An agreed percentage paid by the publisher to the writer or artist for each copy of work sold.

SASE. A self-addressed, stamped envelope. Sent for the postage-paid return of materials or reply to a letter or inquiry.

Signage. Posters, banners—any graphic essentially designed to be viewed from a distance.

Simultaneous submission. Submission of the same material at the same time to more than one publisher, agent or potential buyer.

Slant. The subject matter, approach or style of a story or illustrations that will appeal to readers of a specific magazine. For example, if a magazine wants only cartoons on "golf," their "slant" is golf.

Speculation. Creating material with no assurance that the buyer will purchase it or reimburse expenses in any way, as opposed to creating work on assignment. Sometimes called creating work "on spec."

Spot illustration. Often just called spots. A small drawing used to break up an otherwise gray, boring, solid block of copy.

Stat. A photoprint, similar to a PMT or Velox.

Storyboards. Comprehensive color marker drawings plotting the various scenes of animation, film or video production.

Tearsheets. Published prints of your work as they appeared in a publication.

Thumbnail. A rough layout done in smaller than actual size.

Transparency. A photographic positive film such as a color slide.

Velox. Photoprint of a continuous tone subject that has been transformed into line art by means of a halftone screen.

Wash. Thin application of transparent color or watercolor black for a pastel or gray tonal effect.

Work-for-hire. An agreement which essentially transfers all rights of one's creative product to the buyer. Often involves transfer of the copyright to the buyer.

Zip-a-tone. Trade name. See Benday.

Subject Index
Book Publishers

This subject index is set up to help you more quickly locate the book markets that publish the type of humorous material you write. Read each listing carefully and follow the publisher's specific information about the types of manuscripts each prefers to read.

Relationships
Great Quotations
Page One Publishers & Bookworks, Inc.
Price Stern Sloan
Shapolsky Publishers, Inc.

Religious
American Atheist Press
Behrman House
Harvest House Publishers
Pacific Press Publishing Association
Shapolsky Publishers, Inc.

Science/Medicine
Rutgers University Press

Self-Help
CCC Publications
Grapevine Publications, Inc.
North Light Books
Piccadilly Books
Price Stern Sloan

Shapolsky Publishers, Inc.
Warner Books
Workman Publishing

Senior Citizen/Retirement
Great Quotations

Special Interest
American Atheist Press
American Council for the Arts
Catbird Press
CWW Publications
New Victoria Publishers
Players Press Inc.
Speech Bin, Inc., The
Wescott Cove Publishing Co.

Sports
Aegina Press, Inc.
Great Quotations
Laffing Cow Press
Menasha Ridge Press

Subject Index
Publications

This subject index is set up to help you more quickly locate the magazine and newspaper markets that publish the type of humorous material you write. Read each listing carefully and follow the publisher's specific information about the type of manuscripts each prefers to read.

Animals/Pets
Cat Fancy
Chronicle of the Horse, The
Diversion Magazine
Dog Fancy
Kentucky Afield, The Magazine
Mountain Family Calendar
Rotarian, The
Saturday Evening Post, The
Western Horse, The

Business
Good Reading for Everyone
Home Office Opportunities
Management Accounting
Manhattan Magazine/New World
  Journal
Rotarian, The
Small Business Opportunities

Computers
Collegiate Microcomputer
Computer Shopper
Link-Up
Online Access

Education
Forum
Phi Delta Kappan
World and I, The

Entertainment/Games
Dragon Magazine
Just for Laughs
Paintball
TV Time Magazine
Winning!

Environment
Environment
Final Edition, The
Kentucky Afield, The Magazine
Manhattan Magazine/New World
  Journal
Mother Earth News
Mountain Family Calendar
Outdoor America
Rotarian, The

Ethnic
Aboard
Automundo Magazine

Family
Catholic Digest
Diversion Magazine
Fairfield County Woman
Good Housekeeping
Good Reading for Everyone
Housewife-Writer's Forum
Laf!
Lion Magazine, The
Our Family
Parish Family Digest
Saturday Evening Post, The
Today's Christian Woman
Virtue
Virtue
Woodmen of the World Magazine

Fantasy/Sci-Fi
Abyss Magazine
Amelia Magazine
Omni

Farm/Rural
Farm & Ranch Living
FFA New Horizons
Mother Earth News

Feminism
Women's Glib™

General Interest
Aardvark Enterprises
Amelia Magazine
American Legion Magazine
Better Homes & Gardens
Cracked
Good Housekeeping
Home
Laf!
Monthly Independent Tribune Times
  Journal Post Gazette News Chron-
  icle Bulletin, The
Monthly, The
Mountain Family Calendar
Penthouse
Radiance, The Magazine for Large
  Women
Spy
Woman's World Magazine

Health Fitness
American Fitness
Catholic Digest
Health
Health Journal and Digest
New Living
Nutrition Health Review
Prevention Magazine
Womens Sports & Fitness

Interviews
Bassin'
Better Homes & Gardens
Cartoonist Magazine, The
Casino Digest
Cleaning Business
Collegiate Insider
Complete Woman
Currents
Final Edition, The
Funny Times, The

Gem Show News
High Society Magazine
Juggler's World
Just for Laughs
Laf!
Mature Years
Minne Ha! Ha!, The Twin Cities
  Sorely Needed Humor Magazine
Modern Drummer
Mountain Family Calendar
New Woman Magazine
Paintball
Racquetball Magazine
Senior
Snow Country
Suds 'n Stuff
Swank Magazine
Thrasher Magazine & Thrasher Com-
  ics
TV Time Magazine
Women's Glib™
World and I, The
Writer's Guidelines Magazine

Juvenile
Boy's Life
Highlights for Children

New Age
Phenomenews

Parenting
Childsplay
Fairfield County Woman
Grand Rapids Parent Magazine
Housewife-Writer's Forum
Parentguide News
Today's Christian Woman
Woman's World Magazine

Political
California Journal
Casino Digest
Current
Funny Times, The
Living Among Nature Daringly
Manhattan Magazine/New World
  Journal
Metro

National Review
Penthouse
Random Lengths
Realist, The
Women's Glib™

Relationships
Catholic Digest
Fairfield County Woman
FFA New Horizons
Manhattan Magazine/New World
  Journal
New Woman Magazine
Nutrition Health Review
Radiance, The Magazine for Large
  Women
Today's Christian Woman

Religious
American Atheist
American Baptist, The
Catholic Digest
Clergy Journal, The
Leadership
Lutheran, The
Mature Years
Messenger
Our Family
Parish Family Digest
Today's Christian Woman

Satire
Light Quarterly
Living Among Nature Daringly
Metro
Random Lengths
Realist, The
Spy

Science/Medicine
Catholic Digest
Nutrition Health Review
Sciences, The

Secretary, The

Self-Help
EAP Digest
Health Journal and Digest

Senior Citizen/Retirement
Alive! A Magazine for Christian Se-
  nior Adults
Mature Years
Outdoor America
Senior Edition USA

Sex/erotica
Gallery/Fox
Genesis
High Society Magazine
Penthouse
Swank Magazine
Women's Glib™

Slice-Of-Life
Accent on Living
Bassin'
Bird Talk
Campus Life
Casino Digest
Cat Fancy
Catholic Digest
Cleaning Business
Collegiate Insider
Complete Woman
Final Edition, The
Forum
Gem Show News
Golf for Women Magazine
Good Old Days
Good Reading for Everyone
High Society Magazine
Housewife-Writer's Forum
International Bowhunter Magazine
Kentucky Afield, The Magazine
Laf!
Long Island Update Magazine
Lutheran, The
Mature Years
Metro
Minne Ha! Ha!, The Twin Cities
  Sorely Needed Humor Magazine
Mother Earth News
Mountain Family Calendar
National Review
New Living
New York Update Magazine
NW Kitchen & Bath Quarterly

Online Access
Our Family
Paintball
Parish Family Digest
Racquetball Magazine
Radiance, The Magazine for Large Women
Rotarian, The
Scuba Times Magazine
Senior
Senior Edition USA
Suds 'n Stuff
Swank Magazine
TV Time Magazine
Virtue
Weight Watchers Magazine
Winning!
Wisconsin, The Milwaukee Journal Magazine
Women's Glib™
Woodmen of the World Magazine
World and I, The
Writers Digest
Writer's Guidelines Magazine

Special Interest
AIM
American Atheist
Atlantic City Magazine
Automundo Magazine
Balloon Life
Bassin'
Bicycle Guide
Bird Talk
Bird Watcher's Digest
Bostonia
California Highway Patrolman, The
Cartoon Markets
Cartoon World
Cartoonist Magazine, The
Casino Digest
Casino Player
Chesslife
Cleaning Business
Construction Publications
Electrical Apparatus
Fairfield County Woman
Family Motor Coaching
Flower & Garden Magazine

Freedonia Gazette, The
Funny Times, The
Gem Show News
Glass Factory Directory
Heaven Bone Magazine
High Performance Pontiac
Instrumentalist, The
Japanophile
Journal of Reading
Judicature
Juggler's World
Just for Laughs
Kashrus Magazine
Lutheran, The
Mangajin
Modern Drummer
Muscle Mag International
Now and Then
NW Kitchen & Bath Quarterly
Optometric Economics Magazine
Overseas
Pennsylvania Magazine
Radiance, The Magazine for Large Women
Road King Magazine
Satellite Retailer
School Mates
Skydiving
Suds 'n Stuff
Tech Directions
Thrasher Magazine & Thrasher Comics
Tole World
Truckin
Vette
Weight Watchers Magazine
Wisconsin, The Milwaukee Journal Magazine
Workbench
Writers Digest
Writer's Forum
Writer's Guidelines Magazine
Yankee Magazine/The Old Farmers Almanac

Sports
Basketball Digest
Currents
Dakota Country

Diversion Magazine
Field & Stream
Football Digest
Golf for Women Magazine
Golf Journal
Good Old Days
Good Reading for Everyone
Hockey Digest
International Bowhunter Magazine
North American Hunter
Outdoor America
Pennsylvania Sportsman
Racquetball Magazine
Rotarian, The
Scuba Times Magazine
Snow Country
Soccer Digest
Tennis Magazine

Teen/Young Adult

Campus Life
Collegiate Insider
FFA New Horizons
Florida Leader
Listen
Student Assistance Journal

Touring America

Trade

Military Market

Travel

Aboard
Diversion Magazine
Family Motor Coaching
Mountain Family Calendar
Winning!

Women's

American Woman
Complete Woman
Fairfield County Woman
Golf for Women Magazine
Good Housekeeping
Housewife-Writer's Forum
New Woman Magazine
Today's Christian Woman
Virtue
Wisconsin, The Milwaukee Journal
    Magazine
Woman's World Magazine
Women's Glib™
Womens Sports & Fitness

General Index

Check the "Changes . . ." lists following each section for alphabetical lists of those companies which were in the 1991 Humor and Cartoon Markets but do not appear in the 1993 edition.

Check the "Changes . . ." lists following each section for alphabetical lists of those companies which were in the 1991 Humor and Cartoon Markets but do not appear in the 1993 edition.

Check the "Changes . . ." lists following each section for alphabetical lists of those companies which were in the 1991 Humor and Cartoon Markets *but do not appear in the 1993 edition.*

Other Books of Interest

NOW, get 15% off these companion books to the *1993 Humor & Cartoon Markets*:

How to Write & Sell Greeting Cards, Bumper Stickers, T-Shirts & Other Fun Stuff, by Molly Wigand
Molly Wigand, a successful freelancer and former staff writer for Hallmark, shares valuable advice on how to write for and sell to the profitable "social expression" market. Learn how a greeting card company works, plus how to build the writing skills and marketing savvy to produce greetings, slogans and fun ideas that sell. 176 pages/paper/$15.95 now $13.55

1993 Artist's Market, edited by Lauri Miller.
Expand your market base with 2,500+ places to sell your illustrations, greeting cards, cartoons, posters and prints listed in this annual directory. 1993 Artist's Market also offers "Close-Up" interviews with top professionals in their field including Gail Machlis, one of only 10 women cartoonists syndicated in the U.S. 672 pages/$22.95 now $19.50

Comedy Writing Secrets, by Mel Helitzer
Funnyman Mel Helitzer covers the basics of comedy writing, the anatomy of humor, and how to turn a comedic talent into a well-paying pursuit in this comprehensive guide to writing, selling and performing all types of comedy. Includes comments, advice, gags and routines from dozens of top comedians. 336 pages/paper/$15.95 now $13.55

The Complete Guide to Caricature, by Bob Staake
This fun-to-look-at book is a comprehensive guide to caricature drawing, and includes extensive samples from top professionals including David Levine, Mort Drucker and Ralph Steadman. Combined with step-by-step lessons and exercises, this is the definitive book on caricatures. 144 pages/$18.95 now $16.10

The Complete Guide to Greeting Card Design & Illustration, by Eva Szela
Former Hallmark design manager Eva Szela shows how to create and execute designs for every greeting card style and subject using a variety of media and techniques. Complete with 12 step-by-step demonstrations and illustrations of 140 published cards. 152 pages/$29.95 now $25.50

How To Draw & Sell Cartoons, by Ross Thomson & Bill Hewison
Caricatures, political satire, visual jokes, comic strips—whatever the style, this book is for you! Learn how to develop a distinctive style, create ideas and sell your work . . . plus how to prepare your cartoons for submission and get them published. 144 pages/$19.95 now $16.95

How to Draw & Sell Comic Strips, by Alan McKenzie
This guide is packed with information that can take most cartoonists a lifetime to acquire! Learn how to transform your three-dimensional ideas into two-dimensional comic strips and books—and then market and sell them to a growing (and profitable) industry. 144 pages/$19.95 now $16.95

Other Market Books
Children's Writer's & Illustrator's Market, edited by Lisa Carpenter (paper) $17.95
Novel & Short Story Writer's Market, edited by Robin Gee (paper) $19.95
Photographer's Market, edited by Michael Willins $22.95
Poet's Market, Edited by Michael Bugeja $19.95
Songwriter's Market, edited by Michael Oxley $19.95
Writer's Market, edited by Mark Kissling $26.95
Guide to Literary Agents & Art/Photo Reps, edited by Roseann Shaughnessy (paper) $18.95

General Writing Books
Annable's Treasury of Literary Teasers, by H.D. Annable (paper) $10.95
Beginning Writer's Answer Book, edited by Kirk Polking (paper) $13.95
Discovering the Writer Within, by Bruce Ballenger & Barry Lane $16.95
How to Write a Book Proposal, by Michael Larsen (paper) $11.95
On Being a Writer, edited by Bill Strickland (paper) $16.95

Pinckert's Practical Grammar, by Robert C. Pinckert (paper) $11.95
The 29 Most Common Writing Mistakes & How to Avoid Them, by Judy Delton (paper) $9.95
Word Processing Secrets for Writers, by Michael A. Banks & Ansen Dibell (paper) $14.95
The Wordwatcher's Guide to Good Writing & Grammar, by Morton S. Freeman (paper) $15.95
The Writer's Book of Checklists, by Scott Edelstein $16.95
The Writer's Digest Guide to Manuscript Formats, by Buchman & Groves $18.95

Fiction Writing

The Art & Craft of Novel Writing, by Oakley Hall $17.95
Best Stories from New Writers, edited by Linda Sanders $16.95
Characters & Viewpoint, by Orson Scott Card $13.95
The Complete Guide to Writing Fiction, by Barnaby Conrad $18.95
Creating Characters, by Dwight V. Swain $16.95
Dialogue, by Lewis Turco $13.95
Handbook of Short Story Writing: Vol 1, by Dickson and Smythe (paper) $12.95
Manuscript Submission, by Scott Edelstein $13.95
Plot, by Ansen Dibell $13.95
Theme & Strategy, by Ronald B. Tobias $13.95

Special Interest Writing Books

How to Write Horror Fiction, by William F. Nolan $15.95
How to Write Mysteries, by Shannon OCork $13.95
How to Write Romances, by Phyllis Taylor Pianka $15.95
How to Write and Sell True Crime, by Gary Provost $17.95
How to Write Tales of Horror, Fantasy & Science Fiction, edited by J.N. Williamson (paper) $12.95
Successful Scriptwriting, by Jurgen Wolff & Kerry Cox (paper) $14.95
Hillary Waugh's Guide to Mysteries & Mystery Writing, by Hillary Waugh $19.95

The Writing Business

Business & Legal Forms for Authors & Self-Publishers, by Tad Crawford (paper) $15.95
The Writer's Guide to Self-Promotion & Publicity, by Elane Feldman $16.95
Writing A to Z, edited by Kirk Polking $24.95

To order directly from the publisher, include $3.00 postage and handling for 1 book and $1.00 for each additional book. Allow 30 days for delivery.

Writer's Digest Books, 1507 Dana Avenue, Cincinnati, Ohio 45207
Credit card orders call TOLL-FREE
1-800-289-0963
Prices subject to change without notice.

Write to this same address for information on *Writer's Digest* magazine, *STORY* magazine, Writer's Digest Book Club, Writer's Digest School, and Writer's Digest Criticism Service.

1993 Close-up Personalities

Illustrator: Bob Staake

Marty Chapo
Art Director
Page 46

Doug Gamble
Humor Writer
Page 144